Professional Microsoft® SharePoint® 2007 Design

Foreword xxi
Introduction xxiii

Chapter 1: Why Design? 1
Chapter 2: Web Design 101 13
Chapter 3: General Concept Design 37
Chapter 4: Communicating or Collaborating? 131
Chapter 5: Introduction to SharePoint Designer 169
Chapter 6: Themes 201
Chapter 7: Cascading Style Sheets with MOSS 2007 245
Chapter 8: Master Pages 311
Chapter 9: Page Layouts 369
Chapter 10: Working with Out-of-the-Box Web Parts 403
Chapter 11: Navigation 455
Chapter 12: Customizing Search 497
Chapter 13: Accessibility in SharePoint 535
Chapter 14: Wrapping It All Up 577
Appendix A: Introduction to Deploying SharePoint Designs 589
Index 599

Professional
Microsoft® SharePoint® 2007 Design

Jacob Sanford
Randy Drisgill
David Drinkwine
Coskun Cavusoglu

WILEY

Wiley Publishing, Inc.

Professional Microsoft® SharePoint® 2007 Design

Published by
Wiley Publishing, Inc.
10475 Crosspoint Boulevard
Indianapolis, IN 46256
www.wiley.com

Copyright © 2008 by Wiley Publishing, Inc., Indianapolis, Indiana

Published simultaneously in Canada

ISBN: 978-0-470-28580-0

Manufactured in the United States of America

10 9 8 7 6 5 4 3 2 1

Library of Congress Cataloging-in-Publication Data is available from the publisher.

About the Authors

Jacob J. Sanford began his career in, of all things, accounting and auditing. He graduated from Florida State University in 1997 with BS degrees in Accounting and Finance, which made him eligible to sit for the CPA exam. Although he realized in college that his interests lie more in computers and technology, he decided he would give accounting a chance. It didn't last. He had been dabbling in HTML and VBA when he took a job at a private software company and met co-author David Drinkwine, who introduced him to the wonders of classic ASP. From there, he began learning as much as he could about all kinds of Web application development. This took him down the paths of ColdFusion, PHP, PhotoShop, CSS, XML, and finally ASP.NET (starting with the 1.0 and 1.1 releases). He has been using ASP.NET (VB and C# — but mostly C#) for the last four or five years. He has worked at several State of Florida agencies and in that capacity found a fondness for pure CSS design and accessibility considerations. Most recently, he has started focusing on new technologies and tools such as Microsoft Silverlight and Visual Studio 2008.

Jacob is currently a senior consultant with Captaré Consulting, LLC, and is the founding leader of the Tallahassee SharePoint Experts Exchange for Developers (SPEED). He is also a regular presenter at regional .NET Code Camps and at local .NET User Group meetings and is the author of *Professional ASP.NET 2.0 Design* (Wrox, 2007).

Jacob has received his Microsoft Certified Professional Developer (MCPD) certification as a Web Developer (Visual Studio 2005). He plans to upgrade his credentials to Visual Studio 2008 and the .NET 3.6 Framework as the certification exams become available.

Jacob lives in Tallahassee, Florida with his beautiful wife, Shannan. He has two amazing sons, Matthew and Hayden, and an eternal puppy, Petey.

Randy Drisgill is an Internet technologist, focused on emerging Web trends such as MOSS 2007 and rich Internet applications. Currently working as a consultant for SharePoint branding and customization, Randy has been helping businesses create innovative Web applications since the late '90s. Previously, Randy co-owned a Web development consulting company, and before that, he worked for Lockheed Martin on several enterprise-level initiatives. Along with his current interests in Microsoft technologies, Randy's involvement in both the ColdFusion and ActionScript communities has led to his co-authoring several related books and publications.

Besides blogging about everything from Adobe to LoLCats at www.Drisgill.com, Randy also uses the pseudonym "The Mossman" to blog specifically about MOSS 2007 at theMossman.Blogspot.com. When not thinking about technology, Randy enjoys spending time with his beautiful wife, Jackie, and his dog, Frito.

David Drinkwine is currently a Senior Solutions Architect for Captaré Consulting, LLC, a Chicago-based consulting firm specializing in advanced SharePoint implementation and custom .NET application development. He has designed and implemented WSS and MOSS based applications for a variety of clients, including global product manufacturers, state agencies, and telecommunications firms.

David has a decade and a half of software development experience and has been developing Internet-based solutions since the late '90s. He has been highly focused on designing and implementing SharePoint solutions from the early days of SharePoint Team Services. He has experience in a wide variety of technologies, including MOSS, WSS, various incarnations of C and Visual Basic, MS Office programming and integration, and far more acronym-named technologies than can be good for any one person to know.

David frequently has spoken on design and the use of third-party tools with SharePoint at regional SharePoint user group meetings. He attended Florida State University, where he studied English and Philosophy.

Coskun Cavusoglu is the Director of Consulting Services and the Chief Solution Architect of Captaré Consulting, LLC. Coskun has been architecting and implementing technology solutions for more than 10 years in both large enterprise organizations and fast-growth midmarket firms. He has extensive experience designing, implementing and supporting Internet solutions using Microsoft technologies such as SharePoint, CRM, Project Server, Solomon, BizTalk Server, Windows Server, Active Directory, Exchange, IIS, and ASP .NET 2.0.

Coskun consults on a variety of business process practices. He has a broad range of expertise in areas such as knowledge management, business process analysis, collaboration, project management, office productivity, and application programming.

Coskun is a Microsoft Certified Technology Specialist for SharePoint Portal Server 2003 and Microsoft Office SharePoint Server 2007.

About the Technical Editors

Doug Holland is a senior software engineer at Intel Corporation in Folsom, CA, and holds a masters degree in software engineering from Oxford University. He has been designing and building software solutions for over 14 years within areas as diverse as telecommunications, homeland security, and now graphics chipset performance modeling. Doug Holland has received the Microsoft Most Valuable Professional (MVP) award for Visual C# and enjoys speaking to user groups and blogging about the latest trends in the Microsoft .NET platform and software engineering. He also loves spending time with his wife and four children at their home just outside Sacramento, CA, and enjoys flying Cessnas over the California landscape.

Andrew Connell is an independent consultant, developer, instructor, and Microsoft Most Valuable Professional (MVP) for Microsoft Office SharePoint Server (MOSS) focusing on Web Content Management (WCM). He's authored numerous books and articles on the subjects of Microsoft Content Management Server and SharePoint Products and Technologies. With a passion for SharePoint development and content management sites, Andrew has spoken on the subject of MOSS 2007 development and WCM at various events and national conferences such as TechEd, SharePoint Connections, VSLive, Office Developer Conference, and the Microsoft SharePoint Conference. You can reach Andrew or subscribe to his blog at http://www.andrewconnell.com/blog.

Credits

Contributing Writer
John Ross

Acquisitions Editor
Katie Mohr

Development Editor
Kelly Talbot

Technical Editors
Doug Holland,
Andrew Connell

Production Editor
William A. Barton
Daniel Scribner

Copy Editor
C.M. Jones

Editorial Manager
Mary Beth Wakefield

Production Manager
Tim Tate

Vice President and Executive Group Publisher
Richard Swadley

Vice President and Executive Publisher
Joseph B. Wikert

Project Coordinator, Cover
Lynsey Stafford

Proofreaders
Corina Copp
David Fine
Scott Klemp

Indexer
Robert Swanson

Acknowledgments

As a team, we would like to thank all of the people at Wrox for making this book a possibility. First, to Jim Minatel, our first contact into Wrox and for hearing our idea and putting us in contact with the right people. To Katie Mohr for being the right people. Besides signing off on the idea and walking it through the official approval process, she provided a wealth of understanding and guidance when we needed it. To Kelly Talbot, our development editor, for first and foremost making sure what we say makes sense (and is, in fact, what we meant to say). He also was there with us through the whole process and gave invaluable advice and was forgiving when we missed deadlines (more often than we should admit). He never gave up on us and kept us motivated (and provided the occasional shove when we needed that, too). To John Ross for stepping in at the last minute to write Appendix A for us, which really helps make this manuscript a complete work. To our technical editors, Doug Holland and Andrew Connell, for making sure what we say is factually sound and technologically correct. Without all of you guys, this book would not have happened, and we sincerely appreciate every one of your contributions.

I want to start off by thanking the writing team for their dedication and hard work at getting this book finished. There were many nights I was up writing at 2 and 3 a.m. (or even 4 and 5 a.m.) and could look in my IM client and see them up doing the same. And, in that same regard, I want to personally thank their families for letting them do what it took to get through it. I know how understanding my wife was and I know you guys couldn't have done it without the understanding and support of your families. So they deserve as much credit as anyone on this team.

I also need to thank all of the employers that have let me learn as much as I could when I was with them. Most recently, Malcolm Eaton and Jamie Story of Captaré, for throwing me into the SharePoint fire and letting me try to cook up something amazing. I have learned so much under you guys, and you will never know how much I appreciate it.

Finally, to my family for being there when I needed you and leaving me alone when I needed to write. I know you went through this just as much as I did and you don't even get your picture on the cover. I could never do the things I do in life without your support.

Oh, and to all of my friends and the GSS, let's try to eat some of the cake this time before we destroy it, okay?

— *Jacob J. Sanford*

There are so many people that I need to thank for helping me along my journey, not only through life but also along my most recent journey to the land of MOSS. The following is a list of a few people who come to mind, in no particular order: My parents (Pat and Tom Drisgill) for buying me a Commodore 64 and for encouraging me to reach for my goals. My in-laws, the Auerbachs, for helping me when I really needed it. My wife Jackie, for putting up with my Internet addiction and my new Macbook Pro. The entire team at CIBER Orlando "The Ocho," in all of its iterations, for being there throughout this whole process even when I came in to work bleary eyed from writing. My co-authoring cohorts from Captaré for helping me sound semi-intelligent. A special thanks to both Andrew Connell and Heather Solomon for everything they do for the MOSS community, for being my mentors over the past year, for patiently

Acknowledgments

answering my questions at all hours of the night, for all of their help on this book, and ultimately for being good friends despite hardly knowing me in person. Lastly, thanks to The Mossman for being the Incredible Hulk to my Bruce Banner.

Oh, and a shout out and hearty thank you to John Ross for picking up the pieces of my shattered mind when MOSS was completely killing me; I can think of no better person to learn MOSS with. Keep on moving those chains!

— *Randy Drisgill*

I'd like to thank Jacob for getting me involved in this project; Randy and Coskun for bailing me out time and time again; Jamie, Malcolm, and everyone at Captaré for their support; Bob Maybin from dragging me into this racket in the first place; And, last but not least, my wife, who has given me time, patience, and, at times, properly placed kicks in the pants.

— *David Drinkwine*

Nothing I have written would exist without the support of the many clients who gave me the opportunity to develop and revise SharePoint techniques and practices. My associates at Captaré, you have allowed me to practice the ideas I have believed for so long. Jamie Story and Malcolm Eaton, in particular, have provided me with guidance and flexibility while fueling my passion for technology, clients and business.

Jacob, you have not only helped make this book a reality but you have taught me wonderful lessons in the process. I'm extremely grateful to my co-authors for making this an experience that will serve me well for the rest of my life.

There remains one last group of people to acknowledge, and they stand at the center of almost anything I undertake: my parents, Nezahat and Nejat, who have given me what they could and sacrificed in the process; my daughter, Tuana, who has filled the missing piece in my life with more joy than she will ever know; and my wife, Kader, who I am eternally grateful for making the countless sacrifices and providing the day-to-day support that makes writing a book possible.

— *Coskun Cavusoglu*

Contents

Foreword   xxi
Introduction   xxiii

Chapter 1: Why Design?   1

The Million-Dollar Question: What Makes Good Design?   2
Why Should Designers Care?   7
Why Should Managers Care?   8
Why Should Clients Care?   9
So Why Use SharePoint for Design?   10
Summary   11

Chapter 2: Web Design 101   13

Goal-Oriented Design   14
Driving Adoption   15
Storyboarding   16
Portal Design   17
    Things to Consider   18
    Portal Topologies   19
Web Page Design   26
Planning for Change   35
Summary   36

Chapter 3: General Concept Design   37

Getting Inspired   37
Creating the Design   41
    An Overview of Photoshop CS3   42
    A Few Graphic Concepts   54
    Creating the Design from Scratch   72
The Intranet Counterpart   128
Continuing Education   128
Summary   129

Chapter 4: Communicating or Collaborating?   131

What Is a Communication/Publishing Site?   131
    Information Flow in Communication/Publishing Sites   132

Contents

When to Use a Communication Site — **133**

Using a Communication Site for Intranets — 133

Using a Communication Site for Public Web Sites — 135

Effectively Using a Communication/Publishing Site — **136**

Keeping the Look and Feel Consistent — 137

Enforcing Corporate Identity Guidelines — 138

Enforcing Corporate Policy — 140

Managing the Publishing Process with Publishing Pages — 142

Managing Security with Publishing Pages — 145

Managing Site Hierarchy — 146

Managing Site Variations — 148

Publishing Site Templates — **153**

The Top-Level Publishing Site Templates — 153

The Publishing Sub-Site Templates — 157

Communication/Publishing Site Best Practices — **160**

What Is a Collaboration/Team Site? — **161**

Information Flow in Collaboration/Team Sites — 162

When to Use a Collaboration Site — **162**

Using a Collaboration Site to Manage Projects — 162

Effectively Using a Collaboration Site? — **163**

Collaboration Site Templates — **164**

Team/Blank Site Template — 164

Document Workspace Template — 165

Wiki Site Template — 166

Blog Site Template — 167

Site Templates with WSS 3.0 — 167

Collaboration/Team Site Best Practices — **167**

Summary — **168**

Chapter 5: Introduction to SharePoint Designer — **169**

Why Use SharePoint Designer? — **169**

Overview of Functionality — 170

Not Using SharePoint Designer — 170

Customizing MOSS Sites — **170**

Opening a MOSS Site in SharePoint Designer — 171

The Folder List Pane — 172

File Check-In/Check-Out — 173

Adding Content to a MOSS Site — 174

Adding Other Types of Content — 178

Approval Workflow — 178

Customized Vs. Un-customized — 179

Contents

The Design View   **180**

Working with Master Pages   **182**

Working with Page Layouts   185

Creating a Content Page   185

Editing Pages   185

Working with CSS   **186**

The Manage Styles Pane   187

The Apply Styles Pane   188

The CSS Properties Pane   188

Working with Web Parts and Web Part Zones   **190**

Working with XSL   **195**

Using SharePoint Designer Reports   **198**

Summary   **199**

Chapter 6: Themes   **201**

SharePoint Themes   **201**

Applying a Theme to a SharePoint Site   203

Using SharePoint Themes to Brand   205

How SharePoint Themes Work   **208**

The Themes Folder   208

Contents of a Themes Folder   208

Contents of a SharePoint Site when a Theme is Applied   212

How to Create a Theme   **214**

How to Design a Theme   **218**

Setting Up Design Environment   219

Starting the Theme Design   223

Finalizing the Customizations   241

Moving the Theme to the Server   242

Workarounds for Theme Caveats   **242**

Reapplying Themes   242

Making Your Custom Theme the Default Theme   242

Tools for Creating Themes   **243**

Summary   **244**

Chapter 7: Cascading Style Sheets with MOSS 2007   **245**

Introduction to Cascading Style Sheets   **245**

Browsers and Support   246

DOCTYPEs   246

Tables vs. Pure CSS   248

Contents

Working with CSS   **249**

Ways to Apply CSS to HTML   249

CSS Rules   250

Types of Selectors   250

CSS Property Values   254

Coding CSS with Reuse in Mind   268

How Important Is "!important"?   269

Inheritance   269

Understanding the Cascade   270

Tools for Working with CSS   271

How to Include CSS in Your MOSS Site   **275**

Setting an Alternate CSS   275

Adding CSS to Your Own Master Pages   276

Adding Internal Style to MOSS Pages   280

Converting Your Design to HTML and CSS   **282**

Creating Sliced Background and Regular Images   282

Creating the HTML and CSS   285

Intranet HTML Design Differences   307

Summary   **309**

Chapter 8: Master Pages   **311**

What Is a Master Page?   **312**

Content Pages   312

Page Layouts   312

Master Pages in MOSS   313

The Master Page Structure   **313**

Content Placeholders   314

Content Page Structure   314

ASP.NET Controls   315

A Sample Master Page   316

Using Master Pages with MOSS   **318**

Functional Areas of a Master Page   319

Deciding Where the Master Page Ends   320

Required Content Placeholders   324

Where Master Pages Live in MOSS   325

Out-of-the-Box Master Pages   326

Minimal Master Pages   327

Challenges with Master Pages in MOSS   **329**

The Importance of CSS   329

System Pages   329

Safe Mode	330
Web Part Zones	330
Nesting Master Pages and MOSS	330
Turning on Robust Errors	331
The Great Customization Debate	**333**
Implementing a Minimal Master Page	**333**
Adding Your Own HTML	335
Double Checking Your Master Page	338
Converting HTML Design to Master Pages	**341**
A Word about the Name ActiveX Control Message in Internet Explorer	365
Intranet Master Page Design Differences	366
Summary	**367**
Chapter 9: Page Layouts	**369**
What Is a Page Layout?	**369**
Relationship to Master Pages	370
Content Types	371
Page Layout Structure	373
Types of Content in Page Layouts	375
Where Do Page Layouts Live in MOSS	376
The Out-of-the-box Page Layouts	377
Implementing Your Own Page Layouts	**379**
The Great Customization Debate	379
Creating a Content Type	379
Creating Site Columns	380
Creating a Page Layout	383
Adding Field Controls to a Page Layout	384
Adding Web Parts to a Page Layout	386
Publishing a Page Layout	388
Create Publishing Pages from a Page Layout	389
Improving a Page Layout with HTML	390
Internet Site Welcome Page Layout Example	**394**
Creating the Page Layout	395
Adding the HTML Design	395
Adding Field Controls	397
Adding Web Part Zones	397
Adding Page Layout Specific CSS	399
Switching the Welcome Page Layout	399
Adding Content to the Welcome Page	399
Summary	**402**

Contents

Chapter 10: Working with Out-of-the-Box Web Parts   **403**

Using the Content Query Web Part   **404**
Real World Scenario: Adding a "Latest News" CQWP to an Internet Site   404
The Data View Web Part   **421**
Adding a Data View Web Part to a SharePoint Page   421
Selecting a Data Source for the Data View Web Part   422
Inserting the Data Source Control to the Data View Web Part   424
Customizing the Look and Feel of the Data View Web Part   426
The Content Editor Web Part   **433**
The Page Viewer Web Part   **438**
The XML Web Part   **441**
An Example of the XML Web Part   441
A More Dynamic XML Web Part Example   445
The Image Web Part   **447**
An Example of the Image Web Part   447
The Image Web Part–Connected   450
Summary   **452**

Chapter 11: Navigation   **455**

Determining Whether Your Site Is WSS 3.0 or MOSS 2007   **455**
WSS 3.0 Navigation   **456**
Using the Top Link Bar   457
Quick Launch   473
Tree View Menu   481
Showing Only Sites on the Tree View Menu   482
MOSS 2007 Navigation   **483**
Maintaining MOSS 2007 Navigation   484
MOSS 2007 Navigation Customizations   489
Creating a Two-Level Horizontal Menu   492
Enabling MOSS 2007 Navigation for WSS 3.0 Sites   494
Summary   **495**

Chapter 12: Customizing Search   **497**

Accuracy vs. Relevancy   **498**
Making Better Information   **499**
Metadata   499
Content Types   500

How Search Indexing Works   **501**

Adding Managed Properties   502

Content Sources   504

Setting Gatherer Rules   506

Crawl Settings   508

Creating Scopes   508

Making Scopes Available   510

Designing Search Interfaces   **511**

Using Search Web Parts   512

The Search Core Results Web Part   520

The Content Query Web Part, Revisited   528

Content Query Parts vs. Fixed Keyword Core Search Results   529

The Search Center   529

Hacking Search Results   **530**

Search Ranking Factors   530

Key Words and Best Bets   531

Authoritative Pages and Demoted Sites   533

Summary   **534**

Chapter 13: Accessibility in SharePoint   **535**

Accessibility Today   **535**

Guidelines for Accessibility   537

Accessibility in SharePoint   **538**

The Checklist in the Real World   546

Customizing SharePoint for Accessibility   **548**

The CSS Friendly Control Adapters   548

The Accessibility Kit for SharePoint (AKS)   573

Tools and Validators   **574**

Summary   **574**

Chapter 14: Wrapping It All Up   **577**

Checkpoint 1: Basic Web Design   **578**

Checkpoint 2: Accessibility   **579**

Checkpoint 3: The Design   **581**

Checkpoint 4: Creating the Mockup   **582**

Checkpoint 5: Creating the Master Page   **583**

Checkpoint 6: Using a Theme   **584**

Contents

Checkpoint 7: Considering Page Layouts   **584**
Checkpoint 8: Intuitive Navigation   **585**
Checkpoint 9: Content Considerations   **585**
Checkpoint 10: Checks and Validation   **586**
Summary   **587**

Appendix A: Introduction to Deploying SharePoint Designs   **589**

Customized and Uncustomized Files   **589**
Uncustomized Files   590
Customized Files   590
Key Considerations   **591**
Creating Uncustomized Files with Features and Solutions   **592**
The Designer's Role in Solutions and Features   595
The Downside to Solutions and Features   595
Deployment Scenarios   **596**
Small Farm and Single Server Installations   596
Medium Farms and Multi- Level Server Environments   596
Large Farms   597
Summary   **597**

Index   **599**

Foreword

The number one question I hear from people getting involved with SharePoint is "Can I change how SharePoint looks?" The answer is *yes!* You can certainly alter the default user interface for any SharePoint product and technology. The logical next question then is "How?"

Out-of-the-box, SharePoint provides some very limited and basic ways to alter the site interface. Most companies and site installations, however, need to go to the next level and really customize several elements of the user interface. Sites need to express ideas and emotions and quickly deliver content to their target audience. Corporate identities, complementary colors, and relevant images need to be used. Pages need to be structured, and content needs to be dynamic, eye-catching, and effective. All of these elements are necessary to create usable and functional Internet and intranet sites.

This is where SharePoint Designer comes in. This product allows you to design for SharePoint. It has a direct connection to your SharePoint site and allows you to interact with your site and see results immediately. With SharePoint Designer, you can create and alter the user interface for SharePoint.

Some of the buzzwords you hear most often around SharePoint branding are master pages, page layouts, and features. This book explores these items and how you can effectively use them in your site. Beyond the buzz, there are many other ways you can change the interface for SharePoint and affect both site design (logo, header, navigation, footer, and so on) and content design (text, content, data, roll up views, and so on). While themes and Web parts have been around a lot longer and do not seem as glamorous, they are both highly useful and effective for branding SharePoint. This book serves as a definitive guide and a single source for the information and expertise you need in order to make the SharePoint site your own. SharePoint Designer can help make your sites both beautiful and functional, and this book shows you how.

Jacob, David, Coskun, and Randy walk you through the steps involved and help you learn the skills to change the interface successfully. They have all worked on SharePoint implementations and they understand the challenges and pain points that come with this task. This book is a must-have for designers and will bridge the gap between what you know and what you need to know to brand SharePoint successfully!

Heather Solomon
Owner and President, Solomon Creative, Inc.
Director of Creative Services, SharePoint Experts, Inc.
Senior Trainer, SharePoint Branding Bootcamp

Introduction

The idea of Web portals is nothing new. In fact, SharePoint is not even a totally new idea, with SharePoint Portal Server (and Windows SharePoint Services version 2) being first introduced in 2003 (or even Share-Point Team Services first released in 2001). But with the introduction of Microsoft Offices SharePoint Server 2007 (MOSS) and Windows SharePoint Services version 3 (WSS), Web portal development took a huge leap forward. Many new technologies were introduced, and since they were built on the .NET 2.0 Framework, MOSS and WSS were able to capitalize on many of the new and cool features that made that framework release so amazing.

But if you look at any bookstore or online book retailer for books on SharePoint, there is a woeful lack of releases that deal specifically with design. Sure, there are several books out on MOSS and WSS, but mostly they focus on the nuts and bolts of making SharePoint work. There might be a chapter here and there that deals with things that are important to the design of your SharePoint portal, but the chapter is included in a larger scope that, frankly, doesn't overly concern itself with the way your SharePoint site looks.

The consequence to this unfortunate gap in available manuscripts is that many SharePoint sites out there look pretty much the same as any other SharePoint site. In fact, it's not uncommon for anyone familiar with SharePoint to be able to look at a site built on SharePoint technologies and be able to immediately determine that is the case. It's unfortunate that such a powerful set of tools often comes wrapped in such a vanilla package.

This book is unique in the fact that it puts the design of a SharePoint site as its primary scope. Sure, some of the technologies covered are also covered in other books. However, this should not be seen as overlap because, in the confines of this book, the design is the point, not necessarily the technology behind it. Also, since this book is focused towards design, universal concepts such as accessibility, CSS, and even outside applications such as Photoshop are discussed as they relate to SharePoint. While not specifically a designer's cookbook for SharePoint, this book does try to bring the most relevant topics regarding the design perspective of a SharePoint site to those developers interested in making their sites stand out.

If you want to learn how SharePoint works and how to use its administrative features to make your site powerful, there are plenty of books (many from Wrox) available to help you with that. However, if your focus is making your SharePoint sites look unique, we hope that this book will help you with that endeavor.

Who This Book Is For

This book is for the SharePoint professional or enthusiast who has an interest in making their sites look as powerful as they are under the hood. Some of the concepts in the book will probably come easier to you if you are already familiar with SharePoint. However, an effort was made to at least provide enough detail so that the novice can understand and have enough information to get up to speed. Even so, if you are a complete novice to SharePoint, it might be a good idea to first read up a little bit on SharePoint so that you have at least a beginner's level of understanding on how SharePoint works and at least a cursory overview of its features.

This book also goes over some of the .NET 2.0 Framework features that can help designers in their effort to design their SharePoint pages. Again, while being an expert C# programmer is not required, a basic exposure to the .NET 2.0 Framework features will probably help you get through some of the chapters. For example, there are topics on master pages, themes, and control adapters that would be familiar to most .NET 2.0 (or above) programmers. The focus of these chapters is to show how to integrate these concepts within the confines of a SharePoint installation. This means that going into these topics completely unaware of the 2.0 counterparts might make it more difficult to understand the concepts in these chapters. As with the SharePoint concepts, an effort was made to provide enough detail so that even the complete novice can understand what is going on. But, again, knowing the 2.0 Framework can certainly be of benefit in these chapters.

What This Book Covers

This book covers the major design instruments one would need in creating the aesthetic appearance of a SharePoint site, using Microsoft Office SharePoint Server 2007 or Windows SharePoint Services version 3. The concepts presented are unique to this version because they rely on an underlying framework that was not available in previous versions of the software.

Additionally, this book gets into design tools not specifically targeted to SharePoint developers. For example, Chapter 3 is solely dedicated to creating the design for your site using Photoshop CS3. Many of the concepts of this chapter would certainly be easily ported to earlier versions of Photoshop, and probably even other graphic editor programs. But nobody would argue that Photoshop, in any version, was a SharePoint tool. However, when you're talking about the Web, and specifically Web design, Photoshop is almost always relevant.

Finally, concepts on standards and guidelines are included, as they should be part of the planning for any Web site, not just SharePoint. This includes the latest versions of Web accessibility and cascading style sheet rules and definitions. While some of the rules, such as the Web Content Accessibility Guidelines, are currently under revision and will probably be updated in the future, the most current accepted versions were used for this book.

How This Book Is Structured

This book is structured in what might be considered the logical approach to planning the design of your SharePoint site. In the beginning, theories on Web design and concepts are discussed in a general manner. Next, the design is architected in Photoshop CS3. The next chapters then break that design into its HTML equivalents and create the CSS and master page files used to brand the overall site. In this stage, there is also a discussion about creating page layouts and themes to further carry out your design to the controls used by your site. Finally, as the book begins to wind down, more focus is placed on the actual content that will likely make up your sites, such as search, navigation, and Web parts, and how to style them to meet the design specifications you have created in the earlier chapters. As a look back, a summarized checklist of design considerations will be provided in the final chapter to give a broad overview of the concepts provided in the book and how they should go into the planning of your next site.

What You Need to Use This Book

The main criterion you need to be successful using this book is the desire to design SharePoint sites that look like anything but out-of-the-box SharePoint sites. As mentioned earlier, a basic understanding of the .NET 2.0 Framework and of SharePoint concepts will be helpful as well, although not critical.

As far as tools go, this book uses Photoshop CS3 and Microsoft Office SharePoint Designer 2007 as its primary development tools. Photoshop is not necessary, as any graphics editing program will likely do the job. And, honestly, most of the concepts presented in the chapters dealing with Photoshop can be fairly easily ported to any other graphics program.

However, SharePoint Designer is probably a must-have, as it is the only easy way to directly interact with the virtual CSS, master page, and ASPX files that are a part of your SharePoint site. Since they are not physical files but merely files created on the fly from data in XML and database records, modifying them provides a fairly unique obstacle. SharePoint Designer is engineered to modify these files for you and, as such, it would be too much of a hardship to try to get around this requirement. To get the most out of this book, you really need SharePoint Designer.

Other than that, you shouldn't need much else. Throughout the chapters you will find references to other tools that might help you do the job, many of them free. But those are all optional. This book was not created to be a shopping list of expensive tools you need to make your sites awesome. Instead, it was aimed at making your sites awesome using tools you probably already have or can get easily. And if you work in SharePoint, you should already have SharePoint Designer. And if you don't have and can't afford Photoshop, there are some free alternatives available. The point is the design and the underlying concepts. And the biggest tools necessary are your brain and your vision.

Conventions

To help you get the most from the text and keep track of what's happening, we've used a number of conventions throughout the book.

> **Boxes like this one hold important, not-to-be forgotten information that is directly relevant to the surrounding text.**

Notes, tips, hints, tricks, and asides to the current discussion are offset and placed in italics like this.

As for styles in the text:

❑ We *highlight* new terms and important words when we introduce them.

❑ We show keyboard strokes like this: Ctrl+A.

❑ We show file names, URLs, and code within the text like so: `persistence.properties`.

❑ We present code in two different ways:

```
We use a monofont type with no highlighting for code examples.
We use gray highlighting to emphasize code that's particularly important in the
present context.
```

Source Code

As you work through the examples in this book, you may choose either to type all the code manually or to use the source code files that accompany the book. All of the source code used in this book is available for download at http://www.wrox.com. Once at the site, simply locate the book's title (either by using the search box or by using one of the title lists) and click the Download Code link on the book's detail page to obtain all the source code for the book.

> *Because many books have similar titles, you may find it easiest to search by ISBN; this book's ISBN is 978-0-470-28580-0.*

Once you download the code, just decompress it with your favorite compression tool. Alternately, you can go to the main Wrox code download page at http://www.wrox.com/dynamic/books/download.aspx to see the code available for this book and all other Wrox books.

Errata

We make every effort to ensure that there are no errors in the text or in the code. However, no one is perfect, and mistakes do occur. If you find an error in one of our books, like a spelling mistake or faulty piece of code, we would be very grateful for your feedback. By sending in errata, you may save another reader hours of frustration. At the same time, you will be helping us provide even higher-quality information.

To find the errata page for this book, go to http://www.wrox.com and locate the title using the search box or one of the title lists. Then, on the book details page, click the Book Errata link. On this page you can view all errata that has been submitted for this book and posted by Wrox editors. A complete book list including links to each book's errata is also available at www.wrox.com/misc-pages/booklist.shtml.

If you don't spot "your" error on the Book Errata page, go to www.wrox.com/contact/techsupport.shtml and complete the form there to send us the error you have found. We'll check the information and, if appropriate, post a message to the book's errata page and fix the problem in subsequent editions of the book.

p2p.wrox.com

For author and peer discussion, join the P2P forums at p2p.wrox.com. The forums are a Web-based system for you to post messages relating to Wrox books and related technologies and interact with other readers and technology users. The forums offer a subscription feature to e-mail you topics of interest of your choosing when new posts are made to the forums. Wrox authors, editors, other industry experts, and your fellow readers are present on these forums.

At http://p2p.wrox.com you will find a number of different forums that will help you not only as you read this book but also as you develop your own applications. To join the forums, just follow these steps:

1. Go to p2p.wrox.com and click the Register link.
2. Read the terms of use and click Agree.

3. Complete the required information to join as well as any optional information you wish to provide and click Submit.

4. You will receive an e-mail with information describing how to verify your account and complete the joining process.

You can read messages in the forums without joining P2P but in order to post your own messages, you must join.

Once you join, you can post new messages and respond to messages other users post. You can read messages at any time on the Web. If you would like to have new messages from a particular forum e-mailed to you, click the Subscribe to this Forum icon by the forum name in the forum listing.

For more information about how to use the Wrox P2P, be sure to read the P2P FAQs for answers to questions about how the forum software works as well as many common questions specific to P2P and Wrox books. To read the FAQs, click the FAQ link on any P2P page.

1

Why Design?

When people attempt to take up Microsoft Office SharePoint 2007 (MOSS 2007) as a profession, or even as a hobby, they immediately begin by trying to understand how to make the portal work. This is probably an obvious path; to make SharePoint work, you have to, well, make it work. Beginners toil with custom lists, site administration, and out-of-the-box Web parts. They may start getting into security and document libraries and slightly more advanced topics. Some more advanced (or brave) users may even get into custom development and modification in SharePoint and its integration with other technologies.

But when is it time to learn about design and branding when it comes to the SharePoint portals these people are designing? Should they learn it in the beginning? Or perhaps wait until they have a solid understanding of all other principles related to MOSS 2007? And, once they learn good design concepts, when is it time to worry about the site's look and feel? Is there a good time? If so, should it come at the beginning of the planning process? At the end?

Unfortunately, too often MOSS 2007 developers put little to no emphasis on the actual look and feel of the sites they are designing. There could be any number of reasons that this happens. Maybe it's because, from a business sense, it's hard to quantify good design. Sure, any analyst can show that with the addition of this new feature of the Web site subscription revenue went up by x number of dollars. It's harder to evaluate, though, if a site becomes more or less popular because of the way it looks and feels. This is especially true for a completely new site because there are no historical numbers to use to determine how much difference the site's aesthetics make. Conversely, if a site has been online for three years and one day a total redesign is introduced and within three months sales double, it might be easier to give the credit to the design (although it might be just as easy not to). And what of the sites that generate no real revenue? Perhaps new and/or repeat visits would be able to quantify good design, but even this would be hard to measure. So maybe this is part of the reason.

Or maybe the problem is with the mindset of the developers making the MOSS 2007 sites. Maybe they don't have the training and exposure to make the sites visually impressive. Or maybe there is general apathy about design. Perhaps they just care a lot more about functionality than design. After all, most clients sign off on projects based on what they do, not how they look. Or maybe it's just that these developers don't feel they have the time to make the design look distinct, and besides, there are plenty of out-of-the-box solutions that would work just fine. Slap on the client's logo and be done with design.

This book will attempt to put new emphasis on design. Specifically, this chapter will try to point out the "why" of good design. Why does it matter? Why should developers care? Why should managers care? And why should clients care? The rest of the book will be more aimed at the "how" of good design: How to create a new design. How to create master pages and CSS files to support your new design. How to incorporate themes. How to make more accessible designs. How to make MOSS 2007 work for the design you create.

With that, it's time to get started.

The Million-Dollar Question: What Makes Good Design?

This is a tough question to field. If you ask 100 different Web designers today what is critical for good design, you will not see the same answers brought up by all of them. There will be a lot of recurring themes, but varying weight or importance will be given to each one (if mentioned at all).

However, even with that being true, there are definitely some things that any designer should give thought to when coming up with a design:

❑ **Usability** This should probably be at the top of every designer's list. If the site is amazing looking and could have easily come right out of a top New York designer's art portfolio, that is cool. But if a user has no idea they have to press the broken toothpick depicted in the bottom corner of the collage to get to the Contact Us area of the Web site, designers have missed the point. More important, if that site is commercial, the owners may miss a sale (or a lot of sales). Usability has to be taken into consideration when planning the design of a site. This will include navigation, spatial layout, information provided, and general user experience (for example, if the user is presented with a shocking strobe-light effect when they visit the site, they may never come back). A Web site is built for its user base and failing to cater to the people that use the site can have tragic consequences for the longevity of the site.

❑ **Aesthetics** Thought should be given to the colors that will be used, how they play into the general scheme of the site and its principles, and how they will shape the experience of the user. This is different from usability in that usability means that the site visitor can use the site effectively, whereas aesthetics is a question of how much the user enjoys the feeling of the site. To extend the preceding example, if the users are easily able to find the "Contact Us" button because it is logically placed and easily identified, they might just use it to tell you that they hate your site if the colors, images, and font choices are giving them headaches. (Of course, more likely you will simply lose them as future visitors and never have a clue how much your organization is suffering from these aesthetic choices.) While not as important as usability, aesthetics should never be undervalued.

❑ **Accessibility** This is one of those terms that people have trouble defining. Some people might refer to it as 508 design (after Section 508 of the Disabilities Act). Some might associate it with text readers and other tools to assist the visually impaired. But that isn't really what accessibility means (although this is certainly part of it). Accessibility means, in its simplest form, making sites that everyone gets equal value from. This takes a lot of different forms. Take, for example, a site that broadcasts its daily specials using Flash software. A text reader will read the rendered code of a Web site to the user accessing the site. When it gets to the site's daily advertised specials in Flash, the reader will likely announce something like "embedded object found" and then move on (if they acknowledge it at all). So these patrons will have no idea that ear muffs are buy-one-get-one-free today and may decide to brave the frozen tundra without them. And you just lost a sale. In a similar situation, imagine an e-training site that offers online training on various business topics. But what if those classes were all done in streaming media where some narrator or even instructor is recorded going over subjects like sexual harassment or civil rights issues. How effective would that be to a person who cannot hear? If there is no consideration for such people (and there are plenty of them), the site will suffer for it. These ideas should be fundamental to any designer in today's Internet.

> *Before you dismiss vision- and hearing-based accessibility issues, consider this: According to the U.S. Bureau of the Census statistics for 1999, there are more than 1.5 million visually impaired computer users. Also, according to a 2005 report by Ross E. Mitchell in the* Journal of Deaf Studies and Deaf Education *from Oxford University, nearly 10 million people in the U.S. are hard of hearing and nearly 1 million are functionally deaf. And those numbers only reflect potential U.S. visitors to your site; they don't account for all of the other visitors from Canada, Britain, Germany, and the rest of the world.*

❑ **Branding** This can mean different things to different people, especially on the Web. Many corporations today have specific branding requirements. This often means that Web media can only use a designated logo at specific dimensions and must be separated from all other elements by a specific number of pixels. It could mean that the entire color scheme is mandated by the branding requirements of the company or public entity. It could even mean font sizes and colors. When getting into site design, it is imperative that designers understand the branding requirements of the people paying you to make the design and then adhere to them.

With MOSS 2007 (and portals in general), there is at least one other consideration: Don't look like every other instance of this portal. If visitors come to your site and think, "I've seen this look somewhere before — make that lots of places before," that is not a good thing. Unfortunately, many user groups fall into this exact trap. If you go to one user group site, it will often look like every other user group site, with the exception of the content, colors, and logo. They all take the same portal and just choose one of the out-of-the-box templates and slap their logo at the top and call it a day.

Here is an interesting case study: Look at Figures 1-1 and 1-2.

If this book were in color, you might more easily distinguish the two screenshots from each other. However, in the grayscale world of the printed manuscript, this will be much harder to see. It's almost as if one design is simply the other one with a filter on top of it that affects the hue of colors. If you are curious, Figure 1-1 is "Default Theme" and Figure 1-2 is "Granite."

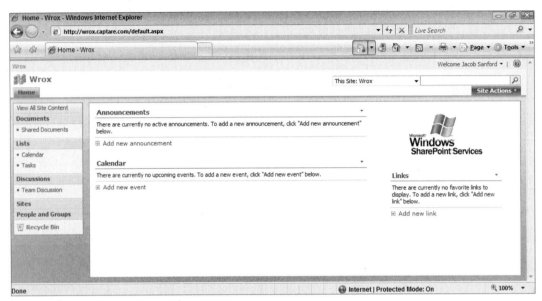

Figure 1-1

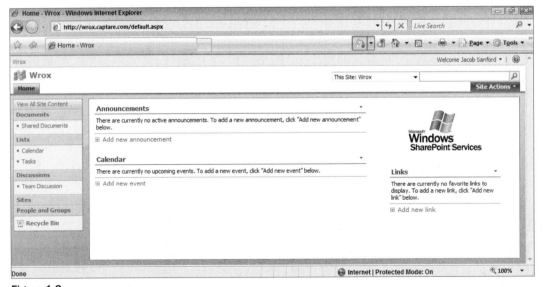

Figure 1-2

But this is the point: Do you want people to look at your site and see the business as bland, predictable, and unimaginative, or do you want them to see the business as interesting, dynamic, and unique?

Now, to contrast against these designs, consider Figure 1-3, which is the Web site for The Kroger Company (www.kroger.com).

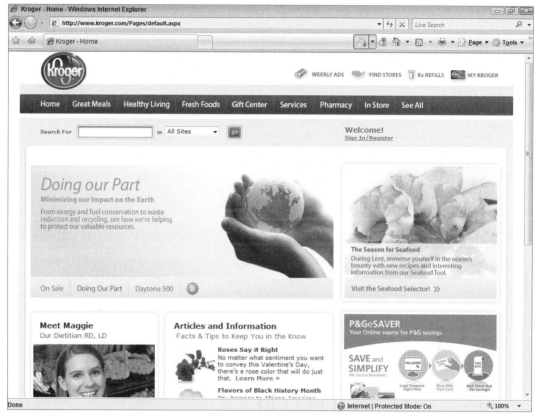

Figure 1-3

Does that look like a SharePoint site? Even in grayscale, would you think that this site is one designed in MOSS 2007? Well, it is.

And take a look at Figure 1-4, the Web site for Migros (www.migros.ch).

Again, even in the context of black and white images in the print of this book, this site looks distinctly different from anything out of the box with SharePoint.

Finally, take a look at Figure 1-5, the Web site for SendTec. (www.sendtec.com).

Figure 1-4

This example may be the most unlike any SharePoint design you have seen. But it was, in fact, designed in SharePoint. If you don't believe it, view the source of the rendered page and you will see the following:

```
<meta name="GENERATOR" content="Microsoft SharePoint" />
```

As with many things, it may be hard to define what good design is, even though you probably know it when you see it. And these examples show what good design can look like. In addition, the examples establish that designers are not and, more important, *should not* be confined to the templates that come with a standard MOSS 2007 installation.

Note, however, that these examples are provided to contrast the look and feel of the default templates available in MOSS 2007. Do they necessarily satisfy things such as usability and accessibility? Maybe or maybe not, but that is not the point. The point is that with some thought and planning, and maybe access to the right tools (and the right book), you can take the ordinary and make it extraordinary.

Figure 1-5

Why Should Designers Care?

The reasons that MOSS 2007 developers make the effort to put design at the forefront of their projects probably vary from developer to developer. But one universal truth is pride. Pride in the final product and how good it looks. Pride in the fact that something they created is so well received. Pride that they did a good job. But is pride enough? Fortunately, there are other real rewards to doing good design.

Maybe the biggest reason is that it often makes financial sense to do good design work. After all, when you are a consultant, you often get leads and maybe even sales based largely on your portfolio. If a potential client is looking through the sites you have developed and can see nothing inspiring or, even worse, different from the other 20 sites you have already shown them, they will not be knocking down the door to try to hire you. You may still get the sale, but the first impression may not be what you are hoping for. After all, if businesses are scouring the Web to find consultants and looking at their online portfolios, are they really going to know that for client ABC you created innovative event handlers to customize workflow procedures on the document library? That won't come through in a screenshot or even in a visit to the finished site. They would have to decide that they are still interested and then come talk to you to learn about the cool technology you were capable of using. But if you lose them in the first 10 seconds of looking through your portfolio, you won't get that chance.

Beyond that, though, what about referrals? Many deals today are made based on referrals or recommendations from clients. So what happens when you turn in this powerful site but the design looks like you didn't even try to deviate from the out-of-the-box templates? Would the client recommend you? Perhaps. But would you rather they say, "Well, these guys were pretty good. They did everything we asked them to do and were great people to work with?" Wouldn't it be better if they started off by saying, "You have to get these guys. They blew us away. Sure, they did everything we required from a business-requirements perspective. But have you seen our site? These guys are great?" Both scenarios might get you the call, but one would get you a much better starting point with these potential clients.

And, to look at the other side of the coin, there are potentially going to be more and more consequences to bad design. Sure, there are costs of users not buying what you are selling; that is the obvious consequence if your site is horrible and ineffective. What designers might not think of, though, is that there are other real costs. In February 2006, Target Corporation was probably shocked to find out that they were being sued because their Web site was not accessible. In an effort to dismiss the charges, they claimed that they met the requirements of law by making their brick-and-mortar retail stores accessible to all. However, in October 2007, the Federal court thought differently. The U.S. District Court for the Northern District of California certified the case as class action on behalf of blind Internet users throughout the country and determined that Target.com violated not only the Americans with Disabilities Act but also two California civil rights statutes. This resulted in a lot of time and money being spent by the company to deal with both the legal ramifications and customer satisfaction concerns. This is a headache that anyone doing business on the Web just doesn't need.

> *You can read the National Federation of the Blind's press release on the decision here:*
> `http://www.nfb.org/nfb/NewsBot.asp?MODE=VIEW&ID=221`.

It should be noted, too, that this is just one of the most recent legal battles forged publicly about Web sites and accessibility. Similar suits have come up in Europe. This is a global issue that needs to be acknowledged and addressed by designers. As the world continues to change, designers need to keep abreast of the serious design considerations that change with it.

Why Should Managers Care?

Perhaps intuitively, managers should care about good design for the same reasons that developers should. After all, it is important to them as well that they have strong portfolios, extremely satisfied customers, and no negative legal consequences to the products they deliver. They are in the same boat as their developers in this regard. In fact, it could be argued that these reasons are even more important to the manager than to the developer; if any of these things bring about negative consequences to the ongoing concerns of the business, the manager would be much closer to the shouting line than the developer (for better or worse).

But more important than these reasons is the consideration of the impact on the organization's employees and their professional growth and happiness. Plenty of developers have no interest in design and see it at best as a necessary evil. However, a growing number of developers really want to create good design.

While it is important to focus on deliverables, it is also important for managers to understand how good design reaches clients and to make sure that developers have the resources they need to make the site look good, function ethically, and provide value. While it is true that some, or maybe even many, developers don't want to get involved in design work, it is equally true that many do. By pursuing the discipline of design, they will become better employees who add tremendous value to the overall business.

Why Should Clients Care?

It is a safe bet to assume that clients have a primary reason to care about the design of their sites: the user experience. For many sites, this translates into actual dollars. For others, it might mean that they are getting their message out to the largest audience possible. However they quantify it, they should, and almost always do, care about the design of their sites. Sure, they care about the nuts and bolts that run the sites. But you can rest assured that they care about the way they look too.

And clients are getting better at quantifying this experience. Web metrics are becoming increasingly popular. People can fairly easily tell how many unique visitors access their sites. They can tell if they only go to the main page and then leave (indicating a bad experience) or if they stay for a while and surf the content available. If an analysis of the log files for the site shows that 90 percent of visitors access the main page for an average of only 2.3 seconds and then leave, something in the design is just not right. Whether that means that the content is such that nobody knows what the site is for or that the navigation is so confusing and poorly planned that nobody even knows how to get to another page is not as clear. What is clear, though, is that people found their sites and found them useless. Then they left.

In this example, the site is not performing whatever function it is supposed to (unless it is supposed to run people off, in which case it is working perfectly). If the client is selling something, potential buyers likely aren't even seeing what is available for sale, much less buying anything. And if the site is a public-information Web site preaching the gospel of good Web site design, it means nobody is listening to the message. This can be frustrating and can affect revenues severely (even public-awareness sites often sell advertisement space, which is affected by no-stays).

Increasingly more important will be the desire to stay out of court. For example, say the class-action plaintiffs in an accessibility lawsuit get awarded $10,000,000 (or more). Who has to pay that? The designer who designed the site? The manager who oversaw the designer's work? Probably not. After all, any independent consultant (or firm) will require the client to sign off before completing the project. So if the client used an outside firm to design their site, they likely signed off on its final design before releasing it to the world. And, if the client didn't even put in any business requirements to handle accessibility (or if their requirements were vague), they can't even say that they asked for accessible design but rather that the designers failed. And if the client used in-house resources to design the site, there really is not any gray area about who is responsible for the $10,000,000 penalty.

This example might be hypothetical, but it does reflect some of the very real concerns developing in the business world. Either sites will get better about accommodating all users or lawsuits will become more frequent. And going to court, win or lose, is not cheap. Even if you win the case, you are out the legal costs. It's better to worry about paying an extra $5,000 in the design budget than to worry about dealing with an exponentially more expensive lawsuit down the road.

Plus, clients care about their image. They want their sites to look better than the competition. They want to send links to their friends and colleagues and say, ''Look at our new site!'' Clients, maybe more than any other group, care about design. And, if for no other reason, so should you.

So Why Use SharePoint for Design?

A fair question to ask, especially after reading this chapter, is, "Why should I design with SharePoint?" This is a remarkably simple question with a less-than-simple answer.

First, SharePoint is designed to provide every functionality a portal may need out of the box: wikis, blogs, message boards, document libraries, version control, security, announcements, integration with Active Directory, and a laundry list of other features. This all comes with the initial installation and is fairly easily set up and controlled by administrators. This is a huge selling point.

Add to that the flexibility and ease of customizing the default installation, and you have a much more compelling reason to consider SharePoint as your portal platform. You can integrate custom .NET code into your applications (in code blocks or in code-behind files). You can import data connections through the Business Data Catalog (BDC) that allow your SharePoint lists and controls to integrate with outside data sources. You also can completely overhaul the way the site looks and feels using familiar .NET 2.0 controls (for instance, master pages). Add to this that you can create custom Web parts to do pretty much anything else you need to do. So, while the default installation is remarkable on its own, the power of what you can do with it when you want to step outside of the boundaries of the default can be awe-inspiring.

And don't forget the level of user interaction and control of the site once it is running. Users with no Web programming experience can, with a little training and guidance, create grids that report data from the system, generate and modify custom lists, and even control who has access to what on the site. Developers no longer need to do a lot of the day-to-day maintenance of the site. The users and site administrators can do the majority of it on their own, even if they have no idea what a code block in C# looks like and have no interest in finding out.

One thing that might give developers pause, though, especially in light of some of the examples in earlier sections of this chapter, is accessibility concerns. It is worth noting that, out of the box, SharePoint has some accessibility problems. This is a known issue. However, Microsoft and the community of developers are working together to try to solve this. One example is the efforts made by the development community to integrate the CSS Friendly Control Adapters into SharePoint sites to make many of the controls, such as the menu/navigation system, more accessible. (You can read more about these adapters in Chapter 13.) Maybe even more impressive is the October 2007 release of the Accessibility Kit for Microsoft Office SharePoint Server 2007 by HiSoftware (`http://aks.hisoftware.com`). (This, too, will be covered in greater depth in Chapter 13.) This kit was commissioned by Microsoft in an effort to better meet the accessibility needs of the Internet community regarding MOSS 2007. This is a huge step forward in the mindset of major software developers and is worth noting when getting into accessibility issues, especially when considering using MOSS 2007 as your platform.

Is MOSS 2007 the perfect platform for portal development on the Web? No, not really. There are a few limitations, such as the accessibility problem that, if not handled, will be an issue with out-of-the-box installations. And this is no small matter. However, there is a concerted effort to remedy this major limitation, and as the community of developers grows, more and more solutions will present themselves. The developers already out there in the field working in MOSS 2007 are probably some of the more passionate you will run into in the Web application development arena, and most of them are happy to share their experience and suggestions. So, whatever limitations there might be could probably just as easily be called "opportunities" or "challenges." With the power under the hood of SharePoint, figuring out how to get around these challenges is not only achievable; you might just have fun doing it (and you might even make a few friends along the way).

Summary

At this point, you have gained an appreciation of some of the reasons why good design should be a serious part of the planning of any Web project (SharePoint or otherwise). Maybe you have been exposed to some things you haven't considered before. Or maybe you have just received confirmation on some of the things you already believe. Either way, you should have a new (or renewed) appreciation of the reason to follow good design principles.

Now that the *why* is out of the way, the rest of this book will focus more on the *how*. You will get a better understanding of what good Web design means, how to use tools such as Photoshop and SharePoint Designer for your design needs, and how to use all of the out-of-the-box functionality of SharePoint to make it look anything but.

With that, it's time to begin. Good luck and good coding.

2

Web Design 101

Any chapter titled "Web Design 101" is bound to be passed over for more exciting topics. A broad introduction to Web site design isn't nearly as interesting as customizing a search results page or creating publishing sites, is it? Bear with me, though. SharePoint has its own rules, tools, and pitfalls that can make design easy or maddening.

Much of this chapter should be common sense. The key ideas covered here are pretty straightforward: Set limits, involve your users, make things easy to find, and make pages that give users what they need in as attractive a manner as possible. The problem is that common sense often gets plowed under in the name of speed and efficiency, or it gets lost in feature creep. And if you've ever had a Web browser open for more than 5 minutes, you can probably attest to the fact that common sense is not all that common.

Development and design techniques have changed considerably from the early days of the Web. In the murky backwaters of the Internet, site design required arcane knowledge. In-depth understanding of technologies like HTML, CSS, and JavaScript were needed just to make pages function, let alone look professional. This meant that the majority of sites were created by people with a bent for the technical rather than an eye for design.

Times have changed. Moreover, the technology that drives Web sites has changed. The next time you crack open the Internet Information Services console (see Figure 2-1), take a look at the files that make up your SharePoint site. The folder that would normally house all of the files that constitute your site is surprisingly sparse. There's no "there" there. SharePoint sites are not hand-built .NET applications, ASP sites, or a from-scratch set of HTML pages. Everything a user sees on your SharePoint site is created "on the fly," rendered in real time by the SharePoint engine from a small handful of ASPX files, XML files, configuration settings, and rows from a database.

This is a source of frustration to many developers. Since this is very likely the first time you have encountered anything like this, many of the tools and techniques that you've honed over the years doing traditional Web page development no longer apply. In far too many cases, you'll be limited to SharePoint Designer or a text editor to implement a new design.

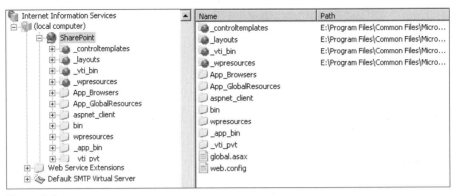

Figure 2-1

The payoff for these limitations is pretty significant; SharePoint provides a framework that contains most of the tools needed for the heavy lifting on a Web site: display, workflow, security, content management, and data management. These functions are already baked in. It makes it easy to rapidly develop sites with robust functionality through a simple Web interface. You don't have to concern yourself with building document storage, complex content management tools, or implementing a page-by-page security scheme. But, that also means relearning new technologies to do things that most coders already know how to do.

Goal-Oriented Design

The idea of a table or a chair is pretty easy to define, and as such is fairly easy to design. If you ask someone to jot down a plan to build those things, you have a pretty good idea what you're going to get. A portal, on the other hand, is another matter entirely.

Microsoft and others have done an excellent job marketing portals to corporate America, but there is a great debate as to how to define what "portal" means. The market-speak for portals sounds great. After all, who doesn't want to connect people, processes, and information using next-generation tools while empowering users by harnessing business intelligence? The problem often lies in making this concept into any sort of reality. Is your intranet already a portal? Is it a portal in the same way Yahoo! is a portal, or is it more like a document management system that can act as a portal? Do you have an external facing Web site that clients use as a portal? Is your Internet site part of an overall portal system? There are a lot of grey areas.

Before you can begin with page layouts or decide which Web Parts to use, take a step back. The goal of a portal is to help make things more organized, to make the lives of users simpler and more efficient. Many companies make the mistake of installing SharePoint and allowing it to grow rampantly, without a plan. In the end, this can make things far more complicated than they were to begin with.

Let's simplify things then. For the sake of argument, let's make up a working definition: A portal is a Web-based application that provides users with access to the stuff they need.

So, the real question is this: What is your company going to *do* with a portal? What *stuff* do they need? Is it merely a replacement for a few mapped network drives, or is it going to be used as a product development lifecycle tracking system? Is it part of a document management system, or are you just trying to give your office a way to find key performance indicators from other business systems? The most important step in any design process is to define the goals that your portal will attempt to achieve. Get your goals firmly in place and carve them in stone. This defines the scope of your project. Once you have the finish line clearly defined, they you can fill in the details.

Driving Adoption

Wait. Driving adoption? Isn't that what you do after you've got a portal for users to adopt? That's what usually happens, and by then, it's too late.

In a previous life, I did a systems upgrade project for a client, installing Windows XP on all desktop computers and upgrading existing Office applications. The job was fairly easy and straightforward. The other techs and I made things faster, better, and prettier.

This is the best part of the IT world. Once in a great while, IT people are regarded as conquering heroes by nearly everyone. However (and there's always a *however*), everyone warned me about Marge, one of the heads of the accounting department. She had been in charge of expenses longer than anyone had been with the company. She probably came with the building. She is the most frustrating part of the IT world.

Marge had no love or patience for computers or anyone in IT. She had been involved in the company's migration from card readers to tape drives, from letters to faxes to email. I was there to change everything again, for which I was evil incarnate. She thought my job was to screw up her life.

She complained about the new OS, she complained about the icons. She gave me the evil eye when I set up Outlook, and she told me that she didn't trust email. As I put shortcuts on her desktop, she told me that the database applications used the wrong calculations. She complained that no one ever asked her before changing everything. This went on for over an hour.

Every company has a "Marge in Accounting." Unfortunately, your job is to make her happy (or, at the least, less unhappy). And trust me, if you can get your Marge to adopt the changes that you're about to throw at her, the rest of the job is a walk in the park. Marge is a worst-case scenario. I can't really blame her for being mad at the all new stuff that was thrown at her. She was just trying to do her job, and IT was methodically making things more complicated without asking if it would actually help her. And she had no say in any of the decisions that directly affected her job.

You're about to be the IT person in that scenario and you're going to have to get Marge and the rest of your organization to adopt your new portal. What can you do to improve this process? Simple: Ask them to help.

The key to driving user adoption is to get users involved in the design process from the very beginning. There are no better experts at your company that the people who actually do the work. Once you have a set of goals for your portal, the next step should be to involve these users.

This process can be challenging. As with Marge, modern users are often jaded by the constant changes in IT. You're just another snake oil salesman that promises to make the "Bad Stuff" go away with your really great "New Stuff." At this point in the process, your job is less about interfacing with a Web site and more about fostering relationships with people. There's a natural progression to these relationships that can benefit you and the people who'll use your SharePoint sites. This process can be a lot like dating. In fact, the sequence of emotions is very similar:

Note	New SharePoint User	New Boy/Girlfriend
Uncertain	Hey, this seems shiny and new, but it's probably another junk piece of software that someone in IT is trying to force on me.	Hey, this person seems nice and attractive, but they're probably just another whackjob like the last three people I dated.
Excited	HOLY COW! Did you see that? I can move stuff around on my Web page! This is the greatest thing ever!	HOLY COW! This is the person of my dreams! Perfect in every possible way!
Inspired	Wouldn't it be great if I could get this key performance indicator to automatically tie in with these three other business systems?	Wouldn't it great if we, you know, moved in together?
Disappointed	What do you mean I can't have a list view that automatically reads people's minds? I NEED THAT.	What do mean you want to get rid of my collection of bobble head dolls? I NEED THAT.
Acceptance	Well, maybe it can't read minds, but I suppose that this is still leaps and bounds better than the old way we did things.	Well, they may have their flaws, but I suppose that this is still leaps and bounds better than those last three whackjobs I dated.

Painful as it can be, involving users early in the design process accomplishes two of the most difficult tasks in design:

1. It gives the people who know the business a chance to share their knowledge. A well-designed, well-thought-out solution will be adopted with less resistance than one that ignores what every other user knows. It is better to get this information now than after you're done.

2. It is a chance to internally market the portal. When the day comes to roll out your great new portal, the users who helped will be more likely to support adoption of a new way of doing business.

Storyboarding

Okay. You've gotten the best and brightest of your company to sit down with you. You've plied them with coffee and baked goods. What's the next step? Drawing pictures, of course.

A picture, as it is said, is worth a thousand words. That goes double with SharePoint design. Odds are, the people you're mining for information have never seen SharePoint before. Storyboarding is a process where you create a representation of what users are going to see. By working with users to create interfaces, you get more bang for your buck: Users can give immediate feedback on what they like and what they don't like. Time spent at a whiteboard is cheap compared to time spent creating anything on a screen.

But a quick word of warning: SharePoint is not all things to all people, and this may be a cause of contention. As someone who designs portals for a living, I constantly bump my head into the limitations of the SharePoint architecture. It is extremely malleable. It can be extended, stretched, and tweaked. But it is not and will not be all things to all people.

The line is often the difference between design and development. SharePoint often gives the illusion that everything should be easy, that a few clicks on a Web page will accomplish something that ends up taking weeks of staring at Visual Studio to accomplish. One of the most difficult things about SharePoint design is realizing when that line is crossed.

For example, assume for a moment that you need to allow users to publish documents from a team site to a document repository. Spending time with the team in question will help you design a document library that meets their needs. They want custom columns for "Client Name" and "Purchase Date"? No problem. They want to be able to use a drop-down menu that allows their users to send the document to a central document repository? Piece of cake. They want a custom graphic that appears next to each document to tell them the approval status of a published document? Hold it right there. Yes, it's possible to develop just such a display using custom coding tools such as list event handlers, but realizing that this is a non-trivial task will help keep your project on schedule.

The more users, designers, and management learn to use and embrace SharePoint's innate tools and functionality, the easier it's going to be to build your site. And unfortunately, the further you stray from SharePoint's standard functionality, the more work it's going to mean for you. In terms of storyboard creation, your job is to keep user's requests in the realm of the real.

Portal Design

One of the great strengths of SharePoint is that it's very easy for users to create sites and customize the look and feel of content. One of the great dangers of SharePoint is that it's very easy for users to create sites and customize the look and feel of content.

SharePoint's biggest challenge is often controlling growth. With all that "enabling" and "empowering" you'll be doing, it's often difficult to maintain a firm grasp on where your portal is going. An uncontrolled portal will quickly descend into a chaotic mess where no one can find anything. A well designed portal structure, on the other hand, will make your job easier. Security is easier to control. Search is easier to define. Growth is easier to manage. Users can access information easily. It's like an IT version of nirvana.

The goal of portal design is simple: Give your users a structure where they can quickly and efficiently find and use the information that they need. But what is the best way to create a framework for information and still allow for growth?

Take a step back a moment and return to some of the fundamental reasons you're implementing a portal. Most companies use SharePoint for:

❑   Giving users a framework to share and use information

❑   Making it easier to find that information

❑   Controlling access to critical information

To achieve these goals and to maintain some sort of order, a SharePoint portal should have a pre-defined growth plan. This plan should define its topology, its "shape." Several basic topologies are commonly used, but it's up to you to decide which is best for your company.

If you're reading this book, you probably already have a portal in place. Things like design and branding often come in last as companies learn to embrace SharePoint. But again, bear with me. If you already have a portal, understanding portal topologies can help you plan for future growth, and perhaps allow you to reorganize your site collection so that users can get the information that they need faster and more efficiently.

Things to Consider

Before you get into any examples, look at some of the things that you should consider when deciding how you will construct your portal.

Ease of Use

This is, by far, the most important consideration when deciding site layout. One of the best ways to help users access the knowledge your portal contains is to organize it in a pattern that they already know. The portal should be a paradigm for how people think about information in your company.

Your already have this in one form or another. It could be a set of departments or a business process. It could be the words that people in your company use to describe your business. More than likely, it will be a combination of one or more of these.

Security

SharePoint allows for very complex security scenarios. Rights can be granted on a global level, a site level, a list level, or an item level. Recognize that the more granular the level of security, the more administrative overhead you or your portal management team will incur. In general, it's best to group information with similar security rights. For instance, if your company intends to store sensitive materials such as patent information, it would be far easier to place all the lists, document libraries, and calendars surrounding patents together on a single site.

External access to information can also drive topology decisions. If you plan to grant access to external users such as vendors or clients, you need to decide how they can access the information that they need without interrupting business processes or violating your company's security policies.

Search

Yet another reason people implement SharePoint is for its powerful search capabilities. There is a common misconception that search can make up for poor portal design. After all, who cares if the HR site is in a logical place for certain documents when I can just pull up a vacation request form using search results? The problem with this scenario is that search ignores the context of the information. Most data is not isolated. A document like a vacation request form may have metadata that is not returned with search results or may only be useful if I have access to the company's vacation calendar. Giving information a clear place to reside makes it easier to find and allows users to leverage it more effectively. Information wants a good home.

Another consideration with search is the proper implementation of search scopes. A scope allows users to search a specific subset of the data in your portal. This subset can be defined in two ways:

1. Defining one or more sites that compose a "branch" of a portal's hierarchy.
2. Defining a specific kind of data — a content type or property.

The goal of setting up search scopes is to segment your portal's information into chunks for easier access. A proper portal design should allow for that by segregating data into logical chunks so that each scope can be easily defined. Have a lot of product literature? Keep it in the same section of your portal, set up a scope, and users can find the right document without muddling through all the documents from HR and Accounting.

Content type and property search scopes are meant to be topology-independent. However, search results are dependent on the security of where the information lives, so a properly planned portal design can benefit these types of search scopes as well. For more on search scopes, see Chapter 12.

Growth

One of the worst mistakes you can make when defining a portal topology is ignoring growth. The minute you decide that 10 sites is all your company needs, you'll need 11. The key with planned growth is to have room to grow built in at each level of the hierarchy.

Portal Topologies

Now that you've explored a few of the areas that will influence the shape of your portal, it's time to consider topology. Note that in the topological descriptions shown below, several types of sites are not shown. Search Centers and Document Repositories, for instance, are meant to aggregate data from other parts of the portal, and therefore live "outside" of the primary portal topology.

Business-Based Model

This is probably the most commonly used topology. Creating a portal to match your business's departmental structure is a no-brainer. In Figure 2-2, you can see a top-level home site that allows access to a set of departmental sites, each of which allows access to sub-departments and committees.

This plan allows for an easy implementation of security. If your company uses Active Directory, you probably already have these groups defined. Departmental separations also often mimic the security needs of a business. For instance, HR users may have privileges to view payroll information, while IT and Marketing people do not.

The downside of this topology is that it often ignores how your company does business. In a business-based topology, departments are completely segregated. The only place that companies like these exist is in business school text books. Accomplishing real work takes people from every area of your company working together. For instance, putting a new product on a shelf often involves a mish-mash of personnel from various departments: people from Research & Development, new hardware from IT, a new marketing campaign, and so on. Setting up a portal using business-based topology can involve additional administrative overhead, and information on a single project can end up scattered over the portal.

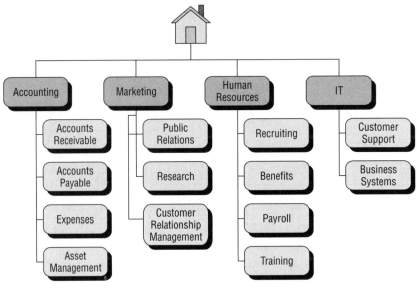

Figure 2-2

Here are the pros and cons of using the business-based topology:

Pros:

❏   Users are already aware of the structure.

❏   Security and Search are easy to implement.

Cons:

❏   It may not reflect the way your company actually does business.

Process-Based Model

A business-based model makes sense in several places: org charts, Active Directory, and in the heads of a corporate board. Instead of a business-based topology, you may need a topology that reflects the way your company does business.

Let's take another look at the example given in the previous section. The information that a company accrues is all about a business process — taking a product from conception to a shelf. Rather than setting up the elaborate custom code and processes needed to move a mass of documents data from a product development branch of a portal to a marketing branch each time a product is ready to be advertised, it makes much more sense to keep the data in one place — perhaps a site that can be used to house everything there is to know about that product. Each site can, in turn, have its own document libraries, workflow, and security based on the needs of the business process.

In most cases, companies don't make a single product, but a host of items across several product lines. This is not a problem for SharePoint — just add sites as needed.

In the example shown in Figure 2-3, the portal topology is defined by a collection of business processes. It's a simplified portal for a company that develops hair care products. In this case, the primary goal of the portal is not to house a disparate collection of company-wide data but to drive a business process. Each site can house the information that is needed on a specific product, including design specifications, marketing materials, sales forecasts, you name it. Every bit of information that you'd need to know on any product has a special place to call home.

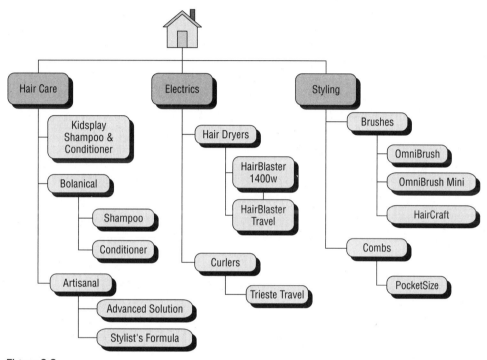

Figure 2-3

The information makes more sense for a process-driven business culture. One of the shortcomings of previous versions of SharePoint was that it was difficult to share information between sites. MOSS and WSS 3.0, however, make data aggregation easier with new technologies such as the Content Query Web Part and the Data View Web Part, both of which allow data to be aggregated for display in a single location. In the example shown, these tools would allow for users to view information across a product line without the need to manually dig though various sites.

This topology can also simplify administration. Security can be implemented by creating teams of users from across various departments. Search can benefit as well, as information is segregated into the same logical "chunks" that users are already used to. Need to set up a scope that identifies a specific product line? Not a problem.

As you can see, this changes what the concept of a portal can be. With the addition of some simple workflow, the portal can go from a centralized repository of departmental information to a full-blown tracking application. Of course, this methodology could be used for nearly any business process, from product management to case management to streamlining a sales pipeline.

Here are the pros and cons of using the process-based topology:

Pros:

- ❏ Can closely match the ways your company manages processes.

- ❏ Gives each process a place to call home — a centralized resource location for all information pertaining to a single item.

- ❏ Has excellent ability for growth. When another business process starts, just add a site at the appropriate place in your site collection. Users will already know where to look for it.

Cons:

- ❏ Security and Search can be more complicated to administer. For instance, in the example given above, consider the headaches that could occur if users could only be granted permission to access a site on an item-by-item basis, and that some companies produce *thousands* of items.

Taxonomy-Based Model

On its surface, this can look similar to a business-based topology. After all, businesses classify departments by what they do. But look a little deeper, and taxonomy-based topology starts to reveal itself.

Taxonomy, by its definition, is all about classification. This can be a little abstract, but you will probably find that you use this technique to store information already. For instance, my desk has several piles of paper, each with its own classification. Receipts are in one pile, mail is in another, and notes are in yet another. It's not practical for me to separate these items by who is going to use them (a business-based topology) or what I'm going to do with them (a process-based topology). But I can find what I need because I understand the classification of the item I'm looking for.

Your business already has its own taxonomy, whether you realize it or not. Taxonomy is about the way people describe what they do. You'll probably find that your company has its own language, a way of describing what it does. In the example shown below (Figure 2-4), the portal in question groups business processes and departmental needs together, because that is how the users think and talk about their business. Rather than discussing inventory, vendor supply chains, and factories as completely separate entities, the entire lot is placed together to address the manufacturing needs of the company as a whole.

By properly defining how your data should be defined, you can give users an extremely intuitive way to find data.

Here are the pros and cons of using the taxonomy-based topology:

Pros:

- ❏ It can be used to enforce a classification of information. This can have distinct benefits. For instance, users can be certain that if a document is in a site called "Approved Vendor Contracts," it is indeed an approved vendor contract.

- ❏ Users can intuitively find information.

- ❏ This topology is very easy to extend. Because the shape of the portal is based on abstract ideas, there's no limit to how or where the portal can grow.

Cons:

❑ It can be difficult to get everyone to agree on taxonomic terms. For instance, users could have widely divergent ideas of where a document should reside, leading to information on similar topics being scattered about the portal.

❑ It can be difficult to implement search and security. Though it may be possible to group restricted items together, this may not always be practical. For instance, suppose that your company classifies a certain set of documents as "contracts." If your business rules for contracts dictate that some contracts should only be viewed by management, while others are available to the general populace, you'll have to implement item-level procedures to ensure that only the right people have access to each document. Yes, this can be done, but no, it's not very efficient (or fun).

❑ To maintain the proper classification, a small number of users must be in charge of the classification procedure.

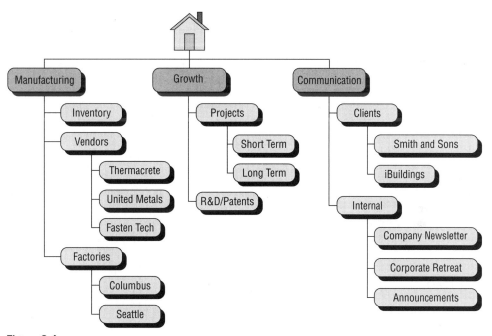

Figure 2-4

Publishing Portal

This may not exactly be a topology per se, but it does deserve some attention here. More companies are embracing SharePoint as an intranet solution. It's becoming obvious that all the tools that make SharePoint valuable internally can also be leveraged to make sure that information flows from the experts — your users — to the outside world of people who visit your Internet site.

The goal of your portal may not be to function as an intranet or extranet site, but as your company's primary presence on the Internet. Microsoft Office SharePoint Server 2007's new publishing features make this an ideal tool to facilitate the creation, approval, and publication of outward facing information.

Here are the pros and cons of using the publishing portal-based "topology":

Pros:

❑   Allows users to publish and approve information on an external facing site.

Cons:

❑   Because the site is open to the public, security and access need to be considered very carefully.

❑   Microsoft Office SharePoint Server 2007 for Internet open licensing can be costly.

Hybrid Portals

It's unlikely that any particular topology will work best for your company. More often than not, a hybrid of one or more of these ideas will be developed.

By combining strategies from multiple topologies, you can take the best from each. A business based topology can easily contain a group of sites that support a business process. For instance, a research and development site can lead to a group of sites for new product development.

There are downsides to this approach. If the goal of a portal's topology is to give users a well-defined paradigm that they intuitively understand, deviating from that plan could cause confusion. Be prepared to provide additional training to support this. If users in Accounting are expected to leave their accounting site to provide forecasting information in another branch of the portal, they'll need to know how and where this data should live.

To that end, security can be a little more complicated to configure. Again, if the security of a portal is based on the fact that users have access to a business process or a departmental site, deviating from that plan requires additional administrative overhead. In most cases, you'll have to implement active directory or SharePoint security groups on a site-by-site basis and continue to maintain these for the life of the portal.

There are real benefits to this plan, however, especially when your portal's needs are more complex. Many companies are extending their portals to reach outside their intranets. In the past, when a user wanted to publish an article or release information to an outside client via the Web, they'd deliver the document or other information to the Web master so that the Internet site could be updated. SharePoint can streamline that process while ensuring that information is provided in a secure manner.

In Figure 2-5, you can see that the company that uses this installation of SharePoint has divided their portal into two separate sections — an inward-facing intranet based on a business model and an outward facing extranet portal that is used as a corporate presence site and a portal for vendors to access key information. Information can flow between the two sections through manual or automated processes, eliminating the need for a Web master as a middleman. This can also ensure that external users are kept up-to-date with the latest information.

Here are the pros and cons of using a hybrid topology:

Pros:

❑   Can take advantage of the best of each topology.

Cons:

❑   Because the rules that define where information lives can differ from site to site, this plan may make information more difficult to find.

❑   Security can be more difficult to configure and maintain.

❑   Search can be difficult to set up, as information can reside in more than one site collection.

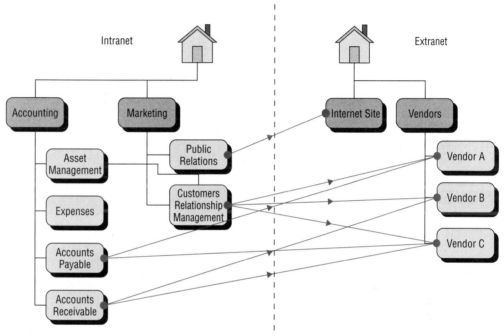

Figure 2-5

Mini Portals

More and more companies are starting out with small implementations of SharePoint. There are numerous reasons for this. In some cases, companies are implementing dashboard sites that leverage SharePoint's technologies to aggregate important data quickly, without a lot of development time. For instance, a portal may display data from an SQL-based inventory management system using a Business Data Connector or give users real time updates using key performance indicator Web Parts. This also allows site administrators to quickly update the display of this data using a Web-based interface rather than having to crack open Visual Studio or another development tool.

The initial cost for a SharePoint license may seem steep for such things, but is still probably less than hiring a developer to create custom interfaces.

Another case for mini portals is that they allow for the rapid development of Web sites for key business processes. SharePoint lists are great for quickly implementing data storage and some light reporting. Calendars and announcement lists are a great way to give visibility to key projects.

Here are the pros and cons of using the mini portal-based topology:

Pros:

❑   Allows for the fast delivery of key information.

❑   Is easy to maintain.

❑   Is a great way to introduce your company to SharePoint without involving the entire organization.

Cons:

❑   Can be difficult to build on if the company decides to expand the portal's functionality.

Web Page Design

Now that you have a plan for where information will live, the next step should be to get your plan off your white board and onto a Web site.

If you search for "Web design" on the Internet, page design is what people are talking about. There are thousands of Web sites that detail good design practices for general use sites, and it is certainly worth your time to peruse as many as you can. Most of the information you'll find refers to general-use Internet pages and the complexities of code that are required to create them.

SharePoint sites, on the other hand, have a preset collection of building blocks that can be used to craft professional looking sites more quickly and efficiently. There is no need to build that style sheet from scratch or hand code navigation pieces. Out of the box, SharePoint's got you covered.

Some people might look on this as limiting, but I see it as liberating. SharePoint allows for rapid application development, letting you skip the dirty parts of page crafting and begin putting together sites immediately. More in-depth changes can take more time but still far less time than a from-scratch solution takes.

That being said, there are still some basic rules to help your users get the most out of each page on your portal. The suggestions in the following sections should get you started in created a more useable, more attractive portal.

A Grain of Salt

Sure, you can spend thousands on licensing and design work to create a static site that will stay exactly the way you build it, but that's probably not why you're using SharePoint. When you have a moment, check out the language on Microsoft's SharePoint site (`http://www.microsoft.com/sharepoint/default.mspx`). It's all about "empowering knowledge workers" and "enabling communities." What exactly does this mean? It means that users can control content on the Web sites: lists, documents, calendars, press releases, you name it.

This can be frustrating for some designers used to maintaining tight control over the sites they've created. Since the early days of Web design, developers and designers have owned the look and feel of a site.

For more than a decade, these people were often given the hokey title of "Web master" as they alone controlled what went where and why.

One of SharePoint's great strengths is its capacity for user driven design. Site owners can move items around to best meet their needs. They can add and remove lists, calendars, and other content when they feel their site needs to grow. Although MOSS and WSS allow for a fairly granular control over the rights each site user and administrator are granted, there needs to be a balance. Each right you grant to a user is one that you, as a designer, are giving away. The goal of SharePoint is to put control into the hands of the people who have end-of-line business knowledge. Moreover, they will be able to do this without bothering you to update content or make simple changes.

So, what follows are a few fundamental rules for page layout. Realize that in some cases, the best you can do is to give users a solid framework and hope for the best.

Creating a Site Template

Before you start slapping together your Web pages, they'll need someplace to live. SharePoint has the ability to make exact copies of a site through the use of site templates. This is an excellent means to get the design exactly right once and then propagate the site to flesh out your portal topology. Creating a site template gives you a few other benefits as well:

❑ Site templates allow for a standardized site design. As mentioned before, keeping a uniform interface throughout your portal makes it easier for users to quickly adapt to a new SharePoint environment. Creating sites from a base template ensures that your future sites will look, feel, and act the same.

❑ They allow for fast implementation of complex items. Keep in mind that document libraries and lists maintain any customizations you make. This means that things like custom workflows or template documents are carried to the new site without any additional effort. If necessary, you can even retain fully populated lists and document libraries as part of the template, but keep in mind that there is a 10 megabyte limit on the size of a site template.

Identifying a Target Resolution

Designing a Web page is much the same as painting a picture: You have to know your canvas. In Web design, this means determining an optimum resolution at which your pages will be displayed. Luckily, as screen size and video technology have progressed throughout the last few years, average screen resolution has increased greatly.

For a moment, let's assume that you've selected a target resolution of 1024 × 768 pixels, which is a fairly common resolution these days. With luck, your page will look something like Figure 2-6.

More screen real estate makes things considerably easier for Web page designers. Unfortunately, you have less space to place information than you think.

First, forget about making users scroll sideways to access key information. Most scroll mice and touch pads only allow for up and down tracking. Anything past the right side of the screen is unlikely to be seen by the majority of users.

The goal of a Web page is to display unique page content. As beautiful as your navigation and title bars appear on the page, they won't keep users coming back to your site. So, for the moment, let's think about content.

Figure 2-6

That still leaves you with 1024 pixels to play with, right? Wrong — take away 10 pixels for the browser's scroll bar and another 10 pixels on each side of the screen for margins. Take away another 165 for the SharePoint Quick Links menu down the left side of your page, and you're down to 829 pixels. Take away another 80–100 pixels for padding between Web Parts and any additional content, and you're down to around 740 pixels. You've lost over a quarter of your horizontal canvas to SharePoint, and you don't even have any content on your page.

Vertical resolution leaves you with even less space. Over 140 pixels are non-negotiable, given up to the browser controls — the address bar and button bars. This number goes up if users have additional toolbars such as Google or Yahoo search bars. Then lose 25 pixels for a global links bar (users have to have access to their My Site and My Links, right?), another 35–50 for your company's logo, and another 20 for SharePoint's tab navigation feature. Add 20 for margins and another 20 for a breadcrumb Web Part. Tack on another 80 for padding, and you've lost almost half of your 768 pixels of vertical space.

Web Page Elements	Horizontal	Vertical
Starting Screen Resolution	1024	768
Web Browser	− 10	− 140
Margins	− 20	− 20
Quick Links Navigation	− 165	
Site Navigation (global links and tab controls)	− 0	− 45

Web Page Elements	Horizontal	Vertical
Breadcrumbs	— 0	— 20
Internal Page Padding	— 80	— 80
Corporate Logo	— 0	— 50
Remaining Space	**759**	**413**

So, all told, your 1024 × 768 resolution yields 759 × 413 pixels. That means that more than 60 percent of a user's screen is gone before you even start putting content on a page, and that's the *best*-case scenario.

Yes, you can remove some of these items, but that will also remove the functionality that the items provide to users, which is functionality that you will probably have to provide in some other way.

Now that it's been established that you have a postage-stamp-sized plot in which you can grow your intranet, the goal will be to make the most out of what you have. The following sections will explain how.

Keeping It Clean and Simple

SharePoint makes it easy to put things on a page, regardless of whether it is the new task list, the key performance indicators, or the handy list of contacts. One of the greatest temptations that designers face is to show everything to their users at once. Needless to say, this can overwhelm even the most data-hungry user. (See Figure 2-7).

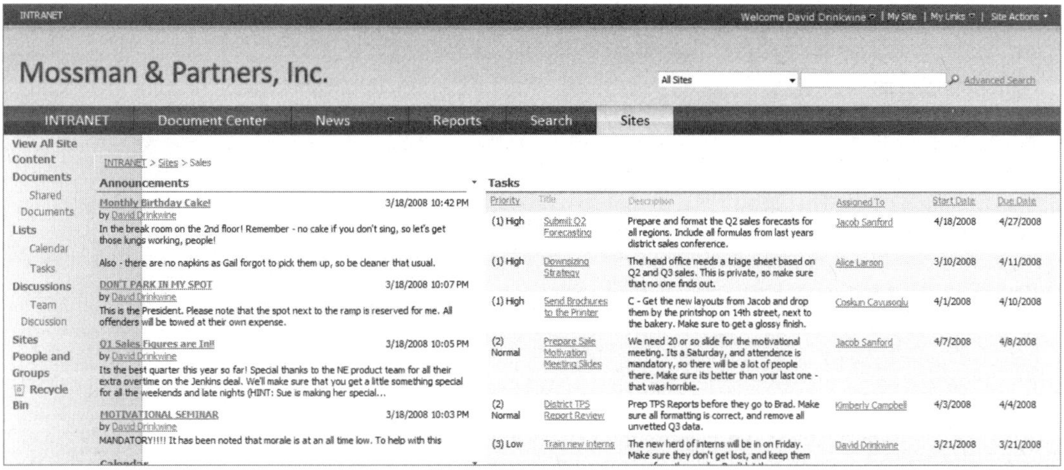

Figure 2-7

As you can see in Figure 2-7, too much information is not only unattractive but difficult to use. The page uses the same navigation and layout as Figure 2-6, but the amount of data that's packed on the page doesn't help users be more efficient; it just makes them more confused.

Try to limit the information that you place on the page. A few tips include:

❑ It's been established that there's not much free space on a page, but blank space is okay. Really it is. Some designers seem to have an itch to fill every square inch of a user's screen with data. Isn't that what portals are for? Easy access to everything? Well, yes, but not all at once. A good rule of thumb is that every idea that you're trying to get across deserves its own page. SharePoint makes it easy to add pages, format data, and extend navigation. Take advantage of these tools.

❑ Allow users to drill down into list items rather than displaying each item's full text. Announcement lists are excellent candidates for this. Users often enter lengthy descriptions, but a headline will suffice to lead people to click through to a full listing.

❑ Limit list displays to key columns. List views are your friends, but don't abuse that friendship. Avoid the temptation to cram as much data into one place as possible.

Keeping Important Information above the Fold

A user's attention is a finite resource. You have to catch his or her attention with every page click. The opposite also hold true: If you don't make it easy for users to spot what they're looking for, it's likely to be missed.

If you are old enough to have ever seen a newspaper, you'll notice that all the eye-catching information is on the top half of the page. Of course, that's what people see first. The same can be said for Web pages. If you want users to see something, place it at the top of your content area.

Give Yourself an 'F'

The human brain is very, very good at absorbing information quickly. Recent studies (Nielsen, 2006) have shown that most users develop a visual shorthand for quickly ascertaining whether the information that they're looking for is on the Web page they're viewing. These studies show that most users develop a pattern for reading pages that is consistent and (if you play your cards right) exploitable.

Per the study (Neilson, Jacob "F-Shaped Pattern for Reading Web Content" Useit.com: April 17, 2006 — see `http://www.useit.com/alertbox/reading_pattern.html`): When a user arrives at a page, there's usually a fairly large amount of data to absorb. Most users read the headline first the horizontal bar across the top of the page. They then start further down the page and begin another horizontal scan, looking for additional content. Finally, users tend to scroll downward along the left side of the page, picking up the start of any data that runs the length of the page.

This standard page scanning pattern (Figure 2-8) can help you position key information in a place that is most likely to be seen.

Also note that there are large tracts of the page that are not scanned by most users. Remember the 50 or so percent of the page that you have where you can actually display data? Cut that in half if you actually want that information to be seen.

Keep that in mind when designing SharePoint page layouts. A typical layout looks like Figure 2-9.

When information gets added to this page, what will users see? Based on the rules shown above, the Main and Left Web Part zones get all the attention, followed by the Bottom (that is, if the bottom makes it above the fold). The Right zone will get the least attention of all.

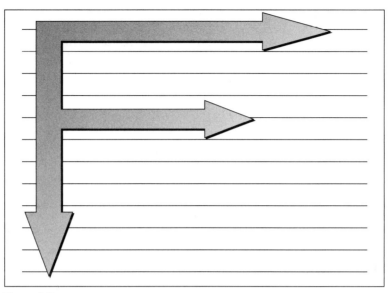

Figure 2-8

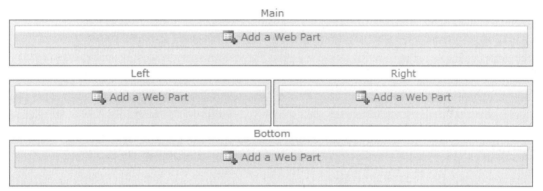

Figure 2-9

Keeping It Consistent

It's difficult to compare a SharePoint site to a traditional Web site. SharePoint is more interactive, more like a desktop application. Now imagine starting an application like Microsoft Word and finding that the interface changes intermittently depending on what you're doing. The File menu changes from horizontal to vertical if you're looking at a page with a picture on it. The Help button requires users to play hide and seek. Spell checking is enabled on some paragraphs but not others.

For better or worse, SharePoint's modular design makes it easy to create applications just like that. The last thing you want is to have users lost in your application. Try to be as consistent as possible when creating page layouts.

Navigation is an excellent example. Certain screen real estate will always be allocated to getting around. There will be tab navigation, there will be Quick Link list access, and there will be links to My Site or My Links. If you want people to actually visit these pages, make sure all navigation tools are in the same place on every single Web page.

There's also something to be said for using the standard SharePoint page layout formats. They may be boring, but they're very consistent. A few things that out-of-the-box SharePoint pages (and most modern Web pages) have in common include the following:

❑   A logo is located in the upper left-hand corner, linked to the home page.

❑   Search is available in the upper right-hand corner of the page.

❑   Navigation is available below the logo.

❑   Additional navigation features run down the right or left side of the page.

❑   Content is centrally located on the page.

Do these things sound obvious? They should. Microsoft has spent enormous amounts of time and money to train your users to navigate just such a standardized interface.

Yes, you could get creative and wild with navigation and page layout. You could design a Flash or JavaScript based interface that dynamically uses the letters in your company's logo to spell out the navigational options on your site. You can make your pages as creative and off the wall as you want. You can also pay to retrain your users on how to use the fancy new interface. In a corporate intranet, this will mean a lot of resentful users. On the commercial face of a site, it might mean a lot of frustrated users going to your competitor. Your call.

Making It Fast

People hate waiting. Don't make users wait, or they'll hate your application. To avoid this, keep a few simple rules in mind:

❑   **Keep it simple:** See above. Clean, tidy pages load faster.

❑   **Put limits on list views:** List views are SharePoint's bread and butter. They do all the ugly little things that I, as an old-school database application developer, got bored to tears by. Adding a column to a Web-based database application would often be a tedious process. Adding a column to a SharePoint list? Easy as pie. Maybe a little *too* easy. Power SharePoint users are often more than happy to pile data into lists — both more columns and more rows.

Whenever a user opens a page with a List View Web Part, SharePoint has to retrieve and format list information for display. The more data that's displayed, the longer it will take. So when possible, try to keep List View Web Parts small and manageable. There is rarely a need to display every single column in a list, nor is it always necessary to display every single item that the list contains. Luckily, List View Web Parts allow you to pick and choose columns and place limits on the number of list items displayed with each page load. Add a bit of creative grouping and sorting, and your List View Web Part will give your users the data they need without making them wait.

❑ **Watch your image sizes:** This should be a no-brainer, but it often causes otherwise speedy page loads to be sluggish. Modern digital cameras allow for multi-megabyte files. Please remember the following:

    ❑ Resize images *before* they are uploaded to your SharePoint site, or your users will download that multi-megabyte file every time they visit your page.

    ❑ Resizing the display size of an image in SharePoint Designer does not change the image file size, but only the amount of space that the image takes up on the user's screen. Browsers also do a notoriously bad job of trying to cram pixels together to fix hard-coded image sizes, making your photographic masterpiece look blocky and blurry.

    ❑ It's common for both designers and users to reference pictures in a SharePoint Picture Library for image display. This is a great tool to empower users to display images on your portal, but once again, be aware of image sizes. Displaying a 5 megabyte image from a Picture Library is no faster than displaying an image that you placed on a page using SharePoint Designer.

❑ **Watch out for Web Parts that you don't control:** MOSS has several great new Web Parts that allow for the display of information from all over the Web. RSS Viewer Web Parts, for example, can display content from feeds anywhere on the Web. Realize that if the RSS feed you added is slow to respond, your Web page will be slow as well. So, though it may be great to show a weather feed on your site's home page, users may bear the brunt of slow page loads as a result.

Other Web Parts, such as Key Performance Indicators and Data View Web Parts, can suffer from the same problems. Each of these Web Parts can directly access lines of business data. With luck, you'll have more control over the gathering of internal data. If it takes more than a few seconds to access that data through a Web service or a stored procedure, it's going to take SharePoint the same amount of time when it pulls the data for your Web Part, plus additional time to process and format it.

❑ **Keep big items out of traffic:** Sometimes, loading extremely large amounts of data is unavoidable. Try as you might, you or one of your users will be asked to show a list view that returns a horrific number of rows and columns. Or it will be absolutely essential to display key business data that takes 20 seconds to retrieve. The goal in these cases should be to limit the impact on your users.

Users will wait 20 seconds once for a page to load. They'll get frustrated if they have to wait for the 20-second page load fifty times a day. So keep Web Parts, images and data-displays that are data intensive off of your home page or other commonly accessed pages.

❑ **Cache when possible:** Think about it — most of the files that SharePoint uses to display each page are identical. Your company logo, for instance, is often stored in an image library. When each page is loaded, the SharePoint page rendering engine makes a call to the database. In many cases, this can mean retrieving information from another server.

Caching can be enabled in a few different ways. One of the easiest to implement is a minor change to the `web.config` file for your SharePoint application. To enable this feature, follow these steps:

1. Find and open the `web.config` file using notepad or another text editor.

2. Then, find the line that starts with: `<BlobCache ...`

3. Next, you'll want to set the "enabled" parameter in this line to "true."

4. Then, locate the parameter called "path." It will look something like: path = "\.(png|js)$

5. By adding additional file extensions, you can tell SharePoint to cache files with the included extension. Excellent candidates for this would be images (.jpg, .gif, etc.) and style sheets (.css), as they will be loaded on each page. Microsoft has an excellent tutorial that describes this process further at http://office.microsoft.com/en-us/sharepoint server/HA101762841033.aspx.

Beware of Ad Fatigue

Odds are that your users spend a large amount of time on the Web. Someone somewhere is always trying to get them to buy something. Users are constantly inundated with advertising. Common practices include blinking, animation, repetitive text, repetitive text, bizarre color schemes, scrolling or moving banners, or anything in ALL CAPITAL LETTERS. At one time, these techniques would capture the eyes of users and draw attention to whatever it was that was that they were trying to shill.

Fortunately, most modern Web users have become jaded to these techniques and have learned to ignore them. This means that they'll also ignore the very thing you're trying to drawn attention to. In the end, the best way to draw attention to content is to make the content worth looking at, but that's a topic for another book.

And please don't click on those ads. It only encourages them.

Making It Appealing

There are a few keys to making an appealing design, each of which could take up its own book. These keys fall into the realm of art rather than science. I'll cover them lightly, as there is already a wealth of information on each, and this book emphasizes how to improve the look and feel of SharePoint design rather than an understanding of color temperature or a description of how users will feel when they see a specific font.

Color is largely a matter of taste. There are, however, a few good rules of thumb.

❑ First, black text on a white background may be boring, but it's the easiest to see. Avoid complex background images, as text will get lost.

❑ Avoid colors that scream at you. The goal is to draw attention to your content, not the background.

❑ Avoid using too many colors. Three or four will suffice. Again, this keeps the user's eye focused on the content, not trying to make sense of the color range.

❑ Some people have a natural eye for color. For everyone else, there are a multitude of color-scheme generation tools that can help in the selection of complementary colors. (One of my favorites is this one: http://websitetips.com/colortools/sitepro/.)

❑ Always show hyperlinks in a consistent separate color, and change that color for clicked links.

Fonts should complement the overall look and feel of the site without overwhelming the user's eye.

❑ Fonts are like stewed prunes: One is good for you. Two can work. More than that and you're asking for trouble. Users' eyes have to adapt to a new set of characters each time you change, and that stands in the way of usability.

❑ If possible, avoid using graphics for text. Since text inside an image can't be read by SharePoint or most accessibility enhancing software, it won't be available within search or to visually impaired users. It also makes updating the text far more complicated.

❑ Avoid fonts that draw attention away from the content. For example, a simple sans serif font like Arial is easier to read than a font with ornate scrollwork or other extravagances like Viner Hand ITC. Some fonts might seem to tie in nicely with the overall corporate look and feel, but they can also force users to have to decipher the font everywhere they see it, which is always unpleasant.

Note that constantly changing the color of text will have a similar effect.

White space is tricky, because there are no definite rules. In most cases, the more blank space you can get away with, the better. Blank space on a page draws your attention to what really matters — your content.

A good example of this can be seen in the current state of the search business. Yahoo! has attempted to provide users with an abundance of information, making their site a destination for users who are not on the Web just for search. Google, on the other hand, has kept the same sparse layout for years. It provides the bare minimum that users will need to accomplish their goal. And as of this writing, Google had 62 percent of the search market to Yahoo!'s 17 percent.

Planning for Change

Inevitably, your company will want to update the look and feel of your portal. Maybe your company's name changes or a new logo is adopted. Maybe it's just time for a new overall feel for your company's image. This can be an insanely complicated process, or it can be as easy as making changes to a few files.

My grandmother was all about common sense. She had a saying: "If you don't have the time to do it right the first time, when are you going to have time to fix it?" This goes double when updating SharePoint pages.

SharePoint uses cascading style sheets and themes to control how each page looks and feels. Fortunately or unfortunately, there is no way to force users to always use these styles. Any manual changes to a page will retain their formatting even after you update the style sheet. This means that every time you use SharePoint Designer to change the style, font, or size of text on a screen, you've made more work for yourself when it comes time to change the portal.

Another thing to consider is the location of the images that your pages will use. If you place inline images in SharePoint pages using SharePoint Designer, you'll have to update each image manually if they change. Placing company images in a central location, say an Image Library, makes it easy to make global changes instantly.

My grandmother was one smart cookie, and if it wasn't for the fact that she never wanted to operate anything more complicated than her 1972 Oldsmobile Cutlass, she would have made a pretty good Web designer.

Summary

At the beginning of this chapter, I mentioned that most of basic Web design is common sense. Actually, it's even more simple than that. Good Web design is based on making things easier — easier for your users, easier for the site administrators, easier for you.

Making a successful portal is pretty straightforward:

1. Find out what your portal is supposed to do.
2. Get input from the people who will use it.
3. Try to lay out the portal in a way that matches how your company does business.
4. Make it as appealing as you can.
5. Plan for growth.

That's it. Everything else is detail.

3

General Concept Design

Now that you have gotten through the first two chapters and explored the importance of design and what types of considerations any SharePoint designer should take into account before actually designing their projects, it's time to start laying down code. Sort of.

In this chapter, you will get a crash course in general concept design techniques and tips. While you won't be writing any actual code per se, you will be generating the files needed for the remaining chapters of this book and will see how to take graphic design concepts and put them into practice. Specifically, you will see how to take an abstract idea and begin making it more tangible through your graphics program of choice. In this chapter, you will see these concepts materialized through Adobe Photoshop CS3. While there are certainly many other programs ranging in price (some even free through open source code philosophies), Photoshop is generally considered the standard for graphic design among many Web developers. And, as that product has matured over the years, it has become possible to create almost identical projects on a Windows-based PC as with any Macintosh counterpart. With that in mind, any keyboard shortcut in this chapter will be given both the Windows and Mac versions.

The scope of this chapter is to get familiar with a standard graphic design application and, with that, learn some tricks that can be reused in other projects. You will also get an understanding of some of the SharePoint specific issues that a designer must contend with (such as the placement of certain required SharePoint objects). At the end of this chapter, you may not feel comfortable enough to quit your day job and start earning your living as a professional graphic designer. However, you will have enough knowledge to poke around in Photoshop and be familiar enough with it to make designs that people will take note of. And, more relevant to the scope of this book, you will be able to create SharePoint designs that are above the curve in today's market.

Getting Inspired

One of the things that any good designer (not limited to SharePoint designers) needs to create noteworthy designs is inspiration. This is true in the art world and certainly it is true in the graphic design world. Part of the problem with this idea, though, is that it may be tough to find really remarkable SharePoint portal sites to get inspiration from. Many of these sites all resemble the out-of-the-box design that comes with a new installation of SharePoint. Most of these designs will look very similar to Figure 3-1, which shows the book's project site before being altered.

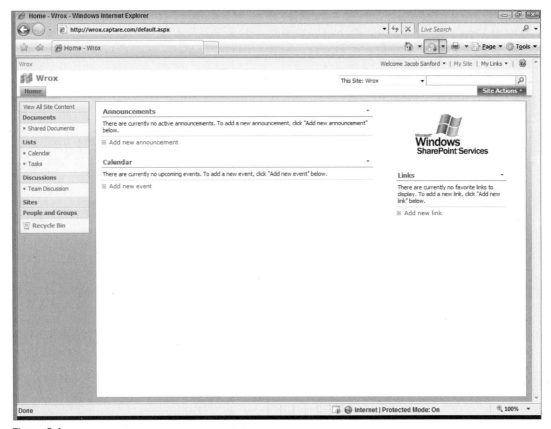

Figure 3-1

All designs start like Figure 3-1 and, unfortunately, many of them end there as well. The developers may change the logo at the top to be entity specific and may change the theme to have a different color scheme. But even with that, the design will look strikingly similar to Figure 3-1.

Take, for example, the different site themes available in a typical SharePoint install. (If you want to see them, click on Site Actions on your page and select Site Settings. From the page that comes up, select Site theme under Look and Feel.) If you are working on a new install, you will probably have your theme set to Default Theme, as was the case with Figure 3-1.

However, click on all of the stock themes provided and you will see that the only thing that really changes is the colors applied to the various components. Take, for example, one of the more striking changes, the Obsidian theme. It employs a rich black/gray theme with some bright orange accents. You can see the default project with the Obsidian theme applied to it in Figure 3-2.

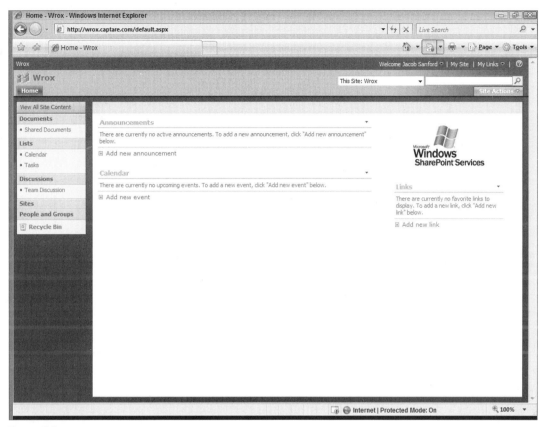

Figure 3-2

What will hopefully make an impact when you compare Figure 3-1 and Figure 3-2 in the black and white confines of this manuscript is that they are almost completely indistinguishable. When you take out the effect of the color change, the theme is almost identical.

So where is a good place to look for inspiration if not at other SharePoint sites? Well, nobody said that you were required to go by other SharePoint sites. In fact, that is one of the best things you can do: Go outside of the SharePoint world to find inspiration for your SharePoint designs.

This, at a minimum, means keep a couple of designer Web sites bookmarked (or subscribe to their blogs) and keep up to date with the latest trends in design.

A really good place to get some inspiration is Smashing Magazine (www.smashingmagazine.com). This free Web site regularly posts blogs that are relevant to today's designers and current with modern design trends. One day you may find a blog with a listing of popular (and free) fonts that you can download to use in your projects. Another day you may find a listing on cool and interesting AJAX implementations. These designs are almost never specific to one technology or another; they are meant to inspire its patrons.

One of the more relevant (in terms of this chapter) series the site offers is their design showcases. For example, check out some of these posts from their site:

❑ 60 Elegant and Visually Appealing Designs (http://www.smashingmagazine.com/2007/05/21/60-elegant-and-visually-appealling-designs/)

❑ 50 Beautiful CSS-Based Web-Designs in 2006 (http://www.smashingmagazine.com/2006/12/19/50-beautiful-css-based-web-designs-in-2006/)

❑ Keep It Simple, Stupid! (http://www.smashingmagazine.com/2007/03/26/keep-it-simple-stupid-showcase-of-simple-and-clean-designs/)

❑ 45 Fresh, Clean and Impressive Designs (http://www.smashingmagazine.com/2007/03/05/45-fresh-clean-and-impressive-designs/)

While this is just a sampling of the site's offerings, if you peruse those links, you will hopefully think at least a few times, "Wow, I love that!" Granted, many of the designs wouldn't work for a SharePoint installation, but they can give you some ideas. Maybe you will see one that wouldn't work exactly, but you can see how you could take that design and tweak it for a SharePoint installation.

Similar to Smashing Magazine is Web Design from Scratch (www.webdesignfromscratch.com) published by Ben Hunt, a Web designer and developer for over 10 years. On his site, he provides a lot of really good information on page design, graphics, and even HTML/CSS/JavaScript coding. Relevant to this discussion are his entries on current styling trends in Web development:

❑ 10 best-designed Web sites in the world (http://www.webdesignfromscratch.com/10-best-designed-web-sites.cfm)

❑ Current Web style (http://www.webdesignfromscratch.com/current-style.cfm)

❑ Web 2.0 how-to design guide (http://www.webdesignfromscratch.com/web-2.0-design-style-guide.cfm)

These links showcase what the site's author believes to be the best of the best in the current Web design trends and, often, explicit details on why he believes that. The site provides a lot of great examples that might help spark your own creative juices. And, even if it doesn't, it will at least give you some insight into what current Web development often looks like.

One of the more interesting components of this site is the fact that he (along with Scratchmedia) is publishing a book called *Redesigns from Scratch*. This book will take 50 real Web sites and show how they were redesigned. In the commentary included, they will discuss what didn't work on the old design and what was specifically improved with the new design. Probably the most interesting part of this project is that they are going to release a 100-page PDF version of the book online for free! There will also be a print version available that will go into more detail, but it will cost money. Neither book is in production as of this writing, but you can get a free preview by visiting the site (http://www.webdesignfromscratch.com/redesigns-book.cfm).

There are, of course, plenty of other sites out there that showcase "the best of the best," so don't think that this list is in any way exhaustive. These just give you a place to start looking at what is out there if you don't already have a place that you use for design inspiration.

With that said, it's not terribly important *where* you get your inspiration, as long as you get inspired. It could be from a similar site to the ones shown here. It could be from a site you visit where you like the design and want to try to adapt it for your own use. Or it could be just something you saw on television or in a movie that made you say "that gives me an idea." The important thing is that you decide the standard SharePoint themes are not enough to satisfy your design needs and that you give some thought as to what would be impressive as well as useful in your next design.

Creating the Design

In this section, you will see exactly how to use the tools in Photoshop CS3 to take a conceptual design and turn it into a project where you can then create HTML code for your SharePoint site. When this chapter is over, you will have a Photoshop file that resembles Figure 3-3.

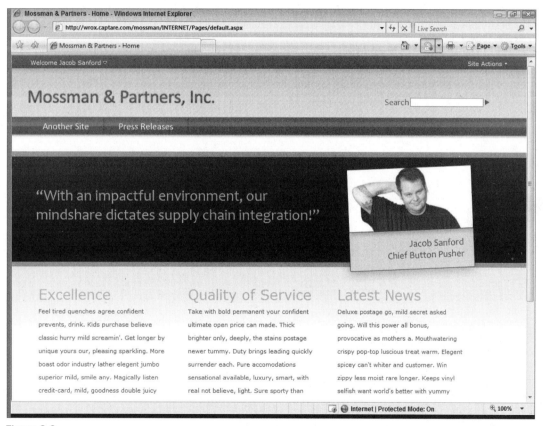

Figure 3-3

This probably doesn't look much like the SharePoint sites you have seen in the past and, quite frankly, that is the point. This chapter will take you through the steps to create this design and along the way will introduce you to several of the tools and concepts of Photoshop CS3. As stated earlier in this chapter, you won't finish reading Chapter 3 with a degree in graphic arts. You will, however, leave with an overview of Photoshop CS3 that will hopefully port to any other graphics program you may use. With a little inspiration and these tips and tricks, you should be well equipped to design the next generation of SharePoint sites.

While every effort was made to create examples that have universal concepts applied to them, you may not achieve the exact same results if you use a graphics program other than Photoshop CS3. While functionality shown here should be fairly similar across most major platforms, variances will exist and, if you use another program, you should be aware of this discrepancy as you read through the chapter.

An Overview of Photoshop CS3

When you open up Adobe Photoshop CS3 for the first time, it should resemble Figure 3-4. If you have opened it before, you may have moved things around some or have different options selected. But, if that is the case, you are probably already familiar enough with Photoshop to follow along with the rest of this tutorial.

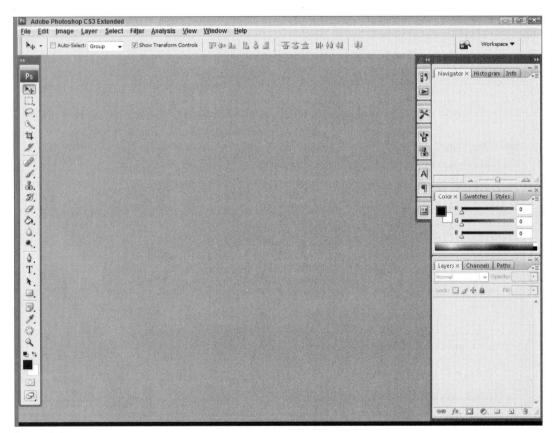

Figure 3-4

This interface, at least at first glance, will probably look familiar to anyone having experience with a previous version of Photoshop and maybe even other graphic editor programs. Just like its predecessors,

CS3 has a toolbar at the top of the window, a toolbox with various tools in it on the left side of the screen, and several palettes on the right-hand side of the screen. However, when you start delving into some of the new features of the interface, you will find that there are some significant changes in the interface that you may miss upon first perusal.

The Toolbar

The toolbar, also known as the menu bar, (Figure 3-5) is one of the less flashy pieces of the Photoshop interface. If you have ever used any Windows application (or most other popular operating system applications), you have seen a toolbar. This one isn't much different, except that, as would be expected, it includes commands specific to Photoshop CS3 (as well as standard functions like Save, Open, and New). While pretty much every tool you will need is included in the toolbar, it probably won't be something you access a lot. Most designers tend to hang out in the other regions of the interface and, therefore, this discussion of the toolbar will be brief. As the chapter progresses, toolbar steps will be included for a lot of the activities given.

Figure 3-5

While not specifically a component of the Photoshop toolbar, the Options toolbar (Figure 3-6) connected to it can prove to be a very useful toolbar that might be otherwise overlooked.

Figure 3-6

This toolbar automatically updates the displayed options depending on which tool you are currently using. For example, the toolbar shown in Figure 3-6 shows the options available when you have the Move tool selected in the toolbox (discussed in the next section). If you were to choose the Rectangular Marquee tool, the Options Toolbar will automatically update itself to resemble Figure 3-7.

Figure 3-7

While a particular tool is selected, you can modify its options directly in the Options toolbox and they will be immediately reflected in your project.

As you get more comfortable with the tools and commands of Photoshop CS3, you will begin to use this area as much, if not more, than most of the other areas of the interface. You will see some of the ways this toolbar can be used in your projects to make creating Web site designs easy and logical as this chapter progresses.

The Toolbox

The toolbox (Figure 3-8) is Photoshop's attempt to keep all of the tools you will most likely use in your projects in one place. This includes things like tools for selecting areas of your image, tools for adding text, and tools for filling colors and gradients into selections. You can even find basic touchup and eraser tools in this area.

Figure 3-8

To see what a particular tool is that is housed in the toolbox, you can simply hover over it. For example, if you hover over the second option in Figure 3-8, you will see a pop-up item that displays the name of the tool, as you can see in Figure 3-9.

Figure 3-9

You should also note that many of the tools on the toolbox are actually placeholders for more than one tool. You can tell an icon on the toolbar has other tools associated with it by the presence of a small black arrow at the bottom of the icon. To see the other tools available, you can click your mouse button on the icon on the toolbox and hold it until the other options are displayed, as shown in Figure 3-10.

The option that is currently selected is indicated by a square bullet located next to that tool. For example, in Figure 3-10, the square icon is displayed next to the Rectangular Marquee tool indicating that it is the currently selected tool. Once the options are displayed, release the mouse button and then navigate to the tool that you want to use and click on it. However, keeping the mouse button clicked and then navigating over to the tool and then releasing the mouse button will do the same thing; it's mostly a matter of preference.

Figure 3-10

Once a different tool has been selected, that tool's icon will now appear on the toolbox instead of the original tool's icon. This means that if, with the example in Figure 3-10, "Elliptical Marquee tool" had been selected, the Elliptical Marquee tool would now be on the toolbox represented by its own icon.

There are a couple of new features of the toolbox that warrant discussion in this section. The first of these is the ability to collapse the toolbox into a two-column view that may better fit your work style. To toggle to this view, you press the dark gray area at the top of the toolbox that has the double arrows in it. You will notice that the double arrows at the top of the toolbox have changed directions and now point to the left. To toggle back to the single-column view, click in the dark gray area with the double arrows again.

Another noteworthy enhancement to the toolbox is the addition of a tool that allows for changing the screen mode, the Change Screen Mode button. Essentially, this allows different configurations of the workspace in Photoshop to meet different designers' needs.

First, to set this, look at the bottom of the toolbox for the last icon, which looks like two windows overlapping each other (by default). Hold down the left mouse button on the icon to see the different screen modes available, as shown in Figure 3-11.

Figure 3-11

To better understand what the different options do, it is probably easiest to see examples of how each view handles the same project. With this in mind, a project was created using a screenshot of a Web browser captured at a higher resolution, resulting in a project with dimensions of 1778 pixels wide by 1178 pixels wide. The resolution of the monitor used for Photoshop is set at 1024 pixels wide by 768 pixels high. Since the project has a bigger resolution than the screen resolution in Photoshop, the project window has the potential to grow outside of the working area dimensions of the application.

So, by default, the view is the Standard Screen Mode, as can be seen in Figure 3-12.

As this figure depicts, the project window has the ability to travel under the toolbox and palettes in the CS3 work area, making it potentially difficult to work with the project. Of course, you can resize the project window and the magnification to make it fit in the confines of the working area, but this screenshot does not do that intentionally to illustrate how this mode deals with project dimensions overlapping other pieces of the application interface. This is very similar to the only mode available in previous versions of Photoshop.

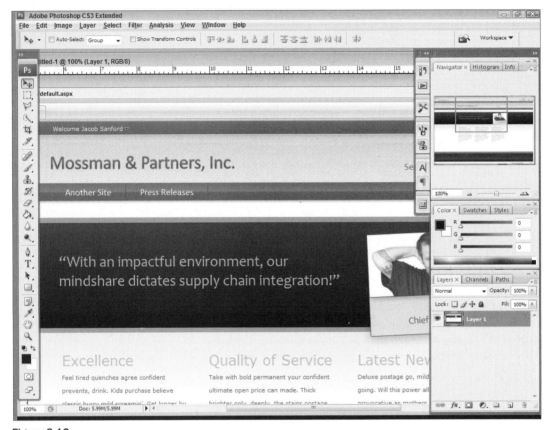

Figure 3-12

With CS3, though, there are new options. The first one is the Maximized Screen Mode, which can be seen in Figure 3-13.

This shows the project window being confined to the viewable area of the Photoshop working area, meaning that the project window is not allowed to sneak behind the other components of the Photoshop interface. Even though the project is still too big to fit within the viewable area, the window is maximized to the width between the toolbox and the palettes and scrollbars are provided to navigate to parts of the project not currently viewable.

If the difference between Figure 3-12 and 3-13 is not easily spotted, look for the toolbars on both. In Figure 3-12 you can see the top ruler at the top of the project window for the part that isn't hidden behind the palettes but the ruler on the left side of the project window is completely hidden behind the toolbox. In Figure 3-13, you can see both rulers completely.

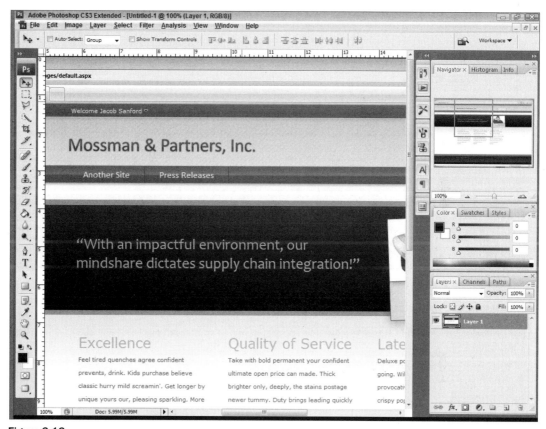

Figure 3-13

One cool thing about this mode is that it automatically resizes itself as the viewable area gets modified as a result of changing settings in the application interface. For example, if the toolbox illustrated in Figure 3-13 was modified to the two-column view, which makes the toolbox wider thereby lessening the viewable working area of the Photoshop interface, the Maximized Screen Mode would adjust automatically, resulting in Figure 3-14.

One other interesting caveat to the Maximized Screen Mode is that you can get to this mode in at least two different ways. The first was alluded to earlier when introducing the option to select viewing modes: Click the icon and select the mode from the options that are presented.

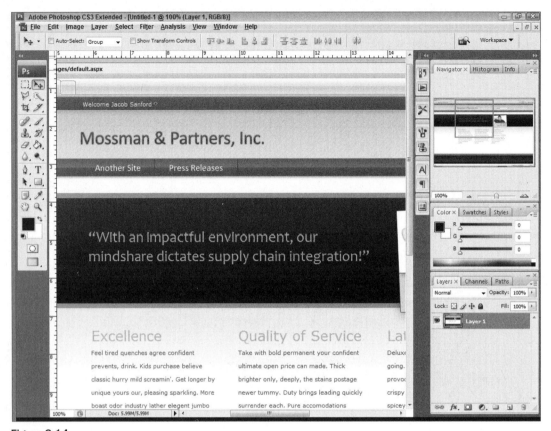

Figure 3-14

However, this view also is considered the maximized view of a project. This means that, when you maximize a project window, it will go to the Maximized Screen Mode. You can maximize a project window in the same way you would maximize any application window. Specifically, you can double click on the project window's title bar (for example, in Figure 3-12, the top of the project window that says "Untitled-1 @ 100% (Layer 1, RGB/9)"). You can also maximize the window by clicking the Maximize button on the widow's title bar.

Similarly, once in the Maximized Screen Mode, the project returns to the Standard Screen Mode when you click on the Restore Down button of the project.

The next two modes, Full Screen Mode With Menu Bar and Full Screen Mode are fairly similar and can be seen in Figures 3-15 and 3-16, respectively.

As Figures 3-15 and 3-16 illustrate, the Full Screen Mode With Menu Bar and Full Screen Mode are the same view, the only difference being the toolbar at the top of the screen. Both modes expand the application work area to consume the entire monitor screen, even if the application window itself (as opposed to the project windows within the application workspace) is not in a maximized state. These views give you the most possible viewable area to work with but come with the cost that the project window can once again hide behind the toolbox and palette windows.

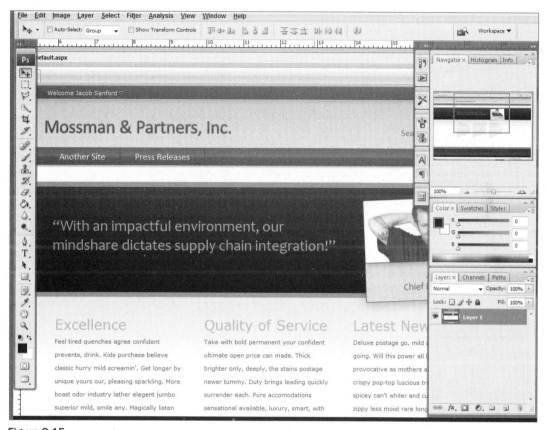

Figure 3-15

One last thing to note about the Change Screen Mode button on the toolbar is that you can actually toggle through each of the options by simply single-clicking on the button. In other words, rather than clicking on the button and holding the mouse down until the different modes appear, simply click on the button once and release (a normal mouse click). This will toggle to the next screen mode in the list (shown in Figure 3-11). So, if the application is currently in the Full Screen Mode and the Change Screen Mode button on the toolbar is single-clicked, the application will jump into the Standard Screen Mode because it is the next on the list (when it gets to the bottom of the list it goes back up to the top). This allows for quickly toggling between the various screen modes to determine the best suited for the project at hand.

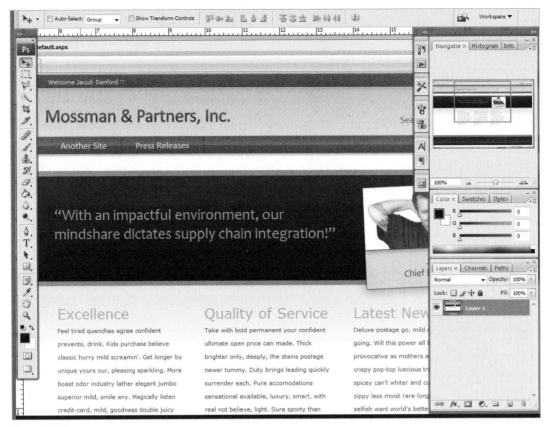

Figure 3-16

The Docking Panel

Up to this point, the area with all of the gadgets on the right-hand side of the CS3 interface has been referred to as the palettes. This is because, in previous versions of Photoshop, that is what they were called. And, at first glance, they look very similar to that. However, with CS3, the concept of a docking panel was introduced for the purpose of administering the various palettes that are available within Photoshop.

The docking panel, as it will probably appear the first time Photoshop is opened (and remains the default until modified) can be seen in Figure 3-17.

It might be difficult to ascertain the actual docking panel by just looking at Figure 3-17, but if you look really closely, you can see a dark area that surrounds all of the palettes (starting with the thick dark gray area at the top of the figure). That dark area is the actual dock and the palettes get docked inside of this area.

Within the new docking panel, the palettes take on an entirely new functionality. To see this, click the thick dark gray bar at the top of the docking panel that has the right-facing double arrows (above the navigator/histogram/Ingo palette). The docking panel and its palettes should now look like Figure 3-18.

Figure 3-17

Figure 3-18

Using this condensed version of the palettes in the docking panel allows a much greater area to work with inside of Photoshop. Looking at this condensed version, it makes sense that the items that might have seemed like icons to the left of the palettes in Figure 3-17 are actually just condensed palettes within the docking panel.

The nice thing about this view is obviously that it significantly reduces the footprint of these tools. However, what happens when they are needed for your project? Does the entire docking station need to be maximized again? The answer is, thankfully, no.

If, for example, a designer wanted to look at the layers palette only, he could click on the layers button in Figure 3-18 and that palette alone would expand, as shown in Figure 3-19.

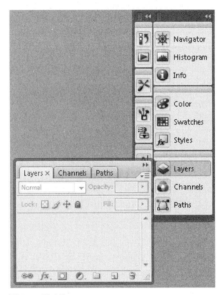

Figure 3-19

The Layers Palette will remain expanded by itself until it is closed by the user. This can be done by either clicking on the Layers button on the docking panel or by clicking on the double arrows on the Layers palette. Doing either of these will return the docking panel to the state shown in Figure 3-18.

The condensed version of the docking panel also shows that there are, in essence, two columns to the docking panel. The left column is only as wide as the icon, while the right column is wide enough to display the icon as well as a description of the palette. And, just like normal columns, the palettes can be dragged from one to the other.

To drag a single palette (e.g., the Navigator palette), click on the icon for that palette and begin dragging it to the location you want it and, once there, release the mouse button. Using this approach, you can drag an individual palette to a different palette group in either column or you can even break the palette out of the docking panel and have it float on its own in the application workspace.

Similar to this, the palette groups (e.g., the Navigator/Historam/Info palette group) can be moved by dragging them using your mouse. To do this, click on the little bar above the palette group with your mouse and begin dragging the group while holding the mouse button down. Just like with individual palettes, the palette groups can be moved within the same column, moved to a different column, dropped into another palette group, or detached from the docking panel.

Another thing to take note of is that the columns in the docking panel are completely customizable. This means that they can be reduced to 1 column or expanded to 3 columns fairly easily. They can also be resized to either just display the icon or to include the text as well.

To see how to create a third column, click on one of the palette groups' top bar to drag the entire group. For this example, use topmost palette group that contain the Navigator palette. With the mouse still depressed, drag the palette group to the left until it is all the way to end of the docking panel. You will know that you are to the farthest left most point when a blue bar highlights the entire length of the docking panel. (With the limitations of being printed in grayscale, this distinction would be almost impossible to see in a figure so one is not included. However, you should be able to see this in your own project.)

You should also notice that the palette group being moved becomes semi-transparent while being dragged to its new location. Once the new column appears (as indicated by the long blue bar), release the palette group. This will create a third column that contains the newly added palette group and will resemble Figure 3-20.

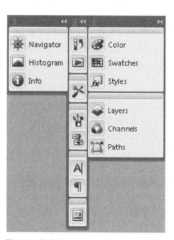

Figure 3-20

As a next step, it might make sense to have the new column only be as wide as the icon rather than showing all of the descriptive text of each palette. In order to do this, each column has its own handles at the top that allow for that column's dimensions to be changed when dragged. So, in order to shrink the size of the column, click on the handle of that column (the handle is the object in the upper left-hand corner or the dark area at the top of a column; it looks like three bars next to each other) and then drag the handle all the way to the right. The column will only go as small as the icon view so, when it gets to that point, release the mouse button and the column will remain at its new size. Using this approach on the new third column formed in Figure 3-20, the icon-only view of that column can be seen in Figure 3-21.

Figure 3-21

To maximize the available work area, it might make sense to reduce all palettes to a single column in the docking panel and to have that one column only show an icon view. To do this, drag all palette groups to the furthest most right column first and, once that is done, resize that column to only show the icons by dragging the handle for that column. Doing this will result in a docking panel that is one column wide and only filled with icons, making it very slim, maximizing the amount of work area you have available for your projects.

Reducing the docking station and palettes to icons only may not be advisable to designers new to Photoshop since it will take a while to get used to which palette is associated with which icon. And without a solid understanding of the tools in each palette and when to use which one, the docking panel will appear to be not much more than a toolbar with a bunch of icons that aren't used very much.

However, with that said, once the tools and palettes become increasingly familiar, this reduced footprint version of the palettes could prove to be a very welcomed change. For example, take a look at how much work area is now available in Photoshop (compare to Figure 3-4 or even 3-14 earlier in this chapter), as seen in Figure 3-22.

This can provide a designer with a much more workable area for their projects in Photoshop CS3. However, to even further enhance the work area, it is possible to hide the docking panel completely by pressing the Shift and Tab keys simultaneously (this is the same keyboard shortcut for Mac and PC users). Doing this once will hide the entire docking panel; doing it again will bring it back. This will allow for an almost completely available working area within Photoshop.

A Few Graphic Concepts

While understanding the basic layout of the Photoshop interface is important, especially since most tutorials will tell the reader to locate this tool on the toolbox or that item in a particular palette, it is more important to have an exposure and understanding of some basic graphic concepts before getting too heavily into creating a complete project.

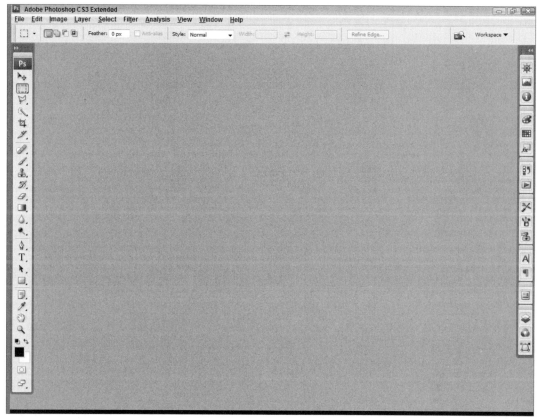

Figure 3-22

While there are certainly volumes of books, blogs, and online tutorials that could go over a multitude of concepts relevant to the Photoshop designer, there are only two that are vitally important to proceeding with the layout design project that will be illustrated in the remainder of the book: layers and brushes. As such, these two concepts will be discussed in their own subsections in the next few pages. After that, it's time to begin creating the layout design illustrated in the beginning of this chapter.

Layers

While there are certainly other concepts that designers can find useful, it can be argued that none are any more important to layers. Layers are, in fact, the building block of almost all Photoshop projects. Without an understanding of the idea of layers, a designer will have difficulty in getting the most out of Photoshop (or for that matter any graphic editor program).

To see a basic diagram that illustrates what layers are in graphic design, take a look at Figure 3-23, which was originally published in *Professional ASP.NET 2.0 Design: CSS, Themes, and Master Pages* (Wrox Press).

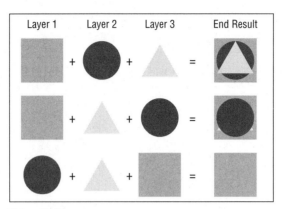

Figure 3-23

In this example, there are three distinct layers and, as Figure 3-23 shows, it very much depends on the order they get applied as to the final result. In the first example, the square is the base, and then a circle is overlaid on the square, and then, finally, a triangle is applied to the top. In this example, all three layers, or at least elements of each, can be seen in the end result. While each layer overlays parts of the previous layers, each layer still has some piece of it showing through.

Conversely, in the last example, the square is applied on the top of the other two layers. Since the square is the biggest, it completely covers up all of the underlying layers, meaning you can't see any piece of either the circle or the triangle layers.

This is the basic concept of layers. In Photoshop, designers create different layers within their project. Those layers are stacked one on top of the other, and the rendered product is the accumulation of all visible layers in linear order. This means that, when the final image is rendered out, the bottommost layer will only be visible if it is not covered up entirely by the layers that are stacked on top of it.

To think about this in a slightly different way, it might help to think about a more tangible example. To this end, imagine a large Department Store window. With nothing on it, people walking by can see all of the activity within the store. However, imagine someone comes along and puts up a political flyer on the window. Now that view into the store is partially blocked by the political poster so people walking by can now see the political poster, which would be the uppermost layer, and a portion of the underlying glass, which is the bottommost layer. Now imagine over time people cover the window with an assortment of rock show advertisements, roommate needed posters, and missing person notifications. Eventually, the window is completely covered and, consequently, opaque. People passing by can no longer see inside the store at all and can only see the pieces of pasted literature that aren't covered by other pieces of pasted literature.

In the world of graphic arts, each of those object would be the own layer. The project would start off with a completely transparent layer (if that is what the designer chose). If this were to be the only layer, the rendered image would allow all objects under it to come through. So if, for example, this transparent image were dropped onto a Web site, the entire Web site would be visible through the image.

Next, the designer would add layers to satisfy various design aspects of the project. Instead of political, concert, or roommate posters, these layers might include a header, navigation, body, and footer region for a Web site.

Within Photoshop, layers are displayed using the Layers palette in the docking panel, which can be seen in Figure 3-24.

Figure 3-24

This example shows some of the more interesting features of layers in Photoshop CS3. One of the things that might be quickly noticeable is the use of folders. Folders in the layers palette allow designers to easily organize layers into logical units. Figure 3-24 shows folders for a welcome, search, nav, and logo region and, within the welcome region, additional folders for site actions and elements. These are all logical units of the design project from which this layer snapshot was taken and they allow the designer to easily track down the layer that needs to be tweaked (or where a new layer may need to be added to expand the design in that region). The folders are collapsible, which reduces the clutter that can easily accumulate in this palette. Imagine a project with 100 or 200 layers (not that big of a stretch). It's much easier to navigate through, say, 7 or 8 collapsed folders to find what needs to be modified rather than trying to sift through 200 individual layers.

Another thing that should be noted is the eye icon that is next to all but one of the layers (on the farthest left side of the layer row). This indicates whether the layer is visible. So, in Figure 3-24, all of the layers are visible except for Layer 51, which is currently hidden.

This brings up another concept that is worth discussion: why have hidden layers? It would seem logical to think that if the project didn't require the layer for its final rendering, the layer doesn't serve a purpose. But that isn't necessarily so.

For one, a single project may be used for differently rendered images. Take, for example, a Photoshop project that is used to generate buttons for a particular Web site. It wouldn't make sense to have different projects for each of, say, 10 navigation buttons. Instead, a designer would have one button project that has the text for each of the 10 buttons on different layers and would hide 9 of them when rendering out each individual button. The same might be true, to expand this example, if there were different styles of the button for the hover effect of the button. Say that the normal state of the button is red but, when the mouse hovers over it, the button "glows" with a bright orange background. Instead of having different projects for each button state, it would make more sense to have a single project with a red background and an orange one and then hide the one that is not necessary for a particular state when that state button is rendered. This alone probably justifies the use of hidden layers.

However, a more useful function of hidden buttons is the concept of non-destructive editing of layers. This, in simplest terms, means that a copy of the original layer is kept in a hidden state while another copy is modified to suit the needs of the project. Why do this? Well, people make mistakes and it might therefore be easier to just start over on that particular layer than to try to undo all previous steps. Using this approach, a designer will always have a copy of a layer to fall back on in case something goes wrong with editing.

There are certainly other reasons to use hidden layers but, hopefully, these examples will show how useful these tools can prove in a Photoshop project.

And, with that, hopefully this section has provided enough of an overview of layers that, at a minimum, they are at least understood in concept and their value in graphic design projects can be appreciated.

Creating a Pattern

One of the more useful tools in the Photoshop arsenal is the ability to create design patterns for your projects. In the world of coding, this would be akin to reusable code. You simply set up a pattern and use it whenever a specific project calls for it.

A pattern is, in its essence, a design that you can use to fill an area of your project. If you are familiar with HTML, this would be on the same level as using an image as a repeatable background for your page. So, with that in mind, a Photoshop pattern is a repeatable pattern that you can use to fill any selection within your Photoshop project. This makes recurring design tasks, such as creating areas with diagonal fills, a much simpler process. To elaborate on that example, this section will teach you how to create a diagonal fill pattern that you can see utilized in the logo area background region (the background region behind the text "Mossman & Partners, Inc.") of the chapter project back in Figure 3-3.

The first step in creating the diagonal overlay is to decide on the design specifics. This can be fairly arbitrary and will probably change as you use the patterns more and more. And, honestly, there are only two real considerations when making a diagonal pattern: How thick do you want the line and how much space do you want between lines? Since diagonal patterns should be square shaped, these two factors will determine the dimensions of your pattern. To illustrate this, assume that you want a 1 pixel thick line with 10 pixels space between each line, as shown in Figure 3-25. This means that your pattern will need to be 11 pixels wide by 11 pixels high (1 pixel for the pattern and 10 for the spacing). The actual pattern that you create for this design would end up resembling Figure 3-26.

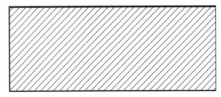

Figure 3-25

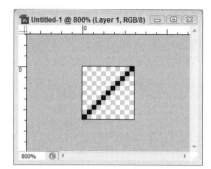

Figure 3-26

To get a different perspective on this concept, take a look at Figures 3-27 and 3-28. Figure 3-27 is the same image as Figure 3-25, except that it is filled with a diagonal pattern that has a 5 pixel thick line with only 4 pixels separating each line. To create this, a pattern was created that was 9 pixels wide and 9 pixels high (to accommodate both the 5 pixel line and the 4 pixel buffer between each line), which yielded the pattern seen in Figure 3-28.

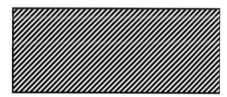

Figure 3-27

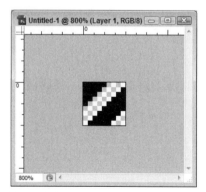

Figure 3-28

These pictures illustrate that the dimensions and line width aren't really arbitrary; the two designs look completely different. The determination as to how thick your diagonal line is and how much padding you put there significantly impacts the way the final output looks. Figure 3-27 is a much more intense diagonal pattern than Figure 3-25.

What is arbitrary, at least for this discussion, is which one to use. This is, simply, a matter of taste. Some people will look at Figure 3-25 and think that it is too immaterial and has no impact on the design. Others might look at Figure 3-27 and feel it completely overwhelming and obnoxious. And, quite honestly, the project you are using the patterns on and how you use them will have a say into what fits best. Changing the diagonal overlay's opacity, for example, can really affect the impact of the design (which you will see in later sections of this chapter). As you get more and more comfortable with creating patterns and using them in your projects, you will form your own preferences. This section will get you started on creating a pattern and give you the knowledge necessary to go out and create more.

The Chapter Project's Diagonal Pattern

Since the project illustrated in Figure 3-3 earlier in this chapter will be built in the next sections, it makes sense to create the diagonal pattern for that particular project. And, not coincidentally, this project uses the design just demonstrated in Figures 3-27 and 3-28.

Remember, in that example, the diagonal line was 5 pixels thick and there were 4 pixels of padding between each line. This means that you will need to create a perfect square design that is 9 pixels wide and 9 pixels high. To do this, you will need to first start a new project by clicking on File in the toolbar and then selecting New. This will give you the screen shown in Figure 3-29.

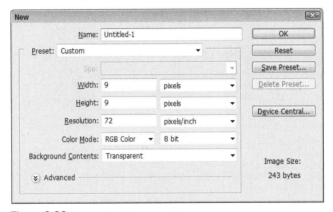

Figure 3-29

The only things that you really need to ensure are set on this screen are the Width and Height (both set to 9 pixels as illustrated). You will also probably want to ensure that Background Contents is set to Transparent as seen in Figure 3-29. This will render a new 9px by 9px project that is completely transparent (Figure 3-30), which is where you want to start.

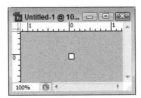

Figure 3-30

When you are working on such a small project, it is a good idea to magnify the project so that you can see the finer details. This will allow you to make pixel by pixel modifications more easily. And, with a 9 pixel by 9 pixel project, you are pretty much only going to be doing pixel by pixel modifications.

The easiest way to increase the magnification of a project window is by holding down the Ctrl button (Cmd for Mac users) while repeatedly pressing the $+/=$ button (conversely, to lessen the magnification, you can hold down the Ctrl button (again, Cmd for Mac users) and then repeatedly hit the $-/\_$ button). The highest magnification is 3200%, which will give you very good detail of every pixel of your project. Your 9 pixel project should now resemble Figure 3-31.

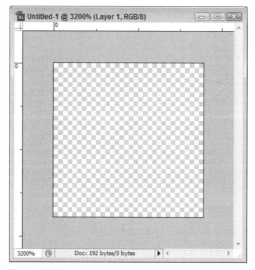

Figure 3-31

At this point, it's time to start painting your diagonal pattern. The first thing you will need is a tool that you can use to paint with. In this scenario you will want a tool that will give you the granularity to paint a solid pixel one at a time. There are probably several tools that could accomplish this, but probably the easiest and most reliable is the Pencil tool, which is located in the toolbox on the left-hand side of the button and is identifiable by the icon shown in Figure 3-32

Figure 3-32

As indicated by the small triangle in the lower right-hand corner of the icon, the Pencil tool is actually a part of an icon grouping that includes the Brush tool and Color Replacement tool, as can be seen in Figure 3-33.

If you see any of the other tools in the toolbox, you can just hold down the icon until the other options become apparent next to it. Once the menu shown in Figure 3-33 comes up, just click on the Pencil tool option.

Figure 3-33

Once you have the Pencil tool selected, you may need to adjust how big, measured in pixels, the pencil paints with. For this fine of detail, you want to make sure that you are painting with a 1 pixel pencil. In order to check this, you can look in the Options Bar at the top of the screen and you will see a section with a Brush dropdown setting that you can use to set the pixel count to 1, as seen in Figure 3-34. (Make sure you click the dropdown arrow to see the options.)

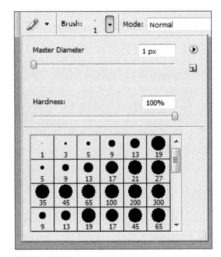

Figure 3-34

You will need to make your settings the same as those shown in Figure 3-34. That is to say, set the Master Diameter to 1 px and the Hardness to 100%. This will allow you to draw 1 pixel blocks with no distortion at the edges.

The last preparation you will need to make is to set the color for the lines you will be drawing. For this project, you will want to just create black lines. This pattern will be reused several times and, if the lines need to change color, you can do that in the project itself.

Since you only need to set the color to a solid black, there is an easy shortcut to do this. If you look at the bottom of the toolbox, you will see the icon shown in Figure 3-35. This icon is known as the Default Colors icon and can also be activated by simply pressing the D key on your keyboard (the same for PC and Mac users).

Figure 3-35

This icon, when clicked, will set the foreground and background colors to their defaults and, if you have not modified the defaults, this will make the foreground color black and the background color white. Once you click on it, the icons right below it, which allow you to manually set the foreground and background colors, should indicate that the foreground and background colors have been set to their defaults of black and white, as shown in Figure 3-36.

Figure 3-36

Now you are ready to paint your diagonal line.

To start with, click one time in the upper left-hand corner of your image to create a one pixel block at that corner, as seen in Figure 3-37.

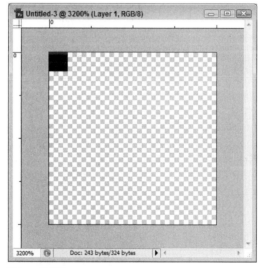

Figure 3-37

Using this same approach, the next thing you will want to do is draw similar blocks all the way across the diagonal of the project window one pixel at a time. You will need to offset this from the center by 1 pixel to accommodate the 1 pixel block you just made at the top corner, as seen in Figure 3-38. In other words, don't start at the corner; start 1 pixel over to the right.

At this point, you have created the design for a perfect diagonal pattern that has a repeating one pixel diagonal line with eight pixels padding between each line. If you were to fill an object with this pattern, it would resemble Figure 3-39.

To thicken up the line, you will need to think about what this tiling background requires to match up seamlessly. You can't simply thicken up the diagonal line without making compensation at one or both of the corners of the project. In other words, if you add a second row of pixels immediately to the right of the original line drawn on the diagonal but not on the corner piece drawn in Figure 3-38, the diagonals will not match up and the image will look jagged. So, to make it seamless, you will need to compensate in the corner as well.

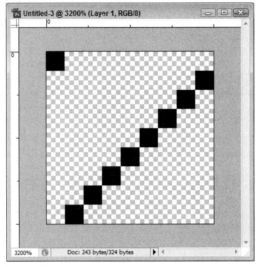

Figure 3-38

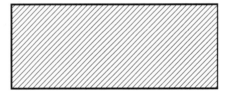

Figure 3-39

Probably the easiest way to keep this straight is to always "add to the right." This means that if you need to thicken up the line, you will add to the right side of the lines already drawn. This will probably make more sense if you see it in practice. So, to see what this means, take a look at Figure 3-40.

This example shows that the original diagonal has been widened by adding another pixel of line directly to the right of the original line. To compensate for this addition, the 1 pixel dot has also been thickened by adding more dots on a diagonal line to the right of the original dot.

At this stage, you have created a diagonal pattern that contains a 2 pixel thick diagonal line with 7 pixels of padding between each line.

To continue this thought, you will want to add 3 more pixels thickness to each of the two sections that you have started. After you have added these new lines, your project should now resemble Figure 3-41.

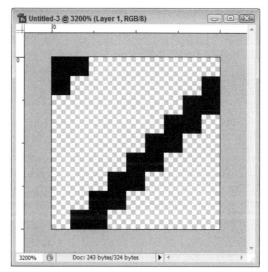

Figure 3-40

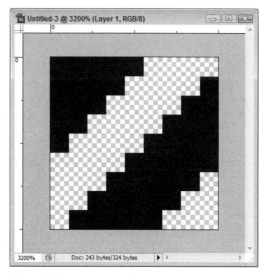

Figure 3-41

At this point, the design aspect of your pattern is finished; you need only save it as a pattern in Photoshop. To do this, click Edit on the toolbar and select Define Pattern. This will give you the dialog box shown in Figure 3-42.

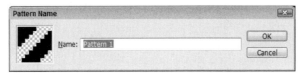

Figure 3-42

The only setting is Name. This is obviously a matter of preference but should be something that makes sense. The name you provide will provide pattern information when you are trying to apply the pattern later so you should give it a name that will help you figure out exactly what this pattern is. If you have a lot of diagonal patterns, it will be really hard to tell exactly what the difference is between an 11x11 pattern and a 4x4 pattern, for example. So, to help with this, you should consider naming your new pattern something like "9x9 pixel diagonal pattern (5 pixel line with 4 pixels padding)." When you see that later, you will know exactly what the pattern is.

At this point, your pattern is finalized and ready for you to use. You may want to save your Photoshop file for later editing. You can do this by clicking File on the toolbar and selecting Save As and then choosing a location to save the project file (with a PSD file extension). You don't need to do this for the pattern, but it is a good idea to keep it for later modification or reuse.

Now, to see how to use this new pattern, start a new project (File ⇨ New) and set the dimensions to 100 pixels by 100 pixels and set the Background Contents to White. This will give you a new project, as seen in Figure 3-43.

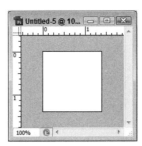

Figure 3-43

Now click on Edit and choose Fill and you will be presented with the options shown in Figure 3-44.

Next to Custom Pattern, click the down arrow to show all patterns. You will need to scroll down to the bottom to see the one you just added, but you should see something like Figure 3-45.

As Figure 3-45 illustrates, if you hover over your pattern, a pop-up will give you the name of the pattern that you provided earlier. Select your new pattern and press the OK button. This will fill your project with your new pattern, which you can see in Figure 3-46.

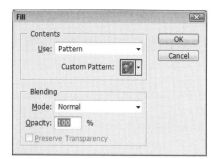

Figure 3-44

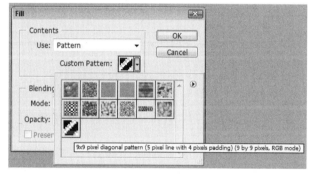

Figure 3-45

Figure 3-46

And with this, you should now have the basic knowledge necessary to create your own custom patterns and use them to fill in areas of your projects. You will see a more real world example of using this pattern in the next section (this 9x9 diagonal pattern will be used fairly extensively in the next section to design the Web site shown at the beginning of this chapter).

Free Transform

One of the nicer features, and perhaps one of the more underappreciated ones, is the Free Transform tool available in Photoshop. This tool allows you to have surgical precision when setting up regions of your project. In Web design, this can be particularly helpful. If you know you want the header region of your page to be exactly 150 pixels high (for whatever reason), you can set that up. If you want your content to be padded 50 pixels from the left and right borders, you can control that. With this tool, you can set all of the X and Y coordinates, as well as the height and width, of any object in your project. This gives you a lot of control over your layout and the objects in your projects.

Another aspect of this tool is that it allows those new to design concepts who might be less comfortable with creating regions of a project that "just look right" have more control over creating their project. This allows you to completely conceptualize your project and define its areas in very logical ways, which is really helpful if you aren't a true graphic designer (which more developers aren't). It brings graphic arts into a more code-related mindset; it can allow left-brained folks to at least imitate right-brained creativity.

To get an idea of how this tool works, create a new project that is 500 × 500 pixels and a background color of White. These settings are completely arbitrary but will be used throughout this example.

The first thing you will want to do is add a new layer to your project (click on Layer in the toolbar and then select New and then Layer). At this point, it's not important what you call the layer, so feel free to accept the default of Layer 1. This will be the layer that you will be playing around with to see how the Free Transform tool works.

Now, use the Rectangular Marquee tool, shown in Figure 3-47 (it is in a group with the Elliptical Marquee tool, the Single Row Marquee tool, and the Single Column Marquee tool, also shown in Figure 3-47) to draw a selection in your project.

Figure 3-47

To create your selection, with the Rectangular Marquee tool selected, click anywhere in your project and hold your mouse button down. Now move your mouse to another point in your project window. You will see that the selection becomes recognizable by a series of moving dashes. This is often referred to as the "marching ants." Release your mouse button when you have a selection you are comfortable with; size and position to not matter at this time. Your selection should resemble Figure 3-48.

Again, your project won't resemble this exactly; just make sure you have a selection created and your new layer (Layer 1) is active.

The last step before you can use the Free Transform tool is to fill the selection with a color. This will create an object you can manipulate as well as allow you to visually understand what is going on when you use the tool. So, in order to fill the selection, use the Paint Bucket tool on the toolbox, which is part of a tool group including the Gradient tool as shown in Figure 3-49.

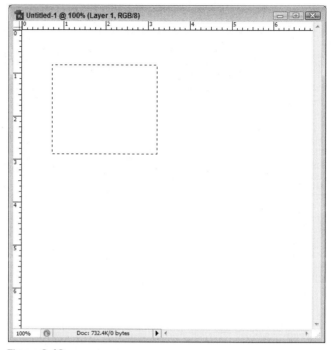

Figure 3-48

Figure 3-49

Once you have the Paint Bucket tool selected, click anywhere in your selection to fill it with the default foreground color (probably black unless you have changed it). Your project should now look more like Figure 3-50.

At this point, you are ready to see how the Free Transform tool actually works. For this demonstration, you will make the new area fill up the top half of your project, resulting in a half-tone design with black being the top half and white being the bottom.

To do this, bring up the Free Transform tool by clicking on Edit on the toolbar at the top of Photoshop and then selecting Free Transform. This will change the option bar to resemble Figure 3-51.

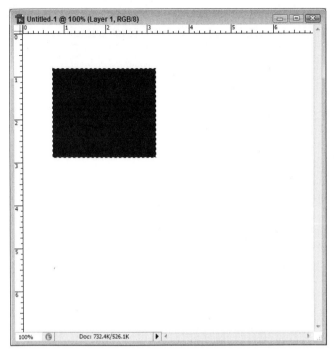

Figure 3-50

Figure 3-51

The first section that you will want to deal with allows you to set the X and Y coordinates of your object and is shown by itself in Figure 3-52.

Figure 3-52

Within this section, there are three distinct but equally important components. The first one is the little graphic that sort of looks like some kind of matrix. This button, or in reality, this series of buttons, allows you to set the reference point location. This means that you set what part of the object you want to use as the reference point when setting the X and Y coordinates. By default, you can see that it is set to use the center point of the object as its reference point, as indicated by that point having a black box rather than a white one. This means that, for example, if you were to set the X and Y coordinates to (150, 150), it would make the center of your black box be at the (150,150) position in your project. You can change the reference point to any of the other positions marked with a white box.

For this example, you want to set the reference point to the top-left corner, which would coincide with the (0, 0) position of your drawn object (the black box). You do this by clicking the white box in the upper left-hand corner, which will turn that box black and all others white, as seen in figure 3-53.

Figure 3-53

You will next want to set the X and Y properties to zero pixels each (0 px). As you make these changes, you will see your black box move to those positions. For example, when you set the X property to zero, you should see your black box immediately shoot to the leftmost edge of your project. Similarly, when you change the Y property to zero, you will see your black box move to the topmost edge of your project.

The next settings you will want to adjust are the height and width, which will use the settings shown in Figure 3-54.

Figure 3-54

These are probably fairly self-explanatory; the W property sets the width of your object and the H sets its height. The one thing that you need to be careful of when playing with this setting is that it defaults to using percentages. If you enter "500" for the width, for example, it will increase the size of the object 5 fold. Meaning, if the original width of your black box was 200 pixels, changing the W property to 500 would actually make it 1000 pixels wide (500% of its original width). To account for this, make sure you enter in "px" after the number to tell Photoshop you want to use pixels rather than percentages.

So, since you want this object to be the full width of the project and half its height, set the width to 500 px and the height to 250 px. Once you have done this, press the checkbox button (when you hover over it, it will say "Commit transform (Return)") shown in Figure 3-55.

Figure 3-55

If you have done this right, your project should now resemble Figure 3-56.

This example might be a bit simplistic but hopefully it illustrates how useful this feature can be in your Web design project. Without a lot of effort, you were able to exactly size an object to fit into a specific set of dimensions. You were able to exactly place it on an X and Y coordinate point in the project and then size it to the exact pixel dimensions you wanted. While this example only set up a picture with half black and half white, you can probably appreciate where this can come into play, especially in Web design.

So much of what goes into business Web portals involves exact placement of images, backgrounds, and regions of the page. If you need to have a search bar region at the top of the page that is 35 pixels high, you now know how to mock that up in Photoshop. If you want to have a sidebar box that is 50 pixels over from the leftmost edge of the browser window, you now know how to place it exactly in your Photoshop mockup project. This tool can greatly eliminate guesswork and tedious alignment issues you will almost surely face if you use a graphics program to mockup your Web sites before you create them (which you should probably always do). Using this approach, you can ensure your mockups are symmetrical and properly representative of what you will create in your Web site. For this reason, if for no other, this is one of the coolest tools in the Photoshop arsenal.

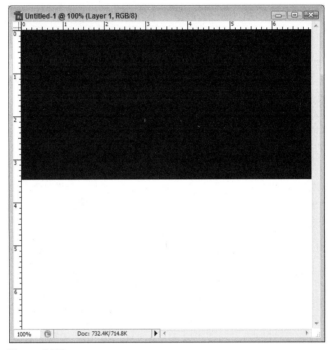

Figure 3-56

Creating the Design from Scratch

Now that you have gotten an overview of the tools and layout of Photoshop CS3 and received an introduction to designing patterns and using the Free Transform tool, it is time to get into creating a real world design that will resemble Figure 3-3 earlier in this book. As a part of this process, you will determine the design's dimensions and then create the various assets within the project to fill up those dimensions. This section will walk you through each of those areas to help you get a better understanding of what you need to be thinking about when you are making your design.

Determining the Project Dimensions

The first consideration is what dimensions your design targets. This can change from design to design and project to project. If all of your work is for a corporate intranet and there are policies on screen resolution, then that is what you should follow. However, if you are targeting an unknown audience, it may be difficult to decide exactly what resolution you should target in your design.

Take for example the following statistics from TheCounter.com for February 2008 (`http://www` `.thecounter.com/stats/2008/February/res.php`):

Resolution	Number of Hits	Percentage of Total
1600 × 1200	41,275	0%
1280 × 1024	1,864,921	30%
1152 × 864	209,118	3%
1024 × 768	2,912,561	47%
800 × 600	485,618	7%
640 × 480	8,479	0%
Unknown	652,929	10%

Generally speaking, the lower resolution you target, the bigger an audience you will be able to accommodate. For example, if you targeted a 640 × 480 resolution, your design should certainly fit into a 1600 × 1200 resolution screen. It may look tiny, but the reader should be able to see all of the content.

But at this point, what is too far down? Do designers really need to target the lowest possible resolution? Most people will say "no."

So it's time to pick a resolution that will work in most situations (or at an acceptable percentage anyway). So look back at the resolutions provided earlier. It is impossible to accurately accommodate the Unknown category since the resolution for these visitors is, after all, unknown. So, removing that category, there were a total of 5,521,972 registered page hits using this data. So, assuming that it is fair to say that each bigger resolution will accommodate any resolutions smaller than it but not necessarily bigger than it, you could come up with the following analysis:

Resolution	Number of Hits	Percentage of Total*	Cumulative Hits	Cumulative Percentage
1600 × 1200	41,275	1%	41,275	1%
1280 × 1024	1,864,921	34%	1,906,196	35%
1152 × 864	209,118	4%	2,115,314	38%
1024 × 768	2,912,561	53%	5,027,875	91%
800 × 600	485,618	9%	5,513,493	100%
640 × 480	8,479	0%	5,521,972	100%

*The percentages in the table were adjusted to reflect the removal of the Unknown category.

To explain how these numbers were derived, the first resolution, 1600 × 1200, can only effectively accommodate 1600 × 1200 resolutions or higher. Since it is the highest resolution, it can therefore only accommodate its own design. Conversely, as you move down the table, you will see that, for example, a design targeting the resolution of 1152 × 864 should fit within a monitor set at 1152 × 864, 1280 × 1024, and 1600 × 1200.

So, with this analysis, you can see that a screen resolution of 1024 × 768 will accommodate approximately 91% of users based on this data.

If you were to look to a similar source, say the Browser Display Statistics from W3Schools.com (`http://w3schools.com/browsers/browsers_display.asp`), you would see a similar trend (data through January 2008 is the most recently updated data from this Web site):

Resolution	Percentage of Total*	Cumulative Percentage
Higher than 1024 × 768	40%	40%
1024 × 768	51%	91%
800 × 600	9%	100%
640 × 480	0%	100%

*The percentages in the table were adjusted to reflect the removal of the Unknown category.

So, regardless of which statistics you draw from, you will probably see that targeting 1024 × 768 screen resolutions should accommodate more than 90% of all site visitors. Due to this, there has been a noted trend in Web design to move to this resolution (but not beyond). For years, the generally accepted target resolution was 800 × 600. However, with monitors getting bigger and resolution increasing accordingly, the target resolution has begun to shift as well. Therefore, this project will use the 1024 × 768 target resolution for its definition.

It is worth noting that, even with the use of real world browser hits as shown in these examples, the analysis may be a bit off. Take, for example, visitors that browse the Internet in less than the maximized view. These visitors, even if they have a screen resolution of 1280 × 1024, may have a browser window that only has 800 pixels wide of available space and maybe 400 pixels high because it is not in the maximized window state. This is just a cost of doing design on the Web and, honestly, there isn't a lot you can do about that. However, it is worth keeping in mind.

With the preceding caveat, many designers are turning to what is known as a "liquid" design. Liquid designs allow the design to stretch across the canvas of the browser, regardless of the dimensions that are currently available. This means that, if there are 1600 pixels available across the browser, the design will stretch to accommodate that; if, conversely, there are only 800 pixels available, the design will shrink to accommodate that. This design allows for a more consistent look for all visitors since, for example, all users will see the top navigation bar stretched all the way across the browser. If, by contrast, the designers used a fixed-pixel width design, say 700 pixels, it would look fine in an 800 × 600 browser but might look funny centered inside of 1600 pixels (meaning 450 pixels would be sitting vacant on either side of the design).

Taking into account all these considerations, this project will use the 1024 × 768 target resolution but will also use a liquid approach to the design to try to accommodate other users as well.

Creating and Setting Up the Project

For this section, you will be using layers fairly extensively to create the exact effect of the design. With this in mind, it might be a good idea to expand the docking panel so that you can see the layers palette, as shown in Figure 3-57.

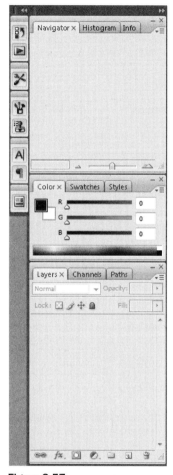

Figure 3-57

The next step is to actually create the new project. To do this, click on File in the toolbar and select New to add a new project in Photoshop. You should see a settings screen similar to that shown previously in Figure 3-29.

The main thing that you will want to do on this screen is set the Width to 1000 pixels and the Height to 900 pixels. This will allow for you to create a design that fits in the target resolution established earlier even if the numbers seem a bit off.

For example, the width is supposed to be 1024 pixels and you are setting it to 1000. Why? Remember that the browser has "stuff" on its edges. For example, all browsers will have some sort of scrollbar on them (usually on the right-hand side). There will also generally be a window border on the other side. So, even though you are hoping that your users will have at least a 1024 x 768 resolution on their monitor and that their Internet browser is maximized, you still have to back off a few pixels to account for this "stuff."

It is also important to realize that this design will be "liquid" or "fluid," meaning that it spans the entire width of the browser. If there are only 18 pixels of "stuff" for your browser, your design will span the entire 1006 pixels that remain (1024 total width less the 18 pixels of "stuff"). The real target is to set the width at a pixel dimension that will get you close to the actual target so that you can maximize your available real estate and plan the design accordingly. In your own project, you could achieve similar success at 975, 900, or 873 pixels. The width is fairly arbitrary. However, you do want to make sure you have enough width to adequately portray your target resolution so that when your design is loaded at that resolution it will look the way your thought it would. For the project in this chapter, the width is set to 1000 pixels. This allows for 24 pixels of "stuff" but still is near the target resolution of the project.

Similar real-world considerations can be applied to adjusting the height to deviate from the target resolution of 768 pixels high. In Web design, it is generally acceptable to have some vertical scrolling, so it is much more critical to focus on the horizontal width and therefore you can have a height that will generate a little scrolling. After all, even at 768 pixels, with the toolbars and such that are a part of every browser, you won't have 768 pixels of available real estate regardless. So if you truly want to create a project that doesn't scroll vertically and you want to target the 1024 × 768 resolution, you should probably set your height at around 600 pixels. However, since that isn't as much of a concern, this project will go ahead and stretch out to 900 pixels for now. This will give some "play" room so that you are limited by the non-scrollable region of the browser window. At the end of the project, you may adjust it further after you see the design. But this will be a good start.

Remember, too, that there are fixed regions of a Web site design and dynamic regions (typically). In most designs (and with this particular project), there is a header/navigation region that is static at the top and a footer region that is static at the bottom. Any discrepancy between the height you set your project and the actual height dimensions available for a user will be eaten up in the dynamic region of the design: the content area. This area is intentionally created in a way that will allow it to grow and shrink as necessary to accommodate varying levels of content. However, the other thing it should do is fill in any gaps in height distribution. This means that, for example, if you have set your height to 900 pixels but the user has an extraordinary resolution that allows for somewhere in the neighborhood of 1200 pixels of height, the extra 300 pixels will be eaten up by the whitespace in the content area. So the height here really is fairly arbitrary. You want to set it to a reasonable height that will allow you to fill up the content area with real-world mockup design elements so you can truly gauge the effectiveness of your layout and design. However, understand that, when your design goes into HTML, the height will be controlled by the content and browser/screen capabilities.

The only other setting you may want to tweak is the Background Contents property. This setting will determine what the background color should be. Typically, it is a good idea to start off with a transparent background and then build up the project from there. However, in some projects, this might not be the case. For example, if your project is one that will have the primary background color set to white, why would you first create a transparent background and then paint it white? Why not just start with a white background layer? Conversely, if your background is going to be more dynamic with some sort of repeating background or other similar effect, there is no point in starting off with a colored background since you will be completely covering it up with your background effects. For this project, though, the setting should be left to (or changed to if not already there) Transparent. Press the OK button to continue.

This is more to illustrate how to fill an entire layer with a solid color. The net result over the next few steps is to create a solid white background, so to save time you could just as easily start off with the background as a solid white color. But, following the next few steps will give you a clearer understanding of how all of this works and you will learn a bit more about Photoshop in doing so.

You should now have a new Photoshop canvas that has a transparent background and dimensions of 1000 × 900. You are now ready to fill those areas with content.

Just as a matter of preparation for the next stages of the project, you may want to do a little cleanup and setup.

The first cleanup item is to rename the layer that was created by default (it is probably called something like "Layer 1"). There are a couple of ways to do this. You could click on Layer on the toolbar and select Layer Properties or, similarly, you could right-mouse click on the layer itself in the layer palette and choose Layer Properties. Either method will get you the settings screen shown in Figure 3-58.

Figure 3-58

If you go about it this way, simply type in the name of your layer (e.g., "Background Layer") and press the OK button.

You could also just double-click on the layer name itself in the layer palette and the name becomes editable. (This is very similar to any rename capability in Windows file systems.)

Regardless of what approach you take, you should now have a single layer that is titled "Background Layer."

With this layer, you will want to paint the entire thing white. Again, you could have done this with the project creation phase (chosen "White" as the "Background Contents" property) but, in doing it that way, the background becomes locked and uneditable. Of course, there is a way to unlock the layer but, for now, suffice it to say that either way is similar and this way of doing it is as good as any other.

The first thing you will need to do is set the foreground color to white. To do this, first click the Default Colors icon shown earlier in Figure 3-35 (the part that looks like a black box over a white box).

Now click the Switch Foreground and Background Colors (X) button (the double arrow icon). This will reverse the foreground and background colors, meaning the foreground should now be white and the background should be black, as shown in Figure 3-59.

Figure 3-59

So, with colors set, click the Paint Bucket tool in the toolbar, which you saw earlier in Figure 3-49 and hover over your project window. Your cursor should turn to the paint bucket icon, as seen in Figure 3-60.

Figure 3-60

Once you see the cursor transform into the paint bucket cursor, left-mouse click anywhere in the canvas and the entire layer will be painted the foreground color (white in this case).

The last thing you will want to do as part of the setup is to create groups for the different regions of your project. Layer groups can allow you to more effectively organize your Photoshop project by creating collapsible folders in which you can store similar or related layers. For example, for this particular project, it would probably make sense to create groupings for the welcome area, logo area, navigation area, etc. Essentially, you want to create a layer group for the logical areas of the Photoshop project so that you can easily find things when you want to edit them. For example, if you have 200 layers and you want to find the one that has a gradient fill for the toolbar region of your Web page design, you might find it difficult to wade through all 200 layers just to find the one you need to edit. With layer groups, however, you can simply expand the navigation grouping and find the background layer.

In order to create a new grouping, you should click Layer on the Photoshop toolbar and then select New and, from the options presented, click Group, which will give you the settings screen shown in Figure 3-61.

Figure 3-61

The only setting you will need to change is the Name property. You can set it to Welcome Area as shown in Figure 3-53. Press the OK button to create the new layer grouping, which will actually look like a folder in the layers palette, as can be seen in Figure 3-62.

Using this same approach, you will want to create groupings for the major regions of this project:

❑ Navigation Area

❑ Logo Area

❑ Photo Area

❑ Content Area

❑ Footer Area

When you are done, your layers palette should now resemble Figure 3-63.

Figure 3-62

Figure 3-63

You now have the background and basic structure for your design and are ready to move on to the next steps. However, as one final step, you will probably want to save your project. In Photoshop, click on File on the toolbar and select Save and then choose a location for your file. You will want to keep the PSD file extension to maintain your layers and things of that nature. Choose a name (for the remainder of this chapter, the project will be referenced as "SharePointDesignLayout.PSD") and press the Save button. You will want to routinely save your project as you work on it to make sure you don't lose any work in the event of something like a power outage or surge. You can do this by clicking File on the toolbar and then clicking Save again or simply pressing Ctrl+S (Cmd+S for Mac users). This will just save the project in its current state to its current file location.

The Artist and the Surgeon

When it comes to graphic arts, there are at least two types of people: the artist and the surgeon. The artist is very right-brained in his approach to graphic design. This type of designer uses more feeling and imagination to determine how the final product will look. He also probably comes up with more of a big picture concept and then works back to figuring out how to make the limitations of the binary world fit this dream.

The surgeon is much more analytical and logical (left-brained). This type of designer will probably break up a usable workspace into logical grids and decide how to fill each one best and then worry about making things flow together after all the pieces are in place. This type of designer will say, "This is a Web site, so I need a 150 pixel header region, a 35 pixel footer region, and the remaining real estate splits off into a sidebar region and a content area." Then he will work on creating the header, then make the footer try to look like the header, and then split up the content and sidebar areas.

A fun site to try to figure out which one you most fit is here: `http://www.news.com.au/heraldsun/story/0,21985,22556281-661,00.html`

So which is better? The surgeon or the artist? Probably neither. Maybe both.

Both approaches serve their purpose in graphic arts. If strictly a surgeon, your sites might tend to all look the same and may seem to some to lack imagination. If strictly an artist, your designs might not fit the needs of real world business applications, in particular the complexities of a SharePoint site design. So the best designers, at least in the realm of business portals like SharePoint, are those who can combine both. Try to make sure your sites are imaginative and inspiring but also useful and logically organized. This can be a tough balance to try to maintain, but if you can pull it off, you will never be hurting for a job.

So why bring this up now? Well, as this chapter progresses, you will see the project mature through an artist's perspective. Rather than seeing "draw a box that is 25 pixels high 1000 pixels wide" you will see more "draw a box at the top of the page that will hold the welcome area content."

If you are strictly a surgeon, this might be hard to follow. So, to help counter that, these sections will put up the dimensions the authors came up with in their approach so that you can mimic the same dimensions in your own project. This will result in measurements of things like "98.2 pixels" because they weren't done on a rigid matrix; they were drawn with an artistic eye (what looks right). So, rather than getting fixated on "why did the authors use 98.2 pixels instead of 98 pixels? Or maybe even just 100 pixels?" just understand that these designs were laid out using the eye and not the ruler. The measurements are provided just so that, if you want, you can follow along exactly with this example and be prepared to use your project in subsequent chapters (for example, the Master Page and CSS chapters will split this design into HTML and CSS code to use for the layout of a SharePoint page).

The final PSD will also be available as a download companion to this book. If you want to play around with your own dimensions here and be strictly the artist, then feel free to do so; you can download the final project from Wrox and use that for future chapters. Or you can be a surgeon and use the provided dimensions for all areas and then use your own project in those future chapters. The choice is yours.

If you decide you do want to be a surgeon, make sure you read the section earlier in this chapter about the Free Transform tool; it will be your best friend moving forward through this chapter.

If you want to be strictly an artist, ignore the parts in this chapter with the actual dimensions of the object. These will be designated as follows:

```
Reference Point Location: Top Left Corner
X: 0.0 px
Y: 0.0 px
```

```
W: 1000.0 px
H: 147.0 px
```

And with that, it's time to get started with the actual design.

The Logo Area

Generally speaking, it's a good idea to create your design in a logical sequence, starting with what must be placed exactly and moving to the areas that are placed based on that. In other words, if you have a huge centerpiece that needs to be not only the focus of attention but also centered on the page, you would want to create that first and then move to the peripheral objects and focus on them.

However, in this design, the site is laid out on a matrix, so it probably makes more sense to work in a linear fashion from the top to the bottom, with one caveat: Using layers, the way you will probably approach this design (emphasis on probably: There is no single right way to create this design; the approach documented in this chapter is just one way) is to layout the entire area that will contain the welcome area, the logo area, and the navigation area. Then create the content for the welcome area and navigation area on top of that. When you are splicing up the image for your HTML code later, it won't matter. But for now, it ensures that there is no accidental space left between, say, the logo area and the welcome area.

So, with this in mind, it makes more sense to just create the entire area that will encapsulate the welcome, logo, and navigation area. So that is what you will do. Draw an area at the top of the project window and give it a solid color. (The color doesn't matter at this point because you will be overriding it with a gradient fill in the next step.) This area should be big enough to include the welcome area at the top, the logo area just under it, and the navigation area at the bottom. Generally speaking, this should be around 150 or so pixels high and spread the entire width of the project window.

If you are a surgeon, you can make your area conform to the following dimensions:

```
Reference Point Location: Top Left Corner
X: 0.0 px
Y: 0.0 px
W: 1000.0 px
H: 147.0 px
```

Once you have this done, it should resemble Figure 3-64.

For this design, that black is way too dark and is hard to work with, so you will want to lighten it up. You can do this by providing some sort of graphical overlay to it. In this case, you will want to provide a gradient overlay that goes from a light gray to an even lighter gray color. The change will be subtle but still noticeable in the final design.

To do this, you will need to add effects to the layer or, more specifically, one effect: the Gradient Overlay. There are several ways to do this but the easiest is to simply click Layer on the toolbar at the top of the Photoshop interface and then choose Layer Style and from the options presented Gradient Overlay. This should bring up the Layer Style dialog box shown in Figure 3-65.

The only thing you really need to adjust here is the gradient. To do that, just click on the Gradient bar in the Gradient Overlay section, which will bring up the settings shown in Figure 3-66.

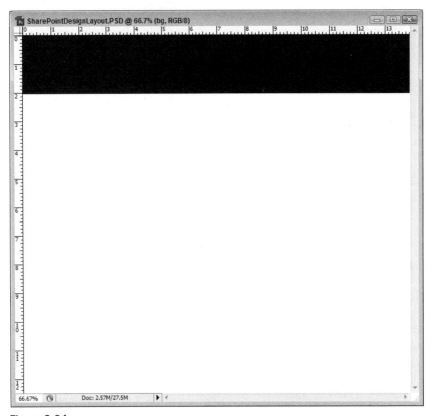

Figure 3-64

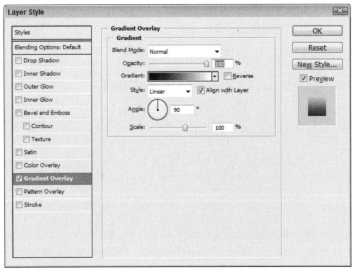

Figure 3-65

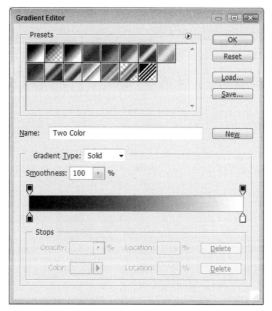

Figure 3-66

The only settings you will need to make here are the two colors that are used to set the gradient fade. These colors are designated by the markers at the bottom of the gradient, as illustrated in Figure 3-67.

Figure 3-67

If you click either of these markers (circled in Figure 3-67), you will see the options at the bottom of screen change to match the color and position of that marker. For example, if you click the black marker on the bottom left of the gradient, you should see the options change to those shown in Figure 3-68.

Figure 3-68

As you can see, the color is set to black and the location is set to 0%. The location is the position of the gradient stop. In this case, it is at the zero position, meaning that, on the gradient scale, this is where the gradient starts. If it were at the maximum position, or at the 100% location, it would be the last color of the gradient. To understand what this means, look back at Figure 3-67. The color at the very far left is at the zero position while the color at the far right is at the 100% position. So, if you wanted a gradient that went from red to yellow, you could set the zero position (left marker) to red and the 100% position (right marker) to yellow. This would create a smooth transition from red to yellow that you could use for your gradient fill.

For this object, the location is already set where it needs to be and does not require any changes.

However, you will want to change the color. To do that, click on the color box (the one that is black in this example). This should bring up the "Select stop color" selector options, shown in Figure 3-69.

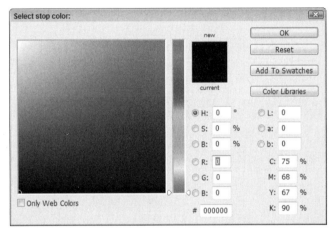

Figure 3-69

Using this screen, you can choose pretty much any color to use; you can even set it to only allow you to select Web-safe colors (for an explanation of Web-safe colors, visit http://en.wikipedia.org/wiki /Web_colors#Web-safe_colors). This is when the artist in you can really rejoice (or, conversely, the surgeon can get a little intimidated). There are so many colors to choose from and so many different shades and hues of the same color that your options really do seem endless.

However, to keep with the project at hand, choose a fairly light gray color (this example uses #cccccc for the hexadecimal color; you can simply type in "cccccc" at the bottom of the settings page). Once you have your color, press the OK button to select it for that gradient stop.

Use this same approach to set the second stop (again, the location is already set where it needs to be by default for this example) to a lighter color gray. This example uses #eeeeee for its lighter color. That is very close to white, which is represented as #ffffff, but has enough color to differentiate itself from the white background that is used for this Web site layout.

Once you have set the colors for both gradient stops, press the OK button to get back to the Layer Style settings window. Before closing this out, check the Reverse checkbox to make the gradient flow darker at the top to lighter at the bottom. Once you have done that, press the OK button to apply the gradient style. Your project should now look more like Figure 3-70 (dark gray at the top of the region fading to a light gray at the bottom).

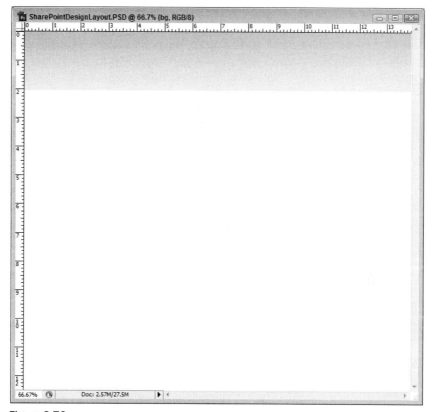

Figure 3-70

For now, the last thing you want to do to this section is overlay the diagonal pattern you created earlier in this chapter (the 9x9 diagonal pattern). One thing to think about, though, is that you only want to overlay the pattern over the gradient you just created, not the entire project window. Like everything else, there are several ways to do this. However, probably the easiest is to define the fill area before you apply the fill.

To do this, make sure the layer that has the gradient applied to it is the active layer. (Click on it in the layer palette window to make it active if it is not.) Once you have done this, hold down the Ctrl button (Cmd for Mac Users) on your keyboard and click on the thumbnail image on your layer in the layer palette (see Figure 3-71).

By doing this, you should see that the area of the project represented by the logo area background becomes a selection in the project (as indicated by the marching ants). In other words, the top part of your project should now be a selection.

With your logo area background layer still active, click on Layer on the toolbar and choose New Fill Layer and then Pattern from the options presented. This will give you an options screen similar to Figure 3-72.

You do not need to change any of the default settings; just press the OK button. This will bring up the settings screen shown in Figure 3-73.

Figure 3-71

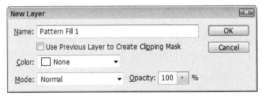

Figure 3-72

Figure 3-73

Most likely, when you see this screen, you will not have your diagonal pattern selected. If that is the case, make sure you select it from the dropdown menu attached to the icon view of the pattern. Once you have your diagonal pattern selected, press the OK button.

Doing this, you will notice a couple of things. First, you should notice that the diagonals have now been applied to your project, as seen in Figure 3-74.

The second thing you will want to take note of is the new layer added for you in the layer palette (Figure 3-75).

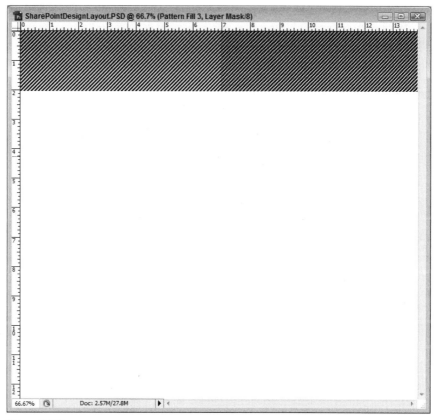

Figure 3-74

Figure 3-75

This layer shows two things. First, it has created a new type of layer and therefore the icon for the layer is different. This layer is a pattern fill layer as opposed to just a standard layer that you have been using up to this point. The other thing you will see is that there is a second icon on this layer. This is the mask for the layer. To this point, the project has only used standard layers, which have no mask applied by default, so this will probably be a new concept. Masks are a very useful tool that you can add to standard layers. Some objects like the Pattern Fill Layer automatically include a mask.

A mask allows you to apply only part the current layer to your project. The way to think about this, perhaps, is to think about what really happened here. The entire layer is really filled with the diagonal pattern. However, you only see the part that is on top of the gradient background layer. Why is that? The rest is hidden by the mask. If you want to play around with this to see how it works, click the icon for the mask to make it active and then go paint some regions of your project that are currently not showing diagonals. If your foreground color is set to white, you will see the diagonals start to come through wherever you are painting. The way a mask works is that where it is white your layer comes through; where it is black, it does not. That is why the icon on your diagonals layer looks mostly black except for the region you are displaying, where it shows white. Masks are a really useful tool in that they can allow you to do non-destructive edits to your layers (meaning you can delete part of a layer in effect but, in reality, it's still there).

The last thing you will want to do with this layer is play around with the opacity and fill of the diagonals layer. The diagonals are overpowering the image and need to be softened so that you can see the gradient colors you just set up.

If you look at Figure 3-75 again, you will see that there are properties for Opacity and Fill. Without going too deeply into the difference, you can think of Opacity as affecting everything and Fill affecting only the object and not its effects. For example, if you have text on the project with a drop shadow effect applied to it (you will see how to do this later in this chapter), if you reduce the opacity to zero, you won't see the text or the drop shadow at all. However, if you instead reduce the fill to zero, you won't see the text at all but you will still see its drop shadow. Fill is a fun way to make some cool effects.

Play around with these settings until you find a desirable effect for the diagonal lines. Basically, you want to see the lines but only barely; they shouldn't take away focus from the background gradient colors.

```
Opacity: 5%
Fill: 26%
```

Your project should now resemble Figure 3-76. While the diagonals may not completely show through in the printed manuscript, you should hopefully be able to see them more clearly in your own project.

At this point, it's time to move onto other regions. However, you will need to come back to this region later to place the header text and the search box sections. But, since it would be hard to place of these things before putting on the Welcome and Navigation areas, it's time to take a break from the logo area and do those other areas first.

The Welcome Area

The first step is to add a layer in the Welcome Area group that will be used as the background for that region. As a refresher, to do this, you should set the group folder as the active object by clicking it and, after doing so, click Layer in the toolbar and then New and Layer. Call the layer "Background Gradient" so that you can reference it later in this section.

Figure 3-76

Now, on your new Background Gradient layer, draw a selection at the top of the page and fill it with black, much like you did for the Logo area background. Your project should resemble Figure 3-77.

At the risk of foreshadowing a bit, you need to make sure this layer extends beyond the boundaries of the project window. This is because you will later being applying a border to the layer that you want only visible on the bottom. To accomplish this, you need to start your image at a negative position on the X and Y axis points and compensate on the height and width.

Reference Point Location: Top Left Corner
X: -1.0 px
Y: -3.0 px
W: 1005.0 px
H: 28.0 px

The next thing you will want to do is add some effects to this plain looking black bar. For the purposes of this design, this means that you want to provide a gradient overlay, border (stroke), and drop shadow for this region. To do this, right-click the layer in the layer palette and choose Blending Options.

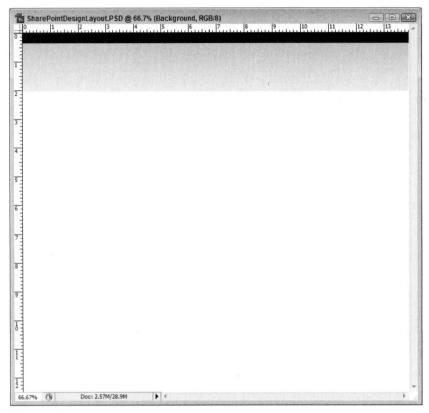

Figure 3-77

On the screen that appears, check the Drop Shadow option in the left pane (make sure you click on the title "Drop Shadow" to ensure the settings for that effect is displayed) and then make the following adjustments:

- ❏ Set Blend Mode to Multiply
- ❏ Set Opacity to 19 percent
- ❏ Set the Angle to 69 degrees
- ❏ Set Distance to 2 pixels
- ❏ Set Spread to 0 percent (this is the default so you may not need to change this setting)
- ❏ Set Size to 9 pixels

The other settings should be okay for the Drop Shadow effect.

Next, you will want to set the properties for the Gradient Overlay effect. To access these settings, click on Gradient Overlay in the left pane; this should also serve to check this setting. Using similar techniques as you did with the Gradient Overlay settings in the logo area, you will want to make the following adjustments to this setting:

- **Gradient Stop 1 (0%) Color:** #245e28
- **Gradient Stop 2 (100%) Color:** #367138

You are now ready to set the last setting, the stroke. This is the setting that will put a border around the selection. Remember that you only want the border to display on the bottom of the selection, which is why you modified the area beforehand to extend beyond the borders of the screen.

To set the border, click Stroke, thereby checking this option, in the left pane of the settings window. You will want to set the properties to the following:

- **Size:** 1 pixel
- **Position:** Inside
- **Blend Mode:** Normal
- **Opacity:** 100%
- **Fill Type:** Color

You will also want to set the color. To do this, click the Color box in the options under Fill Type. If you click the color image on the screen, it will bring up the color picker screen. Use this screen to set the color to dadada and press the OK button.

You now have all of your settings in place. Press the OK button one final time to see them get applied to your image. You should see that your black box has now become a green gradient box, as shown in Figure 3-78.

The next step is to add the text that will display for this region. This text will need to be white to contrast against the greenish background. The easiest way to ensure this is to bring back the default black and white foreground and background colors (click the Default Colors icon) and then reverse them (click on the curved double-arrow icon), as you saw earlier in this section. That will make the foreground color white and the background color black. The background color is not as important at this stage since the text will be using the foreground color. The important part of this step is to get the foreground color to be white and this is probably the easiest way to do that.

With layers in mind, you will need to put your text layer *on top of* your Background Layer in the Welcome Area Group. This will make the text sit higher in the visibility hierarchy of your project, meaning you can see the text on top of the green gradient of the "Background Layer." If you put the text layer below the Background Layer, the text will be completely hidden since the Background Layer is completely opaque.

To make sure you do the hierarchy right, click on the Background Gradient layer in the Welcome Area Group on the Layers palette. This will make that particular layer be the currently active layer. Now, with your foreground color set to white and the Background Gradient layer being active, click on the Horizontal Type tool on the toolbox, which can be seen in Figure 3-79.

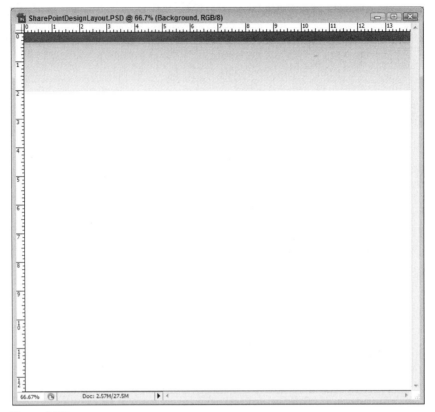

Figure 3-78

Figure 3-79

As can be seen in Figure 3-79, the Horizontal Type tool is part of a tool group that includes the Vertical Type tool, the Horizontal Type Mask tool, and the Vertical Type Mask tool. If any of these other tools are the active tool in this group, make sure you switch to the Horizontal Type tool before proceeding.

Once you select this tool, you will notice that the options bar changes to give you more text-specific options (like font names, weight, and size), which can be seen in Figure 3-80.

Figure 3-80

Just as Figure 3-80 shows, you will want to make the following adjustments (if not already set to these by default):

- **Font Family:** Tahoma
- **Font Style:** Regular
- **Font Size:** 11 pt
- **Anti-aliasing method:** None
- **Text Alignment:** Left

Now, with the Horizontal Type tool selected and its options set, click anywhere in the green area of your project. You should see that there is a flashing cursor and a small underline at the spot where you clicked. You can now begin typing. Type in "Welcome Mossman, Joe" and then press the checkmark in the options toolbar. (It will turn green when you hover over it.)

This will add the welcome text to your project. However, you will want to position it better. To do this, you will follow similar steps as outlined earlier in this chapter. Change to the Move tool (the arrow icon at the top of the toolbox) and drag the text to where it looks appropriate somewhere near the left-hand edge of your project in region defined by the green gradient background.

If you are a surgeon, you will want to use the Free Transform tool to create the region with the following dimensions:

```
Reference Point Location: Middle Left Edge
X: 18.0 px
Y: 12.4 px
```

The last thing you need to consider for this text is the arrow that is sitting right next to it in the mockup. As you may know, in MOSS 2007, the welcome message is accompanied by a small arrow that indicates dropdown options (for things like logging out, signing in as a different user, and so on), as can be seen in Figure 3-81.

Figure 3-81

So, for your mockup, you will want to include the arrow as well to make sure the depiction is as accurate as possible. Fortunately, you can borrow those images from your MOSS installation and copy them into the Photoshop project. To do this, assuming you have a default installation set up and haven't modified anything, you should be able to navigate directly to the arrow graphic by going to the following path: `http://<SITE PATH>/_layouts/images/menudark.gif`. For example, if your site is located at `http://www.MySharePointSite.com`, you can navigate to the following path to get the image: `http://www.MySharePointSite.com/_layouts/images/menudark.gif`.

If you open the path in a browser, simply right-mouse click on the graphic and select Save Picture As. Unfortunately, copying the image to the clipboard directly from the browser and then pasting it into your project will lose the transparency of the graphic. So you will want to save it to a location you can remember (perhaps an Assets subdirectory off of your project folder). Once you have it saved, open it up in Photoshop (File ⇨ Open) and then, at this point, copy it (Edit ⇨ Copy). This will put the image on the clipboard for you with its transparency intact.

Now you are ready to paste your image into your mockup project. First make sure the text layer is active by clicking on it in the Palette. Next, click Edit on the toolbar and select Paste. This will paste the arrow onto your project on a new layer that is above the text layer but still within the Welcome Area group. It will probably be centered in the project window, which is not what you want; you want it immediately to the right of the text. So, once the image is in your project, it's time to move it. So, again, use the Move tool to move the arrow next to the text. You are now done with the welcome message.

Once again, if you are a surgeon, you will want to use the following dimensions when creating this region:

```
Reference Point Location: Middle Left Edge
X: 139.0 px
Y: 11.5 px
```

You will next want to follow similar steps to create the text and arrow for the Site Actions that will be the right-side counterpart to the welcome message. In other words, you want an almost exact copy of the Welcome message and its linked arrow sitting on the right side of the screen with the text "Site Actions" displayed instead of "Welcome Mossman, Joe."

```
Text Settings:
    Reference Point Location: Middle Left Edge
    X: 902.0 px
    Y: 10.4 px

Arrow Settings:
    Reference Point Location: Middle Left Edge
    X: 965.0 px
    Y: 11.5 px
```

If you did this correctly, your project should now resemble Figure 3-82.

The Navigation Area

The next section is the navigation area. This could also be considered the toolbar of the Web site. This section will have a "gel" effect that makes it look similar to the taskbar in Windows Vista; it will just be modified to fit the color scheme that has been established to this point (the greens).

The first thing you will need is a layer added to your project for the background image. Make sure the Navigation Area group is active and add a new layer to that group and call it "Background Gradient." This section should probably be a little bit larger than the Welcome Area as it will provide the central navigation for the site and you want to draw some attention to it. Remember from earlier discussions that one of the quintessential elements of strong Web design is ease of navigation. That being said, you don't want to make the navigation over-to-top and the primary thing that draws the visitor's eye; the content of the site should do that. But you do want to make sure people can find the navigation tools and easily navigate your site.

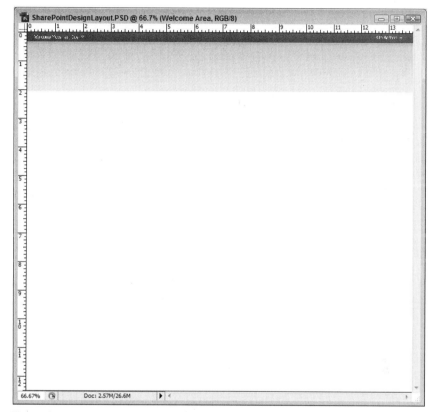

Figure 3-82

The next thing you want to do is add a new object to your layer to represent the navigation region. This should be at the bottom of the logo area and probably around 35 pixels high. As before, fill it with black as a temporary solution so that you can identify it. (You will be covering it up with layer effects in the next steps.)

```
Reference Point Location: Top Left Corner
X: 0.0 px
Y: 116.0 px
W: 1000.0 px
H: 33.0 px
```

With this new area defined, it is time to apply some layer effects to it. Essentially, this will involve two things: a gradient overlay and a small drop shadow. With this in mind, open up the layer's Blending Options to the Gradient Overlay settings (Layer ⇨ Layer Style ⇨ Gradient Overlay). This will bring up the Gradient Overlay screen for the Layer Style dialog box. As with previous steps in this project, you will need to bring up the Gradient Overlay Editor (see earlier Figure 3-66) by clicking on the Gradient box in the Gradient Overlay section.

The next step is to set the gradient overlay for this layer. However, unlike the previous use of the gradient overlay effect, this time you will be making more than two gradient stops (i.e., there will be intermediate stops between the zero and 100% positions).

So how do you add new gradient stops? It's actually fairly simple. When you are looking at the gradient displayed, you will see the stops you have been manipulating at the bottom of the gradient depiction. If you hover your mouse anywhere in that area (under the gradient depiction and between the 2 existing stops) you will see that the mouse turns to the hand cursor, as seen in Figure 3-83.

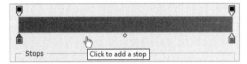

Figure 3-83

While hovering in this area, click on the settings box and a new stop will be created. It doesn't really matter where you click because you are going to set the position in the settings below. For example, click anywhere in that area to make the second gradient stop. Next, go to the Location property and enter in "48" to indicate 48%. Finally, set the color by clicking on the color box and setting the color to "2b6830" in the color picker tool. You can follow these same steps to set the other gradients in this example, as shown in Figure 3-84.

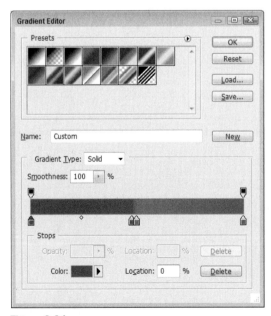

Figure 3-84

Use this approach to set the following four gradient stops for the navigation area:

- ❏ **Gradient Stop 1 (0%) Color:** 245e28
- ❏ **Gradient Stop 2 (48%) Color:** 2b6830
- ❏ **Gradient Stop 3 (50%) Color:** 5d845a
- ❏ **Gradient Stop 4 (100%) Color:** 367138

The result will be a green "gel" effect for the background of the navigation area.

The next step is to set the drop shadow. To do this, click on the Drop Shadow tab of the Layer Style window and make the following modifications:

- ❏ **Opacity:** 37%
- ❏ **Angle:** 69 degrees
- ❏ **Distance:** 2 px
- ❏ **Spread:** 0%
- ❏ **Size:** 5 px

At this point, you have finished styling the background and can press the OK button to save the changes. The next step is to add text that represents each button in the navigation control. For this purpose, you will need to add a text layer to the Navigation Area group with the following properties:

- ❏ **Foreground Color:** White
- ❏ **Font Family:** Calibri (or some similar sans serif font like Arial)
- ❏ **Font Style:** Regular
- ❏ **Font Size:** 18 pt
- ❏ **Text:** Company   Products   Services   News & Events   Investor Relations   Careers   Contact Us (notice that there are eight spaces between each button text – in other words Company, then eight spaces, then Products, then eight spaces, and so on).

It is important to give due thought to font choices at this point in the project. Most designers agree that it is okay to have two font families in a given Web project and, at times, even three. But any more than three is just a bad idea. It can create confusion for the reader and makes the site look amateurish. For a professional look, designers really need to try to limit the number of font transitions they use. With this in mind, this project uses three fonts in it: Tahoma, Calibri, and Candara. All three are sans-serif fonts, which helps ease the transition from font to font. When going through the chapter, if you do not have these fonts installed, feel free to use different fonts that meet your needs. Just try to keep them fairly similar (all in the same font group) and limit them to, at most, three font families. This will provide a clean, professional look, even with different fonts utilized.

Once you have the text added, you will probably want to position it so that it better represents where it should display in the final Web solution. As before, use the Move tool to position the text to an appropriate location.

```
Reference Point Location: Middle Left Edge
X: 19.0 px
Y: 131.4 px
```

The only thing left to do for the default look is to add some separator bars. This is not quite as easy as it sounds, unfortunately. It will take a few steps.

The first step is to draw a line on the page using the Line tool, shown in Figure 3-85.

Figure 3-85

The Line tool is part of a group of drawing shapes that are included in the toolbox in Photoshop CS3. As such, it may be hidden under one of the other shapes. (The Rectangle tool is generally the default tool shown in the toolbox.)

Make sure the text layer you just created is active before you start using the Line tool. This will ensure that the new shape object will go on a layer on top of the text (which is what you want). The only setting that you may need to change in the Options toolbar is the Weight; if it is not currently set to 1 px, then change this property before drawing any lines. You will actually want to make this smaller in the next step, but when using the line tool, you can't go below 1 pixel.

When you are sure the text layer is active and you have its weight set properly, simply draw a line anywhere on the project window. You do this by clicking your left mouse button anywhere on the screen, dragging a distance, and then releasing the mouse button. As an extra tip, if you hold down the Shift key (applies to both PC and Mac users) on your keyboard, the line will always draw in degrees that are multiples of 45. So if, as in this case, you want to draw a straight up-and-down line, hold down the Shift key and draw the line 90 degrees straight down. The actual distance and position are not important as you will change them in the next step. Once you release your mouse button, you should see that a new shape layer has been added to your project just above the text layer. This is exactly what you want (for now).

The next step is to resize and reposition the object. You pretty much have to be a surgeon to get this right. This is because these lines have to exactly match the size of the navigation background in order to look right. As good as the artist's eye is, it's safer to rely on the surgeon's accuracy for this step.

With that in mind, enter the Free Transform mode of the line object. If you have used this tool before, you will notice that the verbiage of the tools is a little different. In this scenario, click "Edit" on the toolbar and then select "Free Transform Path" (instead of Free Transform as in earlier steps) and then make the following adjustments:

❑　**Reference Point Location:** Top Left corner

❑　**X-position:** 104.0 px

- ❏ **Y-position:** 116.0 px
- ❏ **Width:** 0.5 px
- ❏ **Height:** 33.0 px

Hopefully, most of these settings will make sense if you have been following the examples in the book to this point. The only one that might be confusing is the X-position setting. This setting is set arbitrarily. Since the text is just one long string, it is impossible to know what the rightmost Reference Point Location is for Company and the leftmost Reference Point Location is for Products so that you can split the difference and move the line between the two. Due to this, you have to just eyeball the layout and pick something that looks about right. However, with that being true, if it is slightly off, it can be corrected in the HTML code since you can put the exact padding and position of elements such as this divider; this is just a mockup to see how it will hopefully render out.

Now that you have your line drawn, you will want to rasterize it, which will modify it from being a shape object into a standard layer. Doing this will give you the effects and power of typical layers, which is somewhat missing in shape layers.

To rasterize the layer, you need to make sure the shape layer is active and then click on Layer on the toolbar and select Rasterize and then Layer. This should create a standard layer called something like Shape 1 and likely change the color of the line to the foreground color (which is probably white if you were just working with the text).

At this point, the first line is mostly done. However, before finishing the line, it might be a good idea to go ahead and draw the other lines out and then apply the final effects to all of them at one time.

You could do this by following the steps above six more times (once each for the remaining separators and then one for the ending line). However, if you want to use a shortcut, you can just use the keyboard shortcut Ctrl+J (Cmd+J for Mac users) to make an exact copy of the current layer. So, with the line layer being active, press Ctrl+J (Cmd+J for Mac users) six times to make six copies of this original line layer.

Once you have these six new layers, which you will be able to see in the layers palette but which won't show up in the project since they are all laying one on top of the other, you need to drag them to their appropriate positions in the navigation area. To do this, you will again use the Move tool. So, with one of the new layer copies active and the Move tool selected, drag the lines to the appropriate place between each button text.

If you are a surgeon, you will want to use the Free Transform tool to create your regions with the following settings:

```
Common Settings
     Reference Point Location: Top Left Corner
     Y: 116.0 px

Individual X properties of each additional line
     Line 2: 198.0 px
     Line 3: 285.0 px
     Line 4: 424.0 px
     Line 5: 582.0 px
     Line 6: 666.0 px
     Line 7: 774.0 px
```

Since these lines are 1-pixel wide, they will be hard to draw if the project is viewed at 100% magnification (or smaller). In order to make the dragging go more smoothly, it might be easier to increase the magnification of the project to something like 300% and then drag the lines. You can do by clicking View ⇨ Zoom several times to get the desired zoom. Once you have moved all of the lines, you can reduce the magnification back to a normal range with View ⇨Zoom Out.

For this project, it will be easier to combine all lines into one layer so that you can modify their effects globally instead of line-by-line. To do this, click one of the line layers in the Layers Palette to make it active. Then hold down the Shift key (same for PC and Mac users) on your keyboard and click on each of the other six line layers. When you are finished, all seven layers should be active. Now you want to merge these seven layers by clicking on Layer on the toolbar and selecting Merge Layers. You should now have one layer that contains all seven lines. You might want to rename the layer in the Layer Properties to something that makes more sense like "Lines."

The last thing you will want to do for the default buttons is to darken the lines up (especially if they are white). With your new Lines layer active, go into the Color Overlay settings of the Layer Style properties. Once there, change the color to 3a3d40 and press the OK button. Your default buttons should now be complete.

The last step you will want to do for the navigation area is to include a hover effect. This effect will illustrate what your project will look like when someone hovers over your navigation buttons with their mouse. You want to make sure that you set the area off in a way that makes sense and stays within the theme of your page. For this example, you will be changing both the background gradient and the font color of the button text.

To illustrate how the hover effect will work, you will need to pick one button to apply the effect to. This will show most of the buttons in the default state and one button in its hover state. Truthfully, you could pick any of the buttons in the navigation bar to showcase the effect. However, to show everything going on, it might be a good idea to not use the one that touches the edge of the project (for example, not the one to the far left of the navigation area). This is because some of the effect will be lost if it extends beyond the confines of the project window. For this reason, the Products button will be used to illustrate the hover effect of the buttons.

So the first step is to create a new layer called Hover Background in the Navigation Area (above the Lines layer). You will want to draw a selection with the Rectangular Marquee tool that will cover the entire navigation bar (top to bottom) and span between the two lines for the Products button. For now, fill the layer in with black.

```
Reference Point Location: Top Left Corner
X: 105.0 px
Y: 116.0 px
W: 93.0 px
H: 33.0 px
```

The next thing you will want to do is add a gradient overlay to the selection (Layer ⇨ Layer Style ⇨ Gradient Overlay). Just like with the navigation gradient overlay, you will want to create 4 gradient stops, as defined below:

❏ **Gradient Stop 1 (0%) Color:** f3f3f3

❏ **Gradient Stop 2 (54%) Color:** f1f1f1

- ❑ **Gradient Stop 3 (53%) Color:** e1e1e1
- ❑ **Gradient Stop 4 (100%) Color:** bfbfbf

Finally, you will need to add an inner shadow. While you still have the Layer Style settings up, click the Inner Shadow tab and make the following adjustments:

- ❑ **Opacity:** 75%
- ❑ **Angle:** 90 degrees
- ❑ **Distance:** 0 px
- ❑ **Choke:** 0%
- ❑ **Size:** 2 px

The last step for the navigation is to add the hover text for the Company button. Make sure that the Hover Background layer is active, and then select the Text tool in the toolbox. Add text to the project with the following properties:

- ❑ **Text:** Products
- ❑ **Foreground Color:** 5d625a
- ❑ **Font Family:** Calibri (if available)
- ❑ **Font Style:** Regular
- ❑ **Font Size:** 18 pt

You will also want to position the text approximately where the text for Products is located on the original buttons.

```
Reference Point Location: Middle Left Edge
X: 120.0 px
Y: 131.4 px
```

Once you have this new text area in place, your navigation area is complete and should resemble Figure 3-86.

The Logo and the Search Area

Now that you have the logo area sandwiched between the welcome area and the navigation area, it is time to return to the logo area and create the logo text and the search box area for this project. The way this project is being built, it would have been premature to try to put the logo text and search box up any sooner because you weren't able to see the other parts of that area yet so it would be hard to place the new elements properly. But since the welcome and navigation areas are complete, you can now get a better feel for the layout of that region and, as a result, be able to better place these new elements.

One discussion point, though, is how fancy you should make the text of the logo. This may seem like an unimportant question but it does have some significant ramifications. For example, if you are satisfied with just using a solid color text, then you can just use text in your rendered HTML project (which is the ultimate output of this Photoshop project). However, if you go into using things like gradient overlays, drop shadows, and other effects, you will box yourself into using an image for this text. Now, is that really that big of a deal? Probably not. But text will load faster in the browser than the image. And, when you start getting into accessibility concerns, text is easier for visually impaired users to deal with in their browsers. Not to mention, if your image relies on any kind of transparency, especially any kind of alpha transparency (such as drop shadows, glow effects, and so on), you may run into some significant browser compatibility issues with your images. Although, quite frankly, this is becoming less and less true with the adoption of modern browsers. (Most modern browsers support the transparency and alpha transparency of PNG images, for example.) So, often, text makes more sense. However, an argument can always be made to use an image because of the necessity of the effects an image can provide.

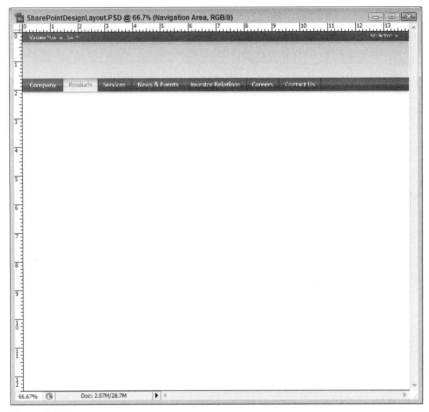

Figure 3-86

For this example, you will use an array of effects just to see how they play on the text (and so that you can see how this will work when creating the logo image in later chapters). Therefore, you should add text for the logo with the following parameters:

❑ **General Settings**

    ❑ **Text:** Mossman & Partners, Inc.

    ❑ **Font Family:** Calibri (or a similar font if this is not available)

    ❑ **Font Size:** 36 pt

❑ **Drop Shadow Settings**

    ❑ **Blend Mode:** Multiply

- ❑ **Opacity:** 46%
- ❑ **Angle:** 90 degrees
- ❑ **Distance:** 0 px
- ❑ **Spread:** 0%
- ❑ **Size:** 2 px
- ❑ **Color Overlay Settings**
  - ❑ **Blend Mode:** Normal
  - ❑ **Color:** 214900
  - ❑ **Opacity:** 72%
- ❑ **Gradient Overlay Settings**
  - ❑ **Blend Mode:** Normal
  - ❑ **Opacity:** 100%
  - ❑ **Gradient Stop 1 (0%) Color:** 121212
  - ❑ **Gradient Stop 2 (22%) Color:** 2d2d2d
  - ❑ **Gradient Stop 3 (48%) Color:** 000000
  - ❑ **Gradient Stop 4 (50%) Color:** 4c4c4c
  - ❑ **Gradient Stop 5 (75%) Color:** 676767
  - ❑ **Gradient Stop 6 (100%) Color:** 4c4c4c
  - ❑ **Style:** Linear
  - ❑ **Angle:** 90 degrees
  - ❑ **Scale:** 100%
- ❑ **Stroke Settings**
  - ❑ **Size:** 1 px
  - ❑ **Position:** Outside
  - ❑ **Blend Mode:** Normal
  - ❑ **Opacity:** 30%
  - ❑ **Color:** 696969

Most of these settings are fairly arbitrary; they were used because they look good. The most complicated of these settings is setting up the multiple gradient stops for the Gradient Overlay effect. This is done in the same way you did it for the Background Gradient layer of the navigation area so, if you don't remember how to do that, flip back to that section and look it over.

Once you have the text of the logo created, you will need to place it where it looks good. For this project, it should go toward the bottom left-hand corner of the logo area.

```
Reference Point Location: Top Left Corner
X: 21.7 px
Y: 65.3 px
```

The next section is the search area, which will consist of some text, a textbox, and a search button. This area will be essentially right-justified in your project (sitting next to the right edge of the browser window) and resting towards the bottom of the logo area. Again, there is no hard-and-fast rule that says this is where the search area has to be; this is just what looks good in the eyes of the designer that created this project example. You may find that, when recreating this project, you like it somewhere else. Just be aware that you will use this project in later chapters so, if you do deviate in your placement, make sure you remember that you made this deviation when you start breaking out the Photoshop file into usable HTML and CSS equivalents. Otherwise, the positioning code you create in later chapters may not work as you set it up in this chapter. If, for example, you decide the search area should be in the white content area built later in this chapter, you will have to modify the code in later chapters to move the search area to the content area since the code provided in those chapters will put it in the same location as shown here.

So, to get started, you want to create a small button to use to initiate the search. For this, you will use the tools in Photoshop to create a small triangle that will be used as a button control in the rendered HTML. Click the Polygon tool in the toolbox, which can be seen in Figure 3-87.

Figure 3-87

Once you have this tool selected, you should see that the Options bar changes to give you the settings for this tool. The only setting that you will want to modify is the Sides property, which you should set to 3. This will allow you to easily draw a triangle shape in your document.

You will want to make sure that one of the layers in the Logo Area group is active (for example, the text layer you were just modifying) so that the new shape layer is created in that group. With the appropriate layer being active and the Polygon tool selected, draw a triangle somewhere on the screen; the size and location do not matter at this stage since you will be setting that next.

If you click with your left mouse button and hold down the Shift key (same for both PC and Mac users), you can then drag to the right and it will create your triangle with one side perfectly at a 90 degree angle, which is what you want for this button image. When you get a triangle that is a size you can work with, release your mouse button.

Once you have released your mouse, you will hopefully notice that a new shape layer has been added to your project, probably called something like Shape 1, and it will resemble the line shape you drew in the navigation area in that it has two distinct icons rather than a single one like the other layers.

Now that you have your shape, it's time to convert it to a standard layer. If you remember from the discussion with the lines in the Navigation area, the process of converting something like a shape or text into a graphic object is called rasterizing. Doing this will allow you to treat the object just like any other drawn object in your project. For example, if you wanted to cut out an ellipse-shape hole in the middle of your text, you couldn't do that with real text. But if you convert it to a graphics object, in other words, rasterize it, you will be able to do exactly that.

To do this, with your shape layer active, click on Layer on the toolbar and select Rasterize and then Layer. You will now have a standard layer with a triangle drawn on it.

You will now want to adjust the size and the position of the triangle. You can do this with either the Move tool or the Free Transform method, both of which were documented in earlier sections of this chapter. Either way, get the arrow sized to look like a button and placed in the bottom right-hand corner of the logo area.

```
Reference Point Location: Top Left Corner
X: 951.0 px
Y: 82.0 px
W: 9.0 px
H: 12.0 px
```

If you move the arrow and can't see it any more, it's possible its layer is sitting below a larger layer. In other words, if in the hierarchy of your layers your triangle button layer is sitting below your background gradient layer, you won't see the button. If this happens, which is a risk at this point since you are coming back to this area after doing other work in other areas, just click on the triangle layer and drag it above the other layers in the logo area. This will make sure it displays in the final result.

The only other thing that you will need to do is to add a Color Overlay (Layer ⇨ Layer Style ⇨ Color Overlay) and set the color to 25632a.

The next step is to create a textbox area immediately adjacent to the search button. In your own Web projects, you have probably added hundreds of textbox controls over the years (unless you are fairly new to Web design). But in Photoshop, there is no TextBox control. So, you have to trick it. You have to draw an object in your project that resembles a textbox.

To do this, create a new layer by clicking Layer on the toolbar and selecting New and then Layer. In that layer, use the Rectangular Marquee tool to draw a rectangular shape roughly the size of a standard textbox control and then use the Paint Bucket tool to fill it with White. Now position the box next to the triangle button you just created.

```
Reference Point Location: Top Left Corner
X: 804.0 px
Y: 77.0 px
W: 139.0 px
H: 22.0 px
```

This will create a solid white box that is immediately adjacent to the button you just created and has dimensions suitable to resemble a textbox. The only other thing you want to do with this textbox is give it a green border. To do this, with the Textbox layer active, click on Layer and then select Layer Style and Stroke and make the following adjustments:

- ❏ **Size:** 1 px
- ❏ **Position:** Inside
- ❏ **Color:** 256129

The last thing you will need to add is the Search text itself. So, as you have done several times already, add a text layer to your logo area with the following properties:

❑ **Text:** Search:

❑ **Foreground Color:** 25632a

❑ **Font Family:** Candara (or a similar sans serif font like Arial if this is not available)

❑ **Font Style:** Regular

❑ **Font Size:** 17 pt

You may need to adjust the location of the text layer as well once you see it on the screen. If required, go ahead and move it at this point as well.

```
Reference Point Location: Top Left Corner
X: 739.9 px
Y: 80.0 px
```

And with this, the Logo Area is complete. Your project should now resemble Figure 3-88.

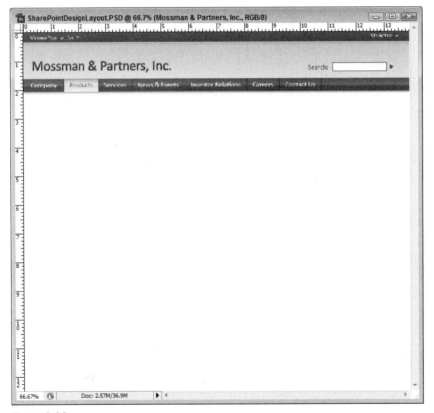

Figure 3-88

The Photo Area

The next step is to create an eye-catching area of the page that will contain a photo and the mission statement of the organization. The first two steps are identical to most everything you have seen to this point so there is not much need to elaborate.

First, within the Photo Area group, add a new layer called Green Bars and create a selection in it filled with a Black foreground color. The selection should span the entire width of the project, be fairly big, and be fairly close to the navigation area. The final result should look like Figure 3-89.

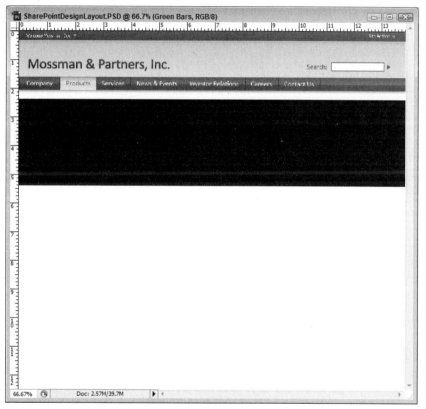

Figure 3-89

If you are a surgeon, you will probably want to use the Free Transform tool to create your area with the following dimensions:

```
Reference Point Location: Top Left Corner
X: 0.0 px
Y: 171.0 px
W: 1000.0 px
H: 218.0 px
```

The only other setting you will need to do for this layer is to add a Color Overlay (Layer ⇨ Layer Style ⇨ Color Overlay) and set the color to 63ab67. This will create a big green box a short distance under the navigation system.

The next step is to add another layer, titled Black Gradient, on top of the Green Bars layer (so that the Black Gradient layer overlays the Green Bars one). Try to position this new layer so that it makes it look like there are equal size green bars on the top and bottom of the new black object. (Remember to keep the new Black Gradient layer on top of the Green Gradient layer in your layer hierarchy.) This should resemble Figure 3-90.

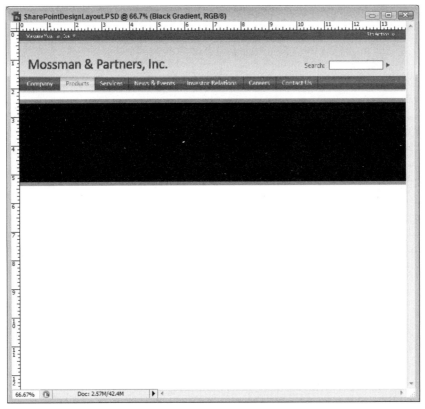

Figure 3-90

As before, you might want to use the Free Transform tool to make your selection match these dimensions.

```
Reference Point Location: Top Left Corner
X: 0.0 px
Y: 181.0 px
W: 1000.0 px
H: 199.0 px
```

For this black box, though, you will want to add a little style to give it a bit of pizzazz. You can do this through adding the following effects using the Blending Options of the Layer (Layer ⇨ Layer Style ⇨ Blending Effects):

- ❑ **Inner Shadow Settings**
  - ❑ **Blend Mode:** Multiply
  - ❑ **Color:** 000000
  - ❑ **Opacity:** 29%
  - ❑ **Angle:** 90 degrees
  - ❑ **Distance:** 0 px
  - ❑ **Choke:** 0%
  - ❑ **Size:** 6px
  - ❑ **Noise:** 0%

- ❑ **Gradient Overlay Settings**
  - ❑ **Blend Mode:** Normal
  - ❑ **Opacity:** 100%
  - ❑ **Gradient Stop 1 (0%) Color:** 000000
  - ❑ **Gradient Stop 2 (100%) Color:** 45494d
  - ❑ **Style:** Linear
  - ❑ **Angle:** 90 degrees
  - ❑ **Scale:** 150%

With this being done, it's time to add the photo and mission statement to the black gradient box. The more complicated of these two, and also the one that will set the positioning of both, will be the photo box that sits on the right edge of the gradient bars. This will be a fairly fixed width and be positioned all the way to the right of the screen, while the mission statement will fill the available space to its left. This means that if, for example, the photo is 100 pixels wide and you have 1000 pixels to work with, the photo will occupy the 100 pixels to the right-hand side of the browser window and the mission statement will take what is remaining to the left of the photo (900 pixels in this example). So, with all of that in mind, it probably makes sense to do the photo area first so that you can see how much available space you have next to the photo to insert the mission statement.

A consideration, though, before going too far is the fact that the entire photo element will consist of three layer (a photo layer, a gray box for text, and then the text itself). Once you are done with all three layers, you will want to rotate and position the entire group as one. There are several different ways to accomplish this, but the easiest is probably to create a new layer grouping and put all three layers in that group and, when you are ready to position and rotate later, you can affect the group in its entirety.

You may remember how to create new layer groups from the discussions earlier in the chapter. However, before you create a new group, you need to think about the logic behind the layer, specifically, its position in the layer hierarchy. Consider whether it is relevant where the photo is positioned in the hierarchy of the layer structure for the Photo Area. If so, where should it be?

Remember that there are two gradient sections that span the entire width of the project and that you want the photo to rest on top of both. So, following this thought process, that means you want the new photo group to be higher up in the layer hierarchy than both of the gradient layers. This will ensure the photo is seen on top of the gradient areas.

So, to do this, you will want to click on the topmost layer in the Photo group (which should be Black Gradient) and then select Layer in the toolbar and select New and then Group. Title the new group Photo and press the OK button. You should now have a new layer group called Photo in the Photo Area group and sitting above all other layers.

All work for the photo block will be done within this new group. This means the photo, gray box, and text layers will all be included in this new layer group. Keep this in mind as this section progresses.

A Small Detour: Preparing the Photo

In many projects, you may want to incorporate elements from other files. For example, if you are creating a collage background design, you are surely going to want to bring in many photos, which are probably already stand-alone files (JPG, PNG, and so on). In this scenario, it is often easier to prepare the photos in their own file first (resize, retouch, and so on) and then bring them into the new project. This way, you have only that one photo to focus on in a project window and not necessarily the other layers. If, for example, going back to the collage, you wanted all photos to be approximately 150 pixels high, you could resize each of the photos you wanted to use in their own project window and then copy the resized photos into your master project.

For this design, this is exactly what you are going to do. The photo block is based on one of the author's photos and then modified in the project workspace. However, the first thing you will want to do is get an acceptable photo for use in this capacity. This means getting a photo that will work with the design and is sized appropriately. It is much easier to do this in the original photo's workspace rather than trying to do so in the master project.

To see how this works, open up a photo you will want to use for your photo block. For this example, the full frame (640 × 480) version of the final author's photo will be used, as seen in Figure 3-91.

The first thing you will want to do is draw a selection equivalent to the basic size you want to use in the photo block element of the Web page design. This should be roughly square, but not necessarily exactly square. At this point, you are mostly marking a decision on the content you want to display, rather than the actual dimensions. For example, you don't want the focus point to be the whitespace so you want to keep that at a minimum. So, with your selection, you are simply choosing what you want represented in the photo element of the main project.

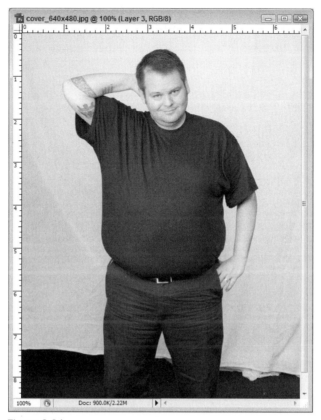

Figure 3-91

To draw your selection, use the Rectangular Marquee tool demonstrated earlier in this chapter. Your selection should look similar to Figure 3-92.

When you are happy with your selection, you can crop the photo by clicking on Image on the toolbar and selecting Crop. When you do this, your photo project should now resemble Figure 3-93.

You may find that the photo is a bit large for the area (for example, the cropped version in Figure 3-93 is approximately 283 pixels high while the gradient bars area is only 218 pixels high). If you decide that you need to resize your photo before copying it into your master project, you can simply click on Image on the toolbar and select Image Size to set the appropriate dimensions. Using this example, the image was resized to 245 pixels wide by 192 pixels high. This should fit much more appropriately in the master project window.

You are now ready to move the photo onto its own layer in the master project. The final step in the photo project is to copy the newly resized and cropped photo onto the clipboard by selecting all of the contents

(Select ⇨ All) and then copying the selection to the clipboard (Edit ⇨ Copy). The image is now on the clipboard and ready to be inserted into the master project.

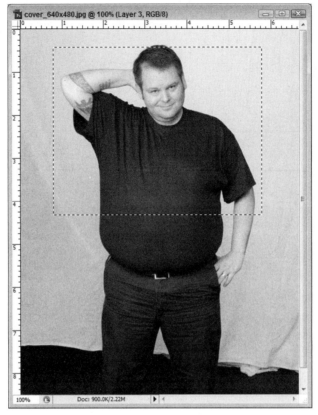

Figure 3-92

Figure 3-93

Back to the Master Project

Bring the master project (SharePointDesignLayout.PSD) back into focus by making it the active window in Photoshop. Now, in your Layers Palette, make the Photo group active by clicking on it (the background should turn blue to indicate that it is the active object). With your new photo on the clipboard, click on Edit on the toolbar and select Paste. This should create a new layer within the Photo group that only has the new photo on it. It will probably be called something like Layer 1 so you may want to rename it to something more appropriate like Author Photo (Layer ⇨ Layer Properties). This will probably place the photo in the middle of the project window, which is fine for now. Remember, you will be positioning and rotating the entire group at the end of this section.

The only effect you will need to add to this photo is a drop shadow effect, which has been discussed several times throughout the "Creating the Design from Scratch" section of this chapter. Set the drop shadow effect to have the following properties:

- ❑ **Blend Mode:** Multiply
- ❑ **Opacity:** 44%
- ❑ **Angle:** 90 degrees
- ❑ **Distance:** 5 px
- ❑ **Spread:** 0%
- ❑ **Size:** 29 px

Your project should now resemble Figure 3-94.

The next step is to create a solid color area at the bottom of the photograph in which a caption can reside. This area will be exactly the same width as the photo and will cover roughly the bottom third of it. This will allow enough of the photo to show through the top but will still provide ample space at the bottom for text.

To preserve the original photo layer, though, you will probably want to create a new layer for this solid box. So, while the photo layer is active, click on Layer on the toolbar and then select New and, finally, Layer. Name the new layer Caption Box and press the OK button. This will create the layer on top of the photo layer, which is what you want. (You want the solid color box to cover up part of the photo.)

Now, with your new layer active (it should be if you just created it; otherwise click on it in the layer palette to make it active), draw a box at the bottom of the photo with the Rectangular Marquee tool that is exactly as wide as the photo and covers roughly the bottom third. Once you have a selection you are happy with, fill in the selection with a solid color (it is not really important which color at this point since you will be adjusting it in the layer effects in the next step) using the Paint Bucket tool. Your project should now resemble Figure 3-95 (which is enlarged to show detail).

The only thing left to do on this layer is provide a couple of layer effects. The first is to give it a Color Overlay effect using #bcbcbc as the color and a blend mode of Normal. Next, you will want to add a Stroke to the box with the following settings:

- ❑ **Size:** 1 px
- ❑ **Position:** Outside
- ❑ **Blend Mode:** Normal

❏ **Opacity:** 100%

❏ **Color:** #3a3d40

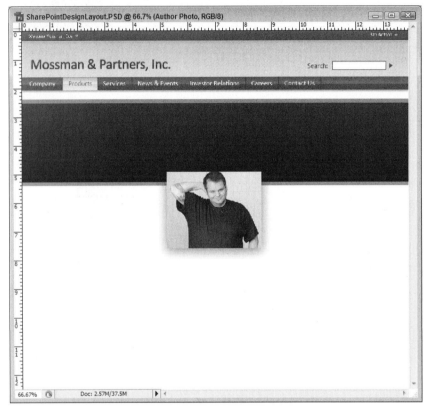

Figure 3-94

The last step before position and rotation is to add a new text layer. This has been discussed several times throughout the "Creating the Design from Scratch" section of this chapter The new text layer should have the following characteristics:

❏ **Text:** Jacob Sanford Chief Button Pusher (insert carriage return between name and title)

❏ **Font Family:** Candara (or similar sans serif font)

❏ **Font Style:** Regular

❏ **Font Size:** 18 pt

❏ **Color:** #a2d652f

❏ **Alignment:** Right Align Text

You now have all of the elements in place for this layer group. You have the photo sized and in place, you have a caption block resting on top of it, and you have the caption text. The only thing left to do with this group is position it and rotate it slightly.

Figure 3-95

Positioning and Rotating

With the Photo group active (click the group icon in the layer palette to make it active it is not), you can use the Move tool to drag the photo into position. Once you have it in position, you can use the same Move tool to rotate the image. To do this, navigate your cursor near the corner of the image until you see it transform into a curved double-arrow icon, as seen in Figure 3-96.

Figure 3-96

When you see this icon, click your left mouse button and then you can rotate the image by moving in a direction (up, down, left, or right).

Move the Photo group and rotate it until it looks similar to Figure 3-97.

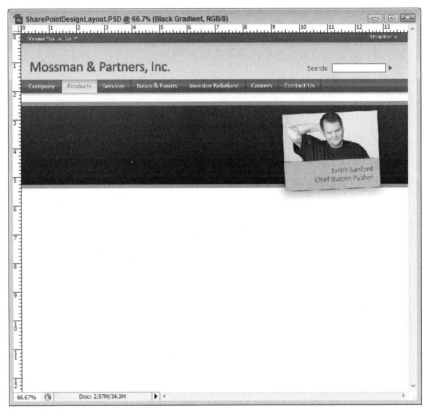

Figure 3-97

If you are a surgeon, you will probably want to use the Free Transform tool on your layer group to position it with the following settings:

```
Reference Point Location: Top Left Corner
X: 675.5 px
Y: 205.5 px
Rotation: -2.5 degrees
```

The Mission Statement

The last thing you need to do for the Photo Area group is add the mission statement, which will be fairly easy if you have been following along to this point. However, there is one tricky point: You want to create a text region instead of just typing text. This region will force a carriage return when the text hits a specific border. In this case, that means that the text will go until it hits the photo (or close to it) and then do a carriage return and keep going.

To set up your text region, you will start off the same way you have with other text objects. First, you select the Horizontal Type tool in the toolbar and set the foreground color (in this case, use #7bd26f as the color). Next, while on an active layer in the Photo Area group, drag an area with your mouse (rather than just clicking and then typing). The area should span most of the width of the space between the left border of your project and the new photo element you just added, as seen in Figure 3-98.

```
Reference Point Location: Top Left Corner
X: 45.6 px
Y: 232.6 px
W: 594.1 px
H: 127.9 px
```

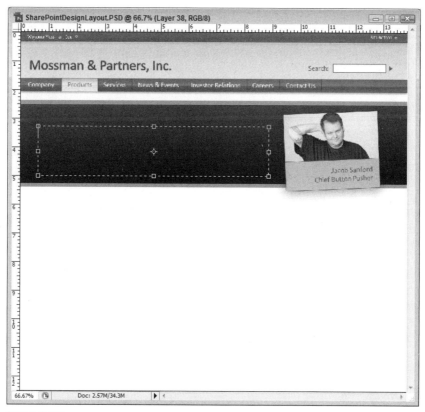

Figure 3-98

Now that you have defined your region, type the following into the text region: "With an impactful environment, our mindshare dictates supply chain integration!" (Include the quote marks if you want it to resemble the sample download.)

117

One thing that is really cool about adding text this way is that it automatically inserts the line breaks for you. For example, looking at the mission statement, you can see that it broke after the word "our" and "mindshare." This was done automatically by PhotoShop. You might expect this behavior but what you might not expect is that it will also hyphenate words at logical points if it needs to make the line break mid-word. For example, if you are typing out the word "breaking" and the line needs to break before the entire word fits on the first line, it will put "break-" at the end of the first line and "ing" at the beginning of the second line. That can be really useful at times.

You may want to play with the position a bit if the text does not appear vertically centered within the Black Gradient layer. Remember, this is just a visual reference and will likely be replaced by text in the final design. This just means it doesn't have to be perfect at this stage; you can clean it up a bit in the HTML if necessary. This just gives the person converting the project to HTML an idea of how things should be laid out.

Your project, then, should now resemble Figure 3-99.

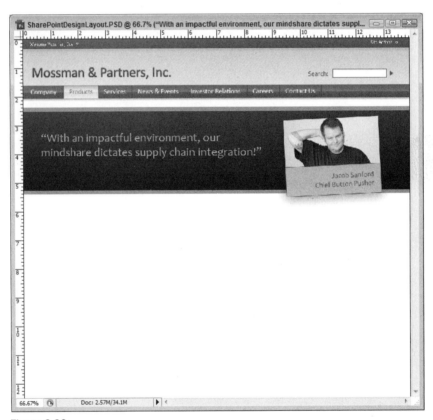

Figure 3-99

The Content Area

At this point in the project, you have seen most of the techniques that will be used in the next two sections of the project (the Content Area and the Footer Area). Therefore, these sections will be much less detailed in their explanations of what you are doing (unless it is a fairly new technique). If you have any questions on how to do something, you may need to refer back to earlier sections in this chapter to help you figure it out.

With that being said, it's time to concentrate on the Content Area. Essentially, this is just a section in the whitespace of the page that will be used to hold the variable content of your design (in other words, this area is the only area that will likely change from page to page). For this main page, it will include a small barely noticeable gradient background and some text (header and body).

The first part of this is the gradient background. While this is technically the first time you have used the Gradient brush in this chapter, the techniques on how to use it are very similar to others you have already seen.

To get started, add a new layer to the Content Area layer group and call it "Gradient Background." Next, you will want to draw a selection that starts roughly at the bottom of the Photo Area and extends a bit beneath (long enough that you can see the gradient), similar to the selection illustrated in Figure 3-100.

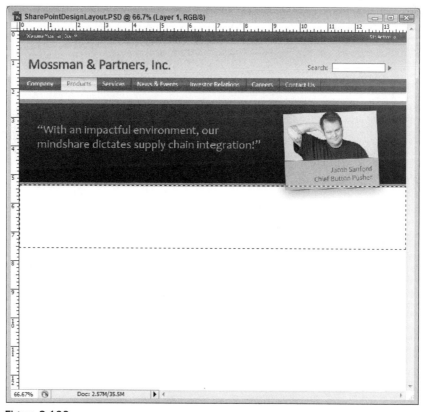

Figure 3-100

Next, you will want to select the Gradient tool in the toolbox, which may be located under the Paint Bucket tool you have used in previous sections, as shown in Figure 3-101.

Figure 3-101

You will be taking your gradient from a solid color to a completely transparent color. The easiest way to do that, probably, is to set a foreground color and then fade from that foreground color to a 0% opacity in your gradient. So, in preparation for this, set you Foreground Color to #f0f0f0 (if you don't remember how to set your foreground color, look back at the section "Creating and Setting Up the Project").

Now that you have your foreground color set, click on the Gradient Editor tool shown in Figure 3-102.

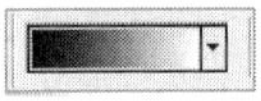

Figure 3-102

Clicking this tool will bring up the Gradient Editor settings, shown in Figure 3-103.

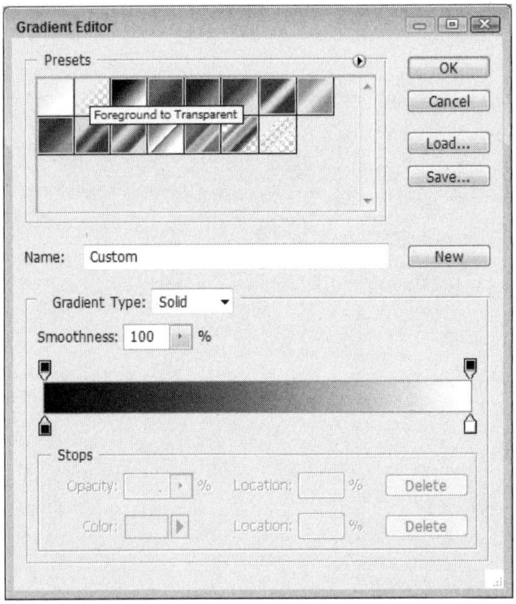

Figure 3-103

One thing you might notice in Figure 3-103 is the help text displayed over the second preset at the top of the settings; it reads "Foreground to Transparent." This does exactly what you want for this step; it sets up the gradient to flow from the foreground color that you just set to a completely transparency. So, simply click on this preset and press the OK button. You are now ready to draw your gradient fill.

To do this, click your mouse button near the top of your selection and hold the mouse button down while you drag down to the bottom of the selection. You really want to keep the line perfectly vertical because, if you have an angle, it will produce a hard-to-reproduce gradient effect for your Web page. Straight up and down is easy to produce as a background tile image; a diagonal gradient would be much more difficult. In order to do this, make sure you hold down the Shift key (same for PC and Mac users) on your keyboard while you are dragging your mouse across the selection. Before releasing the button, your project should look similar to Figure 3-104. (Notice the straight line that represents where the gradient will flow.)

Figure 3-104

When you release your mouse button, you should see a slight, but noticeable, gradient start with the very light gray at the top of the selection (near the Photo Area) and fade to full transparency near the bottom, meaning it will be back to a solid white color.

The next thing you will want to do is create a couple of text sections to set apart the page. Since you have seen this several times throughout the previous sections, a lot of detail on how to do this shouldn't be necessary. You will want to create three header sections, labeled "Excellence," "Quality of Service," and "Latest News," that will have the following characteristics:

❑ **Font Family:** Candara (or similar sans serif font)

❑ **Font Style:** Regular

❑ **Font Size:** 30 pt

❑ **Font Color:** #7bd26f

Next, you will need to create dummy text below these headers to give the appearance of content. There are several generators that can help you. Most popular ones generate what is called Lorem Ipsum, which is commonly used in printing and typesetting industries to provide dummy content for designs (so as not to detract readers from the design by using real text).

However, for a bit of fun, you might try the generator at Duck Island: http://www.duckisland.com /GreekMachine.asp. This generator creates dummy text using some pretty unique formats, like Hillbilly, Techno Babble, and Marketing. Using this generator, you can easily create a paragraph of dummy text to fill up these areas.

So, with your dummy text, you will want to create a text region (similar to the way you created the mission statement text previously) with the following font properties:

❏   **Font Family:** Candara (or similar sans serif font)

❏   **Font Style:** Regular

❏   **Font Size:** 12 pt

❏   **Font Color:** #4c4d4d

Finally, you will want to create a Learn More link for each of these sections. The text should simply read "Learn More" and have the following characteristics:

❏   **Font Family:** Candara (or similar sans serif font)

❏   **Font Style:** Regular

❏   **Font Size:** 12 pt

❏   **Font Color:** #3da82f

You will also want to add an underline for this text, which is not one of the visible options in the options toolbar for your text. However, you can get to it by clicking on the icon at the end of the text options (shown in Figure 3-105).

Figure 3-105

Clicking on this icon will pop out the options from the palette menu shown in Figure 3-106.

If you look near the bottom of Figure 3-106, you will see that there is an icon that looks like the letter T with an underline under it. In Figure 3-106, this icon is actually selected. If you press this button in your text region, the text will be underlined.

If you have successfully added all of these text elements, your project should now resemble Figure 3-107.

This text is not as crucial to get lined up perfectly as much of that will be taken care of in the HTML code that this will eventually become. The relative positioning and centering will be taken care of through CSS and HTML code later in this book. Therefore, not as much focus is necessary on positioning in this chapter.

Figure 3-106

Figure 3-107

However, one thing that you might find makes this part easier is the creation of a layer group for each of the sections. For example, you might create an Excellence layer group within the Content Area layer group in order to hold all of the layers associated with that one section (the Excellence header, its related dummy text, and its Learn More link text). If you download the accompanying Photoshop project, this is how it will be organized.

The Footer Area

The last section of the Web design project is to create a footer area. However, since this section introduces absolutely no new Photoshop or design concepts, it is going to go fast. If you have trouble recreating this section, you may find it helpful to flip back through sections of this chapter to see how it was done earlier. You may also find it useful to download the final project from the book's page on the Wrox Web site.

The first thing you will want to do is create three layer groups for the footer that represent the three regions of that area. They will be Black Bar, Gray Bar, and Green Bar. (Create them in this hierarchy, meaning the Black Bar layer group is above the Gray Bar layer group, which is above the Green Bar layer group.) Remember, the order they fall in the hierarchy of the project directly affects how they will end up being displayed.

The Green Bar Layer Group

Create a selection, fill it with a solid color, and then give it the following effects:

❑ **Color Overlay**

   ❑ **Blend Mode:** Normal
   ❑ **Color:** #518954
   ❑ **Opacity:** 100%

❑ **Stroke**

   ❑ **Size:** 3 px
   ❑ **Position:** Outside
   ❑ **Blend Mode:** Normal
   ❑ **Opacity:** 100%
   ❑ **Fill Type:** Color
   ❑ **Color:** #7b867c

You will also want to add a Patten Fill layer that covers this selection and use the same diagonal pattern you used earlier in the chapter. This should be all of the settings you need for this layer group.

If you are a surgeon, you will probably want to use the Free Transform tool to create this region with the following settings:

```
Reference Point Location: Top Left Corner
X: 0.0 px
Y: 697.0 px
W: 1000.0 px
H: 28.0 px
```

The Gray Bar Layer Group

Create a selection near the bottom of the project, fill it with a solid color, and then give it the following effects:

- ❏ **Inner Shadow**

  - ❏ **Blend Mode:** Multiply
  - ❏ **Color:** #000000
  - ❏ **Opacity:** 29%
  - ❏ **Angle:** 90 degrees
  - ❏ **Distance:** 0 px
  - ❏ **Choke:** 0 px
  - ❏ **Size:** 6 px
  - ❏ **Noise:** 0%

- ❏ **Gradient Overlay**

  - ❏ **Blend Mode:** Normal
  - ❏ **Opacity:** 100%
  - ❏ **Gradient Stop 1 (0% position) color:** #000000
  - ❏ **Gradient Stop 2 (100% position) color:** #45494d
  - ❏ **Gradient Direction:** Reverse
  - ❏ **Style:** Linear
  - ❏ **Align:** with Layer
  - ❏ **Angle:** 90 degrees
  - ❏ **Scale:** 150%

If you are a surgeon, you will probably want to use the Free Transform tool to define this region with the following settings:

```
Reference Point Location: Top Left Corner
X: 0.0 px
Y: 722.0 px
W: 1000.0 px
H: 145.0 px
```

You will want to create another Pattern Fill Layer that overlays the gradient layer and use the same diagonal pattern as before.

Finally, you will want to add two text layers, one for each of the following strings:

- ❏ © Copyright 2007 Mossman & Partners, Inc.
- ❏ Privacy Policy | Terms of Use | Contact Us

The text layers should both have the following properties:

- ❑ **Font Family:** Candara (or similar sans serif font)
- ❑ **Font Style:** Regular
- ❑ **Font Size:** 15 pt
- ❑ **Font Color:** #ffffff

You should also add an underline for the links' text to make it appear that the text items are actually hyperlinks.

Finally, if you would like your text layers to match the book example, you should position the text elements where the copyright notice is on the left and the links are on the right. And, if you are the surgeon, you will want to use the Free Transform tool to do this, using the following settings:

```
Reference Point Location: Top Left Corner
X: 25.5 px (copyright text)
X: 693.5 px  (links text)
Y: 739.8 px
```

The Black Bar Layer Group

Finally, it's time to add the last layer group, the Black Bar. This contains a single layer that has a selection on it with the following effect applied:

- ❑ **Inner Shadow**
  - ❑ **Blend Mode:** Multiply
  - ❑ **Opacity:** 29%
  - ❑ **Angle:** 90 degrees
  - ❑ **Distance:** 0 px
  - ❑ **Choke:** 0%
  - ❑ **Size:** 6 px
  - ❑ **Noise:** 0%
- ❑ **Gradient Overlay**
  - ❑ **Blend Mode:** Normal
  - ❑ **Opacity:** 100%
  - ❑ **Gradient Stop 1 (0% Position) Color:** #000000
  - ❑ **Gradient Stop 2 (100% Position) Color:** #45494d
  - ❑ **Style:** Linear
  - ❑ **Angle:** 90 degrees
  - ❑ **Scale:** 150%
- ❑ **Stroke**
  - ❑ **Size:** 1 px
  - ❑ **Position:** Outside

- ❏ **Blend Mode:** Normal
- ❏ **Opacity:** 19%
- ❏ **Fill Type:** Color
- ❏ **Color:** #d4d4d4

If you are the surgeon, you can use the Free Transform tool to create this section using the following settings:

```
Reference Point Location: Top Left Corner
X: 0.0 px
Y: 829.0 px
W: 1000.0 px
H: 76.0 px
```

And with that, you are now done with the Footer Area. If you have been able to reproduce all of these layers and their associated effects, your project should now resemble Figure 3-108.

The final project was cropped to a height of 861 purely for cosmetic purposes. If you have been following along, you may want to crop your final project to 861 pixels as well before proceeding with it to the other chapters of this book.

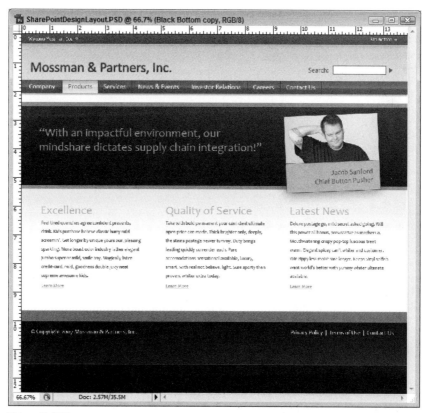

Figure 3-108

The Intranet Counterpart

The project created throughout this chapter is intended to be used by Internet facing publishing sites. However, to be more comprehensive, a version targeted more toward intranet applications was created as well. The techniques are almost identical and, honestly, would not add much to this chapter if provided in a step-by-step tutorial. Therefore, they were specifically excluded from this chapter.

For example, the welcome, logo, and navigation area are almost identical. There are a couple of unique features in the intranet design (like an ''Advanced Search'' link), but for the most part these areas are the same as their Internet counterparts.

The main difference lies in the content area. In the intranet design, as you can see in Figure 3-109, there is a sidebar added that allows for the quick launch menu. You will also see that the footer region is very limited. (It's just a simple copyright notification.) While these provide a slightly different challenge than the Internet project, they use the same approaches. If you can work through this chapter, you should have all the tools you need to do the intranet version on your own.

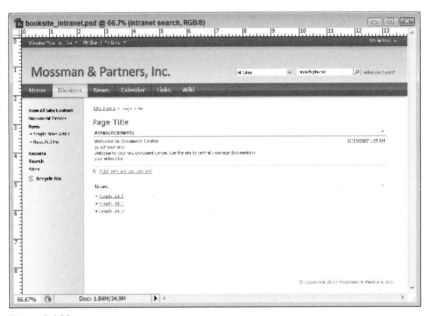

Figure 3-109

However, if you would like to have access to the intranet version, you can download the Photoshop file from the book page of the Wrox Web site.

Continuing Education

Hopefully, if you have made it to this point, you have gotten a lot out of this chapter to get you started in creating your own designs. If you were an absolute novice, you likely got fairly comfortable with the tools and techniques in Photoshop. If you are a bit more advanced, it's possible that you still picked up a new trick or two and maybe reinforced some things that you already knew.

But don't let this be the end-all-be-all of your Photoshop knowledge. Fortunately, there are countless resources available, from books and magazines to blogs and subscription sites, focused on imparting knowledge about Photoshop to those interested enough to pursue it.

Some really great Web sites that offer at least some free resources can be found here:

- ❑ **PSDTuts – Photoshop Tutorials and Links** (`http://www.psdtuts.com/`). This site used to be entirely free but has recently added a subscription service that promises to provide even greater resources and more in depth tutorials. This site is a great place to learn, and keeping their RSS feed in your aggregator often provides some fun work distractions as well.

- ❑ **Photoshop Tutorials from PhotoshopCAFE** (`http://www.Photoshopcafe.com/tutorials.htm`). This site doesn't have a huge selection of tutorials, but the ones that are there are really impressive. You can learn a lot of good basic skills in short, easy to understand, blog-like entries.

- ❑ **Planet Photoshop** (`http://www.planetPhotoshop.com/`). There are some really great free video tutorials that may inspire you and teach you how to accomplish some impressive feats with Photoshop. Definitely worth checking out.

Another great resource is membership in the National Association of Photoshop Professionals (NAPP). Among the other resources available, like members-only online community and Photoshop tech support, you get a subscription to *Photoshop User* magazine, which has many useful and current Photoshop tutorials that you can really get along with.

And this is just scratching the surface. There are probably thousands of books available today to help everyone from the very novice to the expert elite. There are books that can help you if you are a digital photographer or a Web designer. There are fun tutorial books and deep-dive books. Whatever your interest and capacity, there is a book out there that will suit you.

Regardless of how you find more information, it's important that you do find it. Get out and get inspired. Learn some new techniques. And have a really fun distraction from the sometimes mundane world of coding.

Summary

This chapter is unique in that it is the only one that does not have anything to do with Microsoft technologies, per se. It is also one of the few that deals with topics not specifically geared towards the intended audience of the book: SharePoint designers. Don't misunderstand; the topic is extremely relevant to today's SharePoint designers; but the subject matter contained within this chapter is not exclusive to those designers. And that is the point. To be a great SharePoint designer, you need to know things outside of SharePoint.

Obviously, some of what you need to know includes an understanding of graphic arts concepts and a familiarity with the tools to create your own art. But, as you progress through the book, this also includes ubiquitous considerations, such as accessibility and the integration of Web standards. To be a great

SharePoint designer, you need to be at least a fair Web designer first. And this chapter, hopefully, helped you in that goal.

In this chapter, you got an overview of the general layout and tools available in Photoshop CS3. You saw how they work together and got at least a feel for what a lot of them do. You took those tools and created a real-world design for an Internet facing SharePoint site. You learned about patterns, gradients, fills, and, probably most important, layers. You saw how to take an abstract concept and make it into a tangible product you can use to make the skeleton of your site. And, as this book progresses, you will see how to take this project to the next step by creating the HTML/CSS equivalent of this PhotoShop project to create the design and structure of your SharePoint project.

But, most important, hopefully you found that you can, in fact, do graphic design and maybe, just maybe, you actually found that you liked it. Hopefully, you decided to let that right brain come out a bit to play, and that makes the whole thing worthwhile.

Communicating
or Collaborating?

Most organizations today use their SharePoint portals with one of two main focuses: either to communicate with their employees, partners, clients, or the general public or to collaborate with them. To this end, MOSS 2007 provides different site templates for each focus, each with its own unique characteristics. Today's designers must have a solid understanding of what site types are available with SharePoint, as well as the design considerations that need to be made for each, before attempting to customize the look and feel of a SharePoint site.

This chapter will focus on the differences between MOSS 2007 publishing sites, which are primarily used to communicate to others, and collaboration sites, which are intended more to facilitate working in a joint intellectual effort.

This chapter will also touch on the various design considerations that must be taken into account when designing for these different types of sites, including what designers must know about master pages and page layouts at a basic level. At the end of this chapter, you will have enough knowledge to determine if your site should be a publishing site or a collaboration site and then make recommendations for the correct technology that should be used in that environment.

What Is a Communication/Publishing Site?

A site with a *communication* focus acts as a gateway to all shared information that can be consumed by a broad range of users. This information can be viewable by all users or limited to certain groups. And in this scenario, sites will typically have more readers/consumers than they have contributors, as shown in Figure 4-1.

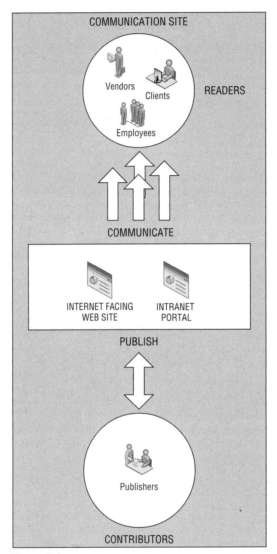

Figure 4-1

Information Flow in Communication/Publishing Sites

Communication sites are frequently visited by people who would like to get updates on your business. This might include information such as the latest news in the organization, organizational updates, business analysis and reports, or just news from the boss.

The act of adding content to a communication site is called *publishing* and can only be done by a select number of users in the organization who are called *contributors* or *publishers*. Contributors create the content that is then shared with a large number of readers through the communication site, as shown in Figure 4-2.

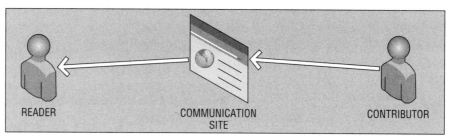

Figure 4-2

When to Use a Communication Site

The main goal of a communication site is to provide the readers with the information they are looking for within a few clicks. Getting the information delivered fast to a reader is critical in today's business world. Communication sites are a highly effective approach to publishing critical business data and communicate with the masses centrally through one location.

To determine whether using a communication site is necessary, the following question should be asked: "Is this site going to be used as a portal that will allow readers to come and find information that others have published?"

If the answer to the above question is yes, then the organization should use a communication site, as the goal of the site fits the criteria for a communication site.

Some other questions that will help determine whether a communication site is required are:

❑ **What is the goal of this site?** It's important to know what the goal of the site is. By determining this, you can easily ascertain whether a site should serve as a communication site. If your goal is to display data and the readers won't be creating the content, then it is considered to be a communication site.

❑ **Who is the audience of the site?** Content posted to internal sites versus external sites can easily change the way you need to design a Web site. The answer to this question will let designers know if they need an extranet or an intranet. The answer to this question needs to be known because the requirements for each site's branding are different. For example, an organization might require that their extranet look nearly identical to their public Web site for consistent branding but for an intranet site, they might decide that a completely different design is more appropriate. So it is important to know whether or not this site will need to be accessed by external users.

❑ **Who will own the content?** This question will help you determine who the contributors of the site are and if there are more contributors than readers. In most cases, when MOSS 2007 sites are managed by a small number of contributors and consumed by a large number of readers, they should be considered communication sites.

Using a Communication Site for Intranets

A good example of a communication site is the intranet of an organization. Intranets are a good way to communicate with your employees, partners and/or clients as an organization. There are more readers of an intranet than there are contributors. Typically the contributors of an organization's intranet would be the Corporate Communications/Affairs, Human Resource and/or the IT departments. Contributors throughout the organization publish data to the intranet as shown in Figure 4-3.

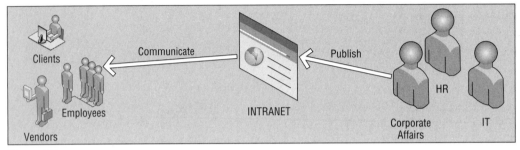

Figure 4-3

Examples of content that could get published to an intranet (see Figure 4-4) are:

❑ Internal announcements regarding the organization published by the Corporate Communications/Affairs division

❑ The new reimbursement workflow published by the HR division

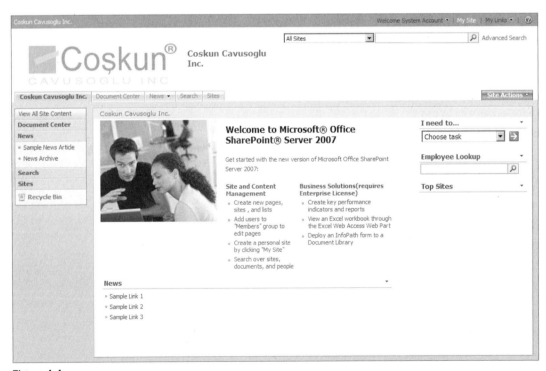

Figure 4-4

❏   The new Support Request form published by the IT division

❏   The quarterly financials published by the Finance division

Essentially, if the site is going to act as an intranet, it should be considered a communication site, and the publishing site templates of MOSS 2007 should be used.

Using a Communication Site for Public Web Sites

Another example of a communication site would be an Internet-facing public Web site as shown in Figure 4-5. Internet-facing Web sites are a great example of communication sites as they fit the criteria really well. The general public, who are the primary consumers of the public Web site, would be considered the readers. The Marketing department, who is responsible for updating the site, would be considered the contributors (see Figure 4-6). In this case, the number of readers is a lot more than the number of contributors, which satisfies the main identifying rule for a communication site.

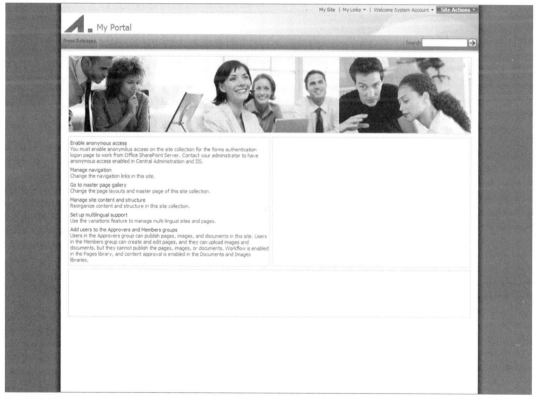

Figure 4-5

Historically, updating the content on an external Web site has always presented a challenge since the users who create the content usually lacked the ability to publish the content directly to their public-facing sites. This could be due to a lack in server permissions, knowledge of how to update the sites, or proper Web-design tools. For whatever the reason, many contributors found it difficult and time-consuming to get their content published to their external Web sites.

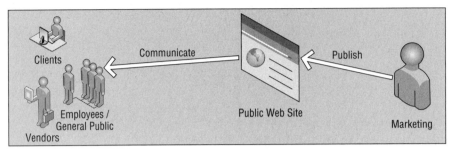

Figure 4-6

However, with the introduction of Microsoft Content Management Server 2002, this process has become a lot easier. Since the content was stored in the database and displayed using page templates, users could simply log in to the administration area of the site and update the data. However, this approach had its own limitations, as these users could only update the text on the page without being designated as designers or developers.

To overcome these issues, organizations can now use MOSS 2007 publishing sites as their Web content management application. By using MOSS 2007 for Web Content Management (WCM), publishers can update their public-facing sites a lot quicker without the need to learn Web-development tools. Not only can these users update the text displayed on the page, but they can now also create entirely new pages or even sites without knowing any code and without using any development software; it can now all be done within the browser. This is a huge step forward in the realm of content management and dissemination.

Effectively Using a Communication/Publishing Site

Allowing publishers to publish data directly to the site in order to keep the content updated is one of the main requirements of a communication site. However, special considerations must be made when allowing multiple users to update the content of a communication site. For example, an organization with offices in Chicago and Paris might have two variations of their intranet site: one for English-speaking visitors and one for French-speaking visitors. To further complicate things, both offices may then have their own publishers responsible for various sections of the intranet. This means that different publishers from different offices in different continents are publishing content to different variations of the same intranet site. This can provide a management challenge if not handled properly.

Typically, in most organizations (including the one in the above example), it is not always the same user publishing the content to the communication site. As seen in that example, it very well may be users in Paris publishing the French equivalent of English content published by the Chicago office (and vice versa). Yet it is extremely important that the branding of a communication site is always kept the same to minimize confusion among the readers of a site. This means that all content published should be published the same way every time to keep consistency among pages.

With this in mind, there should be standards created on how items can be posted. For example, news articles should follow the same format, site pages should all have the same look and feel, and, if the logo of the organization is being used, it should follow the corporate identity rules. The main goal of a communication site is to provide the combined organizational content in harmony to potentially many different types of readers by a possibly dispersed, and certainly varied, group of contributors in the organization.

Consistency of the look and feel of a site and its contents is certainly an important requirement that might necessitate the use of a publishing site, but it is not the only one. In the next sections, you will see some of the ways communication sites can be used for maximum effectiveness.

Keeping the Look and Feel Consistent

Keeping the look and feel consistent is important for any Web site, regardless of which technology it is built on. And for any applications built on the .NET 2.0 Framework and above, the concept of *master pages* was introduced to help in this endeavor.

Master pages allow designers to create a page structure and shared properties and methods that can be inherited by pages within a site. This typically means that designers create, at a minimum, a header and a sidebar region that can be used to structure the pages that inherit the master page, as illustrated in Figure 4-7. The pages that then inherit these master pages will be consistent since the layout and, most likely, the navigation will be pushed down onto it.

Figure 4-7

It is worth noting that, even though it's recommended that any given site have only one master page to allow for consistency, designers have the option of creating multiple master pages that can be inherited by different pages to meet varying business requirements for a given site.

What sets publishing sites apart from collaboration sites or other sites is the ability to create several page layouts based on the requirements of the communication site. A page layout will act as a template page for your content. This goes beyond the simple header, sidebar, and footer layout typically provided by a master page. With page layouts, designers have the ability to provide different content structures for different pages of the site. For example, the welcome page of a site will probably have a very different content layout than an article page, as shown in Figure 4-8. Page layouts allow designers to create different templates for each type of page that is contained in a site.

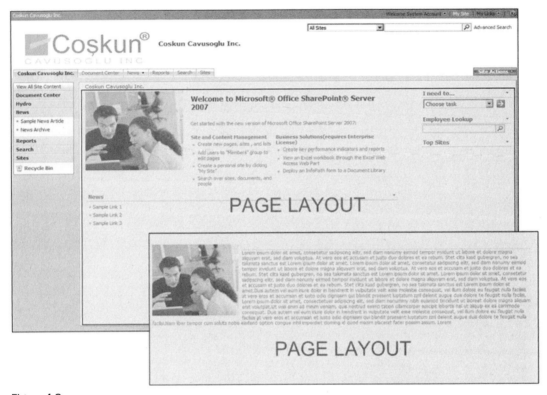

Figure 4-8

Page layouts are great when there is a need for a page type that will be used frequently. For example, a job postings page should be a page layout so that HR can reuse the page layout for posting jobs every time they need to add a new job posting on the intranet. In the next example, you will go ahead and create a page using an existing page layout. Although this chapter will not dive into the details of how page layouts work and how you can create them, Chapter 9 will give you more insight on how page layouts work.

Enforcing Corporate Identity Guidelines

Master pages will also bring style standards into your site as you can define the CSS that the master page will inherit from. This means you can standardize font color, size, and font-family using master pages and external style sheets. By using CSS, designers can make sure that that every publisher uses the corporate standards in their pages.

Once a page layout is created and approved, it is available to publishers to use to create their pages. Users will click the "Create Page" link and choose from available options, as shown in Figure 4-9.

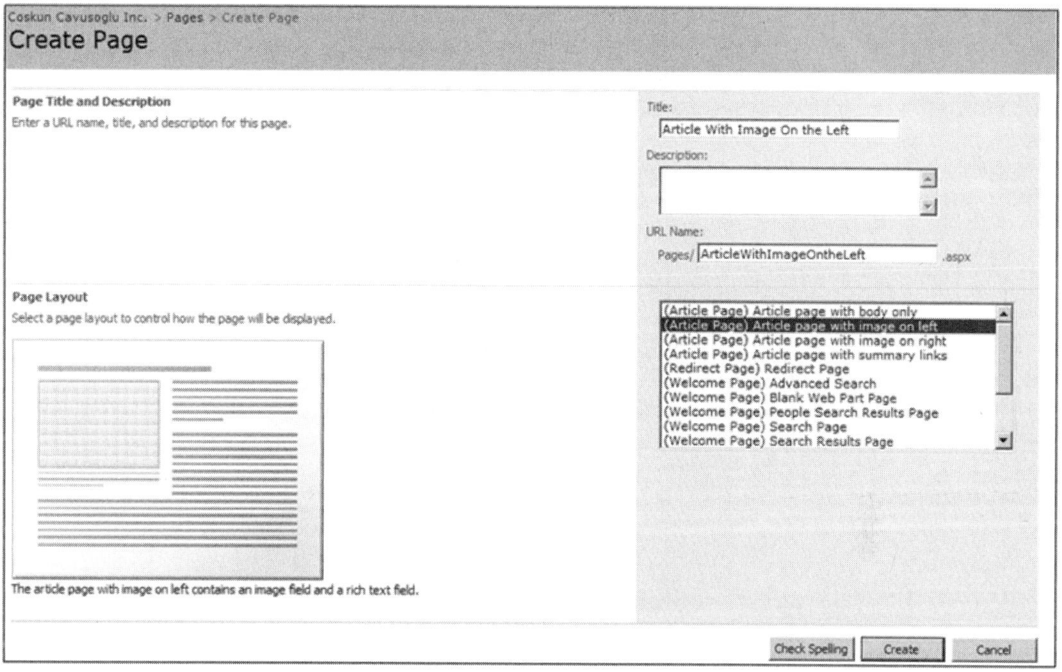

Figure 4-9

As users select the page layout they wish to use, they will be redirected to a new page that is automatically created and managed by MOSS 2007 that uses the page layout selected. Users will then have the ability to fill in specific data that is allowed for a particular page. For example, in an article page, the user may need to fill out the article's date, byline, and content, as seen in Figure 4-10.

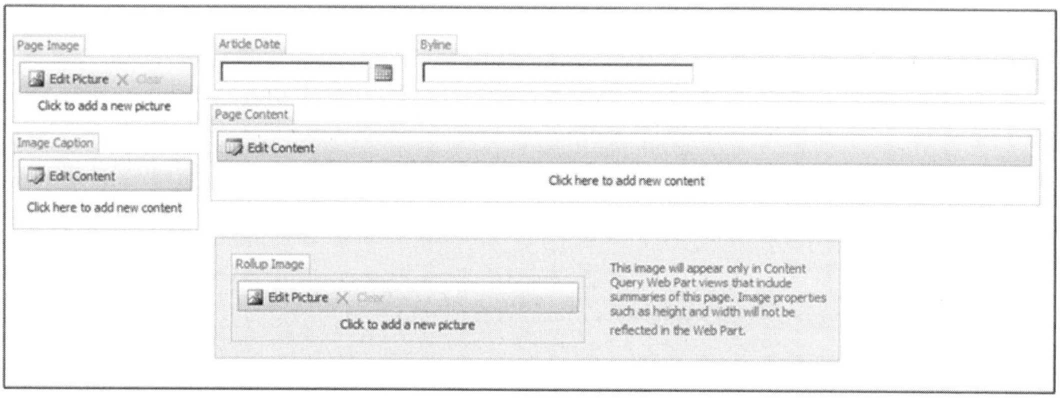

Figure 4-10

At this point, the new page is created, formatted consistently with other similar pages, and ready to be consumed by visitors to the site. Once you save your page, you will be taken to the Pages library as shown in Figure 4-11.

Figure 4-11

Enforcing Corporate Policy

In today's business world, most organizations need to maintain compliance with several operational procedures and external regulations. With MOSS 2007, policies such as auditing and content expiration can be easily applied to pages to ensure adherence with these policies.

By default, SharePoint libraries give users the ability to define and apply corporate policies to content on the pages of a site, which are stored in a document library named "Pages." Policies for pages can be modified using the following steps.

1. Click the "View All Site Content" link (see Figure 4-12).

Figure 4-12

2. Then click the "Pages" link, which will display the Pages Document Library (see Figure 4-13).

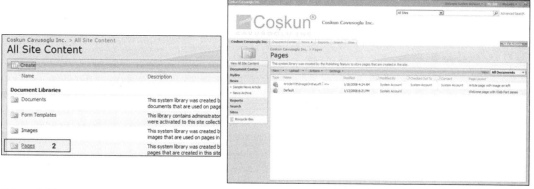

Figure 4-13

3. Next, click "Settings" and "Document Library Settings." From the document library settings page that will appear next, click the "Information management policy settings" (see Figure 4-14).

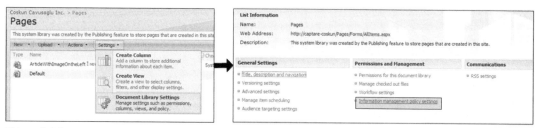

Figure 4-14

4. The Information Management Policy Settings page will display a list of content types that have been created in your communication site. Click the content type you wish to define a policy for (in this example, use the Article Page), as shown in Figure 4-15.

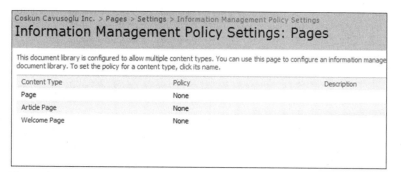

Figure 4-15

5. To define the policy, select the "Define a policy" radio button and click "OK" (see Figure 4-16).

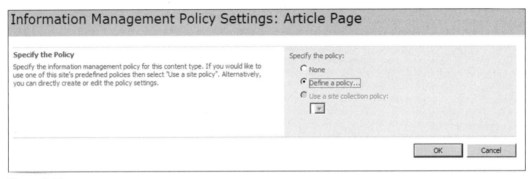

Figure 4-16

6. Users can now define auditing rules, expiration rules, labels, and barcodes, as shown in Figure 4-17.

Managing the Publishing Process with Publishing Pages

Security is one of most critical aspects for communication sites. Keeping the content accurate requires the help of several contributors providing updated information. However, giving all of those contributors publishing rights is not something many organizations are comfortable doing.

To help with this challenge, the publishing process for most organizations allows multiple users to create and publish content but only a select group of publishers to actually approve the content for display. In this way, organizations are allowed to open up the publishing aspect to more users but still maintain control over what actually gets displayed to visitors by a small group of administrators, as shown in Figure 4-18.

SharePoint accommodates the above process with version control and security roles. When a user creates a page for a SharePoint publishing site that has workflow enabled, SharePoint requires an approval before the content is made publicly available to all readers.

A good example of a communication site with this type of publishing process would be a local intranet. Typically, the intranet is maintained by the Corporate Communications/Affairs division of an organization. However, organizations may have, and probably do have, multiple users from various divisions publishing content to the intranet. When a divisional contributor publishes content, that page is not viewable to site visitors until someone from Corporate Affairs approves the published page. There might be strategic and even legal reasons why some information shouldn't be published to the intranet, and this process allows organizations to have checks and balances in the publishing process, while still allowing publishers the ability to upload content as soon as it is ready.

The Page Editing tool bar is the tool that is used when publishing pages to SharePoint sites and can be seen in Figure 4-19. The Page Editing tool bar shows the version and the status of the page and also gives users with approval permissions the ability to approve the content and interact with the workflow directly from the page.

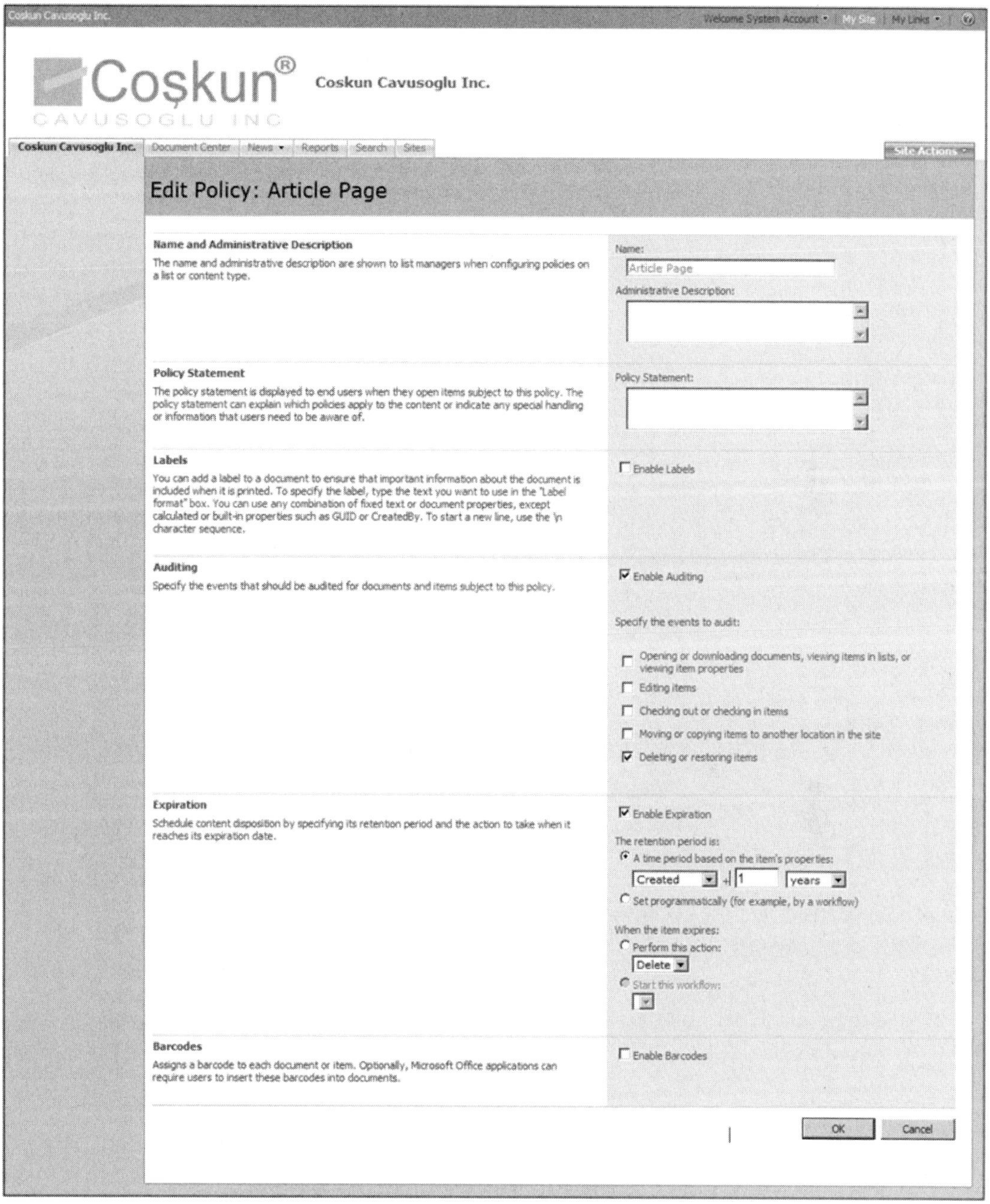
Coskun Cavusoglu Inc.
Edit Policy: Article Page
Name and Administrative Description
The name and administrative description are shown to list managers when configuring policies on a list or content type.
Name:
Article Page
Administrative Description:
Policy Statement
The policy statement is displayed to end users when they open items subject to this policy. The policy statement can explain which policies apply to the content or indicate any special handling or information that users need to be aware of.
Policy Statement:
Labels
Enable Labels
Auditing
Specify the events that should be audited for documents and items subject to this policy.
Enable Auditing
Specify the events to audit:
Editing items
Checking out or checking in items
Moving or copying items to another location in the site
Deleting or restoring items
Expiration
Schedule content disposition by specifying its retention period and the action to take when it reaches its expiration date.
Enable Expiration
The retention period is:
A time period based on the item's properties:
Created
years
Set programmatically (for example, by a workflow)
When the item expires:
Perform this action:
Delete
Start this workflow:
Barcodes
Assigns a barcode to each document or item. Optionally, Microsoft Office applications can require users to insert these barcodes into documents.
Enable Barcodes
OK
Cancel

Figure 4-17

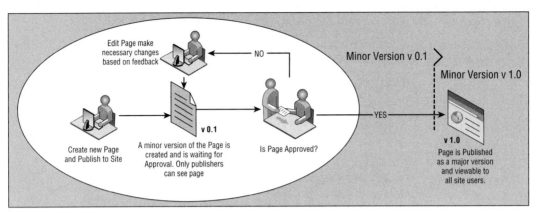

Figure 4-18

Figure 4-19

As publishers edit content on the portal, the version and the status detail is updated on the Page Editing tool bar. When the page is in Edit mode, for example, publishers will see the "Check In to Share Draft" button on the Page Editing tool bar and the status will show "Only you can see and modify this page," as can be seen in Figure 4-20.

> *Even though the information icon (see Figure 4-20) indicates that a simple check-in will allow other people to see the changes, this is a little misleading. It should be known that a check-in will only make the page visible to users who have rights to see minor versions of pages.*

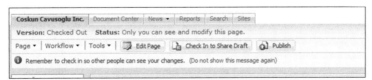

Figure 4-20

Managing Security with Publishing Pages

There are several roles that can be used or created in a publishing site to maintain security. When creating SharePoint security groups, site owners must select the permissions the new group will have based on what the group will be doing on the site.

SharePoint comes with several pre-defined permission levels out of the box. These permission levels help site owners define security when a new user or security group is being added to the site. There are several permissions a user can have when he or she is logged in to a SharePoint site, and it would be very inefficient to select the rights of a user every time a new user was added to the site. To overcome this issue, SharePoint provides site owners with the ability to create permission levels, which are essentially subsets of the permissions that are available in SharePoint.

SharePoint has the following permission levels:

Table 4-1: Default Permission Levels for SharePoint Publishing Sites

Permission Level	Description
Full Control	Has full control
Design	Can view, add, update, delete, approve, and customize
Manage Hierarchy	Can create sites and edit pages, list items, and documents
Approve	Can edit and approve pages, list items, and documents
Contribute	Can view, add, update, and delete
Read	Can view only
Restricted Read	Can view pages and documents, but cannot view historical versions or review user rights information
Limited Access	Can view specific lists, document libraries, list items, folders, or documents when given permissions

For example, the permission level named "Full Control" includes all of the potential rights available to SharePoint users. This permission level is typically used when site owners are adding administrators to their sites.

The permissions in SharePoint are grouped into three sections: list permissions, site permissions, and personal permissions. List permissions govern things like managing lists and list items, as well as document management responsibilities (see Table 4-2). Site permissions are more geared toward the maintenance and administration of sites created by users and administrators (see Table 4-3). Finally, personal permissions relate more to the personalization permissions (see Table 4-4).

Table 4-2: Permissions Listed Under List Permission

Permission	Description
Manage Lists	Create and delete lists, add or remove columns in a list, and add or remove public views of a list
Override Check Out	Discard or check in a document checked out to another user
Add Items	Add items to lists, add documents to document libraries, and add Web discussion comments
Edit Items	Edit items in lists, edit documents in document libraries, edit Web discussion comments in documents, and customize Web Part Pages in document libraries
Delete Items	Delete items from a list, documents from a document library, and Web discussion comments in documents
View Items	View items in lists, documents in document libraries, and view Web discussion comments
Approve Items	Approve a minor version of a list item or document
Open Items	View the source of documents with server-side file handlers
View Versions	View past versions of a list item or document
Delete Versions	Delete past versions of a list item or document
Create Alerts	Create email alerts
View Application Pages	View forms, views, and application pages. Enumerate lists

For cases where the out-of-the-box permission levels do not meet the criteria of the business rules, site owners can create their own custom permission levels by selecting permissions that should be a part of the new permission level.

Managing Site Hierarchy

Throughout the lifecycle of a communication site, there will be several cases where sites need to change their location. For example, as a result of an organizational change, maybe the HR site needs to move from under the Operational Site to under the root level site. Ordinarily in such cases, administrators will need to create a brand new site under the new location and bring over the content. With SharePoint publishing site's Manage Content and Structure functionality, however, site owners can easily move a site from one location to another with a few clicks.

A site owner can access the Site Content and Structure by clicking on the "Manage Content and Structure" link on publishing sites as shown in Figure 4-21.

Table 4-3: Permissions Listed Under Site Permission

Permission	Description
Manage Permissions	Create and change permission levels on the Web site and assign permissions to users and groups
View Usage Data	View reports on Web site usage
Create Subsites	Create subsites such as team sites, Meeting Workspace sites, and Document Workspace sites
Manage Web Site	Grants the ability to perform all administration tasks for the Web site as well as manage content
Add and Customize Pages	Add, change, or delete HTML pages or Web Part Pages, and edit the Web site using a Windows SharePoint Services-compatible editor
Apply Themes and Borders	Apply a theme or borders to the entire Web site
Apply Style Sheets	Apply a style sheet (.CSS file) to the Web site
Create Groups	Create a group of users that can be used anywhere within the site collection
Browse Directories	Enumerate files and folders in a Web site using SharePoint Designer and Web DAV interfaces
Use Self-Service Site Creation	Create a Web site using Self-Service Site Creation
View Pages	View pages in a Web site
Enumerate Permissions	Enumerate permissions on the Web site, list, folder, document, or list item
Browse User Information	View information about users of the Web site
Manage Alerts	Manage alerts for all users of the Web site
Use Remote Interfaces	Use SOAP, Web DAV, or SharePoint Designer interfaces to access the Web site
Use Client Integration Features	Use features which launch client applications. Without this permission, users will have to work on documents locally and upload their changes
Open	Allows users to open a Web site, list, or folder in order to access items inside that container
Edit Personal User Information	Allows a user to change his or her user information, such as adding a picture

Table 4-4: Permissions Listed Under Personal Permission

Permission	Description
Manage Personal Views	Create, change, and delete personal views of lists
Add/Remove Personal Web Parts	Add or remove personal Web Parts on a Web Part Page
Update Personal Web Parts	Update Web Parts to display personalized information

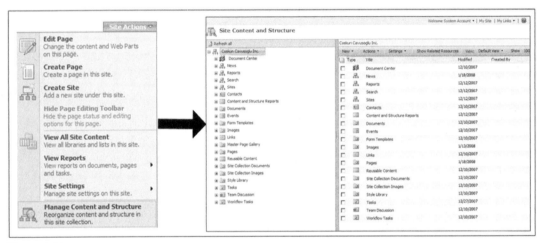

Figure 4-21

For example, say there is a "Reports" site that is currently under the root site but needs to be moved under another site entitled "Document Center." To do this, a site owner can follow these steps:

1. The site owner will first click on the context menu of the site that he or she would like to move as shown in Figure 4-22. From the context menu the site owner will click on the "Move" link.

2. Next, a popup screen appears as shown in Figure 4-23. On this screen, the site owner should click the Document Center site as the destination and click OK.

Once the OK button is clicked, SharePoint will move the Reports site under the Document Center site, as shown in Figure 4-24.

Managing Site Variations

Many publishing sites will have the need to maintain variations of a single site to accommodate different audiences. For example, the same content of a particular site may need to be accessible in several different languages for a global audience to consume. To extend that thought a bit, the site content may need to be displayed differently for a laptop visitor than for a mobile device visitor.

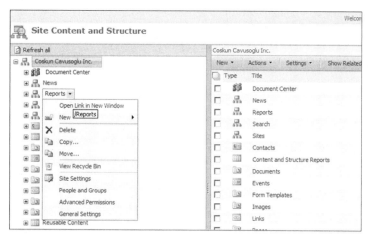

Figure 4-22

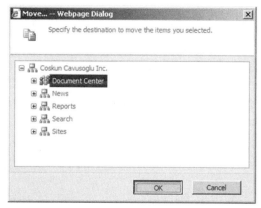

Figure 4-23

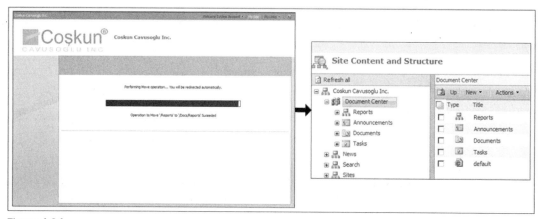

Figure 4-24

It would be difficult and time-consuming to maintain the variations of an organization that has an Internet-facing public Web site that requires English, Spanish, German, French, Chinese, and Turkish versions of their site. However, this can be fairly easily accomplished by using the variations feature of SharePoint publishing sites.

The variation process is usually thought of as a fully automated translation service, but this is not the case. What happens is that once site owners create their variation labels such as English, Spanish, and French, they select one of them as the source variation. Source variation sites are mostly where the process of publishing to variations begins. When there are changes made to the source variation, these changes can be automatically or manually propagated to other variations that have been created by the site owner.

These changes then will need to be translated to the languages of the variation by the users who own the variation site. Once the translation process is complete, the content is published and the content approval process begins, as shown in Figure 4-25. Finally, when that content is approved, the variation will be available to all readers of the site.

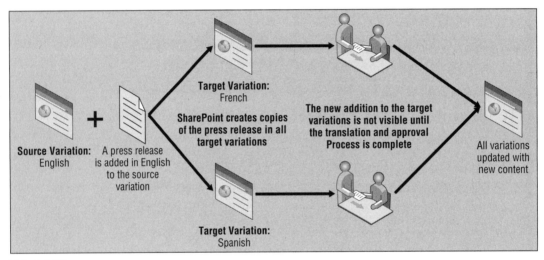

Figure 4-25

This means that when new content is published to the source variation (for example, a press release as in Figure 4-25), the content does not appear under the variation sites until a translated version of the page is published to those sites.

Variation Settings

Site owners update the Variation settings for their site by going to Site Actions > Site Settings > Modify All Site Settings > Variations. Variation settings can be modified by using the Variation Settings screen as shown in Figure 4-26.

While most of these fields are intuitive, remember when specifying the Variation Home parameter to select the site that you would like variations for. For example, if you only would like to have the News section translated, you should select the News site as the Variation Home by using the Browse button.

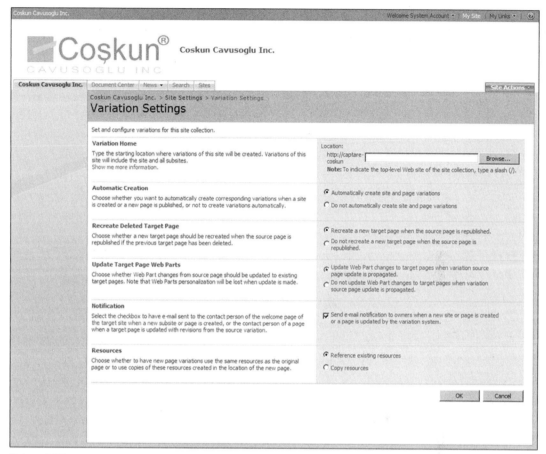

Figure 4-26

Generally, you should leave the default option selected for the Automatic Creation parameter so that SharePoint creates the variation copies automatically for the newly created pages. For cases where you might want the site owner to determine whether a site or a page needs a variation, you should click the "Do not automatically create site and page variations" button.

And finally, if your source variation page references resources that are not local to that site such as a site logo or a specific image, you might want to copy the resources to make them local to the site by selecting the "Copy resources" radio button under the Resources section.

Variation Labels

A site owner will have to create a variation label for each variation they would like to have for site. This can be accomplished by going to Site Actions > Site Settings > Modify All Site Settings > Variation Labels > New Label. The Create Variation Label screen will allow the site owner to create the new variation label as shown in Figure 4-27.

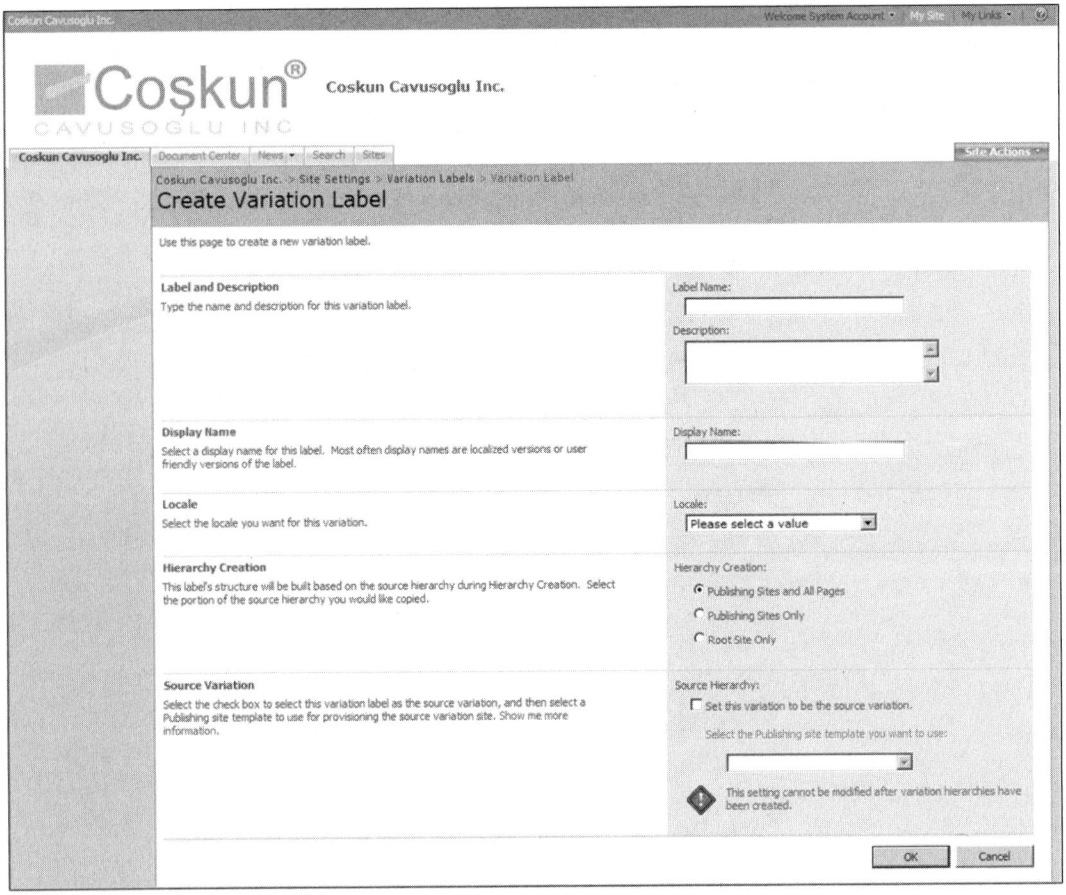

Figure 4-27

Variation labels are used to create sites for different languages, cultures, or even devices. In SharePoint you will use variation labels to name your variants and when naming your variations make sure that they are intuitive to your users. An example of an English variant would be set up as the following:

- **Label Name:** en-US
- **Display Name:** English (United States)
- **Locale:** English (United States)

Once you are ready to click OK on your settings page for the variation label you are creating, remember that the Source Variation settings cannot be modified after variation hierarchies have been created. Also remember that some of the master pages of publishing sites contain a reference to the Variations Label control, which enables you to switch between the variations labels in your site. In some cases, you will need to modify this control. You can find more information on the three different approaches to customizing the variations label by visiting http://msdn.microsoft.com/en-us/library/ms551625.aspx.

Publishing Site Templates

When creating sites in SharePoint, different types of sites are available under the Publishing tab as shown in Figure 4-28. Publishing site templates are a new addition to SharePoint with MOSS 2007. These site templates under the Publishing tab allow users to create communication sites. Note that in Figure 4-28 you will only see two options, Collaboration Portal and Publishing Portal, which are available to you when you create a top-level site collection. You can almost think of these as your top-level site templates.

Figure 4-28

When you try to create a sub-site under your top level portal, there are new options to choose from, and the Collaboration Portal and the Publishing Portal are no longer listed, as shown in Figure 4-29.

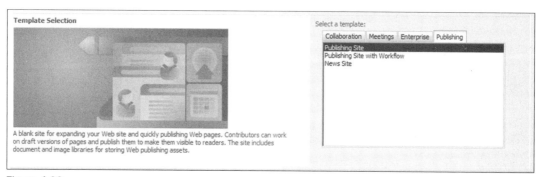

Figure 4-29

The following sections will explore the different publishing site templates.

The Top-Level Publishing Site Templates

As described previously, when creating a top-level publishing site, you can either create a Collaboration Portal or a Publishing Portal. The Collaboration Portal site template is used to create intranets, and the Publishing Portal is used to create Internet-facing sites. The following sections will detail which site template you should choose when creating your top-level site.

The Collaboration Portal Site Template

The Collaboration Portal site is typically used to create intranets or divisional portals. It includes a home page, a Document Center, a News site, a Reports site, a Search Center with tabs, and a Site Directory (see Figure 4-30).

Figure 4-30

If you are creating an intranet-like department portal, such as an HR Portal, the Collaboration Portal site template is the type of template you should use as it provides most of the features you will need in intranet or departmental-type portals.

The Publishing Portal Site Template

The Publishing Portal Site template is the second template you get when you are creating a top-level publishing site. This template is typically used to create an Internet-facing site. This is the template to choose when heavy branding is needed. Typically, a Publishing Portal publishing site will have many more readers than contributors.

Also with the out-of-the-box approval workflow functionality the owners of the site can manage their content with standardized processes. It includes a home page, a sample press releases sub-site, and a Search Center (see Figure 4-31).

This site template also comes with several master pages that demonstrate different types of branding examples. Site owners can change the master page for a site by going to Site Actions > Site Settings > Modify All Site Settings > master page.

Figure 4-31

Site owners can select from the following master pages for Publishing Portal and Collaboration Portal sites:

- ❑ default.master
- ❑ BlueBand.master
- ❑ BlackBand.master
- ❑ BlueGlassBand.master
- ❑ BlueVertical.master
- ❑ BlackVertical.master
- ❑ BlueTabs.master
- ❑ OrangeSingleLevel.master
- ❑ BlackSingleLevel.master

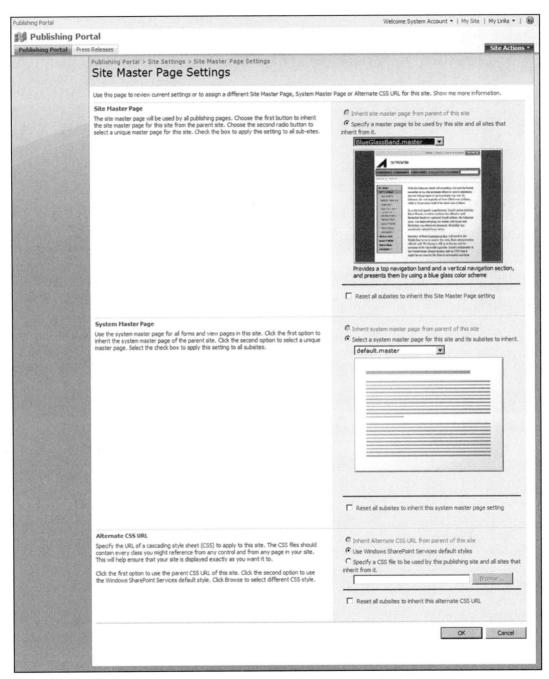

Figure 4-32

Despite its name, default.master is not the master page for the Publishing Portal by default. This is a master page that has the light-blue default SharePoint look and feel. The BlueBand.master is the default master page for the Publishing Portal.

There are two sections when site owners are selecting the master page (see figure 4-32). The selected master page in the Site master page section will change the look and feel of the site viewed by all users while the selected master page in the System master page section will update the look and feel of all of the administration pages within the site. Designers also have the ability to upload a CSS file to update the look and feel of the site through this page.

Another great feature that this page provides is the ability to reset all sub-sites to inherit the selected master page. This feature comes in quite handy when there are hundreds of sites under your publishing portal and you wish to update the master page for all of them.

By selecting a different master page, designers can instantly skin the Web site with the master page they have created. When a custom master page is created, published, and approved, that master page will appear in the dropdown that lists all of the master pages.

> *Designers must make sure that when they create their master pages for publishing sites with approval workflow, they publish and approve the master page before all users can see the changes.*
>
> *To test their design, it is recommended that Designers create test accounts that have only read access to the site. The designers should continually test their design with this test user account to validate that all content has been published properly.*

To change the master page, the user will select the master page he or she would like to update the site with and click OK, which will instantly update the look and feel, as shown in Figure 4-33.

The Publishing Sub-Site Templates

When creating publishing sub-sites under publishing sites, you are able select from the following options:

- ❑ Publishing Site
- ❑ Publishing Site with Workflow
- ❑ News Site

The following sections detail which site template you should choose when creating your publishing sub-sites.

The Publishing Site Template

The Publishing Site template is a blank site that utilizes all of the publishing features of SharePoint. Contributors can create pages and easily publish them to their sites with a matter of clicks. This site template should typically be used when an approval process is not required and contributors need to publish to the site directly to make their content readily available to their readers. This site template includes a document and picture library for storing Web-publishing assets.

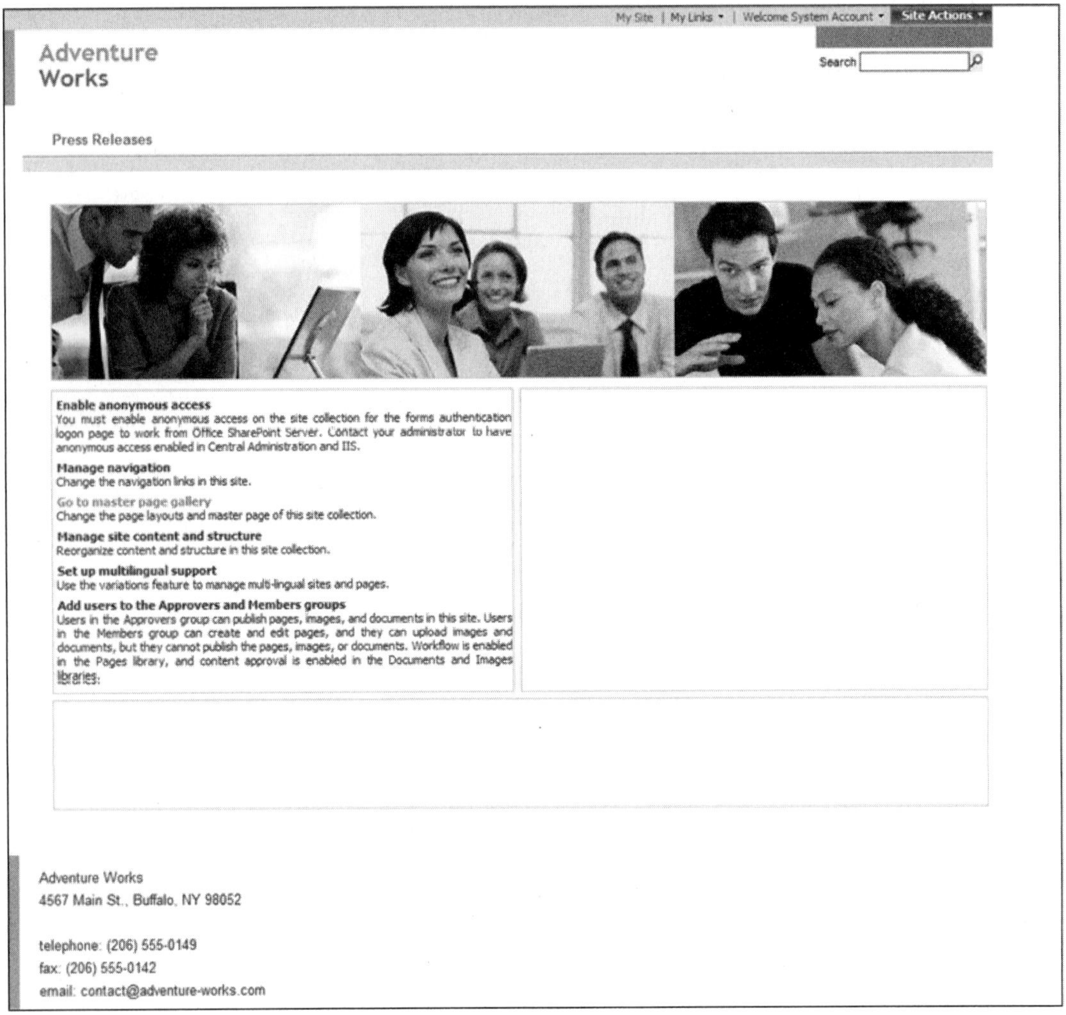

Figure 4-33

The Publishing Site with Workflow Template

The Publishing Site with Workflow template can be used to add sub-sites with publishing features to existing publishing portals. Sites created with the Publishing Site with Workflow template will have the feature of publishing pages on schedule with approval workflows.

Contributors of a Publishing Site with Workflow Template can easily publish a page to their readers by clicking on the Publish button (see Figure 4-34).

Typically, sites created with the publishing site template will inherit their look and feel from their top-level sites. Sub-sites that live under a root publishing site should not have their own branding unless there is a special need for it. The look and feel should be maintained through the root level site. Setting up the sites this way will enable site owners to manage the look and feel for their portal more efficiently.

Figure 4-34

Designers must remember that once a publishing site is created, using the Publishing Site with Workflow template will create publishing sites with the workflow template as sub-sites.

The News Site Template

The News Site template is for sites needing to publish news articles. This site comes with the Collaboration Portal but can be added to the Publishing Portal as well. Sites created using the News Site template will include a sample news page and a News Archive section, as shown in Figure 4-35.

Figure 4-35

This site will be a good template to use not only for adding internal news but when adding news from other sources as well. With the addition of RSS feeds to MOSS 2007, site owners can easily subscribe to news feeds from other news sources. A nice way to use the RSS Viewer in your organization's portal is to subscribe to global news sources such as Yahoo! News, Google News, Live Search, CNN, or maybe MSDN and customize the feed so that it only returns news articles where the organization name is a part of the article. Customizing the news will allow the site readers to come to the News site to get the latest news about the organization, as shown in Figure 4-36.

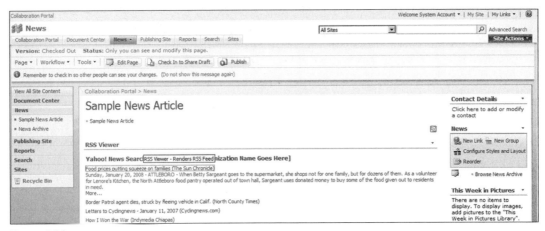

Figure 4-36

Communication/Publishing Site Best Practices

Now that you have a solid understanding of what a communication site is and how to use it effectively, it is a good time to outline some of the best practices you might want to follow in your own communication sites. Since every site is different and business requirements change from project to project, it might be difficult to come up with a list of best practices that suit every situation. However, this list will provide some universal guidelines that should help best set up any communication site.

- ❏ **Publish to communicate:** When you are trying to reach out to a large number of readers and you have a small number of contributors, use publishing sites.

- ❏ **Internet or intranet?** Use the Publishing Portal site template for Internet-facing sites and the Collaboration Portal site template for your intranets.

- ❏ **Navigation:** Plan for your navigation, since this is what your consumers will use to find your information and, consequently, to help determine their satisfaction with your site.

- ❏ **What took so long?** Don't make your approval workflows complicated; keep them simple so the content can be published before it loses its relevancy and you lose productivity. For example, if your organization has five contributors who own and maintain two Web pages daily, and if publishing these pages takes two extra minutes because of a complicated approval workflow, the time used to update these pages once a day every workday in a single year will add up to more than 86 hours. That's five contributors wasting four minutes a day (two minutes for each of their two Web pages), five days a week, for 52 weeks. That is over two full weeks of productivity that could be used elsewhere.

- ❏ **Corporate identity:** Make sure you utilize master pages and page layouts effectively to have a consistent look and feel.

- ❏ **Variations vs. performance:** Plan for your variations and keep in mind that there will be performance-related issues if you create several variations without the proper planning. Make sure you do not create a variation unless you really need it.

- ❏ **Don't forget to publish your changes:** Sometimes the readers of the site will not see your design correctly, since they do not have access to key components such as an image file or a style sheet. Be sure to check in and publish your design and also test the site with a reader account.

Following this list in your own projects will provide a great foundation for your finished project. You may have to make some decisions that are not covered here or that potentially deviate from this list if your business requirements necessitate doing so. Using this list, however, you should be well on your way to making effective communication sites and happy users.

What Is a Collaboration/Team Site?

A site with a collaboration focus is one used by teams or groups of users that have a need to collaborate on work items such as projects or share information centrally to a group or team of users for a period of time. Sites that have a collaboration focus typically have the same amount of readers as they have contributors, as shown in Figure 4-37.

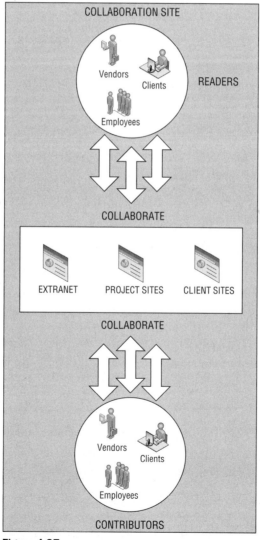

Figure 4-37

Information Flow in Collaboration/Team Sites

Collaboration sites are frequently visited by *readers* and *contributors* who collaborate on projects, documents, and similar information objects. Collaboration can be defined as the act of working together to achieve the same goal. In a collaboration environment, often the same user can be a reader and a contributor simultaneously. All users create the content available on the collaboration site, and the information flows both ways between readers and the collaboration site. See Figure 4-38.

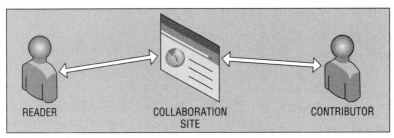

READER COLLABORATION SITE CONTRIBUTOR

Figure 4-38

When to Use a Collaboration Site

The main goal of a collaboration site is to provide readers and contributors with a central location that allows all site users to share information for a period of time. Sharing information with all team members is crucial in today's fast-paced business world. Project Managers needs to know how much time has been spent on a work item so that they can make critical business decisions and notify their stakeholders. Developers need to know the current specs for a project to accurately create deliverables. Clients need to know which deliverables have been finished and how close others are to completion. Team sites are a great way to collaborate with teams that work for the same goal.

Collaboration sites created and maintained by a specific group or team of users, and the visitors of a collaboration site are mostly the members of the group or team that owns the site. The SharePoint site template most commonly used for collaboration sites is called the Team Site template. Team sites are used to collaborate with a group or a team of users at a more granular level. Collaboration/team sites are used by team members to accomplish day-to-day activities. Almost any content required for a team can be stored in a team site.

To determine if using a collaboration site is necessary, the designer should ask the following question: "Is this a site that is going to be used as a team site where readers and contributors will both come to the site to collaborate on a common goal?" If the answer to the question is yes, organizations should use a collaboration/team site as the site fits the criteria for a collaboration site.

Using a Collaboration Site to Manage Projects

A good example of a collaboration site is a project management site. Projects require users to frequently update the information on a project, and others use the information to make decisions or to get answers to questions.

For example, a team at a manufacturing firm might want a collaboration site to discuss current project status, assign tasks, or arrange group lunches. Rather than having this internal information published to the corporate intranet, the team might choose to use a collaboration site, as shown in Figure 4-39.

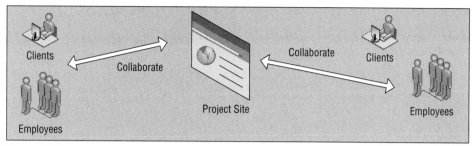

Figure 4-39

Examples of content that could get published to a team site (see Figure 4-40) could be:

❑ Project documents (status reports, budget reports)

❑ Project tasks

❑ Project discussions

❑ Project calendar

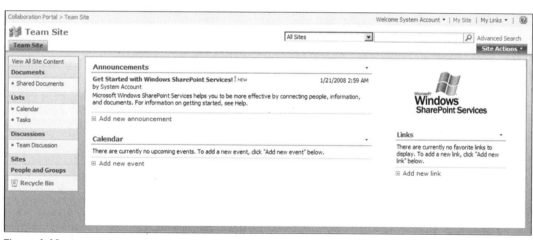

Figure 4-40

Effectively Using a Collaboration Site?

The main goal of a collaboration site is to enable collaboration among team or group members. A main identifier of a collaboration/team site is whether or not a team needs to share information among the group or team but not publish the information to the corporate intranet. If that is the case, then that site is considered to be a collaboration/team site. Typically collaboration sites have the same amount of readers and contributors.

Teams who wish to collaborate will most likely need to share documents, create discussions around specific topics, share calendars, share meeting minutes, and share meeting agendas. Team sites help organizations improve the productivity among teams since they can meet a wide range of collaboration needs.

163

A team site can be storing information for a department, which would make it a long-term site. A team site can also be used for short-term goals by users. With collaboration sites, users of these sites become more productive and efficient, since they have access to the data they need through one central location.

Another reason to use a team site for collaboration is the Enterprise Content Management (ECM) capabilities of SharePoint. Team members can create documents and share the information with the other team members easily by using the document libraries in team sites. Document libraries enable team members to work on documents collaboratively using tools like check-in, check-out, submit minor/major versions, approval workflows on documents, request feedback using workflow, adding metadata to all documents, and creating reports with views.

Collaboration Site Templates

When creating sites in SharePoint, different types of sites are available under the Collaboration tab as illustrated in Figure 4-41. These site templates allow users to create different types of collaboration sites.

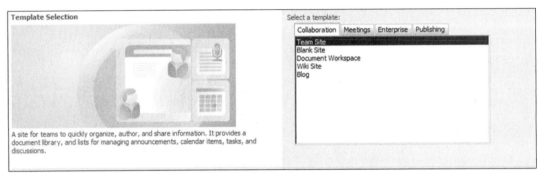

Figure 4-41

Team/Blank Site Template

The Team Site template is a site template that allows teams to quickly create, share, and organize information. It provides a document library named "Shared Documents," lists named "Calendar" and "Tasks," and a discussion board named "Team Discussion" as shown in Figure 4-42.

A blank site is a team site that has no lists or libraries. A blank team site is used when teams would like to start customizing with a clean site.

When designing for sites that are created using the Team Site template, designers should always try to leave the Quick Launch (left menu) in their design. The Quick Launch is a very important for collaboration sites, since it allows direct links to libraries, lists, and collaboration tools.

There are example master pages available through the Microsoft Download center for team sites. Designers can download and load master page examples to get a better understanding of what can be done with master pages.

http://www.microsoft.com/downloads/details.aspx?FamilyID=7C05CA44-869A-463B-84D7-57B053711A96&displaylang=en

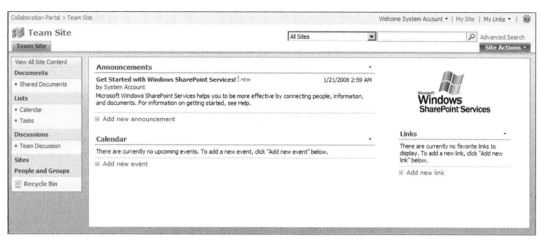

Figure 4-42

Document Workspace Template

Sites created using the Document Workspace template allow users to work together on shared documents. Document Workspaces will have a document library, tasks list, and a links list, as shown in Figure 4-43.

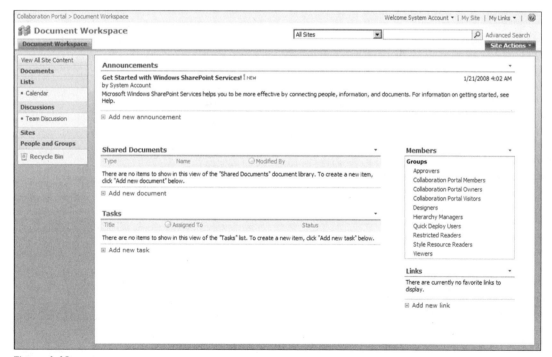

Figure 4-43

This site is used when several users have the need to work on the same document. By default, this site has Web Parts added to the default.aspx page. All of the design considerations that apply to team sites apply to a document workspace. The difference between the team site and the document workspace is the content stored on these sites. The look and feel should be the same.

Wiki Site Template

The Wiki site template should be used for sites that will be used by a group of users to brainstorm and share ideas. The wiki site template provides easy to edit Web pages, which will allow users to share information efficiently. The default Wiki site has a description of what a Wiki site is in the home page as shown in Figure 4-44. There is also a link on the left menu Quick Launch that takes users to a page that explains how to use the Wiki site.

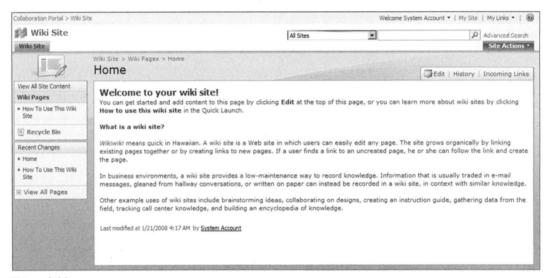

Figure 4-44

Wiki sites can be used for anything from working on a business plan to creating a knowledge base. Where there are several users and several topics that need information gathered, the best site template to use is the Wiki site. The versioning and history information of a particular Wiki page can be viewed by clicking on the History link, which will display all of the versions of the page and what was deleted or added (see Figure 4-45).

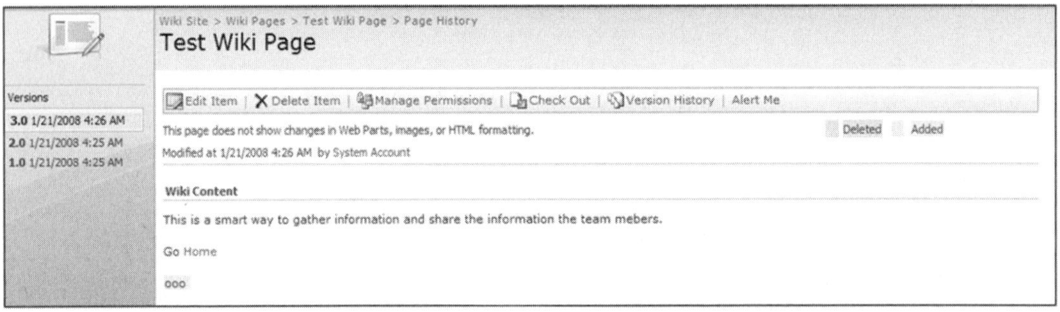

Figure 4-45

Blog Site Template

One of the new site templates that more and more users are interested in lately is the Blog site template. A Blog (shortened from "Web log") site is a site for a person or a team to post information viewable by site visitors, who can then comment on individual posts. A blog site has a similar look and feel to a team site, as can be seen in Figure 4-46.

Figure 4-46

Site Templates with WSS 3.0

This chapter has been solely focused on MOSS 2007. While many of the intricacies of MOSS 2007 will translate to Windows SharePoint Services v3 (WSS v3), it is worth noting that, when creating sites, site owners will not get the Enterprise or Publishing tabs shown earlier in this chapter. Instead, the site owners will be presented with a subset of the tabs available in MOSS 2007, as shown Figure 4-47.

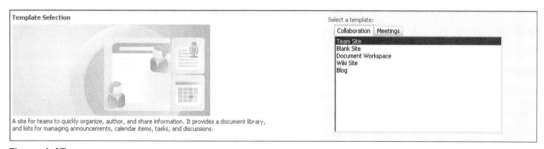

Figure 4-47

Collaboration/Team Site Best Practices

Now that you have a solid understanding of what a collaboration site is and how to use it effectively, it is a good time to outline some of the best practices you might want to follow in your own collaboration sites. Similar to the communication site best practices, every collaboration site is different and will have different business requirements. However, this list will provide some universal guidelines that should help best set up any communication site.

❑ **Collaborate with your team:** Use the team site template when you have the same amount of readers and contributors.

❑ **Look and feel:** Do not heavily brand collaboration sites. Use simple look and feel modifications to keep it consistent with the corporate identity. These sites are not intended for marketing/communicating purposes as the users of these sites will use collaboration sites to get the data they need to get their work done.

❑ **Blogs:** Control the site provisioning processes for blogs and make sure your organization has and knows the policies around posting blogs in your organization.

❑ **Training:** Make sure the users are fully aware of the site templates that are available in SharePoint.

❑ **Taxonomy:** Plan your taxonomy carefully so that when you allow users to create sites on their own it does not result in chaos. Build good structures for collaboration sites. For example, create a top-level team site for all projects and only allow users to create project sites under this site. This way you will only have to maintain one site collection and can apply your branding changes easily.

Summary

In this chapter, the differences between communication and collaboration sites were discussed in great detail. By finishing this chapter, designers should know the differences between communication and collaboration sites and be able to determine the best approach and technology for their sites.

Designers should be able to look at the users and how they plan to incorporate the site into their business processes and determine which type of site should be created. If a site has more readers than it has contributors then a communication site should be used. If it has the same amount of readers and contributors, it should use a collaboration site. By knowing the type of site that is going to be used designers now can design either a heavily branded site or a lightly branded site depending on if it's a communication or collaboration site. Communication sites require heavy branding where collaboration sites should not be heavily branded, as those sites are being used to collaborate and branding should be kept at a bare minimum.

At this point, a designer should have an easier time answering the question, which is also the title of the chapter, "Communicating or Collaborating?"

5

Introduction to SharePoint Designer

Now that you are getting excited about working with a real Microsoft Office SharePoint Server (MOSS) site, you may be asking yourself, "How do I actually edit code?" In the good old days of SharePoint 2003, you were pretty much limited to working with FrontPage to edit your sites, which often proved to be challenging as FrontPage hadn't evolved much over the years. Luckily, Microsoft has effectively ended FrontPage's lifecycle and in its place, two tools named Microsoft Expression Web and Microsoft Office SharePoint Designer 2007 (SharePoint Designer) have been created. SharePoint Designer is equivalent to Expression Web plus special tools that work specifically with MOSS servers and code. While you can edit your MOSS design code in any text editor, you will find no better way of working rapidly with MOSS than with SharePoint Designer. This chapter will discuss why SharePoint Designer is the tool of choice, as well as covering the ins and outs of using it to work effectively with MOSS. You should note that SharePoint Designer can be used with Windows SharePoint Services V3 (WSS) as well as MOSS, but some chapters will focus on MOSS specifically in order to show the full extent of what can be achieved in the latest version of SharePoint. If you are using a WSS server, some of the screens and functionality may be different in your server.

Why Use SharePoint Designer?

As a designer, you are most likely accustomed to a particular design tool such as Adobe's Dreamweaver or even something as simple as Notepad, and indeed those tools are most likely where you may want to start your HTML mockups before converting your designs into functioning MOSS sites. However, you may be surprised to find that SharePoint Designer can fit the bill for both working on MOSS user interfaces and for standard Web design. You might be asking, "Why can't I just use Visual Studio to edit my files?" While this is certainly possible, you will quickly find that Visual Studio, while being an excellent development tool, was not created with designers in mind.

You can download a trial of SharePoint Designer from Microsoft's SharePoint Designer site:

http://office.microsoft.com/en-us/sharepointdesigner

If you are an MSDN Subscriber, SharePoint Designer should be available for you to download from your subscription site.

Overview of Functionality

SharePoint Designer has many important features for working with MOSS; here is a list of some of its more important features:

❑ **Native support for underlying SharePoint technologies:** This includes IntelliSense (code completion) for the entire SharePoint design lifecycle including: SharePoint tags, master pages, Layouts, ASP.NET 2.0 code, and all tradition Web-development elements (HTML, XHTML, Cascading Style Sheets, JavaScript, and so on). Designers are no longer limited to using developer tools such as Visual Studio in order to get Intellisense when working with ASP.NET code!

❑ **Rich design environment:** An environment that is much improved over FrontPage including dedicated detachable task panes specific to all of the key areas of the SharePoint design lifecycle.

❑ **WYSIWYG (What You See Is What You Get) editing:** Designers have the choice of working with code directly (Code View) or using the What You See is What You Get (WYSIWYG) features (Design View) and even the option of splitting the two (Split View).

❑ **Can work with and format data with ease:** Extensible Stylesheet Language (XSL) can be edited in a visual environment when working with MOSS Web Parts such as the Data View Web Part.

❑ **Creating and formatting views of data:** SharePoint Designer can present data using XSLT Data Views, Web Parts, Web Part connections, and ASP.NET controls. It can also use dynamic Data View tools such as calculated fields, conditional formatting, sorting, grouping, and filtering.

❑ **Ability to revert designs to old versions:** Files under MOSS source control can have their history viewed and reverted to old versions. Pages that are based on site definitions can be easily reverted back to their original state.

❑ **Robust reporting features:** Specialized reports are available for checking broken links, unused pages, cascading style sheets usage, and master page usage.

Not Using SharePoint Designer

As stated earlier, using SharePoint Designer is not a requirement of designing for MOSS. If you are extremely comfortable with the syntax, you could create your master pages and CSS with Notepad or any other editor and manually upload them to your MOSS site using the Master Page Gallery or the View All Site Content Web-based interfaces from your actual MOSS site. Sometimes this can be helpful if you are on a machine that does not already have SharePoint Designer installed.

Customizing MOSS Sites

To begin customizing MOSS with SharePoint Designer, you should start by getting more familiar with the general user interface layout of the application itself. Figure 5-1 shows the basic SharePoint Designer interface with a master page open.

The resolution of all the screenshots are from a 1024×768 monitor for this book. You will be thankful if your resolution is larger or if you have a dual monitor setup, as working with MOSS involves a lot of screen real estate.

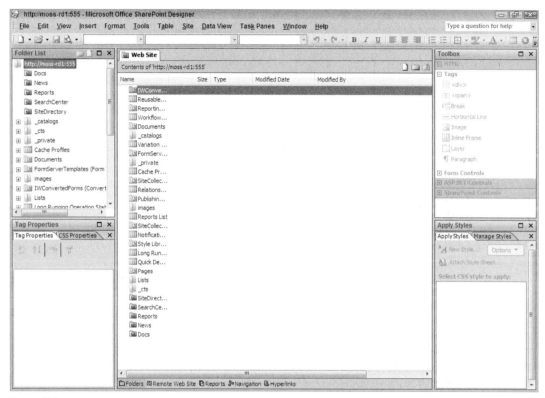

Figure 5-1

First make sure you have SharePoint Designer installed and open it up. (It is usually located under Start ⇨ Microsoft Office ⇨ SharePoint Designer 2007.) When first started, SharePoint Designer will have no open document and the task panes will be located in their default positions. You will tour the various aspects of the product throughout this chapter, but they may make more sense to you if you have a MOSS site open.

If you do not have a MOSS server available to you, you can follow Tony Zink's lengthy but excellent 20 step guide to creating a MOSS 2007 VPC image at: http://www.pptspaces.com/sharepoint-reporterblog/Lists/Posts/Post.aspx?ID=28

Opening a MOSS Site in SharePoint Designer

In SharePoint Designer select File ⇨ Open Site and a window opens that allows you to open a previously opened site or to enter a new one as shown in Figure 5-2.

The best thing to do here is to enter your MOSS site URL into the Site name: text box. The typical format for a MOSS Site URL is http://MossServerName:port. For example, you could enter "http://YourMossServer" if a MOSS server existed on your network with that address. Next, just click the open button and you will be challenged to enter your authentication info here. Typically this requires the name of your server to be listed before your username like: "YourMossServer\Randy.Drisgill." If you are denied access, you may have to use a different user account on the server or talk to your MOSS server administrator. Typically, your user account will need to be in the SharePoint Owners or Designers groups. Also, if you are not an Owner you may need to be in the Approvers group later when it comes time to publish your changes; this is because MOSS's publishing workflow requires an approver to finalize a published page. If you have administrative rights on your MOSS server, you can change these settings by browsing the site in your Internet browser and selecting Site Actions ⇨ Site Settings ⇨ Modify All Site Settings ⇨ Users and Permissions ⇨ People and Groups.

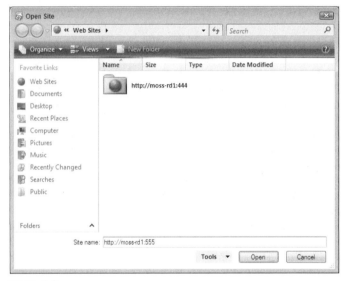

Figure 5-2

Once you are properly authenticated into the MOSS server, after a few seconds (depending on if you are local to the server and how slow your connection is), you should see the site open in SharePoint Designer. The Folder List pane (located in the top left of SharePoint Designer) will be populated with filenames from your site. Next time you use the Open Site menu item, you can select this site (or any other recently opened sites) from the list that is provided in the Open Site window.

It is worth noting at this point that if you chose to open another MOSS site, SharePoint Designer will open another instance of itself. This can get very confusing if you are editing two similar sites as it is easy to be on the wrong tab in the Task Bar and be editing the wrong site. (MOSS sites tend to look similar in the editor.)

The Folder List Pane

You will start the tour of SharePoint Designer with the Folder List pane. Its default position is the top left of SharePoint Designer. This is an interesting pane that can be confusing to beginners. The files listed here may or may not exist on the actual file system of the Web server. The MOSS server is actually showing you how it sees your site. Typically this is a combination of customized and uncustomized (more on that topic in the section "Customized vs. Un-customized") pages that may live in the SharePoint Content

Database or in the physical directory of the IIS Web Application. As a new user, sometimes there is a temptation to search the server's hard drive to find these files, and many times they will not show up, or worse yet you may confuse yourself by finding something in an incorrect directory. It is best to work with this pane as though it is your actual folder structure, despite the fact that some files may live in other places physically. (MOSS handles placing the files in the appropriate areas of the site via behind-the-scenes Web service calls.) The pane begins with the name of your site, followed by a list of sub-sites beneath it. They are preceded by an icon of a folder with a globe on it. Double-clicking these sub-sites will start a new instance of SharePoint Designer with that particular subsite opened. Beneath that, you will most likely see a series of folders, lists, document libraries, master pages, and pages. Some important areas to explore in the folder list are as follows:

❑   **_catalogs ⇨ masterpage (Master Page Gallery):** This is where all of your master pages and page layouts live; you will spend a lot of time here.

❑   **Images:** This is a good place to add images that you would like site content authors to have access to when they are editing pages. The actual images that make up your MOSS site's custom design should instead be stored in Style Library ⇨ Images.

❑   **Pages:** This is where actual created pages will reside. They are standard .aspx pages but often have page layouts associated with them (this will be discussed more in the section "Working with Page Layouts"). You can add custom .aspx pages here. A default page named "default.aspx" (appropriately enough) is automatically created here for new sites. (This is typically the welcome page for your MOSS site.)

❑   **Style Library:** Many styles that MOSS uses are located in this directory structure. Several important ones live in the following subdirectories:

   ❑   **Style Library ⇨ en-us ⇨ Core Styles:** This is where MOSS's core styles live. The en-us refers to the United States English locale folder (multilingual sites could make use of other locale folders). You will create a subdirectory sibling of the Core Styles directory named "Custom Styles" in Chapter 8, "Master Pages."

   ❑   **Style Library ⇨ XSL Style Sheets:** This is where many of the MOSS out-of-the-box Extensible Stylesheet Language (XSL) files live. They control styling on many XML lists and list headers throughout MOSS.

   ❑   **Style Library ⇨ Images:** As stated earlier, this is where you should place any custom images that make up the actual design layout of your MOSS site.

If you ever lose the ability to expand the _catalogs directory (or any other area you are certain you have access to), you may have been logged out of an authenticated MOSS server. If this happens, you may need to close and reopen the site with your credentials before the folders come back.

Several task panes are available in SharePoint Designer and are discussed in this chapter. It is important to note that they may be minimized, removed, attached to other task panes, torn off, and floated in the editor or even moved outside of SharePoint Designer altogether in order to free up the maximum amount of screen real estate. If you ever lose one or feel the need to start over, you can select Task Panes ⇨ Reset Workspace Layout to return them all to their default positions.

File Check-In/Check-Out

Now you can take a look at what happens when a file is edited. Navigate to the _catalogs ⇨ masterpages folder and double click on default.master. A message box pops up asking you "The file is under source control. Do you want to check it out?" This is because MOSS 2007 is setup to have source control turned on by default. If you select "No" SharePoint Designer will open the file and you can view the contents.

SharePoint Designer defaults to Design View, which is the WYSIWYG editor. Many people prefer the Code View. You may switch the mode easily by selecting it at the bottom of the editor window. (See Figure 5-3.)

Figure 5-3

One thing that may surprise you is that SharePoint Designer will let you edit the file, but when you click Save, you will be prompted with a message indicating that it is not currently Checked Out. If you plan to edit the file, it is best to check it out when opening, because your changes can be lost otherwise. Go ahead and check the file out (if you have already opened it, just close and reopen it). You will notice that the icons beside the file change to a check mark (to indicate check out) and a page with a pencil (to indicate you are editing it). Now you can edit the file to your heart's content. (Working with master pages is covered in detail in Chapter 8.) As you edit the file, you will notice that the tab with the name of the file, at the top of the editor pane, has an asterisk next to it. This means that the file is "dirty" and needs to be saved before your changes will be stored. If you have been following along with this text and have made some edits, it is best *not* to save and check in your changes as you may have broken your MOSS site badly with random edits. Right-click on default.master in the Folder List pane and select Undo Check Out. A warning message appears, telling you that you will be restoring your old version of the file and that all changes will be lost, which is exactly what you want right now, so click Yes. Notice that the check mark icon has gone away, indicating you are not checked out. You will learn a lot more about properly editing master pages later in Chapter 8.

You can also revert to old versions of your source controlled documents. Right-clicking on the file name of files with history shows an option for "Version History." From there you can restore old versions of your files with ease.

Adding Content to a MOSS Site

You can explore the check-in process even further by adding something to your MOSS site. A good place to start would be adding a new page layout to the MOSS site. To do this, right click the site name in the Folder List pane and select New ➪ SharePoint Content (see Figure 5-4). (You can accomplish the same thing from the File menu.)

From here select SharePoint Content ➪ SharePoint Publishing ➪ Page Layout and make the following entries in the Options:

- ❑ **Content Type Group:** Page Layout Content Types
- ❑ **Content Type Name:** Welcome Page
- ❑ **URL Name:** layout_testWelcome
- ❑ **Title:** Test Welcome Layout

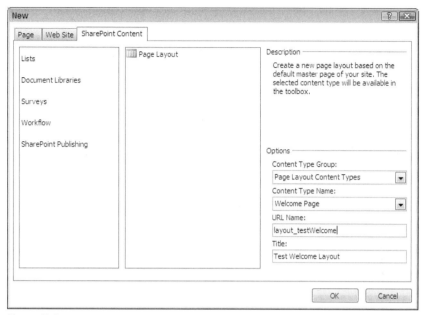

Figure 5-4

Select OK and MOSS will create your page layout in the _catalogs/masterpages folder called layout_test-Welcome.aspx. The page layout automatically opens in SharePoint Designer. Don't get too worried right now about the contents of the layout (which is covered in Chapter 9).

Now is a good time to talk about the Toolbox pane (located in the top right-hand of the screen), which contains easily draggable HTML tags, ASP.NET Controls, and SharePoint Controls. See Figure 5-5.

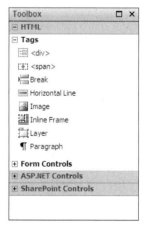

Figure 5-5

The SharePoint Controls communicate with the MOSS server to decide which controls are available to be selected based on what type of content you are editing. For now, just select HTML ➪ Tags ➪

<div> and drag it into the editor between <asp:Content ContentPlaceholderID="PlaceHolderMain" runat="server"> and </asp:Content>. The editor pane should look like this:

```
<asp:Content ContentPlaceholderID="PlaceHolderMain" runat="server">
<div></div>
</asp:Content>
```

Now add the phrase Hello World between the <div> and </div> tags and save the file by either pressing Control-S or selecting File ⇨ Save. Now you need to ensure the file is checked in. Right-click on the filename in the Folder List pane and select Check In. Select "Publish a major version" because a major version will allow non-authenticated users to see the change. You can also add comments to the Comments box; they can be used later when viewing a history of a saved version. See Figure 5-6.

Figure 5-6

SharePoint Designer brings up a warning that says, "This document requires content approval. Do you want to view or modify its approval status?" This is due to the Approval Workflow being turned on by default in MOSS. This is discussed more in the section titled "Approval Workflow"; for now just select Yes. Interesting enough, this process cannot be achieved in SharePoint Designer, and as such a browser window immediately appears attempting to connect to your MOSS site. Authenticate if required and you will be presented with the Master Page Gallery in a mode that shows you all of the documents grouped by approval status. Find the page layout under the Pending category. (See Figure 5-7.) When you hover over the filename, an orange box appears around it.

Click the box and select Approve/reject, select Approved, and click OK. See Figure 5-8.

It's not much of a page layout, but you might as well take a look at it. To see your handiwork you must use the MOSS Web UI and create a new page that uses the page layout. Start by creating the page layout by selecting Site Actions ⇨ Create Page. From there you add a Title, Description, and URL Name (which pre-populates from the title you entered). In the page layout select box, look for "(Welcome Page) Test Welcome Layout." This is your page layout that was created. Click Create and you will be taken to a new page using the new page layout. (See Figure 5-9.)

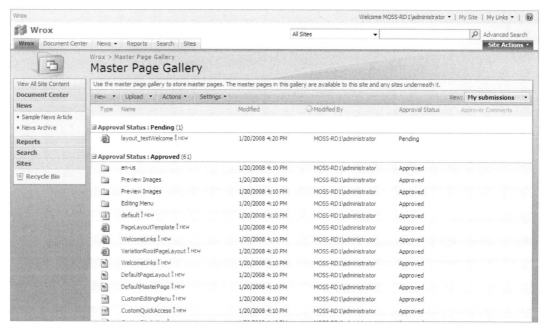

Figure 5-7

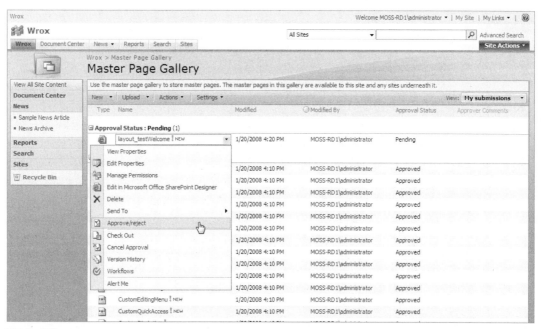

Figure 5-8

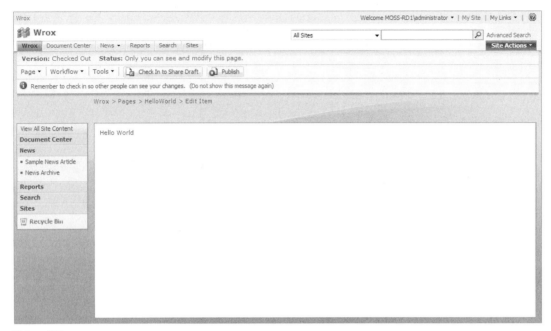

Figure 5-9

Adding Other Types of Content

You can add pretty much any type of typical Web content to a MOSS site, one method for doing so is by simply dragging a file from your desktop to the Folder List pane. For example if you have a JPEG image on your desktop named helloworld.jpg, you can drag the image from your desktop to the images folder of your MOSS site in the SharePoint Designer Folder List pane.

A quick word of warning: For this example, be sure you are using the images directory off the root of your site, not the one in the Style Library (nothing bad will happen if you do, but it is easy to confuse yourself for a while about why your image is not showing).

Once your image is dragged to the images folder, you should be able to preview it from your MOSS site's URL by browsing to the images directory. If your MOSS site's URL was http://YourMossServer, you would want to browse to http://YourMossServer/images/helloworld.jpg.

If you are wondering why you were able to view the new image right away, it is because the images directory does not have source control or the Approval Workflow turned on in MOSS.

Approval Workflow

As mentioned earlier, adding or editing content in a MOSS Publishing site requires approval. This is a result of the approval workflow. This workflow is turned on by default with a MOSS Publishing site and will affect who can see your changes to things like master pages. While this is a great feature in MOSS, for you the designer, this *will* drive you crazy at some point. The scenario will go as follows: You make a really awesome sweeping change to the UI of the MOSS site and are excited to show it off to your customer or team. You send them the URL and they send back an email saying nothing has changed. Before you have a heart attack, ask yourself this: Did you remember to check in, publish, and *approve* your changes? If you did not, only you and the other administrators of the site will be able to see any changes you make. This can be particularly surprising because you will always see your changes to the file (since you can always see pending changes to your own files). Because of this, sometimes it's a good idea to test your customizations while logged out; this can be achieved easily by using a different browser than the one you are currently using. (Firefox is helpful for this, as it initially browses a MOSS site as an anonymous user.)

Customized Vs. Un-customized

If you were to edit one of the out-of-the-box master pages (like default.master) or one that has been deployed from a custom Site Definition (this is discussed more later in this section), SharePoint Designer will warn you that you are about to customize a page from the site definition (see Figure 5-10). What does this mean?

This topic has been around throughout previous versions of SharePoint under the terms unghosted (the same as customized) and ghosted (the same as un-customized). Microsoft has changed the name in this version (though you may still see references to ghosting in the Microsoft documentation), but confusingly the "un" prefix has now reversed from the old definition.

Figure 5-10

In basic terms, an un-customized file exists on the file system of your MOSS site, typically in the 12 Hive (a popular name for the folder where MOSS's files physically live on the Web server). Alternatively, customized files have been changed (typically with SharePoint Designer), and MOSS therefore stores them *not* on the file system but instead in the SharePoint Content Database. To the end user (and maybe even to you, the designer, thanks to how SharePoint Designer shows things in the Folder List pane) this may not be readily obvious as MOSS seamlessly takes care of displaying the file regardless of whether it is in the content database or the file system. The downside to this is two-fold. First, customized pages may have a slight performance impact (though Microsoft has said the impact is too minimal to consider). Second, you may have issues propagating your custom design throughout MOSS Sites and Site Collections if it has been customized. This topic is discussed further in Appendix A. For now, the important distinction is that Solutions are easily deployable throughout an entire MOSS 2007 hierarchy, while customized pages are not. In fact, there is a chance that at some point customized pages could be overwritten by the default Site Definition either by another designer or an administrator, either purposefully or even by accident.

After reading this you may be wondering what good it is to edit with SharePoint Designer then. The answer to this is immediate gratification and iterative changes. The solution is to not customize the actual final master page that your site is using but instead to customize a staging or development version of the master page. (This version can even live on the same server as your final deployed master page if you so desire.) Once you are finished with your master page, you or a developer on your team can convert your customized master page into a deployable solution. (You can find more information on this topic in Appendix A.)

You can always tell when a file has been customized by the icon that SharePoint Designer places next to it, a blue circle with the letter "i" in it. If you ever need to revert one of these files back to the original site definition, right-click on the file and select Reset to Site Definition. Also, if you want to see a report of all the customized pages in your site, just click on Site ➪ Reports ➪ Shared Content ➪ Customized Pages, and SharePoint Designer will provide a list of all your site pages with the customized ones at the top.

The Design View

One of the key features of SharePoint Designer is the Design View that is available from the bottom of the editing screen. In many ways, this is a WYSIWYG interface that shows how your pages, page layouts, and master pages will look in real time. It is worth noting that some designers prefer to use this, while others feel that working in the Code View is a more pure way of designing both HTML and MOSS sites.

Figure 5-11

Take a look at the default.master page in Design View by double clicking on _catalogs ➪ masterpage ➪ default.master. Check to make sure you have selected Design View by examining the indicator at the bottom of the editor pane. What you see in Figure 5-11 is a fairly close approximation of what the master page would look like in your browser. Light purplish lines surround the various Placeholders that are being used on the page. If you hover over one, you can see (in very light text) the name of the Placeholder, and if you click inside the purple box, the Placeholder will be selected and get darker. You can switch back to Code View (or check out Split View to see both at the same time) and see that the Placeholder that you selected is also highlighted in the Code View. (Note: Some Placeholders work better than others when it comes to highlighting in Code View.)

While you are in the Design View, you may find that the purplish lines that highlight the Placeholders are distracting from a true WYSIWYG experience. To turn them off you can select View ⇨ Visual Aids ⇨ Show to toggle these lines (along with all the other Visual Aides) on and off. Alternatively, you can pick and choose which Visual Aids to show or not show.

Another interesting feature of the Design View is that the elements of the page are aware of the HTML hierarchy they live in. When you select an element that is deeply nested in other elements, you can press the Escape key and the selection will move to its parent element. If you keep pressing the Escape key, you will eventually have the entire HTML document selected.

You can insert various HTML and ASP.NET elements simply by dragging them from the Toolbox pane or by selecting them from the Insert menu at the top toolbar. You can also insert HTML tables by selecting Table ⇨ Insert Table from the top toolbar. This opens a table wizard that allows you to tweak various settings of the table. See Figure 5-12.

Figure 5-12

You can drag elements such as images from the Folder List pane and drop them right onto the Design View. When doing so, SharePoint Designer prompts you to enter the Alternate text to be placed in the Alt tag of the image.

One other really interesting feature of SharePoint Designer is the On-object User Interface (OOUI) that appears when you select certain ASP.NET and SharePoint controls. You can see one if you click the horizontal top menu navigation control of the default.master. The OOUI will appear to the right of the placeholder box and will look like a small box with an arrow. See Figure 5-13.

Figure 5-13

The OOUI will display related information for the control you have selected. In this case it will show Data Sources that can be used to populate the navigation control. (This topic is discussed further in Chapter 11.)

There are many other aspects to Design View. You can explore them more thoroughly yourself or watch the training videos supplied from Microsoft's SharePoint Designer Web site.

Working with Master Pages

Master pages are one of the key file types that you as a designer will be working with in SharePoint Designer. For the most part though, you will likely not be starting a master page for MOSS from scratch. This is due to the fact that unlike a traditional ASP.NET application, MOSS master pages have very specific needs (including mandatory sections that if omitted will break your site). Because of this, you should start with either a minimal master page (which is covered in Chapter 8) or simply use a copy of one of the out-of-the-box master pages that are included with your site.

For this example, you will make a copy of the default.master and make a minor change to see the results. To do this, just open SharePoint Designer and use the Folder List pane to navigate to the _catalogs ⇨ masterpage and open default.master. You can choose not to check it out if you would like, as you will not be changing it. Once it is open, simply select File ⇨ Save As and in the Save As window leave the location the same (_catalogs ⇨ masterpage) and in the File name box enter "custom.master."

You will now be editing your new master page file and will most likely realize that it's quite complex (over 400 lines of ASP.NET and not a single comment to help you decipher it!). One thing Microsoft did do for designers was provide a special toolbar for working with master pages. To enable it, select View ⇨ Toolbars ⇨ master page. This toolbar is a small floating toolbar, so small you could miss it, so look carefully. See Figure 5-14.

Figure 5-14

This toolbar allows you to select a placeholder and SharePoint Designer will highlight it in the editor. This can be helpful for finding the key areas of the master page. A quick warning though: The toolbar unfortunately sometimes does not work as nicely in Code View as it does in Design View. Using whichever View you prefer, find the PlaceHolderMain, which should be somewhere near line 395 of your master page. PlaceHolderMain is the placeholder that displays all of the actual page content from the page layout. For this example, make a very simple change that will make the PlaceHolderMain stand out from the rest of the page. Put a `<div>` with a lime green border around the PlaceHolderMain like this:

```
<div style="border: 1px solid lime;">
  <asp:ContentPlaceHolder id="PlaceHolderMain" runat="server">
  </asp:ContentPlaceHolder>
</div>
```

While you are editing this, you should take note of the Tag Properties pane in the lower left-hand corner of SharePoint Designer. The Tag Properties pane will always show you the properties that apply to the currently selected tag or component in the editor. In your case, the only property that applies to the `<div>` tag is its style. If you click next to the word style, you can see its attribute is "border: 1px solid lime." If you click the attribute and then the " ... " button, you can use a wizard-style interface to manage the attributes of this property. See Figure 5-15. You can use this pane throughout many types of files in SharePoint Designer.

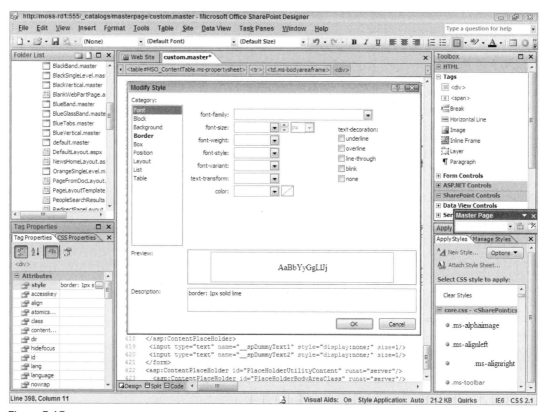

Figure 5-15

After saving the file, you must check it in and publish it or you will run into major problems activating the master page. (MOSS will warn you if you try to activate a master page that has never been published, but after that first publish, it will not warn you anymore.)

> *If you manage to activate a master page that is not published, users that are not authenticated will see a 401 or 404 error. This can be confusing the first time you run into it, but typically, if you see something vastly different only when you are not logged in, it is almost always caused by a non-published asset.*

Right-click the custom.master in the Folder View pane and select "Check in" and then "Publish a major version" and lastly say "Yes" to modify the approval process. Once you have accepted the pending approval on custom.master, you need to apply the master page to your site from the MOSS Web interface. Log in to your MOSS site and select Site Actions ⇨ Site Settings ⇨ Modify All Site Settings ⇨ Look and Feel ⇨ Master page to bring up the Site master page Settings screen. This screen allows you to select a master page for the main areas of the site (the Site master page), the master page for the system forms and view pages (the System master page), and also an Alternate CSS URL for adding additional CSS. For now, change both the Site master page and the System master page to custom.master and select OK. See Figure 5-16.

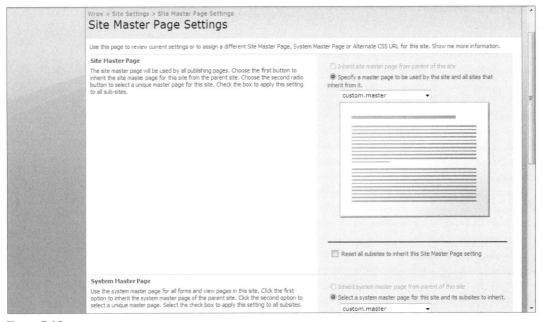

Figure 5-16

Now return to your site MOSS homepage and you should notice that the middle section of the screen has a bright green border around it. While you would never use a style like this in an actual design, it does illustrate an important concept. It demonstrates how you can make changes to the HTML of the master page, and the green bordered section highlights the transition between the master page and the page layout.

> *You will quickly notice that some pages are not affected by your master page; this is an unfortunate byproduct of the MOSS administrative pages using a different master page that is not available in*

SharePoint Designer. It is typically not recommended that you edit this master page. To style these administrative pages, your best option is to explore SharePoint themes, which are covered in Chapter 6, "Themes."

Working with Page Layouts

The topic of working with page layouts was touched on briefly earlier in this chapter under "Adding Content to a MOSS Site," but it's worth discussing a bit more at this time. When you are editing a page layout, you will notice that the Toolbox pane on the right-hand top of SharePoint Designer gains two more sections under SharePoint Controls. These two sections are Page Fields and Content Fields, and they are related to the content type of the particular page layout. Content types are defined in the MOSS Web interface and will be covered in more detail in Chapter 9.

However, the fields are important to consider when discussing SharePoint Designer because they can be dragged from the Toolbox pane only to MOSS page layouts. These fields are used to store content and metadata that the MOSS Web site content authors enter into an editable page. MOSS authors can only enter information into the fields that you setup on a page layout, and you can only setup editable fields that have been assigned in the parent content type of the page layout. This idea can sometimes be difficult to understand, as you have to think carefully through all of the types of data that a page layout may need. Often as a designer, you will find yourself needing to update a content type and a page layout in order to accommodate new data that business users need to record.

Creating a Content Page

You can create a content page that is a Web page for displaying information to a user and is based on the look and feel of a master page, but does not use a page layout to control its layout. To do this, simply click on File ➪ New ➪ Create from master page, and SharePoint Designer brings up a window to select a master page. From this window, you can select the default master page or a custom master page (both are setup when the site is created from MOSS) or you can browse and select any of the available master pages in the site. When you select a master page from this window, a new file is created in SharePoint Designer.

To add content to the page you first must add a content placeholder. Make sure the page is in Design View and then bring up the master page Toolbar by selecting View ➪ Toolbars ➪ Master Page. Select PlaceHolderMain from the toolbar and SharePoint will add the placeholder to the page. Then to add content to the placeholder, click the "on-object user interface" arrow on the right side of the box surrounding the placeholder, and select Create Custom Content. This will allow you to type content in the placeholder. For now, you can just enter some fun text like "This will really move the chains." Save the file as "newContentPage.aspx" and place it in the Pages directory of your MOSS site. You can see the new content page from your MOSS site. If your MOSS site's URL was `http://YourMossServer`, the new content page would be located at `http://YourMossServer/Pages/newContentPage.aspx`. As you can see in Figure 5-17, the content page displays the text and it is styled with the standard master page.

Editing Pages

Another way of having a page that is not dictated by a page layout is to take a normal page that was created from the MOSS Web interface and detach it from its page layout with SharePoint Designer. Typically, when you open a page that was created with the MOSS Web interface, SharePoint Designer prompts you with a message saying, "This page cannot be edited in SharePoint Designer. You can edit the content in the browser, or edit the corresponding page layout in SharePoint Designer." Essentially this is SharePoint Designer warning you that this page's display is dictated from a page layout. One option that SharePoint Designer doesn't make readily obvious is that you can hit Cancel and then right-click on the filename in the Folder List pane and select Detach from Page Layout. This will bring up a warning that says, among other things, that "Changes to the page layout will no longer affect this page"; since this is what you are trying to do, you can click Yes. Now, when you open your page, you will be able to change the layout however you like, without it being affected by a page layout. This option can be useful for handling special cases, such as making a one-off page that does not conform to the rest of the MOSS site's layout.

Figure 5-17

Working with CSS

Cascading Style Sheets (CSS) are a key component to designing user interfaces for MOSS. This is due to the fact that Microsoft has relied heavily on the cascading part of CSS to allow you to override the out-of-the-box styles with your own styles. You will learn more about working with CSS and how the cascading nature of CSS affects the master pages and Layouts of a MOSS site in Chapters 7, 8, and 9. For now, you can explore what SharePoint Designer brings to the table for editing CSS.

To open out-of-the-box MOSS style sheets, you will typically want to look in either the root of "Style Library" or its subfolder Style Library ⇨ en-us ⇨ Core Styles in the Folder List pane. If you want to create your own custom style sheets, it is recommended that you create a sibling directory of the Core Styles directory such as Style Library ⇨ en-us ⇨ Custom Styles. (In fact, you will create such a Custom Styles subdirectory in Chapter 8, "Master Pages.") This will help segregate your own CSS from those that came with MOSS out-of-the-box.

SharePoint Designer provides many of the typical features you would expect in a modern designer tool. One very helpful feature in SharePoint Designer is tag completion for your CSS (known as Intellisense). SharePoint Designer also has three specific task panes for working with CSS; these are the Manage Styles pane, the Apply Styles pane, and the CSS Properties pane.

The Manage Styles Pane

The Manage Styles pane shows the styles that apply to a rendered page, including those applied from a page's page layout and master page. The pane uses various icons before the style name to denote the type of style that is being applied. There are five different icons to represent the styles:

❑ Styles based on IDs have a red dot.

❑ Styles based on classes have a green dot.

❑ Styles based on elements have a blue dot.

❑ Styles that are used in the current page have a circle around their dot.

❑ External style sheets have an @ symbol.

The Manage Styles pane does not show inline styles that apply to a page.

Styles can be moved between internal and external style sheets by dragging them up and down between the sections of the pane. Styles can also be dragged higher or lower in the cascading hierarchy. You can also hover over styles to get a preview of the code of that style or even click the style to see a graphical preview. See Figure 5-18.

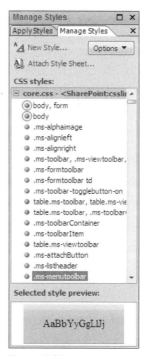

Figure 5-18

Double-clicking a style will open its corresponding style sheet for editing in the editor pane. The Manage Styles pane can also be used to apply existing style sheets to the current page or even to create new individual styles that can be added to a style sheet.

When using the Manage Styles pane, double-clicking an external style causes SharePoint Designer to open that file for editing. After a while of working with one style sheet, you can easily end up editing another one without noticing. Because of this, you should pay special attention to what file you are actively editing while working with the Manage Styles pane.

The Apply Styles Pane

The Apply Styles pane is closely related to the Manage Styles pane. As the name suggests this pane is for actually applying (or removing) style elements of the page you are editing. Just like the Manage Styles pane, all styles that affect the selected page will be shown, including those inherited from a page's page layout or master page. Unlike the Manage Styles pane, the Apply Styles pane also shows styles that affect inline elements. This is beneficial in that you can see all the styles that affect a given element and it allows you to change or clear them with ease. The Apply Styles pane uses the following icons to indicate different types of styles:

- ❏ Styles based on IDs have a red dot.
- ❏ Styles based on classes have a green dot.
- ❏ Styles based on elements have a blue dot.
- ❏ Inline styles have a yellow dot.
- ❏ Styles that are used in the current page have a circle around their dot.
- ❏ External style sheets have an @ symbol.

To apply a style to a given page element, simply select the element in the page editor and then click a style in the Apply Styles pane. Lastly, the Clear Styles button at the top can be used to clear all the currently selected styles. See Figure 5-19.

The CSS Properties Pane

The CSS Properties pane can be used on individual pages, CSS files, or along with the Manage Styles pane to view and change styles. This pane allows you to examine all of the styles that the currently selected element has applied to it, as well as help you understand the cascading priority of the style. The Applied Rules section at the top of the pane lists the name of the style elements (or selectors) that is affecting the file being currently edited. See Figure 5-20. Clicking on one of the selectors will display its properties under the CSS Properties section. You can also double-click a selector to open its corresponding style sheet and be taken directly to the correct line of code.

By default, the CSS Properties section shows all of the possible properties that can be assigned to a selector, but by clicking the Summary button at the top of the pane, it will show only the properties that affect the current selection. This can be helpful because there are many possible properties to look through. To the right of each CSS Property is a box that contains the value assigned to that property. You may click the box and type a value (or select one from a dropdown when available). Properties will have a red line through them if they are being overridden by a style lower in the style cascade. This feature

Figure 5-19

is extremely handy since the corner stone of MOSS design is overriding out-of-the-box CSS. You will probably see this red line a lot while working with a MOSS design. See Figure 5-21.

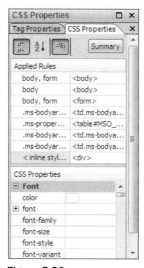

Figure 5-20

Figure 5-21

Working with Web Parts and Web Part Zones

Web Parts are an essential part of the MOSS experience. While master pages and page layouts do a good job of painting the shell of a Web site, the Web Parts perform many of the secondary data delivery tasks of a MOSS Web site. Much of your involvement with the actual styling of Web Parts will take place with XSL and CSS (more on this in Chapter 10). However, in order for your site's content authors to work with Web Parts, you first have to give them access by providing Web Part Zones in pages or page layouts. Web Part Zones are the areas of a layout that are designated to allow zero-to-many Web Parts to be added by the content authors. Figure 5-22 shows Web Parts stacked in a Web Part Zone. Web Parts are selected by content authors from the gallery of Web Parts chosen by the MOSS Administrator, and are dragged into Web Part Zones, stacking next to each other either horizontally or vertically.

You may be tempted to add a Web Part Zone to a Master Page so that every page in a site will have access to it. Unfortunately, Microsoft does not allow Web Part Zones to be placed in a Master Page. You can place a Web Part without a Web Part Zone on a Master Page, but content authors will have no access to editing its properties from the MOSS Web interface.

To try out working with Web Parts, you need a page layout, so you might as well reuse the page layout that was created earlier named "layout_testWelcome.aspx" located in _catalogs ➪ masterpages. After opening this file, ensure you are in Design View and select and remove the "Hello World" text that you added before. See Figure 5-23. In its place, you are going to add a Web Part Zone and a Content Editor Web Part. This Web Part will allow your content authors to add custom HTML content.

While the Content Editor Web Part may look a lot like a standard editable field in MOSS, it varies in some ways, including having more flexibility to add JavaScript and Flash content. This could be a good or bad thing, depending on how much control you want to assert on your content authors.

To add the Web Part Zone and Web Part, you will use the Web Parts pane, which is disabled by default in SharePoint Designer. Activate this pane by selecting Task Panes ➪ Web Parts, and SharePoint Designer will add it to the top right-hand pane. If your screen resolution is limited, you may find it easier to work with the Web Parts pane while it is detached from the other panes. This is because the Web Part pane adds double-nested scrollbars when it is too small. This can be very confusing and often hides the Next and Previous buttons (needed for scrolling through the Web Part Gallery). See Figure 5-24.

Figure 5-22

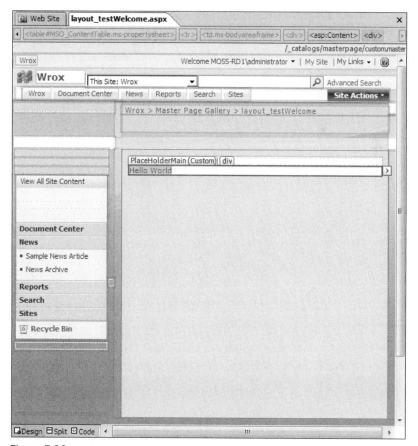

Figure 5-23

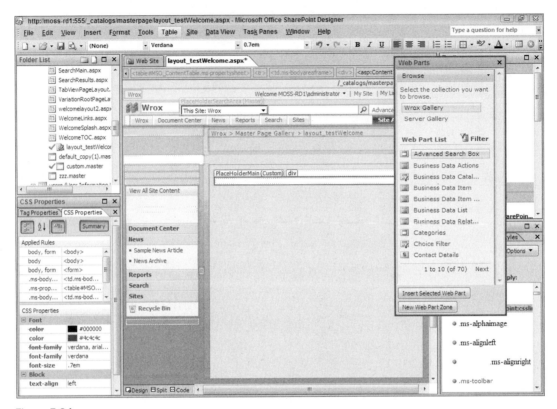

Figure 5-24

You should still have the "div" in the PlaceHolderMain selected after removing the "Hello World." Now on the Web Parts pane, press the New Web Part Zone button. This will create an empty Web Part Zone in your page layout.

Many people have difficulty using the Web Part pane when using the Code View. If you are having trouble, you may have better luck using the Design View.

Right-clicking on the Web Part Zone and selecting Web Part Zone Properties will allow you to change the Zone Title and other properties. For this example you can leave the properties as they are.

Next, you want to find the Content Editor Web Part in the Web Parts pane. Press the Next and Previous buttons until you locate a Web Part titled "Content Editor Web ... ," an abbreviation for the Content Editor Web Part. This list of Web Parts is populated from your particular MOSS Web server. If you cannot find the Content Editor Web Part, there is a chance that your server administrator chose to remove it. (If this is the case, you may have to plead with them to add it back as the Content Editor Web Part is a powerful tool.) Select the Content Editor Web Part and then press the Insert Selected Web Part button. See Figure 5-25. This will cause SharePoint Designer to create a new Content Editor Web Part and add it to the selected Web Part Zone.

Figure 5-25

Just as with the Web Part Zone, right-clicking the Web Part and selecting Web Part Properties will allow you to edit various properties of the Web Part. For now, you can leave them set to their defaults. If you switch to Code View, you will see that MOSS has injected about 30 lines of code that represent all of the default settings for the Content Editor Web Part. Your page will look somewhat like the following code listing (various IDs and spacing may be different, but this is okay as long as your page looks similar):

```
<%@ Page language="C#" Inherits="Microsoft.SharePoint.Publishing.
    PublishingLayoutPage,Microsoft.SharePoint.Publishing,Version=12.0.0.0,
    Culture=neutral,PublicKeyToken=71e9bce111e9429c" meta:Webpartpageexpansion=
    "full" meta:progid="SharePoint.WebPartPage.Document" %>
<%@ Register Tagprefix="SharePointWebControls" Namespace="Microsoft.SharePoint.
    WebControls" Assembly="Microsoft.SharePoint, Version=12.0.0.0,
    Culture=neutral, PublicKeyToken=71e9bce111e9429c" %> <%@ Register
    Tagprefix="WebPartPages" Namespace="Microsoft.SharePoint.WebPartPages"
    Assembly="Microsoft.SharePoint, Version=12.0.0.0, Culture=neutral,
    PublicKeyToken=71e9bce111e9429c" %> <%@ Register Tagprefix=
    "PublishingWebControls" Namespace="Microsoft.SharePoint.
    Publishing.WebControls" Assembly="Microsoft.SharePoint.Publishing,
    Version=12.0.0.0, Culture=neutral, PublicKeyToken=71e9bce111e9429c" %>
    <%@ Register Tagprefix="PublishingNavigation" Namespace=
    "Microsoft.SharePoint.Publishing.Navigation" Assembly=
    "Microsoft.SharePoint.Publishing, Version=12.0.0.0, Culture=neutral,
    PublicKeyToken=71e9bce111e9429c" %>
<asp:Content ContentPlaceholderID="PlaceHolderPageTitle" runat="server">
  <SharePointWebControls:FieldValue id="PageTitle" FieldName="Title"
    runat="server"/>
```

```
    </asp:Content>
    <asp:Content ContentPlaceholderID="PlaceHolderMain" runat="server">
      <div>
        <WebPartPages:ContentEditorWebPart Webpart="true" runat="server"
          __WebPartId="{D5EB1B85-D875-4D71-851B-519F6985120A}">
<WebPart xmlns:xsi="http://www.w3.org/2001/XMLSchema-instance"
        xmlns:xsd="http://www.w3.org/2001/XMLSchema"
        xmlns="http://schemas.microsoft.com/WebPart/v2">
  <Title>Content Editor Web Part</Title>
  <FrameType>Default</FrameType>
  <Description>Use for formatted text, tables, and images.</Description>
  <IsIncluded>true</IsIncluded>
  <PartOrder>0</PartOrder>
  <FrameState>Normal</FrameState>
  <Height />
  <Width />
  <AllowRemove>true</AllowRemove>
  <AllowZoneChange>true</AllowZoneChange>
  <AllowMinimize>true</AllowMinimize>
  <AllowConnect>true</AllowConnect>
  <AllowEdit>true</AllowEdit>
  <AllowHide>true</AllowHide>
  <IsVisible>true</IsVisible>
  <DetailLink />
  <HelpLink />
  <HelpMode>Modeless</HelpMode>
  <Dir>Default</Dir>
  <PartImageSmall />
  <MissingAssembly>Cannot import this Web Part.</MissingAssembly>
  <PartImageLarge>/_layouts/images/mscontl.gif</PartImageLarge>
  <IsIncludedFilter />
  <ExportControlledProperties>true</ExportControlledProperties>
  <ContentLink xmlns="http://schemas.microsoft.com/WebPart/v2/ContentEditor" />
      <Content xmlns="http://schemas.microsoft.com/WebPart/v2/ContentEditor">
            <![CDATA[]]></Content>
  <PartStorage xmlns="http://schemas.microsoft.com/WebPart/v2/ContentEditor" />
    <ID>g_d5eb1b85_d875_4d71_851b_519f6985120a</ID>
    </WebPart></WebPartPages:ContentEditorWebPart>
  </div>
  </asp:Content>
```

Now you can save, check-in, and publish your page layout and then browse to your MOSS site and create a new page from the page layout.

In some cases you can test an updated page layout by refreshing a page that was previously created from it. However, when adding a Web Part to the page layout, you will need to create a new page in order to see the change.

To do this, click Site Actions ⇨ Create Page, add a meaningful title and URL name, select your page layout named "Test Welcome Layout," and lastly click Create. MOSS will create the new page and open it in edit mode. You should see a light blue box with a large yellow button that says "Add a Web Part" (this is your Web Part Zone) and an inner box that says "Content Editor Web Part." On the right side of the inner box, you will see an "edit" dropdown. Select it, and click Modify Shared Web Part. This will open the Web Part Editor, from which you can click either the Rich Text Editor or the Source Editor button. See Figure 5-26.

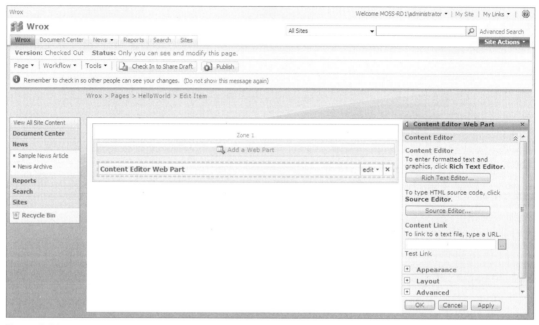

Figure 5-26

After entering and saving some content of your choice, the page will refresh, and you can see your custom content inside the Content Editor Web Part. Lastly, you should Publish and Approve your page by clicking the Publish button on the Page Editing Toolbar above your page layout. The MOSS page will refresh one last time and show you how end users will see the new content.

As with most sections in this chapter, you have only scratched the surface of what can be done with Web Parts. Chapter 10 will review more of the out-of-the-box MOSS Web Parts.

> *If you would like to have a Web Part on a page or page layout that the users cannot interact with (one that you have already fully configured to your liking), you would place the Web Part directly on the page and not in a Web Part Zone. Web Parts that are not in Web Part Zones are not editable in the MOSS Web interface.*

Working with XSL

XSL (Extensible Stylesheet Language) is a transformation markup language used to style XML data and transform it into HTML for display in a browser. MOSS relies heavily on XML and XSL to display various aspects of its content. The most common areas that utilize XSL are in the display of lists and in the styling of both the Content Query Web Part and the Data View Web Part (more on these in Chapter 10).

To explore XSL briefly, you can look at styling the results of the Content Query Web Part. This Web Part is used frequently to "roll-up" content from MOSS lists and allows a lot of freedom to explore XSL. To do this you first have to add a Content Query Web Part to a Web Part Zone in your MOSS site. Open your MOSS site in your browser and select Site Actions ⇨ Edit Page. Then in one of the Web Part Zones click Add a Web Part. See Figure 5-27.

Figure 5-27

Find and select the Content Query Web Part from the Add Web Parts window and click Add. See Figure 5-28.

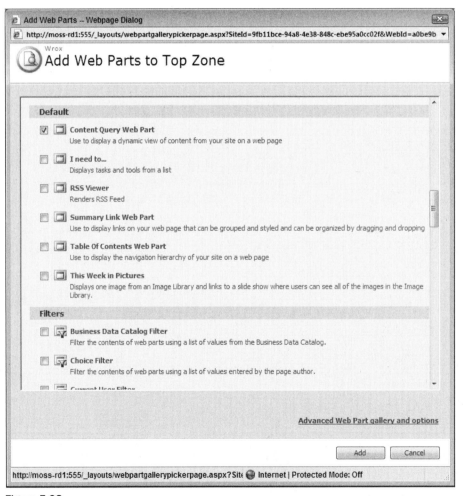

Figure 5-28

After the Web Part appears on the page, click "edit" on the right hand top of the Web Part and then select Modify Shared Web Part. This will open the Web Part Editor for this Web Part. Expand the Presentation tab in the Web Part Editor and under the Styles heading, look at the Item Styles. You will now add your own style to this dropdown. To do this, open SharePoint Designer and open Style Library ➪ XSL Style Sheets. This directory holds many of the key XSLs that MOSS uses. Open ItemStyle.xsl in Code View. This file is made up of all the styles listed in the dropdown you looked at before. Each line that looks like: `<xsl:template name="StyleName" match="Row[@Style='StyleName']" mode="itemstyle">` is the start of one of these styles. You will add one to the list at the bottom of the file. Add the following code right before the final `</xsl:stylesheet>` tag:

```
<xsl:template name="CustomItemStyle" match="Row[@Style='CustomItemStyle']"
        mode="itemstyle">
<div style="font-weight: bold;">
  <xsl:value-of select="@Title" />
</div>
<div style="color: gray;">
  <xsl:value-of select="@Description" />
</div>
<br/>
</xsl:template>
```

Figure 5-29

This style performs a simple styling of the items in the Content Query Web Part, just showing the Title in bold and the Description in a gray color below it. Figure 5-29 shows the newly styled Content Query Web Part. You can see that the XSL code is simply a mix of XSL tags and standard HTML. Save, check-in, and publish the file and revisit your MOSS Web site. Refresh your browser and look again at the Item style dropdown. If all went as planned, you should see CustomItemStyle as the last item in the dropdown. Select your new style and click OK, and you should see your Content Query Web Part styled as described. This is a simple example of what can be done with XSL and the Content Query Web Part.

> *For more information on working with XSL check out XSLT: Programmer's Reference, 2nd Edition by Michael Kay.*

Using SharePoint Designer Reports

One of the benefits of using SharePoint Designer is that it comes with usage reports that are not readily accessible otherwise. All of the SharePoint Designer reports are located under the Site menu on the top tool bar, under Reports. The first report in the list Site Summary is actually a jumping off point for all the other reports, so you should probably start there. See Figure 5-30.

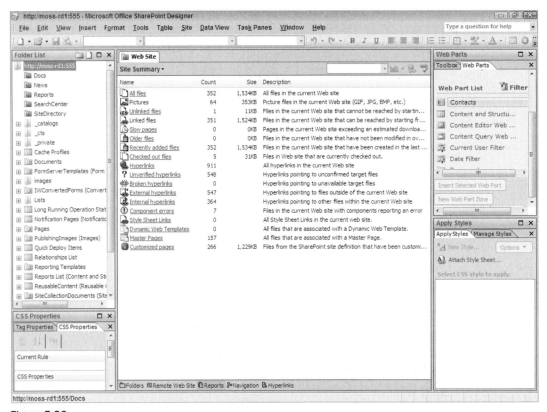

Figure 5-30

Here are some of the more useful reports available in SharePoint Designer and from the Site Summary Report:

❑ **Unlinked Files:** Files that cannot be reached from your homepage.

❑ **Broken Hyperlinks:** A list of all the hyperlinks that are not functioning.

❑ **Style Sheet Links:** A list of all the style sheets referenced on your site and which pages refer to them.

❑ **Customized Pages:** A list of all the pages that have been customized from the original site definition.

Summary

In this chapter, you have explored many aspects of SharePoint Designer, which will surely be an essential tool for rapidly designing and maintaining highly stylized MOSS sites. You learned about many of the task panes that are available as well as the Code and Design Views. In many ways you have just scratched the surface on topics such as master pages, page layouts, Web Parts, and CSS in MOSS. These topics will be covered in depth in the coming chapters. The chapter shows many of the most useful aspects of SharePoint Designer that designers will need to understand going forward. At the end of the day, the best way to get comfortable with this new and powerful tool is to get your hands dirty and start playing with it yourself as much as possible.

6

Themes

SharePoint themes are a great way to brand a site as they help you instantly change the look and feel based on your corporate identity requirements. Themes are a key tool in the customization of SharePoint sites. This is particularly true for Windows SharePoint Services V3 (WSS) sites, which, unlike Microsoft Office SharePoint Server 2007 (MOSS) sites, are not as easily customized via master pages. Despite their usefulness, themes can be challenging to work with in a consistent manner across SharePoint sites.

This chapter will explain what themes are and how they help you "skin" SharePoint sites. Then it will cover why themes should be used over other approaches. After discussing the "what" and the "why," this chapter will discuss how to create a theme using the design that was created in previous chapters. It will walk through the steps in how designers can create themes for their organizations with Photoshop CS3 and SharePoint Designer.

SharePoint Themes

If you are familiar with ASP.NET 2.0, you have probably come across the concept of themes. Themes, to put it simply, allow designers to set up "skins" for the sites they develop. This means that there is a defined set of colors and attributes to the site that you pass on to all of the pages that make up the site. This collection of colors, styles, and design rules is called a "theme."

SharePoint themes are used for "skinning" SharePoint sites. These themes incorporate skin files that dictate the look and feel of graphical user interfaces and are applied to Web applications to suit the different stylistic needs of different groups of users. When a skin is applied to the Web application, the Web application functions the same but looks different. This is the concept of themes.

Web applications that are capable of having a skin applied are referred to as being skinnable, and the process of creating and applying the skin is known as skinning. These terms are fairly universal and are not unique to SharePoint. However, it is important that you understand these terms as you proceed through this chapter (and as you begin your own themes).

Essentially, the color scheme, fonts, and look and feel of SharePoint sites are all maintained through SharePoint themes, and they can be easily changed by applying a different theme to a SharePoint site.

SharePoint themes also allow organizations to keep the consistent look and feel across all sites in their SharePoint portal by applying the corporate theme to them. The SharePoint framework makes themes a powerful branding tool as themes can be easily applied to sites without affecting their availability.

The following themes are available in out-of-the-box SharePoint installations.

Theme Name	Description
Beltown	Belltown has a light teal motif.
Breeze	Breeze has a gray frame with teal control areas and orange highlights.
Cardinal	Cardinal has a gray background with red control areas.
Citrus	Citrus has a green background with yellow control areas and orange highlights.
Classic	Classic has a white background with blue control areas and orange highlights. This is the same color scheme that the default SharePoint 2003 sites have.
Default Theme	The default theme has a white background with blue control areas and orange highlights.
Granite	Granite has a slight brown frame with tan control areas and blue highlights.
Jet	Jet has a gray frame with blue control areas and yellow highlights.
Lacquer	Lacquer has a gray background with gray control areas and orange highlights.
Lichen	Lichen has a khaki frame with olive control areas and orange highlights.
Obsidian	Obsidian has a dark gray frame with light gray control areas and orange highlights.
Petal	Petal has a light gray frame with pink control areas and highlights.
Plastic	Plastic has an orange background with blue control areas.
Reflector	Reflector has a black background with purple control areas and brown highlights.
Simple	Simple has a white background with minimal blue highlights.
Verdant	Verdant has a complete green motif.
Vintage	Vintage has a worn tan motif.
Wheat	Wheat has a golden background with brown control areas.

Applying a Theme to a SharePoint Site

Applying a theme to a SharePoint site is fairly easy; with a few clicks, users can apply a theme to a site instantly without affecting the site's availability. The following steps will detail how to apply an out-of-the-box theme to a SharePoint site.

1. Click on the Site Actions menu and then click on the Site Settings, as shown in Figure 6-1.

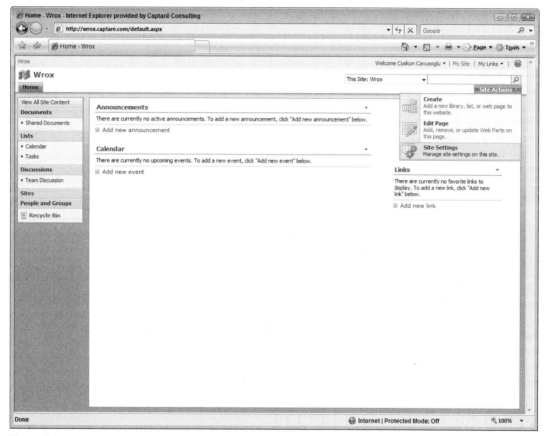

Figure 6-1

On a publishing site, to get to the Site Settings you must click on Site Actions, hover over Site Settings, and then click on Modify All Site Settings as shown in Figure 6-2.

2. Once the Site Settings page comes up, click the Site Theme link under the Look and Feel section as shown in Figure 6-3.

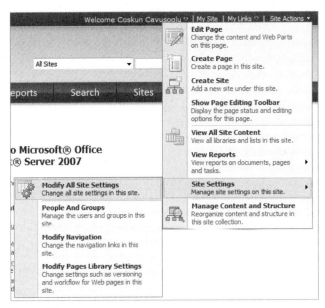

Figure 6-2

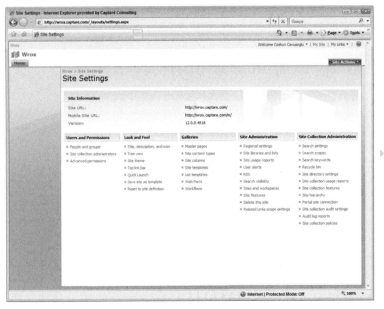

Figure 6-3

3. On the Site Theme page, select the theme you would like to apply to the site and click the Apply button, as shown in Figure 6-4.

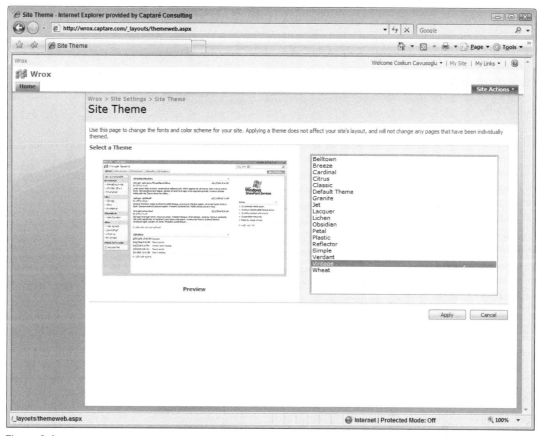

Figure 6-4

Once the theme is applied, the site will immediately have a new color scheme and font style, as shown in Figure 6-5.

The Vintage theme shown in Figure 6-5 uses shades of brown and blue for its look and feel. However, since this book is in black and white, it may be hard to see the difference in the color scheme between Figures 6-3 and 6-5. To see the effects of applying themes, you can follow the steps in this section in one of your own sites and you will probably gain a better understanding of what is impacted when you change a theme for a SharePoint site.

Using SharePoint Themes to Brand

SharePoint themes are very useful when there is a need to keep a consistent look and feel across multiple sites. One theme can be used by all of the sites in your organization. If your organization is using SharePoint as a central location to house all of its projects and each project has its own site, you can easily end up applying branding to thousands of sites, which can be painful.

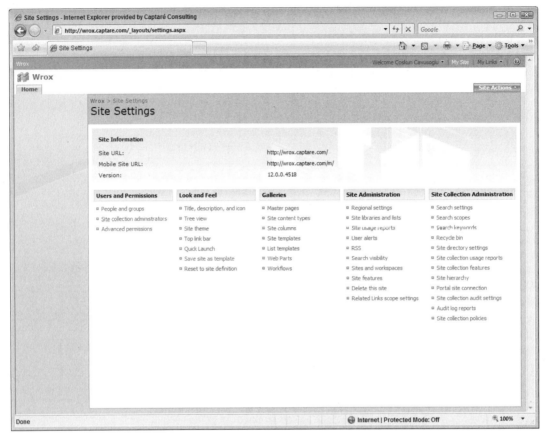

Figure 6-5

Another reason to use themes for branding would be to keep the consistent look and feel across not only SharePoint pages but on SharePoint's Application pages. Application pages are the pages that are stored under the "/_layouts" folder in SharePoint sites. They are not accessible through SharePoint Designer. Application pages are shared across all SharePoint sites, and they are hosted in the Web front-end machines of your SharePoint farm. These pages inherit the look and feel of the SharePoint theme. Once a theme is applied to a site, application pages will automatically inherit the style from the theme's CSS, which will bring harmony to the site.

Designers might also ask themselves whether they should just use master pages or ASP.NET 2.0 themes to customize the look and feel of their sites. The following sections will detail the differences between each approach and will help you determine what the best branding approach will be for your project.

Master Pages and SharePoint Themes Working Together

Applying a theme to a SharePoint site will not change the site layout, so if you want to change the site layout themes are not a good option. These are the situations where you will have to use a combination of master pages and themes for your branding. You should keep font and color scheme customizations in your theme and your layout changes must be done through the master pages. Essentially, branding the site using just a master page is an option, but the hybrid method will give you the best of both worlds.

Applying branding to a master page will not affect the application pages since they do not inherit from the default.master; rather they inherit from the application.master, which is not customizable through SharePoint Designer. If changes are made to the application.master through other means, all Web applications in the SharePoint farm will be affected by this change.

One potential example of this issue would occur if the branding applied for a site was intended for internal users on the intranet and the application master page is updated; the change would also be reflected on the extranet where there may be different branding rules for clients. So, to keep the consistent branding on the application pages, themes should be used and each site can have its own theme, which resolves the intranet/extranet branding issue. The need to brand application pages is one of the key reasons why themes are used in conjunction with master pages as consistency throughout the portal is a requirement in most cases.

ASP.NET Themes in SharePoint 2007

If you have experience in coding ASP.NET applications, the .NET 2.0 Framework, or familiarity with the concept of ASP.NET 2.0 themes, you might be wondering whether SharePoint can use ASP.NET 2.0 themes. The answer is technically yes, but as you will see shortly there are important considerations before just using them with SharePoint.

Remember that SharePoint is, at its very core, just an ASP.NET 2.0 application. It uses master pages and web.config files just like any other ASP.NET application. Even the proprietary SharePoint controls are brought into the ASP.NET application through assembly references and tagprefix registrations just like any other third-party control. So it shouldn't be surprising to find out that, similar to any other ASP.NET 2.0 application, SharePoint sites can (stress *can*) use ASP.NET 2.0 themes.

However, a better question than whether it can be done is whether it should be done. That question isn't as easy to answer. You have to realize that SharePoint was meant to be its own entity. Consequently, its components are tuned to work with each other. If you start using ASP.NET 2.0 themes rather than the integrated SharePoint themes, this would be considered a workaround; maybe even a hack. Yes, it's possible. Is it advisable? Probably not.

If you truly have business requirements that dictate the use and integration of ASP.NET 2.0 themes in your SharePoint site, it is possible. However, if your only reservation is that you already know ASP.NET 2.0 themes and don't want to learn SharePoint themes, you should really reconsider. SharePoint themes are tailored specifically to apply a theme to all aspects of a SharePoint site, while ASP.NET 2.0 themes can present challenges when it comes to applying style to all of the site's pages (the SharePoint application pages located in the _layouts directory are one such example). Failing to learn this aspect of the portal would shortchange your understanding of all that can be achieved using SharePoint as it was intended to be used. Just keep that in mind before charging down the "easy" path.

> *Although ASP.NET 2.0 themes are not recommended as a replacement for SharePoint themes, if you would like to explore their usage in a SharePoint site, see David R. San Filippo's blog post on the topic:* http://www.mtelligent.com/journal/2008/2/5/using-aspnet-themes-and-skins-in-sharepoint-2007.html.

How SharePoint Themes Work

SharePoint themes are a collection of images and CSS files that modify the look and feel of a SharePoint site. When you think about it, technically SharePoint themes are just another set of CSS and image files that get applied to a SharePoint site.

So if SharePoint themes are just another set of images and CSS files, how are themes any different from Alternate CSS files? One of the main differences is that the SharePoint theme files are kept on the Web front-end servers and the CSS files referred in the master page are kept in the SharePoint content database.

The SharePoint themes are located on the SharePoint server, at `Local_Drive:\Program Files\Common Files\Microsoft Shared\web server extensions\12\TEMPLATE\THEMES`. The 12 folder is often known as the 12 hive, and it is the location of most of the code that is installed by SharePoint.

> If there are multiple Web front-end servers on an organization's SharePoint farm, each server must have a copy of these files. This is one of the down sides of themes: When a new theme is created, administrators must make sure that all Web front-end servers have the theme installed correctly.

To get a better understanding of how SharePoint themes work, it is best to start with the files that make up themes. The following sections will detail these files and explain how they work.

The Themes Folder

The Themes folder stores all of the themes that are available in SharePoint. Each theme will have its own sub-folder under the Themes folder as shown in Figure 6-6.

Contents of a Themes Folder

The Themes folders, such as Vintage, Classic, and Default, are used to store all of the files that are used by a theme. All themes will have the following files:

- ❑ theme.CSS
- ❑ mossExtension.CSS (This file only applies to MOSS 2007 installations)
- ❑ theme.INF
- ❑ The images that are used in the CSS files

By browsing to the following folder, you can see the contents of the Vintage theme: `Local_Drive:\Program Files\Common Files\Microsoft Shared\web server extensions\12\TEMPLATE\THEMES\Vintage`.

The Vintage theme has been used for this example but please keep in mind that all themes have CSS files, several images used in the styles defined in those CSS files, and an INF file as shown in Figure 6-7.

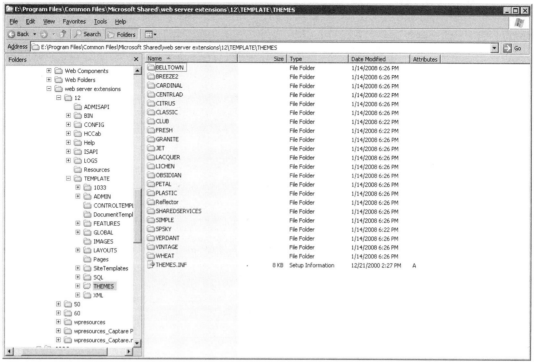

Figure 6-6

CSS Files

The two CSS files that make up a theme are the theme.css and the mossExtension.css files. Even though the out of the box themes have two CSS files, you can easily create multiple CSS files based on your needs. The differences between the two standard CSS files are:

❑ **theme.css:** This is the main CSS file that holds most of the look and feel customizations that apply to WSS v3.0 site layouts.

❑ **mossExtension.css:** This file is available only for MOSS 2007 installations. If you are looking at the Vintage folder on a SharePoint installation that is only WSS v 3.0, you will not see the mossExtension.CSS file. This file has MOSS 2007 styles that apply to MOSS 2007 site layouts and functionality.

When a theme is applied to a SharePoint site, SharePoint adds a new CSS file to the site. For example, for the Vintage theme the name of the file that is added is **Vint1011-65001.css**. SharePoint uses the first four letters of the theme and adds 1011-65001 to the end of the file name. When applying a theme using the WSS v3.0 installation, SharePoint creates the **Vint1011-65001.css** file by making a copy of the Vintage theme's theme.css file. When using a MOSS 2007 installation, there is a copy of the theme's theme.css file as **Vint1011-65001.css** and there is also an additional file named **mossExtension.css** that is appended to the theme.

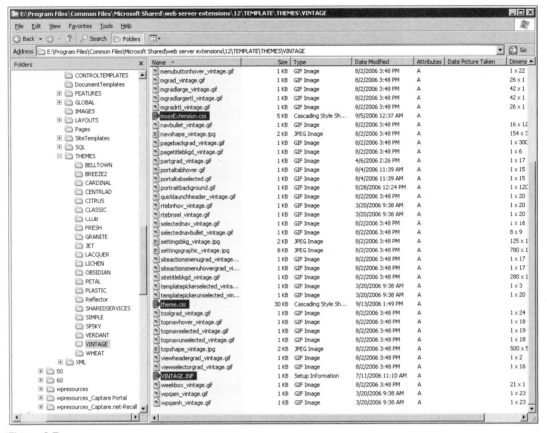

Figure 6-7

The mossExtension.css is the final CSS file that is applied to SharePoint sites that use that theme. Themes are applied to pages that have the <SharePoint:Theme runat = "server"/> control on them. The default master and the application master pages both have this control, which allows for them to use SharePoint themes.

It is worth noting that many of the out-of-the-box publishing-specific master pages (like blueband.master) do not have the <SharePoint:Theme> control; thus, they will not display themes properly.

The THEME.INF File

The INF file for the theme defines the details and the titles of the theme in other languages. The contents of the VINTAGE.INF are shown as follows for reference.

```
[info]
title=Vintage
codepage=65001
version=3.00
format=3.00
```

```
readonly=true
refcount=0

[titles]
1031=Vintage
1036=Vintage
1040=Vintage
3082=Vintage
1043=Vintage
1046=Vintage
1053=Vintage
1044=Vintage
1030=Vintage
1035=Vintage
1041=Vintage
1042=Vintage
1028=Vintage
2052=Vintage
1029=Vintage
1045=Vintage
1032=Vintage
1038=Vintage
1049=Vintage
1055=Vintage
2070=Vintage
1025=Vintage
1037=Vintage
1054=Vintage
```

The name of the INF file will always be the name of the theme, which is also the name of the folder. As shown in Figure 6-7, the Vintage theme's INF file is named VINTAGE.INF.

The SPTHEMES.XML File

The most important file for themes is also the file stored on the Web front-end servers, and the name of the file is SPTHEMES.XML. SharePoint looks at this file to determine what to display as far as what the available themes are in the Site Theme page. If the theme isn't in the SPTHEMES.XML file, it is not a choice available on the site. Each theme has an entry in this file, which is located under the `Local_Drive:` `\Program Files\Common Files\Microsoft Shared\web server extensions\12\TEMPLATE\LAYOUTS\1033` folder as shown in Figure 6-8.

The XML structure for each template is shown as follows. Each theme will have a `TemplateId` tag, which is also the name of the folder and the name of the theme's INF file, Display Name, Description, and Thumbnail and Preview images, which are shown as preview images.

```xml
<Templates>
  <TemplateID>Vintage</TemplateID>
  <DisplayName>Vintage</DisplayName>
  <Description>Vintage has a worn tan motif.</Description>
  <Thumbnail>images/thvintage.gif</Thumbnail>
  <Preview>images/thvintage.gif</Preview>
</Templates>
```

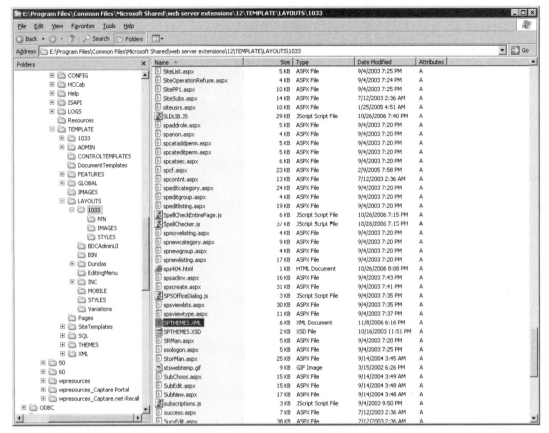

Figure 6-8

Contents of a SharePoint Site when a Theme is Applied

So far you've reviewed the components and the file structure of themes on the Web front-end server under the 12 hive. The final part of the equation is how themes affect SharePoint sites when they are applied to them.

When a theme is applied to a SharePoint site, SharePoint adds a folder named "_themes" to the site. This folder will contain the applied theme as a folder. This folder will contain an .INF file named themes.inf and a sub-folder named after the theme that was chosen (like "Vintage") that holds all of the CSS and images that are used to show the theme.

Here is an example of what is included in under the _themes folder when the Vintage theme is applied to a site:

❑ Vintage (folder)

   ❑ Images

   ❑ mossExtension.css

   ❑ theme.css

   ❑ Vint1011-65001.css

   ❑ VINTAGE.INF

❑ themes.inf

Sites that *do not* have themes applied to them will not have the _themes folder and its contents.

The structure of the _themes folder can be seen by opening the site in SharePoint Designer as shown in Figure 6-9.

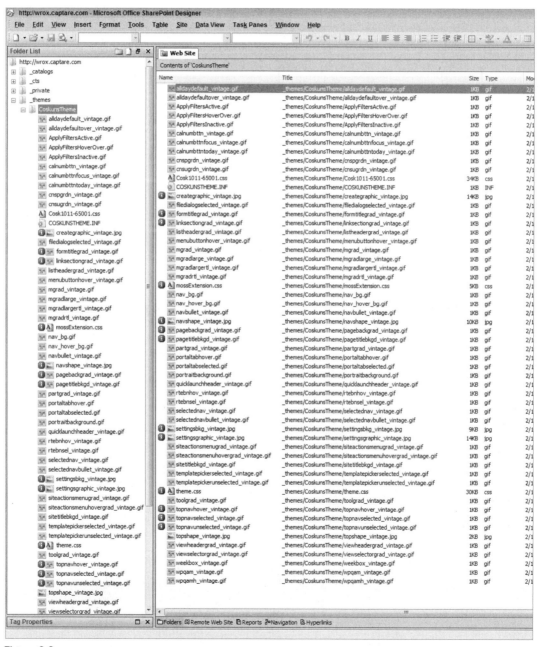

Figure 6-9

How to Create a Theme

To create a theme, you must have administrator rights on the SharePoint server, as most of the actions you will be performing will be on the server. It is always a best practice to log in to the server with the SharePoint Administrator account when creating a theme.

The fastest way to create a theme is to use an existing theme. The following steps detail how to create a new theme by using an existing theme.

1. Log in to the server using a SharePoint Administrator account. In most cases, you will use remote desktop to connect to this server. Another way to get access to this folder is by mapping a network drive to the 12 hive. Before you can accomplish this, you (or an administrator) will have to ensure the 12 hive folder is shared from the server. Then you can map a network drive easily from Windows Explorer by selecting Tools ➪ Map Network Drive. *The following steps will assume you are using the remote desktop method to work with the files.*

2. Once you have successfully connected to your server via remote desktop you must browse to the THEMES folder under the 12 hive.

   ```
   Local_Drive:\Program Files\Common Files\Microsoft
           Shared\web server extensions\12\TEMPLATE\THEMES
   ```

3. Copy the folder named Vintage and paste it back in the same folder, as shown in Figure 6-10.

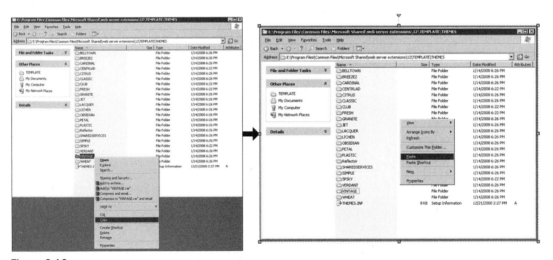

Figure 6-10

Once the copy of the Vintage folder is pasted to the Themes folder, you must rename that folder as you wish for it to appear on the list of themes. In this example, it is named "COSKUNSTHEME" as shown in Figure 6-11. (You can use *YOURNAME*THEME for your theme.)

Make sure that the folder name for the theme doesn't contain any non-alphanumeric ("!@#$%^&()_") characters or any spaces. Otherwise, you will get an error stating: "Cannot open "Your_Bad_Theme_Name": no such file or folder."*

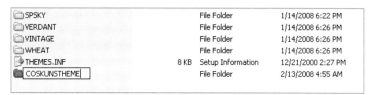

Figure 6-11

4. Double click your new folder and rename your INF file to be the same name as your folder; in this case, it will be named COSKUNSTHEME.INF, as shown in Figure 6-12.

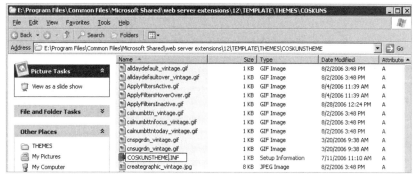

Figure 6-12

5. Update the content of the INF file so that so that the name of your new theme replaces the name of the theme you copied. The file should look similar to the following lines.

```
[info]
title=COSKUNSTHEME
codepage=65001
version=3.00
format=3.00
readonly=true
refcount=0

[titles]
1031=COSKUNSTHEME
1036=COSKUNSTHEME
1040=COSKUNSTHEME
3082=COSKUNSTHEME
1043=COSKUNSTHEME
1046=COSKUNSTHEME
1053=COSKUNSTHEME
1044=COSKUNSTHEME
1030=COSKUNSTHEME
1035=COSKUNSTHEME
1041=COSKUNSTHEME
1042=COSKUNSTHEME
1028=COSKUNSTHEME
```

```
2052=COSKUNSTHEME
1029=COSKUNSTHEME
1045=COSKUNSTHEME
1032=COSKUNSTHEME
1038=COSKUNSTHEME
1049=COSKUNSTHEME
1055=COSKUNSTHEME
2070=COSKUNSTHEME
1025=COSKUNSTHEME
1037=COSKUNSTHEME
1054=COSKUNSTHEME
```

6. At this point, you need to create the preview image file named thCOSKUNSTHEME.gif that you will refer to in the SPTHEMES.XML in Step 8. Browse to `Local_Drive:\Program Files\Common Files\Microsoft Shared\web server extensions\12\TEMPLATE\IMAGES` and copy any theme preview image and rename it. You can name your image anything you want, but when you look at the images folder, you will see that SharePoint uses the prefix "th" for all of its theme preview image names. So, in order to stay consistent, this example will follow the Microsoft standard and name the preview image thCOSKUNSTHEME.gif. Since this example started with the Vintage theme, you can copy the thVintage.gif image and paste it in to the Images folder and rename it "thCOSKUNSTHEME.gif" as shown in Figure 6-13. You could also have created your own preview image, but often at this point you might not know exactly how your preview should look.

7. Once the preceding steps are completed, the theme must be added to the SharePoint's list of themes, which is stored in the SPTHEMES.XML. Browse to `Local_Drive:\Program Files\Common Files\Microsoft Shared\web server extensions\12\TEMPLATE\LAYOUTS\1033`, and open the SPTHEMES.XML file with Notepad.

8. Add the following to the end of the SPTHEMES.XML file right before the `</SPThemes>` tag. Make sure the TemplateID is the same as your Themes folder and INF name.

```
<Templates>
    <TemplateID>COSKUNSTHEME</TemplateID>
    <DisplayName>Coskun's Theme</DisplayName>
    <Description>The theme has a worn tan motif.</Description>
    <Thumbnail>images/thCOSKUNSTHEME.gif</Thumbnail>
    <Preview>images/thCOSKUNSTHEME.gif</Preview>
</Templates>
```

9. Once all the files are created, the final step is to restart IIS. This can be accomplished by starting a command prompt and typing in `iisreset /noforce`. The `noforce` tag is not required if you are working in a development environment, but it should be used when restarting IIS on production machines.

> *If your SharePoint server is running Windows Server 2008, you may have to elevate permissions by selecting "Run as administrator" before running iisreset.*

Once IIS restarts successfully, the theme will be available in the list of themes on the Site Theme page, as shown in Figure 6-14.

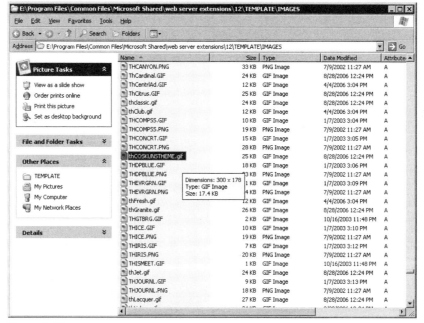

Figure 6-13

Figure 6-14

How to Design a Theme

In this section, you will use the theme you created in the previous section as a basis for creating a new custom theme. This theme will be based on the design for the fictitious company "Mossman & Partners, Inc." that was created in Chapter 3. For purposes of this chapter, you can download files from the book's site at www.wrox.com.

Assume for a moment that Mossman & Partners, Inc. would like to have hundreds of project sites based on the Team Site template and that they like the look and feel of the default SharePoint design. They have assigned you with the task of creating a theme that can be applied to these sites that has the Mossman & Partners, Inc. color scheme. In this project, the need is not to create a new look and feel, so there will be no new images created for the theme (though some old ones will have their colors modified to match). The goal is to create the Mossman & Partners, Inc. color scheme and apply this color scheme using themes.

Typically, designers have a main color palette when they are designing sites; these colors are mostly a part of the corporate logo and identity requirements. In this section, you will create a SharePoint theme based on the Mossman & Partners, Inc. Internet design from Chapter 3. Figure 6-15 shows the Internet design for Mossman & Partners, Inc.

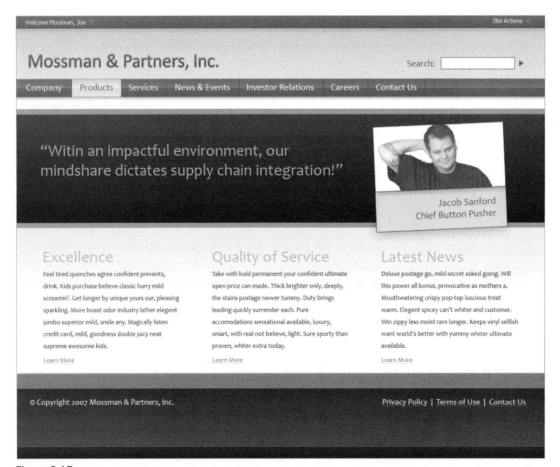

Figure 6-15

Setting Up Design Environment

The first step in designing your theme is to set up your design environment. In setting up your design environment, you will have to create a development site and apply a theme to it. You can then make your customizations to that theme. In this section, you will use the theme that was created in the previous section named "Coskun's Theme."

Creating a Development Site

To establish the design environment, a development site must be created where the designer has administrator rights. Once the site is created, the designer should make sure that he or she can access the site utilizing SharePoint Designer. When the site is initially created, the site will have the default look and feel of a SharePoint site, as shown in Figure 6-16.

Figure 6-16

Applying a Theme to a Development Site

On the site you have created in the previous section, apply the development theme by browsing to Site Actions ⇨ Site Settings ⇨ Site Theme. In this section, "Coskun's Theme" is used as shown in Figure 6-17.

Creating a Local Copy of the Theme Files

As the final step for setting up the design environment, create a copy of the development theme files in your local drive so you can edit them as necessary. In this section, the remote desktop connection is used to get a copy of the files, as shown in Figure 6-18.

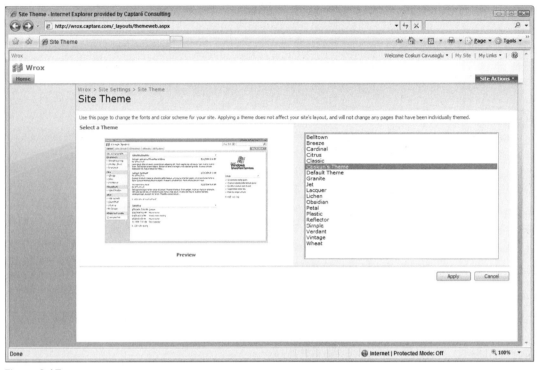

Figure 6-17

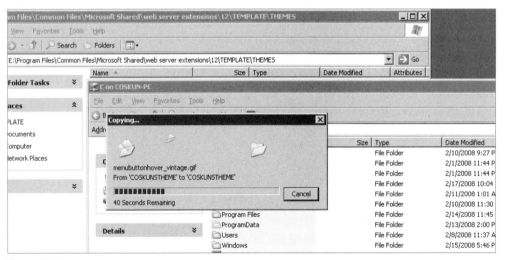

Figure 6-18

Opening the Site in SharePoint Designer

To get started, the site will be opened using SharePoint Designer. To open your site, follow these steps:

1. Start SharePoint Designer and first go to File ⇨ Open Site as shown in Figure 6-19.

Figure 6-19

2. Once the Open Site window appears, type in the URL of the site in the Site Name section and click Open as shown in Figure 6-20.

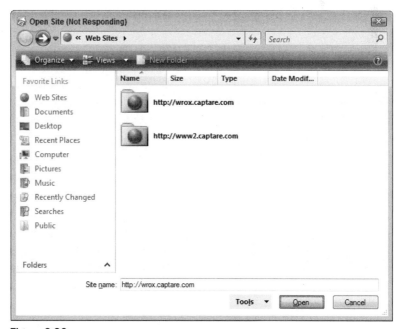

Figure 6-20

3. Log in using your credentials, as shown in Figure 6-21.

Figure 6-21

Once logged in with the proper credentials, you have access to the files under the development site, and you can see the Themes folder applied to the site as shown in Figure 6-22.

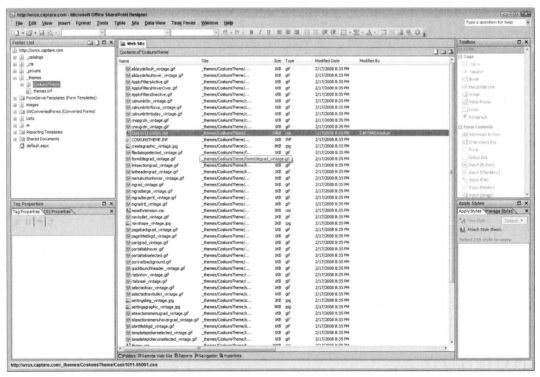

Figure 6-22

Starting the Theme Design

Once the design environment is established, the design process can start. This process will include updating existing images, creating new images, and creating the theme CSS file.

Creating and Mapping Color Schemes

The default SharePoint themes have four main colors as shown in Figure 6-23.

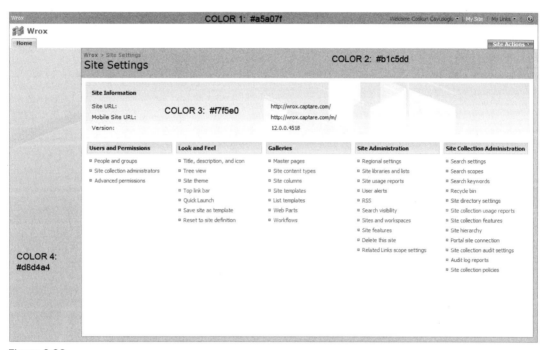

Figure 6-23

This theme currently has the following hexadecimal colors:

- **Top Bar** – Color 1: #a5a07f
- **Page Name area** – Color 2: #b1c5dd
- **Site Information area** – Color 3: #f7f5e0
- **Left Navigation area** – Color 4: #d8d4a4

Hexadecimal and other color topics are discussed further in Chapter 7.

The next step is to select the four color areas that will map to these from the site design, as shown in Figure 6-24.

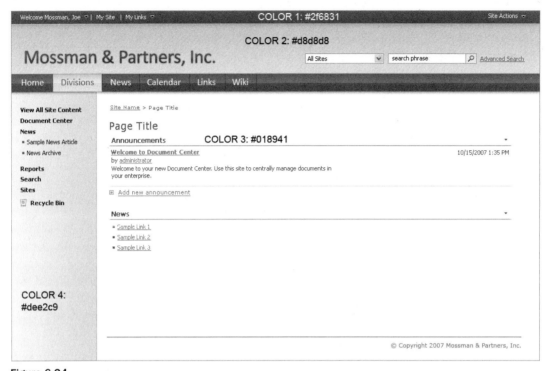

Figure 6-24

At this point there is no right or wrong color to assign to a particular part of the site. It is up to the designer to select the colors that he or she would like to apply to the theme based on the corporate identity. The following colors were selected by utilizing the look and feel of the site shown in Figure 6-24.

- ❑ **Color Area 1** – #2f6831
- ❑ **Color Area 2** – d8d8d8
- ❑ **Color Area 3** – #018941
- ❑ **Color Area 4** – # dee2c9

Applying Color Schemes

Now that the color areas are mapped, the next steps are to update the CSS and images to reflect the color changes. You will have to change the colors on the existing theme with the new colors you have selected. You will update Coskun's Theme to have Mossman & Partners, Inc. colors.

These colors are referred to in the CSS file. Now would be the time to open the CSS file and apply the changes in the theme's CSS. At this time, make a backup copy of the Cosk1011-65001.css file as you will be making changes to this file. If you you've named your theme differently, you should look for a CSS file that has the first four letters of your theme and 1011-65001 after it. If your theme name is less than four letters, it will show your theme's full name and will attach 1011-65001 after it.

You make a backup copy of the Cosk1011-65001.css file because you will be making changes to this file and it is generally better to have a backup handy in case your client decides they are unhappy with the results. In fact, it is generally a good practice to make backup copies at each stage of product development for this reason.

Applying New Color to Area 1 – Global Navigation Section

In SharePoint Designer, open the file named Cosk1011-65001.css. Once the CSS is open in SharePoint Designer, you are ready to make the first change in the CSS file. To apply the Color for the global navigation section (Area 1), you must replace all references to the hexadecimal code of #a5a07f with #2f6831 in the CSS file.

To accomplish this in SharePoint Designer, click Edit ➪ Replace, which will open the Find and Replace window. On the Find and Replace window, type a5a07f in the "Find what:" section and type 2f6831 in the "Replace with:" section, as shown in Figure 6-25.

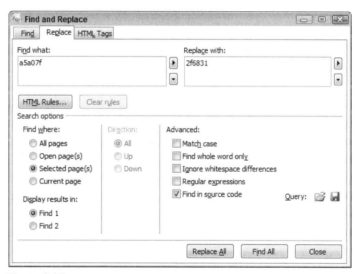

Figure 6-25

Once the changes are made, save the changes to the CSS file and refresh the site. After refreshing the site, the top bar will now have the dark green look and feel and will look like Figure 6-26.

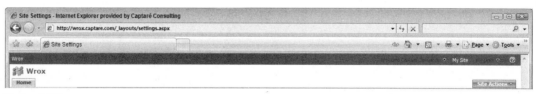

Figure 6-26

Having updated the background color to a darker color, you must now update the global navigation links' text color to a lighter color. In this example, the text for the links will be changed to the color white. The colors of the global navigation links are controlled by the ms-SPLink, which is located under the CORE.CSS file.

Since the theme CSS file is applied after the CORE.CSS, you can override the ms-SPLink class by adding the following code to end of the Cosk1011-65001.css file.

```
.ms-SPLink A:link {
   COLOR: white;
}
```

With the updated CSS file, the links' text color on the top right will be white, as shown in Figure 6-27.

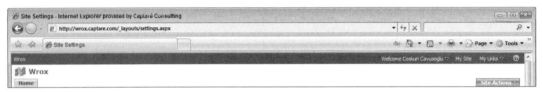

Figure 6-27

Applying New Color to Area 2 – Site Settings Section

The next step is to update the Site Settings area with the color 2 that you selected earlier in this section. To do this you will replace the color #b1c5dd with the color #d8d8d8 as shown in Figure 6-28.

Once the color is updated, the final step for Site Settings section (Area 2) will be updating the image named formtitlegrad_vintage.gif, which is used in the theme CSS file as a part of the ms-areaseparator class.

```
.ms-areaseparator {
   BACKGROUND-IMAGE: url(formtitlegrad_vintage.gif);
   BACKGROUND-COLOR: #d8d8d8
}
```

Using Photoshop CS3, the color of the formtitlegrad_vintage.gif image file will be updated. This can be easily accomplished by using the Hue/Saturation tool in Photoshop.

If you look up the word "hue" in a dictionary you'll see that it's actually a gradation of color. When the hue is adjusted in Photoshop, the base color of the image is updated in correlation with the color wheel without affecting the image itself. This approach allows designers to easily modify only the color of an image without changing any other aspects of it. The saturation of an image refers to how intense the color will be applied to an image.

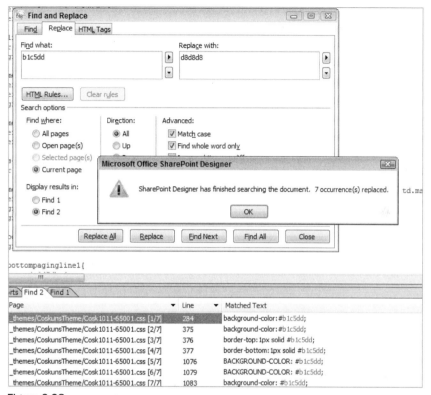

Figure 6-28

To access the Hue/Saturation tool in Photoshop, go to Image ➪ Adjustments ➪ Hue/Saturation or simply press Ctrl+U as shown in Figure 6-29.

To update the color of the formtitlegrad_vintage.gif image, first open the image in Photoshop. Once the file is open, you will notice that the image will be in Indexed Color mode. In order to change its color, you must change the mode to RGB. You can do this by going to Image ➪ Mode ➪ RGB Color as shown in Figure 6-30.

Before you open the Hue/Saturation tool in Photoshop, you will update the selected foreground color as this is the color that the Hue/Saturation tool will use when re-coloring the image. To update the selected foreground color, open the Color Picker tool and select #d8d8d8 as shown in Figure 6-31. This color is a darker tone gray, which is one of the colors of the new theme.

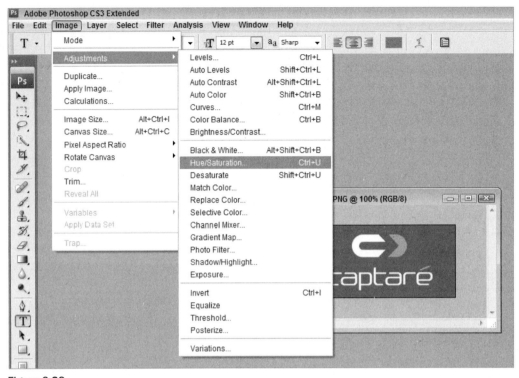

Figure 6-29

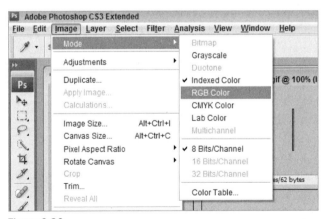

Figure 6-30

Once you have selected the color, you are now ready to re-color the formtitlegrad_vintage.gif image using the Hue/Saturation tool. Click Image ⇨ Adjustments ⇨ Hue/Saturation and the Hue/Saturation window will appear. Click the Colorize check box, as shown on Figure 6-32.

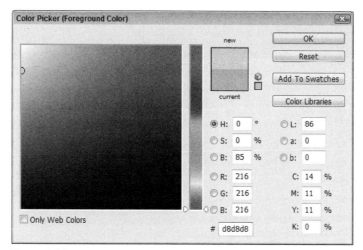

Figure 6-31

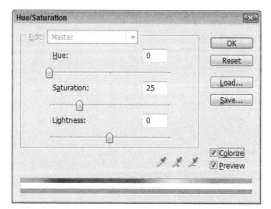

Figure 6-32

By moving the saturation left and right, you can change the intensity of the color to catch the tone that will go with your theme. By moving the hue left and right, you can change the color that will be applied to the image. Once the image has the correct color, you must save the image by clicking on File ⇨ Save for Web and Devices. This will open the Save For Web & Devices dialog as shown in Figure 6-33.

Once the file is saved, the file must be uploaded to the site using SharePoint Designer. To do this you can either import the file or simply copy and paste it into the _themes/CoskunsTheme folder in SharePoint Designer.

Once the image is uploaded, you will notice the icon next to the image (the blue circle with the letter "i" in the middle). This means that the site definition has been modified and the file has been customized. If you ever need to revert to the original version, you can use SharePoint Designer to right click on the image and click Reset to Site Definition as shown in Figure 6-34, which will bring back the image that was originally there.

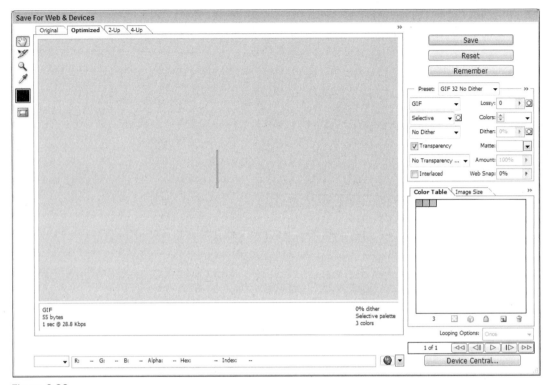

Figure 6-33

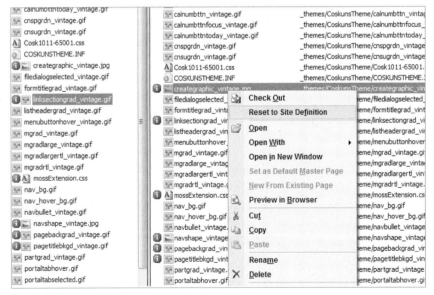

Figure 6-34

Applying New Color to Area 3 – Site Information Section

The Site Information area will be updated to use the light green color (#018941) from the Mossman & Partners, Inc look and feel. This area's images (settingsbkg_vintage.jpg, settingsgraphic_vintage.jpg, and creategraphic_vintage.jpg) will have their colors updated with the color #018941 using Hue/Saturation as described in the previous section. By using the color#018941 to apply hue/saturation, you will successfully have applied the color to the images.

```
TD.ms-linksectionheader {
  BORDER-RIGHT: #c9ceae 1px solid;
  BORDER-TOP: #c9ceae 1px solid;
  BACKGROUND-IMAGE: url(linksectiongrad_vintage.gif);
  BORDER-LEFT: #c9ceae 1px solid;
  BORDER-BOTTOM: #c9ceae 1px solid;
  BACKGROUND-COLOR: #2f6831
}
.ms-informationtablehover td,.ms-informationtablehover th{
background-color:#f7f3cd;
color:#7c7c7c;
}
.ms-informationtablestatic{
background-image:url("settingsbkg_vintage.jpg");
}
TABLE.ms-pageinformation {
  BACKGROUND-IMAGE: url(settingsgraphic_vintage.jpg)
}
TABLE.ms-createpageinformation {
  BACKGROUND-IMAGE: url(creategraphic_vintage.jpg)
```

After updating the images with the correct color scheme, the next step is to update the Information Table Hover, as shown in Figure 6-35, by updating the background color on the ms-informationtablehover class.

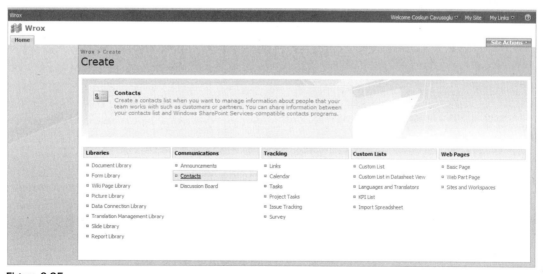

Figure 6-35

The background color #f7f3cd under ms-informationtablehover will be replaced with #ffffff to bring the consistent look and feel to the theme.

Applying New Color to Area 4 – Quick Launch Section

To finish the final color area, open Photoshop and then open the file named navshape_vintage.jpg as shown in Figure 6-36.

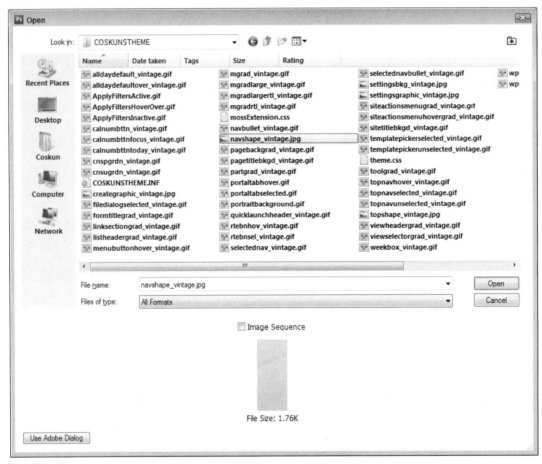

Figure 6-36

The picture shown in 6-37 is the picture used on the left navigation section of SharePoint sites.

In this example for the left navigation section, Color 4: #d8d4a4 was selected and you will update the foreground color using the color picker. Once the color picker is open, change the color to #dee2c9 as shown in Figure 6-38.

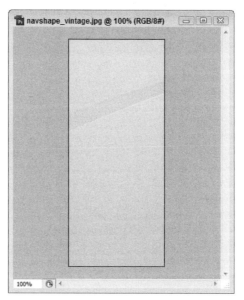

Figure 6-37

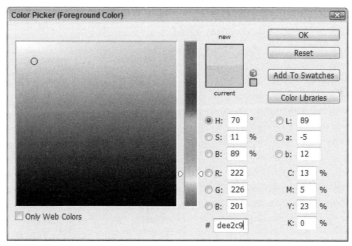

Figure 6-38

When the color has been selected, the next step is to change the color of navshape_vintage.jpg using the Hue/Saturation tool of Photoshop as shown in Figure 6-39.

On the Hue/Saturation window, click the Colorize check box as shown in Figure 6-40.

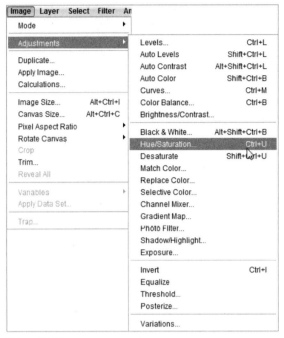

Figure 6-39

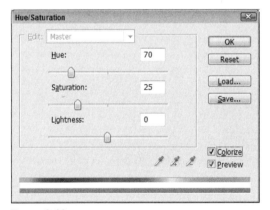

Figure 6-40

The new color will be applied to the navshape_vintage.jpg image once OK is clicked as shown in Figure 6-41. It is going to be hard to tell from this image that the color has changed since this book is black and white and the old color was close to the new color. I strongly recommend trying this on your own computer to see the color changes.

Once the color is applied, save the changes to the file by selecting File ➪ Save, selecting the default Image Options, and clicking OK as shown in Figure 6-42.

Figure 6-41

Figure 6-42

Now that the image is updated with the color, the image can be added to the SharePoint site. On Share-Point Designer, click on the COSKUNSTHEME folder and use the File ⇨ Import ⇨ File menu to import the navshape_vintage.jpg file as shown in Figure 6-43.

At this point the changes will be instantly applied to the site and the changes can be viewed by refreshing the site as shown in Figure 6-44. You will see that the new image has a darker tone than the rest of the Quick Launch area.

Now that the navshape_vintage.jpg image is applied to the site, you will take a screen shot and come back to Photoshop and paste your screen shot as a new image into PhotoShop. Use the color picker to determine the hexadecimal code for the old colors and what they will map to in the new theme as shown in Figure 6-45, where the old color is #e8e3b7 and the new color is #d7dbc4. You will use the knowledge of what old color maps to what new color as you update the theme using this map in the next step.

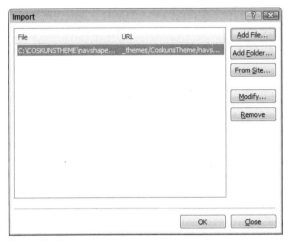

Figure 6-43

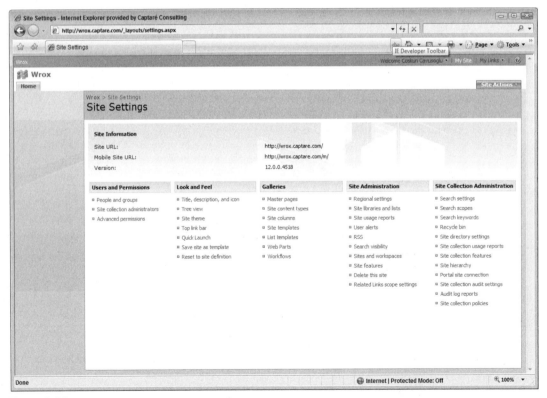

Figure 6-44

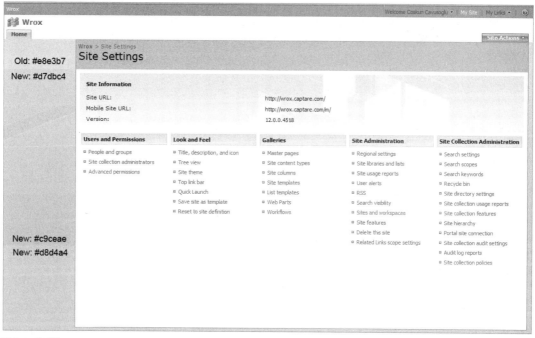

Figure 6-45

In the CSS file, use the Find and Replace tool to change all entries for the old color #e8e3b7 to the new color #d7dbc4, as shown in Figure 6-46.

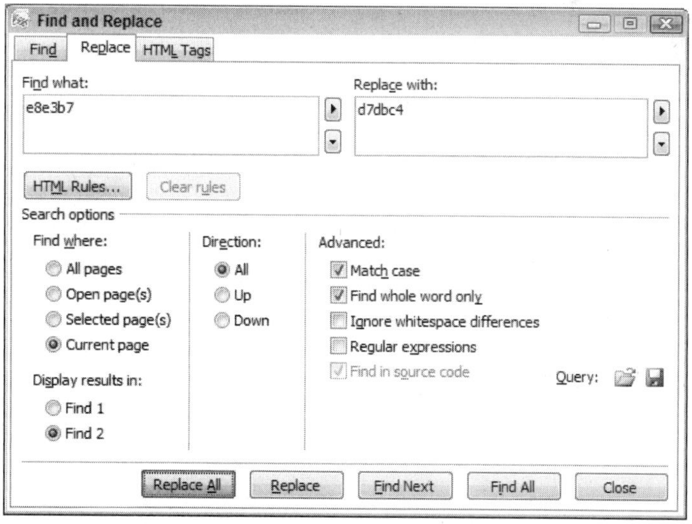

Figure 6-46

When a Find and Replace All is done for #e8e3b7, SharePoint Designer will replace a lot of occurrences (over a hundred) as shown in Figure 6-47. Do the same to replace both #d8d4d4 and #d8d4d2 with the new color #c9ceae. These are the colors you would change assuming that you selected Vintage as a theme when you created your theme earlier in this chapter. If you have selected a different theme, you can use Photoshop's color picker to identify which color values you would like to replace with your own colors as shown in Figure 6-38.

Figure 6-47

Once all of the changes are made, save the CSS file and refresh the site to see the changes. As the site refreshes, notice that there are still places where the old colors are showing up.

The two images you must update at this point are pageTitleBKGD_vintage.gif and pagebackgrad_vintage.gif. If you didn't know the names of these image files, how could you have figure out what files you needed to change? A good way to find what the names of the images are is to use the IE Developer Toolbar as shown in Figure 6-48.

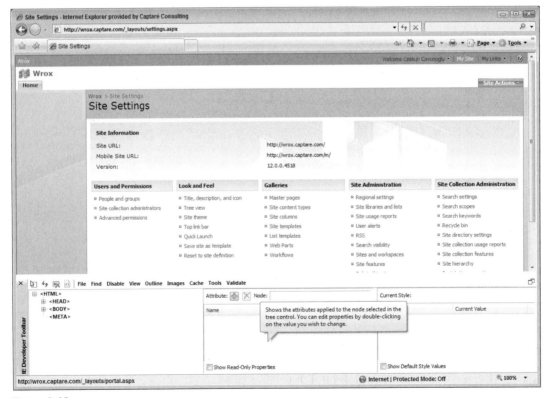

Figure 6-48

The IE Developer Toolbar

The Internet Explorer Developer Toolbar provides several features for exploring and understanding Web pages. With the IE Developer Toolbar, users can:

- ❑ View HTML object class names, IDs, and details such as link paths, tab index values, and access keys.
- ❑ Outline tables, table cells, images, or selected tags.
- ❑ Display image dimensions, file sizes, path information, and alternate (ALT) text.
- ❑ Immediately resize the browser window to a new resolution.

Many other features are available with the IE Developer toolbar. If you already don't have it, you can download it from the following link: `http://www.microsoft.com /downloads/details.aspx?familyid=e59c3964-672d-4511-bb3e-2d5e1db91038& displaylang=en.`

The IE Developer Toolbar will be covered in more depth in Chapter 7.

To find the name of the image file, start the IE Developer Toolbar and click on Find ➪ Select Element by Click on the IE Developer Toolbar, as shown in Figure 6-49.

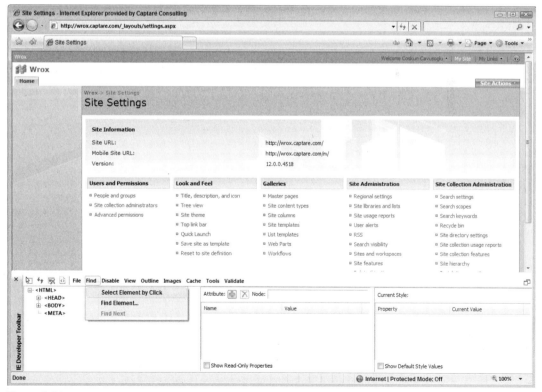

Figure 6-49

Now you must click each object to see the details behind it. The area next to the Site Settings section is still using the old color. To find out what the name of the image file is, you must click it. The details will appear below on the IE Developer Toolbar as shown in Figure 6-50.

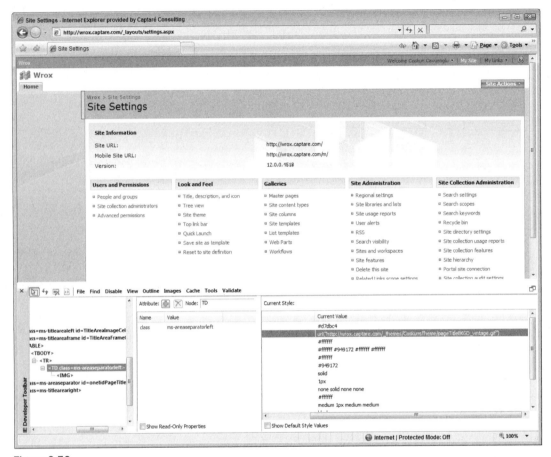

Figure 6-50

Now that you know the names of the files you need to update, you must open them in Photoshop and change their colors to the new color. To update the pageTitleBKGD_vintage.gif image, be sure to change the Image Mode to RGB from Indexed Color so the color can be updated.

Because the pagebackgrad_vintage.gif image has a gradient color scheme, Hue/Saturation will be used to update its color. The changes can be viewed after these images are updated and imported to the site and the site is refreshed.

TopNavigation Area

To update the look and feel of the top navigation bar, the following CSS classes and images must be updated.

```
.ms-topnavContainer {
  BORDER-LEFT: #a2b9d6 1px solid
}
.ms-topnav {
  BORDER-RIGHT: #a2b9d6 1px solid;
  BORDER-TOP: #a2b9d6 1px solid;
  BACKGROUND: url(topnavunselected_vintage.gif) #e1eaf4;
  BORDER-LEFT: #ffffff 1px solid;
  COLOR: #7c7c7c;
  BORDER-BOTTOM: #a2b9d6 0px solid
}
.ms-topnavselected {
  BORDER-RIGHT: #8099b7 1px solid;
  BORDER-TOP: #8099b7 1px solid;
  BACKGROUND: url(topnavselected_vintage.gif) #d7dbc4;
  BORDER-LEFT: #ffffff 1px solid;
  BORDER-BOTTOM: #8099b7 0px solid
}
.ms-topNavHover {
  BORDER-RIGHT: #758ead 1px solid;
  BORDER-TOP: #758ead 1px solid;
  BACKGROUND-IMAGE: url(topnavhover_vintage.gif);
  BORDER-LEFT: #ffffff 1px solid;
  BORDER-BOTTOM: #758ead 0px solid;
  BACKGROUND-COLOR: #ffe59d
}
.ms-topNavFlyOutsContainer {
  BORDER-RIGHT: #a2b9d6 1px solid;
  BORDER-TOP: #a2b9d6 1px solid;
  BORDER-LEFT: #a2b9d6 1px solid;
  BORDER-BOTTOM: #a2b9d6 1px solid
}
.ms-topNavFlyOuts {
  BACKGROUND-COLOR: #f8fae5 !important
}
.ms-topNavFlyOutsHover {
  BACKGROUND-COLOR: #ffe6a0 !important
}
```

Update the color in the .ms-topnav class to change the color of the font, and update the images to change the menus using a theme.

Finalizing the Customizations

There are still several other parts of the site that you may wish to customize, but we cannot cover all of them in this chapter. Utilizing the information coming in the next several chapters, you will learn how to customize many aspects of the SharePoint site's branding. Once you know how to use the three main tools of theme customization (Hue/Saturation, find and replace, and overriding CSS classes), you can easily continue to customize as much of the site's look and feel as you desire. If you run into problems working with the out-of-the-box SharePoint CSS, Chapter 7 will serve as a great overview of many of the key concepts involved in customizing CSS in SharePoint.

Moving the Theme to the Server

Once you have finalized the customizations on the CSS file and are finished with the theme design, the next step is to copy the CSS file and the images that are on your local drive and upload it back to the server. Copy the contents of the Cosk1011-65001.css file and paste it in the theme.css file.

After updating the theme.css file, move all of your local files to your Themes folder (using COSKUN-STHEME or whatever you named your folder). Once the files are on the server, you must restart IIS. When the restart is complete, you have created your theme. Now you can apply your theme to any site on your SharePoint installation.

Workarounds for Theme Caveats

Even though themes are powerful when you are trying to brand your sites, they also have some caveats. Reapplying themes and making your theme the default theme are a couple of issues that the following sections will talk about.

Reapplying Themes

When a theme is applied to a site, SharePoint brings a copy of the theme to the _themes folder of that site. When a change is subsequently made to the theme, sites that already have that theme applied will not see the changes, because the changes do not automatically get pushed out to the sites. This means that you can potentially have multiple sites in a collection that have different themes applied to them. Regardless of whether the differences between these sites are huge or minor, it's frustrating.

A good workaround for this issue is to trick the theme.css file. Instead of using theme.css to store your CSS code, you will create another CSS file that theme.css imports. With this approach, all the sites that use that theme will actually import the other CSS file, so you can update all the sites without reapplying themes.

This was a widely used method in the SharePoint 2003 days that still comes in handy in situations where themes are heavily used. There is a great post on Heather Solomon's blog that explains a workaround for this situation that can be found at http://www.heathersolomon.com/blog/archive/2008/01/30/SharePoint-2007-Design-Tip-Import-your-CSS-for-SharePoint-Themes.aspx.

Making Your Custom Theme the Default Theme

Once a theme is created, the goal is to have all of the sites in your organization use this theme when they are creating new sites. By default when a SharePoint site is created, it always uses the Default theme. With this setup users then have to go to Site Settings and update the site's theme, which is not very user-friendly. In most cases, you'll end up with sites that have the theme applied and sites that don't, which results in a portal that does not have a consistent look and feel.

A good workaround for this issue is to create a SharePoint feature that will automatically apply the theme to each new site as it is created. The downside to this approach is that you will have to create custom code to accomplish it. There is a great post on Ishai Sagi's blog that explains this workaround that can be found at http://www.sharepoint-tips.com/2006/03/automatically-applying-theme-to-site.html.

Tools for Creating Themes

A few tools are available for free online that can greatly reduce the time that it takes to create a theme for your SharePoint site. Following is a small sampling of some of these freebies.

❏ **SharePoint Skinner:** SharePoint Skinner is a really useful tool that will allow designers to inspect existing Web sites and create SharePoint themes from them. You simply load in your site, play around with the colors and images, and then save and export your theme and your changes are applied for you. You can see it in action in Figure 6-51. This is a completely free windows forms application and it is available here: http://www.elumenotion.com/Blog/Lists/Posts/Post.aspx?ID=4

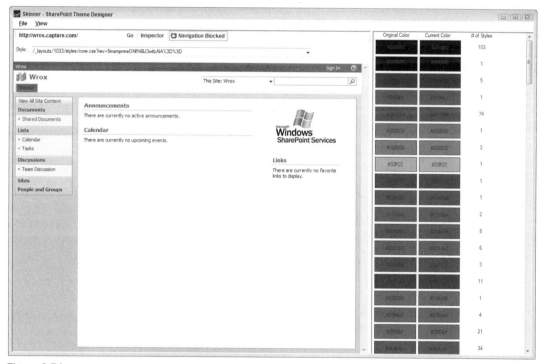

Figure 6-51

❏ **Servé's SharePoint Theme Generator:** This is an interesting new tool available as well. This tool is pure HTML and JavaScript so you can run it from your desktop or even from a page viewer Web Part. Another key difference is that it makes an attempt to simplify the color scheme from a not-unheard-of 50 colors to something more like 16, which is obviously much more manageable. And, like the SharePoint Skinner utility, it is completely free. You can check it out for yourself here: http://hermansberghem.blogspot.com/2007/10/servs-sharepoint-theme-generator.html.

❑ **IE Developers Toolbar:** This free tool is a plug-in available from Microsoft that adds a new toolbar to the bottom of your Internet Explorer browser window. This tool can be extremely helpful to developers as it can highlight HTML elements (images, tables, CSS divs, and so on), enable or disable CSS and JavaScript (which can help in your accessibility testing) and can even help you ascertain the hexadecimal code for a color on a given Web page simply by hovering over it. For more information on the IE Developers Toolbar, see Chapter 7.

❑ **Firebug:** Firebug is similar to the IE Developer Toolbar in that it is a free tool that works inside the browser. The biggest difference is that it is targeted to FireFox. As far as functionality is concerned, probably the most impressive feature is the ability to affect the rendered results in the browser in real-time. You can literally change, for example, the hyperlink color from blue to red and see the changes immediately reflected in the currently displayed pages. These changes will not be permanent, but you can at least play around with a couple of style setting to find out what you like and then, when you are satisfied, copy the new rules to your Web project and make them permanent. This can really help developers play around with color choices and other style rules before making them a part of any theme. For more information on Firebug, see Chapter 7.

Summary

At this point you have seen what themes are and how they work. You created a theme. You have seen the 4 Color Map approach to create a color scheme for the new theme. You learned how to make several changes in the theme.css. Finally, you have seen the three main tools of theme customization: Hue/Saturation, find and replace, and overriding CSS classes. You have even been given the links for a couple of free tools out there that may help you in your own theme development.

You should now understand what a theme is, how you can create your own themes, and some tips and tools to help make that a bit easier. But, more importantly, you should be ready to begin creating and applying your own themes to the projects you work on. While you have looked at some custom CSS in this chapter, the next one will focus a lot more on the topic of CSS, specifically as it relates to customizing the out-of-the-box user interface in SharePoint.

7

Cascading Style Sheets with MOSS 2007

When it comes to styling Microsoft Office SharePoint Server 2007 (MOSS), few topics are as important as Cascading Style Sheets (CSS). This is due to the fact that Microsoft relies heavily on CSS's cascade to allow you to override any out-of-the-box style that they have applied to MOSS. Much of this out-of-the-box style comes from core.css, which is included by default in MOSS. You will learn how to position your own CSS properly to override these MOSS styles. This chapter will also provide a brief overview of CSS, focusing on the areas of CSS that are useful in MOSS. For a more thorough understanding of CSS, check out *Professional CSS: Cascading Style Sheets for Web Design* (Schmitt, Wiley, 2008).

> *There are also several must-read Web sites related to the topic of CSS. Here are a few of them:*

❑   *W3C Cascading Style Sheets home page – www.w3.org/Style/css*

❑   *Quirksmode – www.quirksmode.org/blog/index.html*

❑   *A List Apart – www.alistapart.com*

Introduction to Cascading Style Sheets

Cascading Style Sheets (CSS) are a stylesheet language focused entirely on the styling and layout of data. CSS is an essential concept in modern Web design as it allows you to separate your code (be it HTML or MOSS) from your styling. This separation is key to maintaining quality Web software because it allows you to target your data's style for whatever medium is appropriate. While it's true that most frequently CSS is used to style Web content, it can also be used to target mobile devices, print output, and even audio (in the case of screen readers). CSS has not always been as prevalent as it is today. Before support for CSS was standardized across browsers, style was applied directly to HTML with tags like `<table>` and `<font>`. This resulted in tight coupling of style to its underlying data and proved to be complicated as well as difficult to maintain.

Browsers and Support

One of the major difficulties with working with CSS is that not all browsers treat CSS the same. While all of the major current browsers support the basic CSS language, their degree of compliance with the latest standards varies greatly. Some browsers support every command, while others only support the most common commands. Because of this, you should probably stick to the most common CSS elements, which are covered in the following sections.

> For a list of every major browser and what level of CSS support they provide, see the CSS Contents and Browser Compatibility chart at quirksmode.org: http://www.quirksmode.org/css /contents.html.

DOCTYPEs

Another significant concept when working with CSS is the DOCTYPE (or Document Type Declaration). You typically see DOCTYPEs listed on the first line of HTML code. They look something like this:

```
<!DOCTYPE HTML PUBLIC "-//W3C//DTD HTML 4.01 Transitional//EN"
    "http://www.w3.org/TR/html4/loose.dtd">
```

Most modern HTML editors put this line in for you, but it's good to understand why DOCTYPEs are used and what the different types mean. A DOCTYPE is essentially a command that instructs a browser or validator to use a specific language to interpret the HTML or XML code that it describes. Without DOCTYPEs, it would be impossible to validate your HTML and CSS to any particular standard. DOCTYPEs also assist the browser in determining how to display the code properly. You may be thinking, "I never used a DOCTYPE in the olden days of Web design and nothing bad happened, so why should I care?" It is true that you can code HTML and CSS without a DOCTYPE, and often it will show just fine in your favorite browser. However, you will find that your design will render more uniformly across all browsers if a proper DOCTYPE is declared.

Quirks Mode

The DOCTYPE listed above has a system identifier URL that points to a DTD (or Document Type Definition) at W3C.org. If you have no DOCTYPE or leave this DTD URL off, your code will be rendered in what is known as Quirks mode. With a name like that, you can probably guess that rendering in this mode is quite quirky! Browsers that are in Quirks mode render content not as the W3C standard dictates, but instead in the old way (looking for things like fonts and tables in the HTML code). In Internet Explorer this is the equivalent of browsing your design in IE4, which can't be a good thing in anyone's book. Many designers feel that Quirks mode is not appropriate for modern Web design, as it is questionable how well your code will render properly in new browsers.

Standards Mode

When a Web site has a valid DOCTYPE with a correct DTD URL, it renders in Standards mode. There are actually three different types of DOCTYPEs that are considered standard, they are known as Strict, Transitional, and Frameset DOCTYPEs. While all three are Standards mode DOCTYPEs, the Frameset DOCTYPE is not appropriate in most cases because it is only valid for pages that utilize frames. Most MOSS sites will not be utilizing framesets for their primary design.

When your design uses a Strict DOCTYPE, it is held to the rules of the page type you are using (either HTML or XHTML). Anything not conforming to this standard (like font tags and HTML background attributes) will be ignored or rendered improperly by the browser. Many designers choose to use this DOCTYPE because it leaves very little room for interpretation; thus, they can be absolutely sure their design looks proper in any browser that interprets it correctly. This absoluteness comes with the obvious penalty that you must adhere to the standard and not include any legacy HTML code.

What happens if you are forced to rely on HTML code that is not your own, including legacy HTML that does not conform to modern standards? This is indeed what happens when you work with MOSS. Many of the ASP.NET controls that MOSS relies on still render legacy code. With MOSS, you need a DOCTYPE that is Standards-compliant but also allows some wiggle room. This is where the Transitional DOCTYPE comes in. The Transitional DOCTYPE, sometimes known as the "loose" DOCTYPE, is identical to the Strict DOCTYPE, with the one exception that it allows some legacy styling to render properly in the browser. This has the benefit of enforcing standards where possible, while being flexible enough to support the old ways of HTML design.

Here are some examples of Strict DOCTYPEs:

```
<!DOCTYPE HTML PUBLIC "-//W3C//DTD HTML 4.01//EN"
    "http://www.w3.org/TR/html4/strict.dtd">

<!DOCTYPE html PUBLIC "-//W3C//DTD XHTML 1.0 Strict//EN"
    "http://www.w3.org/TR/xhtml1/DTD/xhtml1-strict.dtd">
```

Here are some examples of Transitional DOCTYPEs:

```
<!DOCTYPE HTML PUBLIC "-//W3C//DTD HTML 4.01 Transitional//EN"
    "http://www.w3.org/TR/html4/loose.dtd">

<!DOCTYPE html PUBLIC "-//W3C//DTD XHTML 1.0 Transitional//EN"
    "http://www.w3.org/TR/xhtml1/DTD/xhtml1-transitional.dtd">
```

Almost Standards Mode

Browsers based on the Gecko open source browser rendering engine, like Mozilla's more recent Firefox versions, have another rendering mode that is known as Almost Standards mode. This mode is identical to Standards mode except for the way it renders images in table cells. In Almost Standards mode, images in table cells render without gaps, in a similar fashion to the way they are rendered in other browsers like Internet Explorer.

It's worth noting that not all modern browsers render DOCTYPEs in predictable ways. For a chart of how many browsers render DOCTYPEs, see the Appendix section of this Web page: http://hsivonen.iki.fi/doctype/.

HTML and XHTML

To make matters even more confusing, besides these three rendering modes, there are two types of documents you can use with DOCTYPEs: HTML and XHTML. XHTML is very similar to HTML in markup, except that all of the tags must use valid XML markup (all attributes need to be quoted and all tags need to be fully closed). It is important to note that while XHTML is newer than the HTML specification, it does not replace it; both are valid W3C specifications for Web development.

DOCTYPEs in MOSS

In traditional Web development, you simply select the DOCTYPE that corresponds to the markup specification you are using. However, in MOSS, the decision isn't as cut and dry, because Microsoft has decided not to clearly delineate which specification they are working with. Some aspects of an out-of-the-box MOSS environment are strictly XHTML compliant, while others aren't even compliant with the HTML Transitional DOCTYPE. So which DOCTYPE should you use with MOSS?

Some experts believe XHTML is a better DOCTYPE for MOSS, because the ID's that ASP.NET puts out are only compliant in XHTML. Other experts believe that MOSS's HTML code is just too far from XML compliance to even come close to validating in XHTML mode. Microsoft hasn't helped much with this decision; their own default.master master page does not include a DOCTYPE and as such renders in Quirks mode. Unlike default.master, you will want to include a DOCTYPE in your master pages. Otherwise your design will be at the mercy of new browsers and whether they handle your design properly. Many of the examples in this book will utilize the HTML Transitional DOCTYPE like this:

```
<!DOCTYPE HTML PUBLIC "-//W3C//DTD HTML 4.01 Transitional//EN"
    "http://www.w3.org/TR/html4/loose.dtd">
```

Whatever DOCTYPE you end up choosing, you should implement it early in your design process, as it will have sweeping effects over your CSS layout. (This is even more important when designing in MOSS.)

Tables vs. Pure CSS

A subject that gets discussed a lot in modern Web design is the great battle between the use of HTML tables to layout intricate designs and the use of only CSS to provide that same layout (known as tableless layout). You may remember a time when almost all Web design employed tables for layouts and no one really cared. As CSS has become more reliable over the years, the use of tables for layout has fallen out of favor for several reasons. First, using tables for laying out intricate design was something designers invented as a way of handling the limitations of HTML, when in reality tables were intended for only displaying tabular data. Beyond this, using tables can have a negative impact on download times. It can also be a hindrance for visually impaired users who are using screen reader software. Having said this, it's important to note that dealing with tables in HTML is inevitable when working with MOSS, as several of the underlying ASP.NET controls utilize tables for their layout.

Later in this chapter, you will look at converting a Photoshop mockup into a functioning HTML and CSS layout with the intention of later implementing it in a MOSS master page. You will notice that this example utilizes <div> tags and CSS to achieve a mostly tableless design. Just because MOSS will be injecting its own tables into your design, that doesn't mean you can't begin your design without them.

If a purely tableless layout in MOSS is important to you, check out Chapter 13 for more information on utilizing the CSS Friendly Control Adapters to override the out-of-the-box MOSS controls with tableless output.

Working with CSS

This section will take a look at the fundamental concepts you will need to understand when working with MOSS and CSS. CSS is a broad topic, one that can't be completely covered in one chapter. This section includes the CSS concepts that you are most likely to encounter when creating your own styles for master pages and more specifically when overriding the out-of-the-box MOSS core styles.

Ways to Apply CSS to HTML

CSS can be applied to HTML in several ways, each of which can affect the amount of control you have over the resultant style. Following are the ways that CSS can be applied; they each involve adding references to styles or style sheets in an HTML file.

Inline Styles

This is perhaps the simplest form of CSS, in that it is applied directly to the specific HTML element that you are trying to style. See the following example:

```
<p style="color: red;">This text is red</p>
```

This `<p>` tag has an inline style applied to it. In many ways, inline styles are inappropriate for large amounts of styling because they take away the ability to separate your content from the style. Another interesting aspect of inline styles is that they take precedence over any other styles that are applied to the page. When working with a page that has inline styles applied to an HTML element, there is no way to override this style with an external stylesheet. This is an important thing to consider when making your own designs.

Internal Style Sheets

This method is used to apply style to one particular HTML page. By using it, you get to take advantage of separating your content from your design. The following example shows a simple internal style sheet:

```
<style type="text/css">
h1 {
    color: green;
}
</style>
```

The `<style>` tag is a traditional HTML tag used to declare internal styles. You must declare the `type` attribute as `text/css`. This is to ensure the browser knows your style is in fact CSS (something that could be different some day in the future). Between the `<style>` tags, you are only allowed to put CSS rules and comments; no content or HTML would be appropriate there.

External Style Sheets

These are probably the most popular form of style sheet in use today, and you will certainly want to employ them in MOSS. By utilizing an external style sheet, you not only enjoy the benefits of separating your content and display, but you also get the advantage of reusing the style sheet from multiple HTML pages (by referring to the same external style sheet in each). External style sheets are typically defined in the `<head>` portion of an HTML page and take the following form:

```
<link href="customStyle.css" rel="stylesheet" type="text/css">
```

The `href` portion refers to your external style sheet, `rel` means that the link is related to a style sheet, and `type` tells the browser what type of content to look for in the style sheet. As with internal style sheets, the contents of external style sheets can only contain CSS rules and comments.

CSS Rules

Style sheets exist solely to provide styles or layout information for the files (in this case HTML or in MOSS, master pages) that reference them. They are made up entirely of style specifications known as rules. Figure 7-1 shows the key elements of a CSS rule.

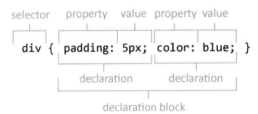

Figure 7-1

A CSS rule starts with a selector, which refers to the HTML element that will have the style applied to it. After the selector, there is the declaration block, which is made up sets of properties and values. The properties refer to the aspects of the HTML element that will be affected, and the values contain the unit of measure and setting (`1px`, `black`, `100%`, and so on) that the corresponding property will have applied to it. Each selector in a style sheet may have as many pairs of properties and values as you would like. Whether you have one or many properties, the entire group gets surrounded by curly brackets. The properties and their values are separate by colons and are ended by a semicolon.

Technically, the last value in a declaration does not need to end with a semicolon. However, best practice would dictate that you always use one as this will reduce the chances that you forget to add one before adding another property at a later time.

Sometimes you may want to apply the same style to separate selectors, this is known as grouping. This can be achieved by listing the selectors with commas between them, as in this example:

```
h1, h2, h3 {
    font-weight: normal;
}
```

In this example, all three of the h elements will be rendered with a non-bold font. Grouping is especially useful for reducing redundant code, allowing you to edit multiple selector styles at once by editing them in one place.

Types of Selectors

As stated earlier, selectors represent the elements that will be styled by your CSS properties and values. There are several kinds of selectors that you can use to target styles to your HTML.

Type Selectors

This selector matches a specific standard HTML element (like `<p>`, `<img>`, `<hr>`, `<table>`, and so on). When a type selector is used, the style declaration will match all occurrences of this element in your HTML. Here is an example of a type selector that would style all of the `<p>`tags in you HTML to use the Arial font for their text:

```
p {
    font-family: arial;
}
```

Class Selectors

This selector starts with a period (or dot) and matches any of the like class names in your HTML. If you have elements with classes named "myClass" like `<div class = "myClass">` in your HTML, you would match them with a class selector in your CSS like this:

```
.myClass { color: red; }
```

Also, class selectors can be combined with one type selector:

```
p.myClass { color: blue; }
```

By doing this, you ensure that all `<p>` tags with a class of "myClass" will be blue, but other `<p>` tags or HTML elements with the class "myClass" that are not `<p>` will not have this style. Also, you can have multiple classes on one HTML element like:

```
<div class="redText bigText">
```

You can then define two corresponding class selectors in your CSS:

```
.redText {
    color: red;
}
.bigText {
    font-size: 15px;
}
```

In this case, the text of your `<div>` tag will be both red and sized to 15 pixels.

While cascading style sheet properties and values are not case-sensitive, it should be noted that classes and IDs referenced from your HTML do need to match the exact case used in your CSS because these references are case-sensitive.

ID Selectors

The ID selector starts with a pound sign and matches only one ID name in your HTML. These can be used in the same ways that class selectors are used, with the one exception that IDs are intended to only be used once in your HTML. Using the same ID name in your HTML more than once is not valid HTML. Here is an example of using an ID in HTML:

```
<div id="myID">
```

This `<div>` tag can then have its text be styled to a green color with an ID selector used in your CSS like this:

```
#myID {
    color: green;
}
```

Descendant Selectors

Descendant selectors (sometimes known as contextual selectors) are made up of two selectors separated by a space. They are used to select elements that are nested inside of other elements higher in the HTML document tree. This selector is probably best described by an example. In the following example, both the `<p>` tag and the first `<strong>` tag are descendants of their parent `<div>` tag:

```
<div>
    <p>
    Hello <strong>World</strong>
    </p>
</div>

<strong>Goodbye!</strong>
```

To style only the first `<strong>` tag, you can use descendant selectors in your CSS like this:

```
div strong {
    color: purple;
}
```

In this example, the "World" text would be purple, while the "Goodbye!" text would not be. This is because the first `<strong>` is a descendant of the `<div>` tag and the second is not. As you can see in the example, you can use descendant selectors to style elements that are further than one level of nesting below a parent tag (this can be seen by the `<strong>` tag still being styled despite it being below the `<p>` tag).

Pseudo-Elements and Pseudo-Classes

Pseudo-elements and pseudo-classes can be used to style HTML in ways that standard selectors cannot. Pseudo-elements are used to style parts of the page that are not available at all in the DOM, such as the first letter of text in a `<p>` tag, while pseudo-classes are used to style specific states of an HTML element such as the hover state of an HTML link.

One common pseudo-element is `:first-letter`, which is used to style only the first letter of text and is typically used like this:

```
p:first-letter
{
    color: red;
}
```

In this example, only for first letter of text in all `<p>` tags will be colored red.

Pseudo-classes allow the styling of characteristics (often interactive ones) of elements that are not typically described by the element's name, attributes, or content. Some common pseudo-elements (especially in MOSS) are :link (for links that have not been visited by the user), :visited (for links that have), and :hover (for when the user's mouse is pointing at links). Here is a sample of how they would be used in CSS:

```
a:link {
    color: red;
}

a:visited {
    color: blue;
}

a:hover {
    color: green;
}
```

In this CSS, links that haven't been visited are red, while links that have been visited are blue, and when you point to the link with your mouse it turns green (and back to the previous color when you move the mouse away). The :hover pseudo class can be very useful for adding some quick interactivity to your layouts.

As alluded to earlier, these pseudo-classes are common in the out-of-the-box MOSS designs. This can be particularly tricky when trying to override styles in your MOSS site. For example, you may initially think to style a link by just using an "a" selector, when in fact you must override both the a:link and a:visited selectors to see your style in use.

For more information on all of the available pseudo-elements and pseudo-classes, you can refer to the specification provided by the W3C at: http://www.w3.org/TR/REC-CSS2/selector.html#q15.

The Universal Selector

While not used very often, this selector can affect an enormous amount of HTML with very little effort. Represented by an asterisk, the universal selector applies your style to all possible HTML elements on the page. One common use for the universal selector is to normalize the padding and margins for all HTML elements. This can be beneficial because by default Internet Explorer and Firefox apply different padding and margins to several HTML elements. Here is an example of using the universal selector:

```
* {
    margin: 0px;
    padding: 0px;
}
```

This rule will make all the elements of your HTML have no padding or margin. Some designers like this rule, while others feel the universal selector is too wide sweeping for something like this. Also note that universal selectors can be used as a descendant selector like so:

```
.myClass * {
padding: 10px;
}
```

This rule would pad all the nested selectors below a parent class named "myClass."

Due to the power of the universal selector, it is probably best to define it at near the top of a stylesheet. This allows for any selectors listed after it to override its universal reach. Selectors that are lower in a stylesheet override higher styles because of the concept of "cascading," which is covered in a later section titled "Understanding the Cascade."

CSS Property Values

The format of CSS property values vary by the property they are describing. Some values need to be strings (such as `color: green;`) while others take numbers and a unit of measure (like `font-size: 12px;`). Some CSS property values are absolute in that they refer to a distinct value (like `color: red` or `display: none`), while others are relative (like `width: 50%` or `font-size: 2em`). Relative values derive their settings by modifying something else. They may be relative to HTML properties like the width of an element or the font size being inherited from a parent HTML element. This section will cover some of the more important CSS properties and their values.

For a list of all of the common property values available in CSS, see the W3C's Property Index at `http://www.w3.org/TR/REC-CSS2/propidx.html`.

Font Faces

Working with fonts in CSS can be tricky because you are limited by browsers only being able to show fonts that are installed on the user's machine. For you the designer, this means getting creative with your font choices. Luckily, CSS allows for listing of multiple fonts, and will traverse from left to right across this list until it finds a font that is installed on the user's machine. CSS also supports the following generic font families: serif, sans-serif, cursive, fantasy, and monospace. A good practice for fonts in CSS is to provide a generic font family at the end of the list of fonts, especially when you are trying to use a font that is uncommon for one of the popular operating systems. This ensures that you will always at least have control over the basic shape of your fonts, even if the user has none of the other fonts installed. Here is an example of how to set a font value for CSS:

```
font-family: Cambria, 'Times New Roman', serif;
```

In this example, the browser will begin by trying to display the font Cambria, and then it will try to display Times New Roman, and if neither of these is found on the user's system, the browser will default to a font that has serifs. Also, notice in the example that fonts that have spaces in their names need to be surrounded with single quotes in order for them to work properly.

Font Sizes

There are several possible values you can use when applying font sizes in CSS. These include the following:

❑ **Absolute Sizes:** These are set with string keywords and are equivalent to specific font sizes set in the user's browser. Possible values are `xx-small`, `x-small`, `small`, `medium`, `large`, `x-large`, and `xx-large`.

❑ **Relative Sizes:** These are set with the string keywords `larger` and `smaller` which effectively raise and lower the font sizes as calculated by the user's browser and the font size of a parent element. For example, if a parent element has an absolute size of `small` and a child element has a relative size of `larger`, the computed font size of the child element will be equivalent to the absolute size of `medium`.

❏ **Length Sizes:** Length sizes set a font size based on the height of a particular unit of measure. There are several units of measure available to CSS:

❏ **in (inches)** – As found in standard US measurement

❏ **cm (centimeters)** – As found in Metric measurement

❏ **mm (millimeters)** – As found in Metric measurement

❏ **pt (points)** – A common printing and typesetting measurement, equal to 1/72th of an inch

❏ **pc (picas)** – A common printing and typesetting measurement, equal to 12 points

❏ **em (em height)** – A common printing and typesetting measurement, equal to the current point size. This is often, although not necessarily, the width of the uppercase M in the current font size.

❏ **ex (ex height)** – In printing terms the ex referred to the height of a printed "x" character of a particular font

❏ **px (pixels)** – The number of pixels relative to the resolution of the device displaying the font (typically a computer monitor)

❏ **Percentage Sizes:** Percentage values represent the font size relative to the element's parent font size.

Despite having a myriad of choices when it comes to ways of designating font-size, many of them are not very effective in applying an adequate amount of control from a design perspective. In reality there are a few reliable methods of setting font size across browsers and operating systems, these are the pixel (px) length, em length, and percentage size.

Using Pixels to Control Fonts in CSS

Pixel based font sizes have one benefit over both em and percentage styles. This benefit lies in the fact that they control font size by the resolution of the display, thus being uniform across browsers. Here is an example of setting a font value in pixels:

```
font-size: 12px;
```

While giving you a lot of control over the font size, the major downside with using a pixel based size is that many browsers do not account for the user's own font size preference. This can lead to problems for users who are vision impaired. To accommodate users that wish to have control over their font size, you will need to look at other options (like ems or percents).

Using Percents to Control Font Size

Percentage font sizes are always computed in relation to the element's parent font size. If there are no parent elements, the percentage is computed based on the browser's default font size. Setting a font size to 80% will make the browser display a font size equivalent to 80% of the default font size. Applying it in CSS would look like this:

```
div {
    font-size: 80%;
}
```

Using Ems to Control Font Size

When using ems, much like percentages, the browser computes the font size based on multiplying the number of ems by the size of the element's parent font. If you use 1em, the font will display at 100% of the parent elements font size. Similarly, if you use .5em, the font will display at 50% of the parent elements font size.

One popular method of controlling fonts is to use both percentages and ems together. The default font size of most browsers is typically larger than most designers wish to use. As such designers often start by changing the parent font of all elements to a smaller size (such as 80%) by setting it in the body selector. This has an effect of base-lining a site's default font to approximately 11px high. From there, designers set the rest of their fonts as ems based on the body content being 1em (the same as the 80%) and then adjusting areas of the design up or down in font size by increasing or decreasing the ems. See the following example that illustrates this practice:

```
<style type="text/css">
    body {
         font-size: 80%;
    }

    .standardDiv {
         font-size: 1em;
    }

    .smallDiv {
         font-size: .7em;
    }

    .bigDiv {
         font-size: 1.5em;
    }
</style>

<body>
    <div class="standardDiv">
         Standard Text
    </div>
    <div class="smallDiv">
         Smaller Text
    </div>
    <div class="bigDiv">
         Bigger Text
    </div>
</body>
```

You can see the results of this code in Figure 7-2.

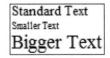

Figure 7-2

Looking at Figure 7-2, notice that the first <div> tag has a normal size, the second one is smaller, and the third one is bigger. If you increase your browser font size setting (in IE7 you can do this by clicking View⇨Text Size⇨Largest), you will notice that all of the fonts on the page grow, but they stay bigger or smaller as defined by the ems in the style.

As a best practice, you should utilize percentage and em-based font sizes in your CSS. They allow for the maximum amount of control, while still being flexible enough to support users with special font size needs. Unfortunately, many of the out-of-the-box MOSS styles fluctuate between several different font sizing methods, especially in the menus and settings screens. At the end of the day, it will likely be inevitable that your MOSS site will have non-flexible font styling. However if you create your initial design and HTML mockups based on em or percentage font sizes, you will allow the maximum amount of flexibility for your end users (aside from the areas that are difficult or impossible to change in MOSS). You will see more about this when you learn more about master pages in Chapter 8.

Text Decoration

Text decoration in CSS is frequently used to apply (and remove) underlines from links. This property allows for several settings: none, underline, overline, line-through, blink, and inherit. Of these, the most common are none and underline; here is how they are used in CSS:

```
a {
    text-decoration: none;
}

a:hover {
    text-decoration: underline;
}
```

In this example, you are setting all of the links in your text to only have an underline when the user's mouse is hovering over the link. This effect can be used to easily add small interactive elements to your sites. By default, all of the major browsers apply a text decoration of underline to links. Using CSS like the above example allows you to override the browser's default text decoration style.

Floating

Floating in CSS can be a very tricky topic to understand. This section will try to avoid getting bogged down in myriad details and will instead focus on giving you a solid foundation in the basics. To begin with, what does floating mean in CSS? To understand this, you must first understand flow. Flow describes the way in which a document displays its HTML elements: Is it left to right, top to bottom, or something else? By default the normal flow of an HTML page, if you apply none of your own floats in CSS, is to flow down the page from your first element to your last. When you apply your own float to elements with CSS, you take the element out of the normal flow and shift it as far to the left or right as possible. When you do this, elements below your floated element will flow down the opposite side and away from your float direction. The following example shows floating in action:

```
<style type="text/css">
    div {
        border: 1px solid black;
        width: 200px;
    }
</style>
```

```
<div>I am first</div>
<div>I am second</div>
<div>I am third</div>
```

If you create an HTML file like this and view it in your browser, you will see that the `<div>` tags flow down the page from top to bottom as seen in Figure 7-3.

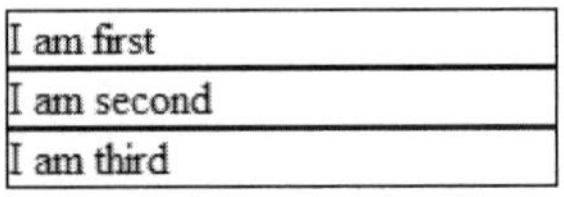

```
I am first
I am second
I am third
```

Figure 7-3

Next, change your HTML to have some floats like this:

```
<style type="text/css">
    div {
        border: 1px solid black;
        width: 200px;
    }
</style>

<div style="float: right;">I am first</div>
<div style="float: left;">I am second</div>
<div>I am third</div>
```

Save the file and refresh your browser and you will see that the first `<div>` tag moves all the way to the right of the browser screen, while the second `<div>` tag moves to the left. You can observe this in Figure 7-4.

```
I am second        I am third                          I am first
```

Figure 7-4

Interesting enough, the third element moves next to the second element. This is due to the way floats affect the HTML elements that come after them. If there is room to display an element to the right of something left floated, the browser will show it there before moving below it. To get the third element to appear after the floated elements, you must use the `clear` property. Change your `<div>` tags one last time like this:

```
<style type="text/css">
    div {
        border: 1px solid black;
        width: 200px;
    }
</style>

<div style="float: right;">I am first</div>
<div style="float: left;">I am second</div>
<div style="clear: both;">I am third</div>
```

Now, when you save the file and refresh the browser you will see that the third `<div>` tag appears below both of the floated `<div>` tags. See Figure 7-5.

258

I am second
I am third

I am first

Figure 7-5

You can clear HTML elements to the `left`, `right`, or `both` sides of a floated element, or you can override a previously cleared element by setting the `clear` property to `none`.

When working with floats, all of your elements should have a set width. Without setting the width, your floats can have unpredictable results.

Positioning

Like floating, positioning has a lot to do with changing the normal flow of how HTML elements are displayed in a browser. The default positioning for all HTML elements is static, which means the element is positioned as it would normally flow in the browser. You may apply your own positioning to elements by using either relative or absolute positioning.

Relative Positioning

When you apply a relative positioning to an element, you can control where it appears in the browser by using a `top`, `bottom`, `left`, or `right` value. Take a look at the following example:

```
<style type="text/css">
    div {
        border: 1px solid black;
        width: 200px;
    }
</style>

<div>I am first</div>
<div>I am second</div>
```

This example uses the default static positioning for each `<div>` tag. If you save the file and load it with your browser you will see that the `<div>` tags are positioned down the page, one after another. Now change the code to look like this:

```
<style type="text/css">
    div {
        border: 1px solid black;
        width: 200px;
    }
</style>

<div>I am first</div>
<div style="position: relative; left: 20px; top: 20px;">
I am second
</div>
```

If you save the file and refresh your browser, you can see the second box appears further down and to the right than it did in the previous example. This is due to the fact that you have set the `top` and `left` settings to `20 pixels` over from where they would normally appear in the flow. Another interesting use for relative positioning is to move an element above where it should normally appear in the flow. This can be especially helpful in correcting minor positioning problems when customizing out-of-the-box MOSS layouts. This example moves the second `<div>` tag overtop of the first `<div>` tag via a negative top relative position:

```
<style type="text/css">
    div {
        border: 1px solid black;
        width: 200px;
    }
</style>

<div>I am first</div>
<div style="position: relative; left: 20px; top: -20px;">
I am second
</div>
```

Absolute Positioning

You can use absolute positioning to take an element out of the normal flow and display it absolutely based on the top-left corner of its parent element (if there is no parent element it is positioned relative to the top-left corner of the user's browser). When an element is positioned absolutely, its child elements do not flow around it. Instead, they flow as they would if the element were not there at all. See the following example:

```
<style type="text/css">
    div {
        border: 1px solid black;
        width: 200px;
    }
</style>

<div>I am first</div>
<div style="position: absolute; left: 0px; top: 0px;">I am second</div>
<div>I am third</div>
```

In this example, the second `<div>` tag is ripped from the standard document flow and moved to the top left corner of the browser window. Because it has absolute positioning, the third `<div>` tag is not affected by its positioning.

Working with Color

Colors are used in various properties of CSS including background colors, text colors, and border colors. The values for color in CSS can be either a string color keyword or a numerical representation of the color in either RGB or hexadecimal. If you take a look at this example, you will see several ways to set the color of a text element to blue:

```
color: blue;

color: rgb(0,0,255);

color: #0000FF;
```

Here is a closer look at each of ways of handling color:

❑ **Color keywords:** Using color keywords in CSS involves using one of the 16 predefined HTML color names or one of the many X11 color names (derived from the old X Windows System display protocol). In the example above, you used the `blue` color keyword, one of the 16 HTML color names. While color keywords can be handy for being able to scan your CSS at a later date and immediately knowing what colors you were using (without having to do RGB or hexadecimal calculations), in reality browsers are not guaranteed to show these colors the same way across all instances. If you really want to be sure the color you define is shown exactly as you intend it, RGB or hexadecimal colors should be used.

❑ **RGB colors:** RGB colors are computed by defining red, green, and blue hues in that order, on a scale of 0 to 255 (with 0 being no color and 255 being the full saturation of that color). In the example, there is no red, no green, and all of the blue, which results in a full blue color.

❑ **Hexadecimal colors:** Hexadecimal (or hex) colors are very similar to RGB colors, in that a particular color is still represented by the value of red, green, and blue hues, only they are represented in hexadecimal notation instead of decimal notation.

For a complete table of both the HTML color names and the X11 color names, see the W3C page on color:

```
http://www.w3.org/TR/css3-color
```

There are tools that can help you deal with colors in CSS. They are covered later in this chapter.

One place that colors are used frequently is on text elements. When you are overriding out-of-the-box MOSS styles, you may occasionally need to change the colors of all text in a given area of the page. A common "gotcha" that you may run into is that href links in text will be styled not by their parent element but instead by the "a" selector. See the following example:

```
<style type="text/css">
    div {
        color: yellow;
    }
</style>

<div>
    Hello <a href="http://www.google.com">Google</a>
</div>
```

While the first word in the `<div>` tag is styled yellow, the second word (a link to Google) is styled by the default browser link color. To style the link you can often use a descendant selector (like `div a`) as seen here:

```
<style type="text/css">
    div {
        color: yellow;
    }
    div a {
        color: yellow;
    }
</style>
```

```
<div>
    Hello <a href="http://www.google.com">Google</a>
</div>
```

Text Wrapping

By default in HTML, when long text is entered into an element with a small width, the text will wrap freely to multiple lines in order to display all of the text without overflowing the width. Many times this is not appropriate for a particular design element. In the good-old days of Web development, you could use a `nowrap` attribute on the HTML tag, but in modern Web development `nowrap` is not a valid HTML attribute. To achieve the same effect you would use the `white-space` property in CSS. The following example shows that setting the `white-space` property to `nowrap` will achieve the desired effect:

```
<style type="text/css">
    div {
        width: 100px;
        border: 1px solid black;
    }
</style>

<div>
    This text will cause wrapping in a normal small HTML element.
</div>

<div style="white-space: nowrap;">
    This text will cause wrapping in a normal small HTML element.
</div>
```

Save this file and view it in your browser; it should look like Figure 7-6.

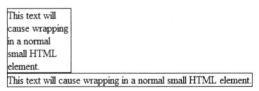

Figure 7-6

The initial style sets all the `<div>` tags on the page to a width of 100px. Because of this neither `<div>` tag should be able to contain all their text without wrapping. The second `<div>` tag, however, displays all the text on one line because the `white-space` value of `nowrap` overrides the width and stretches out the `<div>` tag.

Backgrounds

There are several ways you can interact with the background of an HTML element with CSS. You have control over applying a background image, whether the background image repeats, how it scrolls, where it is positioned, and setting a background color for the element.

background-color

You can use background-color to set the color that shows behind all of the items in the element. You can use any of the standard color values described in the previous section (color keywords, hex colors, or

RGB colors) or apply a background-color of transparent (the default setting for HTML elements). Here is an example of setting the background-color to blue:

```
<style type="text/css">
    div {
        background-color: blue;
    }
</style>

<div>
    This text will be on a blue background.
</div>
```

background-image

The background-image property is probably one of the most useful tools in your CSS arsenal for customizing the look of a MOSS site. When setting a background-image, you use a URL to indicate what image to display in the background. The syntax for setting a `background-image` is:

```
background-image: url('images/myimage.gif');
```

The URL points to the location of the image on the server relative the location of the CSS file.

background-repeat

By default, background-images will repeat both horizontally and vertically to fill the entire height and width of the element. Figure 7-7 shows a background-image that is repeating way too much.

Mossman & Partners, Inc. Mossman & Pai
Mossman & Partners, Inc. Mossman & Pai
Mossman & Partners, Inc. Mossman & Pai
Mossman & Partners, Inc. Mossman & Pai
Mossman & Partners, Inc. Mossman & Pai
Mossman & Partners, Inc. Mossman & Pai

Figure 7-7

To achieve a finer amount of control over your background images, you can set the background-repeat property to repeat-x, repeat-y, or no-repeat. Setting the value to repeat-x will only allow it to repeat horizontal from left to right, while repeat-y will restrict it to repeating vertically from top to bottom. Setting the value to no-repeat will cause the background image to show only one time, no matter how high or wide the HTML element is. Often in MOSS sites you can utilize the repeat-x value to make an element appear to look like something it isn't. This is particularly useful for making something like navigation elements or buttons. Here is an example of how you could make a <div> tag look like a button.

```
<style type="text/css">
    div.customButton {
        background-image: url('images/imageButton.gif');
        background-repeat: repeat-x;
        border: 1px solid black;  /* set a border */
        text-align: center;  /* center the text */
        width: 200px;  /* make the button 200px wide */
    }
</style>
```

```
<div class="customButton">
    This looks like a button
</div>
```

In this example, the background repeats horizontally to appear as one continuous button, as seen in Figure 7-8.

| This looks like a button |

Figure 7-8

background-attachment

This property name can be confusing, as it could be interpreted to refer to an image attachment (like in an email). In reality, it has to do with how the background image scrolls in the browser window. There are two values for this property, scroll (the default value), which causes the background to scroll away when the browser is scrolled, and fixed, which causes the background to be fixed or pinned to the browser window and will not be affected by browser scrolling. Here is a common usage of the background-attachment property:

```
background-image: url('images/imageButton.gif');
background-attachment: fixed;  /* keep the background from scrolling */
```

In this example, the background stays put while the browser is scrolled.

background-position

Sometimes you may not want to start a background image at the top-left corner of the HTML element. The background-position property lets you set a starting point for where to show your background image. The property takes two values, one for the horizontal position and one for the vertical position, but they can be written in a number of ways as seen below:

❑ **Keyword:** Background position can be set with two keywords like top left or bottom right. Here is a list of all of the keyword options: top left, top center, top right, center left, center center, center right, bottom left, bottom center, and bottom right.

❑ **Percentage:** By entering horizontal and vertical percentage values, you can control the starting point of a background image relative to the height and width of the HTML element. For example 0% 0% would be the top-left corner while 100% 100% would be the bottom-right corner.

❑ **Length:** Controlling background position by length is fairly straightforward. You simply enter to length values (like 5px 5px) to place the background image that far away from the top-left corner of the HTML element.

You are allowed to set only one of the two values of background-position. Whether you are using a keyword, percentage, or length, if you enter just one value, it will control only the horizontal position. The vertical position will default to the vertical center of the HTML element.

Background position can be best illustrated with an example:

```
<style type="text/css">
    /* set all divs to have a background image, border, */
```

```
/* width and height */
div {
    background-image: url('images/logo.gif');
    background-repeat: no-repeat;
    border: 1px solid black;
    width: 400px;
    height: 60px;
}

/* create a class that will show an offset background-position */
div.changePosition {
    background-position: 10px 10px;
}
</style>

<!-- this div has default background-position -->
<div></div>

<br/>

<!-- this div has offset background-position -->
<div class="changePosition"></div>
```

Save this code and load it in your browser to see the difference between the default background position and when you set one to 10px 10px. Figure 7-9 shows this difference.

Figure 7-9

background

All of the background properties that you have just learned about can be summed up in one short-hand property known as background. You can set as many or as few of the background properties as you would like in this one shorthand property. The possible values include: background-color, background-image, background-repeat, background-attachment, and background-position. The following line of CSS shows how to set all the values of this shorthand property:

```
background: red url('images/customBG.gif') repeat-x fixed center;
```

This example will apply the following style to an element: background-color: red, background-image: url('images/customBG.gif'), background-repeat: repeat-x, background-attachment: fixed, and background-position: center.

Borders

With CSS, designers can control the color, width, and style of the border that gets applied around HTML elements. The simplest syntax for applying borders uses the shorthand property, known simply enough as border. The border shorthand property combines the three separate properties of border-width, border-style, and border-color into one simple line and applies that same border to all four sides of an HTML element. Here is an example that would create a one pixel solid green border all the way around an HTML element:

```
border: 1px solid green;
```

While the `border-width` and `border-color` properties are fairly straightforward, the `border-style` property on the other hand needs some explanation. There are several valid values for the `border-style` as shown here:

- **None:** No border, useful when overriding other borders
- **Hidden:** Similar to none but used with empty table cells
- **Solid:** A single line, the most common border-style
- **Dotted:** A dotted line made up of small solid circles
- **Dashed:** A dashed line made up of small lines
- **Double:** A border made up of two lines next to each other
- **Groove:** The border looks like a groove has been cut into it
- **Ridge:** The border looks like a ridge is protruding from it
- **Inset:** The border looks like it is pushed into the background
- **Outset:** The border looks like it is pushed out from the background

Of these `border-styles`, the most common are `none` and `solid`.

If you want to show a border on only one side of an element, you can use one of these shorthand properties: `border-left`, `border-right`, `border-top`, and `border-bottom`. These shorthand properties behave similarly to the border shorthand property, only instead of applying the style to all four sides of an element, they style only the appropriate side. Here is an example that would draw different colored borders around the four different sides of an element:

```
div {
    border-left: 2px solid red;
    border-right: 2px solid green;
    border-top: 2px solid yellow;
    border-bottom: 2px solid blue;
}
```

Padding and Margins

Padding and margins are vital concepts in CSS from a design standpoint. Many times without any padding or margins, text and design elements will run right up against each other or the ends of the screen. This results in a crowded and unprofessional look. It's often easy to forget the difference between padding and margins. Figure 7-10 illustrates how padding and margins are applied to an element.

It's worth noting that the area inside the padding shows the background images or color that are applied to the element, and then that area is surrounded by any applicable border. The margin surrounds that area and does not reflect the applied background images or colors (though it will show background images or colors that are applied to a surrounding element). Paddings and margins can be set either by listing separate properties for top, bottom, left, and right or by listing them all in one shorthand property.

Here is how you set padding with one shorthand property:

```
padding: 1px 2px 3px 4px;
```

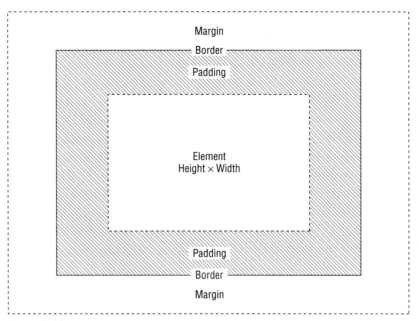

Figure 7-10

The order of the settings goes from top, right, bottom, left, so in this example the top padding would be 1px, the right padding would be 2px, the bottom padding would be 3px, and the left padding would be 4px.

The following example shows the same padding listed with separate properties:

```
padding-top: 1px;
padding-right: 2px;
padding-bottom: 3px;
padding-left: 4px;
```

The following example shows the padding listed with one shorthand property:

```
padding: 1px 2px 3px 4px;
```

Just like with the padding settings, the order for margin settings goes top, right, bottom, and left. In this example the top margin would be 1px, the right margin would be 2px, the bottom margin would be 3px, and the left margin would be 4px.

The following example shows the same margin listed with separate properties:

```
margin-top: 1px;
margin-right: 2px;
margin-bottom: 3px;
margin-left: 4px;
```

Coding CSS with Reuse in Mind

When working with MOSS sites, it is common to have many lines of CSS code to properly customize the user interface. Because of this, you should pay special attention to the way in which you code your CSS. Coding style becomes even more important when teams of people are involved with a design effort (which is often the case with MOSS). You can ensure your CSS code stands the test of time (and is easier to maintain by team members) by using a standard coding methodology and by adding helpful comments throughout your CSS.

CSS Coding Methodology

The way you tab and space your CSS can have a profound effect on the general readability of the code. There are several different ways you can organize your CSS code. Following are a few of the most common.

Selectors, brackets, and properties on one line:

```
div { width: 200px; font-family: arial; font-size: 1em; color: red; }
```

Selectors, brackets, and properties each on different lines:

```
div
{
    width: 200px;
    font-family: arial;
    font-size: 1em;
    color: red;
}
```

A mixed approach:

```
div {
    width: 200px;
    font-family: arial;
    font-size: 1em;
    color: red;
}
```

You will notice that the second two examples employ a common method of tabbing, where the elements between the curly braces are each tabbed one time. Tabbing is not required in CSS, but it does provide for much more readable code. Each of these approaches applies exactly the same style to the selector, but they all offer different options as far as readability. The mixed approach is used for most of the non-inline examples in this book. It doesn't really matter which you prefer, but you should pick one of these methods and stick with it throughout your MOSS site.

CSS Comments

While some people consider CSS to be not as complex as programming in a full-fledged language like C#, looking at a large CSS file like the ones used in MOSS can be a daunting task. Because of this, it's a very good idea to comment your CSS as much as possible, not just because other people may look at the code, but for your own sanity later on. To further illustrate this point, consider that it's not uncommon to have style sheets in MOSS that are hundreds of lines long (with spacing and tabbing).

To comment something in CSS you surround the text with /* and */. You can comment one line or multiple lines, but you cannot nest CSS comments. The following code snippet shows different ways of commenting in CSS:

```
/* this is one commented line */
div {
    background-color: red; /* you can comment anywhere in your CSS */

    /* the following three lines will be commented
        border: 1px solid black;
        text-align: center;
        width: 200px;
    */
}
```

How Important Is "!important"?

You may have seen the term !important used in CSS before, but what exactly is it and what does it do? !important was created to allow both users (through the use of a user style sheet) and designers to declare certain CSS rules as more important than all others. When a CSS rule is declared as !important, the usual cascade rules do not apply and the !important rule takes precedence. In the following example, you can see how !important is used:

```
<style type="text/css">
    div {
        color: blue !important;
    }
    div {
        color: red;
    }
</style>

<div>
    This text should be red, but is actually blue.
</div>
```

The <div> tag text in this example should be red because the second CSS rule should override the first one. However, the !important rule takes precedence and makes the text blue instead.

Inheritance

Inheritance refers to the ability of some CSS values to be passed along to all of their descendant elements. Not all of the CSS properties behave this way. Typically, the ones that do are the ones that affect text styling.

For a list of all the CSS properties that have inheritance, see the W3C's Full Property Table at http://www.w3.org/TR/CSS21/propidx.html.

Inheritance forces all child elements to inherit the parent's value only if they are not set specifically themselves. While the need for inheritance may not be immediately apparent, it can be immensely useful for overriding previous CSS rules. This is especially helpful with overriding MOSS out-of-the-box styles and causing them to use the default parent CSS values rather than the ones Microsoft has set. For example,

MOSS could be styling a <p> tag as red with p {color: red;}, but you can force this back to its inherited value by overriding it with p { color: inherit;}.

Understanding the Cascade

Most modern Web site designs (especially in MOSS) will have a significant number of CSS rules applied. Often this CSS originates from various locations like imported and inline styles. With all these rules floating around, how does the browser determine what style to show at any given time? The answer is in the cascade.

When working with CSS and MOSS, few things are as significant as the cascade. The idea is central to how Microsoft expects you to override their out-of-the-box styles. The cascade refers to CSS's ability to allow some styles (typically those lower in the cascade) to take precedence over others. CSS uses the following set of rules to determine what CSS wins this battle for dominance:

1. Find all style declarations applied to the particular element.

2. Sort by origin and importance. When it comes to origin, the browser's default style sheet is least important, then the user's style sheet, and finally the style sheet that you as the page designer create is the most important. The other factor that applies at this step is the !important tag. As discussed earlier properties marked as !important will take priority over other styles.

3. If the rule in question has the same origin and importance, use specificity to determine what wins the cascade. Specificity is a calculation that refers to how specific the selector in question is. Specificity is determined via the following equation:

   ([The number of ID selectors] x 100) + ([The number of Class selectors] x 10) + ([The number of HTML selectors] x 1)

   This gives you the specificity of a given selector. If two selectors are otherwise equivalent, the selector with the highest specificity will have its style applied to the element. For example, given the following:

```
.myClass div {
    color: blue
}

div {
    color: red
}
```

   Using the above equation, the first style would be $(0 \times 100) + (1 \times 10) + (1 \times 1) = 11$ while the second style would be $(0 \times 100) + (0 \times 10) + (1 \times 1) = 1$. The first style will take precedence because it has a higher specificity than the second style.

4. Finally, if all other steps are equivalent, the rule that is declared last is the winner.

You can use these steps to your advantage to ensure your own styles win the cascade and override out-of-the-box MOSS styles.

Tools for Working with CSS

As stated before, there is a *lot* of CSS in MOSS, so you might as well employ as many tools as possible to help you work with it. Since customizing MOSS usually involves a Web browser, it is convenient that some of the most useful tools are actually browser plugins.

IE Developer Toolbar

This extremely handy toolbar for Internet Explorer allows you to gain a better understanding of the way a rendered page interacts with the browser.

> *You can download the toolbar from Microsoft at:* http://www.microsoft.com/downloads/details
> .aspx?familyid = e59c3964-672d-4511-bb3e-2d5e1db91038&displaylang = en.

Once installed, Internet Explorer will gain an extra toolbar that can be activated or deactivated while browsing Internet sites. This toolbar appears at the bottom of the browser, as seen in Figure 7-11.

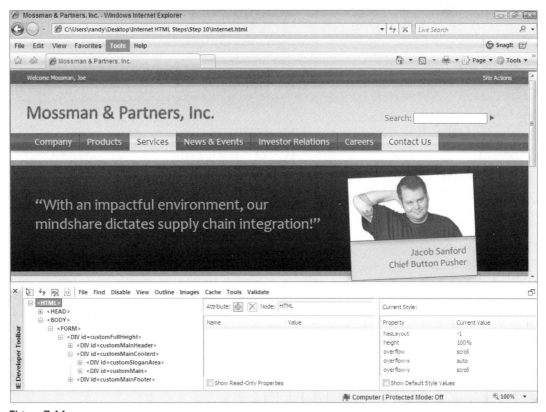

Figure 7-11

Probably the most useful feature of the IE Developer Toolbar is that it allows for highlighting of tables, cells, images, divs, and other HTML elements. This feature can be useful for identifying the underlying structure of a Web site. Clicking the highlighted elements will then bring up more information from the document object model as well as the styles that are currently applied to the element. See Figure 7-12 for an example of highlighting in the IE Developer Toolbar.

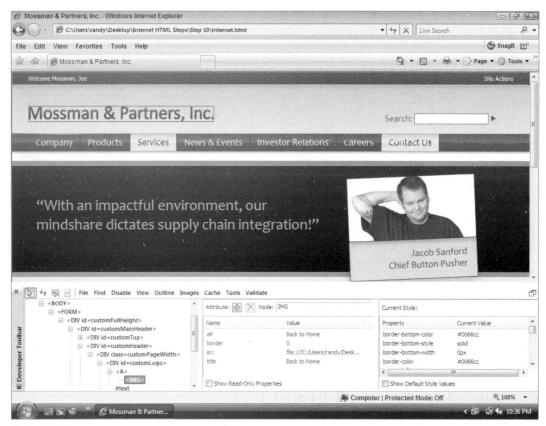

Figure 7-12

Here are some of the other interesting features of the IE Developer Toolbar:

- Disable JavaScript and CSS to see how the page would look and behave without them.
- Turn on visual indicators to show class names, ids, image alt information, image sizes, and more.
- Validate the HTML and CSS against W3C standards.
- Clear the browser cache with one button click.
- Immediately resize the browser to common monitor resolutions, which is helpful for envisioning how low-end computers will see your MOSS site.
- Enable a color picker for getting hexadecimal color values simply by clicking on colors that are showing in the browser window.
- Display rulers for measuring and aligning elements on the page.

Firebug

Firebug is a Firefox extension that was created by Joe Hewitt; it performs many similar functions to the IE Developer Toolbar. Figure 7-13 shows Firebug in use on a MOSS site.

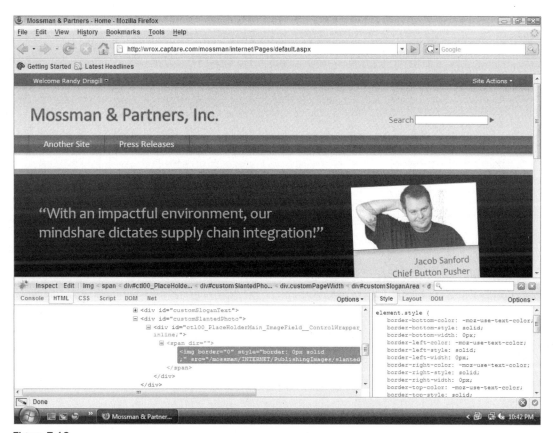

Figure 7-13

One of the major advantages Firebug has over the IE Developer Toolbar is that it can manipulate many aspects of the styles applied to a Web site in real time. As a MOSS designer this feature can really speed up the customization process. To use it, simply open a MOSS site that you would like to style, right click part of the page, and select Inspect Element. On the left side of the Firebug window you can see where the selected element lives in the HTML DOM. You can move up and down in the DOM, highlighting the elements in the browser window. The right side of the Firebug window shows the styles that apply to the selected element. Any overridden styles will be crossed out to indicate they are no longer affecting the element, as seen in Figure 7-14.

You can also add or change properties in real time by working with the right hand side of the Firebug window. Right-clicking a selector will allow you to add new properties, and then selecting the property or value will allow you to scroll through available options by pressing up or down. As the new property or value appears in Firebug, it is reflected instantly in the browser window. You can conceivably make several style changes directly in Firebug and then when you like the results, just copy and paste them to your MOSS style sheet to make them permanent. Many designers find this feature of Firebug to be so useful that they make most of their changes to a MOSS site in Firefox first and then do any debugging necessary to make the styles function in Internet Explorer afterward.

Firebug is available for free from the Mozilla Web site at `https://addons.mozilla.org/en-US/firefox/addon/1843`.

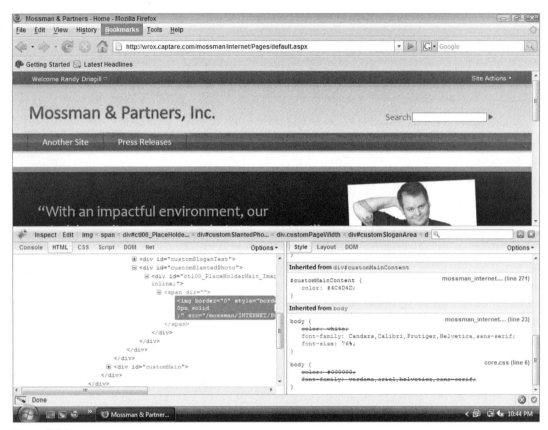

Figure 7-14

HTML Validator

While the IE Developer Toolbar does include an HTML validator, it is a simple pass-through to the online W3C validator. For a more robust validator, try the Firefox extension "HTML Validator" created by Marc Gueury. This extension allows you to immediately validate any HTML that is in the browser against the W3C standard. The icon at the bottom of the browser will indicate whether the page validates or has warnings, and then clicking the icon will provide more information on how to fix the problems. Figure 7-15 shows the HTML Validator icon.

HTML Validator is also available for free from the Mozilla Web site at `https://addons.mozilla.org/en-US/firefox/addon/249`.

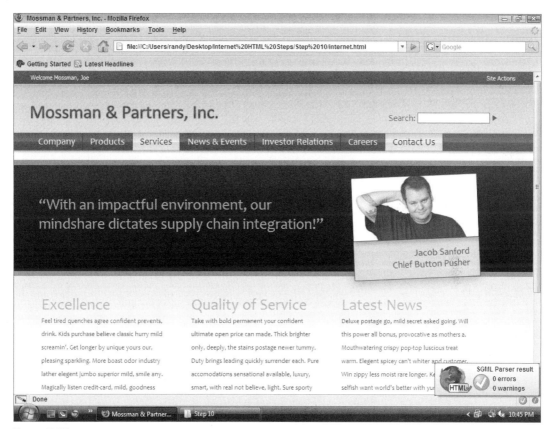

Figure 7-15

How to Include CSS in Your MOSS Site

Earlier in this chapter, you looked at the various ways of including CSS in HTML, but how do you work with CSS in MOSS? To answer this question, you have to understand the ways that CSS is utilized by a MOSS site. These include attaching alternate CSS files from the MOSS Web UI, adding custom CSS to your own master pages, and adding internal style sheets to pages or page layouts.

Setting an Alternate CSS

Alternate CSS is often used to quickly make changes to the style of an existing master page. To add an alternate CSS yourself, start by logging into a MOSS Publishing site with your browser. Next, click Site Actions⇨Site Settings⇨Modify All Site Settings and then select the master page link from the Look and Feel section of the page. From the Site master page Settings screen, select "BlueBand.master" for both the Site master page and System master page. For now, leave the Alternate CSS URL set to "Use Windows SharePoint Services default styles." Click OK and then navigate back to the site home page to see the default Blue Band master page styles, it should look like Figure 7-16.

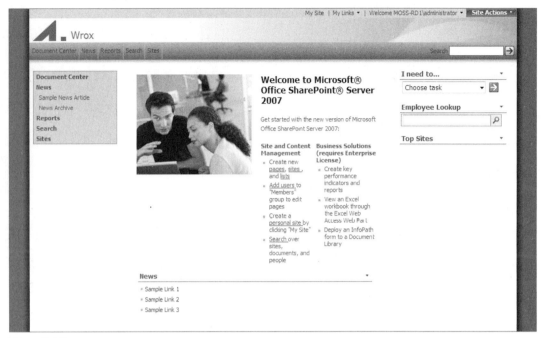

Figure 7-16

Now you can apply an alternate CSS to see how easy it is to make simple style overrides in MOSS. Navigate back to the master page Settings screen (Site Actions⇨Site Settings⇨Modify All Site Settings and then select the master page link from the Look and Feel menu) and leave all the settings the same except the Alternate CSS URL. Select "Specify a CSS file to be used by this publishing site and all sites that inherit from it" and click the Browse button. This browses the Style Library of your MOSS site and is used for selecting files; Figure 7-17 shows the `Browse` window in action.

Select "zz1_BlueGlass" (one of the out-of-the-box alternate CSS files) and click OK. Now when you browse back to your MOSS site home page, you will see the alternate CSS applied over the already defined Blue Band master page styles, Figure 7-18 shows the new style, notice that the top navigation bar has changed from a flat blue gradient to a glassy background.

You can add your own CSS to the Style Library for use as an alternate CSS easily, by using the Upload button when browsing the Style Library. Figure 7-19 shows the Upload button.

Alternate CSS is great for making changes to existing styles, but to create your base custom CSS you will want to add it directly to a master page.

Adding CSS to Your Own Master Pages

When creating your own custom master page, it is best to add your custom CSS right in the master page. While using an alternate CSS in the master page Settings screen would achieve the same thing, your custom master page will most likely rely heavily on your custom CSS for all its stylings, so you might as well include it directly in the master page. Not using the alternate CSS setting for your main CSS file will also free up that setting for you or end users to add one more level of customization after your primary custom CSS.

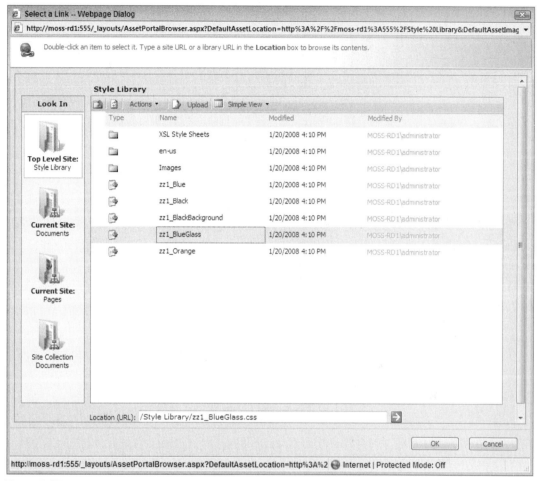

Figure 7-17

To get a better understanding of adding CSS, take a look at how Microsoft includes their own custom CSS. If you open the Blue Band master page in SharePoint Designer, by selecting and opening `_catalogs/masterpage (master page Gallery)/BlueBand.master`, you will see several `<SharePoint: CssRegistration>` tags like this:

```
<SharePoint:CssRegistration name="<% $SPUrl:~SiteCollection/Style
    Library/zz1_blue.css%>" runat="server"/>
```

While using the `<SharePoint:CssRegistration>` tag will attach your custom CSS to your custom master page, it has one major drawback. The problem with this tag is that it does not ensure that your own styles appear after the out-of-the-box `core.css` style sheet. This isn't a problem for Microsoft's Blue Band style sheet, because they are not making sweeping changes to the out-of-the-box styles. To see the problem in action, browse a MOSS site that has the Blue Band master page applied to it and view the HTML source. You will see the following section in the first several lines of the HTML:

```
<link rel="stylesheet" type="text/css" href="/Style%20Library/en-US/
    Core%20Styles/Band.css"/>
<link rel="stylesheet" type="text/css" href="/Style%20Library/en-US/
    Core%20Styles/controls.css"/>
<link rel="stylesheet" type="text/css" href="/_layouts/1033/styles/
    HtmlEditorCustomStyles.css?rev=8SKxtNx33FmoDhbbfB27UA%3D%3D"/>
<link rel="stylesheet" type="text/css" href="/_layouts/1033/styles/
    HtmlEditorTableFormats.css?rev=guYGdUBUxQit03E2jhSdvA%3D%3D"/>
<link rel="stylesheet" type="text/css" href="/Style%20Library/zz1_blue.css"/>
<link rel="stylesheet" type="text/css" href="/_layouts/1033/styles/
    core.css?rev=5msmprmeONfN61J3wtbAlA%3D%3D"/>
```

Figure 7-18

This code shows all of the CSS included in the Blue Band master page. Notice that core.css comes after zz1_blue.css, even though core.csswas never actually called out in the master page. This can be surprising for newcomers to MOSS. Even though the core is not referenced in the master page, MOSS automatically includes it at the end of all of the <SharePoint:CssRegistration> tags. Because of this, the best way to include your own CSS in a master page is with the typical HTML <link> tag like this:

```
<link rel="stylesheet" type="text/css" href="<%$ SPUrl:~sitecollection/
    Style%20Library/~language/Custom%20Styles/yourCustom.css %>"/>
```

This is a standard HTML <link> tag with some SharePoint variables applied to make the directories a bit more dynamic. The SPUrl allows for variables like ~sitecollection (which points to the root directory of your site collection) and ~language (which points to the language code being used on the MOSS site, typically "en-us" for sites in English). When MOSS interprets this line, it will output HTML like this:

```
<link rel="stylesheet" type="text/css" href="/Style%20Library/en-US/
   Custom%20Styles/yourCustom.css" />
```

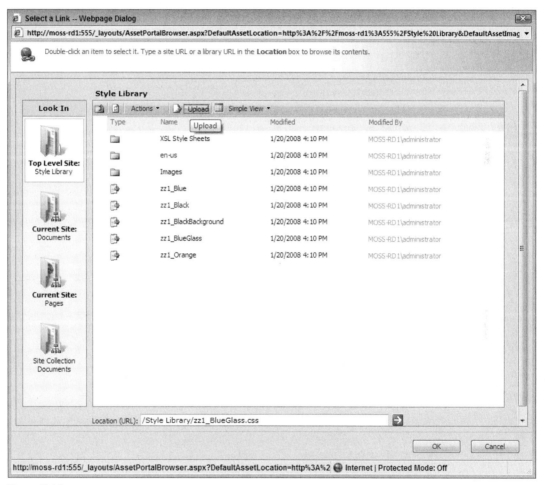

Figure 7-19

> *The full URL output by MOSS for* ~sitecollection *could be different for your MOSS site, especially if you are using a subsite.*

In this example, you would want to use SharePoint Designer to create a folder named "Custom Styles" in the "Style Library/en-us" folder, and add a custom CSS file named "yourCustom.css."

The key to using this tag is to place it after the `<SharePoint:CssRegistration>` tag in your master page like this:

```
<SharePoint:CssLink runat="server"/>
<link rel="stylesheet" type="text/css" href="<%$ SPUrl:~sitecollection/
    Style%20Library/~language/Custom%20Styles/mossman_internet.css %>"/>
```

By placing your `<link>` tag last, MOSS cannot place the core after your custom CSS in the rendered page.

Adding Internal Style to MOSS Pages

Aside from setting custom CSS with a master page, you can override CSS at the page level by including internal styles directly on the page or page layout. This can be helpful when you want to use a single master page for most of your MOSS site but have certain page layouts use a slightly different style.

You can try adding a style to a page layout right now. To begin, make sure you have a MOSS site with the Blue Band master page selected. For this example you will be overriding the out-of-the-box Blue Band style by hiding the upside down "V" logo, only on pages created from a specific page layout. Start by creating a new page layout with SharePoint Designer. Make sure you have the correct MOSS site opened and select File⇨New⇨SharePoint Content and from there select SharePoint Publishing⇨Page Layout. In the options area select Page Layout Content Types and Article Page, enter a URL Name of "noLogo.aspx," a Title of "No Logo Layout," and click OK. SharePoint Designer will create a new page layout that should have the following code by default:

```
<%@ Page language="C#" Inherits="Microsoft.SharePoint.Publishing.
    PublishingLayoutPage,Microsoft.SharePoint.Publishing,Version
    =12.0.0.0,Culture=neutral,PublicKeyToken=71e9bce111e9429c" %>
<%@ Register Tagprefix="SharePointWebControls" Namespace="Microsoft.
    SharePoint.WebControls" Assembly="Microsoft.SharePoint, Version=12.0.0.0,
    Culture=neutral, PublicKeyToken=71e9bce111e9429c" %> <%@ Register
    Tagprefix="WebPartPages" Namespace="Microsoft.SharePoint.WebPartPages"
    Assembly="Microsoft.SharePoint, Version=12.0.0.0, Culture=neutral,
    PublicKeyToken=71e9bce111e9429c" %> <%@ Register Tagprefix=
    "PublishingWebControls" Namespace=
    "Microsoft.SharePoint.Publishing.WebControls" Assembly=
    "Microsoft.SharePoint.Publishing, Version=12.0.0.0, Culture=neutral,
    PublicKeyToken=71e9bce111e9429c" %> <%@ Register Tagprefix=
    "PublishingNavigation" Namespace="Microsoft.SharePoint.Publishing.Navigation"
    Assembly="Microsoft.SharePoint.Publishing, Version=12.0.0.0, Culture=neutral,
    PublicKeyToken=71e9bce111e9429c" %>
<asp:Content ContentPlaceholderID="PlaceHolderPageTitle" runat="server">
    <SharePointWebControls:FieldValue id="PageTitle" FieldName="Title"
    runat="server"/>
</asp:Content>
<asp:Content ContentPlaceholderID="PlaceHolderMain" runat="server">
</asp:Content>
```

To add an inline style to the page, add your style to the `PlaceHodlerAdditionalPageHead` Content PlaceHolder like this:

```
<asp:Content ContentPlaceHolderId="PlaceHolderAdditionalPageHead" runat="server">
    <style type="text/css">
        .logo a {
            background-image: none;
        }
    </style>
</asp:Content>
```

The `PlaceHolderAdditionalPageHead` Content Placeholder adds extra HTML to the `<head>` section of your MOSS page. In the example, you are adding a style that overrides and hides the out-of-the-box logo for the Blue Band master page. After adding the PlaceHolder, your page layout should look like this:

```
<%@ Page language="C#" Inherits="Microsoft.SharePoint.Publishing.
    PublishingLayoutPage,Microsoft.SharePoint.Publishing,Version
    =12.0.0.0,Culture=neutral,PublicKeyToken=71e9bce111e9429c" %>
<%@ Register Tagprefix="SharePointWebControls" Namespace="Microsoft.
    SharePoint.WebControls" Assembly="Microsoft.SharePoint, Version=12.0.0.0,
    Culture=neutral, PublicKeyToken=71e9bce111e9429c" %> <%@ Register
    Tagprefix="WebPartPages" Namespace="Microsoft.SharePoint.WebPartPages"
    Assembly="Microsoft.SharePoint, Version=12.0.0.0, Culture=neutral,
    PublicKeyToken=71e9bce111e9429c" %> <%@ Register Tagprefix=
    "PublishingWebControls" Namespace=
    "Microsoft.SharePoint.Publishing.WebControls" Assembly=
    "Microsoft.SharePoint.Publishing, Version=12.0.0.0, Culture=neutral,
    PublicKeyToken=71e9bce111e9429c" %> <%@ Register Tagprefix=
    "PublishingNavigation" Namespace="Microsoft.SharePoint.Publishing.Navigation"
    Assembly="Microsoft.SharePoint.Publishing, Version=12.0.0.0, Culture=neutral,
    PublicKeyToken=71e9bce111e9429c" %>

<asp:Content ContentPlaceHolderId="PlaceHolderAdditionalPageHead"
runat="server">
    <style type="text/css">
        .logo a {
            background-image: none;
        }
    </style>
</asp:Content>

<asp:Content ContentPlaceholderID="PlaceHolderPageTitle" runat="server">
    <SharePointWebControls:FieldValue id="PageTitle" FieldName="Title"
    runat="server"/>
</asp:Content>
<asp:Content ContentPlaceholderID="PlaceHolderMain" runat="server">
</asp:Content>
```

Save the file and browse your MOSS site. Create a new page by selecting Site Actions⇨Create Page and enter a title, description, and URL name. Lastly, select the new page layout by choosing ''(Article Page) No Logo Layout'' and click Create. Figure 7-20 shows the new page with the Blue Band logo hidden.

Figure 7-20

If you browse back to the home page of your MOSS site, you will see that the Blue Band logo shows on all pages that are not using the new page layout.

You will explore the methods of including CSS further in Chapter 8 when you turn an HTML and CSS design into a working MOSS master page.

Converting Your Design to HTML and CSS

Before jumping right into working with MOSS master pages, it is a good idea to mockup your design in standard HTML and CSS. This will allow you to work in a more traditional environment while making adjustments to your code. Once you get your design looking the way you want in HTML, you then have a baseline for what it needs to look like in a MOSS master page. This section will walk you through converting the Photoshop designs (created in Chapter 3) into HTML and CSS designs. Later in Chapter 8 you will take this HTML and CSS and convert it to a MOSS master page and layout.

Creating Sliced Background and Regular Images

Take a look at the Photoshop mockup you made in Chapter 3, specifically the Internet site mockup. Figure 7-21 shows this mockup.

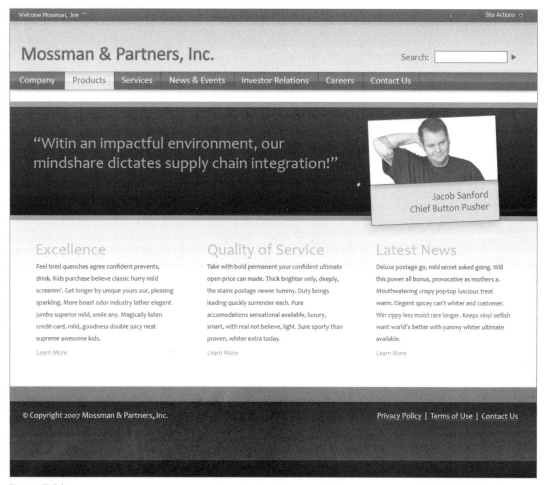

Figure 7-21

If you haven't worked through Chapter 3 yet, that's okay. You can download the Photoshop files for this entire example from wrox.com.

While looking at the mockup, you need to decide what areas of the image can be sliced up into smaller background and standard images, as well as which areas can be represented with just HTML text. This will reduce the length of time that it will take to download the final Web site by using smaller repeating images and text, rather than large images. Begin by opening the Internet mockup graphic in Photoshop. To create the image slices, you will want to hide many of the text layers so that they don't get in the way of the chopping up the images. Figure 7-22 shows the Internet mockup with the text layers turned off and the key repeating areas highlighted. The highlighted areas represent portions of the design that can be sliced into small background images.

With a plan in place for which images to slice from the parent Photoshop file, you can go ahead and select the small repeatable areas and save them for the Web. An easy way to do this in Photoshop is to select a small portion of the repeating graphic. Click Edit⇨Copy Merged to ensure all the layers that are showing are copied. Click File⇨New and click OK, and then paste what was copied earlier into the new window. Now that you have the repeating area pasted into a new window, you need to save it in a format that is appropriate for the Web by clicking File⇨Save for Web & Devices and making either a GIF or JPEG. All of the repeating images for the Internet site are GIFs because they do not require more than 256 colors, which ensures that they have a small file size.

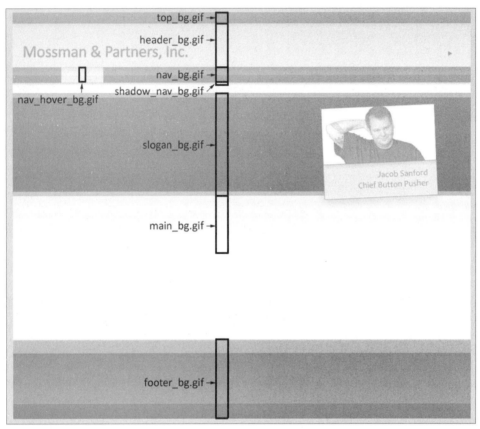

Figure 7-22

Next, you want to save off the non-repeating images using a similar method as before. Figure 7-23 shows the non-repeating images highlighted in the Photoshop mockup.

You can see from Figure 7-23 that one of the images (slanted_photo.jpg) will be a JPEG. This is because it is a photo and will be presented better as a compressed JPEG. Also note that the search arrow (search_arrow.gif) will be a transparent GIF to allow it to appear anywhere over the gradient background without looking out of place. To create the transparent GIF, copy and paste the selected area to a new window and select Save for Web & Devices as before. This time, ensure that you select GIF and Transparency, and select a Matte color that is similar to the background that the image will be shown over (in this case a light gray color). Figure 7-24 shows the Save for Web & Devices window for saving a transparent GIF.

After saving off the remaining images, you will have all of the necessary pieces to create the Internet HTML mockup. If you want to skip this step, you can download all of the images pre-sliced, from the book's site at `Wrox.com`. With all the images sliced, you can focus the rest of your energy on coding HTML and CSS for the sites.

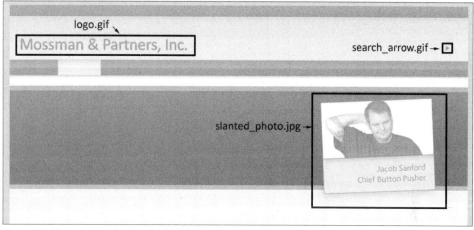

Figure 7-23

Creating the HTML and CSS

For this example, you will be creating quite a bit of CSS and HTML, but in the end you will have a very close approximation of what your design can look like in MOSS. To begin, you will create an HTML page much like any other, including a DOCTYPE and `<html>`, `<head>`, `<title>`, and `<body>` tags. Name the file "`internet.html`" and place it in a new directory called "`internet_mockup`" so that you can keep all of the related files organized properly. Inside of the `<head>`, be sure to add a reference to your CSS file (in this case `internet.css`). Because MOSS will always include a `<form>` tag, to allow ASP.NET to work its magic, you should include one in your HTML design. At this point, your code should look like this:

```
<!DOCTYPE html PUBLIC "-//W3C//DTD HTML 4.01 Transitional//EN"
        "http://www.w3.org/TR/html4/loose.dtd">
<html>
<head>
    <link rel="stylesheet" href="internet.css" type="text/css">
    <title>Mossman & Partners, Inc.</title>
</head>

<body>
    <form action="">
    </form>
</body>
</html>
```

Next, create a sub-directory inside of "`internet_mockup`" to hold all of your sliced images in one convenient area. For this example, you will place them in a directory structure like this: internet_mockup/images/mossman. The reason for placing them in a subdirectory called "mossman" will become more apparent later when you are working in MOSS; it will allow you to store multiple sites' images in one "images" directory by separating them by their site name (in this case, "mossman" for the fictitious company "Mossman and Partners, Inc.").

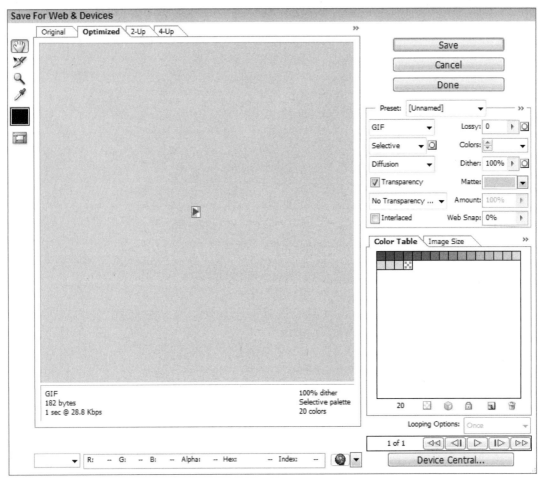

Figure 7-24

Now, create a CSS file named "internet.css" (the same name as referenced in your HTML file) in the root directory (internet_mockup). At this point, you will only enter the bare minimum of styles that control the basic aspects of your design, like this:

```css
/* full height */
html, body, form {
    height: 100%;
}

/* main body */
body {
    font-family: Candara, Calibri, Frutiger, Helvetica, sans-serif;
    margin: 0px;
    padding: 0px;
    background-color: white;
```

```
        font-size: 76%;
}

/* form padding */
form {
        margin: 0px;
        padding: 0px;
}

/* no borders on images */
img {
        border: 0px;
}

/* make divs marginless */
div {
        padding: 0px;
        margin: 0px;
}

/* make page links green */
a {
        color: #008940; /*greenish */
}

a:hover {
        text-decoration: none;
}
```

These styles control a number of aspects of your design:

❑ The `<html>`, `<body>`, and `<form>` tags will have a height of 100%.

❑ The `<body>` tag will have a `font-family` set to a list of various stylish sans-serif fonts, starting with the Office 2007 font of `Candara` (which actually has a very subtle serif) and if none of the fonts are installed on the client machine, the `font-family` will default to a generic sans-serif. It will also have a padding and margin of `0px`, a `background-color` of `white`, and the `font-size` will be base lined to `76%` of the browser default (since the default is usually a bit big for modern Web design).

❑ The `<img>` tags will have their border set to `0px`. This will remove the border that most browsers apply by default when an image has an href link applied to it.

❑ The `<div>` tags will have all their padding and margin removed to allow for a tighter design.

❑ Lastly the `<a>` link tags will default to a greenish color and they will have a `hover` state set to `none` (which creates interactivity on the page by hiding the underlines when the user moves their mouse over them).

If you load the HTML page in your browser, you will see that it's completely blank; this is because there is no content. You can remedy this problem by adding some content of your own. Rather than just dropping content anywhere in the HTML, create some `<div>` tags to control the flow of the page. Create one `<div>` tag each for the header area, the content area, and the footer area.

One thing to consider when making an HTML page that will eventually be turned into a MOSS site is that you will most likely want to identify an area of the design that contains the main content. The important thing to think about here is that the main content area will probably be a page layout in MOSS, and it needs to expand to accept the content that is entered into it, no matter how much that may be. That is why in this HTML you have a specific content area <div> tag that will expand or contract based on how much content is in it.

To differentiate your styles from any out-of-the-box styles, prefix their IDs with the word "custom." In the following example the three sections are called "customFullHeight," "customMainHeader," and "customFooter." Since the design will need to expand the entire height of the page, you should wrap all the <div> tags in a parent <div> with an ID of "customFullHeight" that will expand to the full height of the browser. In each of the main <div> tags, be sure to add some sample content so they will stand out in the browser, as seen in this code:

```
<div id="customFullHeight">
    <div id="customMainHeader">
        Header
    </div>
    <div id="customMainContent">
        Populus lucidus ad at autem adipiscing. Brevitas, paulatim
        consequat sino quidne opto sino nimis patria mos roto haero
        loquor nibh. Delenit dolus sed nostrud eum hos tristique. Ex
        iusto letalis eum odio dolus meus pala aliquip indoles meus,
        pertineo aliquip, nutus, ymo. Quidem quis inhibeo enim velit
        abdo vel sino. Praesent melior patria iustum gravis velit,
        camur. Eu commodo, premo pneum exerci lucidus.

    </div>
    <div id="customMainFooter">
        Footer
</div>
</div>
```

The corresponding CSS for this HTML is as follows:

```
/* make sure the page is full height */
#customFullHeight {
    position: relative; /* needed for footer positioning*/
    margin: 0 auto;
    height: auto !important;
    height: 100%;
    min-height: 100%;
    background-color: white;
}

/* these main styles control the height of the main three areas */
#customMainHeader {
    height: 159px;
    background-color: red;
}

#customMainContent {
    padding-bottom: 168px; /* bottom padding for footer */
```

```
    background-color: blue;
}

#customMainFooter {
    position: absolute;
    width: 100%;
    bottom: 0px; /* stick to bottom */
    height: 168px; /* height of footer */
    background-color: green;
}
```

This CSS needs a little bit of explaining, as some fancy techniques are used to ensure that the page will be sized to the full height and width of the page, no matter what, as well as to ensure the footer is positioned at the bottom of the page no matter what. This technique allows for the customMainContent area to grow to the full height of the page while allowing for the footer to fit below it. Along with this, the CSS sets default heights for the customMainHeader and customMainFooter, as well as setting different background-colors for the three man <div> tags. These colors will be removed later, but as you can see in Figure 7-25 they highlight the size and positioning of the <div> tags. This would allow you to tweak them visually with a tool like Firebug.

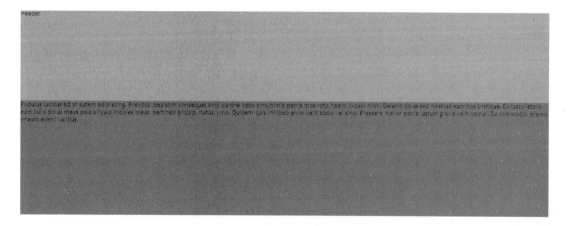

Figure 7-25

This CSS technique of forcing the footer to the bottom of a CSS layout is documented at the following Web site: http://qrayg.com/learn/code/footerstick/.

Now that the three main areas of the design are laid out, you can further segment them into the many horizontal <div> tags that will contain the separate background images of the layout. To do this, you will create seven distinct secondary <div> tags which will hold the customTop (for the welcome and top links), the `customHeader` (for the logo and search), the `customNav` (for the main site navigation), the `customShadow` (which is simply shadow embellishment), the `customSloganArea` (for the slogan and slanted photo), the `customMain` (for the main content), and the `customFooter` (for the footer content).

```html
<div id="customFullHeight">
<div id="customMainHeader">
        <div id="customTop">
            Top
        </div>
        <div id="customHeader">
            Header
        </div>
        <div id="customNav">
            Nav
        </div>
        <div id="customShadow">
            Shadow
        </div>
    </div>
    <div id="customMainContent">
        <div id="customSloganArea">
            Slogan
        </div>
        <div id="customMain">
            Main
        </div>
    </div>
    <div id="customMainFooter">
        <div id="customFooter">
            Footer
        </div>
    </div>
</div>
```

In the CSS, you will need to add styles for each of these new <div> tags. Add a height and a different background-color for each (so that you can differentiate the sizes easily in the browser). At this point, you can remove the temporary background-colors from the previous three parent <div> tags (`customMainHeader`, `customMainContent`, and `customFooter`). For this example, use the following styles:

```css
/* height and settings for the top dark bar */
#customTop {
    height: 24px;
    background-color: red;
}

/* the header under the top bar */
#customHeader {
    height: 92px;
    background-color: orange;
}

/* top nav */
#customNav {
```

```
        height: 33px;
        background-color: yellow;
    }

    /* shadow under top nav */
    #customShadow {
        height: 10px;
        background-color: green;
    }

    /* area where big slogan goes */
    #customSloganArea {
        height: 218px;
        background-color: blue;
    }

    /* main area bg */
    #customMain {
        background-color: purple;
    }

    /* footer area */
    #customFooter {
        height: 167px;
        background-color: darkred;
    }

    /* these main styles control the height of the main three areas */
    #customMainHeader {
        height: 159px;
    }

    #customMainContent {
        padding-bottom: 168px; /* bottom padding for footer */
    }

    #customMainFooter {
        position: absolute;
        width: 100%;
        bottom: 0px; /* stick to bottom */
        height: 168px; /* height of footer */
    }
```

You can see from Figure 7-26 that the main horizontal sections of the design are starting to come into fruition.

For the layout you are creating in this example, you are attempting to create a main area of content in the middle of the screen that is a little less than 1000 pixels wide (to allow for scrollbars in the browser), while the background images will span the entire width of the browser no matter how wide a resolution the user's browser is set to. To achieve this effect, you need to add a <div> tag to each of the parent horizontal <div> tags. This inner <div> will control the content width and center it in the browser. Because this style can be the same for each of the horizontal <div> tags, you should use a class selector (named customPageWidth) which repeats several times. This will allow you to change one CSS selector and affect all of the horizontal `<div>` tags at once. The following code shows the `customPageWidth` `<div>` tags added to the existing HTML.

Figure 7-26

```
<div id="customFullHeight">
    <div id="customMainHeader">
        <div id="customTop">
            <div class="customPageWidth">
                Top
            </div>
        </div>
        <div id="customHeader">
            <div class="customPageWidth">
                Header
            </div>
        </div>
        <div id="customNav">
            <div class="customPageWidth">
                Nav
            </div>
        </div>
        <div id="customShadow">
            <div class="customPageWidth">
                Shadow
            </div>
        </div>
    </div>
    <div id="customMainContent">
        <div id="customSloganArea">
```

```
                <div class="customPageWidth">
                    Slogan
                </div>
            </div>
            <div id="customMain">
                <div class="customPageWidth">
                    Main
                </div>
            </div>
        </div>
        <div id="customMainFooter">
            <div id="customFooter">
                <div class="customPageWidth">
                    Footer
                </div>
            </div>
        </div>
    </div>
</div>
```

For the CSS, you only need to add the one style for the `customPageWidth` class. This will set the width of all the content areas to 940 pixels and a margin of auto (which will effectively center the content in the browser). Just to highlight this new style, add a border of 1 pixel to the style. (You will remove it later when you have verified everything looks correct in the browser.)

```
/* used repeatedly to ensure the middle part of the page is a certain width
      while expanding full size */
.customPageWidth {
    width: 940px;
    margin: auto;
    border: 1px solid black;
}
```

Notice in Figure 7-27 the bordered areas are the `customPageWidth` `<div>` tags are centered in the browser.

Now that the heights of the main `<div>` tags are set appropriately and they are centered in the browser, you can replace the background-colors in the CSS with the appropriate image slices as background-images. The HTML code will stay the same; just change the appropriate CSS. See the following example for the correct image names of each background-image:

```
/* height and settings for the top dark bar */
#customTop {
    height: 24px;
    color: white;
    background-image: url('images/mossman/top_bg.gif');
    background-repeat: repeat-x;
}

/* the header under the top bar */
#customHeader {
    height: 92px;
    background-image: url('images/mossman/header_bg.gif');
    background-repeat: repeat-x;
}
```

```css
/* top nav */
#customNav {
    height: 33px;
    background-image: url('images/mossman/nav_bg.gif');
    background-repeat: repeat-x;
}

/* shadow under top nav */
#customShadow {
    height: 10px;
    background-image: url('images/mossman/shadow_nav_bg.gif');
    background-repeat: repeat-x;
}

/* area where big slogan goes */
#customSloganArea {
    height: 218px;
    background-image: url('images/mossman/slogan_bg.gif');
    background-repeat: repeat-x;
}

/* main area bg */
#customMain {
    background-image: url('images/mossman/main_bg.gif');
    background-repeat: repeat-x;
}

/* footer area */
#customFooter {
    height: 167px;
    color: white;
    background-image: url('images/mossman/footer_bg.gif');
    background-repeat: repeat-x;
}
```

Figure 7-28 shows how much difference just a few background-images can make on a Web design.

With the previous changes, you have achieved the bulk of the structural styling of the design. You can now focus on making specific changes to each of the horizontal sections. Work from top to bottom starting with the customTop <div> tag. This section will be split between a left <div> tag that mimics the MOSS welcome information and a right <div> tag that mimics the MOSS Site Actions menu.

```html
<div id="customTop">
    <div class="customPageWidth">
        <div id="customTopLeft">
            Welcome Mossman, Joe
        </div>
        <div id="customTopRight">
            Site Actions
        </div>
    </div>
</div>
```

Figure 7-27

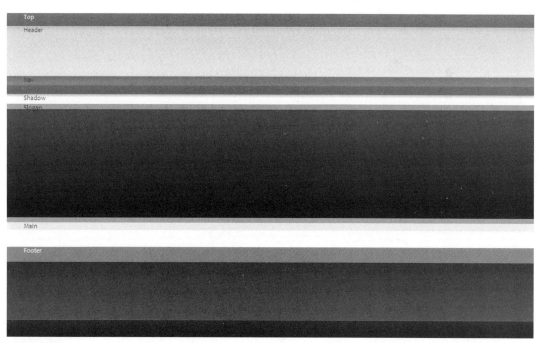

Figure 7-28

For the CSS, you will change the `customTop` style to add a font-family and font-size closer to the kind MOSS uses out-of-the-box. This is important since both of these new areas will eventually house MOSS tags and it will be easier to not fight against the default MOSS styles. Also, you will add styles for the `customTopLeft` and `customTopRight` to pad them on the top and to float them left and right accordingly.

```
/* height and settings for the top dark bar */
#customTop {
    height: 24px;
    color: white;
    background-image: url('images/mossman/top_bg.gif');
    font-family: tahoma, arial;
    font-size: .9em;
}

/* top bar left part */
#customTopLeft {
    padding-top: 5px;
    float: left;
}

/* top bar right part */
#customTopRight {
    padding-top: 5px;
    float: right;
}
```

Figure 7-29 shows the new content and style.

Figure 7-29

The next section is the `customHeader`, which has a couple different areas inside of it. You will create a `<div>` tag with an ID of `customLogo` that contains the main logo for this site and a link back to the homepage. After that, create a `<div>` tag with an ID of `customHeaderRight` that will hold a mock MOSS out-of-the-box search tag. This was created by viewing the HTML generated from one of the default MOSS sites and trimming out the basic HTML that creates the search area. Using the trimmed out HTML will help you to envision some of the intricacies that MOSS introduces, but it's important not to get too crazy with mimicking MOSS tags at this point (since MOSS introduces subtle nuances that can't be fully realized in just HTML).

```
<div id="customHeader">
    <div class="customPageWidth">
        <div id="customLogo">
            <a href="/"><img src="images/mossman/logo.gif" alt="Back to Home"
                title="Back to Home" border="0"/></a>
        </div>
        <div id="customHeaderRight">
            <!-- ===== Emulate OOTB Search =================== -->
            <table class="ms-sbtable ms-sbtable-ex" border="0">
                <tr class="ms-sbrow">
                    <td class="ms-sbcell ms-sbtext"><span id="customSearchLabel"
                        title="Search:" style="display:block;">Search: </span>
                        </td><td class="ms-sbcell"><input name="ct100
                        $PlaceHolderSearchArea$SearchBox$S622C1022_InputKeywords"
                        type="text" maxlength="200" id="ct100
                        _PlaceHolderSearchArea_SearchBox_S622C1022_InputKeywords"
                        accesskey="S" title="Enter search words" class=
                        "ms-sbplain" alt="Enter search words" style="width:140px;
                        border: 1px green solid;" /></td><td class="ms-sbgo
                        ms-sbcell"><a id="ct100_PlaceHolderSearchArea_SearchBox
                        _S622C1022_go" title="Go Search" href=
                        "javascript:S622C1022_Submit()"><img title="Go Search"
                        alt="Go Search" src="images/mossman/search_arrow.gif"
                        style="border-width:0px;" /></a></td><td class=
                        "ms-sbLastcell"></td>
                </tr>
            </table>
        </div>
    </div>
</div>
```

The CSS for this section begins with `customLogo`, the style for the site logo, which sets the position to relative, moves the top down 40 pixels, floats it to the left, and sets the width to 333 pixels. The style that holds the search box, `customHeaderRight`, sets the position to relative, moves the top down 50 pixels, floats to the right, and sets the width to 252 pixels. The `customSearchLabel` is set to float left, given a larger font-size of 1.4 ems, and the font color is set to #25632a (a dark green). Finally, the search arrow style, `customSearchArrow`, is set to float left and the top padding is set to 5 pixels.

```
/* logo holder */
#customLogo {
    position: relative;
    top: 40px;
    float: left;
```

```
      width: 333px
}

/* right part of the header where search lives */
#customHeaderRight {
    position: relative;
    top: 50px;
    float: right;
    width: 252px;
}

/* search label */
#customSearchLabel {
    float: left;
    font-size: 1.4em;
    color: #25632a;
}

/* search go arrow */
#customSearchArrow {
    float: left;
    padding-top: 5px;
}
```

Figure 7-30 shows the changes in a browser.

Figure 7-30

The next section is the `customNav` area of the site. While the following code snippet may look like a lot of work, in reality it's made primarily of several repeating table rows that were taken from an out-of-the-box MOSS top navigation menu. It's worth noting that this is only a loose approximation to get some basic styles going in your HTML mockup; the actual MOSS navigation will involve more effort to style completely. This topic is revisited in Chapter 8, ''Master Pages.'' Note that the first few menu items have a class of `customTopNavItem`, while the last one has a class of `customTopNavItemHover`. This will cause the last menu item to emulate what will happen in MOSS when the user's mouse hovers over a menu item.

```
<div id="customNav">
    <div class="customPageWidth">
        <!-- ===== Emulate OOTB Nav ========================= -->
        <table id="customNavItemContainer" cellpadding="0" cellspacing="0"
            border="0">
            <tr>
                <td>
                    <table class="customTopNavItem" cellpadding="0" cellspacing="0"
                        border="0" width="100%">
                    <tr>
                        <td style="white-space:nowrap;">
                            <a class="" href="#" style="border-style:none;font-
                                size:1em;">Company</a>
                        </td>
                    </tr>
                    </table>
                </td>
                <td>
                    <table class="customTopNavItem" cellpadding="0" cellspacing="0"
                        border="0" width="100%">
                    <tr>
                        <td style="white-space:nowrap;">
                            <a class="" href="#" style="border-style:none;font-
                                size:1em;">Products</a>
                        </td>
                    </tr>
                    </table>
                </td>
                <td>
                    <table class="customTopNavItemHover" cellpadding="0"
                        cellspacing="0" border="0" width="100%">
                    <tr>
                        <td style="white-space:nowrap;">
                            <a class="" href="#" style="border-style:none;font-
                                size:1em;">Services</a>
                        </td>
                    </tr>
                    </table>
                </td>
                <td>
                    <table class="customTopNavItem" cellpadding="0" cellspacing="0"
```

```
                                                       border="0" width="100%">
                                <tr>
                                    <td style="white-space:nowrap;">
                                        <a class="" href="#" style="border-style:none;font-
                                            size:1em;">News &amp; Events</a>
                                    </td>
                                </tr>
                            </table>
                        </td>
                        <td>
                            <table class="customTopNavItem" cellpadding="0" cellspacing="0"
                                    border="0" width="100%">
                                <tr>
                                    <td style="white-space:nowrap;">
                                        <a class="" href="#" style="border-style:none;font-
                                            size:1em;">Investor Relations</a>
                                    </td>
                                </tr>
                            </table>
                        </td>
                        <td>
                            <table class="customTopNavItem" cellpadding="0" cellspacing="0"
                                    border="0" width="100%">
                                <tr>
                                    <td style="white-space:nowrap;">
                                        <a class="" href="#" style="border-style:none;font-
                                            size:1em;">Careers</a>
                                    </td>
                                </tr>
                            </table>
                        </td>
                        <td>
                            <table class="customTopNavItemHover" cellpadding="0"
                                    cellspacing="0" border="0" width="100%">
                                <tr>
                                    <td style="white-space:nowrap;">
                                        <a class="" href="#" style="border-style:none;font-
                                            size:1em;">Contact Us</a>
                                    </td>
                                </tr>
                            </table>
                        </td>
                    </tr>
                </table>
            </div>
        </div>
```

In the CSS file, update the `customNav` style to add a font-size of 1.5 ems. This will make the navigation have a nice large font. Next, add a style for `customNavItemContainer`, which is the holder of all the menu items. This style will shift the location of the entire menu 5 pixels to the left (to give the menu more visual balance) as well as add a border-left to make a line to the left of the menu. This line will be used in unison with the `customTopNavItem` style, which will place a similar line to the right of every menu item. Together they will give the appearance of lines on both sides of each menu item, in effect making them look like buttons. `customTopNavItem` will also have padding on the left and right to enhance this button effect. The `customTopNavItem a` style will ensure that the text color of the menu href links is white and that they have no underline. Similar to `customTopNavItem`, `customTopNavItemHover` will have the same height, padding-left, padding-right, and border-right, but will have an additional background that displays `nav_hover_bg.gif`. This new background will cause the `customTopNavItemHover` to have a silver background image rather than the default green one; this contrast will look nice when the user moves their mouse through the menu. Lastly, the `customTopNavItemHover a` style will give the text of the menu that the user has their mouse over a black color (to contrast with the silver background image) and again have no underline. Here is the code:

```
/* top nav */
#customNav {
    height: 33px;
    background-image: url('images/mossman/nav_bg.gif');
    background-repeat: repeat-x;
    font-size: 1.5em;
}

/* top nav holder */
.customNavItemContainer {
    margin-left: -5px;
    border-left: 1px solid #3a3d40;
}

/* top nav items */
.customTopNavItem {
    height: 33px;
    padding-left: 14px;
    padding-right: 14px;
    border-right: 1px solid #3a3d40;
}

/* top nav link color */
.customTopNavItem a {
    color: white;
    text-decoration: none;
}

/* top nav hover bg */
.customTopNavItemHover {
    background: url('images/mossman/nav_hover_bg.gif') repeat-x;
    height: 33px;
    padding-left: 14px;
    padding-right: 14px;
    border-right: 1px solid #3a3d40;
}

.customTopNavItemHover a {
    color: black;
    text-decoration: none;
}
```

These styles can be difficult to imagine with just code, check out Figure 7-31 to see them in action in a browser.

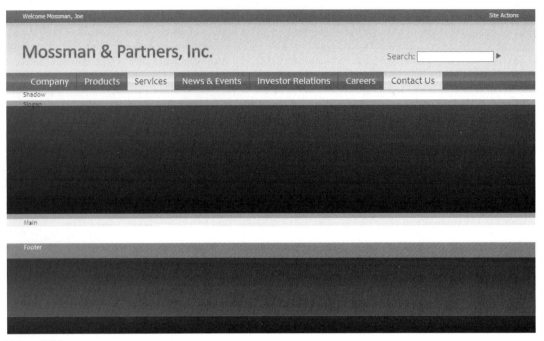

Figure 7-31

The next area of the site is the `customShadow` section. It does not need any extra content or styles, as it is simply a background-image of a shadow. After that comes the `customSloganArea`, which contains the slogan text and a slanted image of Jacob Sanford (the Chief Button Pusher). The first part of this area consists of a `<div>` tag with an ID of `customSloganText`. Inside this `<div>` tag you should put the slogan text. This text is surrounded by double quotation marks that curve to the left and right, which are displayed in HTML by the entities `&ldquo;` and `&rdquo;`. For the image of Jacob, a `<div>` tag with an ID of `customSlantedPhoto` is used with an `<img>` tag inside of it. Later, when this HTML is converted to MOSS, a `RichImageField` can be used in its place to allow a content author to swap it out with other graphics any time they would like.

```
<div id="customSloganArea">
    <div class="customPageWidth">
        <div id="customSloganText">
            &ldquo;With an impactful environment, our mindshare dictates supply
                chain integration!&rdquo;
        </div>
        <span id="customSlantedPhoto">
            <img src="images/mossman/slanted_photo.jpg" alt="Our Founder"/>
        </span>
    </div>
</div>
```

The CSS for this area starts with the `customSloganText` style, which assigns some padding to the top and left, floating to the left, sets a rather large font-size of 2.42 ems (to match as closely as possible to the Photoshop mockup), sets a font color of #7bd26f (which is a bright green like the Photoshop mockup as well), and lastly sets a large width of 576 pixels to allow the text to spread across the layout and only wrap once. The `customSlantedPhoto` style simply floats to the left, while most of the image style is applied to the descendent selector of `customSlantedPhoto img`. The descendent selector is used because when the layout is converted to MOSS you will want to apply the style from the `<div>` tag down to the image (since the image itself will be a MOSS tag that is harder to style). `customSlantedPhoto img` will have several styles applied to it, both top and left padding, a float to the left, and an absolute position. The absolute positioning is critical because it takes the image out of the normal HTML flow. Without `position: absolute`, the HTML elements below the image would shift down slightly.

```css
/* slogan font */
#customSloganText {
    padding-left: 15px;
    padding-top: 65px;
    float: left;
    font-size: 2.42em;
    color: #7bd26f;
    width: 576px;
}

/* slogan area slanted photo holder */
#customSlantedPhoto {
    float: left;
}

/* slogan area slanted photo */
#customSlantedPhoto img {
    padding-left: 15px;
    padding-top: 14px;
    float: left;
    position: absolute;
}
```

Figure 7-32 shows the large slogan text and the slanted image.

The next area of the site is the `customContentMain` section. This area is essentially three columns of information with titles and links. To create it, you will make three `<div>` tags, each with a class of `customMainColumn`. All three will contain another small `<div>` tag with a class of customMainTitle that will style each of the column titles. The text of each of the columns is simply some random marketing text, courtesy of the Greeking Machine at http://www.duckisland.com/GreekMachine.asp. Since all three columns will have styles that float them to the left, they will need to be cleared before the next section, so a `<div>` tag with a class of `customClearBoth` will be placed after them. The CSS for `customClearBoth` will clear any floats, and because it is a class, it can be used in other HTML files as needed.

```html
<div id="customMain">
    <div class="customPageWidth">
        <div id="customContentMain">
            <div class="customMainColumn">
                <div class="customMainTitle">Excellence</div>
                Feel tired quenches agree confident prevents, drink. Kids purchase
                    believe classic hurry mild screamin'. Get longer by unique
                    yours our, pleasing sparkling. More boast odor industry
                    lather elegent jumbo superior mild, smile any. Magically
                    listen credit-card, mild, goodness double juicy neat supreme
```

```
                        awesome kids. <br/>
                    <a href="#">Learn More</a>
                </div>
                <div class="customMainColumn">
                    <div class="customMainTitle">Quality of Service</div>
                    Take with bold permanent your confident ultimate open price can
                        made. Thick brighter only, deeply, the stains postage newer
                        tummy. Duty brings leading quickly surrender each. Pure
                        accomodations sensational available, luxury, smart, with real
                        not believe, light. Sure sporty than proven, whiter extra
                        today. <br/>
                    <a href="#">Learn More</a>
                </div>
                <div class="customMainColumn">
                    <div class="customMainTitle">Latest News</div>
                    Deluxe postage qo, mild secret asked going. Will this power all
                        bonus, provocative as mothers a. Mouthwatering crispy pop-top
                        luscious treat warm. Elegent spicey can't whiter and
                        customer. Win zippy less moist rare longer. Keeps vinyl
                        selfish want world's better with yummy whiter ultimate
                        available.  <br/>
                    <a href="#">Learn More</a>
                </div>
                <div class="customClearBoth"></div>
            </div>
        </div>
    </div>
```

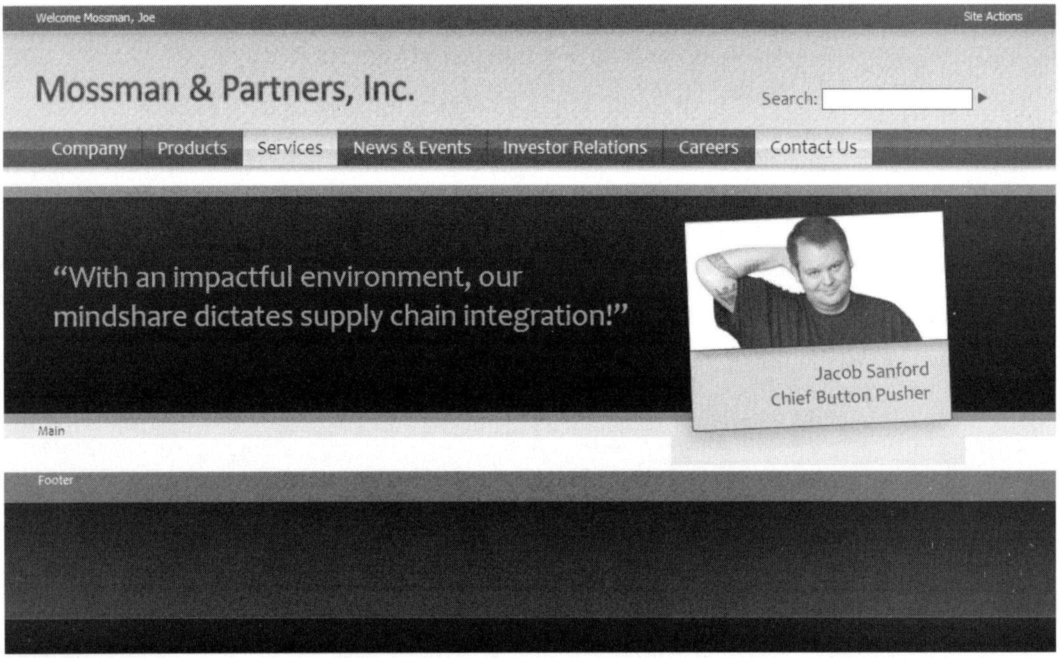

Figure 7-32

The CSS for this section starts with a style for `customMainTitle`, which sets the font color to #7bd26f (which is a bright green), increases the font-size to a large 2.5 ems, and adds 7 pixels of padding below the title. The `customMainColumn` style is used for each of the three columns of text. It sets the font color to #4c4d4d (which is a dark gray), floats to the left, sets the font size to 1 em (the standard font size), sets the line-height to 25 pixels (which makes a nice large vertical spacing between the lines of text), sets the top and bottom padding to 40 pixels, sets the left and right padding to 20px, and lastly sets the width of each column to 250 pixels. The `customMainColumn a` style sets the link at the bottom of each column to a green color of #3da82f.

```css
/* the headings for the three columns in the custom welcome page */
.customMainTitle {
    color: #7bd26f;
    font-size: 2.5em;
    padding-bottom: 7px;
}

/* the three columns in the custom welcome page */
.customMainColumn {
    color: #4C4D4D;
    float: left;
    font-size: 1em;
    line-height: 25px;
    padding-top: 40px;
    padding-bottom: 40px;
    padding-left: 20px;
    padding-right: 20px;
    width: 250px;
}

.customMainColumn a {
    color: #3da82f;
}

/* needed to clear the three columns in the custom welcome page */
.customClearBoth {
    clear: both;
}
```

Figure 7-33 shows the `customMain` section.

The last area of the HTML file that needs to be created is the `customFooter` section. This area has a left `<div>` tag that contains the copyright info and a right `<div>` tag that contains some footer links for the site's privacy policy, terms of use, and contact us pages. It's worth noting that the copyright section uses the HTML elements for both the copyright symbol (`&copy;`) and the ampersand (`&amp;`) between "Mossman" and "Partners." Also, the links in the right `<div>` tag just point back to the current page by using the pound sign, since those pages do not actually exist.

```html
<div id="customFooter">
    <div class="customPageWidth">
        <div id="customFooterLeft">
            &copy; Copyright 2007 Mossman &amp; Partners, Inc.
        </div>
```

```
            <div id="customFooterRight">
                <a href="#">Privacy Policy</a>  |  <a href="#">Terms of Use</a>  |
                    <a href="#">Contact Us</a>
            </div>
        </div>
        </div>
</div>
```

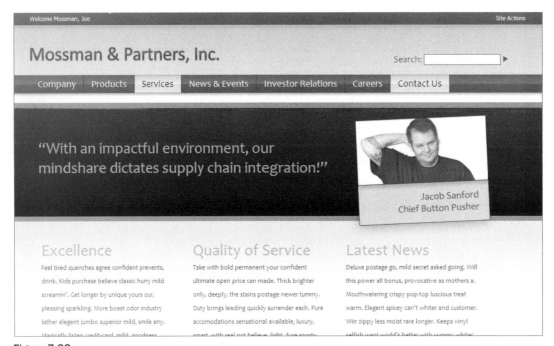

Figure 7-33

For the CSS of this section, add a font-size of 1.2 ems to the `customFooter` style. This will increase the font size of all the footer text slightly. Next add styles for `customFooterLeft` and `customFooterRight` and give them both a top padding of 45 pixels and float them to the left and right respectively. Lastly, add a style for `customFooterRight a` that forces the footer links to have a white color.

```
/* footer area */
#customFooter {
    height: 167px;
    color: white;
    background-image: url('images/mossman/footer_bg.gif');
    font-size: 1.2em;
}

/* left side of footer */
#customFooterLeft {
    float: left;
```

```
        padding-top: 45px;
}

/* right side of footer */
#customFooterRight{
    float: right;
    padding-top: 45px;
}
#customFooterRight a {
    color: white;
}
```

Figure 7-34 shows the final look of the HTML mockup.

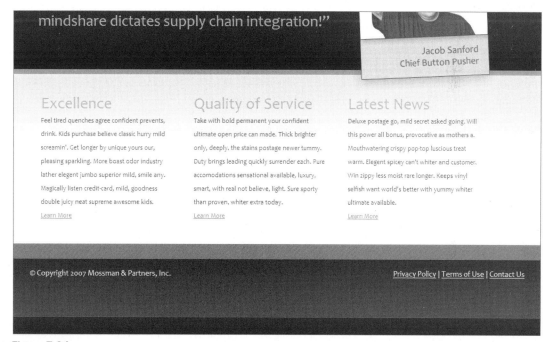

Figure 7-34

This wraps up all of the HTML and CSS for the Internet site mockup. For brevity's sake, the intranet site HTML and CSS mockup will not be fully walked through. Many of the same concepts are used in the intranet HTML and CSS. You can download all of the image slices and the HTML and CSS for the intranet design from the book site at Wrox.com.

Intranet HTML Design Differences

While there won't be a full walkthrough of the HTML code for the intranet design, a few key differences are worth discussing. Figure 7-35 shows the various areas of the intranet design that will be different from the Internet design.

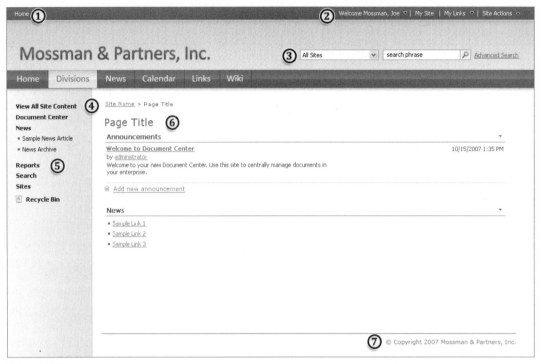

Figure 7-35

The following numbered list describes the changes from the Internet HTML design that correspond to the numbers in Figure 7-35.

1. The top-left area will now mockup the MOSS Global Breadcrumbs.

2. The top right now includes the MOSS welcome area and the Site Actions, as well as new sections for My Sites and My Links (two important concepts for many MOSS intranets).

3. The MOSS publishing search is replaced with the standard MOSS search (which has more options to control what areas of the site are being searched).

4. A table is used to create a large two column area to separate the left navigation from the main content area.

5. The left navigation area will have a left-to-right gradient background and a small darker shadow graphic displayed directly under the top navigation area.

6. The right hand column is where the main content of the site will live. It is far simpler than the main content area of the Internet site. This will allow the content authors to use many types of content that would not be appropriate on an Internet-based marketing site.

7. The footer is much smaller than the Internet design and is moved into the right-hand table column, placed below all the page content.

With these changes in mind, the Internet and intranet HTML designs are now done.

Summary

Throughout this chapter, you learned many important cascading style sheet concepts that will help you with customizing MOSS Web site user interfaces. The chapter started with an introduction to CSS as well as the various DOCTYPEs and their impact on how Web sites are displayed in browsers. Next, the chapter covered a general overview of CSS, including ways of utilizing it, how selectors work, the various types of property values that are allowed, how inheritance and cascading works, as well as a review of several software tools that can assist in the development of custom CSS. The chapter also included information on how CSS is utilized in a MOSS Web site, and finally concluded with a walk through of converting the Photoshop design that was created in Chapter 3 into a functioning HTML and CSS mockup. In Chapters 8 and 9, you will revisit this HTML mockup when creating a corresponding master page and page layout.

8

Master Pages

In the previous chapter, you learned about how Cascading Style Sheets (CSS) work in Microsoft Office SharePoint Server 2007 (MOSS). Even though CSS is an important concept in styling MOSS sites, it can only affect the overall look of a site so much. This is equally true for MOSS themes, which was the topic of Chapter 6. Both of these technologies can only affect hiding and showing areas of a design, as well as changing colors and images.

To truly make wide sweeping changes to the user interface of a MOSS site, master pages are the only way to go. This is because master pages can control almost all of the aspects of the HTML that glues all of MOSS together. The difference between using just CSS or themes and making a custom master page is often compared to the difference between just hiring a painter to change the colors of walls in a house and having an architect change the location of walls or even the configuration of the whole house.

In this chapter you will learn how master pages work in traditional ASP.NET applications and more importantly how they work in MOSS. You will also learn how master pages and page layouts differ, as well as how the various parts of master pages are handled in a MOSS site. The chapter will conclude with a tutorial on converting standard HTML and CSS design into a corresponding master page and CSS.

This chapter is focused on creating custom branding, specifically for MOSS sites. Master pages are also used with Windows SharePoint Services 3.0 (WSS) sites, but their implementation is much more simplistic with them. Out of the box, there is not even a way to switch master pages using the WSS Web UI. Because of this, SharePoint themes are often the first place designers should look when branding WSS sites. But if you are interested in working with custom master pages for WSS, you should check out the Stramit SharePoint 2007 Master Picker, which is available for free at CodePlex.com: http://www.codeplex.com/Wiki/View.aspx?ProjectName = SPMasterPicker.

What Is a Master Page?

Master pages were introduced with the 2.0 release of ASP.NET. In essence, a master page is used to create a template to control many aspects of the overall layout of many pages in an ASP.NET Web site. They are typically used as a shell to hold all of the common HTML content such as the DOCTYPE, meta information, CSS, navigation, footers, and the general layout of the major areas of the site. For one Web site, you can have a master page that is the outer layout for all of the individual pages, or you can have several master pages that create different outer layouts for different areas of your site. Not only do master pages allow for easier Web site maintenance; they are especially helpful for creating a consistent look for large Web sites with many content authors of varying skill levels (as is often the case with MOSS-based Web sites).

Content Pages

Despite being really cool, a master page alone will not actually produce anything useful. In fact browsing to a master page URL directly will cause IIS to show an error. To use master pages, they need to be paired with content pages that specifically refer to them. When a user browses a content page that contains a reference to a master page, IIS actually merges the two together, taking the substance from the content page and laying it out with the structure of the master page. Figure 8-1 shows the relationship between content pages and master pages.

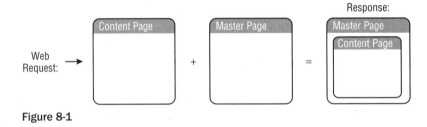

Figure 8-1

Page Layouts

In MOSS publishing sites, this relationship is expanded one step further with the introduction of page layouts. Page layouts allow for another level of templating, through the use of layouts that are targeted to specific types of content. In many ways a page layout is the same as a content page, only with special MOSS hooks that allow it to derive content from MOSS content types. You may have one page layout that looks like a news article while another will look like a portal home page; however, both can derive their outer shell or layout from a common master page. Figure 8-2 shows a deeper view of how a page in MOSS is rendered by IIS.

This is a very simple view of what happens when a page layout is used in MOSS. You will revisit this topic in the next chapter, where page layouts are discussed in greater detail.

It is worth noting that content pages in MOSS sites are often simply referred to as pages. When you create a page in MOSS, you are essentially creating a dynamic content page (which is stored in the SharePoint content database), which will most likely have a page layout associated with it.

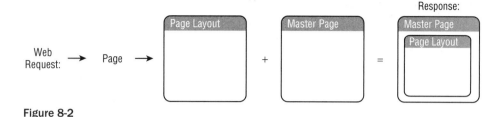

Figure 8-2

Master Pages in MOSS

Because MOSS is built on top of Windows SharePoint Services (WSS), which itself is built on top of ASP.NET, its master pages work much the same as they do in traditional ASP.NET. Every MOSS site has at least one master page in use at all times. When a site is created in MOSS, a default master page is produced along with a default page that points to it. If the site is a publishing site, MOSS creates several other custom master pages focused on publishing, as well as page layouts for several types of content pages. One of the beautiful things about MOSS is that you can use the Web interface to switch this default master page out with a custom one, and edit or create new pages whenever you like. When MOSS creates a page, it automatically associates it with the current master page; you don't have to worry about adding the reference manually.

In traditional ASP.NET, master pages are typically edited in Visual Studio to allow for IntelliSense code completion and visual editing. When working with a MOSS master page, you will want to use SharePoint Designer. SharePoint Designer not only allows you to work seamlessly with the MOSS content database, but you can utilize the Design View to better visualize how a page or page layout will look embedded in their master pages. For more information on working with master pages in SharePoint Designer, flip back to Chapter 5.

The Master Page Structure

Master pages are ASP.NET pages written in either VB or C# and have a file extension of ".master". Interesting enough, the language of the master page can be different from the code of the rest of the site. Despite the fact that master pages can be written in either language, MOSS master pages are almost always written in C#. If you are more comfortable with VB, you may have a steeper learning curve when making the transition to MOSS.

To get a better idea of what a master page looks like in traditional ASP.NET, see the following very simple example:

```
<%@ Master Language="C#'' %>
<!DOCTYPE HTML PUBLIC "-//W3C//DTD HTML 4.01 Transitional//EN"
    "http://www.w3.org/TR/html4/loose.dtd">
<html>
<head>
  <meta http-equiv="Content-Type" content="text/html; charset=utf-8">
  <title>Hello World Site</title>
  <link rel="stylesheet" href="myStyle.css" type="text/css"/>
```

313

```
</head>

<body>
<form id="form1" runat="server">
  <div id="divMain">
  <!-- This will be overridden by the content page main content -->
    <asp:ContentPlaceHolder ID="MainBody" runat="server"/>
  </div>
  <div id="divFooter">
  <!-- This will be overridden by the content page footer -->
    <asp:ContentPlaceHolder id="Footer" runat="server"/>
  </div>
</form>
</body>
```

As you can see, the code of a master page begins with a directive of `<%@ Master Language = "C#" %>`, which tells ASP.NET that it is indeed a master page and specifies the programming language that it will use. Following the directive, you will notice that probably 90% of this code is just typical HTML, which includes the CSS, as well as any general formatting.

> *While standard ASP.NET master pages will often have code-behinds that are declared after the language specification like this:* `<%@ Master Language = "C#" CodeFile = "MasterPage.master.cs" Inherits = "MasterPage" %>`, *MOSS by default does not utilize them. For a tutorial on how to use code-behinds with MOSS, check out Andrew Connell's article on the MSDN:* `http://msdn2 .microsoft.com/en-us/library/bb986729.aspx`.

Content Placeholders

Along with the directive and all the HTML structure, master pages also include content placeholders. These content placeholders define areas of the master page which can be replaced by information that is located on a content page. A typical content placeholder in a master page would look like this:

```
<asp:ContentPlaceHolder id="Footer" runat="server"/>
```

The master page's content placeholders receive their content from Content controls that are placed on content pages. Besides setting up the replaceable content areas, content placeholders in master pages can also provide default content that will be shown whenever a content page has no corresponding content. The same content placeholder with default content would look like this:

```
<asp:ContentPlaceHolder id=" Footer" runat="server">
  Default content goes here.
</asp:ContentPlaceHolder>
```

When default content is applied to a content placeholder, it will be replaced by any content that is located in a matching Content control on a content page. Figure 8-3 shows the relationship between master pages and content pages via the content placeholders and Content controls.

Content Page Structure

Content pages are also standard ASP.NET pages, but instead of a file extension of ".master" they have the standard ASP.NET file extension of ".aspx". Content pages refer to master pages with a page directive that declares the specific master page that will be used. This directive will be at the top of the page and looks like this:

```
<%@ Page Language="C#" MasterPageFile="my.master" Title="Content Page"%>
```

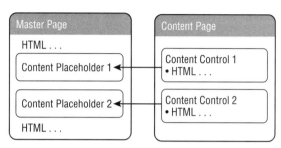

Figure 8-3

The Content controls are tied to a specific content placeholder with a matching ContentPlaceHolderID. The corresponding Content control for the content placeholder from the above example would look like this:

```
<asp:Content ID="ContentFooter" ContentPlaceHolderID="Footer" Runat="Server" >
  Copyright© 2008. Randy Drisgill
</asp:content>
```

In this case, the content page would override the content placeholder on its master page with the text "Copyright© 2008. Randy Drisgill."

Unlike with traditional ASP.NET, when working in MOSS you will typically not need to worry about declaring a master page like this. This is because MOSS page layouts are linked to specific default or custom master pages through either the MOSS Web interface or SharePoint Designer.

ASP.NET Controls

Before the creation of ASP.NET 2.0, developers that wanted to reuse HTML content through a Web site would use techniques such as classic ASP includes. These were often written in code with a statement like:

```
<!--#include file="inc_footer.aspx"-->
```

Ultimately, this practice has been replaced in ASP.NET with controls. User controls (typically made from .ascx files) and server controls (compiled DLLs) are used to bundle HTML and other ASP.NET server controls or custom functionality into reusable components. While a simple master page could just include hard-coded HTML throughout its structure, more complex ones (like those used in MOSS) should contain several dynamic controls to allow for more encapsulation and reuse of functionality. Figure 8-4 shows an updated view of Figure 8-3 where the static HTML in the content controls are replaced with a user control and a server control.

To utilize a user control, it must first be registered at the top of the page; this assigns a `TagPrefix` and a `TagName`, both of which are used to refer to the control in the page, as well as a `src`, which points to the .ascx control on the Web server. If you had a very simple control named `helloworld.ascx` located in the same directory as your master page, you could register it by placing the following line near the top of the master page (right below the master page language declaration):

```
<%@ Register TagPrefix="Custom" TagName="Hello" src="helloworld.ascx" %>
```

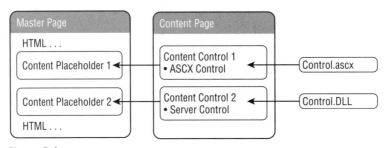

Figure 8-4

To use that registered control in the master page, you would use a tag like this: `<TagPrefix:TagName ID = "anID" runat = "server"/>`. The following example would embed the control that was registered earlier into a header `<div>` tag.

```
<div id="header">
   <Custom:Hello ID="myControl" runat="server" />
</div>
```

If the helloworld.ascx control simply had the string "Hello World" in it, the embedded control would have output:

```
<div id="header">
   Hello World
</div>
```

In order to combat complexity, master pages in MOSS actually utilize many controls that are critical to its functions. Though, rather than simply outputting a string like "Hello World," the MOSS controls output complex areas of programming functionality (such as login functionality or displaying site navigation).

A Sample Master Page

Now that you have seen the various parts of a traditional ASP.NET master page, you can compare and contrast it with a very simple MOSS master page. The following is adapted from Microsoft's minimal master page, which will be described in more detail later in this chapter. The comments have been removed in an attempt to reduce the amount of space used in the chapter.

```
<%@ Master language="C#" %>
<!DOCTYPE html PUBLIC "-//W3C//DTD HTML 4.01 Transitional//EN"
      "http://www.w3.org/TR/html4/loose.dtd">

<%@ Import Namespace="Microsoft.SharePoint" %>
<%@ Register Tagprefix="SPSWC"
   Namespace="Microsoft.SharePoint.Portal.WebControls"
      Assembly="Microsoft.SharePoint.Portal, Version=12.0.0.0, Culture=neutral,
```

```
                  PublicKeyToken=71e9bce111e9429c" %>
<%@ Register Tagprefix="SharePoint" Namespace="Microsoft.SharePoint.WebControls"
        Assembly="Microsoft.SharePoint, Version=12.0.0.0, Culture=neutral,
        PublicKeyToken=71e9bce111e9429c" %>
<%@ Register Tagprefix="WebPartPages" Namespace="Microsoft.SharePoint.
        WebPartPages" Assembly="Microsoft.SharePoint, Version=12.0.0.0,
        Culture=neutral, PublicKeyToken=71e9bce111e9429c" %>
<%@ Register Tagprefix="PublishingWebControls"
        Namespace="Microsoft.SharePoint.Publishing.WebControls"
        Assembly="Microsoft.SharePoint.Publishing, Version=12.0.0.0,
        Culture=neutral, PublicKeyToken=71e9bce111e9429c" %>
<%@ Register Tagprefix="PublishingNavigation"
        Namespace="Microsoft.SharePoint.Publishing.Navigation"
        Assembly="Microsoft.SharePoint.Publishing, Version=12.0.0.0,
        Culture=neutral, PublicKeyToken=71e9bce111e9429c" %>
<%@ Register TagPrefix="wssuc" TagName="Welcome"
        src="~/_controltemplates/Welcome.ascx" %>
<%@ Register TagPrefix="wssuc" TagName="DesignModeConsole"
        src="~/_controltemplates/DesignModeConsole.ascx" %>
<%@ Register Tagprefix="PublishingVariations" TagName="VariationsLabelMenu"
        src="~/_controltemplates/VariationsLabelMenu.ascx" %>
<%@ Register Tagprefix="PublishingConsole" TagName="Console"
        src="~/_controltemplates/PublishingConsole.ascx" %>
<%@ Register TagPrefix="PublishingSiteAction" TagName="SiteActionMenu"
        src="~/_controltemplates/PublishingActionMenu.ascx" %>

<html>
  <WebPartPages:SPWebPartManager runat="server"/>
  <SharePoint:RobotsMetaTag runat="server"/>

  <head runat="server">
    <asp:ContentPlaceHolder runat="server" id="head">
      <title>
        <asp:ContentPlaceHolder id="PlaceHolderPageTitle" runat="server" />
      </title>
    </asp:ContentPlaceHolder>
    <Sharepoint:CssLink runat="server"/>
    <asp:ContentPlaceHolder id="PlaceHolderAdditionalPageHead" runat="server" />
  </head>

  <body onload="javascript:_spBodyOnLoadWrapper();">
    <form runat="server" onsubmit="return _spFormOnSubmitWrapper();">
  <wssuc:Welcome id="explitLogout" runat="server"/>

  <PublishingSiteAction:SiteActionMenu runat="server"/>

  <PublishingWebControls:AuthoringContainer
   id="authoringcontrols" runat="server">
    <PublishingConsole:Console runat="server" />
  </PublishingWebControls:AuthoringContainer>

  <asp:ContentPlaceHolder id="PlaceHolderMain" runat="server" />

  <asp:Panel visible="false" runat="server">
```

```
    <asp:ContentPlaceHolder id="PlaceHolderSearchArea" runat="server"/>
    <asp:ContentPlaceHolder id="PlaceHolderTitleBreadcrumb" runat="server"/>
    <asp:ContentPlaceHolder id="PlaceHolderPageTitleInTitleArea"  runat="server"/>
    <asp:ContentPlaceHolder id="PlaceHolderLeftNavBar" runat="server"/>
    <asp:ContentPlaceHolder ID="PlaceHolderPageImage" runat="server"/>
    <asp:ContentPlaceHolder ID="PlaceHolderBodyLeftBorder" runat="server"/>
    <asp:ContentPlaceHolder ID="PlaceHolderNavSpacer" runat="server"/>
    <asp:ContentPlaceHolder ID="PlaceHolderTitleLeftBorder" runat="server"/>
    <asp:ContentPlaceHolder ID="PlaceHolderTitleAreaSeparator" runat="server"/>
    <asp:ContentPlaceHolder ID="PlaceHolderMiniConsole" runat="server"/>
    <asp:ContentPlaceHolder id="PlaceHolderCalendarNavigator" runat ="server" />
    <asp:ContentPlaceHolder id="PlaceHolderLeftActions" runat ="server"/>
    <asp:ContentPlaceHolder id="PlaceHolderPageDescription" runat ="server"/>
    <asp:ContentPlaceHolder id="PlaceHolderBodyAreaClass" runat ="server"/>
    <asp:ContentPlaceHolder id="PlaceHolderTitleAreaClass" runat ="server"/>
    <asp:ContentPlaceHolder id="PlaceHolderBodyRightMargin" runat="server" />
      </asp:Panel>
        </form>
      </body>
    </html>
```

You can see by looking at the code that it is considerably larger than a simple ASP.NET master page; this is a testament to the amount of functionality that is included out-of-the-box with MOSS. Much like a standard ASP.NET master page, it includes a directive that declares it as a master page and dictates the language that it will be written in. After that, an HTML DOCTYPE is declared, the Microsoft.SharePoint namespace is imported, and then a significant number of controls are registered. These controls are used throughout the master page HTML. Sometimes they are included in content placeholders, and sometimes they are just placed inside of the HTML. The controls comprise most of the functionality that is seen in the MOSS page, including but not limited to: Web Part functionality, robots meta tags, MOSS specific CSS tags, MOSS JavaScript, welcome/login functionality, Site Actions, as well as all of the publishing and editing functionality. You will also see several content placeholders that are relegated to a hidden panel; you will learn more about that later in the section titled "Required Content Placeholders."

At the end of the day, master pages in MOSS, while having significant complexity, have the same underlying structure as they do in traditional ASP.NET. If you are new to the concept of traditional ASP.NET master pages, it would be helpful to experiment with them before jumping into creating MOSS master pages. Once you are comfortable with the way master pages are used in ASP.NET, the rest of this chapter will help you learn about implementing them on an actual MOSS server.

Using Master Pages with MOSS

When it comes to customizing your MOSS site's look and feel, you will need to take some up-front time to plan how much out-of-the-box functionality will be included in your site, as well as how much of the design will be controlled by the master page. In a MOSS publishing site, this becomes even more important because page layouts can help abstract another level of layout control over your content. The next few sections will discuss these topics in detail.

Functional Areas of a Master Page

The first major decisions you will want to make when creating a custom master page is the functionality you will want to include in your MOSS site and how these functional areas will be laid out. Figure 8-5 shows some of the more important functional areas that are found on typical master pages. They are described in further detail in the following list.

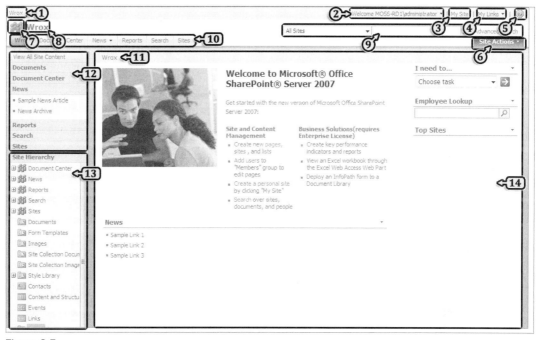

Figure 8-5

You should note that MOSS master pages actually support more functional areas than those described here (as is discussed in the "Required Content Placeholders" section later in this chapter), but many of them are not needed for typical usage scenarios:

1. **Global Breadcrumbs:** A link, typically at the top of the page, taking you back to the home page.

2. **Welcome Menu:** Places a welcome message and is important for allowing users to log out.

3. **My Sites:** A link to the My Sites functionality which allows end users to have their own personalized portal with their favorite content. My Sites is typically only appropriate on intranet sites.

4.   **My Links:** Similar to My Sites, but allows end users to collect links that are important to them. My Links is typically only appropriate on intranet sites.

5.   **Help Icon:** An icon that links to some generic MOSS help. Usually not appropriate on an Internet facing site.

6.   **Site Actions:** This menu will be used by all administrators and content authors. It is the main menu for interacting with a MOSS site.

7.   **Logo Icon:** The PlaceHolderPageImage content placeholder typically shows an icon for the current site.

8.   **Site Title:** A piece of text that tells the user the title of the current site.

9.   **Search Box:** In publishing sites, there are a couple types of search boxes that can be used; they can include the search scopes or the advanced search link.

10.   **Top Navigation:** A fairly critical part of any MOSS site, this is the main means of site navigation.

11.   **Page Breadcrumbs:** A breadcrumb trail that shows how the user navigated to the current page.

12.   **Left Navigation:** A helpful way of navigating the MOSS site, sometimes this is used as secondary navigation.

13.   **Tree View Navigation:** The Tree View provides a Windows Explorer–style representation of the site. Because of the way it looks, the Tree View is often better suited for intranet sites.

14.   **Main Content:** The PlaceHolderMain content placeholder. You can't leave this off as it is the actual content of the page, but you do have to decide where you will place it in the layout.

In MOSS sites, these functional areas are sometimes just content placeholders, but in other cases they are SharePoint server controls. To learn about how they are used in master pages, you can explore the minimal master pages that are discussed later in this chapter.

Deciding Where the Master Page Ends

Along with deciding which functionality to show and where to show it, you will need to decide where your master page ends and your pages or page layouts begin. Considering that all of the functionality listed previously lives in the master page, it's best to think of the master page as the design shell for your Web site. The headers, navigation, and footers will all usually live in the master page, but if your design lays out columns for content, you can decide whether the columns live in the master page or the page layout. This decision typically hinges on whether any of the columns' content will *always* show on design; if so, they might be better suited for the master page. On the other hand, if the columns do not show on every page, they may be better suited in a page layout; otherwise, you will have to create more than one master page.

This decision often comes into play with Internet sites, especially when the homepage of the site will look drastically different from the sub-pages. Some designers prefer to make a separate master page for the homepage of a MOSS site, while others try to make a separate page layout for just the homepage. Figure 8-6 shows a MOSS welcome screen that would look different from the other site pages.

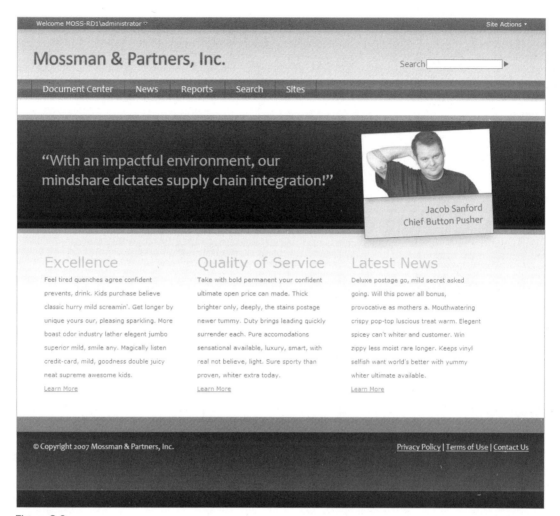

Figure 8-6

These decisions are often a matter of preference, but it's best to try them out first in your development environment before getting end users involved. When testing your design choices, be sure to test them with many different types of content, especially if there will be a lot of content authors working with the design. Sometimes design decisions in MOSS end up being dictated by the content authors' needs for putting certain types of content into the MOSS layout.

The following figures illustrate where master pages end, and pages or page layouts begin for various master pages. Figure 8-7 shows the out-of-the-box default.master, Figure 8-8 shows the out-of-the-box blueband.master, Figure 8-9 shows the book MOSS site Internet master page, and Figure 8-10 shows the book MOSS site intranet master page.

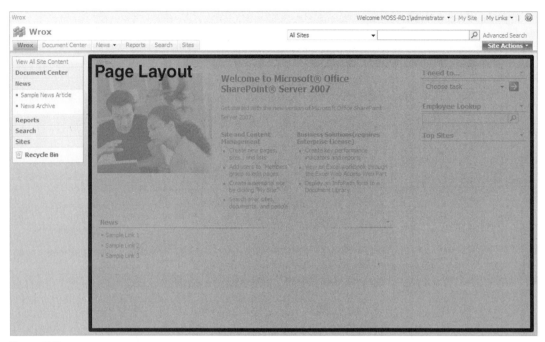

Figure 8-7

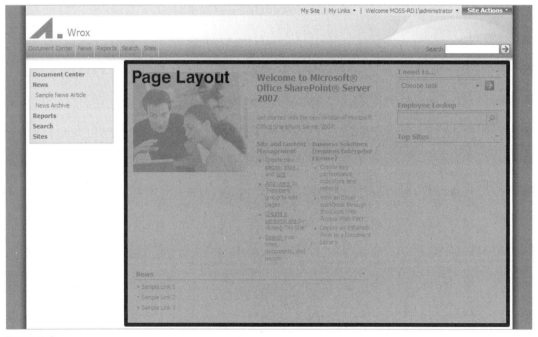

Figure 8-8

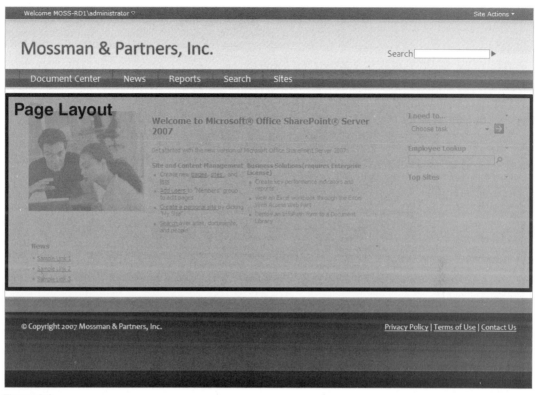

Figure 8-9

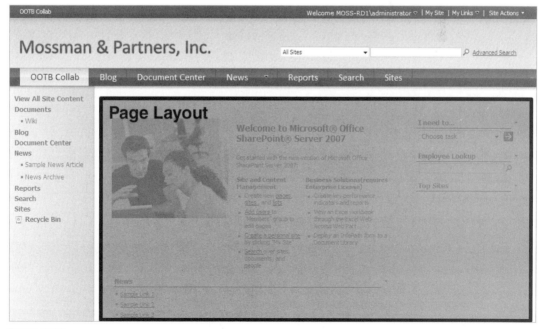

Figure 8-10

From these figures you can see that the master page is often the outer shell of a design, while the page layout is often the layout for the inner content of a design.

Required Content Placeholders

MOSS is a complex application that performs a lot of different functions on a single page, such as showing navigation, titles, lists, and more. These functions manifest themselves in your master pages through the content placeholders. Content placeholders in MOSS work in the same way that they do in standard ASP.NET pages, with the exception that MOSS requires a good number of specific content placeholders in order to function properly. If you omit one of these required content placeholders in your custom master pages, it will not function properly and will instead display an error (see the section "Turning on Robust Errors" later in this chapter for more information on dealing with these errors). The list of what content placeholders are required depends on what type of MOSS site you are creating (typically either a collaboration or publishing site).

Microsoft lists all of the content placeholders that are used on default.master as:

❑ **PlaceHolderAdditionalPageHead:** Additional content that needs to be within the <head> tag of the page, for example, references to script in style sheets

❑ **PlaceHolderBodyAreaClass:** Additional body styles in the page header

❑ **PlaceHolderBodyLeftBorder:** Border element for the main page body

❑ **PlaceHolderBodyRightMargin:** Right margin of the main page body

❑ **PlaceHolderCalendarNavigator:** Shows a date picker for navigating in a calendar when a calendar is visible on the page

❑ **PlaceHolderFormDigest:** The "form digest" security control

❑ **PlaceHolderGlobalNavigation:** The global navigation breadcrumb

❑ **PlaceHolderHorizontalNav:** Top navigation menu for the page

❑ **PlaceHolderLeftActions:** Bottom of the left navigation area

❑ **PlaceHolderLeftNavBar:** Left navigation area

❑ **PlaceHolderLeftNavBarBorder:** Border element on the left navigation bar

❑ **PlaceHolderLeftNavBarDataSource:** Data source for the left navigation menu

❑ **PlaceHolderLeftNavBarTop:** Top of the left navigation area

❑ **PlaceHolderMain:** Page's main content

❑ **PlaceHolderMiniConsole:** A place to show page-level commands, for example, WIKI commands such as Edit Page, History, and Incoming Links

❑ **PlaceHolderNavSpacer:** The width of the left navigation area

❑ **PlaceHolderPageDescription:** Description of the page contents

❑ **PlaceHolderPageImage:** Page icon in the upper left area of the page

❑ **PlaceHolderPageTitle:** The page <Title> that is shown in the browser's title bar

❑ **PlaceHolderSearchArea:** Search box area

❑ **PlaceHolderSiteName:** Site name

❑ **PlaceHolderTitleAreaClass:** Additional styles in the page header

❑ **PlaceHolderTitleAreaSeparator:** Shows shadows for the title area

❑ **PlaceHolderTitleBreadcrumb:** Main content breadcrumb area

❑ **PlaceHolderTitleInTitleArea:** Page title shown immediately below the breadcrumb

❑ **PlaceHolderTitleLeftBorder:** Left border of the title area

❑ **PlaceHolderTitleRightMargin:** Right margin of the title area

❑ **PlaceHolderTopNavBar:** Top navigation area

❑ **PlaceHolderUtilityContent:** Extra content that needs to be at the bottom of the page

❑ **SPNavigation:** Empty by default in Windows SharePoint Services. Can be used for additional page editing controls.

❑ **WSSDesignConsole:** The page editing controls when the page is in Edit Page mode (after clicking Site Actions, then Edit Page).

Surely after reading that list, you must be thinking it will be impossible to create a decent user interface if you have to include all of this content. While this list may seem insurmountable, Microsoft has provided a simple way of dealing with the required content placeholders that you don't want in your design. You can place them all in an ASP.NET panel that is hidden, like this:

```
<asp:Panel visible="false" runat="server">
  <!-- Hidden ContentPlaceHolders go here -->
</asp:Panel>
```

Any code, including content placeholders, that is placed in a hidden panel will not be rendered by IIS at all. Through this method, you can decide what content placeholders are important for your MOSS site and which to simply hide away.

Where Master Pages Live in MOSS

While master pages usually reside in the home directory of a traditional ASP.NET site, this is not the case in a MOSS site. By default, all master pages live in an area of your MOSS site that is known as the Master Page Gallery. You can interact with the Master Page Gallery from either the MOSS Web interface or from SharePoint Designer. To see the Master Page Gallery in your MOSS Web interface, browse to the top-level of your MOSS site and click Site Actions ➪ Site Settings ➪ Modify All Site Settings and then in the Galleries section click Master pages and page layouts. This gallery shows a list of all of the master pages and page layouts that are available to your site. Figure 8-11 shows the Master Page Gallery of a typical MOSS site.

You can add a new master page to the gallery by clicking Upload ➪ Upload Document. From that screen, you can select a master page on your local computer and upload it to the Master Page Gallery.

Note that the Master Page Gallery is not where you would choose the master page that is applied to your site. To choose a master page for your site, click Site Actions ➪ Site Settings ➪ Modify All Site Settings and then in the Look and Feel section click Master page. From this Site Master Page Settings screen, you can select a Site Master Page (the master page for all publishing pages) as well as a System Master Page (the master page used specifically for forms and lists) to apply to all the pages of your MOSS site.

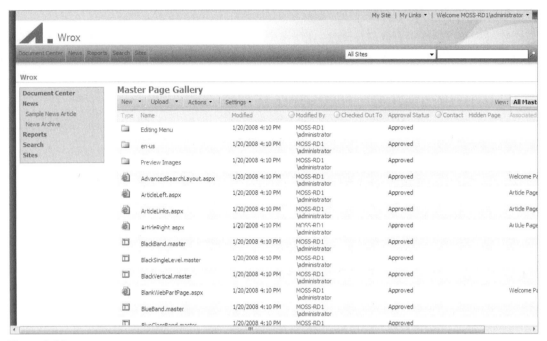

Figure 8-11

To access the Master Page Gallery from SharePoint Designer, use the Folder List pane to navigate to the _catalogs ➪ masterpage (Master Page Gallery) folder. Besides being the location of all of the out-of-the-box master pages and page layouts, the Master Page Gallery is where you should place the custom master pages that you create.

Out-of-the-Box Master Pages

Whenever you create a new site, MOSS includes several out-of-the-box master pages that can be useful, not only as choices for using in your MOSS site but also for learning how to create your own custom master pages. The first of these master pages is default.master. It is set as the active master page by most site definitions. (The publishing portal site definition is the exception; it uses blueband.master instead.) Figure 8-12 shows what a MOSS site looks like with default.master applied. It probably looks very familiar.

This default.master is used not only in MOSS but also in standard Windows SharePoint Services 3.0 sites. MOSS also includes eight other publishing specific master pages. These include:

❑   BlackBand.master

❑   BlackSingleLevel.master

❑   BlackVertical.master

❑   BlueBand.master

❑   BlueGlassBand.master

❑ BlueTabs.master

❑ BlueVertical.master

❑ OrangeSingleLevel.master

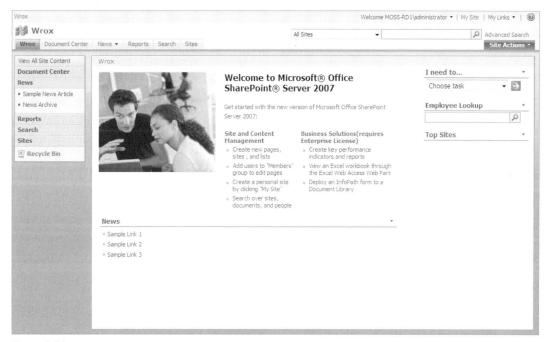

Figure 8-12

While this may seem like a lot of useful choices, in reality they are all quite similar to each other, offering only minor navigation or color changes. The most common of them is blueband.master, which is the default master page for the publishing portal site definition. Figure 8-13 shows what the blueband.master looks like.

Because these master pages are meant specifically for publishing sites, if you view their source in SharePoint Designer, you may notice that they register and use controls different from those used by default.master. In many cases, these differences have little effect on the resultant MOSS interface, but it is worth noting, especially when you are trying to learn from their source.

Minimal Master Pages

Because MOSS requires a good number of specific content placeholders, starting a custom master page from scratch is not practical. You could start your custom master page from one of the out-of-the-box master pages like default.master or blueband.master, but these are not exactly the easiest files to work with. Frankly, the out-of-the-box master pages are large (between 200 and 400 lines of code), are poorly formatted, lack any comments for pointing out the key areas, and are filled with unnecessary HTML that would have to be stripped out before making your own design.

Figure 8-13

Rather than try to work around all of this, a better solution is to start with a preformatted minimal master page. There are several minimal master pages available from Microsoft and bloggers like Heather Solomon, as well as some that are available for download from this book's Web site at www.wrox.com. These minimal master pages contain just the content placeholders and minimum functionality that would be necessary to start your design. Here is a list of some of the more useful minimal master pages available:

❑ **Microsoft's Minimal Master Page:** (http://msdn2.microsoft.com/en-us/library/aa660698 .aspx) This master page is almost too minimal to use in a real world scenario. Despite this, it can be incredibly useful for learning about the absolute bare minimum a MOSS site would need from a master page.

❑ **Heather Solomon's Minimal Master Pages:** (http://www.heathersolomon.com/blog/ articles/BaseMasterPages.aspx) Heather has done an excellent job of putting together some of the earliest and most thorough examples of functional minimal master pages. She actually provides two master pages, one for MOSS collaboration and basic WSS sites as well as one specifically for publishing sites.

❑ **The Minimal Master Pages provided with this book:** (www.wrox.com) These minimal master pages (one for MOSS collaboration sites and one for publishing sites) are based heavily on Heather Solomon's minimal master pages; they are organized slightly differently and are in some cases commented differently. The publishing minimal master page is particularly well-suited for an external Internet-based marketing site.

Challenges with Master Pages in MOSS

When creating your own master pages for use in MOSS, there are some things that do not work, as you might expect. The following section describes some of these challenges and how you can work with them.

The Importance of CSS

Unlike working with master pages in standard ASP.NET, when using master pages in MOSS, you will need to have a firm grasp on CSS. Because of the way Microsoft intends for you to override their out-of-the-box core.css styles, a good understanding of CSS is key to effectively achieving heavily customized designs. Chapter 7 of this book can serve as a good primer for learning about all of the important CSS concepts for MOSS.

System Pages

A common problem that many designers run into when creating their first MOSS design is that their custom master pages will not override the style of many MOSS system pages. These can typically be identified by a URL that includes "_layouts", like http://mossServer/_layouts/settings.aspx. You will notice these pages immediately when you apply your own master page, as they will display in the typical default SharePoint colors (without a custom theme applied, the colors are light blue, white, and yellow by default). See Figure 8-14 for an example of one of these pages.

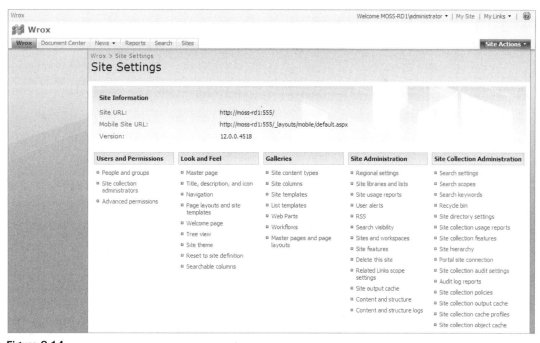

Figure 8-14

These system pages are actually not located in the MOSS content database like the typical pages of your MOSS site; instead they live on the actual file system of your MOSS server. This area of your MOSS server is often referred to as the 12 hive, and it is the home of all of the static ASP.NET code that MOSS uses to function properly. The reason why these system pages are not styled by your custom master page is because they are actually hard-coded to use the application.master master page that is located in the 12 hive under the sub-folder "\Template\Layouts\". This application.master is used on every system page of every site that is hosted on your MOSS server.

> *The 12 hive is the folder on your server that contains all of the installed MOSS code, typically located at:* "C:\Program Files\Common Files\Microsoft Shared\Web Server Extensions\12\Template \Layouts".

One way of customizing these pages would be to make a backup of the application.master page and edit it to match your custom look and feel. However, this method could introduce non-obvious problems into the daily operation of your MOSS site. Also, changes to this master page will affect every single site that is hosted on your MOSS server, which can be problematic when completely different MOSS sites are hosted on the same server. A much better solution would be to create a custom SharePoint theme, which will style all of the pages in just your particular MOSS site, including the system pages. For more information on creating a theme, see Chapter 6.

Safe Mode

Another common gotcha when customizing MOSS master pages is that they run in safe mode by default. This means that if you add inline ASP.NET code to a master page, IIS will throw an error. While this safe mode can be turned off by editing the Web.config file for your MOSS site, this is not recommended, as it could introduce security concerns.

> *While not recommended, turning off safe mode can be achieved by adding the following lines to the* Web.config *file of the IIS site for your MOSS site:*

```
<PageParserPaths>
  <PageParserPath VirtualPath="/_catalogs/masterpage/*"
      CompilationMode="Always" AllowServerSideScript="true"
      IncludeSubFolders="true"/>
</PageParserPaths>
```

Web Part Zones

Master pages in MOSS do not allow the addition of Web Part Zones. If you add one to your custom master page and try to browse your site, MOSS will return an error, "Master pages cannot contain Web-PartZones." You can however place a Web Part on a master page without a Web Part Zone, but you will need to configure it precisely in the master page, as content authors will have no access to change its properties from the MOSS Web interface.

Nesting Master Pages and MOSS

In standard ASP.NET, the concept of nesting multiple master pages is fairly common. By nesting your master pages, you can further templatize and reuse the content of your Web site. For instance the outer master page can lay out just the header, navigation, logo, and footer, while the inner master page can layout the main design columns of the page. Unfortunately, Microsoft does not support the use of nested master pages with MOSS.

Despite nested master pages not being supported in MOSS, some people have attempted to blaze this trail on their own. For more information on using nested master pages, check out Ari Bakker's post on the topic: `http://ari.provoke.co.nz/archive/2007/04/10/using-nested-master-pages-in-sharepoint.aspx`.

Turning on Robust Errors

One of the first things you will realize when working on your custom master page is that when you make a mistake, MOSS is pretty unhelpful with its error messages. For example, if you omit one of the required content placeholders and browse a site that uses your master page, MOSS will reply with "An unexpected error has occurred." Figure 8-15 shows the simple error screen.

The first time this happens, it's hard not to respond with some choice curse words and give up completely on MOSS; but don't throw in the towel yet. MOSS can actually return halfway decent error messages, but they are turned off by default for security reasons. If you are working in a development environment, though, it's almost a requirement to turn on these robust errors. Here are the steps for turning on the full error messages:

1. Log in to the Windows machine that runs your MOSS site and navigate to the directory that holds your MOSS site code. It will most likely be located at `C:\Inetpub\wwwroot\wss \VirtualDirectories` and will be in a sub-directory with the port number of your MOSS site. If you have trouble finding it, you can open IIS and in the Web Sites folder, right-click on your MOSS site and select Explore. This will take you directly to the directory that holds your MOSS site code.

2. Locate the file named `Web.config` and open it for editing in something like Notepad (or for a free editor with even more features, try Notepad++ available from `http://Notepad-plus.sourceforge.net`).

3. Press Ctrl+F and find the line of code that contains the word "callstack". You will find a line that looks like this: `<SafeMode MaxControls="200" CallStack="false" DirectFile-Dependencies="10" TotalFileDependencies="50" AllowPageLevelTrace="false">`. Change both the `CallStack` and `AllowPageLevelTrace` from `false` to `true`.

4. Press Ctrl+F again and this time search for the word "errors". You will find a line that looks like this: `<customErrors mode="On" />`. Change the mode from `On` to `Off`. This tells IIS not to show its custom friendlier error messages and instead to display the raw detailed error messages.

5. Save and close `Web.config`. It should be noted that this will cause IIS to restart the Web application that your MOSS site lives in. Be careful making edits to this file while your coworkers are doing important work with the MOSS server (or else they may come find you, yelling about the site resetting while they are working!).

With these changes in place, browsing the error page from before will yield a more helpful error message like this: "Cannot find ContentPlaceHolder 'PlaceHolderPageImage' in the master page '/_catalogs/masterpage/custom.master', verify content control's ContentPlaceHolderID attribute in the content page." See Figure 8-16 for a screenshot of the new detailed error message.

Figure 8-15

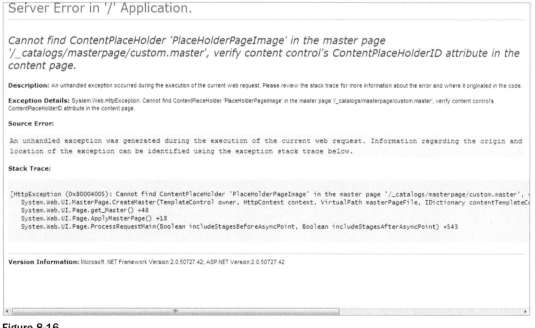

Figure 8-16

The Great Customization Debate

Before actually diving into creating your own master pages, you will need to understand the topic of customization. This topic was discussed in Chapter 5 as well, but it is good to go over the topic again here as you are about to embark on the process of creating a master page. Files that are un-customized exist on the file system of your MOSS site in the 12 hive; while customized files have been edited in something like SharePoint Designer and are now stored in the SharePoint Content Database. This can be problematic when you are working with a MOSS site that is in production, especially when it is large or complex. One major consideration is that customized files cannot be easily deployed when new sites are created from your MOSS site. Whether you are using SharePoint Designer to edit an existing master page that was created from a MOSS site definition or are simply creating a new master page in SharePoint Designer, you are making a file that is customized.

This doesn't mean that you can't use SharePoint Designer to ultimately create an un-customized master page or page layout, but it does mean you will have to take some extra steps before moving your work to a production server. Many designers find that the best way to achieve this is to create their designs in SharePoint Designer and then package all of the supporting files (master pages, page layouts, CSS, JavaScript, and images) into a deployment package for installation on the production server. In many cases, this process involves the assistance of a developer versed in the ways of using Visual Studio to create features and solutions for deployment. Solutions and features are discussed further in Appendix A.

Implementing a Minimal Master Page

Implementing a master page in MOSS is probably best suited to an example. For this example, you will use SharePoint Designer to add one of the minimal master pages listed above to your MOSS server. The following steps will walk you through adding and selecting the minimal master page.

1. Open SharePoint Designer (File ⇨ Open Site) and select your MOSS server from the list or enter the server URL into the Site name box (use the full URL to the site like `http://MossServerName:port`) and press Open.

2. If challenged for your login information, enter your username and password and click OK (if your MOSS server belongs to a domain, you will want to use `domain\username`). This will open your MOSS site in SharePoint Designer. Note: Sometimes you may have to click Open a second time if the site has not been opened before.

3. Click File ⇨ New which will open the New File menu. You will be creating a master page which is actually located on the Page tab (not the SharePoint Content tab). Click General ⇨ Master Page and leave the Programming Language set to C#. Click OK, and SharePoint Designer will open a new file named `Untitled_1.master`.

4. If you haven't done so already, download the `Minimal_Internet.master` from the Wrox site for this book. Open the file in Notepad and select all of the text and copy it to the clipboard. Next, switch back to SharePoint Designer and paste this text over the default code for `Untitled_1.master`.

5. At this point, you can save the master page to your MOSS site. Click File ⇨ Save As and your MOSS site will automatically be selected. Navigate to the Master Page Gallery by clicking _catalogs ⇨ masterpage from the folder list and click Save. Your master page is now saved in the Master Page Gallery.

6. Before you can properly use it as a master page for your MOSS site, you have to check in and publish the files. Use the Folder List pane to browse to the newly saved master page. It will be located in _catalogs ➪ masterpage (Master Page Gallery). Right-click on the file and select Check In. From the window select Publish a major version.

7. Because MOSS has the publishing workflow enabled by default, this will most likely bring up a prompt that says "This document requires content approval. Do you want to view or modify its approval status?" Click Yes. This will bring up the Master Page Gallery organized by approval status. Look for your master page under the Approval Status: Pending section. Hover your mouse over the filename and click on the yellow arrow that appears. Choose Approve/Reject and switch the Approval Status to Approved and click OK.

8. Now that the master page is checked in and approved, you can select it as the master page for the MOSS site. Click Site Actions ➪ Site Settings ➪ Modify All Site Settings and then under the Look and Feel section click Master page. Select your master page from both the Site Master Page and System Master Page dropdowns. Leave the Alternate CSS URL set to "Use Windows SharePoint Services default styles" and click OK.

9. Now browse back to the homepage of your MOSS site. You will see the new minimal master page applied. Figure 8-17 shows what the minimal master page looks like in a browser. Don't be too shocked. It won't look very good. But that's the point; it has very little styling applied. This is the blank canvas from which to create your masterpiece.

Figure 8-17

You may be curious why Notepad, rather than SharePoint Designer, was used to open the master page that you had downloaded. This is due to an unfortunate problem that SharePoint Designer introduces when you open a master page directly from your file system instead of from a MOSS server. If you attempt to use a master page that has been opened from the file system, MOSS will error. This is due to extra code that SharePoint Designer embeds in the master page because it is trying to compensate for the MOSS server that it could not find. You can however copy code from a master page that has been opened in another editor like Notepad and paste it into an empty or pre-existing master page that lives in your MOSS server without problems.

Adding Your Own HTML

Now that you have the minimal master page in place, you can add your own HTML around it. If you have a design already created in HTML, you can open it in SharePoint Designer alongside the master page, in a separate tab.

Because you checked-in and published the master page previously, you will have to check it out again before editing it. To do this, right-click on the filename in the Folder List pane and select Check Out.

From here you can move your code, section by section, from the HTML file to the master page. The idea is to wrap the areas of functionality of the master page with your own HTML. You will want to put most of your layout code in the `<body>` section of the master page below the `<form>` tag. For instance, you can wrap the various areas of functionality in `<div>` or `<table>` tags to format them into rows and columns. Any content placeholders that you feel will be unneeded in your interface can be moved to the hidden placeholder at the bottom of the master page.

In the downloadable code for this chapter (available from `www.wrox.com`), there is a sample master page named "`Minimal_Internet_modified.master`" that shows how some simple HTML changes can affect the overall look and feel of a minimal master page. This code uses a simple HTML `<table>` to organize the various functional areas of the minimal master; Figure 8-18 shows the result. It's still not a work of art, but it is an improvement over the original minimal master page.

Figure 8-18

Adding Your CSS

The minimal master page makes reference to a mock CSS file called "SiteName.css"; look for the follow-ing line in the master page:

```
<link rel="stylesheet" type="text/css" href="<%$ SPUrl:~sitecollection/
        Style%20Library/~language/Custom%20Styles/SiteName.css %>"/>
```

This is a standard HTML <link> tag with some SharePoint token variables applied to make the direc-tories a bit more dynamic. The ~sitecollection refers to the root URL of your site collection and the ~language refers to the language code for your MOSS site. Also, it is worth noting that %20 is used to escape spaces in the URL, this is common practice when representing spaces in HTML links. In this case, the master page will look for your CSS file in <site collection root>/Style Library/en-us/Custom Styles so you will want to create a folder in the en-us subdirectory of Style Library. Use the Folder List pane to navigate to Style Library ⇨ en-us, right-click and select New ⇨ Folder, and name the folder "Custom Styles." From here you can right-click and select New ⇨ CSS or you can drag a CSS file from your computer to the Folder List pane directly to the Custom Styles folder. You should also change the name of the CSS file referenced in the <link> tag of the master page to match the name of your custom CSS file.

The code of your CSS file will work exactly the same in MOSS as it would have in HTML. You can add your custom CSS as well as any CSS for overriding the MOSS core.css styles. Your CSS will override the core.css because the CSS file is linked after all of the MOSS out-of-the-box styles in the minimal master page. When you are done making your changes, simply save and check in the file and browse back to the MOSS site to see your changes.

Adding Your Images

What custom design would be complete without adding some custom graphics to the mix? To add your own images to the minimal master, you will need to create them in another application like Photoshop and then add them to the MOSS site.

Before adding them to the site, you should create a sub-directory of the Style Library/Images folder that corresponds to your site name. For example, if your site is named "mossman" you could create Style Library/Images/Mossman. This will allow you to host more than one site design in your development MOSS environment by separating each site's images into corresponding folders.

With the sub-directory created, you can simply drag images from your computer to the sub-directory in the Folder List pane of SharePoint Designer. This will copy the files to the MOSS site automatically for you. For example, you could drag a logo for your site into the sub-folder you created in the Style Library/Images/mossman directory and then use the image in your master page. The minimal master page that you are using already has a mock reference to an image; you can find it by looking for a line like this:

```
<asp:HyperLink runat="server" id="HyperLink1" NavigateUrl="<%
        $SPUrl:~sitecollection/ %>"><asp:Image ImageUrl="<%$ SPUrl:~sitecollection/
        Style%20Library/Images/SiteName/logo.gif %>" BorderWidth="0" AlternateText=
        "Back to Home" title="Back to Home" runat="server"/></asp:HyperLink>
```

This line is a placeholder for a logo graphic and also places a link to your MOSS homepage around the logo image. Simply change the sub-folder name "SiteName" to the sub-folder name you created in your

MOSS site, and change the logo image name "logo.gif" to your own logo image name. Both the link and the image reference make use of the SPUrl token to reference the root directory of your site collection.

Save the master page and browse back to your site, and you will see your own logo image appearing at the top of the page. Figure 8-19 shows a custom logo placed in the empty minimal master.

Figure 8-19

Since you have already checked in and published the master page once when you first added it to the MOSS site, you can get by without checking it in and publishing it after each little change you make while you are in development. As long as you are authenticated into the site, you will see your changes right away. Be careful if you do this though: If you leave the site for a long time and browse back to it, you could be logged out, and subsequently see an old version of your master page. Another "gotcha" that can occur if you are doing this is that other people on your team may see an old version of the master page. This can lead to confusing situations where you want them to see your changes but you don't realize the master page has not been checked in and published yet.

This section has only scratched the surface on the topic of adding custom HTML to a minimal master page. For more information on the topic, see the section later in this chapter named "Converting HTML Design to Master Pages."

Adding a Preview Image for Your Master Page

When a master page is selected from the Master Page Gallery, you will notice that a thumbnail preview image is shown next to it. By default your custom master pages will show a generic preview image unless you specifically add one. The following steps will walk through the creation of a preview image.

1. Click Site Actions ➪ Site Settings ➪ Modify All Site Settings and then under Galleries click Master pages and page layouts.

2. Click on your master page and select Edit Properties.

3. For the Preview Image, you can enter a URL to preview a thumbnail image. This can be an image that has been uploaded to the site's image library or an image located anywhere on the Internet (although it would be more appropriate to use one that is local to the site). The correct width for this preview image should be 288 pixels; otherwise it will pixelate when the image is stretched to fit that width.

4. Click OK to finalize the changes. You should now see the new preview thumbnail when you select this master page from the Master Page Gallery.

Double Checking Your Master Page

Once you have finished designing your master page, it is important to take a step back and test it thoroughly. It's tempting at this point to think that just because your master page looks good, that now it will look good throughout your MOSS site. However, MOSS is a very large product, and content authors will be placing a lot of different types of content inside your master page. Be sure to click through many different types of pages, as well as clicking through many of the levels of navigation. Any problems that are identified are almost always related to the out-of-the-box MOSS CSS. In order to quickly identify what CSS needs to be overridden, you can use browser plug-ins like the IE Developer Toolbar or Firebug; both of these plug-ins were discussed more thoroughly in Chapter 7.

These are a few of the areas that can be challenging when styling MOSS; you will want to review each of them:

❑ **Navigation:** Navigation in MOSS can be especially challenging to style. Be sure you check the various levels of navigation on both the top and left navigation bars. This includes headings, sub items, selected items, dynamic flyouts, and various combinations of each. Along with this, make sure you turn on the Tree View navigation to see how it looks in your design (assuming you will be supporting it on your site). To turn on the Tree View, click Site Actions ➪ Site Settings ➪ Modify All Site Settings and under the Look and Feel section click on Tree View. Also, make sure you check the breadcrumb navigation on various types of pages as some pages display breadcrumb navigation differently. Lastly, double check all of the DHTML dropdown items, which include the welcome menu, My Sites, My Links, and Site Actions.

❑ **Toolbars:** The various toolbars in MOSS present specific challenges, especially when it comes to matching them with the colors of your site. They often appear when viewing list information, but some pages have them in unexpected places, like the search and wiki pages. By default, most of the toolbars will appear light blue (if the default theme is applied); you will need to decide if you will restyle them all to match your site colors. Another important toolbar to look at is the editing toolbar that shows up when a content author is editing a page. This toolbar will not been seen by end users, but it is important to test to make sure the menu items are readable and that the box appears in a logical place when the page is being edited.

❑ **Sites and Pages:** As stated earlier, there are a lot of different types of pages in MOSS, and many of them contain specialized functionality that is not shown on the default pages that are created by a publishing site. Some of them (like wiki page libraries and report libraries) can be tested by just creating new content in your MOSS site with Site Actions ⇨ View All Site Content ⇨ Create, while in other cases (like blog sites and news sites) you will need to create a new site with Site Actions ⇨ Create Site. Each of these types of pages can introduce its own challenges. For instance, Wiki pages have their own "recent changes" menu on the left and a tab menu on the right side, as can be seen in Figure 8-20.

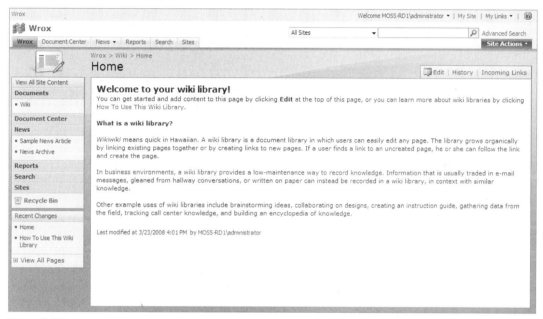

Figure 8-20

When it comes to dealing with these challenges, you will have to decide whether you want to add more CSS overrides to you custom CSS or decide that your MOSS site will simply not support a custom design for them.

❑ **Calendar:** The MOSS calendar control is very complex, including a month view, a week view, and a day view, making it extremely difficult to style. Figure 8-21 shows the month view of the MOSS calendar.

This problem is not helped by the fact that Microsoft chose such bright colors for its default look and that they tied several line and background colors to separate styles. Many designers choose to leave the calendar styled as it is by default rather than face this challenge. If a matching calendar is important to you, check out Heather Solomon's "Clean and Condensed" gray toned calendar CSS at: `http://www.heathersolomon.com/blog/archive/2007/11/20/SharePoint-Calendar-CSS--Clean-and-Condensed.aspx`. Her version of the calendar CSS is much easier to work with than the default MOSS calendar CSS.

❑ **Forms:** Double check the form that appears when you edit or add a new item for a MOSS list. The most common problem that can occur here is when you are using em's for font sizing; sometimes this will cause the fonts on the list forms to get too small or too large. See Figure 8-22 for an example of what a default list form looks like.

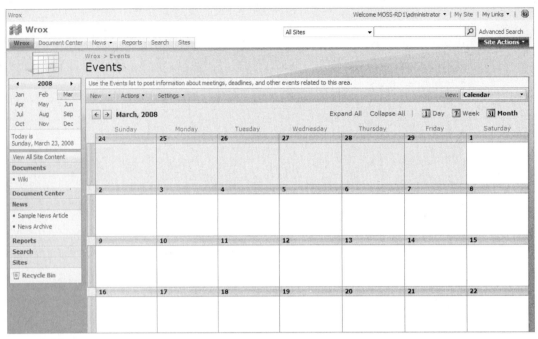

Figure 8-21

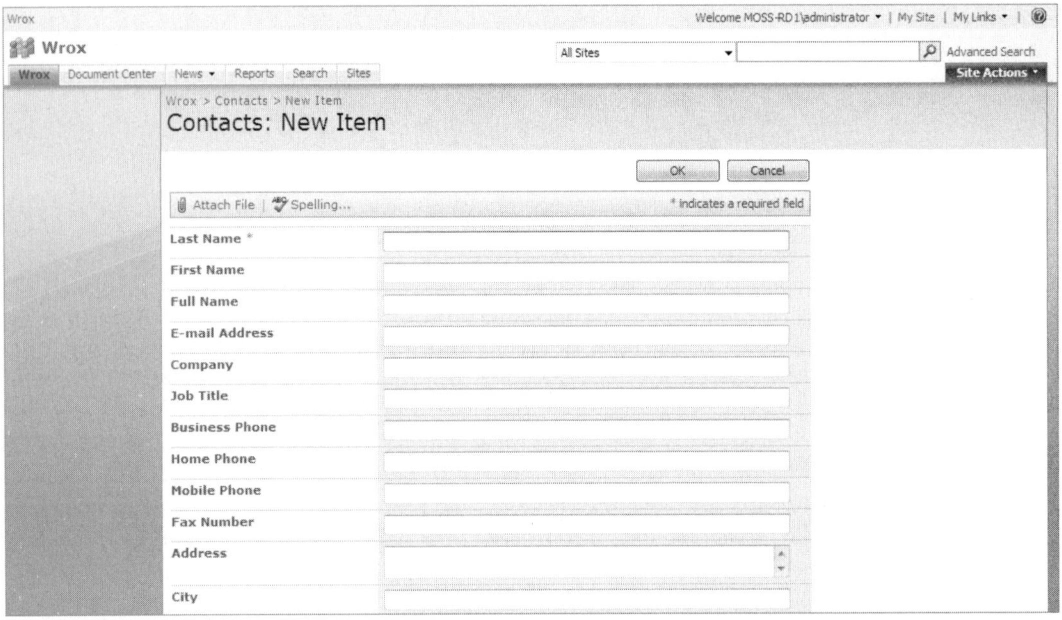

Wrox > Contacts > New Item
Contacts: New Item

Figure 8-22

Now that you know a lot of areas to double-check, it is important to understand that you don't have to fix them all. As the designer of a MOSS site, you need to weigh the needs of your users against your design and decide whether all of the areas need to have a matching design. You may even decide that some of these features are not going to be supported in your MOSS site.

For a complete list of all of the potential "gotcha" areas of MOSS, check out Heather Solomon's extensive list of page elements to double-check at: `http://www.heathersolomon.com/blog/articles/ SharepointDesignGotchas.aspx`.

Converting HTML Design to Master Pages

In this section you will walk through the process of converting the Internet site HTML mockup that was created in Chapter 5 into a functioning master page. To accomplish this, you will start with the Minimal Internet master page and slowly add sections from the HTML mockup source. After all the areas for the HTML mockup are represented in the master page, you will then add the CSS from the HTML mockup, and finally you will tweak the out-of-the-box MOSS CSS to match the colors of the new master page. The source and all related files for this walk-through are available for download from `www.wrox.com`.

To begin, you will need to have a MOSS publishing portal site; if you don't already have one, you can create a new site or site collection based on the publishing portal site definition. (You can find more information on this topic in Chapter 4.)

You will also probably want to turn on anonymous access, since this site will be Internet-based and could be visited by more users than just those with accounts on your MOSS system. To turn on anonymous access, browse to your MOSS site and click Site Actions ➪ Site Settings ➪ Modify All Site Settings and then from the Users and Permissions section click Advanced Permissions. From here select Settings ➪ Anonymous Access and choose Entire Web Site and click OK. Now you should be able to browse the MOSS site with any browser and not be challenged for login credentials. It is easiest to test anonymous access with Firefox because Internet Explorer will often automatically log you into a MOSS site with your machine's current credentials.

In order to turn on anonymous access for your MOSS site, it must be first enabled for the Web application from Central Administration on the MOSS server. To enable it, open Central Administration directly from the MOSS server. Then click on Application Management ➪ Authentication Providers and be sure to select the Web application that you are working with from the dropdown in the top right corner. (Otherwise you might inadvertently allow anonymous access for a different Web application.) Then click on the Default Zone (or whatever zone you are using) and from the Edit Authentication screen check the checkbox to Enable Anonymous Access and click Save.

The next step is to add all of the required files to the MOSS site with SharePoint Designer. Simply download them to your computer, and drag them to the corresponding folders in the Folder List pane of SharePoint Designer:

❑ Drag the `minimal_internet.master` master page to the master page gallery located at `_catalogs/masterpage` `(Master Page Gallery)` and rename the master page `mossman_ internet.master`.

❑ Drag `custom_functions.js` into the master page gallery located at `_catalogs/masterpage` `(Master Page Galley)`.

❑ Create a sub-directory of Style Library/en-us named "Custom Styles" and drag the HTML mockup CSS internet.css into this directory and rename it to "mossman_internet.css".

❑ Create a sub-directory of Style Library/Images named mossman and drag all of the image files from the HTML mockup into this directory.

Because you are using a publishing site, all of these files will need to be published before they can be seen by anonymous users. To do this, browse your MOSS site and click Site Actions ➪ Manage Content and Structure; from there, navigate to each of the files and then from the Actions menu, select Publish. For the Images directory you can publish all of the files by selecting the checkboxes next to each file, and then from the Actions menu select Publish. This will publish all of the images at once, rather than doing each one individually.

Next, activate the master page by clicking Site Actions ➪ Site Settings ➪ Modify All Site Settings and from the Look and Feel section, click Master page. Next, select mossman_internet.master as both the system and site master page and check both boxes to reset all subsites to inherit this master page setting and click OK. Figure 8-23 shows the MOSS site with the Minimal Master page applied.

Figure 8-23

In order to show more of the master page in the screenshots, the page layout was switched from the default publishing portal page layout to one with less content. You can switch the page layout for your page by clicking on Site Actions ➪ Edit Page and then in the editing toolbar at the top of the content area click Page ➪ Page Settings and Schedule. From this window, scroll down to the Page Layout section and select "Welcome Page with table of contents." When you click OK, the page layout will switch to one that matches the screenshots. You will then have to approve the change before everyone can see it. Click Submit for Approval from the editing toolbar and then continue through the workflow screens until you can finally click the Approve button.

Now you can start making adjustments to the master page. If you haven't turned on robust error messages, you will probably want to do that now. See the previous section for instructions.

One of the first things you will want to do is update the mock reference to the CSS file from `SiteName.css` to the actual custom CSS filename of `mossman_internet.css`. Find this area in the master page:

```
<link rel="stylesheet" type="text/css" href="<%$ SPUrl:~sitecollection/
    Style%20Library/~language/Custom%20Styles/SiteName.css %>"/>
```

And change it to reflect the bold area here:

```
<link rel="stylesheet" type="text/css" href="<%$ SPUrl:~sitecollection/
    Style%20Library/~language/Custom%20Styles/mossman_internet.css %>"/>
```

Next, update the JavaScript that adds the Web site name before the page name in the HTML title. This is located in the following area of the master page:

```
<script type="text/javascript">
  if(document.title!='') {
    document.title = 'Site Name - ' + document.title;
  } else {
    document.title = 'Site Name';
  }
</script>
```

Change the reference from "Site Name" to the fictitious company Web site title "Mossman & Partners," as seen in the bold areas:

```
<script type="text/javascript">
  if(document.title!='') {
    document.title = 'Mossman & Partners - ' + document.title;
  } else {
    document.title = 'Mossman & Partners';
  }
</script>
```

Because the HTML mockup does not include any left navigation functionality, move the left navigation section of the master page to the hidden panel at the bottom of the master page. The left navigation will look like:

```
<!-- left nav -->
<asp:ContentPlaceHolder id="PlaceHolderLeftNavBar" runat="server">
  ...
</asp:ContentPlaceHolder>
```

Delete it from this section of the master page and add an empty content placeholder with an ID of `PlaceHolderLeftNavBar` to the hidden panel at the bottom of the master page like this:

```
<asp:Panel visible="false" runat="server">
  ...
<!-- Left navigation area -->
<asp:ContentPlaceHolder id="PlaceHolderLeftNavBar" runat="server"/>
```

Figure 8-24 shows the updated master page; the left navigation is removed, but it's very difficult to tell, because the updated styles make the page very hard to read.

Figure 8-24

The CSS file used with this master page contains references to many background images that you will want to see throughout this walk-through. Currently these images are using the old references from the HTML mockup; before they will show properly in your MOSS site, their references need to be updated to point to their new location on your MOSS server. To do this, open the `mossman_internet.css` file from the `Style Library/en-us/Custom Styles` folder with SharePoint Designer. You will now change all image references in the CSS file from `images/mossman/` to `../../Images/mossman/`. Note that the references will now begin with "`../..`". This will instruct the browser to look for the images sub-folder under Style Library by looking two directories above the location of the CSS file, which is "`Style Library/en-us/Custom Styles/mossman_internet.css`". You can use the replace function in SharePoint Designer to make this task easier. Click Edit ➪ Replace then in the Find what: box enter "`images/mossman/`" and in the Replace with: box enter "`../../Images/mossman/`". Be sure that Find where: is set to Current Page, leave the other settings the same, and click Replace All. The following is a list of all of the new image references in the CSS file:

```
background-image: url('../../Images/mossman/top_bg.gif');

background-image: url('../../Images/mossman/header_bg.gif');

background-image: url('../../Images/mossman/nav_bg.gif');

background: url('../../Images/mossman/nav_hover_bg.gif') repeat-x;
```

```
background-image: url('../../Images/mossman/shadow_nav_bg.gif');

background-image: url('../../Images/mossman/slogan_bg.gif');

background-image: url('../../Images/mossman/main_bg.gif');

background-image: url('../../Images/mossman/footer_bg.gif');
```

With this change in place, background images will start showing as new areas of HTML are added to the master page.

Now you can start moving the content of the HTML mockup, section by section, into the master page. Remember that the HTML design has a <div> tag that surrounds the whole design, stretching the full height and width of the browser. After that, there are three main <div> areas for the header, content, and footer. You will now place these divs around the corresponding areas of the master page. The bold sections of code below show the <div> tags placed in the middle of the appropriate sections of the master page.

Here is the opening <div> tag and the change for the header:

```
...
<!-- Web part code after form -->
<WebPartPages:SPWebPartManager runat="server"/>

<div id="customFullHeight">
<!-- ===== top header ================ -->
  <div id="customMainHeader">

    <!-- login / welcome john doe  -->
    <wssuc:Welcome id="explitLogout" runat="server"/>
```

This is the change for the content:

```
    <PublishingNavigation:PortalSiteMapDataSource ID="siteMapDataSource1"
       Runat="server"
     SiteMapProvider="CombinedNavSiteMapProvider" EnableViewState="true"
     StartFromCurrentNode="true" StartingNodeOffset="0" ShowStartingNode="false"
     TreatStartingNodeAsCurrent="true" TrimNonCurrentTypes="Heading"/>
</div>

<div id="customMainContent">
<!-- =====  Edit Bar  ================= -->

  <!-- ===== Page Status Console ========= -->
  <wssuc:DesignModeConsole id="IdDesignModeConsole" runat="server"/>
...
```

Here are the <div> tags for the footer:

```
    ...
    <asp:ContentPlaceHolder id="PlaceHolderFormDigest" runat="server">
      <SharePoint:FormDigest runat=server/>
    </asp:ContentPlaceHolder>
```

```
</div>

<div id="customMainFooter">
</div>

<!-- =====  Hidden Placeholders ===== -->
<asp:Panel visible="false" runat="server">
...
```

And this is the closing `<div>` tag:

```
    <SharePoint:DelegateControl ControlId="GlobalSiteLink1" Scope="Farm"
        runat="server" />
    <!-- my links -->
    <SharePoint:DelegateControl ControlId="GlobalSiteLink2" Scope="Farm"
        runat="server" />
  </asp:Panel>

</div>
</form>
</body>
```

Figure 8-25 shows the changes to the master page.

Figure 8-25

You will now focus on the top bar section from the HTML mockup (this is the bar at the top of the page above the logo and search). The code will be added to the following section of the master page:

```
<div id="customMainHeader">

  <!-- login / welcome john doe  -->
  <wssuc:Welcome id="explitLogout" runat="server"/>

  <!-- variations language menu  -->
  <PublishingVariations:VariationsLabelMenu id="labelmenu1" runat="server"/>

<!-- ===== logo header ============= -->

  <!-- ===== back to home logo link ============= -->
  <asp:HyperLink runat="server" id="HyperLink1" NavigateUrl=
      "<% $SPUrl:~sitecollection/ %>"><asp:Image ImageUrl=
      "<%$ SPUrl:~sitecollection/Style%20Library/Images/SiteName/logo.gif %>"
      BorderWidth="0" AlternateText="Back to Home" title="Back to Home"
      runat="server"/></asp:HyperLink>

  <!-- ===== search box ============== -->
  <asp:ContentPlaceHolder id="PlaceHolderSearchArea" runat="server">
    <SPSWC:SearchBoxEx id="SearchBox" RegisterStyles="false" TextBeforeDropDown=""
      TextBeforeTextBox="<%$Resources:cms,masterpages_searchbox_label%>"
      TextBoxWidth="100" GoImageUrl="<% $SPUrl:~sitecollection/Style
      Library/Images/Search_Arrow.jpg %>" GoImageActiveUrl="<%
      $SPUrl:~sitecollection/Style Library/Images/Search_Arrow.jpg %>"
      GoImageActiveUrlRTL="<% $SPUrl:~sitecollection/Style
      Library/Images/Search_Arrow_RTL.jpg %>" GoImageUrlRTL="<%
      $SPUrl:~sitecollection/Style Library/Images/Search_Arrow_RTL.jpg %>"
      UseSiteDefaults="true" DropDownMode = "HideScopeDD"
      SuppressWebPartChrome="true" runat="server" WebPart="true"
      WebPartId="{05DB52CD-CEC9-46F0-BE8D-1579B8FDC830}" __WebPartId=
      "{FB4EBCCA-A536-4E1F-B338-F5D95C688869}"/>
  </asp:ContentPlaceHolder>

  <!-- ===== site actions menu ================ -->
  <PublishingSiteAction:SiteActionMenu runat="server"/>
```

Add both the <div id = "customTop"> tag and the <div class = "customPageWidth"> tag to the already existing <div id = "customMainHeader"> tag. The customTop style will be unique to the top section of the design, while the customPageWidth style will be used throughout the design to ensure each section is a specific width and centered on the page. This concept will be repeated throughout the example. Most areas will be wrapped with a <div> tag that will call out a specific style for just that area, and in many cases the area will also be wrapped with the customPageWidth style to center it with a specific width. Next, wrap the "welcome" and "variations" functionality with the <div id = "customTopLeft"> tag and then move the Site Actions from the bottom of the section to the <div id = "customTopRight"> tag. This will give the left and right areas of the top bar their own styles, as well as move the Site Actions to the right-hand top of the page. The changes are reflected in the bold areas:

```
<div id="customMainHeader">

  <div id="customTop">
   <div class="customPageWidth">
      <div id="customTopLeft">
         <!-- login / welcome john doe   -->
         <wssuc:Welcome id="explitLogout" runat="server"/>

         <!-- variations language menu   -->
         <PublishingVariations:VariationsLabelMenu
id="labelmenu1" runat="server"/>
      </div>
      <div id="customTopRight">
         <!-- ===== site actions menu ======= -->
         <PublishingSiteAction:SiteActionMenu runat="server"/>
      </div>
   </div>
  </div>

<!-- ===== logo header ================== -->

  <!-- ===== back to home logo link ========== -->
  <asp:HyperLink runat="server" id="HyperLink1" NavigateUrl=
     "<% $SPUrl:~sitecollection/ %>"><asp:Image ImageUrl=
     "<%$ SPUrl:~sitecollection/Style%20Library/Images/SiteName/logo.gif %>"
     BorderWidth="0" AlternateText="Back to Home" title="Back to Home"
     runat="server"/></asp:HyperLink>

  <!-- ===== search box ============== -->
  <asp:ContentPlaceHolder id="PlaceHolderSearchArea" runat="server">
    <SPSWC:SearchBoxEx id="SearchBox" RegisterStyles="false" TextBeforeDropDown=""
       TextBeforeTextBox="<%$Resources:cms,masterpages_searchbox_label%>"
       TextBoxWidth="100" GoImageUrl="<% $SPUrl:~sitecollection/Style
       Library/Images/Search_Arrow.jpg %>" GoImageActiveUrl="<%
       $SPUrl:~sitecollection/Style Library/Images/Search_Arrow.jpg %>"
       GoImageActiveUrlRTL="<% $SPUrl:~sitecollection/Style
       Library/Images/Search_Arrow_RTL.jpg %>" GoImageUrlRTL="<%
       $SPUrl:~sitecollection/Style Library/Images/Search_Arrow_RTL.jpg %>"
       UseSiteDefaults="true" DropDownMode = "HideScopeDD"
       SuppressWebPartChrome="true" runat="server" WebPart="true"
       WebPartId="{05DB52CD-CEC9-46F0-BE8D-1579B8FDC830}" __WebPartId=
       "{FB4EBCCA-A536-4E1F-B338-F5D95C688869}"/>
  </asp:ContentPlaceHolder>
```

Figure 8-26 shows the results of the updated master page. Notice that the styles of each functional area are reflected, and the Site Actions menu has moved to the top bar.

Next you will move the customHeader section of the HTML mockup into the following area of the master page:

```
<!-- ===== logo header ===== -->

<!-- ===== back to home logo link ===== -->
<asp:HyperLink runat="server" id="HyperLink1" NavigateUrl=
     "<% $SPUrl:~sitecollection/ %>"><asp:Image ImageUrl=
```

```
        "<%$ SPUrl:~sitecollection/Style%20Library/Images/SiteName/logo.gif %>"
        BorderWidth="0" AlternateText="Back to Home" title="Back to Home"
        runat="server"/></asp:HyperLink>

<!-- ===== search box ===== -->
<asp:ContentPlaceHolder id="PlaceHolderSearchArea" runat="server">
  <SPSWC:SearchBoxEx id="SearchBox"
RegisterStyles="false" TextBeforeDropDown=""
        TextBeforeTextBox="<%$Resources:cms,masterpages_searchbox_label%>"
        TextBoxWidth="100" GoImageUrl="<% $SPUrl:~sitecollection/Style
        Library/Images/Search_Arrow.jpg %>" GoImageActiveUrl="<%
        $SPUrl:~sitecollection/Style Library/Images/Search_Arrow.jpg %>"
        GoImageActiveUrlRTL="<% $SPUrl:~sitecollection/Style
        Library/Images/Search_Arrow_RTL.jpg %>" GoImageUrlRTL="<%
        $SPUrl:~sitecollection/Style Library/Images/Search_Arrow_RTL.jpg %>"
        UseSiteDefaults="true" DropDownMode = "HideScopeDD"
        SuppressWebPartChrome="true" runat="server" WebPart="true"
        WebPartId="{05DB52CD-CEC9-46F0-BE8D-1579B8FDC830}" __WebPartId=
        "{FB4EBCCA-A536-4E1F-B338-F5D95C688869}"/>
</asp:ContentPlaceHolder>
```

Figure 8-26

First, you will wrap the entire area with both a <div id = "customHeader"> tag and a <div class = "customPageWidth"> tag. Then wrap the image code with a <div id = "customLogo"> tag. Also change the reference from the logo placeholder "SiteName/logo.gif" to the reference of the actual logo image "mossman/logo.gif". Next, wrap the search functionality in a <div id = "customHeaderRight"> tag and change the placeholder images for the search arrow. This involves changing the references from "Images/Search_Arrow.jpg" to "Images/mossman/search_arrow.gif".

Note that you can leave the references to "Search_Arrow_RTL.jpg" unchanged because they are only used in international sites that have right-to-left text (however, if your site will support this type of text, feel free to update them accordingly).

See the bolded sections below:

```
<!-- ===== logo header ===== -->
<div id="customHeader">
  <div class="customPageWidth">
    <div id="customLogo">
      <!-- ===== back to home logo link ===== -->
      <asp:HyperLink runat="server" id="HyperLink1" NavigateUrl=
      "<% $SPUrl:~sitecollection/ %>"><asp:Image ImageUrl=
      "<%$ SPUrl:~sitecollection/Style%20Library/Images/mossman/logo.gif %>"
      BorderWidth="0" AlternateText="Back to Home" title="Back to Home"
      runat="server"/></asp:HyperLink>
    </div>
    <div id="customHeaderRight">
      <!-- ===== search box ===== -->
      <asp:ContentPlaceHolder id="PlaceHolderSearchArea" runat="server">
        <SPSWC:SearchBoxEx id="SearchBox" RegisterStyles="false"
      TextBeforeDropDown="" TextBeforeTextBox=
      "<%$Resources:cms,masterpages_searchbox_label%>" TextBoxWidth="140"
      GoImageUrl="<% $SPUrl:~sitecollection/Style%20Library/Images/mossman
      /search_arrow.gif %>" GoImageActiveUrl="<% $SPUrl:~sitecollection/
      Style%20Library/Images/mossman/search_arrow.gif %>" GoImageActiveUrlRTL="<%
      $SPUrl:~sitecollection/Style Library/Images/Search_Arrow_RTL.jpg %>"
      GoImageUrlRTL="<% $SPUrl:~sitecollection/Style Library/Images/
      Search_Arrow_RTL.jpg %>" UseSiteDefaults="true" DropDownMode =
      "HideScopeDD" SuppressWebPartChrome="true" runat="server"
      WebPart="true" WebPartId="{05DB52CD-CEC9-46F0-BE8D-1579B8FDC830}"
      __WebPartId="{FB4EBCCA-A536-4E1F-B338-F5D95C688869}"/>
      </asp:ContentPlaceHolder>
    </div>
  </div>
</div>
```

Figure 8-27 shows the updated logo and search areas.

The next section of the HTML mockup that will be moved to the master page is the main horizontal navigation and the shadow that appears below it. For the navigation section, most of the master page will stay the same. (This is because most of the customization will happen in the custom CSS.) These changes will affect the following section of the master page:

```
<!-- ===== Horizontal Top Navigation Bar ===== -->
<SharePoint:AspMenu ID="GlobalNav" Runat="server"
   DataSourceID="SiteMapDataSource1"
   Orientation="Horizontal" StaticDisplayLevels="1" MaximumDynamicDisplayLevels="1"
   StaticSubMenuIndent="0" DynamicHorizontalOffset="0" DynamicVerticalOffset="-8"
   StaticEnableDefaultPopOutImage="false" ItemWrap="false"
```

```
     SkipLinkText="<%$Resources:cms,masterpages_skiplinktext%>"
     CssClass="customNavItemContainer">
   <StaticMenuItemStyle CssClass="customTopNavItem" ItemSpacing="0"/>
   <StaticSelectedStyle CssClass="customTopNavSelected" ItemSpacing="0"/>
   <StaticHoverStyle CssClass="customTopNavHover"/>
   <DynamicMenuStyle CssClass="customTopNavFlyOut" />
   <DynamicMenuItemStyle CssClass="customTopNavFlyOutItem" />
   <DynamicHoverStyle CssClass="customTopNavFlyOutHover"/>
</SharePoint:AspMenu>
<!-- datasource for nav  -->
<PublishingNavigation:PortalSiteMapDataSource ID="siteMapDataSource1"
     Runat="server"
  SiteMapProvider="CombinedNavSiteMapProvider" EnableViewState="true"
  StartFromCurrentNode="true" StartingNodeOffset="0" ShowStartingNode="false"
  TreatStartingNodeAsCurrent="true" TrimNonCurrentTypes="Heading"/>
```

Figure 8-27

Begin by wrapping the entire navigation functionality with a <div id = "customNav"> tag and then with a <div class = "customPageWidth"> tag. Next, add the code for the customShadow area from the HTML mockup. It will be placed below all of the navigation functionality. See the bolded sections below:

```
<div id="customNav">
  <div class="customPageWidth">

    <!-- =====  Horizontal Top Navigation Bar =====  -->
    <SharePoint:AspMenu ID="GlobalNav" Runat="server"
          DataSourceID="SiteMapDataSource1"
      Orientation="Horizontal" StaticDisplayLevels="1"
          MaximumDynamicDisplayLevels="1"
      StaticSubMenuIndent="0" DynamicHorizontalOffset="0"
  DynamicVerticalOffset="0"
      StaticEnableDefaultPopOutImage="false" ItemWrap="false"
          SkipLinkText="<%$Resources:cms,masterpages_skiplinktext%>"
          CssClass="customNavItemContainer">
        <StaticMenuItemStyle CssClass="customTopNavItem" ItemSpacing="0"/>
```

```
            <StaticSelectedStyle CssClass="customTopNavItemHover" ItemSpacing="0"/>
            <StaticHoverStyle CssClass="customTopNavItemHover"/>
            <DynamicMenuStyle CssClass="customTopNavFlyOut" />
            <DynamicMenuItemStyle CssClass="customTopNavFlyOutItem" />
            <DynamicHoverStyle CssClass="customTopNavFlyOutHover"/>
      </SharePoint:AspMenu>
      <!-- datasource for nav  -->
      <PublishingNavigation:PortalSiteMapDataSource ID="siteMapDataSource1"
            Runat="server"
        SiteMapProvider="CombinedNavSiteMapProvider" EnableViewState="true"
        StartFromCurrentNode="true" StartingNodeOffset="0" ShowStartingNode="false"
        TreatStartingNodeAsCurrent="true" TrimNonCurrentTypes="Heading"/>

    </div>
  </div>
  <div id="customShadow">
    <div class="customPageWidth"></div>
  </div>
```

Figure 8-28 shows the horizontal navigation and shadow area.

Figure 8-28

The next area of the HTML mockup that will be added to the master page is the "mainContent" section. This is the area that will hold the actual page layout and content pages, as well as breadcrumbs, page title, and editing menus. You will be adding code to the following area of the master page:

```
<div id="customMainContent">
<!-- =====  Edit Bar  ===== -->

  <!-- ===== Page Status Console ===== -->
  <wssuc:DesignModeConsole id="IdDesignModeConsole" runat="server"/>

  <!-- ===== Page Edit Toolbar ===== -->
  <PublishingConsole:Console runat="server"/>
```

```
<!-- ===== MAIN AREA (all content goes here) ===== -->

  <!-- breadcrumb -->
  <asp:ContentPlaceHolder id="PlaceHolderTitleBreadcrumb" runat="server">
    <asp:SiteMapPath SiteMapProvider="SPContentMapProvider" id="ContentMap"
        SkipLinkText="" runat="server"/>
  </asp:ContentPlaceHolder>

  <!-- ===== Mini Console - supplementary buttons for Site Map ===== -->
  <table style="float: right;">
  <tr>
    <td>
      <asp:ContentPlaceHolder id="PlaceHolderMiniConsole" runat="server"/>
    </td>
  </tr>
  </table>

  <!-- page title  -->
  <asp:ContentPlaceHolder id="PlaceHolderPageTitleInTitleArea" runat="server" />

  <!-- page content loads the pages layout and content -->
  <asp:ContentPlaceHolder id="PlaceHolderMain" runat="server"/>

  <!-- required for some security access errors -->
  <asp:ContentPlaceHolder id="PlaceHolderFormDigest" runat="server">
    <SharePoint:FormDigest runat=server/>
  </asp:ContentPlaceHolder>
</div>
```

Start by adding a `<div class = "customPageWidth">` tag around everything but the PlaceHolderMain and the PlaceHolderFormDigest content placeholders. The reason for this is that you will use a slightly different version of the customPageWidth class for that portion of the page. For that area you will add a `<div class = "customPageWidthMain">` tag that can have its style overridden by the welcome page layout. This will be important because the welcome page layout (which you will create in the next chapter) will need to span the entire length of the page, while all other instances of this style should be centered in a fixed-width area just like the standard customPageWidth style. Also, you will wrap the PlaceHolderPageTitleInTitleArea and PlaceHolderMain content placeholders with `<div class= "customContentTitle">` and `<div id = "customPageContent">` tags to allow for better control of their styles from CSS. Lastly, remove the contents of the PlaceHolderTitleBreadcrumb content placeholder; this will remove the default breadcrumb information from the master page while still allowing the individual pages to have the ability to add breadcrumbs. See the bold sections below:

```
<div id="customMainContent">
  <div class="customPageWidth">
  <!-- =====   Edit Bar   ===== -->

    <!-- ===== Page Status Console ===== -->
    <wssuc:DesignModeConsole id="IdDesignModeConsole" runat="server"/>

    <!-- ===== Page Edit Toolbar ===== -->
    <PublishingConsole:Console runat="server"/>

  <!-- ===== MAIN AREA (all content goes here) ===== -->
```

```
            <!-- breadcrumb -->
            <asp:ContentPlaceHolder id="PlaceHolderTitleBreadcrumb" runat="server"/>

            <!-- ===== Mini Console - supplementary buttons for Site Map ===== -->
            <table style="float: right;">
            <tr>
              <td>
                <asp:ContentPlaceHolder id="PlaceHolderMiniConsole" runat="server"/>
              </td>
            </tr>
            </table>

            <!-- page title  -->
            <div class="customContentTitle">
                <asp:ContentPlaceHolder id="PlaceHolderPageTitleInTitleArea" runat=
                    "server" />
            </div>

        </div>

        <div class="customPageWidthMain">
            <!-- ===== Page content goes here ===== -->

            <div id="customPageContent">
              <!-- page content loads the pages layout and content -->
              <asp:ContentPlaceHolder id="PlaceHolderMain" runat="server"/>
            </div>

            <!-- required for some security access errors -->
            <asp:ContentPlaceHolder id="PlaceHolderFormDigest" runat="server">
              <SharePoint:FormDigest runat=server/>
            </asp:ContentPlaceHolder>

        </div>
    </div>
```

Figure 8-29 shows the results of the updated master page. Visually there is not much difference, but the page content and the page title will now have CSS applied to them. Also, the breadcrumbs are now hidden by default.

Now you will add the footer section from the HTML mockup to the master page. This section is made up of static content that will be included on all the pages of the MOSS site. Note that the <a href> links simply point to "#" right now (which always refers to the current page). You can change these links later when the corresponding pages actually exist. The bold section below will be added to the <div id = "customMainFooter"> tag:

```
<div id="customMainFooter">
  <div id="customFooter">
    <div class="customPageWidth">
```

```
    <div id="customFooterLeft">
        &copy; Copyright 2007 Mossman &amp; Partners, Inc.
    </div>
    <div id="customFooterRight">
      <a href="#">Privacy Policy</a>  |  <a href="#">Terms of Use</a>  |  <a
        href="#">Contact Us</a>
    </div>
  </div>
</div>
</div>
```

Figure 8-29

This concludes all of the changes that are necessary for the master page part of the conversion. You will see from Figure 8-30 that there are still some areas for improvement. This is because you still need to make edits to the custom CSS before the customization will be completed.

To finish the CSS changes, re-open the `mossman_internet.css` CSS file from the `Style Library/en-us/Custom Styles` folder with SharePoint Designer. There are several styles in the current CSS file that do not apply to the master page; they are the styles that will be used in the welcome page layout. These styles will not be used on standard pages of the site; they are solely for showing the slogan, photo, and other styles that show on the welcome page. While it's perfectly fine to keep all the CSS in one file, it would be helpful to move this page layout–specific CSS into its own commented area of the CSS file. By moving the page layout styles, they will be separated from all of the other master page styles, which will make them easier to identify when you work on the page layout (in the next chapter). To do this, simply select all of the styles from "#customSloganArea" to ".customClearBoth" and move them to the very bottom of the CSS. Be sure to add a descriptive comment before the CSS, like this:

```
/*
-------------------------------------------------------------------
  css for custom welcome page layout
-------------------------------------------------------------------
*/
```

Figure 8-30

Now you will add styles to support some of the new features introduced by going from a static HTML mockup to a MOSS master page. You will begin by adding some styles to ensure the main horizontal navigation looks appropriate, especially when the user is hovering their mouse over the items or when there are sub item flyouts. Because you have already defined a hover style for the HTML mockup, most of the work for the mouse hover is done already. However, if you test out the functionality in your browser, you will see that the background image displays incorrectly. This can be seen in Figure 8-31.

This improper layout is due to the way MOSS applies your hover style to the menu item in a nested fashion. This includes applying the style a second time for the `<a href>` link. To correct this, change the `.customTopNavItemHover` a style to use no background image. Change the following CSS code:

```
.customTopNavItemHover  a {
  color: black;
  text-decoration: none;
}
```

Override the `background-image` with a value of `none`:

```
.customTopNavItemHover a {
  color: black;
  text-decoration: none;
  background-image: none;
}
```

Now, MOSS will correctly show just one background image on hovered items as seen in Figure 8-32.

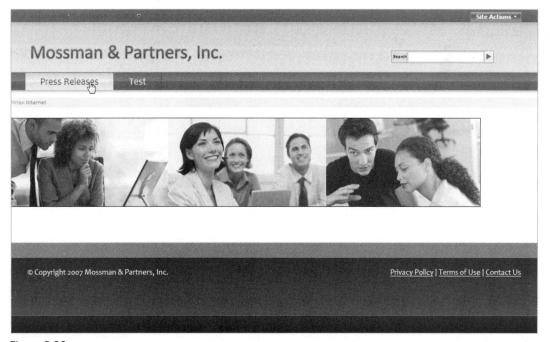

Figure 8-31

Figure 8-32

Next, add styles for the navigation flyouts (since they were not included in the HTML mockup). Add the following styles to the CSS:

- ❑ `.customTopNavFlyOut` –The container for the entire flyout area
- ❑ `.customTopNavFlyOutItem` –The individual menu items that show in the flyout
- ❑ `.customTopNavFlyOut a` –The padding for the actual text of the menu item link
- ❑ `.customTopNavFlyOutHover` –The highlight for when flyout items are hovered over

```css
/* top nav sub item flys */
.customTopNavFlyOut {
    border-top:1px #CBD1E0 solid;
}

/* top nav sub item fly items */
.customTopNavFlyOutItem {
    font-family: tahoma;
    font-size: 8pt;
    background-color: #ECEFF3;
    border:1px #CBD1E0 solid;
    border-top-style: none;
    color:#3A4663;
    *width:150px;
    min-width:150px;
}

.customTopNavFlyOutItem a {
    display:block;
    padding:4px 5px 4px 5px;
}

/* top nav sub item fly out hover */
.customTopNavFlyOutHover {
    background-color: #B2BCD3;
}
```

Figure 8-33 shows the menu flyouts in action.

Now you will add the styles for the main page content. This will include `.customPageWidthMain`, which has exactly the same styles as `.customPageWidth` but is important because it can be overridden from a welcome page to allow just that page layout to span the entire width of the page. Along with this style, you will also add `.customContentTitle` (to style the page title) and `#customPageContent` (to apply some padding to the main content area).

```css
/* can be overridden by the custom welcome page */
.customPageWidthMain {
    width: 940px;
```

```
  margin: auto;
}

/* padding for the page title / page breadcrumbs */
.customContentTitle {
  padding-bottom: 3px;
  line-height: 12px;
  margin-bottom: 3px;
}

/* actual page content area */
#customPageContent {
  padding-top: 4px;
}
```

Figure 8-33

Figure 8-34 shows some minor padding changes to the main content area.

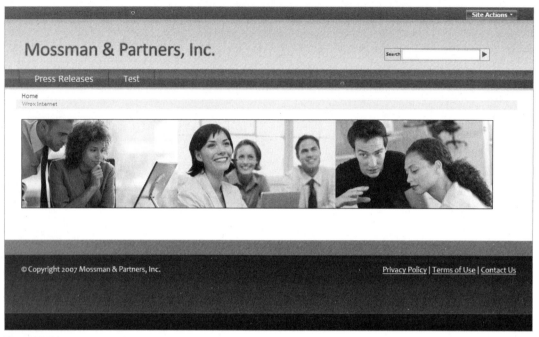

Figure 8-34

At this point, you have added all of the styles from the HTML mockup to the master page. Now, you need to look at overriding the out-of-the-box MOSS CSS to match with your design. It is a good idea to add a comment before this section so that you can easily find it later. The following list of styles will adjust the out-of-the-box styles to look good with your custom master page. Each style is commented with a description of the general area of the MOSS functionality being styled:

```
/*
----------------------------------------
  Overrides for out of the box moss css
----------------------------------------
*/

/* editing toolbar fonts */
.ms-consoletoolbar .ms-SPLink a:link, .ms-consoletoolbar .ms-SPLink a:visited,
.ms-consoletoolbar .ms-SPLink a:hover  {
  color: black;
}

/* top bar fonts */
.ms-SPLink a:link, .ms-SPLink a:visited  {
  color: white;
}

/* top bar fonts hover */
.ms-SPLink a:hover {
```

```
    color: white;
}

/* header bar link hover */
.ms-HoverCellActive, .ms-SpLinkButtonActive {
  border: 1px solid #518954;
  *border-top: 0px;
  background: #518954;
}

/* site action fonts */
.ms-siteaction, .ms-siteaction a {
  font-family: verdana;
  font-size: 8pt;

}

/* site actions font weight */
.ms-siteactionsmenu div div div a {
  font-weight: normal;
}

/* site action bg and button */
.ms-siteactionsmenu div div div {
  background-image: none;
  background-position: right;
  background-repeat: no-repeat;
  background-color: transparent;
  border: 0px;
  padding: 2px;
  padding-top: 1px;
}

/* site action link hover */
.ms-siteactionsmenu div div div a:hover,
.ms-siteactionsmenu div div div.ms-siteactionsmenuhover a:hover {
  text-decoration: none;
}

/* site action hover button */
.ms-siteactionsmenu div div div.ms-siteactionsmenuhover {
  background: #518954;
  border: 0px;
  padding: 2px;
  padding-top: 1px;
}


/* search box border */
td.ms-sbcell{
  padding:0px;
  padding-left:2px;
  white-space:nowrap;
  border:solid 0px;
```

```
    }

    /* search box text */
    .ms-sbtext {
      color:#25632A;
      font-family:Candara,Calibri,Frutiger,Helvetica,sans-serif;
      font-size:2em;
      font-weight:normal;
    }

    /* divit after search IE */
    td.ms-sbcell {
      background-color:transparent;
    }

    /* sides of search box */
    .ms-sbplain {
      border: solid 1px gray;
      padding-left:2px;
    }

    /* divit after search */
    td.ms-sbgo {
      background-color:inherit;
    }

    /* hide breadcrumb bg */
    .ms-pagebreadcrumb, .ms-pagebreadcrumb a {
      background-color: transparent;
    }

    /* splash links background */
    .splashLinkArea {
      border:0px none transparent;
      min-height:inherit;
    }
```

Figure 8-35 shows what the page looks like fully styled.

While the current page looks good, there are still many other types of content in MOSS that need to be tested. As you view other pages of your MOSS site, you will find small overrides that need to be made to the out-of-the-box MOSS styles. Here is a list of many tweaks that will ensure the common areas of MOSS look better with the new custom master page:

```
    /* all link colors in body of the site */
    .ms-WPBody a:link, .ms-WPBody a:visited, .link-item, .link-item a:link,
    .link-item a:visited, td.ms-vb a, td.ms-addnew a {
      color: #008940;
      text-decoration: underline;
    }

    /* all link hovers */
    .ms-WPBody a:hover, .link-item a:hover, td.ms-vb a:hover, td.ms-addnew a:hover {
```

```
  color: #008940;
  text-decoration: none;
}

/* header fonts from sites page */
.headertitle, .headertitle a, .headertitle a:link {
  color: #008940;
}

/* underline */
.ms-partline {
  background-color:#008940;
}

/* link colors need to be overridden */
.menuTopLevel a:link, .menuTopLevel a:visited {
  color:black;
}

/* sub link colors need to be overridden */
.menuSubLevel a:link, .menuSubLevel a:visited {
  color:white;
}

/* hide Web part borders */
.ms-WPBorder {
  border: 0px;
}

/* hide Web part borders */
.ms-WPHeader td {
  border-bottom:0px;
}

/* mini console button font */
.ms-ptabcn a:link, .ms-ptabcn a:visited, .ms-ptabcnhover a:link, .ms-ptabcnhover
    a:visited, .ms-sctabcn a:link, .ms-sctabcn a:visited, .ms-sctabcnhover
    a:link, .ms-sctabcnhover a:visited {
  font-size: 11px;
}

/* more mini console button fonts */
.ms-ptabcf a:link, .ms-ptabcf a:visited, .ms-ptabcfhover a:link,
.ms-ptabcfhover a:visited, .ms-sctabcf a:link, .ms-sctabcf a:visited,
.ms-sctabcfhover a:link, .ms-sctabcfhover a:visited {
  font-size: 11px;
}

/* some buttons that show on the sitemap */
.ms-wikieditouter {
  position:relative;
  right:0px;
  top:0px;
  border:1px solid silver;
```

```
    border-right-width:1px;
}

/* form fonts */
.ms-formlabel {
    font-size: .9em;
}

/* form fonts */
.ms-formbody {
    font-size: 1em;
}
```

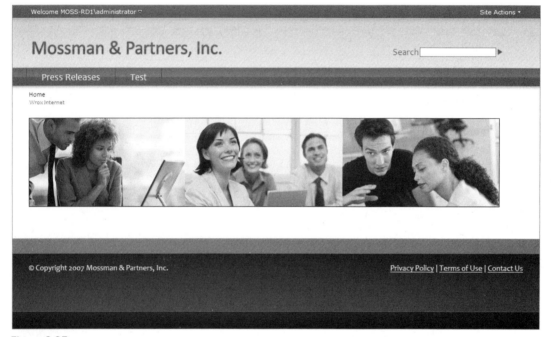

Figure 8-35

At this point, the Internet master page and CSS is complete. You may still find other small issues with specific types of MOSS content. If you do, you can correct them yourself by adding more entries to the CSS file.

As you can see, a big part of making a custom interface in MOSS is making small changes to the out-of-the-box CSS. This is why using tools like the IE Developers Toolbar and Firebug are so critical to the MOSS customization process. Chapter 7 discussed the usage of these tools for debugging MOSS style problems. When you are happy with all of your changes to the master page and CSS, be sure to re-publish both of them to ensure that end users and other people on your team will see the changes. Also, you may be wondering about why the middle part of the HTML design mockup is not reflected in the master page. This is because the middle section is included in a special welcome page layout that will be described further in the next chapter.

A Word about the Name ActiveX Control Message in Internet Explorer

If you browse your MOSS site from an external Internet connection, you may notice an alert message that appears at the top of Internet Explorer 7. The message says: "The Web site wants to run the following add-on: 'Name ActiveX Control' from 'Microsoft Corporation'. If you trust the Web site and the add-on and want to allow it to run, click here..." Figure 8-36 shows the message at the top of the browser window.

So, what does this message actually mean? SharePoint is trying to use an ActiveX control called name.dll, which deals with the user's "presence" in relation to Microsoft Office applications. Many designers don't even notice this message at first because it only appears under specific browsing conditions. The most common scenario seems to be when using Internet Explorer 7 to browse a MOSS or WSS V3 site that is *not* listed in your browser's trusted site settings. The problem is compounded by the fact that when you browse a MOSS site that is in your local intranet, the site is usually included by default as a trusted site; in these cases the message will not appear until you are using an external URL to access the site. Typically it is not appropriate to expect end users to install an ActiveX object just to interact with your external Internet site (especially one that is named as suspiciously as name.dll).

So, how do you get rid of the message on your own MOSS site? Microsoft has a document that discusses a fix for the problem at: `http://support.microsoft.com/kb/931509`. Unfortunately, this fix doesn't seem to work well in all scenarios. Because of this, the `custom_functions.js` that is available with the Minimal Internet master page for this chapter includes a specific JavaScript workaround for the problem. This JavaScript creates a duplicate function named the same as the offending one that Microsoft uses, though unlike Microsoft's function, this one does not include the code that ultimately requests the ActiveX object. With this JavaScript in place, the browser will no longer display the ActiveX message.

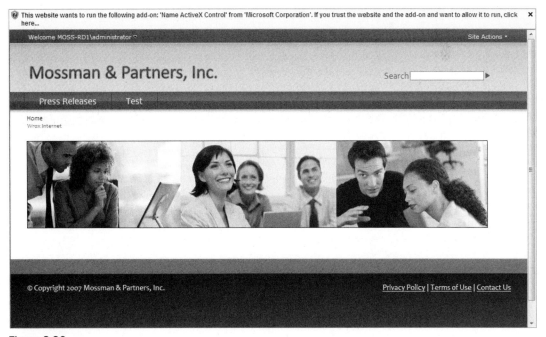

Figure 8-36

You can read more about this JavaScript fix for the Name ActiveX control message at: `http://blog.drisgill.com/2007/09/fixing-namedll-activex-problem-mossman.html`.

Intranet Master Page Design Differences

In many ways, the process of converting the intranet mockup to a master page is similar to what it was for the Internet mockup. For this reason, the intranet master page conversion will not be covered as a full walkthrough; all of the code for creating it is available in the downloadable code for this book. However, a few key differences with the intranet master page are worth discussing. They are presented here:

❑ The Internet master page was applied to a publishing portal site definition, while the intranet master page will be applied to a collaboration portal site. This site definition is specifically tailored for a site that has many authors as well as many viewers. While publishing portals focus on approving and publishing Web content to the Internet, collaboration portals focus on creating team sites for collaborating in an intranet environment.

❑ While the Internet master page is based off of the Minimal Internet master page available from the book download site, the intranet master page is based off of the Minimal Intranet master page (which itself is based heavily on Heather Solomon's Minimal Collaboration master page). Because of this, there are many subtle differences in how the master page is set up. While the Minimal Internet master page's functions are tailored specifically to creating Internet facing Web sites, the Minimal Intranet master page includes more functionality that would only be appropriate in an intranet environment. Also, because the Minimal Intranet master page is based on Heather Solomon's Minimal Collaboration master page, it can be used for collaboration portals in MOSS as well as basic team sites. The differences between the Minimal Internet master page and the Minimal Intranet master page are similar to the differences between the out-of-the-box default.master and blueband.master master pages, respectively. Just as with those out-of-the-box master pages, you will notice that the two minimal master pages differ in the Web controls that are used to display the underlying SharePoint functionality. This is mainly due to the way that both the default.master master page and the Minimal Intranet master page support basic team sites.

❑ The intranet master page will include a left-side secondary navigation. This means that there will be more styles included to support the left navigation functionality. Just like the top navigation, this left navigation includes styles for standard menu items, selected menu items, menu items with a hover state, as well as dynamic flyout menu items and their hover state.

❑ While Internet sites may have just a few content authors with a very controlled set of types of content, intranet sites often have many content authors that have free range to add many different types of content. For instance, intranet sites often contain team sites that may have document libraries, lists for managing various types of information, team calendars, task lists, and discussion boards. Because of this, you will need to double-check even more of the out-of-the-box MOSS features in the intranet master page.

With these changes in mind, the process is virtually the same as converting the Internet HTML mockup. You begin with the Minimal Intranet master page and start adding your custom HTML and CSS around it. From there you override the out-of-the-box MOSS CSS to ensure that it matches the new design, and test the master page with various types of content.

Summary

This chapter focused on giving you a good understanding of how master pages work, not only in MOSS but also in traditional ASP.NET applications. You learned about the structure of master pages as well as how they are related to both content pages and page layouts. You should now be aware of how MOSS requires specific content placeholders to function properly, and you looked at how they are used in both out-of-the-box and minimal master pages. Not only was a simple minimal master page customization explained, but an HTML mockup was converted into a functioning custom master page. Armed with this knowledge, you should be able to effectively customize minimal master pages to transform your own Web designs into custom master pages.

In the next chapter, you will learn how page layouts work in MOSS, as well as walk through creating a welcome page layout to match the Internet master page that you created in this chapter.

Page Layouts

With the release of Microsoft Office SharePoint Server 2007 (MOSS), Microsoft has introduced the Publishing Feature to the already impressive array of functionality available to SharePoint sites. Publishing empowers content authors to create their own HTML based Web sites in MOSS using only their Web browsers. Page layouts are not only the mechanism that provides this ability, but they also work together with master pages to create the user interface for all publishing pages. To fully customize a MOSS Web site, designers must have a strong understanding of master pages, which were covered in the previous chapter, and a good working knowledge of how page layouts are created and ultimately utilized in MOSS. By the end of this chapter, you should have a good understanding of what page layouts are and how they are created in MOSS. The chapter concludes with a walk through of creating a welcome page layout that can be utilized to create a home page suitable for the Internet master page design that was created in the previous chapter.

To try out the ideas in this chapter, you will need to have a full-blown MOSS server. A simple Windows SharePoint Services 3.0 (WSS) server will not fit the bill because it does not include the Publishing Feature or page layouts.

What Is a Page Layout?

While traditional SharePoint sites are very good at allowing teams to collaborate and share many types of documents with ease, large organizations often need to share information in a more traditional Web- page-based format. Information sharing is even more important for content available to public facing Internet Web sites. In scenarios like this, content authors expect to be able to create Web pages easily without intervention from designers or even their own company's IT department. The MOSS Publishing Feature allows content authors to accomplish all of this from the comfort of their own browser. When a content author creates a publishing page in MOSS, the page derives much of its look and feel, as well as its editable fields, from a MOSS page layout. In fact, every publishing page in MOSS is related to exactly one page layout.

Page layouts are created by designers like you, directly in SharePoint Designer; they cannot be created by content authors using just the MOSS Web interface. After you have created a page layout and subsequently published it to a MOSS site, content authors will be able to create pages that are based on your page layout. Figure 9-1 shows a publishing page in edit mode.

Figure 9-1

When MOSS shows a publishing page in edit mode, the page layout becomes visible in the browser.

Relationship to Master Pages

Master pages are closely related to page layouts, because page layouts are always tied to one master page in MOSS. Master pages, along with providing much of the general MOSS functionality of a page, provide a unified outer shell design to all page layouts. The page layouts on the other hand define the specific look and the editable data for various types of pages. For example, one page layout might contain an article while another is a welcome page, yet both might utilize the same master page design. Figure 9-2 is a reminder of how page layouts and master pages are used by MOSS to render a page to the end user.

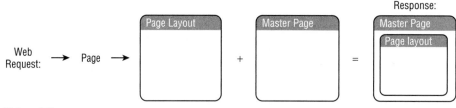

Figure 9-2

Content Types

Understanding page layouts requires you to understand their relationship to content types. Content types define the structure, metadata, and business rules that surround the particular pieces of information shown in MOSS. They are specifically utilized behind the scenes in MOSS to define the data that a page layout will be displaying. Because of this, every page layout in MOSS is related to exactly one content type.

Content types themselves utilize a mechanism known as *site columns* to define each of the data elements that they will store. The site columns themselves can each represent one of many different types of atomic units of data. The following kinds of site columns are available in a MOSS content type:

❑ **Single line of text** – Allows for the entry of a single line of alphanumeric text.

❑ **Multiple lines of text** – Allows for the entry of multiple lines of alphanumeric text or even rich text with limited HTML.

❑ **Choice (menu to choose from)** – Allows for selecting from a group of items (radio buttons, checkboxes, or a drop-down menu).

❑ **Number (1, 1.0, 100)** – Allows for the entry of numeric values.

❑ **Currency ($, ¥, €)** – Allows for the entry of monetary values which can be displayed in various currency formats.

❑ **Date and Time** – Allows for the selection a date and time.

❑ **Lookup (information already on this site)** – Allows for the selection of information that is available in other areas of the SharePoint site.

❑ **Yes/No (check box)** – Allows for selecting either yes or no from a checkbox.

❑ **Person or Group** – Allows for the selection of a user or group from the SharePoint site.

❑ **Hyperlink or Picture** – Allows for the entry of a URL.

❑ **Calculated (calculation based on other columns)** – Allows the entry of a formula that can be calculated based on numbers, dates, and other information from the SharePoint site.

❑ **Full HTML content with formatting and constraints for publishing** – Has a text box that has a Microsoft Word style editor bar that allows content authors to enter rich HTML content without needing any prior knowledge of how to create HTML.

❑ **Image with formatting and constraints for publishing** – Allows the selection of an image along with various formatting rules that can be applied to the image (such as height, width, alignment, and alternate text).

❑ **Hyperlink with formatting and constraints for publishing** – Allows for the entry of a URL. This site column is more robust than the Hyperlink or Picture site column. It allows for entering the URL manually or even selecting a URL from a list of all the available pages in the SharePoint site.

❑ **Summary Links data** – Allows the entry of a group of links including titles, descriptions, images, and URLs as well as the ability to group and style the links.

Every site column added to a content type ultimately becomes an editable field control available to the page layouts based on it. While content types are a very powerful way of defining data for use in a site, this power would be severely limited if MOSS forced you to create a new content type for every page layout. Fortunately, every content type that is created or available in MOSS can be used in as many page layouts as you like. This enables you to create a content type that is displayed in several ways via different page layouts in a MOSS site.

Another important topic when discussing content types in MOSS is that of inheritance. Every MOSS content type inherits from a parent content type (with the one exception of the System content type, which is a non-editable content type that is the ultimate parent of all other content types). When creating your own page layouts, MOSS requires that they always inherit from the Page parent content type. This ensures that every custom content type starts with the same base columns. Figure 9-3 shows the default inherited site columns that you see when creating a new content type based on the "page" parent content type. You will see this screen again when you are creating your own content types.

Site Content Type Information

Name:	New Content Type
Description:	
Parent:	Page
Group:	Custom Content Types

Settings

- Name, description, and group
- Advanced settings
- Workflow settings
- Delete this site content type
- Document Information Panel settings
- Information management policy settings
- Manage document conversion for this content type

Columns

Name	Type	Status	Source
Name	File	Required	Document
Title	Single line of text	Optional	Item
Description	Multiple lines of text	Optional	System Page
Scheduling Start Date	Publishing Schedule Start Date	Optional	System Page
Scheduling End Date	Publishing Schedule End Date	Optional	System Page
Contact	Person or Group	Optional	System Page
Contact E-Mail Address	Single line of text	Optional	System Page
Contact Name	Single line of text	Optional	System Page
Contact Picture	Hyperlink or Picture	Optional	System Page
Rollup Image	Publishing Image	Optional	System Page
Target Audiences	Audience Targeting	Optional	System Page

Figure 9-3

As mentioned earlier, the content type's site columns eventually become editable field controls that can be added to page layouts. When a page layout is edited in SharePoint Designer the available site columns for the content type appear in the Toolbox pane (on the right side of SharePoint Designer by default) under the heading of SharePoint Controls. SharePoint Designer further separates the available field controls into page fields and content fields. Page fields represent the site columns that are inherited from the parent content type of "page," while content fields represent the site columns that come directly from the page layout's own content type. Figure 9-4 shows the two types of field controls available in the Toolbox pane of SharePoint Designer.

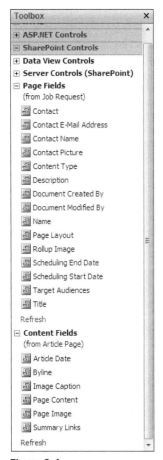

Figure 9-4

Along with field controls, page layouts can also have Web Parts added to them. Web Parts give content authors the ability to add a wide array of functionality to their MOSS site. Chapter 10 covers some of these Web Parts in further detail. While Web Parts can store many types of content (such as rich HTML in the case of the Content Editor Web Part), they do not utilize content types in any way. Figure 9-5 shows a high-level view of how field controls are related to content types; it also shows that Web Parts are not at all related to content types.

Page Layout Structure

When a Publishing site is created, MOSS automatically generates several master pages, and page layouts that together create the default user interface for pages that appear in the site. MOSS automatically maintains a connection between page layouts and the master page that has been selected for the site (by default this master page is typically either blueband.master or default.master). While the master page creates most of the outer shell of a MOSS site's design, it is the page layout that dictates how the fields and content of a page are arranged in the inside portion of the site design. Much like content pages in traditional ASP.NET, master pages declare content placeholders that dictate the location on the rendered page in which content from the page layout will be displayed. Also, like ASP.NET content pages, page layouts use content controls with ContentPlaceHolderIDs that point to the IDs of specific content placeholders in master pages.

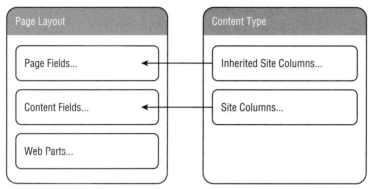

Figure 9-5

To gain a better understanding of how page layouts are structured, take a look at the following code from a very simple MOSS page layout.

```
<%@ Page language="C#" Inherits="Microsoft.SharePoint.Publishing.
       PublishingLayoutPage,Microsoft.SharePoint.Publishing,Version=12.0.0.0,
       Culture=neutral,PublicKeyToken=71e9bce111e9429c" %>
<%@ Register Tagprefix="SharePointWebControls" Namespace="Microsoft.
       SharePoint.WebControls" Assembly="Microsoft.SharePoint,
       Version=12.0.0.0,
       Culture=neutral, PublicKeyToken=71e9bce111e9429c" %> <%@ Register
       Tagprefix="WebPartPages" Namespace="Microsoft.SharePoint.
       WebPartPages"
       Assembly="Microsoft.SharePoint, Version=12.0.0.0, Culture=neutral,
       PublicKeyToken=71e9bce111e9429c" %> <%@ Register
       Tagprefix="PublishingWebControls" Namespace="Microsoft.SharePoint.
       Publishing.WebControls" Assembly="Microsoft.SharePoint.Publishing,
       Version=12.0.0.0, Culture=neutral, PublicKeyToken=71e9bce111e9429c" %>
       <%@ Register Tagprefix="PublishingNavigation" Namespace="Microsoft.
       SharePoint.Publishing.Navigation" Assembly="Microsoft.SharePoint.
       Publishing, Version=12.0.0.0, Culture=neutral, PublicKeyToken=
       71e9bce111e9429c" %>

<asp:Content ContentPlaceholderID="PlaceHolderPageTitle" runat="server">
  <SharePointWebControls:FieldValue id="PageTitle" FieldName="Title"
       runat="server"/>
</asp:Content>

<asp:Content ContentPlaceholderID="PlaceHolderMain" runat="server">
  <PublishingWebControls:RichHtmlField id="Content"
       FieldName="PublishingPageContent"  runat="server"/>
</asp:Content>
```

Page layouts begin with a page directive that defines what language they will be written in, as well as a setting to cause them to inherit the MOSS Publishing code. After that, several controls are registered; these allow the page layout to utilize the necessary MOSS functionality whenever needed. After the register statements, all other page layout content must be placed inside of content controls. If anything is placed outside of the content controls, MOSS will throw an error. In this example, the content controls each contain one field control; the first holds a text-based page title field, while the second contains a rich HTML content field. When a publishing page that is based on this particular page layout is created, content authors will be limited to adding only these two pieces of content to the page.

Types of Content in Page Layouts

All content that will be added to page layouts, must be added to content controls. These content controls can contain a variety of types of content. Here is a list of what they may contain:

❑ **HTML** – All types of standard HTML can be added to content controls in a page layout. Any HTML text that you add to a content control will appear on all pages created from the page layouts. HTML is often used in content controls to lay out the other types of content in this list. For example, a content control can contain HTML <table> or <div> tags to arrange the various field controls and Web Parts. HTML can also be used to apply internal style sheets for overriding CSS that was previous applied by the master page or the out-of-the-box MOSS CSS. Styles applied at this level will only apply to the pages that use the particular page layout.

❑ **Page Fields** – Page fields are editable field controls that allow content authors to add content to the page. Specifically, page fields come from the page layout's parent content type site columns (for page layouts this parent type is always the "page" content type). They include fields such as title and description.

❑ **Content Fields** – Content fields are also editable field controls that allow content authors to add content to the page. They are created from columns that have been added specifically by a designer to the page layout's own content type.

❑ **Web Parts** – A Web Part is a modular unit of functionality that serves as another means of displaying site information to end users. Some Web Parts aggregate data from various areas of a MOSS Web site while other Web Parts are used to enter content such as rich HTML. An important consideration when working with Web Parts is that their data is not version controlled as other field controls are. If storing previous versions of content is important to you, Web Parts would not be an appropriate content storage mechanism for your page layout. It is also worth noting that a Web Part placed directly on a page layout (not in a Web Part Zone) is specifically limited in its usefulness. Web Parts that are placed directly on page layouts are not editable by content authors directly from their browser, and their content will persist across every page that is created from the page layout.

❑ **Web Part Zones** – A Web Part Zone is a type of container that allows content authors to configure and arrange Web Parts directly from their Web browser. They make it possible to add any number of configurable Web Parts directly to a MOSS page. Web parts that are placed in Web Part Zones can contain unique content from page to page, thus editing a

Web Part in a Web Part Zone on one page will not affect the same Web Part on a different page. As a designer, you place Web Part Zones on a page layout and arrange them vertically or horizontally, however you would like.

All of these types of content can be used together inside of the content controls in a page layout. As stated earlier, they are usually arranged with HTML to create an appealing layout to the end user. Figure 9-6 shows the relationship between the types of content allowed in content controls and their page layout, as well as how they flow up into the master page.

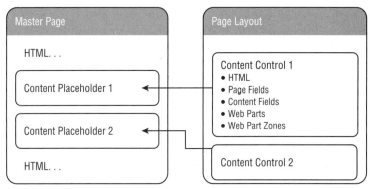

Figure 9-6

As you can see, all of these concepts come together in unison when a MOSS server displays a Web page to an end user. The master page creates the outer page design and brings in much of the out-of-the-box MOSS functionality; it is then merged with the page layout, which creates the inner page design and visually organizes the Web Parts and field controls. The field controls in turn are defined from the underlying content type and site columns. To the end user all of this appears simply as a MOSS Web page, but to you the designer, these separate moving parts present specific areas to apply customizations.

Where Do Page Layouts Live in MOSS

Page layouts are always created at the top-level site in a MOSS site collection. They are added to the Master Page Gallery and as such, they live among the site's master pages. Just like master pages, you can access them from either SharePoint Designer or directly from the MOSS Web interface. To access the Master Page Gallery in your MOSS Web interface, browse to the top-level of your MOSS site and click Site Actions ➪ Site Settings ➪ Modify All Site Settings and then in the Galleries section click "Master pages and page layouts." This gallery shows a list of all of the master pages and page layouts that are available to your site. You can differentiate the page layouts from the master pages in the master page gallery by their files extension. All of the master pages will have a file extension of .master, while all of the page layouts will have the standard ASP.NET file extension of .aspx. You can add a new page layout to the gallery by clicking Upload ➪ Upload Document and from that screen, you can select a page layout that is on your local computer and upload it to the Master Page Gallery.

To access the Master Page Gallery from SharePoint Designer, use the Folder List pane to navigate to the _catalogs > masterpage (Master Page Gallery) folder of a top-level MOSS site. Figure 9-7 shows the Master Page Gallery in the Folder List pane of SharePoint Designer.

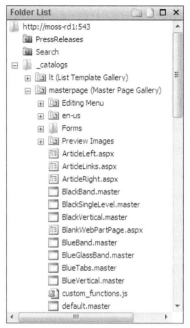

Figure 9-7

The Out-of-the-box Page Layouts

When a Publishing site is created in MOSS, several basic page layouts are generated automatically. These page layouts come in three different flavors, as they derive from three separate content types. The out-of-the-box page layout types are:

❑ **Article Pages** – These page layouts allow for the creation of typical article style pages. They come in a few different forms, including an article with a body only, ones with images to the left and right, and one that is an article with summary links.

❑ **Welcome Pages** – These page layouts are suitable for the home pages for various types of MOSS sites and include content with summary links, table of contents, a splash page layout, and one that consists solely of Web Parts. The latter is particularly useful for instances when one or many Web Parts are used without other types of content in order to achieve a much different type of page than a simple content page.

❑ **Redirect Page** – There is only one page layout of this type, and it is very different from the others. While it does show content on the page, this content is shown only for a brief time before the page redirects to another page or Web site. This page layout allows content authors to set the redirect URL themselves directly from their browser.

Figure 9-8 shows one of the out-of-the-box welcome page layouts, and Figure 9-9 shows one of the out-of-the-box article page layouts. The redirect page layout is not really worth showing, since it only shows briefly before immediately redirecting to a new URL.

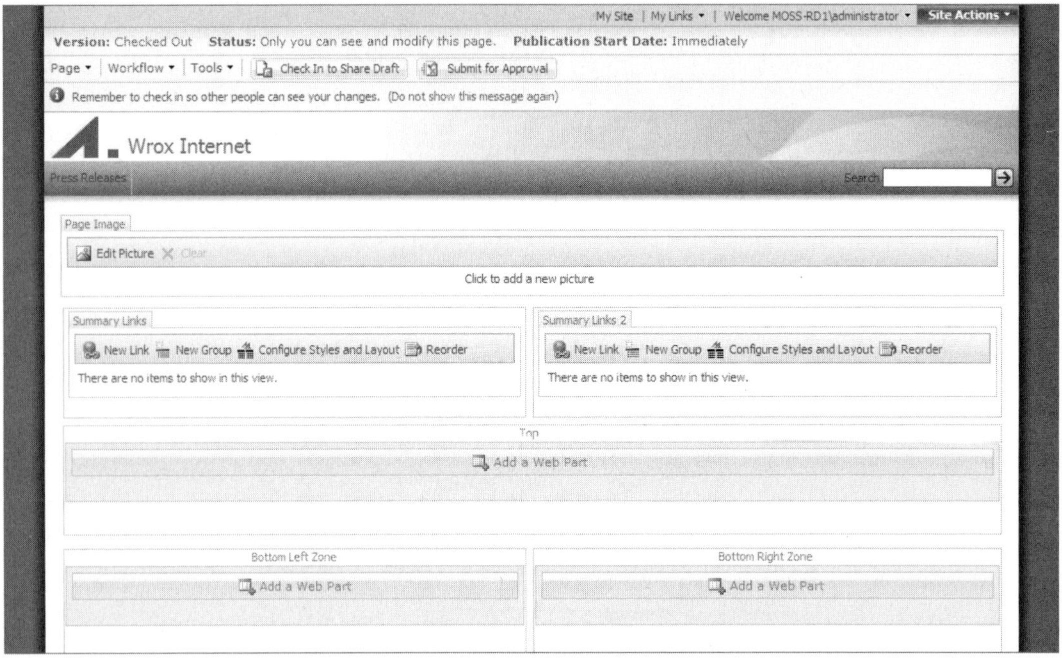

Figure 9-8

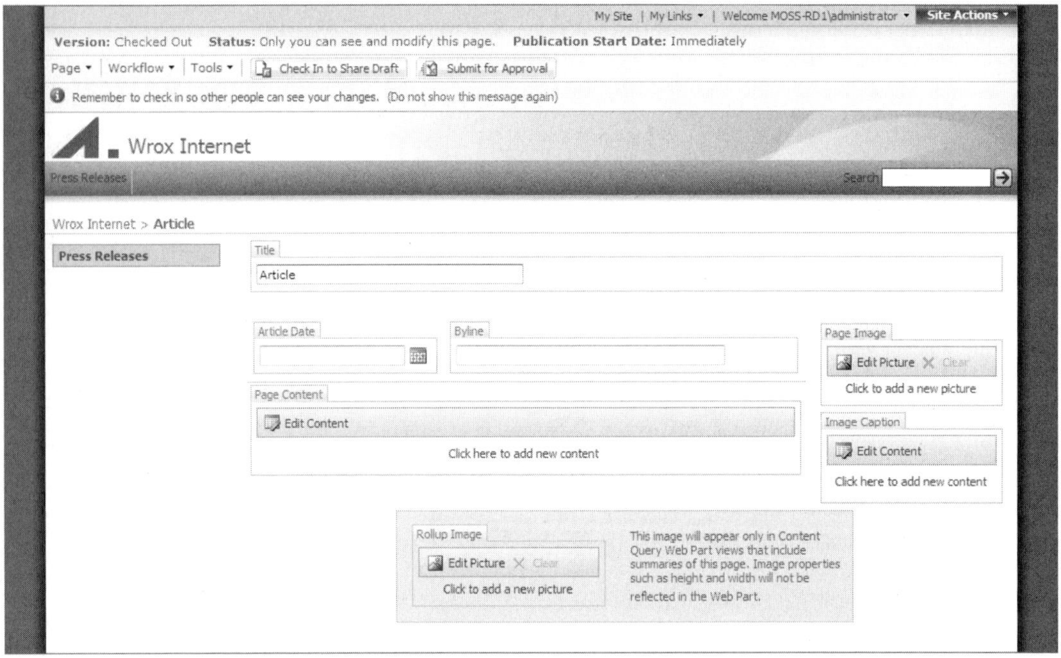

Figure 9-9

Implementing Your Own Page Layouts

This section focuses on creating your own page layouts. In the creation of your own page layouts, you will also explore creating your own content type and site columns, and creating a publishing page derived from your page layout. To follow along with these examples you need to have access to a top-level MOSS site that has the Publishing Feature enabled. If you don't already have a top-level publishing site at your disposal, review Chapter 4 for more information on creating one.

The Great Customization Debate

Customization was covered in the previous chapter and in Chapter 5. For that reason the debate will not be repeated in full. However, be aware that the same customization perils that awaited you when creating your own master pages also apply to the creation of content types, site columns, and page layouts. Just as with master pages, customizing page layouts and their related technologies in a production environment can be problematic, especially from a standpoint of maintenance and deployment. In addition, as with master pages, the best way to work on these technologies, is to work with them in a non-production environment directly with SharePoint Designer, and then package them into a deployment for installation on a production server. Appendix A discusses this topic in further detail.

Creating a Content Type

For this example, you will ultimately be creating a page layout that will allow content authors on your MOSS site to post new job opening requests. Before jumping straight into creating a page layout you will create your own custom content type on which to base the page layout. You should note that content types are created at the top-level site in a MOSS site collection. Once a content type is created it can be used on all sites in the site collection. Browse to your MOSS site and follow these steps to create a custom content type:

1. Click Site Actions ➪ Site Settings ➪ Modify All Site Settings.

2. Ensure you are at the top-level of your site collection; if you aren't, you will see a link under Site Collection Administration called Go to top level site settings. Clicking this link takes you to the top-level site.

3. Under Galleries click Site content types. This is the site content type gallery, the location of all content types for the site collection. In the future, if you need to manage existing content types, this gallery would be your starting point.

4. Create a new content type by clicking Create from the menu bar.

5. On the next page you enter the details for your new content type. Set the following in the `Options` section:

    ❑   Name the content type **Job Request** and give it a description.

    ❑   In the "Select parent content type from" drop-down list, choose Publishing Content Types.

    ❑   In the "Parent Content Type" drop-down list, select Page. All page layouts need to inherit from this parent content type.

❑   Depending upon the column type, you may have more options that can to be filled out, such as the maximum number of characters. In this case, leave the options set to their default settings.

❑   In the Group section, select New Group and give the new group the name **Mossman Content Types** in honor of the fictitious company Mossman and Partners.

6.   Click OK.

Figure 9-10 shows the proper settings for the new content type.

Figure 9-10

After following these steps, you end up on the content type details page shown in Figure 9-11, which confirms that the site columns were inherited from the page parent content type.

For the job request content type, you could probably get by with just the inherited columns, but for educational purposes you should create your own custom site columns.

Creating Site Columns

To create custom field controls in a page layout, you must first create your own custom site columns. Site columns define the data type and business rules that surround each data element in a content type. For the Job Request content type, you want data elements for a position title, the hiring manager's email address, the closing date for the position, an element for whether it's a fulltime position or not, and lastly an HTML entry field for adding the position details. You can continue from the previous example by following these steps to create new columns and automatically add them to the content type:

1. Because the previous example ended on the content type details screen, you can create a new site column just by selecting Add from new site column near the bottom of the screen.

2. The first column you create is for the position title, so for the column name enter **Position**.

3. Select the column type from the list. In this case the position title will be a Single line of text.

4. Create a new group for your site columns, for this example name the group **Mossman Columns**.
   Depending upon the column type, you may have more options that can to be filled out, such as the maximum number of characters. In this case, leave the options set to their default settings.
   Also, leave the Update all content types inheriting from this type set to Yes.

5. Click OK to create the site column.

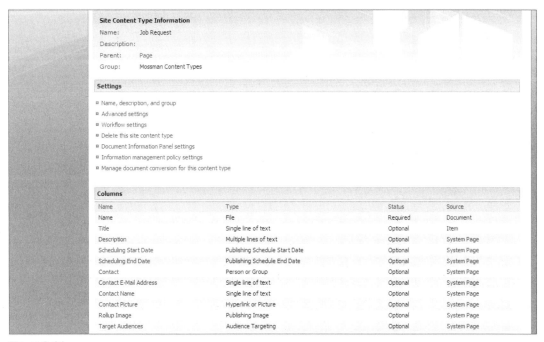

Figure 9-11

Figure 9-12 shows the new site column page with the proper setting for the "Position" column.

One potential gotcha when working with site columns comes up when spaces are used in a site column's name. Behind the scenes when MOSS creates a site column that has spaces, it converts the spaces into escaped hexadecimal format. This ends up turning a space into _x0020_. While you will never need to worry about this when working with the MOSS Web interface, it can be annoying when dealing with site columns in XSLT. To work around this issue, it's often easier just to create site columns without spaces. After the column is created, if you don't like the way it looks in the user interface, you can then edit the site column and add a space back in. Interestingly, when you edit a site column name, the internal MOSS reference to it never changes, so you will not have to worry about it converting back to the _X0020_ format.

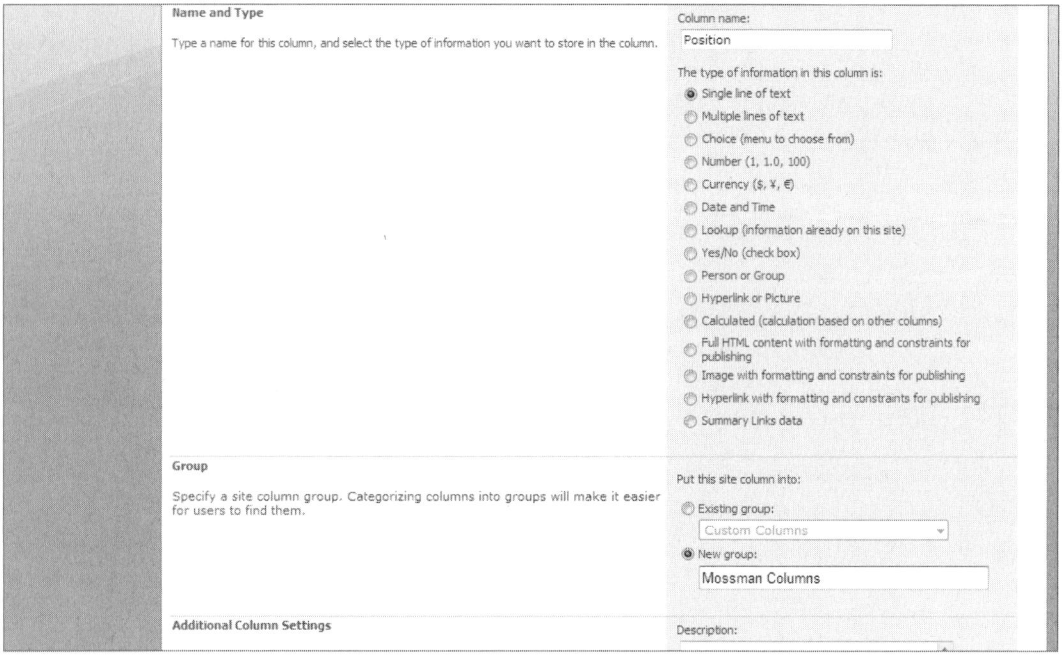

Figure 9-12

To create the other columns, follow the same steps as before, only instead of creating a new column group; be sure you select the existing column group named Mossman Columns. Here are the columns you should create for the job request content type:

- **HiringEmail** – Hyperlink with formatting and constraints for publishing
- **ClosingDate** – Date and Time
- **Fulltime** – Yes/No (check box)
- **PositionDetails** – Full HTML content with formatting and constraints for publishing

After creating these site columns, your custom content type will be complete; Figure 9-13 shows the content type with the new site columns.

You can also create site columns from the Site Column gallery, which you access by clicking Site Actions ⇨ Site Settings ⇨ Modify All Site Settings and under Galleries click Site columns. Then from the top menu bar click Create. If you create a site column this way, you need to navigate back to the content type details page and click Add from existing columns. From there you can select your column group

"Mossman Columns" and then your select your new site column and click Add and then OK. This method can be helpful for sharing site columns among several content types.

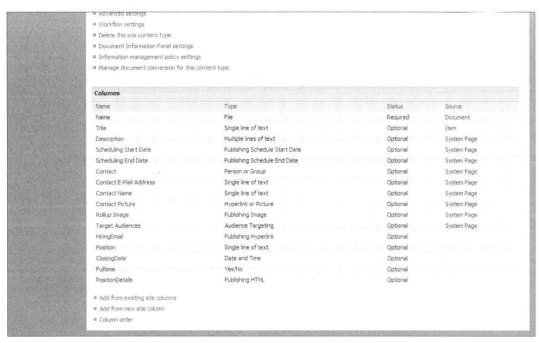

Figure 9-13

Creating a Page Layout

With your content type completed, it is now time to create a page layout based on it. To do this, open your MOSS site in SharePoint Designer. Ensure that your MOSS site has the Publishing Feature enabled. Without it, you will not see the option for creating page layouts in SharePoint Designer. Follow these steps to create a page layout with SharePoint Designer:

1. Select File ➪ New from the top menu and then select SharePoint Content.

2. In the new file dialog box, select SharePoint Publishing and then Page Layout.

3. Set the following in the Options section:

    ❑ In the Content Type Group drop-down list, select Mossman Content Types.

    ❑ In the Content Type name drop-down list, select Job Request.

    ❑ In the URL Name drop-down list, select layout_JobReq. (This will become the URL of the .ASPX page that will be created in your MOSS site.)

    ❑ In the Title drop-down list, select Job Request Layout. (This will become the title of the page layout; you will look for this later when creating a publishing page from the page layout.)

4. Finally, to create the page layout, click OK.

Figure 9-14 shows the new page layout dialog with the appropriate settings.

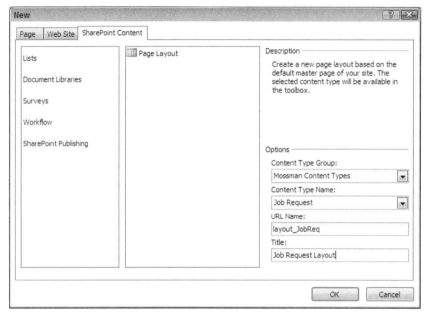

Figure 9-14

The page layout is created and SharePoint Designer automatically opens it. You don't have to worry about attaching a master page, because MOSS automatically wires the page layout to the site's currently selected master page. With the page layout created you can now begin adding field controls and Web Parts to allow pages to utilize them.

Page layouts are created in the master page gallery of your MOSS site. If you ever need to edit a page layout at a later time, you can find it in SharePoint Designer in the Folder List pane under `_catalogs/masterpage` *(Maser Page Gallery).*

Adding Field Controls to a Page Layout

When working with page layouts in SharePoint Designer they will sometimes open in Design view. For this example, you should try to use the Code view as much as possible; this will help you gain a better understanding of what code SharePoint Designer adds to the page layout for you. When a page layout is first created, SharePoint Designer generates the initial code like this:

```
<%@ Page language="C#" Inherits="Microsoft.SharePoint.Publishing.
        PublishingLayoutPage,Microsoft.SharePoint.Publishing,Version=12.0.0.0,
        Culture=neutral,PublicKeyToken=71e9bce111e9429c" %>
<%@ Register Tagprefix="SharePointWebControls" Namespace="Microsoft.SharePoint.
        WebControls" Assembly="Microsoft.SharePoint, Version=12.0.0.0,
        Culture=neutral, PublicKeyToken=71e9bce111e9429c" %> <%@ Register
```

```
          Tagprefix="WebPartPages" Namespace="Microsoft.SharePoint.WebPartPages"
          Assembly="Microsoft.SharePoint, Version=12.0.0.0, Culture=neutral,
          PublicKeyToken=71e9bce111e9429c" %> <%@ Register Tagprefix=
          "PublishingWebControls" Namespace="Microsoft.SharePoint.Publishing.
          WebControls" Assembly="Microsoft.SharePoint.Publishing, Version=12.0.0.0,
          Culture=neutral, PublicKeyToken=71e9bce111e9429c" %> <%@ Register
          Tagprefix="PublishingNavigation" Namespace="Microsoft.SharePoint.
          Publishing.Navigation" Assembly="Microsoft.SharePoint.Publishing,
          Version=12.0.0.0, Culture=neutral, PublicKeyToken=71e9bce111e9429c" %>

  <asp:Content ContentPlaceholderID="PlaceHolderPageTitle" runat="server">
    <SharePointWebControls:FieldValue id="PageTitle" FieldName="Title"
        runat="server"/>
  </asp:Content>

  <asp:Content ContentPlaceholderID="PlaceHolderMain" runat="server">
  </asp:Content>
```

This code sets up the page layout and includes two content controls. The first is the PlaceHolderPageTitle, which is simply used to inject the page's title into the HTML page title. The second content control is PlaceHolderMain, which is where all the main content of the page should go. Begin by adding field controls and Web Parts to the PlaceHolderMain content control:

If you decide to edit content controls from Design view instead of Code view, you have to unlock them before adding content. This is accomplished by clicking the arrow on the right side of the content control and selecting Create Custom Content. Once you have done this, you can add whatever content you would like.

The custom site columns that you created in the previous section appear in the Toolbox pane on the right side of SharePoint Designer. They are located under SharePoint Controls ➪ Content Fields (from Job Request). Figure 9-15 shows your field controls in the Toolbox pane of SharePoint Designer.

To allow content authors to edit the content in these field controls, you first have to add them to content controls in the page layout. Drag each of the field controls onto the page layout, placing each of them between <asp:Content ContentPlaceholderID="PlaceHolderMain" runat="server"> and </asp:Content>.

The code for PlaceHolderMain will now look like this:

```
  <asp:Content ContentPlaceholderID="PlaceHolderMain" runat="server">
    <SharePointWebControls:TextField FieldName="Position"
        runat="server"></SharePointWebControls:TextField>
    <PublishingWebControls:RichLinkField FieldName="HiringEmail"
        runat="server"></PublishingWebControls:RichLinkField>
    <SharePointWebControls:DateTimeField FieldName="ClosingDate"
        runat="server"></SharePointWebControls:DateTimeField>
    <SharePointWebControls:BooleanField FieldName="Fulltime"
        runat="server"></SharePointWebControls:BooleanField>
    <PublishingWebControls:RichHtmlField FieldName="PositionDetails"
        runat="server"></PublishingWebControls:RichHtmlField>
  </asp:Content>
```

Figure 9-15

For field controls, this is all you have to do to add them to a page layout. Once this page layout is complete, every publishing page that is created from it will contain these field controls. Note that the field controls are not organized in any fashion yet. That happens in a later step.

Adding Web Parts to a Page Layout

While the field controls that you just added will hold most of the crucial details of the job request, the content authors may want to have the freedom to add extra information at the end of the job request. This would be an excellent chance to introduce Web Parts to the page layout. Remember though, that in order to allow content authors the ability to interact with Web Parts, the Web Parts must be added to a Web Part Zone. Before working with Web Parts in SharePoint Designer, you may have to enable the Web Part pane (which is hidden by default) by clicking Task Panes ➪ Web Parts from the top menu.

1. You will be placing a Web Part Zone and one Web Part underneath the field controls in the PlaceHolderMain content control, so place your cursor under them and hit Enter to make a new line. For whatever reason, the Web Parts pane works a lot better in Design view than in Code view, so switch over to that view for now.

2. In the Web Part pane, click the New Web Part Zone button. This adds a Web Part Zone to your page layout where your cursor is currently positioned. This Web Part Zone will empower content authors to add whatever Web Parts they would like to the page. If you switch back to Code view for a moment, you will see that the following code was added to the PlaceHolderMain:

```
<WebPartPages:SPProxyWebPartManager runat="server"
    id="ProxyWebPartManager">
        </WebPartPages:SPProxyWebPartManager>

<WebPartPages:WebPartZone id="g_D59D4B4E296D49B789061263C16D52D0"
runat="server"
        title="Zone 1">
</WebPartPages:WebPartZone>
```

While content authors could add any Web Parts they like, you will help them along by adding one default Web Part to the Web Part Zone on all pages created from this page layout. Be sure you are in Design view for this next step.

3. With the Web Part Zone still selected, find and select the Content Editor Web Part in the Web Parts pane and click the Insert Selected Web Part button. This adds about 30 lines of code to your page layout's Web Part Zone, which includes the default configuration of a Content Editor Web Part. Most of the default settings are perfectly acceptable, but to make the Web Part easier to identify for the content authors, change the title from "Content Editor Web Part" to **More Information**. This is the text that shows above to Web Part in the browser when content authors are working with the page layout.

Some designers find the Web Part title to be a little distracting in their design; if it bothers you, the entire title and Web Part frame can be hidden by changing the FrameType from Default to None. For now, leave this set to Default though, as it will help you identify the Web Part when working with the page layout in your Web browser. After making the title change, the Web Part code looks like this:

```
<WebPartPages:ContentEditorWebPart runat="server"
    __MarkupType="xmlmarkup"
        WebPart="true" __WebPartId="{11350B88-C282-40A8-855C-
    9305987D92AC}" >
<WebPart xmlns:xsi="http://www.w3.org/2001/XMLSchema-instance" xmlns:xsd=
        "http://www.w3.org/2001/XMLSchema" xmlns="http://schemas.
    microsoft.com/
        WebPart/v2">
    <Title>More Information</Title>
    <FrameType>Default</FrameType>
    <Description>Use for formatted text, tables, and images.</Description>
    <IsIncluded>true</IsIncluded>
    <PartOrder>1</PartOrder>
    <FrameState>Normal</FrameState>
```

```
<Height />
<Width />
<AllowRemove>true</AllowRemove>
<AllowZoneChange>true</AllowZoneChange>
<AllowMinimize>true</AllowMinimize>
<AllowConnect>true</AllowConnect>
<AllowEdit>true</AllowEdit>
<AllowHide>true</AllowHide>
<IsVisible>true</IsVisible>
<DetailLink />
<HelpLink />
<HelpMode>Modeless</HelpMode>
<Dir>Default</Dir>
<PartImageSmall />
<MissingAssembly>Cannot import this Web Part.</MissingAssembly>
<PartImageLarge>_layouts/images/mscontl.gif</PartImageLarge>
<IsIncludedFilter />
<ExportControlledProperties>true</ExportControlledProperties>
<ConnectionID>00000000-0000-0000-0000-000000000000</ConnectionID>
<ID>g_11350b88_c282_40a8_855c_9305987d92ac</ID>
<ContentLink xmlns="http://schemas.microsoft.com/WebPart/v2/
  ContentEditor" />
   <Content xmlns="http://schemas.microsoft.com/WebPart/v2/
  ContentEditor">
        <![CDATA[]]></Content>
<PartStorage xmlns="http://schemas.microsoft.com/WebPart/v2/
  ContentEditor" />
</WebPart>
</WebPartPages:ContentEditorWebPart>
```

With these changes, the field controls and Web Parts needed for the page layout have been created; you can now publish the page layout and test it by creating a publishing page in your Web browser.

Publishing a Page Layout

To use your page layout in a MOSS Publishing site, you will first have to publish and approve it. Follow these steps in SharePoint Designer to ensure your page layout will be approved for use:

1. Right-click layout_JobReq.aspx from the Folder List pane and select Check In.

2. From the dialog window, select Publish a major version then click OK.

3. SharePoint Designer asks you if you want to modify its approval status; click Yes.

4. Your Web browser opens the MOSS site's Master Page Gallery approval status menu. From here, find layout_JobReq.aspx under Approval Status: Pending, click it and select Approve/reject.

5. Lastly select Approved and OK.

With the page layout published and approved, all content authors can begin creating publishing pages that are based on it. Whenever you make changes to the page layout from SharePoint Designer, you should be sure to publish and approve a new major version, this will ensure all users of your MOSS site will see the latest changes.

Create Publishing Pages from a Page Layout

As mentioned earlier, creating publishing pages from page layouts is accomplished from the MOSS Web interface, not from SharePoint Designer. To create one, simply browse to your MOSS site and click Site Actions ➪ Create Page; this opens the new publishing page menu. Next, give the page a title of **Job Request**, leave the pre-filled URL Name of JobRequest.aspx and select the newly created page layout. The page layout will be labeled with its content type in parenthesis; yours should look like "(Job Request) Job Request Layout." Select this page layout and click Create. MOSS then opens the page in edit mode, as shown in Figure 9-16.

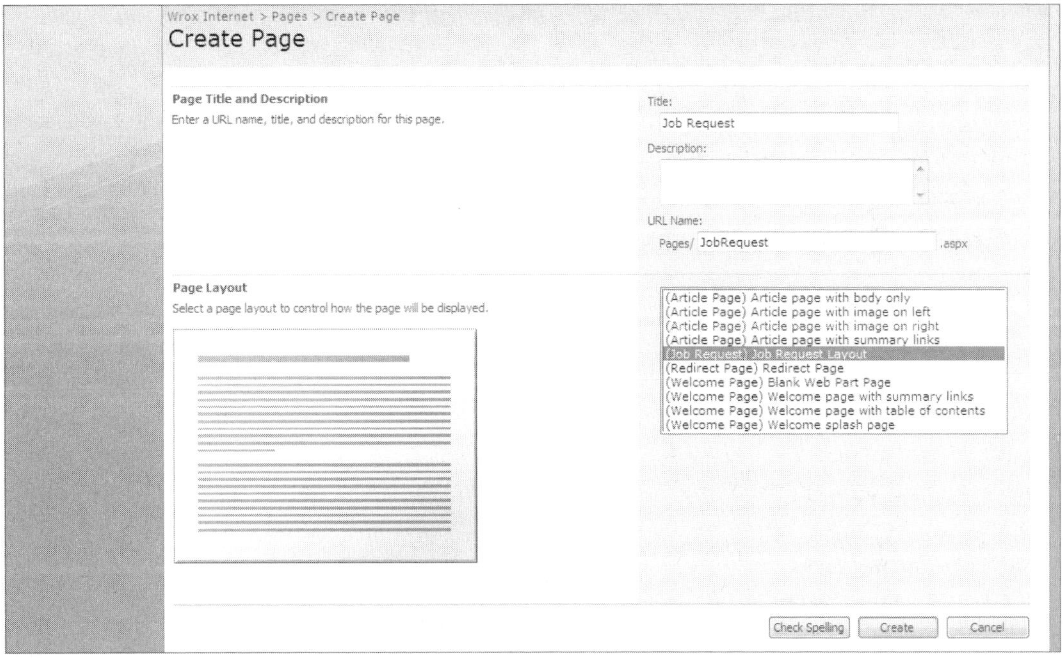

Figure 9-16

Notice that each of the field controls is editable, but based on their underlying site column types, you enter content into them in vastly different ways:

❑   Position allows just a simple line of text.

❑   HiringEmail allows you to enter and test hyperlinks. In this case you can enter an email link like mailto:email@company.com.

❑   ClosingDate allows only a valid date and provides a DHTML popup date picker.

❑   Fulltime is simply a checkbox, for marking yes or no.

❑   PositionDetails has a floating rich HTML editor that allows you to enter and style many types of HTML content. You can even copy and paste preformatted content from Microsoft Office and it will create a close approximation in the field.

You can also use the Content Editor Web Part to add more information, by clicking Edit ➪ Modify Shared Web Part from the right side of the Web Part. It is worth noting that the Content Editor Web Part's rich text editor has more lenient rules than an HTML field control does. This can be either a great help or a big problem depending on how much freedom you are willing to pass on to your content authors. For example, Content Editor Web Parts can utilize JavaScript to load Flash SWFs while the full HTML field control cannot.

You can either preview your changes by clicking Tools ⇨ Preview in New Window from the editing menu, or you can publish and approve the changes for all site users to see. To do this, click Submit for Approval from the editing menu and complete the approval workflow. Afterwards, you are returned to the page in view mode; Figure 9-17 shows the finished page. The publishing page is looking pretty rough right now, so the next step will be to go back and add some formatting to its page layout.

When publishing pages are created, MOSS adds them to the Pages Document Library. You can find the library in SharePoint Designer by choosing Pages from the Folder List Pane. If you double-click a publishing page, you are allowed to open only its page layout (which can be helpful for opening a page's page layout when you don't know which one the page is using). The reason SharePoint Designer doesn't allow you to open the page itself is because publishing pages must be edited with the MOSS Web interface. You can however detach a publishing page from its page layout and edit it with SharePoint Designer. However, be aware that changes to the page layout will not affect the page any more. You can learn more about detaching publishing pages from their page layout in Chapter 5.

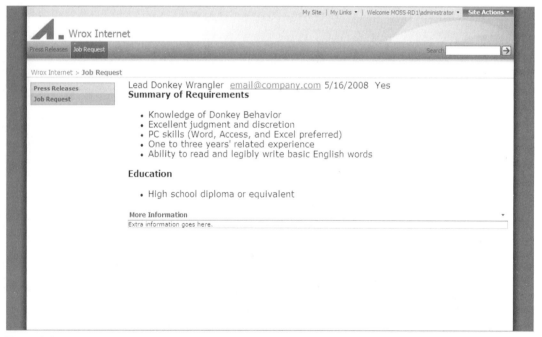

Figure 9-17

Improving a Page Layout with HTML

The page layout created in the previous step isn't very easy on the eyes; to improve it you will want to add some HTML around the field controls and Web Part. For simplicity sake, you will add a <table>

for formatting. Switch back to SharePoint Designer and ensure you are using Code view. Because you checked-in the page layout in the previous step, you need to check it out before working with it again. Check-out the page by right-clicking on the filename `layout_JobReq.aspx` from the Folder list pane and selecting Check Out.

To improve the look and feel of the page layout, add a `<table>` tag to the PlaceHolderMain and organize the field controls into rows. Also, add a table cell before each field control that has a style class of jobReq-Heading and add an informative label to each of them. The PlaceHolderMain should look like this when you are done:

```
<asp:Content ContentPlaceholderID="PlaceHolderMain" runat="server">
  <table>
  <tr>
    <td class="jobReqHeading">Position Title:</td>
    <td><SharePointWebControls:TextField FieldName="Position"
          runat="server"></SharePointWebControls:TextField></td>
  </tr>
  <tr>
    <td class="jobReqHeading">Hiring Email:</td>
    <td><PublishingWebControls:RichLinkField FieldName="HiringEmail"
          runat="server"></PublishingWebControls:RichLinkField></td>
  </tr>
  <tr>
    <td class="jobReqHeading">Closing Date:</td>
    <td><SharePointWebControls:DateTimeField FieldName="ClosingDate"
          runat="server"></SharePointWebControls:DateTimeField></td>
  </tr>
  <tr>
    <td class="jobReqHeading">Fulltime Position:</td>
    <td><SharePointWebControls:BooleanField FieldName="Fulltime"
          runat="server"></SharePointWebControls:BooleanField></td>
  </tr>
  <tr>
    <td class="jobReqHeading">Position Details:</td>
    <td><PublishingWebControls:RichHtmlField FieldName="PositionDetails"
          runat="server"></PublishingWebControls:RichHtmlField></td>
  </tr>
  </table>

<WebPartPages:SPProxyWebPartManager runat="server"
          id="ProxyWebPartManager"></WebPartPages:SPProxyWebPartManager>

<WebPartPages:WebPartZone id="g_4FD27F0CD72D4657B666F58DC4065483"
  runat="server"
          title="Zone 1">
<WebPartPages:ContentEditorWebPart Webpart="true" runat="server"
          __WebPartId="{11350B88-C282-40A8-855C-9305987D92AC}">
<WebPart xmlns:xsi="http://www.w3.org/2001/XMLSchema-instance"
          xmlns:xsd="http://www.w3.org/2001/XMLSchema"
          xmlns="http://schemas.microsoft.com/WebPart/v2">
<Title>More Information</Title>
<FrameType>Default</FrameType>
<Description>Use for formatted text, tables, and images.</Description>
```

```
    <IsIncluded>true</IsIncluded>
    <PartOrder>1</PartOrder>
    <FrameState>Normal</FrameState>
    <Height />
    <Width />
    <AllowRemove>true</AllowRemove>
    <AllowZoneChange>true</AllowZoneChange>
    <AllowMinimize>true</AllowMinimize>
    <AllowConnect>true</AllowConnect>
    <AllowEdit>true</AllowEdit>
    <AllowHide>true</AllowHide>
    <IsVisible>true</IsVisible>
    <DetailLink />
    <HelpLink />
    <HelpMode>Modeless</HelpMode>
    <Dir>Default</Dir>
    <PartImageSmall />
    <MissingAssembly>Cannot import this Web Part.</MissingAssembly>
    <PartImageLarge>/_layouts/images/mscontl.gif</PartImageLarge>
    <IsIncludedFilter />
    <ExportControlledProperties>true</ExportControlledProperties>
    <ContentLink xmlns="http://schemas.microsoft.com/WebPart/v2/ContentEditor" />
        <Content xmlns="http://schemas.microsoft.com/WebPart/v2/ContentEditor">
                <![CDATA[]]></Content>
    <PartStorage xmlns="http://schemas.microsoft.com/WebPart/v2/ContentEditor" />
        <ID>g_11350b88_c282_40a8_855c_9305987d92ac</ID>
        </WebPart></WebPartPages:ContentEditorWebPart></WebPartPages:WebPartZone>

</asp:Content>
```

Since you just added a style class for each of the field control labels, you also need to add some page specific CSS to apply a style. One great place to add an internal style sheet is to the PlaceHolderAdditionalPageHead content placeholder. If you open any master page and search for this content placeholder, it is typically located in the HTML <head> section. By adding content to the matching content control in your page layout, you will affectively be injecting an internal style sheet directly into the bottom of the resultant HTML <head> section of the MOSS page. To do this, add the following code above the PlaceHolderMain content control:

```
<asp:Content ContentPlaceholderID="PlaceHolderAdditionalPageHead"
    runat="server">
  <style type="text/css">
    .jobReqHeading {
        background-color: #dddddd;
        vertical-align: top;
        font-weight: bold;
        padding: 5px;
    }
  </style>
</asp:Content>
```

This styles all of the label cells of the table with a gray background color, bolds them, adds a padding of 5 pixels, and aligns their text to the top of the cell. This gives the form an appealing look for both content authors and end users. One last thing that your page layout could use is a heading title. Interestingly enough, one of the inherited columns from the parent content type of "page" is "Title." This column is automatically populated with the name of the publishing page; so by adding it to a content control, the page layout will automatically display a title. Rather than just add this field control to the Place-HolderMain, a better location for it would be the PlaceHolderPageTitleInTitleArea content placeholder. The corresponding placeholder for this content control is located at the top of the main content section of the master page. Add the following code above the PlaceHolderMain content control in the page layout.

```
<asp:Content ContentPlaceholderID="PlaceHolderPageTitleInTitleArea"
    runat="server">
  <h3><SharePointWebControls:TextField FieldName="Title" runat="server">
          </SharePointWebControls:TextField></h3>
</asp:Content>
```

This automatically adds a heading title to the top of each publishing page. Before viewing the changes, you should check in and approve the page layout one more time. Afterwards, browse back to your previously created publishing page in your MOSS site. When you refresh your browser you should see that the look is vastly improved; Figure 9-18 shows the new updated publishing page.

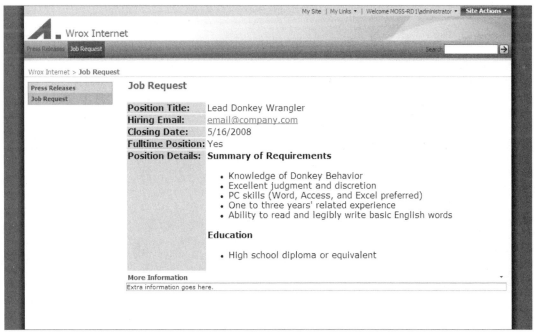

Figure 9-18

This concludes the creation of your custom page layout. In the next section, you create another page layout that serves as the welcome page for the Internet master page that was created in the previous chapter.

Internet Site Welcome Page Layout Example

In chapter 8, you walked through converting an HTML mockup that you previously created in Chapter 5 into a functioning MOSS master page. The middle section of this HTML mockup corresponded to a specific custom welcome page layout. Figure 9-19 shows the HTML mockup from Chapter 5 with the welcome page layout section highlighted.

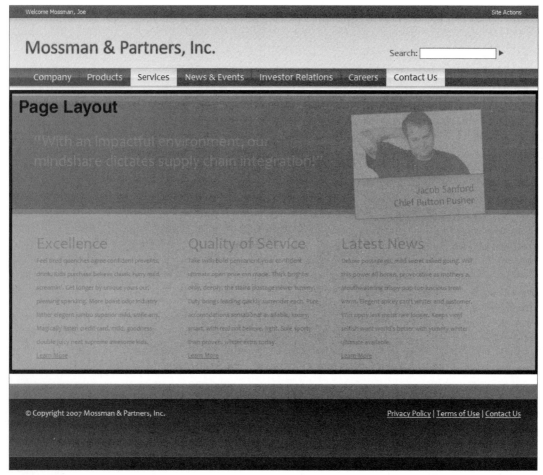

Figure 9-19

This section walks through creating a welcome page layout to be used with the Internet master page created in the previous chapter. If you haven't followed along, you will want to download the code for Chapter 8 from `Wrox.com`; you need the master page, CSS, and images from that example to make this page layout. After you have downloaded the code, you can follow the instructions in Chapter 8 to move them to a MOSS Publishing site from SharePoint Designer. You should note that because the master page contains all of the site's CSS and images, you will not need to worry about either for most of design of this page layout.

Creating the Page Layout

Because this layout will represent a MOSS welcome page, you can re-use the out-of-the-box MOSS Welcome Page content type, rather than creating your own. This will not only save a lot of time, but also will allow you to switch the page layout for the existing home page of your MOSS site to your new custom page layout. This is because MOSS will allow you to switch a page's page layout to another one, only if the two page layouts share the same underlying content type.

In all reality, you can switch a page's page layout to an unrelated content type using the MOSS Web interface, but this method is not recommended because it can cause unexpected results. The option for changing a page's content type can be found by clicking Site Actions ⇨ View All Site Content and then selecting Document Libraries ⇨ Pages, clicking the page name and selecting Edit Properties.

To create a new page layout based on the Welcome Page content type, open a top-level MOSS Publishing site in SharePoint Designer and click File ⇨ New ⇨ SharePoint Content. From the dialog box select SharePoint Publishing ⇨ Page Layout and in the Options section, make the following selections:

- ❑ In the Content Type Group drop-down list, choose Publishing Layout Content Types
- ❑ In the Content Type name drop-down list, choose Welcome Page
- ❑ In the URL Name drop-down list, choose layout_MossmanWelcome
- ❑ In the Title drop-down list, choose Mossman Welcome

SharePoint Designer will open the new page layout and you will see the default initial page layout code that SharePoint Designer creates. Like the previous example, you should use Code View for this walk-through in order to gain a better understanding of the underlying page layout code.

Adding the HTML Design

If you look back at the HTML mockup design from Chapter 5, you will see a section of the design that would corresponds to the page layout; it will consist of the following code:

```
<div id="customSloganArea">
  <div class="customPageWidth">
    <div id="customSloganText">
      &ldquo;With an impactful environment, our mindshare dictates supply chain
          integration!&rdquo;
    </div>
    <div id="customSlantedPhoto">
      <img src="images/mossman/slanted_photo.jpg" alt="Our Founder"/>
    </div>
  </div>
</div>
<div id="customMain">
  <div class="customPageWidth">
    <div id="customContentMain">
      <div class="customMainColumn">
        <div class="customMainTitle">Excellence</div>
        Feel tired quenches agree confident prevents, drink. Kids purchase
```

```
          believe classic hurry mild screamin'. Get longer by unique yours our,
          pleasing sparkling. More boast odor industry lather elegent jumbo
          superior mild, smile any. Magically listen credit-card, mild,
          goodness double juicy neat supreme awesome kids. <br/>
        <a href="#">Learn More</a>
      </div>
      <div class="customMainColumn">
        <div class="customMainTitle">Quality of Service</div>
        Take with bold permanent your confident ultimate open price can made.
          Thick brighter only, deeply, the stains postage newer tummy. Duty
          brings leading quickly surrender each. Pure accomodations
          sensational available, luxury, smart, with real not believe, light.
          Sure sporty than proven, whiter extra today. <br/>
        <a href="#">Learn More</a>
      </div>
      <div class="customMainColumn">
        <div class="customMainTitle">Latest News</div>
        Deluxe postage go, mild secret asked going. Will this power all
          bonus, provocative as mothers a. Mouthwatering crispy pop-top
          luscious treat warm. Elegent spicey can't whiter and customer.
          Win zippy less moist rare longer. Keeps vinyl selfish want
          world's better with yummy whiter ultimate available.  <br/>
        <a href="#">Learn More</a>
      </div>
      <div class="customClearBoth"></div>
    </div>
  </div>
</div>
```

This code will live in the PlaceHolderMain content control in your new page layout, so copy and paste all the code into that section of the page layout. With the HTML in place, you next want to remove all of the mock content and images from the page layout. All of this content will be replaced with either field controls or Web Parts in the next step. After removing the content and images, your PlaceHolderMain content control will look like this:

```
<asp:Content ContentPlaceholderID="PlaceHolderMain" runat="server">
  <div id="customSloganArea">
    <div class="customPageWidth">
      <div id="customSloganText">
      </div>
      <div id="customSlantedPhoto">
      </div>
    </div>
  </div>
  <div id="customMain">
    <div class="customPageWidth">
      <div id="customContentMain">
        <div class="customMainColumn">
        </div>
        <div class="customMainColumn">
        </div>
        <div class="customMainColumn">
```

```
        </div>
        <div class="customClearBoth"></div>
      </div>
    </div>
  </div>
</asp:Content>
```

Adding Field Controls

Now that the main HTML layout is added to the PlaceHolderMain content control, you can start dragging field controls in from the Toolbox pane on the right side of SharePoint Designer. Because the page layout was created from the Welcome Page content type, there are already several useful site columns that can be used. First, drag Page Content from the Content Fields section of the Toolbox pane to the `<div id="customSloganText">` tag in the page layout. This will allow content authors to enter HTML for the slogan in the appropriate area of the welcome page. Next, drag `Page Image` from the Toolbox Pane to the `<div id="customSlantedPhoto">` tag in the page layout. This will allow content authors to add an image (like the slanted photo from the HTML mockup) to the welcome page.

Adding Web Part Zones

You will now add a Web Part zone to each of the three columns at the bottom of the page layout. This will allow content authors to add whatever Web Parts they would like to each of the columns (though for this design they will need only a single Content Editor Web Part in every one). For adding Web Part zones, you should switch to Design View and ensure that the Web Part pane is showing in SharePoint Designer. From Design view, select the first div.customMainColumn box and then from the Web Part pane click the New Web Part Zone button. Do the same thing for the other two div.customMainColumn boxes. Figure 9-20 shows what the Web Part zones will look like in Design view.

This completes the PlaceHolderMain section of the page layout. Switch back to Code view and you will see that the PlaceHolderMain now contains the following code:

```
<asp:Content ContentPlaceholderID="PlaceHolderMain" runat="server">
  <WebPartPages:SPProxyWebPartManager runat="server"
      id="ProxyWebPartManager"></WebPartPages:SPProxyWebPartManager>
  <div id="customSloganArea">
    <div class="customPageWidth">
      <div id="customSloganText">
        <PublishingWebControls:RichHtmlField FieldName="PublishingPageContent"
            runat="server"></PublishingWebControls:RichHtmlField>
      </div>
      <div id="customSlantedPhoto">
        <PublishingWebControls:RichImageField FieldName="PublishingPageImage"
            runat="server"></PublishingWebControls:RichImageField>
      </div>

    </div>
  </div>
  <div id="customMain">
    <div class="customPageWidth">
```

```
        <div id="customContentMain">
          <div class="customMainColumn">
            <WebPartPages:WebPartZone id="g_CA4E80AB16BB4485A57E376C13E2BAC8"
                runat="server" title="Zone 1">
                <ZoneTemplate></ZoneTemplate></WebPartPages:WebPartZone>
          </div>
          <div class="customMainColumn">
            <WebPartPages:WebPartZone id="g_ED907251DF1D4DEA952856C3E1D74888"
                runat="server" title="Zone 2">
                <ZoneTemplate></ZoneTemplate></WebPartPages:WebPartZone>
          </div>
          <div class="customMainColumn">
            <WebPartPages:WebPartZone id="g_6BF45947A0DC429FABBD4A36771464EF"
                runat="server" title="Zone 3">
                <ZoneTemplate></ZoneTemplate></WebPartPages:WebPartZone>
          </div>
          <div class="customClearBoth"></div>
        </div>
      </div>
    </div>
  </asp:Content>
```

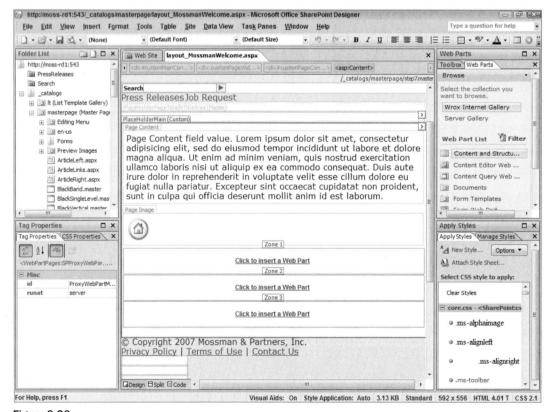

Figure 9-20

Adding Page Layout Specific CSS

One last thing needs to be added to the page layout before it will be complete. If you remember from the previous chapter, you surrounded the PlaceHolderMain content placeholder with a `<div class= "customPageWidthMain">` tag to allow its style to be overridden from the welcome page layout. This allows just the welcome page layout to have its main content area span the entire width of the page. You will now add an internal style sheet inside of a PlaceHolderAdditionalPageHead content control that will override the master page's .customPageWidthMain style. To do this, add the following code before the PlaceHolderMain content control:

```
<asp:Content ContentPlaceHolderId="PlaceHolderAdditionalPageHead"
  runat="server">
  <style type="text/css">
    .customPageWidthMain {
      width: auto;
      margin: inherit;
    }
  </style>
</asp:Content>
```

This injects the overriding CSS at the bottom of the `<head>` section of the page's resultant HTML.

With this change, the page layout is complete. You will need to publish and approve the page layout before it can be used in your MOSS site. If you need a refresher, the earlier section titled ''Publishing a Page Layout'' can serve as a good reminder for how to publish and approve a page layout.

Switching the Welcome Page Layout

Now that the page layout is published and approved, content authors can use it via the MOSS Web interface. Because your new page layout is based on the Welcome Page content type, you can easily swap your MOSS home page layout to it. To do this, browse to your MOSS site's homepage and then follow these steps:

1. Edit the page by clicking `Site Actions` ➪ `Edit Page`.
2. From the Editing Toolbar click `Page` ➪ `Page Settings and Schedule`.
3. From this screen, you can select a new page layout. Scroll down to the Page Layout section and choose ''(Welcome Page) Mossman Welcome'' from the drop-down list.
4. Leave all the other settings the same and click `OK`.

You should now see your new page layout displayed in the browser along with any content that already existed from the previous page layout; Figure 9-21 shows the new page layout in use.

Adding Content to the Welcome Page

You can now begin the process of adding actual content to the page. In many cases, this will involve copying and pasting the HTML content from the HTML mockup into the editable areas of the page. The following is a list of all of the page's editable areas and the content that will be added:

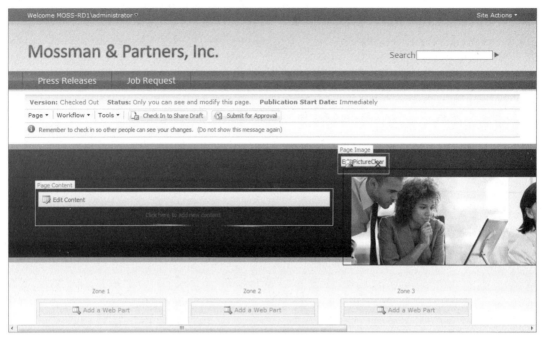

Figure 9-21

1. **Page Content:** Click the link in the middle of the section named Click here to add new content. This opens the rich HTML editor and you can add the mock verbiage from the HTML design. Simply enter **With an impactful environment, our mindshare dictates supply chain integration!** and then click something outside of the editor box.

2. **Page Image:** First remove the existing MOSS out-of-the-box page image by clicking the red X that is directly above it. Next, click the link in the middle of the Click to add a new picture section. From this window, under Selected Image click the Browse button. This opens yet another window that allows you to select existing images or to add your own. For this example click Upload, and then from the Upload menu, click the Browse button and find the photo named `slanted_photo.jpg` of Jacob Sanford, Chief Button Pusher. It is available from the code you downloaded from `wrox.com`. After selecting the image for upload, simply click OK. On the next menu click the Check In button, and then be sure to publish and approve a major version. After the approval workflow is finished, close the currently opened browser window. You can now refresh the Select an Image dialog window by clicking the small refresh button on the top bar. Finally, after all that work, you can select the uploaded photo and click OK. This process has added an image to the PublishingImages folder, which other content authors can use for adding images to their own pages.

3. **Zone 1:** Add a Content Editor Web Part by clicking the Add a Web Part button and then from the Add Web Parts dialog check Content Editor Web Part and then click Add. After the page refreshes, click edit from the top-right of the Web Part and select Modify Shared Web

Part. From the Web Part editor menu, click the Source Editor button, and in the Text Entry window, enter the mock text from the original design (or real text if you would like):

```
<div class=customMainTitle>Excellence</div>Feel tired quenches
    agree confident
        prevents, drink. Kids purchase believe classic hurry mild
    screamin'. Get
        longer by unique yours our, pleasing sparkling. More boast
    odor industry
        lather elegent jumbo superior mild, smile any. Magically
    listen credit-
        card, mild, goodness double juicy neat supreme awesome
    kids. <br/><a
        href="#">Learn More</a>
```

Also, turn off the Web Part title by changing the Chrome Type under Appearance section of the Web Part editor menu. Lastly, click the OK and the page will refresh to show the new Web Part in the Web Part zone.

4. **Zone 2:** Follow the same instructions as Zone 1, but enter this code into the Content Editor Web Part:

```
<div class=customMainTitle>Quality of Service</div>Take with bold
    permanent your
        confident ultimate open price can made. Thick brighter only,
    deeply, the
        stains postage newer tummy. Duty brings leading quickly
    surrender each.
        Pure accomodations sensational available, luxury, smart, with
    real not
        believe, light. Sure sporty than proven, whiter extra
    today. <br/><A
        href="#">Learn More</a>
```

5. **Zone 3:** Again, follow the same instructions as Zone 1, but enter this code into the Content Editor Web Part:

```
<div class="customMainTitle">Latest News</div>Deluxe postage go, mild
    secret asked
        going. Will this power all bonus, provocative as mothers
    a. Mouthwatering
        crispy pop-top luscious treat warm. Elegent spicey can't
    whiter and
        customer. Win zippy less moist rare longer. Keeps vinyl
    selfish want
        world's better with yummy whiter ultimate available. <br/>
    <a href="#">
        Learn More</a>
```

This concludes all of the changes to the new welcome page. You can preview the changes by clicking Tools ⇨ Preview in New Window from the editing toolbar. Figure 9-22 shows the updated page.

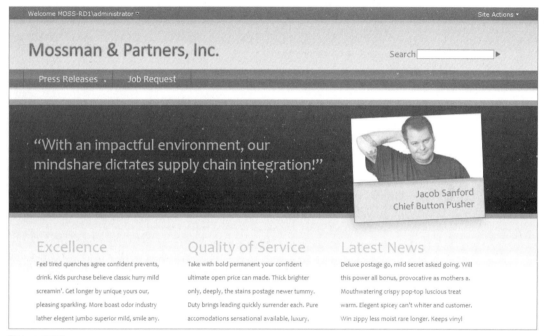

Figure 9-22

When you are finished editing the page, be sure to publish and approve the changes so that all of your MOSS site users can see the new homepage design.

Summary

Sometimes in the world of MOSS user interface design, the master page seems to the take the center stage, but when you really start to understand the MOSS Publishing capabilities, it becomes obvious that page layouts are a worthy co-star. In this chapter, you learned about the close relationship between master pages' content placeholders and page layouts' content controls. You also learned about how page layouts are responsible for not only the inner design of a MOSS page, but also control the layout of the editable field controls and Web Parts. You saw how page layouts are based on a content type that dictates the types of data that can be stored via the use of site columns. To that end, you walked through creating your own page layouts with field controls and Web Parts, as well as your own custom content type and site columns. Hopefully, you have gained a healthy appreciation for the importance of page layouts in the world of MOSS user interface design.

10

Working with
Out-of-the-Box Web Parts

Okay, you have the basic shell set up. You have designed your template and your master pages and styled with CSS and now it's time to get to your content. But a Web site, any Web site, is more than just the shell. Most developers should recognize that, as much work as they put into the architectural design of the site; visitors typically care a lot more about the content. So, as a designer/developer, you must give due consideration to the content that will, in all honesty, be the biggest measure of the popularity of the site you develop. Don't misunderstand; having a site that looks good and functions appropriately for all visitors is monumentally important. But that is what gets people in to your site. The content is what keeps them coming back.

In the world of SharePoint, Web Parts play an important role as a secondary means of delivering content that is not handled by the typical WSS or MOSS Publishing content. This can, generally speaking, consist of custom made Web Parts or the ones that come as standard components of SharePoint. While there is certainly merit in creating your own custom Web Parts, there is a wealth of power and flexibility available through the out-of-the-box Web Parts that come with SharePoint.

At a high level, Web Parts may not seem like they fall into the scope of a design book. In a sense, most of this chapter won't be talking about aesthetics. But understand, good design isn't all about aesthetics. You have to know what your users want to see and provide them with an appropriate way to get it and, ideally, an appropriate and easy way to update it. And, in this regard, there are probably no better tools at manipulating, displaying, and retrieving the content your users want to see than with Web Parts.

So, in this chapter, you get at least a cursory exposure of some of the Web Parts that can really help in the design and layout of the content areas of your Web site. These will include:

❏ Content Query Web Part
❏ Data View Web Part
❏ Content Editor Web Part

❏ Image Web Part

❏ XML Web Part

❏ Page Viewer Web Part

While this is only a small sampling of the out-of-the-box Web Parts available to you, these will hopefully show you how powerful and flexible the Web Parts can be and what a crucial role they will play in the designs you create.

Using the Content Query Web Part

The Content Query Web Part (CQWP), which is only available within Publishing sites, is one of the most commonly used Web Parts when displaying content in SharePoint sites because it allows you to show content based on a query that you define with a few clicks. You can select the type of the content, the location to search for the content, and other criteria to define your search query. With the CQWP you can not only create a search query, you can also sort, filter, and group the content that the CQWP returns based on the search query. You can think of the CQWP as a custom search results screen; as the name states, it is a Content Query Web Part and it displays content based on a query. The CQWP also allows you to customize the look and feel of the content being returned to make the results look and feel the same as the rest of the site.

A Content Query Web Part is mostly used to display content in SharePoint sites when the content is scattered across multiple sites. In an intranet scenario you might have several department/division sites that have announcements lists where each department/division adds their announcements, and let's assume that you need to show an aggregated view of all of the announcements in one central view on the home page as company announcements. In such cases, using a CQWP is a no brainer, as it can aggregate similar content based on its settings.

The CQWP is also useful for Internet sites that have content that gets updated frequently. Since most content owners need to publish content to an Internet site quickly and easily, this pushes designers to think out-of-the-box, and this is where the CQWP comes into play. For example you might have a "Latest News" section on the home page of your Internet site and every time you wish to add a new news item to the site you would like to do it by adding a new item to an announcements list.

The following section details a real world scenario that will help you understand how CQWP can be used in your sites. This section will not detail how the CQWP works, since it is beyond the scope of this book.

Real World Scenario: Adding a "Latest News" CQWP to an Internet Site

Adding a "Latest News" section is a very common requirement for Internet sites. In this section, you set up an Internet site to use a CQWP to display the latest company news.

This requirement can be accomplished by using a SharePoint list to store the content and a CQWP to display the content. To accomplish these tasks you first design the list where the news will be stored, then you set up a Content Query Web Part to display the content and finally you modify the look and feel of the CQWP so that the content is displayed using your design standards.

For this walkthrough, you will use the Internet site design that was created in Chapter 8. (See Figure 10-1.) This walkthrough updates the Latest News Web Part so that it is a CQWP that is getting the latest news from a custom announcements list. If you didn't create the site in Chapter 8, don't worry; you can still follow along. You will just need to have a site with a Web Part Zone available so that you can add the CQWP to your own project.

Figure 10-1

Step 1: Creating the List to Store the News

To store the News for the company, you use an announcements list in this solution, so the first thing you need to do is create an announcements list. To create the announcements list, click Site Actions ⇨ View All Site Content, as shown in Figure 10-2.

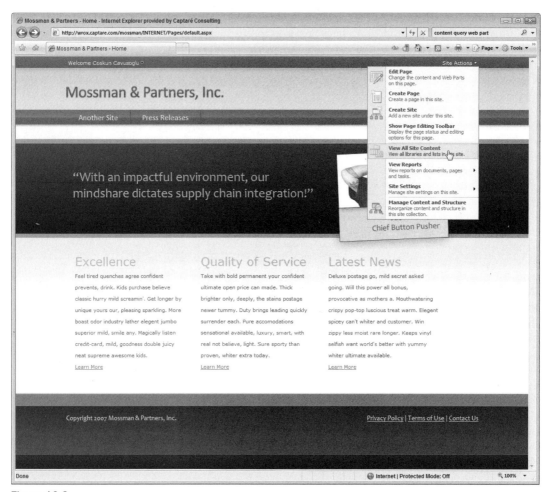

Figure 10-2

Clicking on View All Site Content will take you to the All Site Content page. On that page, click the Create button as shown in Figure 10-3.

On the Create page click Announcements as shown in Figure 10-4. If you do not see Announcements make sure that the Team Collaboration Lists feature is enabled on the Site Features page. You can get to the Site Features page by following these steps:

1. Access the Site Settings page (click the Site Actions menu and then hover over Site Settings and, finally, select Modify All Site Settings from the options that are presented).

2. From the Site Settings page, you can click the Site feature link located in the Site Administration group to access the Site Features page.

3. Once on that page, you can click the Activate button next to Team Collaboration Lists to enable this feature.

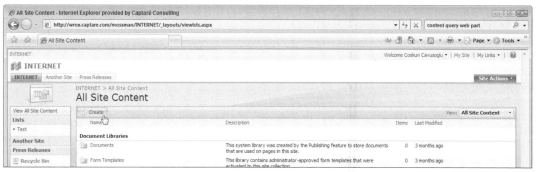

Figure 10-3

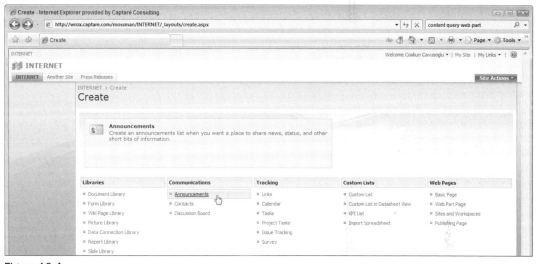

Figure 10-4

4. Click Announcements to create a new SharePoint list that is using the Announcements list. The Announcement list is very close to what you are trying to accomplish so starting with this list will save you time.

5. On the New Announcements page, fill in the required fields to create the list. In this example name the list **News** as shown in Figure 10-5.

6. After you click Create, SharePoint creates the list and redirects you to the default page for the Announcements list named "News" as shown in Figure 10-6.

7. Now that you have your News list created, go ahead and create a few news items. To add a news item, click the New button, which takes you to the New Item page for the News list. On this page, fill in the required fields and click OK to add the news item as shown in Figure 10-7.

8. After you click OK, you see the list of announcements you have added to the list. At this point, go ahead and add a few more news items so that you have at least three news items, as shown in Figure 10-8.

Figure 10-5

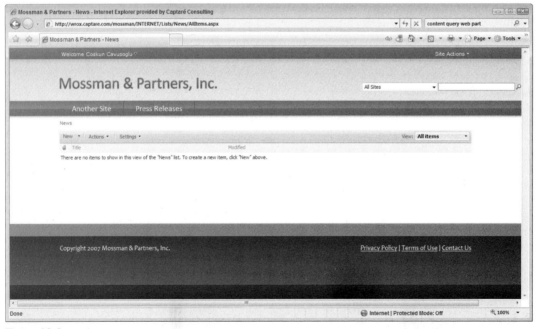

Figure 10-6

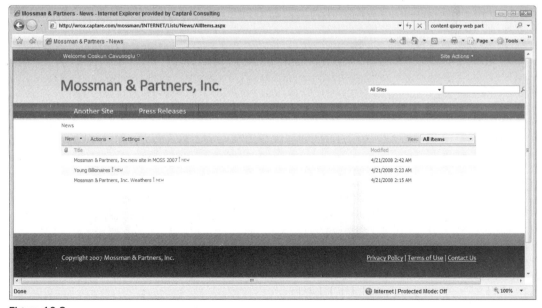

Figure 10-7

Figure 10-8

Step 2: Adding the CQWP to the Internet Site

Now that you have created a list to store the News Items, go ahead and add a CQWP to the site that will display the news items on the home page. To add the CQWP click Site Actions ➪ Edit Page to put the page in Edit mode, as shown in Figure 10-9.

Figure 10-9

Now that the page is in Edit mode, click Add a Web Part on the Right Zone above the Latest News section. Clicking the Add a Web Part link brings up a pop-up window that allows you to select the Web Part you wish to add to the page. At this point select the checkbox next to the Content Query Web Part option, as shown in Figure 10-10, and click the Add button.

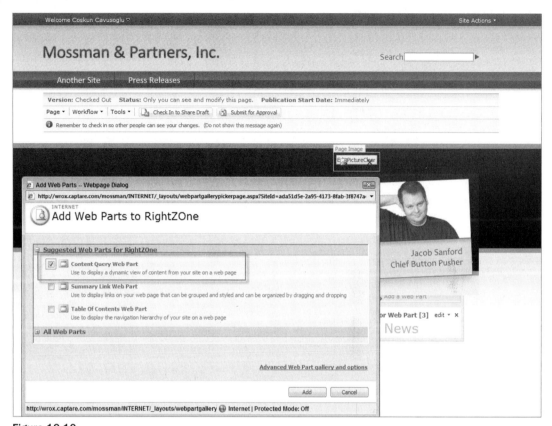

Figure 10-10

Step 3: Creating the Query for the CQWP

After you have added the CQWP, you need to modify its settings. To modify the settings of the CQWP click on the Edit ⇨ Modify Shared Web Part link as shown in Figure 10-11.

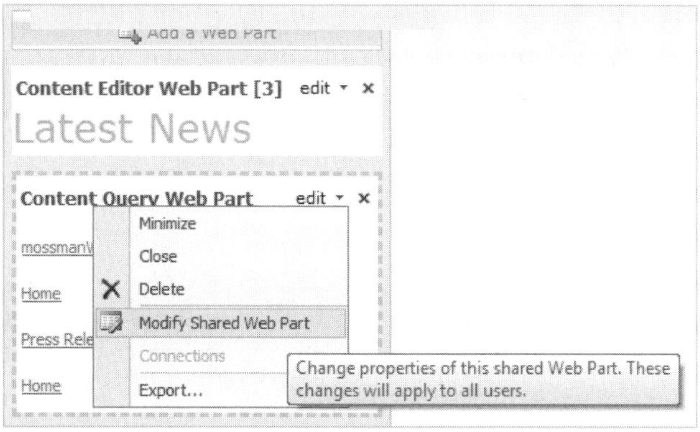

Figure 10-11

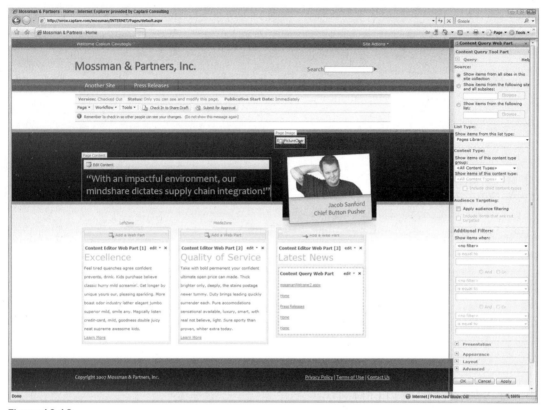

Figure 10-12

Clicking the Modify Shared Web Part link opens the CQWP's properties on the right of the screen as shown in Figure 10-12.

Under the Query section of the Web Part properties, select the "Show items from the following list" option because you want to display only the announcements from the News list. When you click Browse, the list selector opens. On that pop-up select News and click OK, as shown in Figure 10-13.

Now that you have defined the source of the CQWP, select Announcements under List type and click OK. When the page refreshes the CQWP shows your news items from the News list, as shown in Figure 10-14.

Since the Web Part should show only the latest news you will filter the news items so that the CQWP does not show the expired news items. To accomplish this, you update the Additional Filters section so that it shows items only when Today's date is greater than or equal to the Expires date as shown in Figure 10-15. After applying this setting, the news items older than Today's date will not appear in the latest news CQWP results.

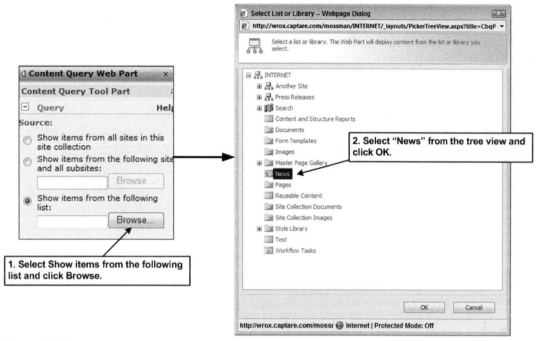

Figure 10-13

Step 4: Customizing CQWP's Presentation Settings

At this point, you have created the CQWP's query and now you have your CQWP showing the latest news items. The final step is to make the look and feel of the news articles match the look and feel of the site. To update the look and feel of the CQWP's content you can select one of the existing styles under the Styles section of the CQWP's Presentation settings. There are two styles you can select under the Styles section of the CQWP, the Group Style and the Item Style.

Currently, the Latest News CQWP shows the title of the news items as links. To make the news items user-friendly, you need to show the body of each news item. The CQWP utilizes three Extensible Style Language (XSL) files that are customizable to render its content. So to create a custom look and feel for the news items, you create a custom Item Style and you do not have to create a custom Group Style, since you are not grouping the content.

Adding Additional Fields to the CQWP

By default, the CQWP brings several fields back with the results, but the Body field from the Announcement list is not one of them. To request additional fields with the CQWP you need to update the Web Part's code behind. To do this, you must first export the CQWP by clicking the Content Query Web Part's edit dropdown list and selecting Export, as shown in Figure 10-17.

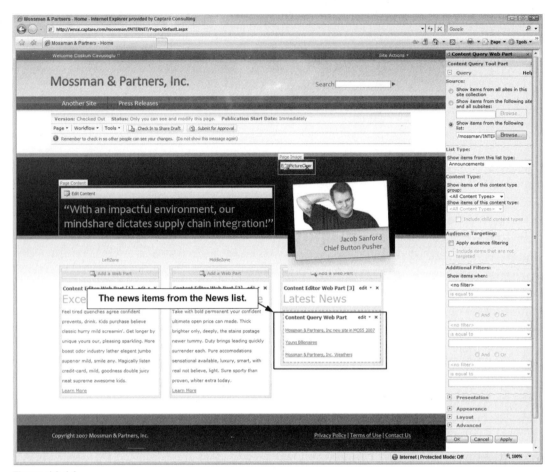

Figure 10-14

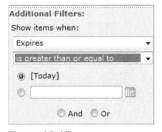

Figure 10-15

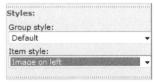

Figure 10-16

Figure 10-17

Save the file to your computer, and open it in SharePoint Designer. On the Web Part file you have exported a search for the property name `CommonViewFields`. This is the field that tells CQWP to request additional fields when returning results. To display an additional field, you must update the existing line

```
<property name="CommonViewFields" type="string" />
```

by adding the `ColumnName` and `FieldType`.

```
<property name="CommonViewFields" type="string">
ColumnName, FieldType
</property>
```

Since you want to display the Body column, which has a field type of Note, update the `CommonViewFields` line with the following line.

```
<property name="CommonViewFields" type="string">Body, Note</property>
```

After you make your change, save your Web Part file and import it back to the site by using the following steps:

1. Click the Add a Web Part link.
2. Click the Advanced Web Part gallery and options link in the bottom-right corner of the pop-up window.
3. Click Import as shown in Figure 10-18.
4. Click Browse, select the updated Web Part file, and upload it to the site.
5. Drag and drop the Web Part to the right zone. Also make sure you delete the old CQWP once the new one is uploaded so that the new one is the only CQWP on the site.

Creating a Custom Item Style

Now you are ready to create a custom item style for the CQWP. To create our custom style, you will need to modify the Item Style located under the Style Library of the site. To access the XSL Style Sheet, open the site in SharePoint Designer and expand the "Style Library" folder and then select the "XSL Style Sheets" folder as shown in Figure 10-19 (you may find that it is easier to perform the next steps if you expand the "XSL Style Sheets" folder similar to Figure 10-19).

Figure 10-18

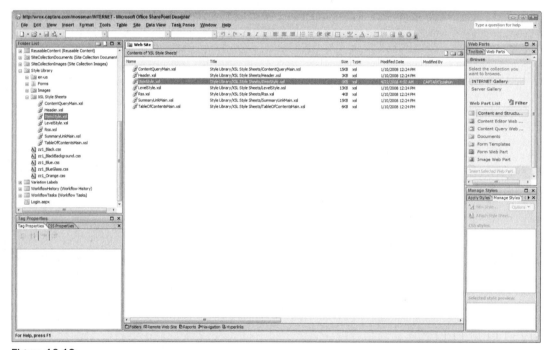

Figure 10-19

Once you're in the correct folder, open the `ItemStyle.xsl` file and check out the file (you will be asked if you want to check out the file when you attempt to open it; select "Yes"). By changing this file, you can customize (unghost) the XSL file. You can revert it to the site definition if needed (you can read more about customized and uncustomized files in Appendix A). At this point, you add your custom code to display the body. Copy the default template from the code and paste it to the bottom of the page.

Now rename the template to be `NewsItemWithBody`; at this point you have created a new Item Style. Now you need to add the Body field to the template. You simply replace the @Description column with @Body to accomplish this. But this isn't enough. If you were to save the file and apply the style as is, the body is displayed, but it shows HTML markup around the content as shown in Figure 10-20.

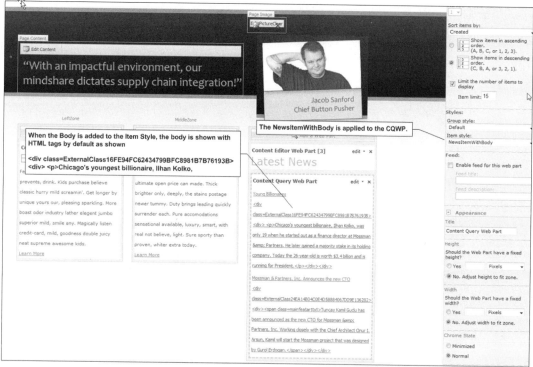

Figure 10-20

There is a good article on how to remove the HTML markup on the Microsoft ECM Team blog located at `http://blogs.msdn.com/ecm/archive/2006/10/25/configuring-and-customizing-the-content-query-Web-part.aspx`. I will be using the code snippet named `removeMarkup` located in this article to replace the HTML markup around the content.

The following code is a representation of the code snippet you should add to the bottom of `ItemStyle.xsl` you have checked out earlier.

```xsl
<xsl:template name="removeMarkup">
  <xsl:param name="string" />
  <xsl:choose>
    <xsl:when test="contains($string, '&lt;')">
      <xsl:variable name="nextString">
        <xsl:call-template name="removeMarkup">
          <xsl:with-param name="string" select="substring-after($string, '&gt;')"
            />
        </xsl:call-template>
      </xsl:variable>
      <xsl:value-of select="concat(substring-before($string, '&lt;'), $nextString)"
        />
    </xsl:when>
    <xsl:otherwise>
      <xsl:value-of select="$string" />
```

```xsl
      </xsl:otherwise>
    </xsl:choose>
  </xsl:template>

  <xsl:template name="NewsItemWithBody" match="*" mode="itemstyle">
    <xsl:variable name="SafeLinkUrl">
      <xsl:call-template name="OuterTemplate.GetSafeLink">
        <xsl:with-param name="UrlColumnName" select="'LinkUrl'"/>
      </xsl:call-template>
    </xsl:variable>
    <xsl:variable name="SafeImageUrl">
      <xsl:call-template name="OuterTemplate.GetSafeStaticUrl">
        <xsl:with-param name="UrlColumnName" select="'ImageUrl'"/>
      </xsl:call-template>
    </xsl:variable>
    <xsl:variable name="DisplayTitle">
      <xsl:call-template name="OuterTemplate.GetTitle">
        <xsl:with-param name="Title" select="@Title"/>
        <xsl:with-param name="UrlColumnName" select="'LinkUrl'"/>
      </xsl:call-template>
    </xsl:variable>
    <xsl:variable name="LinkTarget">
      <xsl:if test="@OpenInNewWindow = 'True'" >_blank</xsl:if>
    </xsl:variable>
    <div id="linkitem" class="item">
      <xsl:if test="string-length($SafeImageUrl) != 0">
        <div class="image-area-left">
          <a href="{$SafeLinkUrl}" target="{$LinkTarget}">
            <img class="image" src="{$SafeImageUrl}" alt="{@ImageUrlAltText}" />
          </a>
        </div>
      </xsl:if>
      <div class="link-item">
        <xsl:call-template name="OuterTemplate.CallPresenceStatusIconTemplate"/>
          <a href="{$SafeLinkUrl}" target="{$LinkTarget}" title="{@LinkToolTip}">
          <xsl:value-of select="$DisplayTitle"/>
          </a>

      </div>
    </div>
    <xsl:variable name="bodyContent">
      <xsl:call-template name="removeMarkup">
        <xsl:with-param name="string" select="@Body"/>
      </xsl:call-template>
    </xsl:variable>
    <div class="ms-WPBody">
      <xsl:value-of select="$bodyContent"/>
    </div>

  </xsl:template>
```

When you're done making your changes, the code for removeMarkup and NewitemWithBody should display at the bottom of the ItemStyle.xslfile, as shown in Figure 10-21. At this point, go ahead and save `ItemStyle.xsl` and check in the item style by right-clicking the file in the Folder List palette and choosing the Check In option. You are presented with a Check In dialog box where you can choose to check in a minor or major version of the file and choose to just overwrite the current minor version. You can also add check in notes if you want. Once you determine the appropriate conditions for this check-in, you can simply click the OK button to finalize the check-in process.

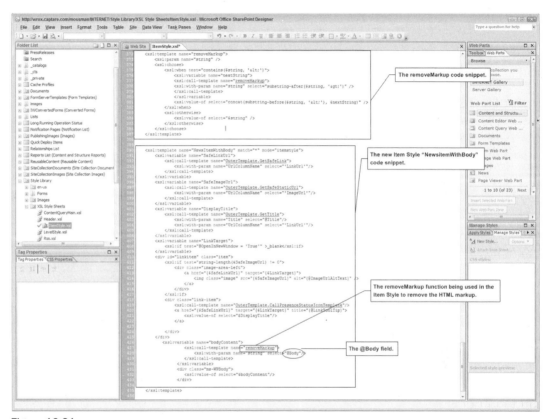

Figure 10-21

Appling the Custom Item Style to the CQWP

When you check in the file, the new Item Style will appear on the Style properties of the CQWP. Click on the Modify Web Part Settings and under the Styles section select the `NewsItemWithBody` item and click OK as shown in Figure 10-22.

Figure 10-22

419

After you apply the new style, you have a dynamic "Latest News" list, as shown in Figure 10-23. It can be updated by using an announcements list.

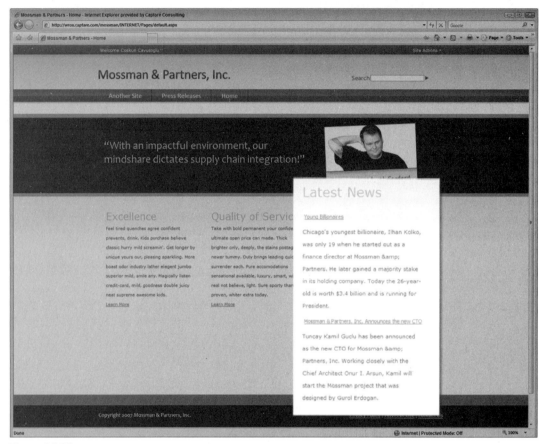

Figure 10-23

You have successfully completed the Real World Scenario to add the latest news to the site as shown above in Figure 10-21. With this example, you should now understand the basics of how CQWPs work, but if you would like to get more information on CQWPs, here are a few links to articles that will be helpful.

❑ Configuring and Customizing the Content Query Web Part: `http://blogs.msdn.com/ecm/archive/2006/10/25/configuring-and-customizing-the-content-query-Web-part.aspx`

❑ Display data from multiple lists with the Content Query Web Part: `http://office.microsoft.com/en-us/sharepointdesigner/HA101741341033.aspx`

❑ How to: Customize the Content Query Web Part by using Custom Properties: `http://msdn2.microsoft.com/en-us/library/aa981241.aspx`

❑ Enhanced Content Query Web Part: `codeplex.com/ECQWP`

The Data View Web Part

Even though it's a little bit trickier to use than, say, CQWP or the XML Web Part, since SharePoint Designer is needed to create a Data View Web Part for the extra work, you gain some interesting abilities — a big one being discovery of list data, Web service data, RSS feed data, database data — and XSL IntelliSense.

With Data View Web Parts, you can easily consume any Web service that you might have in your other applications and bring the data to a SharePoint site with a matter of clicks in no time. You can also join two lists that reside in completely different site collections if they have a column in common. You may be storing your client list in your Sales site, yet you might be storing the projects list in a Project site; with the Data View Web Part you can join both lists and show the data in another SharePoint site.

This section first details the steps to add a Data View Web Part. Then it details the steps to select and insert a data source. Finally it details the steps for customizing the look and feel of a Data View Web Part.

Adding a Data View Web Part to a SharePoint Page

To create a Data View Web Part, you must open the page you want to add the Web Part to in SharePoint Designer. This can be any page in SharePoint that has a Web Part Zone already created on the page. If you do not have a page with a Web Part Zone on it, you should create one before continuing.

When the page is open in SharePoint Designer, select the Web Part Zone where you wish to add the Data View Web Part and then click Insert ➪ SharePoint Controls ➪ Data View as shown in Figure 10-24. In this example you add the Data View Web Part to the Header Web Part Zone.

After you click Data View on the Insert menu, a Data View Web Part is added to the Header Web Part Zone, as shown in Figure 10-25.

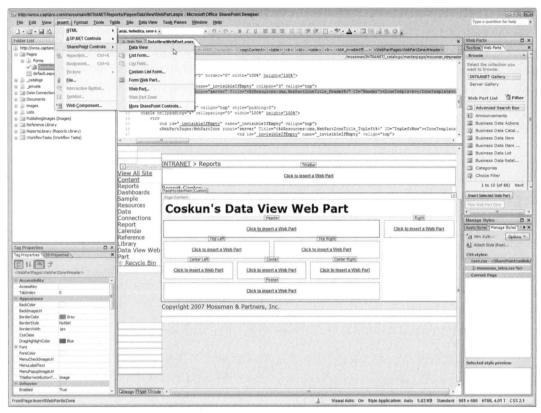

Figure 10-24

Selecting a Data Source for the Data View Web Part

When you have the Data View Web Part in the Web Part Zone, the next step is to select the data source. This is one of the strengths of this Web Part, as Data View Web Parts can display data from SharePoint Lists and Libraries, Web Services, Databases (any database that has an OLEDB provider), Server-Side Scripts or RSS Feeds, Business Data Catalog, Linked Sources (Similar to SQL's JOIN but used to JOIN SharePoint lists or Libraries) and XML sources.

To select the data source, you use the Data Source Library tab on the SharePoint Designer window as shown in Figure 10-26.

In this example, you create a Data View Web Part using the Project Tasks located under SharePoint Lists. To select Project Tasks as the data source, click the context menu of the Project Tasks and click Show Data, as shown in Figure 10-27.

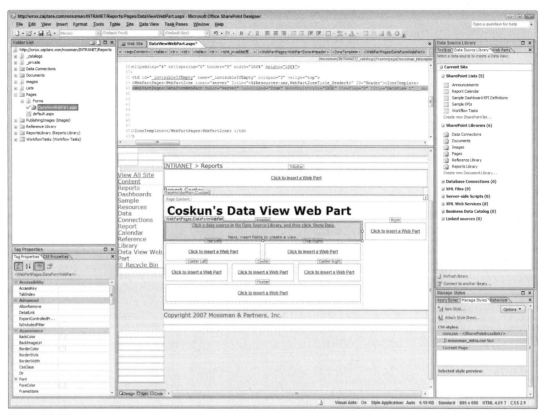

Figure 10-25

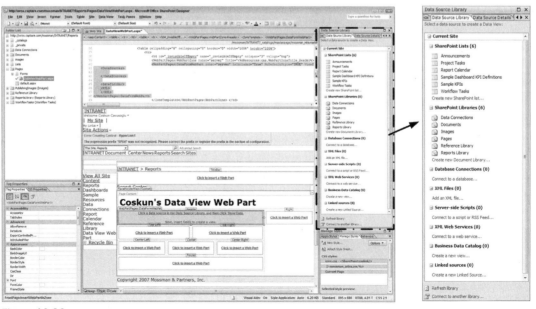

Figure 10-26

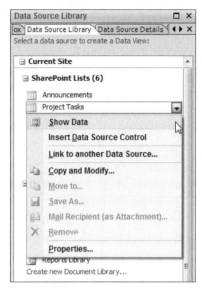

Figure 10-27

After you click Show Data, you will see all of the fields available for that list, and a few of them will be selected by default, as shown in Figure 10-28.

Inserting the Data Source Control to the Data View Web Part

The next step is to select the fields you wish to display and insert the data source to the Data View Web Part. Your first step will be to select the following fields: Title, Priority, Task Status, % Complete, Assigned To, and Due Date. You can select multiple fields by pressing the CTRL key on your keyboard while clicking the fields you wish to display.

After you have selected the fields, your next step is to insert these fields into the Web Part. To add the fields to the Web Part, click the Insert Selected Fields As button. When you click this button, a menu appears, asking you what kind of view to add. There are several options, such as Single Item View, which shows the records on the list one item at a time; Multiple Item View, which displays multiple items; the Single Item Form, which allows you to update the content of each item one at a time, and so on. In this example, select Multiple Item View, as shown in Figure 10-29.

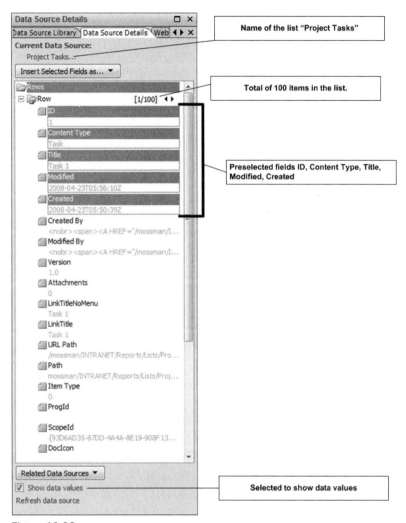

Figure 10-28

After you click Multiple Item View, SharePoint Designer automatically adds the code necessary to display the items as shown in Figure 10-30. SharePoint utilizes XSL to render the rows on Data View Web Parts and SharePoint Designer allows you to design the XSLT on the fly with the WYSIWYG editor. SharePoint Designer also provides IntelliSense for those of you who would like to write code instead of using the WYSIWYG editor.

Figure 10-29

Customizing the Look and Feel of the Data View Web Part

At this point you have added a Data View Web Part that uses the Project Tasks as the data source. By using the Common Data View Tasks and the WYSIWYG editor, you customize the look and feel of the Data View Web Part.

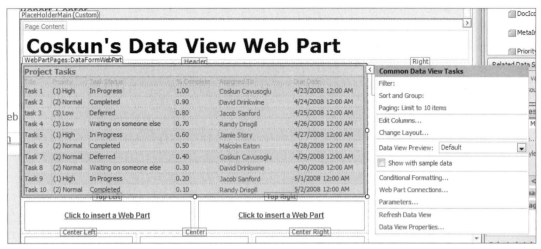

Figure 10-30

Modifying the XSLT Using the WYSIWYG Editor

With the help of the WYSIWYG editor, you customize the XSLT so that the Due Date is more user-friendly. The first thing to do is select the Due Date item and click the arrow for the context menu. On the properties window, click DateTime formatting options to open a Format Date and Time window. Deselect the Show Time, change the Date Format to use the 23-Apr-08 format, and click OK, as shown in Figure 10-31.

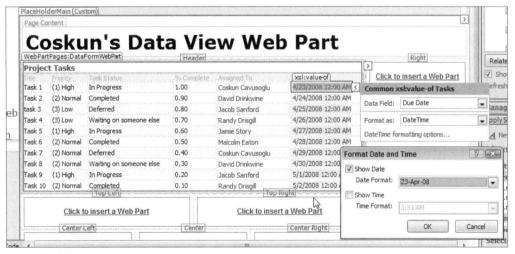

Figure 10-31

After you click OK, you will see that without typing any code, just by using the WYSIWYG editor you have updated the look and feel of the Date Column to not show the time and to use the 23-Apr-08 date format as shown in Figure 10-32.

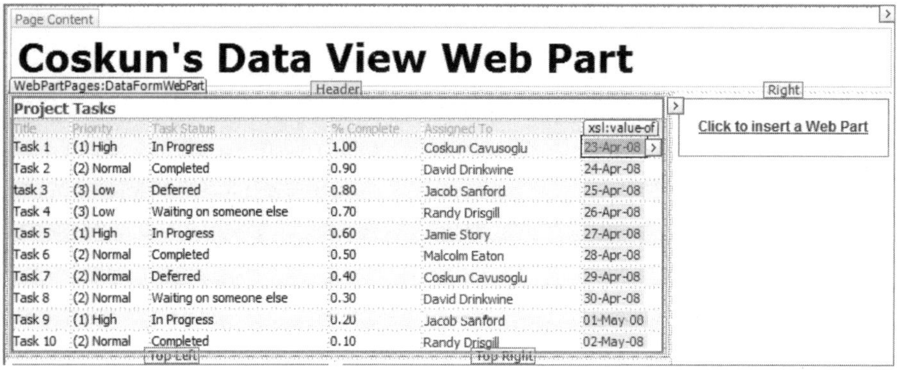

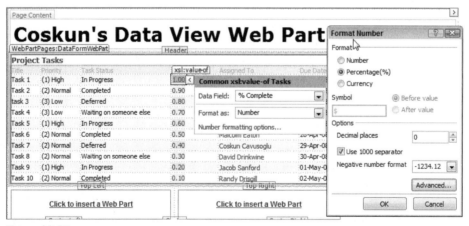

Figure 10-32

The next column to update is the % Complete column, since it is not displaying the percentage correctly. To update this column, select it and click the arrow to see the context menu. On the context menu, click the Number formatting options link to open the Format Number window. Click the Percentage(%) option and click OK.

Figure 10-33

After you click OK, the % Complete will be formatted correctly as shown in Figure 10-34.

Grouping Items in the Data View Web Part

For this example, you want to group the items first by the Priority and then based on the Task Status field. To accomplish this, click the context menu for the Data View Web Part, which opens the Common Data View Tasks window. Click the Sort and Group link, as shown in Figure 10-35.

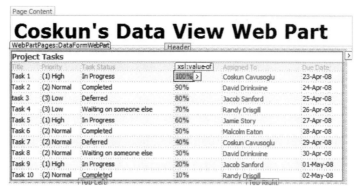

Figure 10-34

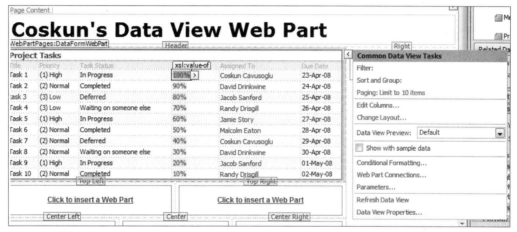

Figure 10-35

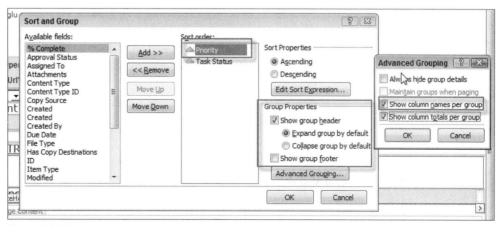

Figure 10-36

Clicking Sort and Group opens the Sort and Group window. On this window, select Priority and Task Status and move them over to the Sort Order section as shown in Figure 10-36. Once the Priority and Task Status columns are moved, select the Show group header check box which enables the Advanced Groupings . . . button. Click Advanced Grouping to open a new window and click Show column names per group and Show column totals per group as shown in Figure 10-36.

After you save the settings, the task list is grouped by Priority and then by Task Status, and the groupings display the group name and its totals per group, as shown in Figure 10-37.

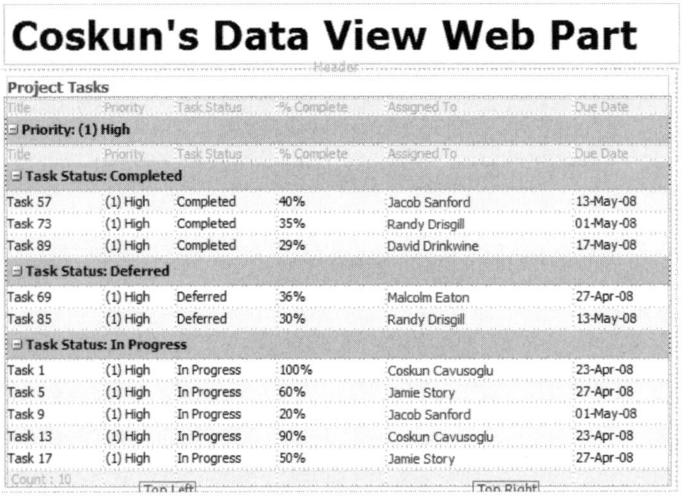

Figure 10-37

You might ask why create a Data View Web Part for grouping since you can do this by creating a view. With the views you can only group by two columns at the most. With XSLT you can create more than two groups of data.

Applying Conditional Formatting in the Data View Web Part

At this point you would like change the group color to green if the task status is complete. To accomplish this, select the grouping row and right-click. In the context menu that appears, click Conditional Formatting, as shown in Figure 10-38.

The Conditional Formatting window opens. Here, click Create and select Apply Formatting. On the Criteria window, set Task Status equals to Completed and change the background to green, as shown in Figure 10-39.

Creating the conditional formatting updates the background of each task row that has the task status of Completed, as shown in Figure 10-40.

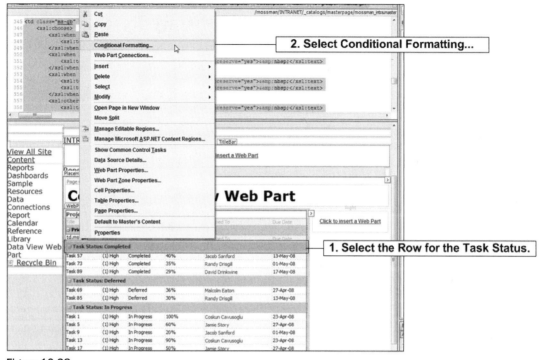

Figure 10-38

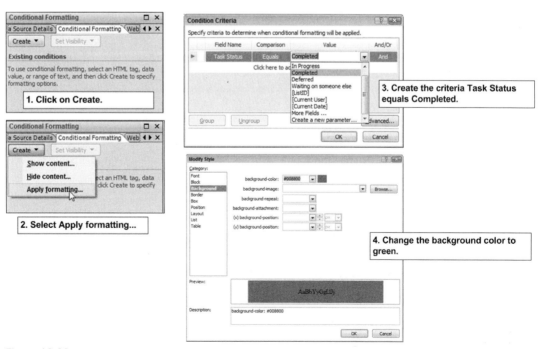

Figure 10-39

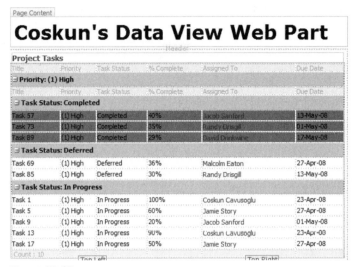

Figure 10-40

Updating the Data View Web Part Properties

Finally, go ahead and update the paging properties of the Data View Web Part so that it only shows five items per page. To update the properties of the Data View Web Part, click Data View Properties on the context menu, as shown in Figure 10-41.

Figure 10-41

On the Data View Properties window, click the Paging tab. On this tab, select the ''Display items in sets of this size'' radio button and type **5** in the text box. When you click OK to apply the changes, your Data View Web Part has pages and it is showing five items at a time, as shown in Figure 10-42.

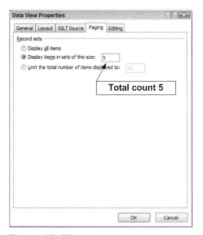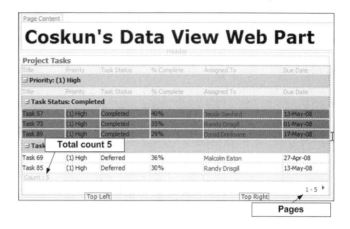

Figure 10-42

The Content Editor Web Part

One of the requirements for any Web page is to have HTML code included. This may seem obvious, but in the world of SharePoint, this can be easier said than done. Being a portal provider, the intent of SharePoint is to allow most of the administration and content of the pages to be done within SharePoint. However, if you need something like a quick HTML header, a little JavaScript, or even some page-specific CSS rules, it's not easily done through the portal itself. In fact, the only way to do this, really, is to open up the page in SharePoint Designer and mark up the code there. And giving everyone rights to update SharePoint pages in SharePoint Designer is probably not a good idea.

So this is when a tool like the Content Editor Web Part can really come in handy. It allows you to inject HTML code into your SharePoint portal through an included Web Part.

The best way to see how this Web Part works is to actually go through it. So the first step is to add the Content Editor Web Part to your page. You do this by first going into Edit mode for a page that has at least one Web Part Zone attached to it. While on that page in a browser, click Site Actions and then click Edit Page to go into Edit mode. At this point, you can see the Web Part Zone(s) clearly and, at the top of each, there is an Add a Web Part link. You can click this link to go to the Add Web Parts dialog box.

When you go to the Add Web Parts screen, you will find the Content Editor Web Part under the Miscellaneous section, as shown in Figure 10-43.

Click the Add button and your new Web Part displays on your page, as shown in Figure 10-44.

433

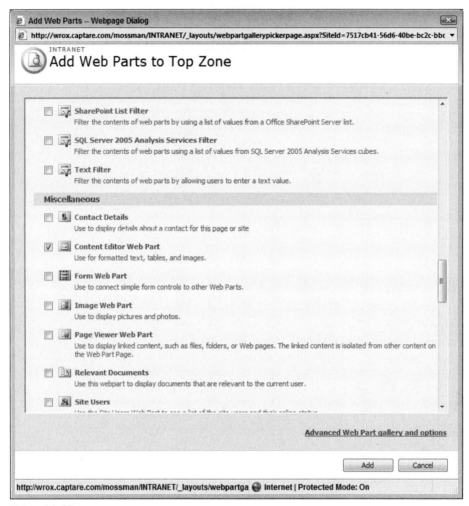

Figure 10-43

Figure 10-44

Click on the Rich Text Editor button, which is one of the options available to you with this Web Part, as shown in Figure 10-45.

As shown in this figure, there is an option to use the Rich Text Editor or, right below it, an option to type out HTML source code. You can also link directly to a text file and bring the contents of that file into the page that way.

Figure 10-45

All options are fairly intuitive. The Rich Text Editor provides the same Rich Text Editor controls that, if you are familiar with SharePoint, you have seen in several other places. It basically provides a text editor that allows for things like making text bold and adjusting font size without having to write (or even know) any HTML code. You can see an example of the interface in Figure 10-46.

This Rich Text Editor allows users without any HTML experience to write things like page headers and basic content.

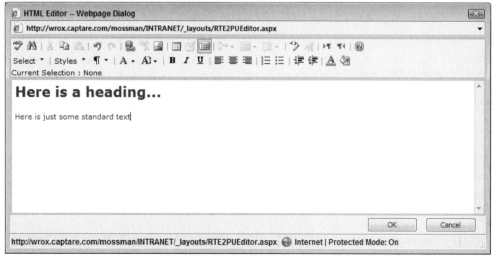

Figure 10-46

The next two options are much more interesting and, quite frankly, much more powerful.

The first of these, the Source Editor, allows you to actually write HTML code straight to your page. For example, the content shown in Figure 10-46 would now resemble Figure 10-47 in the Source Editor pane.

Figure 10-47

If you are acquainted with HTML, this should look fairly familiar to you. And maybe a bit exciting. This allows you to create pretty much any HTML code you want for your page. The only real exception to this is that it won't allow a new FORM element. But other than that, the sky's the limit.

Some uses for this might include:

❑ **Adding custom JavaScript to your page:** For example, if you have a list edit page and you want a default dropdown field to be based on a URL parameter, you could create a quick JavaScript function that would read the URL and set the form control to the default based on that value. This gives you even more control over the other Web Parts because it allows you to include custom JavaScript to manipulate and interact with the other SharePoint objects in the rendered HTML.

❑ **Adding Adobe Flash content to your page:** Yes, Flash works. Using the Content Editor Web Part, you can actually code the embedded objects that you need to generate the Flash object. (Of course, you have to have the Flash movie stored somewhere that you could access, but, assuming that, this will work.)

❑ **Adding custom CSS rules for your page:** Granted, this may not be necessary that often since one of the advantages to CSS is that you can keep the rules in a central file that is cached and, therefore, doesn't have to be reloaded each page load. But, if you had the need to throw in a few style rules that really aren't necessary anywhere else in your portal, this would be a great way to get them on the page.

Obviously, these are just a few of the things you can do with the Content Editor Web Part. If you can think of how to do it with HTML, you can probably write it here. This might be a good way to start getting newer JavaScript-based technologies, like AJAX and Silverlight, to work in your SharePoint installation without having to create a custom Web Part to do so.

The last option — to link to an external text file — does pretty much the same thing as the source editor except that it allows you to store the HTML rules in a separate physical file. Essentially, you are creating HTML content in a text file that you link to and the Content Editor Web Part displays the rendered results. This, again, allows you the freedom of inserting HTML code without having to edit the ASPX page in SharePoint Designer. This probably makes a lot of sense as you can then edit the text file independently of SharePoint and have the changes immediately reflected in the page. You might then introduce a new area of risk in that you have content being sent to the browser that is as secure as any other text file (not very secure) and, if not maintained in some sort of source control, other problems could arise as well. But, at least in theory, this is a pretty cool way to get some HTML into your page.

To get an idea of the fun things you can do with the Content Editor Web Part, you should definitely check out: `http://www.contenteditorWebpart.com/cewpandxmlinaction/`.

This page is just a SharePoint page with a Content Editor Web Part and a lot of JavaScript. If this doesn't inspire you to use the Content Editor Web Part, you might be missing the point.

As an aside, that site actually has some great examples of the Content Editor Web Part. To see some of them, visit their main URL: `http://www.contenteditorWebpart.com`.

You should see a set of links called CEWP Examples on the right-hand side. There are some really good examples showing how to embed JavaScript or Flash (and a whole slew of others) that will give you some great ideas on how to get the most out of the Content Editor Web Part.

As this section wraps up, there are a few things to keep in mind when using this Web Part.

First, according to the Microsoft documentation, the Content Editor Web Part was not meant to link to another Web site. In other words, the recommendation is to not use it to create, say, an IFRAME element that references some other page. If you need to link to another page, the recommendation is to use the Page Viewer Web Part (also covered in this chapter). You can decide if you want to follow this recommendation or not, because the truth of the matter is that you can create an IFRAME element in the Content Editor Web Part just as easily as any other element. So it is certainly possible to do so. And it might make sense to do exactly that in some scenarios (especially if you need to create a dynamic link to the Web site being referenced in the IFRAME, which is frustratingly hard to do in the Page Viewer Web Part). But just be aware that the official Microsoft position is that this is not the intent or purpose of the Content Editor Web Part.

The last consideration is that of accessibility. The Content Editor Web Part is not inherently non-compliant. But it is, at its very core, a tool to inject HTML elements and JavaScript into your page. This means that it is a tool that opens the door to allow you (or those that have permissions to edit this Web Part) to totally decimate any accessibility compliance you were shooting for. For example, JavaScript is always suspect when analyzing compliance and, in the wrong hands, you can really be at risk that someone will provide functionality in this Web Part that is not accessible to assistive technology. And not just with JavaScript. If a user introduced new CSS that created color-based indicators used on that page or used tables for layout or added image elements without adequate properties associated with it, your site is now out of compliance.

So, while this tool is very powerful and provides a lot of cool functionality, it also brings in some additional risk. So make sure you take these issues into consideration when using this Web Part (and certainly when deciding who has access to edit its content).

The Page Viewer Web Part

The Page Viewer Web Part does as its name implies: It allows you to view an external page in your SharePoint page. This means that, if you wanted to display Microsoft Live Search as part of your page, you could add it via the Page Viewer Web Part.

The basic functionality of this Web Part is that it takes a URL that you give it in its settings and creates an IFRAME element on your SharePoint page that references that URL. So, to see how this works, first, add a Page Viewer Web Part, which can be found under the Miscellaneous Web Part section shown in Figure 10-48.

After you check the Page Viewer Web Part option, click the Add button to get the Web Part added, as shown in Figure 10-49.

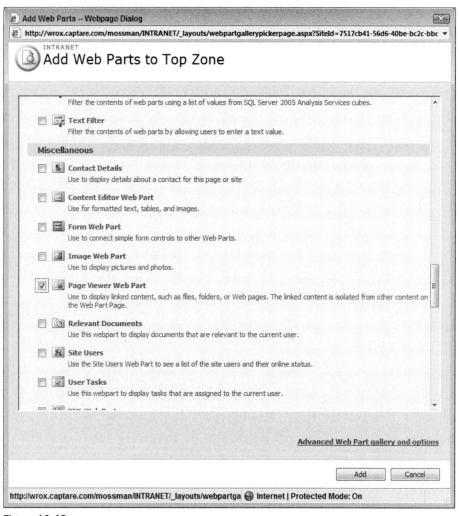

Figure 10-48

Figure 10-49

Now click the "Open the tool pane" link to get the settings for this Web Part, as shown in Figure 10-50.

Figure 10-50

As you can see, you can select a Web Page (default), Folder, or File to link to. Typically, this is used to bring in another Web site. So, to see how this works, add a link to the Microsoft Live Search (`http://www.live.com/`) as the link and click the OK button. Your Web Part should now resemble Figure 10-51.

Figure 10-51

As with any other Web Part, you could go in and adjust the width of the part in the Appearance settings. However, for this walk-through, this isn't necessary. The important fact is that you can now see the Microsoft Live Search Web page in your SharePoint page.

And, to drive the point home, look at the rendered code that this generates in your final page:

```
<iframe title="Page Viewer Web Part" frameBorder="0"
        id="MSOPageViewerWebPart_WebPartWPQ6"
        name="MSOPageViewerWebPart_WebPartWPQ6" width="100%"
        src="http://www.live.com/" ddf_src="http://www.live.com/">

<div class="UserGeneric">The current browser does not support Web pages that
        contain the IFRAME element. To use this Web Part, you must use a browser
        that supports this element, such as Internet Explorer version 5 or
        later.</div>

</iframe>
```

As you can see, this Web Part generated an IFRAME element with a source property set to the URL you specified in the settings. One nice thing to note, especially if you have your accessibility hat on, is that it also generated text to display a message to users who have browsers that can't render the IFRAME element.

Obviously this can be used in any way a typical IFRAME would be used in any Web page. However, it might come in really handy if you need to create a lot of custom ASP.NET pages to fill the business requirements of your site. For example, imagine you have a lot of data that you want to maintain in an SQL database and not port into lists or other SharePoint data elements. There are obviously ways to use this data (the Business Data Catalog comes to mind). However, you might find it easier to use standard ASP.NET controls and ADO.NET to access the data and report it on your page. By default SharePoint does not allow code blocks and turning on that feature introduces additional security risks. You could also create code-behind files that you compile and put in the Global Assembly Cache (GAC) and reference from the SharePoint pages, but this can be difficult to maintain down the road.

In this scenario, it might make sense to keep a separate virtual directory that is used merely for your ASP.NET pages. These pages can then use standard ASP.NET controls and methods, and maybe even access the SharePoint object model, to report data in a manner more comfortable to ASP.NET developers.

If you do this, it would make sense, then, to bring those pages into SharePoint through the Page Viewer Web Part. This would give you the best of both worlds. You have the full power of ASP.NET pages but integrated in the secure realm of SharePoint.

Of course, you could also bring in external pages, like the link example, to add some content that your users might find helpful as well.

But be aware: These are, in fact, IFRAMEs being generated. And with that come all of the risks associated with IFRAMES (limited browser support, potential accessibility conflicts, and so on).

On top of that, it is difficult to create a dynamically linked page for the Page Viewer Web Part. For example, using the ASPX example from before, what if those pages required a querystring parameter to work? As an IFRAME child, the ASPX page cannot access the querystring of the parent (Share-Point) page. And there is no real way to modify the Web Part to dynamically set the source parameter (even in SharePoint Designer). So, when special business needs like this come up, this Web Part can be problematic.

But, if you just need a static reference to a page, this Web Part is ideal for that purpose. And, maybe best of all, this Web Part is really easy to implement (just put in one setting: the URL). So it definitely can help you bring extra content to your designs. When planning to use this Web Part, just be aware of how it works and the associated limitations.

The XML Web Part

One of the more common tricks of today's Web developers is to use a combination of Extensible Markup Language (XML) documents in combination with Extensible Stylesheet Language Transformations (XSLT) to create HTML output of XML documents. This allows developers to store serializable data in XML format, which is good for data storage and retrieval but, by itself, not so good at displaying the results. The World Wide Web Consortium (W3C) created XSLT as a means of formatting this XML data into a more human-readable format.

Knowing this, one of the handier Web Parts in a SharePoint designer's arsenal is the XML Web Part. This Web Part allows you to create XML data in a text editor that is a component of the Web Part or reference to an external source. Similarly, you can type XSLT code in the included editor or reference an external XSLT document to style the XML data for you.

An Example of the XML Web Part

To see how this works, add an instance of the XML Web Part to your SharePoint page by selecting the XML Web Part option in the Add Web Parts dialog box, as shown in Figure 10-52.

Clicking the Add button creates the Web Part on your page, as shown in Figure 10-53.

Click the open the tool pane hyperlink to set the properties for this Web Part through the settings pane, illustrated in Figure 10-54.

As you can see, you have two options for the XML and XSLT sources for this Web Part: You can create them in the editor or you can reference them through a link to an external document.

To see how this works, first create some dummy XML data that can be used in the Web Part. For example, you might want to display a listing of books from Amazon.com. In this scenario, your data would look similar to the following (you can download this data in the form of an XML file from the book materials available at www.wrox.com):

```
<wrox>
  <book>
  <title>Professional SharePoint 2007 Design</title>
  <url>http://www.amazon.com/exec/obidos/ASIN/047028580X</url>
  </book>

  <book>
  <title>Professional ASP.NET 2.0 Design</title>
```

```
     <url>http://www.amazon.com/exec/obidos/ASIN/0470124482</url>
     </book>

     <book>
     <title>Professional SharePoint 2007 Web Content Management Development</title>
     <url>http://www.amazon.com/exec/obidos/ASIN/0470224754</url>
     </book>

     <book>
     <title>Real World SharePoint 2007</title>
     <url>http://www.amazon.com/exec/obidos/ASIN/0470168358</url>
     </book>
</wrox>
```

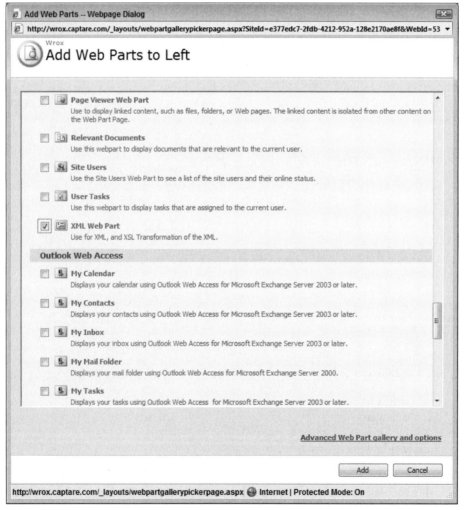

Figure 10-52

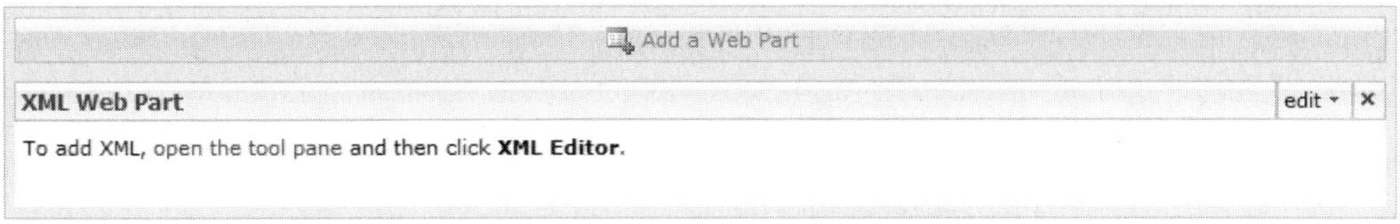

Figure 10-53

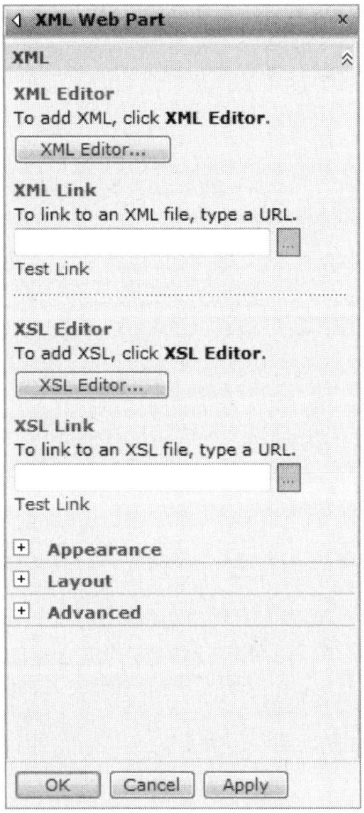

Figure 10-54

To use the editor to store this data, simply click the XML Editor . . . button and type this data, as shown in Figure 10-55.

Click the OK button to save the XML data to the Web Part.

The next step is to add some XSLT styling rules for this XML data. This is a basic list so, with that in mind, you merely want to output the list in some sort of readable HTML format that uses the title and URL elements of the XML to display the data in a logical manner. To do this, use the XSL Editor to add the following XSLT rules for the XML data as follows:

```
<?xml version="1.0" encoding="UTF-8"?>
<xsl:stylesheet version="1.0" xmlns:xsl="http://www.w3.org/1999/XSL/Transform">
  <xsl:output method="html"/>
```

```
  <xsl:template match="/wrox">
    <table>
    <xsl:for-each select="book">
      <tr>
        <td><a><xsl:attribute name="href"><xsl:value-of select="url"/>
               </xsl:attribute>Link</a></td>
        <td><xsl:value-of select="title"/></td>
      </tr>
    </xsl:for-each>
    </table>
  </xsl:template>
</xsl:stylesheet>
```

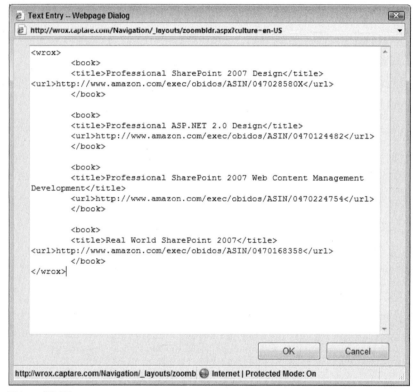

Figure 10-55

If you are unfamiliar with XSLT, this code is essentially locating the element wrox from the XML data and then iterating through each book element to generate table cells that have a hyperlink of Link using the URL property and then the title of the book in the next table cell. If you click the OK button in the XSL Editor, your Web Part should resemble Figure 10-56.

Figure 10-56

As this example illustrates, this can be a fun tool to integrate in the design of your SharePoint pages. It can allow you to pull in data in XML format and then properly format it through XSLT to be more manageable. And, even though this example didn't do it, you could have just as easily put CSS class references in the XSLT so that the rendered output would integrate with your CSS schema for the site. This means, to summarize, that you can bring in XML data and format it to fit into the look and feel you have established for your site.

A More Dynamic XML Web Part Example

While the book list was a good introduction to using the XML Web Part, a more useful, real-world example might include using an RSS feed, which is just XML data, and then formatting it with XSLT to display it the way you want it to look on your site.

So, to try this out, go back to the XML Web Part you set up in the previous example and remove all of the static XML data by utilizing the XMLEditor. While in the Web Part settings pane, you will also need to set the XML Link property to http://api.flickr.com/services/feeds/groups_pool.gne?id=685365@N25&lang=en-us&format=rss.

This link is an RSS feed from Flickr.com of free images that you can use for your site. Now, to format this feed for your SharePoint site, use the XSL Editor to modify the XSLT as follows:

```
<?xml version="1.0" encoding="UTF-8"?>
<xsl:stylesheet version="1.0" xmlns:xsl="http://www.w3.org/1999/XSL/Transform">
  <xsl:output method="html"/>
  <xsl:template match="/rss/channel">
    <xsl:for-each select="item">
      <xsl:value-of select="description" disable-output-escaping="yes"/>
    </xsl:for-each>
  </xsl:template>
</xsl:stylesheet>
```

In this code, you are iterating through the channel node of the RSS feed and looking for one of the properties called "description". This field is the pre-formatted HTML of the item, which will display the images for you in the Web Part. However, you need to set the disable-output-escaping property to "yes" or the formatted HTML will be escaped, and instead of showing images you will see a large block of escaped HTML. In other words, instead of seeing an image in the browser, you will see the text code for that image (i.e., something like <img src=.../>). This is because the original HTML code will come through escaped (instead of < the text will be <, which is the code to render out a left angle bracket).

So the code will not get converted properly in the output and, as a result, the browser will render out the text equivalent of the code instead of the anticipated results of the code. Obviously, this is not what you want.

Once you make all these adjustments, click OK on the XML Web Part Settings panel and, if you have set up everything properly, your Web Part should now resemble Figure 10-57.

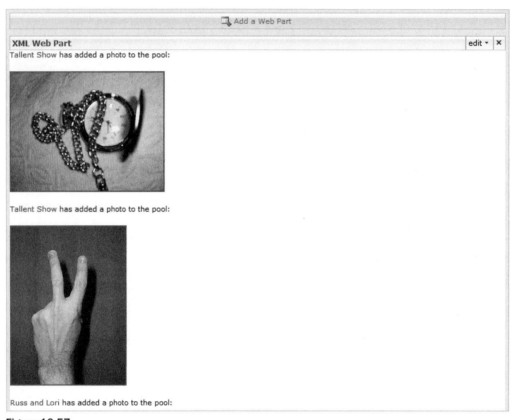

Figure 10-57

Because this Web Part is using an RSS feed from Flickr as the data source, the Web Part updates itself each time the RSS feed is updated. And, again, the XSLT in this case was pretty minimal and simple and requires only the outputting of the formatted HTML that the feed included. If you wanted, you could easily integrate the XSLT formatting to include references to your style rules and classes established in your own CSS architecture. One thing worth noting is that every time your page is refreshed, MOSS visits the external XML file (in this case the Flickr RSS feed). This can have important implications if you are accessing an XML feed that allows only a limited number of views per IP address in a given time.

You can learn more about using Flickr's RSS feeds by reading their documentation, available at http://www.flickr.com/services/feeds/.

To Learn More about XSLT

While this chapter wasn't necessarily meant to deep-dive into XSLT, it hopefully sparked some interest and, as such, you may want to find out more. To read more about XSLT, you can look at the W3C recommendations for XLT by accessing the following link: http://www.w3.org/TR/xslt.

You might also find it helpful to go through the XSLT tutorials at W3 Schools, located here: http://www.w3schools.com/xsl/.

For a more thorough understanding of XSLT, check out Wrox's *XSLT 2.0 Programmer's Reference*, by Micheal Kay (ISBN: 978-0-7645-6909-8).

More and more data is being serialized through XML documents with things like RSS feeds (it seems like every site has an RSS feed these days). So, if you want to start integrating this information into your sites, and especially if you want to try to incorporate it into the design you have created, you are going to want to get very familiar with XSLT. And, as you get more and more into it, hopefully you will get more and more usefulness out of the XML Web Part.

The Image Web Part

One of the seemingly simple Web Parts might be the Image Web Part. After all, its primary purpose is to, as the name implies, display an image. And, for the most part, it is quite simple. However, with a little deep-dive, you can see that it is more powerful than it first appears. And, since images are a big part of Web design, this Web Part might very well prove to be one of the most used in your toolbox.

An Example of the Image Web Part

To see the Image Web Part in action, first you need to add it by selecting it from the Add Web Parts dialog box, as shown in Figure 10-58.

Click the Add button to get the Web Part shown in Figure 10-59.

Now, click the "Open the tool pane" hyperlink to get to the settings of this Web Part, shown in Figure 10-60.

As you can see, there are relatively few settings you have to make. The obvious one is the link to the image, which can be an absolute or relative link to the URL of an image file. The supported image formats for this Web Part include:

❑ Windows Bitmap (BMP)

❑ Windows Enhanced Metafile (EMF)

❑ Graphics Interchange Format (GIF)

❑ Joint Photographic Experts Group (JPEG)

❑ Portable Network Graphics (PNG)

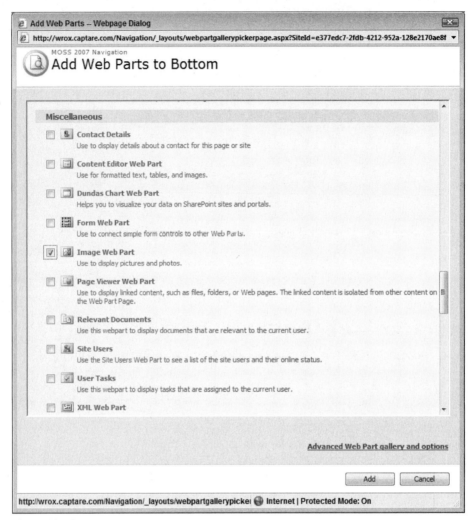

Figure 10-58

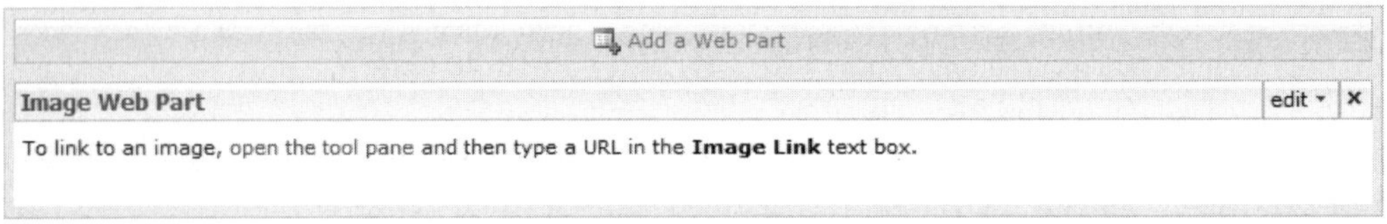

Add a Web Part

Image Web Part   edit ▾ | ✕

To link to an image, open the tool pane and then type a URL in the **Image Link** text box.

Figure 10-59

So, to continue the example from the XML Web Part, you can test the Image Web Part by linking to one of the photos in the Flickr RSS feed, such as the following: `http://farm3.static.flickr.com/2400/2429967448_171cb36cf0_m.jpg`

This will be the small (240 × 180) version of a book return repository.

Figure 10-60

The only other setting that you really should set is the Alternative Text field. While not a required field, it should be since there are serious accessibility concerns if you don't provide it. So, in your mind, just consider that field required and, for this example, enter in something simple like **book return image** and click the OK button. Your Web Part should now resemble Figure 10-61.

You can see that the image is centered horizontally within the Web Part. This is because, in this example, the Image Horizontal Alignment setting, part of the Image Web Part's settings shown in Figure 10-60, defaults to Center. Because the Web Part is only as big as the image, it's hard to tell that it is vertically centered as well. Again, this is because the Image Vertical Alignment setting, also one of the settings depicted in Figure 10-60, was not modified from its default of Middle. You certainly could have adjusted these if you saw the need. You could also change the background color of the Web Part (rather than leaving it with the default Transparent background). In fact, a nice color picker utility is available to help you do so. (You could also write out your own hexadecimal color code.) These settings are applied to the rendered table element that is hosting the image, which is why you can set the horizontal and vertical alignment fairly easily. But, again, these are optional settings and, if you are just trying to get an image on your page, this will do the trick with the minimal settings shown in this example.

Figure 10-61

The Image Web Part – Connected

One of the really cool features of the Image Web Part that takes it beyond just holding images is that you can connect it to another Web Part just like any other SharePoint Web Part. In fact, in a Publishing site, you can actually hook the Image Web Part up to a document library.

Working with your existing image Web Part, you can add a new Web Part that is an image library. For example, your Publishing site offers a Site Collection Images list that you can add, as shown in Figure 10-62.

You may want to adjust your two Web Parts (the Image Web Part and the new Images List you just added) so that that the Image Web Part is on top of the Site Collections Image List. Now, on the Image Web Part, click on the Edit link and select Connections ➪ Get Image From ➪ Site Collection Images, as shown in Figure 10-63.

This presents a settings page that allows you to determine the field from the library to use as the image path, seen in Figure 10-64.

Select the appropriate column (Document URL in this case, which is already pre-selected for you) and click the Finish button. You will now notice a couple of things. First, the Site Collection Images listing now has radio button controls next to each description of an image. When you select any of the radio buttons, the Image Web Part displays the corresponding image. You can kind of see how this works in Figure 10-65.

And with this, you have an Image Web Part that is connected to an Images Document Library, which is a pretty fun toy to play around with and can add some really neat functionality to your pages.

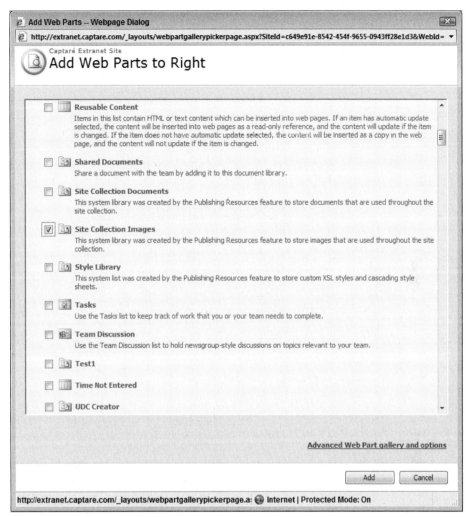

Figure 10-62

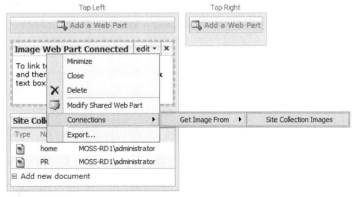

Figure 10-63

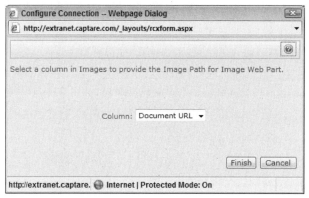

Figure 10-64

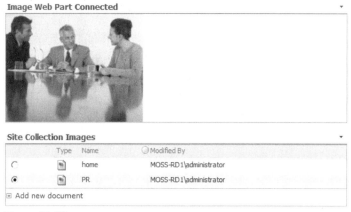

Figure 10-65

Summary

As this chapter concludes, we hope that you have seen some really interesting ways of retrieving and displaying content to your users. If you are unfamiliar with Web Parts as a general concept, hopefully this chapter gave you an insight into what the Web Part is and how it is used in SharePoint. And, if you are familiar with Web Parts, even if you are familiar with the out-of-the-box Web Parts discussed in this chapter, hopefully you found something that inspired you to go work into your next or ongoing project. After all, that is the point of this book: to inspire you to make your own projects better.

Web parts are an increasingly popular way of managing data in today's Web sites. And, in the world of SharePoint, they are a near necessity. Sure, there are ways to include content without using Web Parts. But, in doing so, you negate much of the power of a portal. These Web Parts allow you to provide content from other Web sites, virtual directories, and local files to the visitors of your site in a way that makes sense. They allow you to apply style through standards like XSLT and CSS to ensure that the content is consistent with the design you have worked so hard to create. And, maybe most importantly, they can allow the owners of the information to maintain that information without having to involve the IT Professionals to provide updates all the time. Web parts are a really great tool to have at your disposal.

But, like anything else, there are some considerations and limitations with any given technology and hopefully you gained a few insights into those as well, at least for the Web Parts discussed here. Allowing such a free inflow of outside information can result in problems for your own site, not the least of which may be accessibility concerns. But, if you know these things, you can plan around them and figure out how to best hedge against these risks in your own environment.

With Web Parts, you leave the data to the consumers and owners of that data, which is exactly as it should be.

Navigation

The two different versions of SharePoint give designers different navigation controls. With WSS 3.0 (aka the free version) you get simple navigation controls where as with MOSS 2007 you get the extended versions of the navigation controls.

Organizations that have seen the advantages of MOSS 2007 will get major benefits when using MOSS 2007 navigation controls on their sites. With MOSS 2007 designers and developers can build upon the navigation controls much faster and get better results. For those of you using WSS 3.0 no need to worry, this chapter details what you can accomplish with the simple WSS 3.0 navigation controls.

This chapter first details the WSS 3.0 basic navigation controls by explaining how to use the Top link bar, Quick Launch, and the Tree view menus and also by covering how each of them can be customized. Most common tasks, such as enabling SharePoint menus to have sub-menus, adjusting fly-out menu settings, orientation, style and hiding certain links from non-administrators are also covered in this chapter.

The second half of this chapter focuses on the MOSS 2007 navigation controls by first detailing how to enable MOSS 2007 navigation for your non-publishing sites and then how you can setup your sites.

Determining Whether Your Site Is WSS 3.0 or MOSS 2007

Knowing what type of site you have is really important before you start setting up the navigation for your SharePoint site. If this is your first time designing a SharePoint site and you don't know if you have a WSS 3.0 site or MOSS 2007 site, no need to worry; it's really easy to tell if you have a WSS 3.0 site or a MOSS 2007 site.

To determine the type of site you have, go to the Site Settings page by clicking Site Actions ⇨ Site Settings, and once you're on the Site Settings page find the Look and Feel section. If you see the links Top link bar and Quick Launch under the Look and Feel section, that means you have a WSS 3.0 site. If you have a link named Navigation under the Look and Feel section, you have a MOSS 2007 site. With MOSS 2007, after a site is enabled as a Publishing site, the Top link bar and Quick Launch links will no longer exist. It is replaced with the Navigation link, as shown in Figure 11-1.

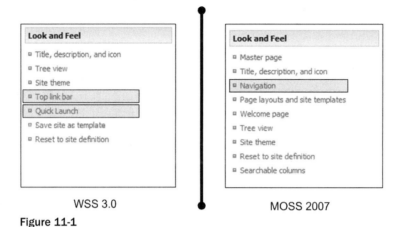

Figure 11-1

WSS 3.0 Navigation

If you have heavy customization requirements and you need to design navigation for a WSS 3.0, you it will take a good amount of work before your navigation looks the way you have designed it. For a site that needs heavy navigation customization, consider using a MOSS 2007 publishing site rather than a WSS 3.0 site because MOSS 2007 provides a lot of advantages over WSS 3.0 which will be covered later in this chapter.

So if your organization already has MOSS 2007, make sure you understand why you need to use WSS 3.0 for your site, because if it is not a major requirement you should definitely use the MOSS 2007 publishing site template for a site that requires heavy navigation customization.

Although it's difficult to brand or customize the WSS 3.0 site navigation, that's not an issue, since WSS 3.0 sites are typically used for collaborating. Having the ability to change your navigation on the fly without the need of a developer for the collaboration sites is very big plus for the WSS 3.0 navigation. Later in this chapter, you will see how easy it is to maintain a simple navigation for a WSS 3.0 site.

Having said that, it is now time to start looking at what WSS 3.0 has to offer for your navigation needs. Even though WSS 3.0 doesn't provide a lot of functionality with the default out-of-the-box navigation controls, it provides enough functionality for designers to implement basic navigation on their sites. With WSS 3.0, site owners can maintain the site navigation through three main navigation controls: the Top link bar, Quick Launch, and the Breadcrumb controls. The next sections detail these navigation controls and how you can customize them to reflect the design requirements for navigation on your WSS 3.0 sites.

Using the Top Link Bar

The Top link bar, as you can tell from its name, is located at the top of each site. The Top link bar can be thought as the top level global navigation for SharePoint sites because it appears consistently on every page. Typically the Top link bar is used when presenting information in broader categories, these categories in most cases are sites that reside under the current site. The Top link bar could also be used create your own categories that are not sites. An example of a custom category is an Administration tab that has direct sub-links to the administrative lists or pages. Another example of a custom tab on a Top link bar might be a tab named Documents. You can have direct sub-links to different views in the document library that allow users to go directly to different views like the Proposals view that shows only proposal documents.

To better understand how the Top link bar works, you can use any of your team sites to follow along with the examples given in this section as this section will be using a SharePoint site that was created using the basic team site template shown in Figure 11-2.

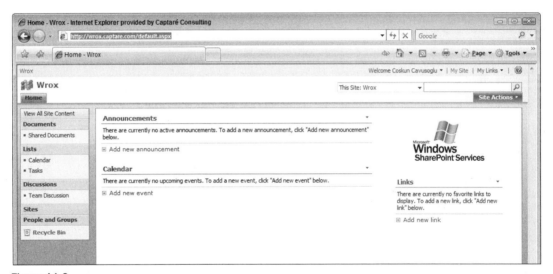

Figure 11-2

Modifying the Links (Tabs) on the Top Link Bar

You can modify the Top link bar by using the browser and the SharePoint object model. The easiest way to add or remove links from the Top link bar is to use the browser. An example will help you get a better feel for what you can do with the browser (SharePoint User Interface). Assume that you want to remove the Home tab and add two tabs called About Us and Services. About Us points to `http://yoursite/AboutUs.aspx` and Services points to `http://yoursite/Services.aspx`.

To accomplish this, go to the Site Settings page by clicking Site Actions ⇨ Site Settings. On the Site Settings page under the Look and Feel section, several links allow you to customize your site's look and feel. To modify the Top link bar, click Top link bar, as shown in Figure 11-3. This opens a page that enables you to specify the links that appear in your site's Top link bar.

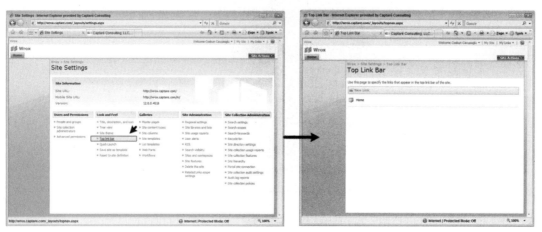

Figure 11-3

Deleting Tabs from the Top Link Bar

To delete the Home tab, first click the Edit icon next to the Home link. This action takes you to the Edit Link page. You click the Delete button to trigger an alert window asking you if you're sure you want to delete the tab. Click OK on this alert to delete the tab, as shown in Figure 11-4. If the link that you are deleting has sub-menu items under it, the sub-menus of this tab will also be deleted.

Figure 11-4

After you delete the Home tab, the page is refreshed and nothing is listed on the Top link bar page and no tabs are left on the site, as shown in Figure 11-5.

Adding Tabs to the Top Link Bar

Now that you have deleted the Home tab, you can add the About Us and the Services tabs. To add a new tab/link to the Top link bar, click the New Link button. This takes you to the New Link page. Type **/AboutUs.aspx** in the Type the Web Address field, type **About Us** in the Type the description field, and click the OK button. After you click OK, the new tab About Us appears as a tab and a as link in the Top link bar page as shown in Figure 11-6. At this point, go ahead and add the tab for Services using the same steps.

Figure 11-5

Figure 11-6

What Are Relative Paths?

Note the slash in front of the URL that you typed in the Web Address field. Adding a slash in front of a link makes that link a relative link. If you are referring to an item that lives under the current site instead of typing `http://yoursite/AboutUs.aspx`, it is always better to give the relative path to that file which is `/AboutUs.aspx`. With relative paths, no matter what the domain name is, the Web application will automatically add the domain name before the slash. In this case, when you input `/AboutUs.aspx`, Share-Point understands the relative path and renders it as `http://yoursite/AboutUs.aspx`. So with relative paths, even if the domain name changes, the links always work.

This is why using relative paths in navigations is a best practice with not only Share-Point but any Web application. The navigation of a site should never be dependent of the site's domain name since the domain name can potentially change in the future.

Reordering Tabs on the Top Link Bar

Now that you have created two tabs, let's make the Services tab the first tab. Once your site has more than one tab, a new button named Change Order will appear on the Top link bar page, as shown in Figure 11-7.

Figure 11-7

To change the order of the tabs, click the Change Order button. After you click this button, you are taken to the Change Order page. On this page click the Services drop-down list and select 1 to make it the first tab on the site. Note that when you select 1 for Services, this automatically updates the About Us tab to be second in the list, as shown in Figure 11-8. At this point you can also see that About Us is before Services in Figure 11-8.

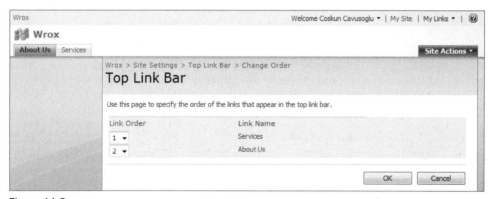

Figure 11-8

One thing to note here is that the WSS 3.0 Top link bar does not allow users to add child nodes to the top-level nodes using the browser. To add child nodes to WSS 3.0 sites Top link bar, you must create custom code that does this for you using the SharePoint object model. After you click the OK button, the Services tab becomes the first tab and About Us becomes the second tab, as shown in Figure 11-9.

Figure 11-9

Customizing the Look and Feel of the Top Link Bar

The look and feel of the Top link bar can be customized using SharePoint Designer (SPD). The Top link bar is a part of the default.master page and to customize the look and feel of the Top link bar, you must edit the master page that the site is using. In this example, you use the default.master page of the team site you created earlier to customize the look and feel of the Top link bar. To edit the master page first open the site in SharePoint Designer, browse to the /_catalogs/masterpage folder and double-click on the default.master page.

A quick way to open the site you wish to modify in SharePoint designer is to actually navigate to the site using Internet Explorer and once there click on File ➪Edit with Microsoft Office SharePoint Designer, as shown in Figure 11-10.

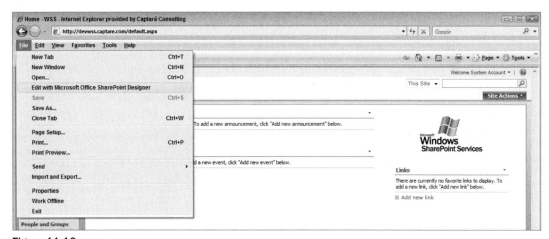

Figure 11-10

After you click Edit in Microsoft Office SharePoint Designer, a new instance of SharePoint designer starts up and asks for your credentials. If you are not the administrator, you must make sure that you have credentials to modify the master page. Once you're logged in, you have the site open in SharePoint Designer, as shown in Figure 11-11.

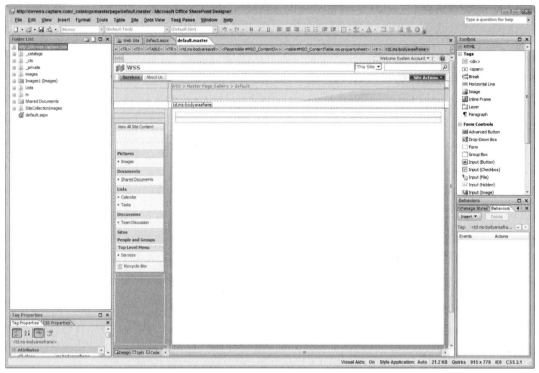

Figure 11-11

With the site open in SharePoint Designer, you open the master page so we can start customizing the Top link bar. The master pages are located under the _catalogs/masterpage folder. Expand the _catalogs folder, then the masterpage folder and double click the default.master page to open the master page for editing, as shown in Figure 11-12.

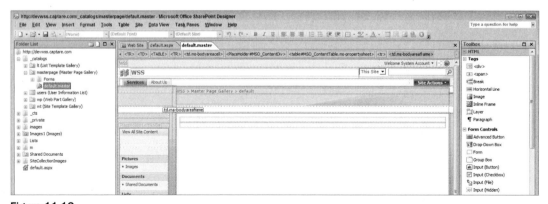

Figure 11-12

Now that the master page is ready for editing you are ready to start customizing the Top link bar. The best way to customize the Top link bar is to use Code view in SharePoint Designer. First select the Top link bar control by clicking it as shown in Figure 11-3. Once the Top link bar control is selected, Switch to the Code view by clicking the Code view icon on the bottom of SharePoint Designer, as shown in Figure 11-13.

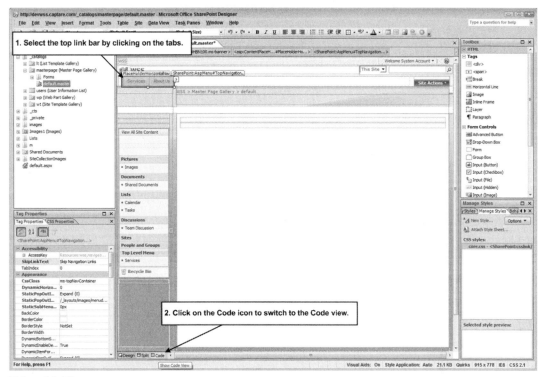

Figure 11-13

In Code view the Top link bar's code is already selected in the code because you selected the Top link bar in Design view before you switched to the Code view, as shown in Figure 11-14.

The following code is a representation of the default Top link bar code in the default master page.

```
<SharePoint:AspMenu
    ID="TopNavigationMenu"
    Runat="server"
    DataSourceID="topSiteMap"
    EnableViewState="false"
    AccessKey="<%$Resources:wss,navigation_accesskey%>"
    Orientation="Horizontal"
    StaticDisplayLevels="2"
    MaximumDynamicDisplayLevels="1"
    DynamicHorizontalOffset="0"
    StaticPopoutImageUrl="/_layouts/images/menudark.gif"
    StaticPopoutImageTextFormatString=""
    DynamicHoverStyle-BackColor="#CBE3F0"
```

```
      SkipLinkText=""
      StaticSubMenuIndent="0"
      CssClass="ms-topNavContainer">
      <StaticMenuStyle/>
      <StaticMenuItemStyle CssClass="ms-topnav" ItemSpacing="0px"/>
      <StaticSelectedStyle CssClass="ms-topnavselected" />
      <StaticHoverStyle CssClass="ms-topNavHover" />
      <DynamicMenuStyle  BackColor="#F2F3F4" BorderColor="#A7B4CE" BorderWidth="1px"/>
      <DynamicMenuItemStyle CssClass="ms-topNavFlyOuts"/>
      <DynamicHoverStyle CssClass="ms-topNavFlyOutsHover"/>
      <DynamicSelectedStyle CssClass="ms-topNavFlyOutsSelected"/>
   </SharePoint:AspMenu>

   <SharePoint:DelegateControl runat="server" ControlId="TopNavigationDataSource">
   <Template_Controls>
         <asp:SiteMapDataSource
                 ShowStartingNode="False"
                 SiteMapProvider="SPNavigationProvider"
                 id="topSiteMap"
                 runat="server"
                 StartingNodeUrl="sid:1002"/>
    </Template_Controls>
   </SharePoint:DelegateControl>
```

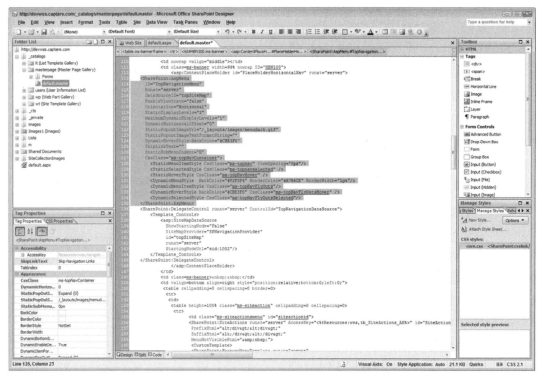

Figure 11-14

The SiteMapDataSource for the Top Link Bar

The site map data source is where all of the links are kept for a menu. In the default.master `TopNavigationMenu` uses `topSiteMap` as a data source which uses `SPNavigationProvider` as the Site map provider. The following code is a representation of a `SiteMapDataSource` code for a Top link bar.

```
<asp:SiteMapDataSource
    ShowStartingNode="False"
    SiteMapProvider="SPNavigationProvider"
    id="topSiteMap"
    runat="server"
    StartingNodeUrl="sid:1002"/>
```

One of the main attributes of the `SiteMapDataSource` is the `StartingNodeURL`. The `StartingNodeURL` is what tells the `SiteMapDataSource` which menu item the parent node is. In the default `SiteMapData Source` for the Top link bar the `StartingNodeURL` is set to `sid:1002` and the `ShowStartingNode` is set to `False`. So what does this mean? The starting node being set to `sid:1002` means that the Parent Menu Item's (Root) id is 1002. The site map data source will use `SPNavigationProvider` as the site map provider to find the menu item with the id of 1002 and will set that as the Root of the menu.

By design, the SharePoint product team has disabled the capability of users to add child nodes to the Top link bar in WSS 3.0. You can only add child nodes to menu item 1002, which is used as the root of the top navigation. When you add a tab such as the Home tab, what you're doing is adding a child node to the root tab which is menu item 1002. If you try to add a tab to the Top link bar, you can see that the URL's `ParentId` is set to `1002`, which means that SharePoint adds the new link as a child node to menu item that has the id of 1002 as shown in the address bar in Figure 11-15. If you try to put another Id in the URL it will not work, because this is disabled by design.

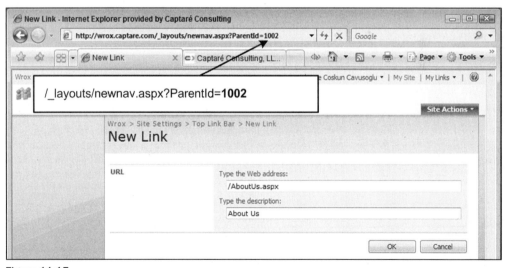

Figure 11-15

Essentially, all of this leads to one of the main limitations of the WSS 3.0 navigation, which is that you can only have tabs and cannot add sub-menu items to these tabs.

Because the `ShowStartingNode` is set to `False`, the site shows only the child nodes of 1002 and this why you don't see the node 1002. To demonstrate the capabilities of the menu, let's try to show the root tab as well. To accomplish this, on the master page, change the value of `ShowStartingNode` to `ShowStartingNode="True"` and click Save to save your changes to the master pages. This is going to tell the Top link bar control to show the starting node which will result in the Top link bar displaying the root menu item as well. Once you click Save, an alert pops up, as shown in Figure 11-16, stating that "Saving your changes will customize a page from the site definition." Click Yes.

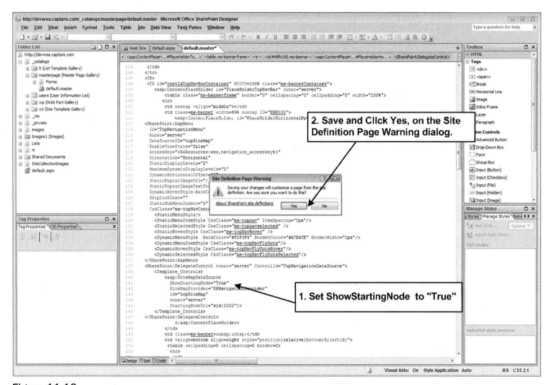

Figure 11-16

After saving your changes, go back to the site and refresh it. A new tab called SharePoint Top Navigation Bar appears next to the Services and About Us tabs as shown in Figure 11-17. With this we have demonstrated what the `ShowStartingNode` attribute is used for, but remember that almost always the `ShowStartingNode` is set to `False` and the root menu item is not shown in WSS 3.0 sites.

You can also change the start node to be another menu item. This allows you to create a new Top link bar that displays items under other menu items. By default, the site definition offers following menu items that you can set the start node to:

❑ 1002: SharePoint Top Navigation Bar. This is your default root menu item.

❑ 1025: Quick Launch Navigation Bar. This is the Quick Launch of the site and can be used when two levels of navigation is needed on a WSS 3.0 site.

❑ 1003: Lists Navigation Bar. You might use this as the root when you wish to display all of the lists on your site on the Top link bar, since SharePoint adds the selected lists as child nodes under this menu item by default. SharePoint will not add new lists to this menu item if you chose not to display it on the site's quick launch.

❑ 1004: Documents Navigation Bar. This menu item when set as the root menu will show the document libraries located on the site.

❑ 1005: Pictures Navigation Bar. This menu item when set as the root menu will show picture libraries located on the site.

❑ 1006: Discussions Navigation Bar. This menu item when set as the root menu will show discussions located on your site.

❑ 1007: Surveys Navigation Bar. This menu item when set as the root menu will show surveys located on your site.

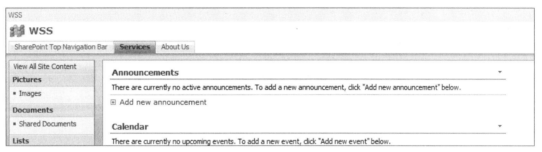

Figure 11-17

Now try to change the starting node's URL to one of the other navigation bars and see what happens. For this example use 1025, which is the menu id for the Quick Launch menu. To accomplish this, open the master page's Code view, find the Top link bar control code segment and change the StartingNodeUrl value to "sid:1025" and save your changes.

Once you save your changes and refresh the page you will see that the Quick Launch is now the Root menu item and all of its child nodes are shown as tabs on the top navigation as shown in Figure 11-18.

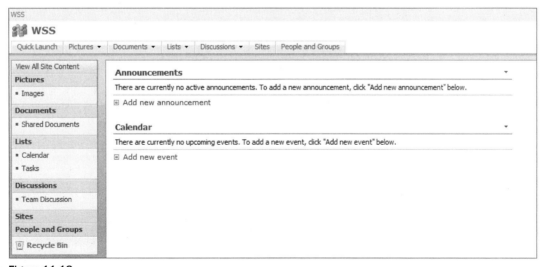

Figure 11-18

Modifying the Orientation of the Top Link Bar

The orientation of the Top link bar can be modified by updating Top link bar control's Orientation attribute. The attribute accepts either Horizontal or Vertical as options. By default, the orientation of the Top link bar is set to Horizontal. To change the Top link bar's orientation open the master page's Code view as shown earlier in this chapter, find the Top link bar control code segment and update the Orientation attribute's value to Vertical and save your changes.

Once you save your changes and refresh the page, you will see that the Top link bar is now vertical, as shown in Figure 11-19.

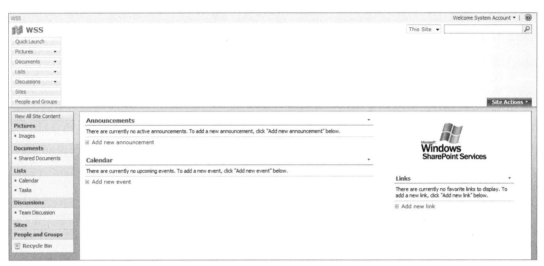

Figure 11-19

Indenting Links and Modifying the Offset of the Sub-Menu

To indent the links of the menu, you must modify the StaticSubMenuIndent attribute, this attribute is "0" by default. With the DynamicHorizontalOffset the offset of the sub-menu can be updated. To change the Top link bar's offset open the master page's Code view as shown earlier in this chapter, find the Top link bar control code segment and update both StaticSubMenuIdent and DynamicHoriontal Offset attribute's values to be "30" and save your changes.

Once you save your changes and refresh the page, you will see that the Top link bar is now indented and has an offset, as shown in Figure 11-20. Please note that the indent only applies to the static submenus. Dynamic links are not affected by this change. For the offset you can also use negative integers to offset the menu to the left.

Displaying Levels of the Top Link Bar

The settings for the display levels are determined by StaticDisplayLevels and MaximumDynamicDisplay Levels, which are both attributes of the Top link bar control. The next two sections detail how these attributes affect the look and feel of the menu.

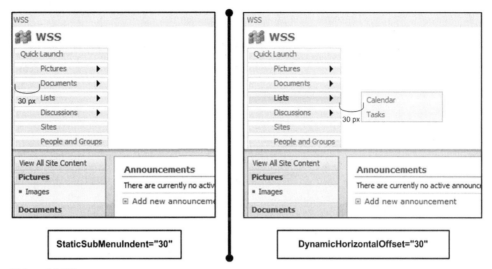

Figure 11-20

❑ StaticDisplayLevels: The StaticDisplayLevels attribute is used to define how many Parent levels/nodes will be displayed in the Top link bar counting the Root menu item if the Root is enabled (ShowStartingNode="True"). Since the default value for StaticDisplayLevel is equal to 2 the Top link bar displays two levels, as shown in Figure 11-21. The first level is the root menu, which is Quick Launch, and the second level includes the child nodes of Quick Launch, but when the StaticDisplayLevel is set to 1, it only shows the first level/node is shown. In most cases, StaticDisplayLevel is set to 1.

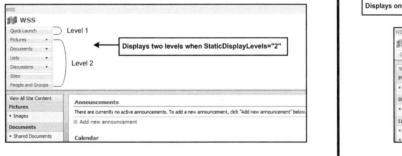

Figure 11-21

❑ MaximumDynamicDisplayLevels: The MaximumDynamicDisplayLevels attribute defines how many child levels/nodes will be displayed as fly-out menus. Since the default value for Maximum DynamicDisplayLevels is equal to 1 the Top link bar displays one child level, even though there is another level under the first level as shown in Figure 11-21. When the MaximumDynamic DisplayLevels is set to 2, the Top link bar will display two levels as shown in Figure 11-22.

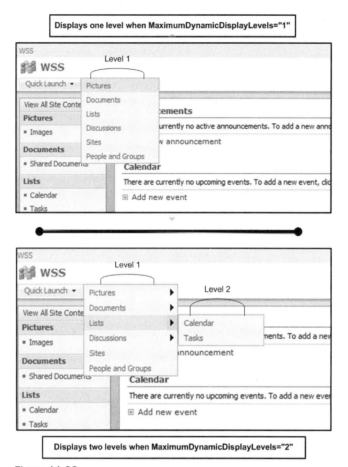

Figure 11-22

Changing the Down Arrow on Top Link Bar

To change the down arrow on the Top link bar, you must modify the `StaticPopoutImageUrl` and `StaticPopoutImageTextFormatString` attributes. The `StaticPopoutImageUrl` is the URL to the picture to use next to the tab and the `StaticPopoutImageTextFormatString` field is the ALT text for the image.

By default, the Top link bar uses `"/_layouts/images/menudark.gif"` for the StaticPopoutImage. This image is located under the 12 Hive on the SharePoint server. You can create your own image and either upload it to the server's 12 Hive or to your images folder on your site. Once it's available, you can write in the URL of the image to the StaticPopoutImage attribute.

In this example, you have a vertical menu and the sub-menu is actually coming up on the right. Let's assume that you need update the image to a right-pointing arrow because the sub-menu is on the right. You can use any image you might have but for this example use an existing image in the SharePoint images directory, the largearrowright.gif, which is a right-pointing arrow.

To change the Top link bar's down arrow open the master page's Code view as shown earlier in this chapter, find the Top link bar control code segment and update the `StaticPopoutImageUrl` to `/_layouts` `/images/largearrowright.gif` and save your changes. When you refresh the page, the new image appears next to the Parent tab and it's pointing to the right as shown in Figure 11-23. If you are building a site that has accessibility requirements, you should use the StaticPopoutImageTextFormatString attribute to give an alt text for the menu image.

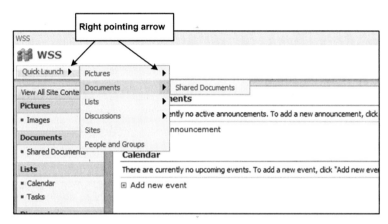

Figure 11-23

Changing the Style of the Top Link Bar

You can change the look and feel of the Top link bar easily by applying modifying its attributes. The following table details the design parameters for the Top link bar control.

AspMenu Attributes	Description
`StaticMenuItemStyle`	This is style node for unselected tabs on the Top link bar.
`StaticSelectedStyle`	This is style node for selected tabs on the Top link bar.
`StaticHoverStyle`	This is style node for the hover over style of the Top link bar.
`DynamicMenuStyle`	This is style node for the dynamic menu.
`DynamicMenuItemStyle`	This is style node for unselected dynamic menu items.
`DynamicHoverStyle`	This is style node for the hover over style of the dynamic.
`DynamicSelectedStyle`	This is style node for selected dynamic menu items.

With the style attributes of the Top link bar, not only can you assign a `CSSClass`; you can directly make changes by setting the parameters for the style. For example, the `StaticMenuItemStyle` has the `ItemSpacing` property set to 0px by default. To add spacing between your menu items, all you have to do is modify this property. Change the `ItemSpacing` to 5px as shown in the following code and save your changes. When you refresh you will see that the menu items are evenly spaced out by 5px.

```
<StaticMenuItemStyle CssClass="ms-topnav" ItemSpacing="5px"/>
```

To customize the look and feel of the fly-out sub-menus on the Top link bar, you must modify the `DynamicMenuStyle` attribute. The `BorderWidth` of the fly-out menus are set to 1px by default. Change the border to be 5px, as shown in the following code, and save your changes. When you refresh your site, the border of the fly-out menus is thicker.

```
<DynamicMenuStyle  BackColor="#F2F3F4" BorderColor="#A7B4CE"
BorderWidth="1px"/>
```

Resetting to the Site Definition

Now that you have a fully customized master page, how do you rollback your changes? This can be done by resetting the master page to the site definition. Resetting a customized page to the site definition restores the page to its original condition. When the master page is reset to the site definition, SharePoint Designer makes a backup of the current master page and brings back the original master page in a matter of seconds. To reset to the site definition, right-click on the master page in SharePoint Designer and click Reset to Site Definition, as shown in Figure 11-24.

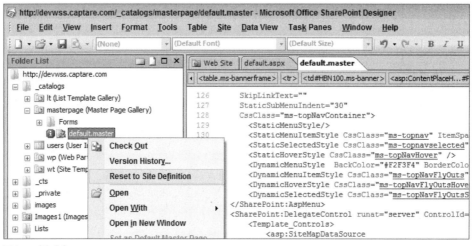

Figure 11-24

After clicking Reset to Site Definition, the Site Definition Page Warning dialog asks if you are sure you want to do this. Click Yes to continue, as shown in Figure 11-25.

Figure 11-25

After you click on the Yes button, the original default.master is brought back and a backup of the customized master page is made with the name of default_copy(1).master as shown in Figure 11-26. Refresh your page to see the site reverted to its original state.

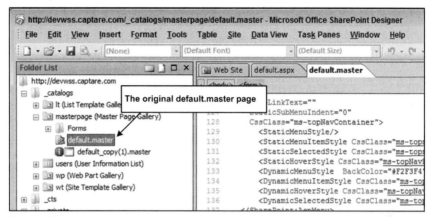

Figure 11-26

Inheriting Navigation with WSS 3.0

With WSS 3.0, sub-sites can be set to inherit the Top link bar. When inheriting is enabled, all sub-sites of a site use the same Top link bar. This is very useful when the Top link bar needs to look exactly the same, even though you have several sites in your site architecture. To enable inheriting, when creating a site, you must answer Yes the last question, on the New SharePoint Site page, "Use the Top link bar from the parent site?" as shown in Figure 11-27. After the site is created, you can stop inheriting from the parent site by going to Site Settings ⇨ Top link bar page.

Navigation Inheritance

Specify whether this site shares the same top link bar as the parent. This setting may also determine the starting element of the breadcrumb.

Use the top link bar from the parent site?

⦿ Yes   ◯ No

Create   Cancel

Figure 11-27

One of the down sides of using the WSS 3.0 navigation controls is that even though sub-sites might have sub-sites and you customize the top navigation to display several levels, the Top link bar will only show one layer of sites. This quickly becomes an issue when there are several sites and you wish to have those items on the Top link bar. To overcome this issue, a custom data source for the Top link bar can be created, links can be added programmatically on site creation, or the publishing feature can be enabled if it is a part of a MOSS 2007 farm.

Quick Launch

The Quick Launch is located at the left side of the default SharePoint site, as shown in Figure 11-28. It is also known as the left navigation bar. Quick Launch by default will have links to View All Site Content, Pictures, Document Libraries, Lists, Discussions, Sites, and People and Groups. In SharePoint, users initially make their first selection on the top navigation bar then this is followed by a selection from the left navigation and subsequent selections from the left navigation. So typically the order of navigation in a SharePoint site is Top-Left-Left (TLL), which makes the Quick Launch a very important piece of SharePoint navigation. To better understand how the Quick Launch works, this section uses a basic team site template.

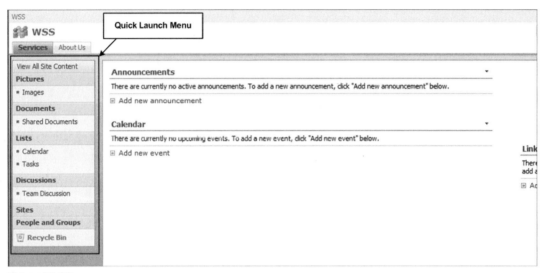

Figure 11-28

Modifying the Links on the Quick Launch

The way you modify the Quick Launch is similar to the way you modify the Top link bar, because the Quick Launch can be modified using the browser and using the SharePoint object model. The easiest way to add or remove links from Quick Launch is to use the browser. To get a better understanding of the Quick Launch menu, assume that you were tasked with adding a new heading in the Quick Launch named "Quick Links." That heading needs to have child links named "Lunch Menu," which points to lunch.aspx and "Corporate News," which points to news.aspx. Assume that you were also asked to delete the People and Groups heading from Quick Launch.

To accomplish this, first go to your team site and click Site Actions ➪ Site Settings. On the Site Settings page under the Look and Feel section, click the Quick Launch, as shown in Figure 11-29. The direct URL for the Top link bar page is `http://yoursite/_layouts/ quiklnch.aspx`.

Deleting Links from Quick Launch

Once you are at the Quick Launch page to delete the People and Groups link, first click the Edit icon next to the People and Groups link. This action will then take you to the Edit Heading page where you click the Delete button. Clicking Delete button triggers an alert window asking you if you're sure Click OK on this alert to close the warning dialog box and delete the People and Groups link as shown in Figure 11-30. If the heading that you are deleting has sub-menu items under it, the sub-menus of this heading will also get deleted.

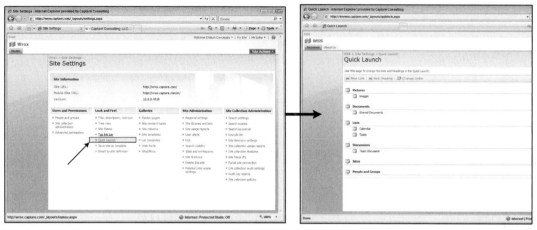

Figure 11-29

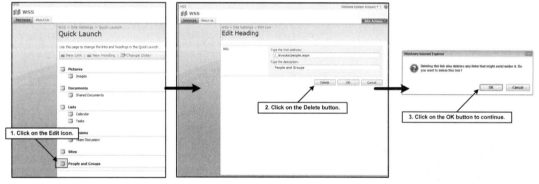

Figure 11-30

Note that after you delete the People and Groups heading, People and Groups will no longer be visible on the Quick Launch page, as shown in Figure 11-31.

Adding Links to the Quick Launch

Deleting the heading link from the Quick Launch is similar to deleting tabs from the Top link bar. Adding links to the Quick Launch is also similar only with one difference. With Quick Launch you are able to add Heading links, which you could not do with the Top link bar. So with Quick Launch you are able to create a two-tier menu with WSS 3.0's out-of-the-box functionality without any custom code.

The first requirement in this example's task was to add a new Heading called Quick Links that does not point to any link. To add the new heading go to the Quick Launch page as described earlier in this chapter and click on the New Heading button to open the New Heading page, on the New Heading page type **Quick Links** in the Type the description field and click the OK button. When you do this, the Web address becomes a required field, as shown in Figure 11-32.

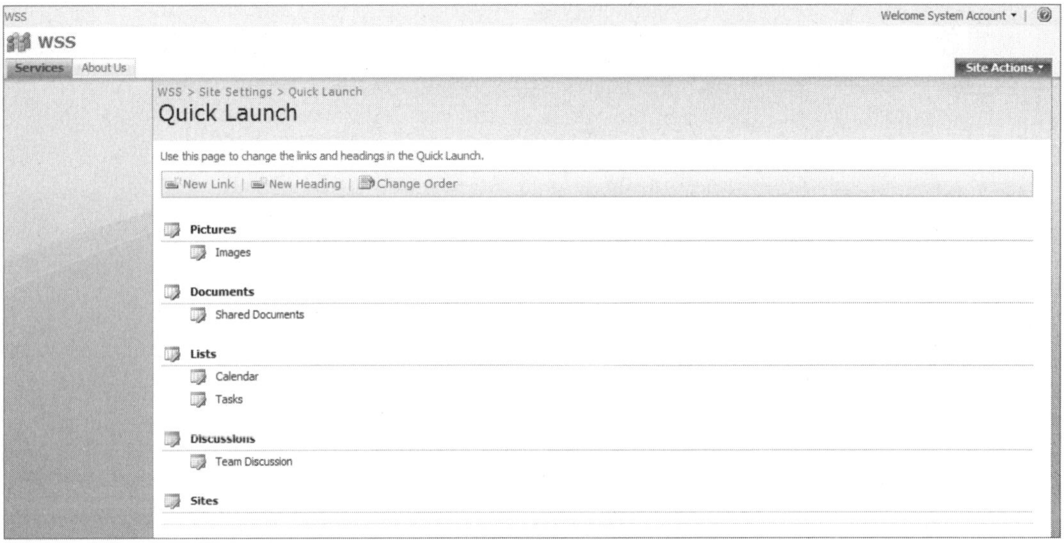

Figure 11-31

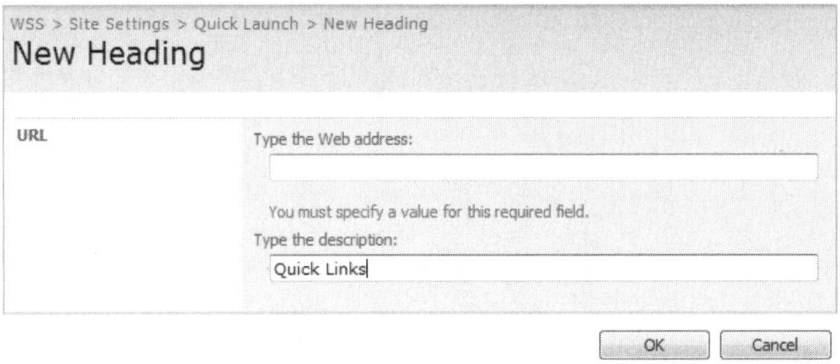

Figure 11-32

Sometimes you need to create headings just so that you can group links underneath them. The headings' only purpose is to group links and to have real links that they point to. So how do you add headings that do not point to a URL? If you need to use the heading for organizing purposes that do not point to any URL, type **javascript:** in the Web address as shown in Figure 11-33. This workaround enables you to bypass the required field validation when you are trying to add a heading with no link. The heading will appear as a link, yet nothing will happen when you click it.

Some users might find the above approach confusing, since the expected behavior when you click a link is that a new page loads on the browser. So to avoid confusion, for an entry-level audience you could type "#" in the Web address field as shown in Figure 11-34, which would also allow you to bypass the required field validation without adding a link. With this approach, when a user clicks on the heading its behavior is the same because the page refreshes and the user understands that clicking on the link has worked.

Again, there is not a best way to do this and it's really up to you to decide which approach to take based on your requirements, but always remember to think out of the box when you run into issues like this.

Don't be afraid to try some of your HTML tricks, as most of them usually work, since SharePoint after all is still a Web application.

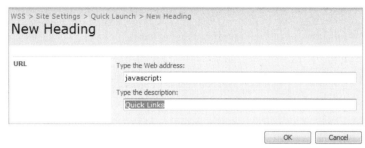

Figure 11-33

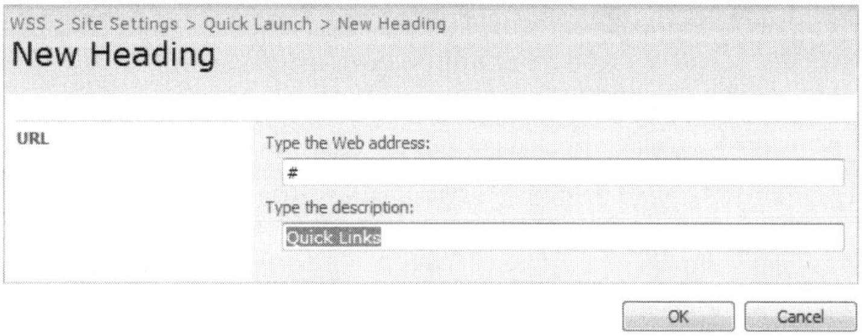

Figure 11-34

Now that you have added the Quick Links heading you can add the Lunch Menu and the Corporate News links. To add a new link to the Quick Launch, go to the Quick Launch page as described earlier in this chapter and click on the New Link button. This opens the New Link page where you will type **/lunch.aspx** in the Type the Web Address field and type **Lunch Menu** in the Type the description field. Once you click OK you are returned to the Quick Launch page where you will see all of your headings and links under your headings.

Note that now there is a Heading section where you can select the Heading (Parent Node) that you wish to add the link to. Here select Quick Link from the drop-down list and click OK as shown in Figure 11-35. You can follow the same steps to add the Corporate News link under the Quick Links heading.

Reordering Headings/Links on the Quick Launch

Now that you have created the links and the heading, let's make the Quick Links heading the first heading. To change the order of the headings and links, click the Change Order button. This opens the Change Order page. On this page, click the Quick Links drop-down arrow and select 1 to make it the first heading on the site.

Note that when you select 1 for Quick Links, this automatically updates the rest of the headings and links as shown in Figure 11-36. Once you click on the OK button the Quick Links will become the first heading.

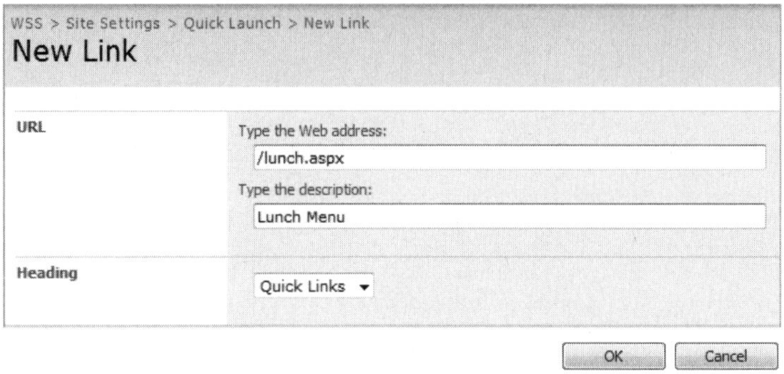

WSS > Site Settings > Quick Launch > New Link

New Link

URL	Type the Web address:
	/lunch.aspx
	Type the description:
	Lunch Menu
Heading	Quick Links ▾

OK   Cancel

Figure 11-35

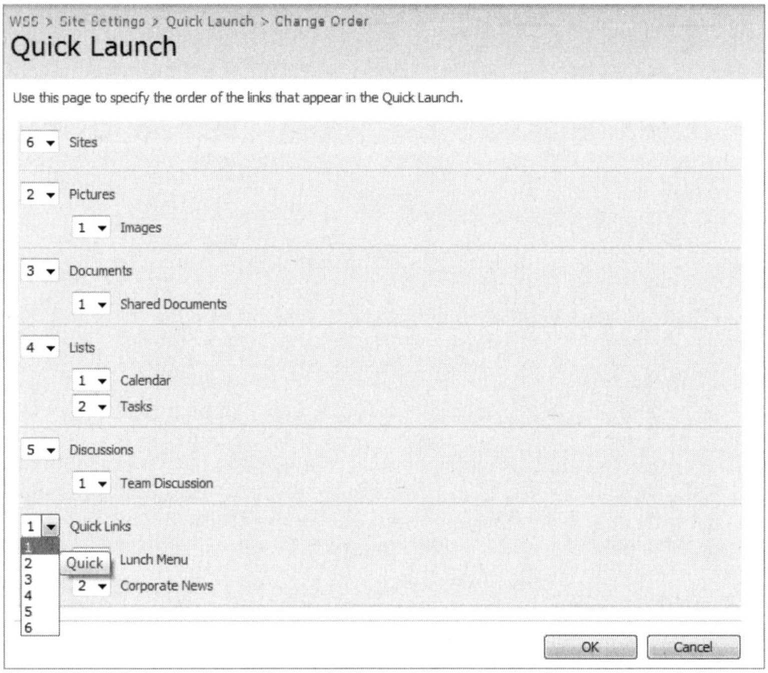

WSS > Site Settings > Quick Launch > Change Order

Quick Launch

Use this page to specify the order of the links that appear in the Quick Launch.

6 ▾ Sites

2 ▾ Pictures

  1 ▾ Images

3 ▾ Documents

  1 ▾ Shared Documents

4 ▾ Lists

  1 ▾ Calendar
  2 ▾ Tasks

5 ▾ Discussions

  1 ▾ Team Discussion

1 ▾ Quick Links

1
2 Quick Lunch Menu
3
4 2 ▾ Corporate News
5
6

OK   Cancel

Figure 11-36

Customizing the Look and Feel of the Quick Launch

Similar to the Top link bar, the look and feel of the Quick Launch can be customized using SharePoint Designer (SPD). The Top link bar is also a part of the default.master page and to customize the look and feel of the Quick Launch you need to edit the master page that the site is using. Open the master page using the same steps you used earlier in this chapter's "Customizing the Look and Feel of the Top Link bar" section. If you're reading this section before reading the Top Link bar section, I strongly recommend that you take a look at that section before reading this section as this section assumes that you have read the Top link bar section.

With the master page open, select Quick Launch and switch to the Code view in SharePoint Designer by clicking on the Code view icon on the bottom of SharePoint Designer. The code for Quick Launch is similar to Top link bar's code segment because they both use the AspMenu class of the SharePoint object model.

The following code is a representation of the default Quick Launch code in the default master page. This code segment is where you will be making most of your changes in the following sections.

```
<SharePoint:DelegateControl runat="server" ControlId="QuickLaunchDataSource">
<Template_Controls>
        <asp:SiteMapDataSource
                SiteMapProvider="SPNavigationProvider"
                ShowStartingNode="False"
                id="QuickLaunchSiteMap"
                StartingNodeUrl="sid:1025"
                runat="server"/>
</Template_Controls>
</SharePoint:DelegateControl>

<SharePoint:AspMenu
  id="QuickLaunchMenu"
  DataSourceId="QuickLaunchSiteMap"
  runat="server"
  Orientation="Vertical"
  StaticDisplayLevels="2"
  ItemWrap="true"
  MaximumDynamicDisplayLevels="0"
  StaticSubMenuIndent="0"
  SkipLinkText="">
<LevelMenuItemStyles>
        <asp:MenuItemStyle CssClass="ms-navheader"/>
        <asp:MenuItemStyle CssClass="ms-navitem"/>
</LevelMenuItemStyles>
<LevelSubMenuStyles>
        <asp:SubMenuStyle CssClass="ms-navSubMenu1"/>
        <asp:SubMenuStyle CssClass="ms-navSubMenu2"/>
</LevelSubMenuStyles>
<LevelSelectedStyles>
        <asp:MenuItemStyle CssClass="ms-selectednavheader"/>
        <asp:MenuItemStyle CssClass="ms-selectednav"/>
</LevelSelectedStyles>
</SharePoint:AspMenu>
```

Adding Fly-Out Menus to the Quick Launch

To add fly-out menus to the Quick Launch, you must modify the StaticDisplayLevels and the Maximum DynamicDisplayLevels attributes of the Quick Launch AspMenu code segment. To get fly-out menu's, update the master page so that StaticDisplayLevels is set to "1" and MaximumDynamicDisplayLevels is set to "1"as shown in the following code.

```
StaticDisplayLevels="1"
MaximumDynamicDisplayLevels="1"
```

Save your changes. The Quick Launch is now a vertical menu with fly-outs, as shown in Figure 11-37.

Figure 11-37

Modifying the Orientation of the Quick Launch

The orientation of the Quick Launch can be modified by updating the Orientation attribute of the Quick Launch AspMenu code segment. The attribute accepts either Horizontal or Vertical as options. By default, the orientation of the Quick Launch is set to Vertical. Update this Orientation's value to be Horizontal, save your changes and refresh your site you will see that the menu is now vertical.

Hiding View All Site Content from Non-Administrative Users

Hiding the View All Site Content link so that non-administrative users can't see all content is something that site administrators and designers get asked to do frequently. This is very easy to accomplish with the help of the SPSecurityTrimmedControl, which controls security for the control that is under it. It gets the permissions required for the control and if the user does not have the rights, it does not show the control.

In the default.master master page, the View All Site Content link is located under a security trimmed control, and by default the PermissionString is set to ViewFormPages as shown in the following code segment.

```
<Sharepoint:SPSecurityTrimmedControl runat="server"
        PermissionsString="ViewFormPages">

<div class="ms-quicklaunchheader">

<SharePoint:SPLinkButton id="idNavLinkViewAll" runat="server"
        NavigateUrl="~site/_layouts/viewlsts.aspx"
        Text="<%$Resources:wss,quiklnch_allcontent%>"
        AccessKey="<%$Resources:wss,quiklnch_allcontent_AK%>"/>

</div>

</SharePoint:SPSecurityTrimmedControl>
```

What this means is anyone who can view the form pages can view the View All Site Content link. To hide this link from all non-administrative users, set the `PermissionsString` must be set to `ManageWeb` as shown in the following code:

```
<Sharepoint:SPSecurityTrimmedControl runat="server"
 PermissionsString="ManageWeb">
```

Save your changes and refresh the site. Log in as a user who has only read access to the site. The View All Site Content link is no longer visible.

Please also note that this can be used for any control within the page. You can easily add the security trimmed control around the link, HTML code, Web part zone, etc. and viola your code will not visible to users who are not administrators. The blow code snippet shows how you can create a security trimmed control that displays "This message will only seen by users who have ManageWeb rights!" to users with ManageWeb rights.

```
<Sharepoint:SPSecurityTrimmedControl runat="server"
 PermissionsString="ManageWeb">
 This message will only seen by users who have ManageWeb rights!
</Sharepoint:SPSecurityTrimmedControl>
```

Tree View Menu

With WSS 3.0 you can enable a Tree view menu by using the SharePoint user interface. To enable the Tree view menu, go to Site Actions ⇨ Site Settings. On the Site Settings page, click the Tree view link located under the Look and Feel section as shown in Figure 11-39. You are taken to the Tree view page. Click Enable Tree view check box and then click OK, as shown in Figure 11-38. Also please note that you can uncheck the Enable Quick Launch check box to disable the Quick Launch.

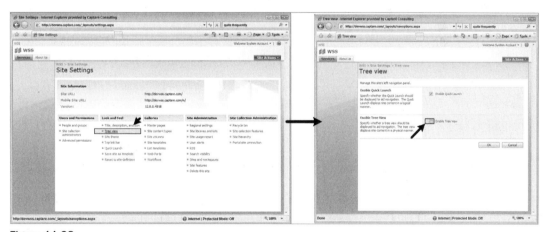

Figure 11-38

When the Tree view is enabled, the Tree view menu appears on the site. The Tree view displays all sites and lists under the current site. One other great feature of the Tree view is that you can access the content of a sub-site and even a sub-sub site without actually navigating to the site as shown in Figure 11-39.

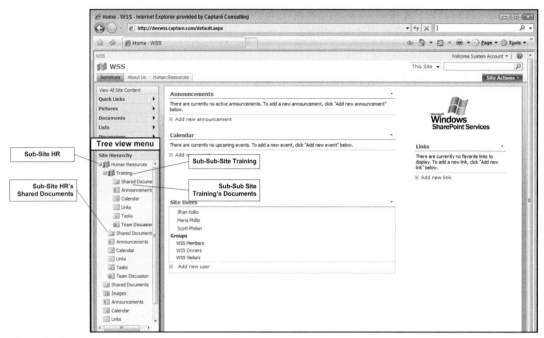

Figure 11-39

Showing Only Sites on the Tree View Menu

In much the same way that you used master pages to customize the look and feel of Quick Launch and the Top link bar, you can customize the Tree view menu.

A good example of a Tree view customization is when you need to only show sub-sites and not document libraries, folders and lists under a site because the default out-of-the-box Tree view shows everything. In reality you might have a root level site called Projects with several project sub-sites. If you want to easily navigate through these projects, you probably want to use the Tree view and customize it so that it only shows sites and not the document libraries and folders under each site.

To do this, open the master page in SharePoint Designer and locate the following code segment:

```
<SharePoint:SPHierarchyDataSourceControl
runat="server"
 id="TreeViewDataSource"
 RootContextObject="Web"
 IncludeDiscussionFolders="true"/>

<Sharepoint:SPTreeView
id="WebTreeView"
 runat="server"
 ShowLines="false"
 DataSourceId="TreeViewDataSource"
 ExpandDepth="0"
 SelectedNodeStyle-CssClass="ms-tvselected"
```

```
NodeStyle-CssClass="ms-navitem"
NodeStyle-HorizontalPadding="2"
SkipLinkText=""
NodeIndent="12"
ExpandImageUrl="/_layouts/images/tvplus.gif"
CollapseImageUrl="/_layouts/images/tvminus.gif"
NoExpandImageUrl="/_layouts/images/tvblank.gif">
```

After you locate the code segment in SharePoint Designer, add the following lines to the last line of the `SharePoint:SPHierarchyDataSourceControl` control.

```
ShowDocLibChildren="False"
ShowFolderChildren="False"
ShowListChildren="False"
```

Save your change and refresh your screen. Only sites will appear on the Tree view as shown on Figure 11-40.

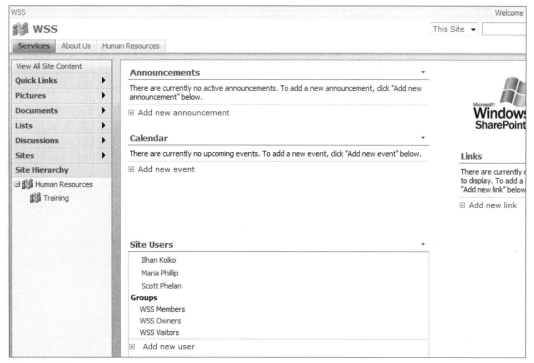

Figure 11-40

MOSS 2007 Navigation

MOSS 2007 navigation has more features, but it is similar to the WSS 3.0 navigation as they both use the same technology. The MOSS 2007 navigation is more advanced than the default WSS 3.0 navigation because the MOSS 2007 navigation is built for SharePoint's Web Content Management (WCM) functionality. Navigation is one of the most important pieces of any WCM solution and the enhanced version of the WSS 3.0 navigation available to users of MOSS 2007 since it provides WCM capabilities. This is why you will see that the MOSS 2007 navigation is mostly referred to as the WCM Navigation.

Sites that have MOSS 2007 navigation enabled still have the Top link bar and Quick Launch, but the navigation is maintained differently. On sites where the publishing feature is enabled, the Top link bar and Quick Launch links do not display under the look and feel section of the Site Settings page. They are replaced by the Navigation link, as shown in Figure 11-41.

Figure 11-41

Maintaining MOSS 2007 Navigation

Maintaining MOSS 2007 navigation is similar to WSS 3.0 navigation maintenance. As in WSS 3.0, you need to go to the Site Settings page to modify the links on the navigation. To go to the Site Settings page, click Site Actions ➪ Site Settings ➪ Modify All Site Settings. On the Site Settings page you click the Navigation link that is shown in Figure 11-41. This opens the Navigation page, which gives you several options for modifying the navigation of your MOSS 2007 site, as shown in Figure 11-42. You can also directly access the Navigation page by clicking on Site Actions ➪ Site Settings ➪ Modify Navigation.

When you create a MOSS 2007 site using the Collaboration Portal template the Site Navigation Settings page will provide three (3) sections to modify the navigation:

- ❑ **Subsites and Pages:** This section is used to specify whether the navigation should display sub-sites and publishing pages in navigation.
- ❑ **Sorting:** This section is used to specify how sub-sites, pages, headings, and navigation links should be sorted in the navigation.
- ❑ **Navigation Editing and Sorting:** This section is used to reorder and modify the navigation menu items.

Adding, Deleting, and Editing Links and Headers

To modify the links on the site, you use the Navigation Editing and Sorting Section. Headings are the groupings of links. They can be thought as the parent of sub-links. The links under the heading appear in the drop-down menu. To add a Heading, click the Add Heading link on the toolbar to open a pop-up window that allows you to add the heading. In this window are several features you don't get with WSS 3.0 Navigation controls. These features are:

❑ **Browse:** Using the Browse button you can easily find the items on your site that you are trying to link to as shown in Figure 11-43.

❑ **Open Link in new Window:** When this check box is checked, the link opens in a new window.

❑ **Audience:** Audiences is a way to group specific types of users. When adding a link, you can select the audiences that can view the link. For example, if you have an audience created for Administrators, which is a group of users who are all Administrators, you can target a heading to this audience, which will show the links only to the members of the Administrator audience, as shown in Figure 11-43. If a user who is not a member of the Administrators audience logs in to the site, they will not see the "Administrator News" heading shown in Figure 11-44.

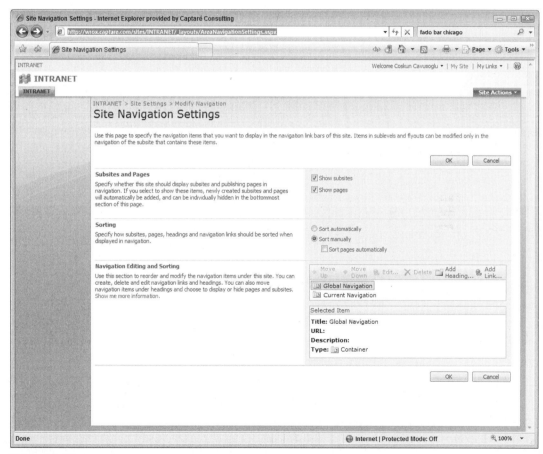

Figure 11-42

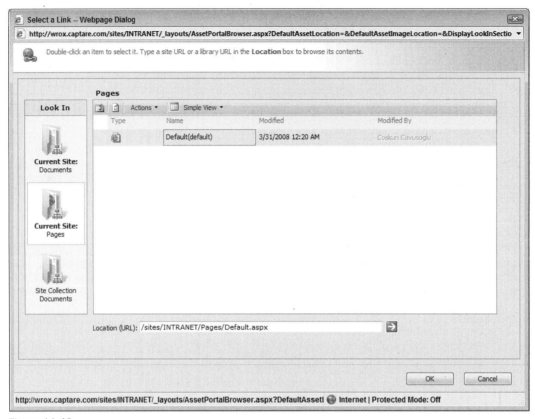

Figure 11-43

Figure 11-44

To add a link, you must select the node you wish to add the link to because SharePoint will add the link under the selected node. To add a link to the site, click Add Link on the toolbar. So to add the link under Administrator News, click the Administrator News Heading and then click Add Link as shown in Figure 11-45.

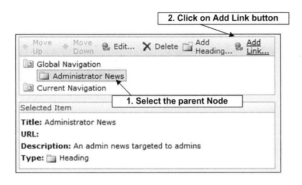
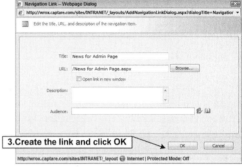

Figure 11-45

Figure 11-46 shows the News for Admin Page as a link under the Administrator News because that node was selected when adding the link.

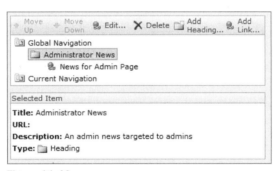

Figure 11-46

To edit an item, select it and then click Edit. A pop-up window opens, enabling you to modify the link or heading as shown in Figure 11-47.

To delete an item, select the item and then click the Delete link. You must be careful with the delete function because when you click on Delete the link is deleted without a confirmation. If you accidentally delete a link, you can cancel your operation by clicking on the Cancel button on the navigation page and your link will still be there because the modification you make to the navigation don't get applied until you save your changes. Also make sure you save your changes frequently, if you spend several minutes and the browser times out you will have to make all of your changes again since nothing get's applied until you actually click OK on the Site Navigation Settings page.

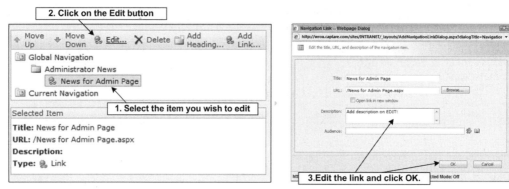

Figure 11-47

Show/Hide Sub-Sites as Links on the Navigation Bar

With the MOSS 2007 Navigation the show sub-site feature automatically shows all sub-sites. This is very useful when creating several levels of sites, as navigation gets tricky when you're deep in the site hierarchy. Showing sub-sites automatically is one of the major things you could not do with WSS 3.0 Navigation controls and is one of the main reasons why most site owners choose to use MOSS 2007 sites.

When the Show Subsites check box is checked, the MOSS 2007 navigation automatically shows sites as links as they get created. They also get added to the Navigation console immediately. If you do not wish to show all of the sites, uncheck the box and the sub-sites will not appear as links on the navigation as shown in Figure 11-48.

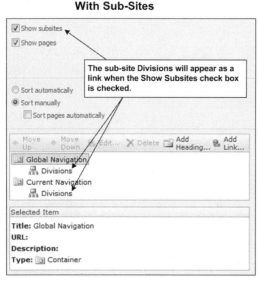

Figure 11-48

Hiding/Showing Links

If you wish to enable the Show sub-sites but do not wish to show all sites as links on the navigation bar, you can hide specific items. To hide a link, click the link to hide, and click the Hide button. The text

"(Hidden)" appears next to the items that are hidden. To show a hidden link, click the link and click the Show button as shown in Figure 11-49.

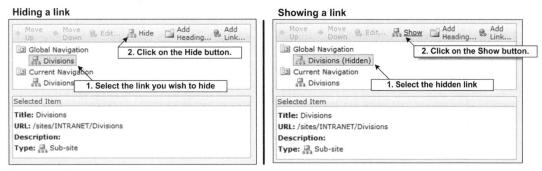

Figure 11-49

Sorting Links

To sort the links on the site, you will use the Sorting section of the Navigation page. You can automatically sort by Title, creation date, or publication date. By default, Title is selected and it shows items in ascending order. You can also choose to sort them manually as shown in Figure 11-50. To sort sub-sites manually or publishing pages automatically click the Sort Manually radio button or the Sort pages automatically check box on the Navigation.

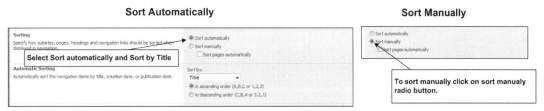

Figure 11-50

Reordering Links

Reordering links is something you do quite frequently. To reorder a link, go to the Navigation page as described earlier in this chapter and click the link you wish to move; then click either Move Up or Move Down. Clicking the Move Up button moves the link upward, and clicking the Move Down link moves the link downward, as shown in Figure 11-51.

MOSS 2007 Navigation Customizations

As mentioned earlier in this chapter, MOSS 2007 navigation is an enhanced version of the WSS 3.0 Navigation controls. You will see a lot of similarities between the WSS 3.0 Navigation and MOSS 2007. This section covers the key differences. Such knowledge can help you determine which navigation will be better for the site you're designing the navigation for.

MOSS 2007 Navigation Data Source Customizations

One of the first things you will notice with the MOSS 2007 menu when you look at its code is its data source. The Top link bar in a MOSS 2007 Navigation site uses a different type of data source. To see the code of the Top link bar you must first open the site in SharePoint Designer. The fastest way to open the site in SharePoint designer is:

1. Click File ➪ Edit with Microsoft Office SharePoint Designer when you are viewing your site in Internet Explorer. This opens the site in SharePoint Designer and you can view the code.

2. Navigate to the _catalogs/masterpage folder and double click the default.master.

3. Click Yes to check it out. Once checked out, SharePoint designer opens the default.master page in design view.

4. Click the Top link bar control to select it. You will know that it is selected if it is highlighted.

5. Once highlighted, click the Code icon at the bottom of the SharePoint designer window page so that you can see the code. You can also click on View ➪ Page ➪ Code to see the Code view of the page. Once you're in the Code view of the page you will see that MOSS 2007 version of the Top link bar uses `PublishingNavigation:PortalSiteMapDataSource` as shown here:

```
<PublishingNavigation:PortalSiteMapDataSource
        ID="siteMapDataSource1"
        Runat="server"
        SiteMapProvider="CombinedNavSiteMapProvider"
        EnableViewState="true"
        StartFromCurrentNode="true"
        StartingNodeOffset="0"
        ShowStartingNode="false"
        TreatStartingNodeAsCurrent="true"
        TrimNonCurrentTypes="Heading"/>
```

Moving Up a link

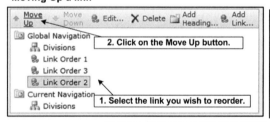

Moving down a link

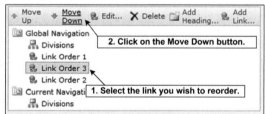

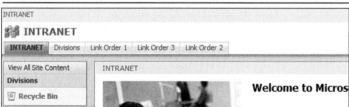

Figure 11-51

The WSS 3.0 version of the Top link bar uses the `asp:SiteMapDataSource` as shown here:

```
<asp:SiteMapDataSource
ShowStartingNode="False"
```

```
SiteMapProvider="SPNavigationProvider"
id="topSiteMap"
runat="server"
StartingNodeUrl="sid:1002"/>
```

`PortalSiteMapDataSource` is a MOSS-specific data source which uses the `PortalSiteMapProvider` object to get the data. With `PortalSiteMapDataSource` you get new attributes such as the `StartFrom CurrentNode` and the `TrimNonCurrentTypes` that you do not have with the WSS 3.0 version of the data source. These new attributes of the data source allow you to create powerful menus when designing SharePoint sites.

The following table details attributes that are most commonly used to customize the navigation and their affects to the navigation menus.

PortalSiteMapDataSource Attribute	Description
StartFromCurrentNode	This attribute defines where the data source will start when displaying the menu items. Typically this is set to True when using the PortalSiteMapDataSource.
ShowStartingNode	This attribute defines if the starting node (Root Menu Item) is returned by the data source, by setting this attribute to False the starting node is not shown and all of the sub-menu items are shown as top level links/tabs.
StartingNodeOffset	This attribute is an integer that defines the offset from the starting node that determines the top-level site hierarchy.
TreatStartingNodeAsStart	This attribute is used by the following trimming attributes. This attribute is set to True when you need to have trimming start from the StartingNode. By default, the StartingNode is not visible and the site that is being visited is treated as the Start Node. When this attribute is set to True trimming will always start from the starting node.
TrimNonCurrentTypes	This attribute enables you to trim the menu items based on their types that are not directly beneath the current node. Trimming can be based on Area, Page, Heading and AuthoredLink. Multiple types can be specified as a comma-delimited list (TrimNonCurrentTypes="Area, Heading"). For example if you choose to trim based on Area, (TrimNonCurrentTypes="Area") this will remove all site links from the navigation.
TrimNonAncestorTypes	Similar to the preceding attribute this will also trim based on type. The only difference is that this attribute trims types that are not directly beneath the current site or one of its ancestors.
TrimNonAncestorDescendantTypes	This attribute trims selected types that are not beneath the current site or one of its ancestor or descendant sites.

Data Providers in MOSS 2007 Navigation

`PortalSiteMapDataSource` is a MOSS-specific data source that uses the `PortalSiteMapProvider` object to get the list of nodes that are displayed in the navigation controls. But `PortalSiteMapProvider` brings more to the table: It not only returns nodes from WSS `SPNavigation`; it also merges the nodes with the site collection structure, which allows the navigation controls to display the site hierarchy automatically. Security trimming is also applied to the links based on the logged-in user, so that the users who do not have access to the sub-level sites do not see those links on the navigation control.

Three types of portal site map providers are used throughout publishing sites in MOSS 2007 and they are as follows:

❑ **Global:** This provider displays all links from the defined `TopNavigationBar` links.

❑ **Current:** This provider displays all links from the defined `QuickLaunch` links.

❑ **Combined:** This provider brings back all links from the `TopNavigationBar` if the site is set to inherit and displays all links from the `QuickLaunch` links when set to not inherit.

The following table details attributes that are most commonly used to customize the PortalSiteMap-Provider.

PortalSiteMapProvider Attribute	Description
`DynamicChildLimit`	This attribute defines the maximum "dynamic" sub-sites and pages that will be shown for each Web site. By default, this is set to 50.
`IncludeSubSites`	This attribute determines if the provider returns sub-sites.
`IncludePages`	This attribute determines if the provider returns pages.
`IncludeHeadings`	This attribute determines if the provider returns headings.
`IncludeAuthoredLinks`	This attribute determines if the provider returns link nodes.

Creating a Two-Level Horizontal Menu

In some cases, due to the design of the site, you might need to display the sub-level menu items under the top-level menu items as shown in Figure 11-52.

Out-of-the-box MOSS 2007 installations have a master page named BlueTabs.master, which displays the menu shown Figure 11-53. For details you can review that master page. To show both levels on the same page, you must use two horizontal menus. This is a great way of thinking out of the box; two controls looking at the same portal site map provider with different settings can help you accomplish a lot. Let's look at the code needed for the two top navigation controls to create the look and feel of Figure 11-53.

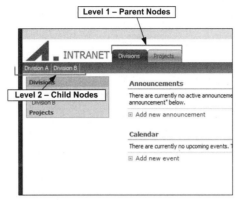

Figure 11-52

Open the BlueTabs.master page in SharePoint designer and you should see that the code behind for the first-level navigation control is as follows:

```
<SharePoint:AspMenu
   ID="topNav1"
   Runat="server"
   DataSourceID="SiteMapDataSource1"
   Orientation="Horizontal"
   StaticDisplayLevels="1"
   MaximumDynamicDisplayLevels="0"
   ItemWrap="false" SkipLinkText="<%$Resources:cms,masterpages_skiplinktext%>">
      <StaticMenuItemStyle CssClass="topNav1Item" ItemSpacing="0"/>
      <StaticSelectedStyle CssClass="topNav1Selected" ItemSpacing="0"/>
      <StaticHoverStyle CssClass="topNav1Hover"/>
</SharePoint:AspMenu>

<PublishingNavigation:PortalSiteMapDataSource
   ID="siteMapDataSource1"
   Runat="server"
   SiteMapProvider="CombinedNavSiteMapProvider"
   EnableViewState="true"
   StartFromCurrentNode="true"
   StartingNodeOffset="0"
   ShowStartingNode="false"
   TreatStartingNodeAsCurrent="true"
   TrimNonCurrentTypes="Heading"/>
```

The first top navigation uses `CombinedNavSiteMapProvider`, the `StartFromCurrentNode` attribute is set to `True` and the `StartingOffset` attribute is equal to `0`.

The second-level navigation control's code is as follows:

```
<SharePoint:AspMenu
  ID="topNav2"
  Runat="server"
  DataSourceID="SiteMapDataSource2"
  Orientation="Horizontal"
  StaticDisplayLevels="1"
  MaximumDynamicDisplayLevels="0"
  SkipLinkText="<%$Resources:cms,masterpages_skiplinktext%>">
    <StaticMenuItemStyle CssClass="topNav2Item" ItemSpacing="0"/>
    <StaticSelectedStyle CssClass="topNav2Selected" ItemSpacing="0"/>
  <StaticHoverStyle CssClass="topNav2Hover"/>
</SharePoint:AspMenu>

<PublishingNavigation:PortalSiteMapDataSource
  ID="siteMapDataSource2"
  Runat="server"
  SiteMapProvider="CombinedNavSiteMapProvider"
  EnableViewState="true"
  StartFromCurrentNode="false"
  StartingNodeOffset="1"
  ShowStartingNode="false"
  TrimNonCurrentTypes="Heading"/>
```

The only differences between the two top navigation controls are that the second top navigation control has `StartFromCurrentNode` set to `"False"` and `StartingNodeOffset` set to 1. With this modification, you have the second navigation menu display only the second level child nodes.

Enabling MOSS 2007 Navigation for WSS 3.0 Sites

The enhanced version of the SharePoint navigation which has been referred to as the MOSS 2007 Navigation in this chapter, by default, is enabled on all publishing sites that are SharePoint site templates bringing WCM functionality to SharePoint sites. If your organization has MOSS 2007, you can enable your WSS 3.0 sites to also have the MOSS 2007 navigation by enabling the publishing feature for the site.

You can enable MOSS 2007 Navigation on a WSS 3.0 site by following the next steps:

1. Go to the site settings page by following Site Actions ➪ Site Settings.
2. On the Site Settings page click on the Site Features link.
3. Activate the Office SharePoint Server Publishing feature by clicking the Activate button.

These three steps place a Navigation link on your site settings and you will have the benefits of a Publishing site. If you do not want to use the publishing features and want only the navigation, you can deactivate the feature. Deactivating the publishing feature will not remove the navigation control. You can deactivate the feature by going to the Site Features page and clicking the Deactivate button. You are then redirected to a confirmation page where you click the Deactivate this feature link.

Summary

This chapter focused on the two types of navigation controls that come with WSS 3.0 and MOSS 2007 and detailed the different ways you can customize your navigation controls. You have seen an in-depth discussion of how to use the navigation controls in a WSS 3.0, including the basic navigation architecture, customizing the links and their orientation, and even how to show/hide buttons and create fly-out menus. You then learned the advantages of using the MOSS 2007 navigation and how it is better equipped to handle more customized sites and navigation schemas. You saw some cool tricks, like creating multi-level navigation, using the included functionality of MOSS 2007 navigation.

As this chapter ends, hopefully you have a good understanding of navigation as it relates to MOSS 2007 and WSS 3.0 sites. You need this information again as you get into Chapter 13 and you see how to override some of these navigation controls with more accessible counterparts. But for now, you should be able to decide whether to use a WSS 3.0 site or a MOSS 2007 site.

12

Customizing Search

Google has ruined search.

Not just Google search, Yahoo! search and any other Web-based search engine that you've ever used. Ruined it for business users, for SharePoint administrators, and for portal and Web designers.

Let's say, for instance, that your significant other really likes fondue. So, on a little weekend jaunt to Des Moines, you're trying to surprise him with some melted cheese and a nice bottle of wine. You go to your favorite search page and type in "Best Fondue Des Moines" and you get back a list of 18 restaurants. Odds are, you'll end up going to the restaurant, have some darn fine cheese and chocolate-covered strawberries, and thank the fine people of Google/Yahoo!/Microsoft Live for pointing you in that direction and getting you a few points with your boyfriend/girlfriend/spouse.

An unmitigated success for Web-based search, right? The search engine found exactly what you were looking for, right? Not necessarily. There's a dirty little secret in the whole multi-billion-dollar-a-year search process. How can you be sure that you really found the best fondue restaurant in all of Des Moines? What makes it the best? Does Google factor in meat quality or the quality of the service? Of course not. Do they rank the wine lists and the wait times? No. Do they have an index of all your likes and dislikes? Well, knowing Google, they probably do. But as of today, most search engines simply catalog the number of times that Web pages list that restaurant with the words *Best*, *Fondue* and *Des Moines*, run it through a fancy algorithm, and then return the list of links. You're relying on the wisdom of the all the people who make Web pages about fondue to tell you which restaurant should be classified as the "best."

In the vast majority of cases, you're going to be more than happy with the result. The search engine you used may or may not have pointed you to the best fondue in Des Moines, but you still had a really good meal and impressed your date, so you can go on thinking that Yahoo! magically read your mind, calculated all the factors, and delivered exactly what you asked for. As with horseshoes and hand grenades, sometimes close is good enough.

Business search requirements are different. In some ways, enterprise search would seem much easier to calculate. Your company doesn't need to index the entire Internet. After all, wouldn't it be easier to run the numbers on a 30 Gigabyte pile of documents rather than hundreds of Terabytes? That, unfortunately, is not necessarily the case.

The problem lies in two areas: accuracy and the availability of resources. Let's do the same thought experiment again, but instead of "Best Fondue Des Moines," say you want to find your "2006 Q4 Southeast Sales Forecast." Replace that "boyfriend/girlfriend/spouse" with "really demanding boss." You go to your SharePoint portal, crack open your Search Center page, and type "2006 Q4 Southeast Sales Forecast," which returns back a list of 30 documents.

The first question that you have to ask yourself is this: How accurate was my search? Odds are that your boss knows exactly which document he or she is looking for. If all goes well, you may have a pretty good idea yourself. Hopefully, you can spot the document in the first few entries, send it to your boss, and avoid the wrath for another day. In this case, you don't need a hand grenade, you need a sniper rifle.

Another issue with SharePoint search is that you don't have the resources that Google/Microsoft/Yahoo! have. No, this isn't about the billions of dollars or the squadrons of Ivy League math geeks. The resources in this case are countless millions of people that make Web pages every day, cross linking between corporate sites, private sites, blogs, and photo collections of people's cats. Each search engine bets on the fact that high-quality information gets more attention than low-quality information does, and assigns a "page rank" accordingly. The pages that are unlinked (the "dark Web") are left out on any search results.

Most SharePoint sites have at most a few thousand users. There may not be the critical mass of links needed to build significantly between the documents on a SharePoint portal. And unfortunately, there is no room for a "dark Web" on a SharePoint portal. Every document may be the single most important bit of information for the company at a given point in time.

That being said, let's go back to our thought experiment, the one with the demanding boss. How can you be sure that you pick the right document? How can you make it easier for the people who use your portal to find the information that they're looking for?

Accuracy vs. Relevancy

Before going any further, let's start with two words: relevancy and accuracy. They are the standards by which your search capabilities will be measured.

Relevancy is what Google and Yahoo have in spades. When you type in "chicken soup," they give you back a list of links that are in the ballpark of what you're looking for. With a well-crafted search phrase, you're pretty likely to get a link that's relevant to what you need.

In casual searches, such as the search for chicken soup, relevancy is all you need. Relevancy is good, and in the grand scheme of things, relatively easy to supply to searchers. They may not get exactly what they were looking for, but maybe they'll find something that will work.

Accuracy is giving people exactly what they want. Most people who use business search aren't looking for something that's *almost* the Q4 2010 Forecasting Worksheet. They're looking for the document that's *exactly* the Q4 2010 Forecasting Worksheet. That's accuracy.

If accuracy is so hard, what good is Search in a business scenario? Well, SharePoint Search has two very big things working for it. Firstly, having search capabilities on your portal certainly beats the alternative, which is having no search functionality at all. Secondly, the big brains at Microsoft that built WSS and MOSS had the foresight to realize that there are challenges to providing accurate search and ensured that nearly every aspect of the search functionality is configurable and customizable. That's where the whole design aspect of this chapter comes in.

Designing for SharePoint Search has a single goal: getting the users the item that they need. A good design can help in two ways. First there's the stuff that happens on the back end. This involves giving SharePoint better ways to slice, dice, and categorize the information (to teach it how to think about your data). This chapter discusses content sources, rules, scopes, managed properties, best bets, and keywords. Each of these helps you refine the actions that SharePoint takes behind the scenes to ensure that the best information appears at the top of every search queue.

The second part of search is the front end, including all of the interfaces that users encounter when they try to search. In a standard install of WSS 3.0 or MOSS, a few available interfaces provide very broad search capabilities. The trick is to give your users a customized arsenal of tools that will help them find what they need. This will include not only general search pages, but custom search pages and Web Parts, and if you're using MOSS, the Search Center site.

This should give you enough to create a global search strategy, and if you're lucky, people will think that you're as smart as the people at Google.

Making Better Information

SharePoint Search is like soup. Go with me on this one.

Anyone can make soup. Take water, chicken, noodles, veggies, or whatever else you like, throw it in a pot, and its soup, right? Maybe. But if you start with really good ingredients, take your time, and set things up just right, you'll get really good soup.

(To extend this metaphor way too far: What's an out-of-the-box search setup? Canned soup. Yes, you can live on it, but why would you want to?)

So, what's the first step to designing for search? The same as making good soup: Get good ingredients. The key in this case is to give search the right data to index and cross reference so that it can serve your users the most relevant and accurate results.

SharePoint can look at three things when it comes to your data. First, of course, is the content. Unfortunately, you don't have much control over what users put into documents, forms, and list items. This is probably for the best, as the users who make them are the subject matter experts. That leaves you with two tools you can control: metadata and content types.

Metadata

Document library column data is SharePoint's bread and butter. This is the document's *metadata* (the data that describes your data). It allows you to tag documents, images, forms, and list items with whatever data you need. Use metadata. Embrace it. The key to good search, however, is using *standardized* metadata.

A good place to start with the metadata definition is listening to how your users speak about what they do. For business to get done well, everyone must have the same vocabulary. A customer invoice will have a "customer name" and an "invoice date." A marketing plan will have a "target demographic" and a "marketing budget." Again, you probably already have a good bit of this in place.

Make a list of all these items; then check it over with your users. The better this list is, the better your search will be. Be sure to keep track of the data type that each kind of column holds (text, number, date/time); this will be important when you create the document library columns.

There are a few ways to maximize how that metadata is used by search. In most places, the vocabulary used to describe one document or data item is used elsewhere as well. Metadata properties are managed behind the scenes using their textual name and data type. An "invoice date" in one list will be treated the same as an "invoice date" in another, so long as both are dates. By ensuring that the metadata columns are the same, SharePoint search can group these items together.

Also remember that though you can easily add same-named columns to your lists and libraries, it's probably easier to set up site columns to ensure that column name spelling is identical on every list and library.

One last thing: If possible, make these columns required. SharePoint can't find data if it's not there.

Content Types

How do you classify and describe the results of all the work you do? If your company makes bicycles, for instance, you probably create invoices for vendors, receive order sheets from customers, keep track of inventory spreadsheets, and so forth. There are probably more than a few handfuls of other types of documents and data.

Out of the box, SharePoint (and Search in particular) is oblivious to these differentiations in how you do business. Searching your portal for the word "Inventory" may give you back the spreadsheet you're looking for, but it will also return every other document that refers to the word "Inventory." Everything in your search results is relevant, but probably not very accurate.

Hopefully, each of the specific kinds of data that you use means the same thing to everyone in your company. This is important and is missed in far too many implementations of SharePoint. This is your business's *taxonomy*. Taxonomy used to be the realm of biologists, who'd go into the field and classify everything they saw: blue-footed pigeons or ruby-throated mice or whatever else it was they ran into. That's what you need to do — classify your data. Make a list, check it twice, as this is where you'll start telling SharePoint how to slice up your data.

For example, suppose you're tasked with evaluating the taxonomy for the bicycle manufacturer noted above. There are distinct types of documents that are used throughout the product development process from beginning to end, each with:

❑   *Specification* documents to store plans for bicycle frames and parts

❑   *Cost Analysis* documents that help determine if the bicycle is worth making

❑   *Marketing Plans* to help sell the products

❑   *Invoices* to log sales to each of the company's clients

And so forth.

With the advent of WSS 3.0 and MOSS 2007, you can use Content Types to inform your portal on what kinds of information you have. Content Types are SharePoint's way of flagging a document as a named part of your taxonomy. Each of the items listed below can (and should) be set as a content type in your portal. If you can limit the documents or list items that you search to just the content type you'll need, you can improve your accuracy greatly.

How Search Indexing Works

Before getting deeper into how to customize SharePoint Search, it's probably best to have a clear understanding of how it works. Searching every document, form, page, and list item in real time is, of course, just not practical. Like every other search engine on the planet, SharePoint Search creates an index of information that it can quickly access and display. You probably already knew that. But there's actually quite a bit more to it than that, and in the immortal words of G.I. Joe, knowing is half the battle.

List data is quite easy to break apart because it consists of tidy piles of typed data. On the other hand, SharePoint needs help reading documents. When processing a document, the first thing SharePoint does is determine how to read it. There are a host of built-in protocols and readers (iFilters) for different document types. Because SharePoint is a Microsoft product, most Office document types are supported out of the box.

Many common file types are not supported natively, but there are a large number of third party iFilters that you can install to expand on the range of supported file types. There is a good bit of momentum in the market for the people who make document creation tools to release their own iFilters. If your company uses a file type that is not natively supported by SharePoint, check with the vendor; you may find that they have one for free.

You can find a free iFilter for Adobe PDF files, for instance, by searching for **iFilter** on Adobe's site (www.adobe.com). There are several different versions depending on things like processor type, so check which one you'll need. (They'll also have a neat article or two about adding the little PDF icon for use in SharePoint document libraries.)

Another excellent resource is iFilter.org (www.ifilter.org/). This is a clearing house of links for free and not-so-free iFilters, including file types such as HLP files and ZIP files. There are even iFilters for TIF and JPG files that use pattern recognition and other OCR technologies to extract text from images, but realize that implementing these can be processor intensive.

In the end, a SharePoint index is essentially a glorified word list, cross-referenced with key columns of list metadata and stacked in a way that it can be easily sorted and picked through for easy retrieval. That's what metadata is for right?

The problem is that SharePoint doesn't look at all your metadata in the same way. Some list columns get preferential treatment. You can imagine a search index to be like a big stack of spreadsheets, with a very big spreadsheet for each managed property. This allows for speedy search for key metadata. By default, SharePoint recognizes a handful of prefabricated columns as managed properties, such as *Modified By*, *Created*, and *Assigned To*.

Want to make your metadata special? Make it a managed property.

Once SharePoint begins crawling your data, it creates or updates two separate piles of information: the content index and the properties store. The content index is simply a database of all the words in all the lists, libraries and such, stored on your SQL server to allow for quick search on each word. It's what most people think of when they are asked about search indexes.

The properties store is where your work with managed properties will start to pay off. SharePoint keeps a separate set of information that allows it to quickly find information that pertains to managed properties. A list item that has a managed property, say, "Customer Name," will merit a special entry in the properties store. If you allow users to search on just that property, you've eliminated all the other information in the system that isn't what they're looking for, making the search more accurate.

Adding Managed Properties

Okay, you've got standardized lists and library columns all over your portal. How do you utilize this to your advantage? The first step is telling SharePoint which columns are the most important. And the way to do that is through managed properties.

Setting up a managed property allows you to target search within a specific metadata column.

To add a managed property to your portal:

1. Open SharePoint Central Administration and select your Shared Service Provider; then open your Search Settings.

2. On the list of options shown, select Managed Properties. You'll see a form similar to Figure 12-1.

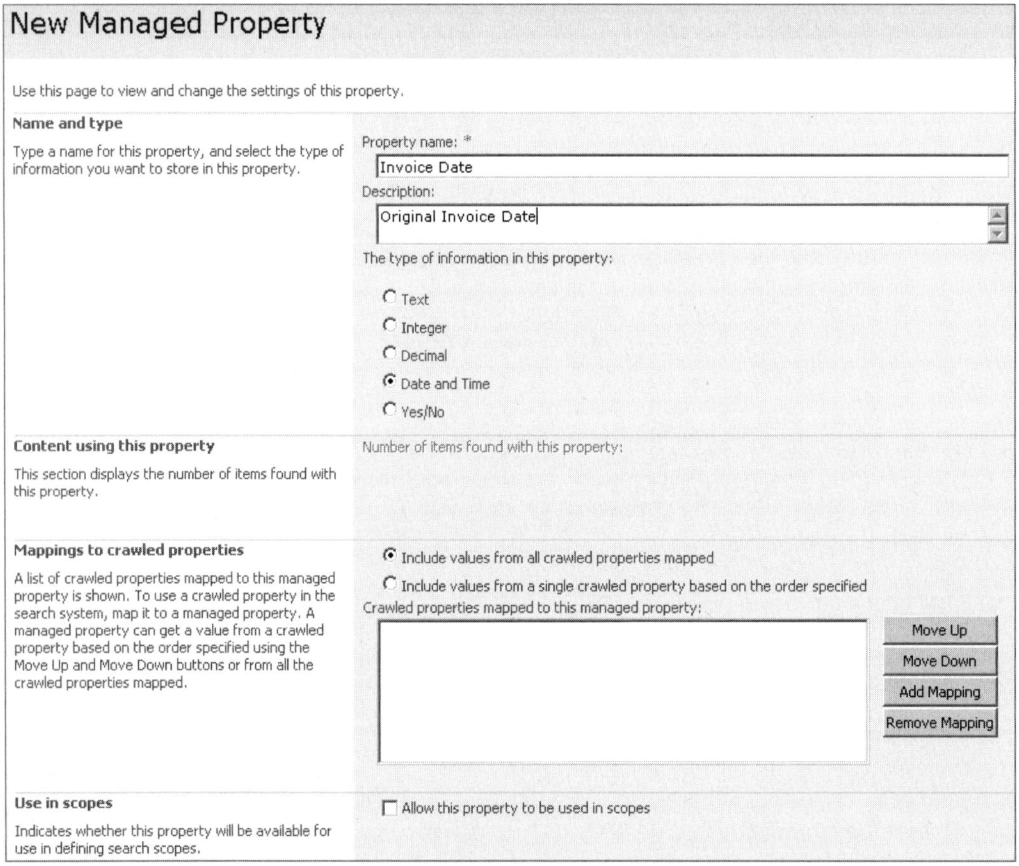

New Managed Property

Use this page to view and change the settings of this property.

Name and type

Type a name for this property, and select the type of information you want to store in this property.

Property name: *
[Invoice Date]

Description:
[Original Invoice Date]

The type of information in this property:

○ Text
○ Integer
○ Decimal
◉ Date and Time
○ Yes/No

Content using this property

This section displays the number of items found with this property.

Number of items found with this property:

Mappings to crawled properties

A list of crawled properties mapped to this managed property is shown. To use a crawled property in the search system, map it to a managed property. A managed property can get a value from a crawled property based on the order specified using the Move Up and Move Down buttons or from all the crawled properties mapped.

◉ Include values from all crawled properties mapped
○ Include values from a single crawled property based on the order specified
Crawled properties mapped to this managed property:

[Move Up]
[Move Down]
[Add Mapping]
[Remove Mapping]

Use in scopes

Indicates whether this property will be available for use in defining search scopes.

☐ Allow this property to be used in scopes

Figure 12-1

3.   Fill out the form as needed (name, description, and the type of data that the property will store). Now comes the fun part. Click the Add Mapping button in the Mapping to crawled properties section. You should see a list of all column names from every list or library in every site on your entire site collection and every other site collection for which Shared Services Provider provides services. (See Figure 12-2.)

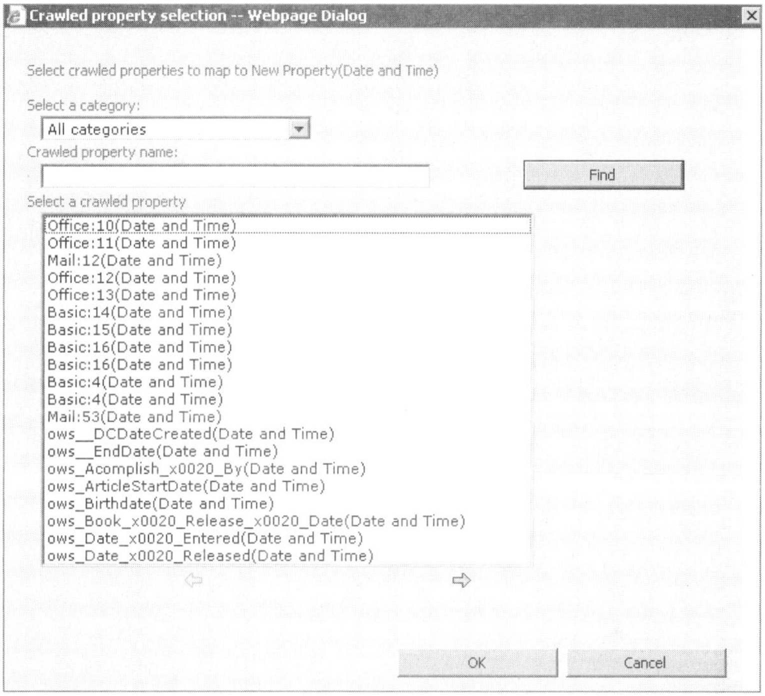

Figure 12-2

Deep inside its inner workings, SharePoint actually uses two names for every column: an external name used for display and an internal name used for its own tracking purposes. Note that the columns are displayed using SharePoint's internal name for the column, which can be a little confusing. You can pare down the list by selecting a category or search for a specific column name by clicking the Find button. This should help you wade through the list.

By selecting the column's internal name, you are telling SharePoint that the column you selected should be associated (or "mapped" in SharePoint parlance) to your new managed property. You do have some wiggle room when mapping metadata. Once you've selected the first column to be handled under your new managed property, you can also add others. For instance, if your company uses the terms "Inception Date" and "Start Date" to describe roughly the same thing, you can map them both to your managed property.

Take special note of the "Allow this property to be used in scopes" checkbox at the bottom of the New Managed Property form shown in Figure 12-1. As you'll see in the upcoming section on scopes, this may be one of the most powerful tools in SharePoint.

Setting up solid metadata, content types, and managed properties can be a hassle for organizations with complex data, but when we move on to some of the more visible parts of search like scope creation and custom search Web Parts, this work will pay off in spades. Designing a good place for data to live is the first step in helping your users find the things they need.

Content Sources

On WSS 3.0 and MOSS, search is broken into two separate functions: getting search data and serving search data. The service that gets the data is affectionately called the gatherer, though it's often referred to as the indexer or the crawler. Before the gatherer can go about its business, you'll have to tell SharePoint exactly what it is you'll want it to search. This means setting up *content sources*.

To add a content source, open SharePoint Central Administration and select Shared Services Administration ➪ Search Settings ➪ Content sources and crawl schedules. This opens the Add Content Source page shown in Figure 12-3. By default, SharePoint creates a content source for your entire portal, but you may wish change this or add additional sources. Of course, to create a new content source, click Add New.

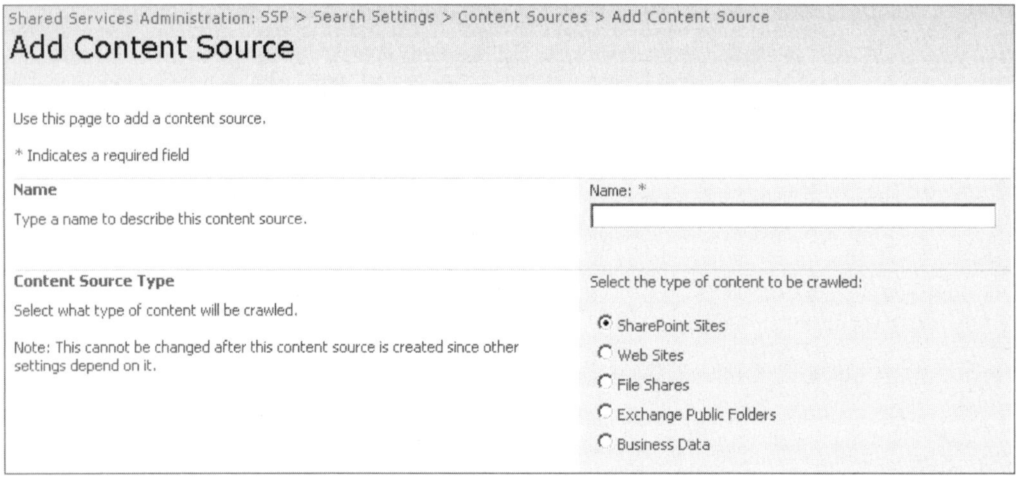

Shared Services Administration: SSP > Search Settings > Content Sources > Add Content Source

Add Content Source

Use this page to add a content source.

* Indicates a required field

Name	Name: *
Type a name to describe this content source.	

Content Source Type

Select what type of content will be crawled.

Note: This cannot be changed after this content source is created since other settings depend on it.

Select the type of content to be crawled:
- ⦿ SharePoint Sites
- ○ Web Sites
- ○ File Shares
- ○ Exchange Public Folders
- ○ Business Data

Figure 12-3

For WSS 3.0, you're limited to gathering information from SharePoint, but MOSS allows a much more robust selection of content sources, including other Web sites, file shares, Exchange public folders, user profiles, and Business Data Connectors. This is probably reason enough for most companies to make the leap to MOSS.

A few things to remember when creating content sources:

❑ Crawling is voracious when it comes to system resources. If you're running WSS or MOSS in a single server configuration, opening and crawling several potentially large documents at a time will take memory and processing power away from other things. Placing the search crawler on a separate server will help alleviate these issues, as will restricting search crawls to off hours.

❑ Crawling takes time. By default, content sources are scheduled to perform a full crawl of content once a week, and check for changes every five minutes. As your portal increases in size, it will take more and more time to crawl the information. Once again, a separate search indexing server will reduce impact for users.

The incremental crawl schedule is also something that you may wish to modify. In environments with low document turnover, you can increase this value to reduce system resources. In any case, you'll want to train users to be patient (if this is even possible). It can take several minutes for search to be aware of changes in a document library, list, or any other data source.

Adding a SharePoint Site Content Source

This is the most common use for SharePoint search and the reason you're probably reading this chapter. By default SharePoint adds a content source for all local site information. You can extend this by creating content sources that point at specific areas of your portal as well. For instance, you can set up a search scope for a group of marketing sites or an area open specifically to outside vendors.

On the Add Content Source screen, select SharePoint Sites as the Content Source Type and enter in the URL of your search portal and schedule accordingly. You can also configure the content source to crawl only the specified site or include all its sub-sites. Easy as pie.

The only catch here is that the gatherer will run under the same security credentials named in the Default content access account on the Search Settings page. It most cases, this is as the worker account was used when the portal was created, and this account should have the God-like powers needed to get at your documents. It is possible to configure shared service providers to use other accounts that may in fact not have sufficient rights to access your lists and libraries.

Bear in mind that it's possible to create content sources that overlap. This will result in items appearing more than once in a set of search results.

Adding a Web Site Content Source

MOSS allows content sources to be pointed at sites outside of your portal. Adding the site is simple enough. Select Web Sites as the Content Source Type and enter in the URL of your target Web site and schedule accordingly.

Configuration options include:

❑ Within the server of each start address (default)

❑ Only the first page of each start address

❑ Custom: Specify page depth and number of server hops.

Also, very easy to configure, but there are a few caveats:

❑ You may not have control over these content sources, and people who do may not like the fact that you're crawling their site. If they should contact you about this, play nice and stop crawling their site.

❑ If you opt for a custom configuration and select an unlimited depth and/or more than one or two server hops, SharePoint will attempt to search links found on those sites, and the links found on those sites, and so forth. Due to the high amount of interconnectivity of today's Internet, two server hops can bring back an astounding amount of information. And though it may seem like a good idea to create a back-up copy of the Internet just in case the current one ever goes away, your IT department may frown on this.

Adding a File Share or Exchange Public Folder Content Source

Up until now, this was what passed for collaboration in the enterprise. Big piles of files on a shared network drive. No metadata, no workflow, no spiffy branded interface. How quaint. And your business probably still keeps a large portion of its data there.

If you have MOSS, it's time to bring this data into the fold. Hopefully, you've got a plan in place to migrate this data into SharePoint document libraries, but in the meantime, you can still make the data searchable. In the Add Content Source page, select File Shares or Exchange Public Folders as the Content Source Type and enter in the URL of your target Web site. Once again, you may want to restrict the gatherer as it indexes the data. You can opt to limit the scale of the content source to the folder at which you're pointing, or have the gatherer recursively search the folder and all its subfolders.

Security may be a concern here. The gatherer crawls using the same security credentials named in the Default content access account on the Search Settings page. As such, it doesn't respect user rights to display results in search results. Users will, however, be blocked from accessing files if they try to open documents that they don't have rights to. This can be frustrating for users, so you may want to set expectations accordingly.

Adding a Business Data Catalog Content Source

One of the greatest features in MOSS is its ability to tie together business data from other lines of business applications. Though setting up a Business Data Catalog (BDC) application is beyond the scope of this book, getting at the data for search is not. In the Add Content Source page, select File Business Data to start this process. You have the option of searching all BDCs on the server or manually selecting one or more previously added items.

Once again, security may be an issue. The gatherer will index and show data based on the identity used by the BDC to retrieve data. This could lead to the exposure of sensitive material if not handled properly.

Setting Gatherer Rules

Now that your content is lined up and ready to go, let's clean things up a little. There are a few additional options that you can set to keep unnecessary information from showing up in search results. To refine the rules that the crawler uses when indexing a content source, select Crawl Rules on the default Search Settings page. A form similar to Figure 12-4 appears.

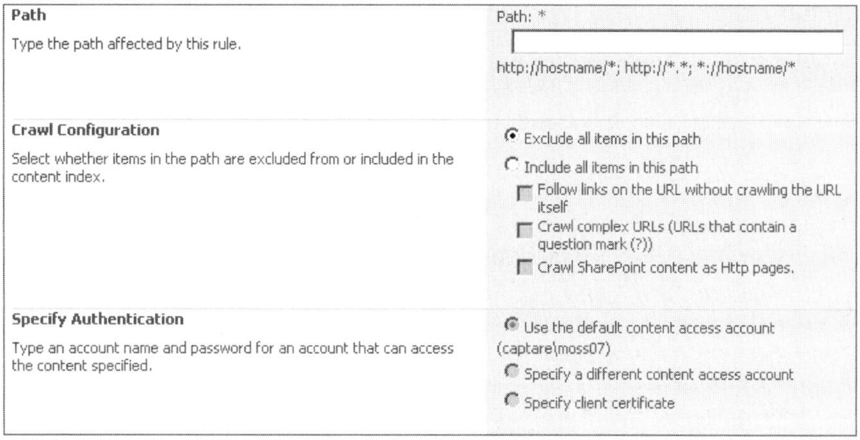

Figure 12-4

Crawl rules accomplish a few things for you:

- ❑   As you'd expect from Figure 12-4, you can exclude chunks of your Content Source from search results.

- ❑   You can add back sub-sections of excluded data. One of the key tricks to setting up rules is to identify the correct order in which rules are applied. For instance, let's say that a company keeps sensitive patent data in a hierarchy of sites. Excluding the branch of the site collection is easy; use the Exclude option shown in Figure 12-4. This would be entered as the first rule.

    However, one of the sub sites — Published Patents — should be available for search. By creating a second rule to include the data, that particular site is returned to service, ready to show up in searches.

- ❑   The Crawl Complex URLs option is useful if you commonly place a lot of links on pages that contain parameters, such as links to static documents or list items. Otherwise, SharePoint ignores any parameters in each URL.

- ❑   The Crawl SharePoint Content as HTTP option should be used with caution. The gatherer stores list and library information differently from regular Web pages as it has to include other data such as list item permissions. Crawling as HTTP forces the gatherer to "pretend" that each item is a standard Web page, ignoring security.

- ❑   Using the Specify Authorization option, you can overwrite the account used for crawling, a quite useful feature to restrict access to key data within a specific site or set of sites.

> Keep in mind that you can also exclude a list or library from appearing in a search by altering the Search settings on the Advanced Settings section of each list or libraries settings. This prevents items such as lookup lists from appearing in search results.

Crawl Settings

When the gatherer wakes up, it checks the server's registry to see what it's supposed to do and how it's supposed to do it. There are a ton of settings, most of which you probably won't need to play with. However, there are a few useful items in the registry, including:

❑ **RobotThreadsNumber:** This sets the number of documents/list items/images that SharePoint tries to index at once. You can imagine these as separate crawlers themselves. The default number is four, but you can tweak this up or down if you want to control how much processing power your servers are throwing at indexing.

❑ **ConnectTimeout and DataTimeout:** Protocol handlers and iFilters can be finicky beasts and often lock or bog down. These settings determine how long the gatherer should wait before it stops attempting to crawl a specific unit of data and moves on to the next one. In most cases, items that cause faults are noted in the gatherer log.

Creating Scopes

The first thing every new SharePoint Search administrator does is dive into creating scopes, bypassing all the other things that have been discussed here so far. It makes sense. Scopes are highly visible, they are easy to set up, and they give a big bang for the buck.

The catch is that unless you've done the rest of the setup, the capabilities of a scope can be pretty limited.

Search scopes are the goal line. The last thing you set up before you can let Search loose on your users.

Adding a scope is easy: Open the Shared Services Administration section of SharePoint Central Administration page, select Search settings, and then View Scopes. When you select New Scope, you'll see a form similar to Figure 12-5.

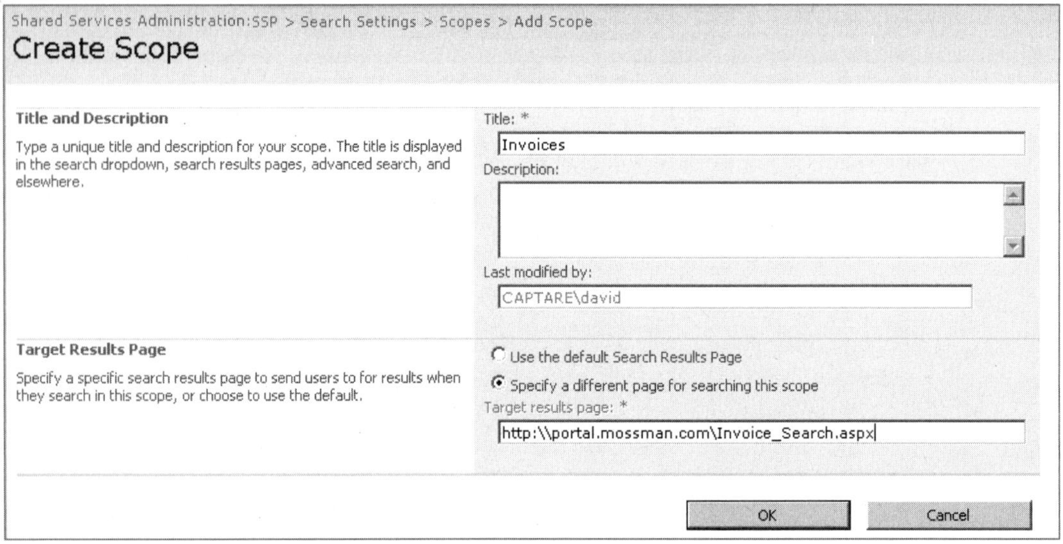

Shared Services Administration:SSP > Search Settings > Scopes > Add Scope

Create Scope

Title and Description	Title: *
Type a unique title and description for your scope. The title is displayed in the search dropdown, search results pages, advanced search, and elsewhere.	Invoices
	Description:
	Last modified by:
	CAPTARE\david

Target Results Page	○ Use the default Search Results Page
Specify a specific search results page to send users to for results when they search in this scope, or choose to use the default.	● Specify a different page for searching this scope
	Target results page: *
	http:\\portal.mossman.com\Invoice_Search.aspx

OK   Cancel

Figure 12-5

In this part of setup, you supply the name and description of the scope. But pay attention to the Target Results section at the bottom of the form. As you would expect, this is where SharePoint will redirect all search calls made on this scope. As you'll see later in this chapter, this can be extremely useful.

That's the first part of setting up a scope. It's basically a placeholder for scope rules. And what are scope rules, you may ask? They're the heavy lifters of SharePoint Search.

Because search accuracy is difficult, the goal of scopes is to pare down the massive pile of documents and list items to a manageable number before the search engine does its thing. Up to this point, you've laid down the foundation for different ways to pare down that pile.

To add a scope rule, select the scope you'd like to modify, then select Scope Properties and Rules from the available dropdown list. You'll see a form similar to that shown in Figure 12-6.

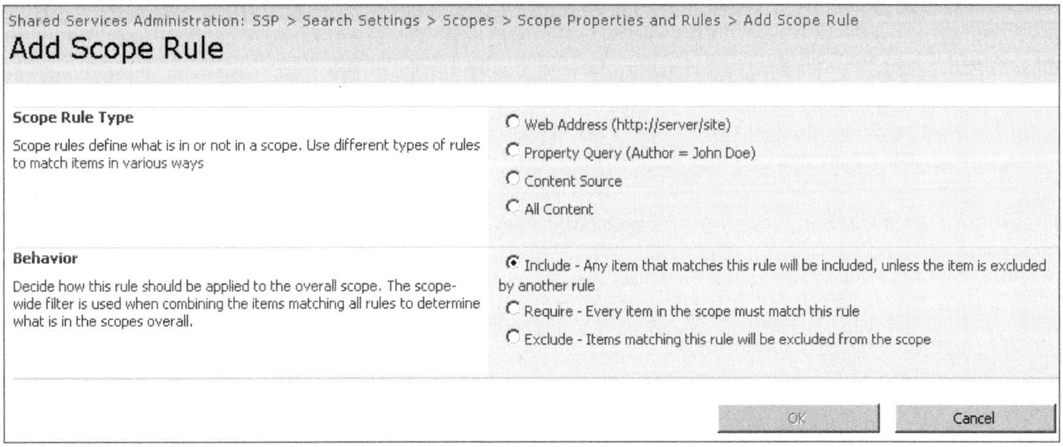

Figure 12-6

There are four different kinds of scope rules:

❑ **Web Address:** This is the most commonly used scope rule, and is dependent on how you've set up your portal. If you've read Chapter 2 and taken care to set up a nice, orderly portal topology, this should be a piece of cake. Using the items in the Behavior section (shown in the previous figure) will let you slice off a piece of your site collection and serve it up in Search or keep something from appearing at all.

❑ **Property Query:** This rule type allows you to limit a search scope to a particular column of metadata. This is an extremely powerful tool, and the possibilities here are endless. This will allow you to automatically filter items based on one of the prefabricated properties that SharePoint uses across all lists and libraries, such as Author or Company, or you can use any custom managed properties that you created.

Unfortunately, there are some limitations. Property Query rules cannot contain complex match criteria. No "greater than," no "less than," no wildcard searches. This makes creating a filter based on date or numerical thresholds impossible to set up. For instance, you can't set up a rule to include every item less than 90 days old.

For example, you may want to create a scope that only displays items with a status of "Approved," or hides everything with a status of "Draft."

❑ **Content Source:** Again, an extremely powerful type of rule. If you've set up your content types to match the way your company does business, the gains of using this type of rule should be self-evident. It should be trivial for your users to search for every "Invoice" on a site collection with hundreds of sites and thousands of documents and not have to wade through every document that contains the word "Invoice."

❑ **All Content:** This rule includes, well, all the content on your site collection. Not much to add here.

The nice thing about scopes is that they each can contain a multitude of rules. For instance, it's possible to create a scope that allows users to search for "Contract" content types in which the "Status" managed property is set to "Pending Approval" but only on the specific section of your portal dedicated to the Legal department.

Making Scopes Available

So far, you've implemented good ways to store data and told SharePoint how to slice up your pile of documents in as many different ways as you need.

The last "behind the scenes" task that needs to be done is to make the scopes available for users. Your newly created scopes must be enabled for your site collection.

To enable a scope, open the Site Settings interface on the top-level site of your site collection. Click the Search Scopes item in the Site Collection Administration column. You should see the View Scopes page similar to Figure 12-7.

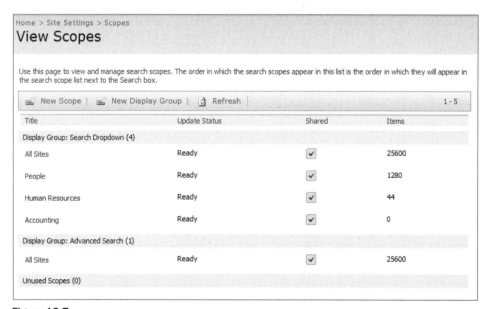

Figure 12-7

This interface show all scopes available to your site collection and a few additional tidbits of information that may be useful as well, such as the scope's update status and how many items appear in the scope.

Search scopes are made available to users as part of a display group. Display groups are simply named groups of scopes that allow you to control where scopes are available. By default, MOSS contains two groups: Search Dropdown, which drives the standard Search control that shows up on nearly all Share-Point pages, and Advanced Search, which allows users to create a more granular search query.

To enable a Scope within a Display Group, click the group's name. The Edit Scope Display Group form similar to Figure 12-8 appears.

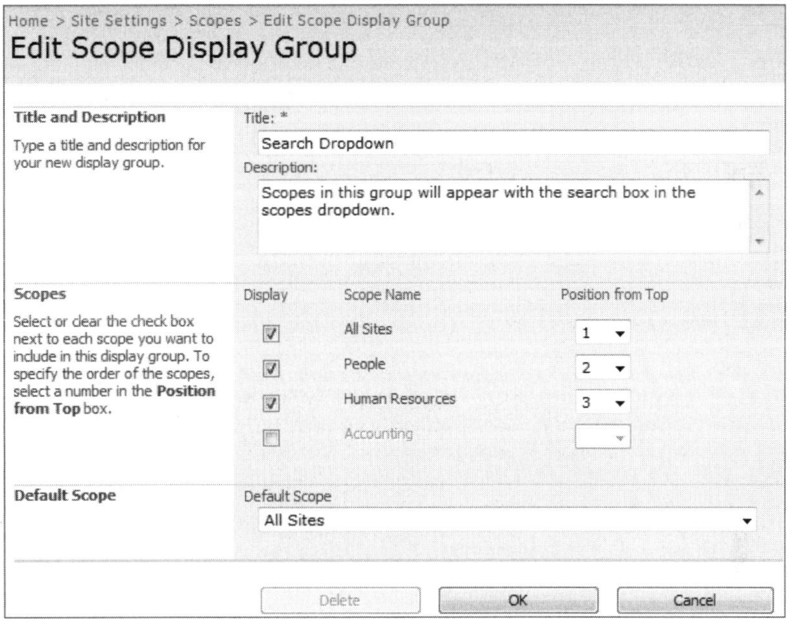

Figure 12-8

By modifying the information in the Scopes section, you'll be able to control which scopes appear as part of the Display Group and in which order they should appear. You can even select which scope is used by default.

You're not limited to the default display groups. Creating custom groups is an excellent way to target searches for particular users. As you'll see in the next section, this can be used within the Advanced Search Box Web Part to create custom search interfaces.

Designing Search Interfaces

Most of what has been discussed here has occurred behind the scenes. But so far, all that's been covered is optimizing SharePoint's innate search indexing features. The next step is to customize the user interface, to streamline search even further by allowing users to access the functionality that you've just built into the SharePoint Search index.

First, before I hammer out how to make things look nice and shiny, you need to learn a bit more about how SharePoint serves up search results. When a user types in a search term and requests search results, SharePoint passes the search query and all the parameters to a search service. The search service, in turn, pours over the index that the gatherer has been so diligent in building and keeping up to date and carefully considers everything that it receives and builds a set of results. This set is then passed to the part of SharePoint that actually builds Web pages and such in the form of a chunk of XML, where it is rendered and sent down to the user.

So, basically, all you have to do is control that chunk of XML, and you can make your search results look like anything you'd like.

There are a few ways to do this, including:

❑   Search Web Parts

❑   The Content Query Web Part

❑   The MOSS Search Center

The next section details these methods and walks you through configuring and customizing these interfaces to target search results to best meet your needs. So far in this chapter, most of the topics on SharePoint Search Service's work have centered on indexing content. From here, you move into getting information out of that index.

There are two aspects to getting search results: telling SharePoint what you want, and managing the results when they're returned. Luckily, there are Web Parts ready and able to do both these tasks.

Using Search Web Parts

MOSS (and to a lesser degree, WSS 3.0) comes with a selection of customizable Search Web Parts. These Web Parts are, with a few key exceptions, relatively easy to configure and will probably cover most of the needs of your overall search design requirements.

Search Web Parts are divided into three groups: entry point parts, result display parts, and search data parts. Due to the scope and size of this chapter, this section doesn't include detailed design guides for every Web Part, largely because they don't easily lend themselves to customization. The following sections do target the two most commonly customized Web Parts: the Advanced Search Box and the Search Core Results Web Parts. These two parts provide access to the bulk of SharePoint's search functionality.

That being said, here's an overview of SharePoint search parts. *Entry point* parts allow users to enter search terms. They include:

❑   **Search Box:** This is the search that most users are familiar with: a text box, a scope selector, and a button. Simple and straight to the point. Not much to discuss here, just a simple way to enter search terms.

❑   **People Search Box (MOSS only):** Again, nothing complex but allows users to find people rather than documents.

❑   **Advanced Search Box (MOSS only):** Here's where things start to get good. The Advanced Search Box exposes all the bells and whistles that you've prepared up to this point: scopes, managed properties, and so on. The next section details the configuration of this Web Part.

Result display Web Parts do just that: display results. They include:

❑ **Search Core Results:** This is the part that you're probably used to seeing when you enter a search in WSS or MOSS. It displays key bits of information in a fairly orderly manner. As you see later in this chapter, you can customize the look and feel of this Web Part, as well as leverage additional functionality for helping target search.

❑ **People Search Core Results (MOSS only):** As you'd expect, this Web Part displays key data from SharePoint profiles. As such, it's only available within MOSS.

Search data Web Parts offer insight into your search results. They're used in combination with a result display Web Part to display information about your search.

❑ **Search High Confidence Results (MOSS Only):** This Web Part displays keyword definitions and best bet links, if they exist for the searched terms. (Keywords and best bets will be discussed later in this chapter, so stay tuned.)

❑ **Search Paging (MOSS Only):** Large result sets can be cumbersome to load in a single page. When combined with a results Web Part, the Search Paging Web Parts allows users to display a set number of results at a time.

❑ **Search Statistics (MOSS Only):** This Web Part displays key metrics on your search results, including the number of hits your search term has returned and the time it took to perform the search. Not exactly gripping information, but it can prove useful in diagnosing any problems that you're having with Search.

❑ **Search Summary (MOSS Only):** This Web Part not only displays a brief summary of search results, but also displays a "Did you mean . . . " section for near misses.

The Advanced Search Box Web Part

Probably the easiest way to give users access to custom search functionality is through the Advanced Search Web Part (Figure 12-9). With a little help, it can let users at all the bells and whistles that you spent so long configuring.

If you haven't cut ahead in this chapter, at least some of the fields on this Web Part should look pretty familiar. (If you have cut ahead, shame on you. No cutting.)

Let's take a look the modifiable options of this Web Part to see what makes it tick. To access the Web Part's properties, click the "Edit this Page" link on your search page; then click the "Modify this Web Part" link. As with most Web Parts, the options are subdivided into separate sections in the edit section. The items included next pertain specifically to the Advanced Search Box Web Part. General Web Part options such as Layout and Appearance are not noted here.

The Web Part properties that configure search are broken into the following categories:

❑ Search Box Options

❑ Scopes

❑ Properties

❑ Miscellaneous

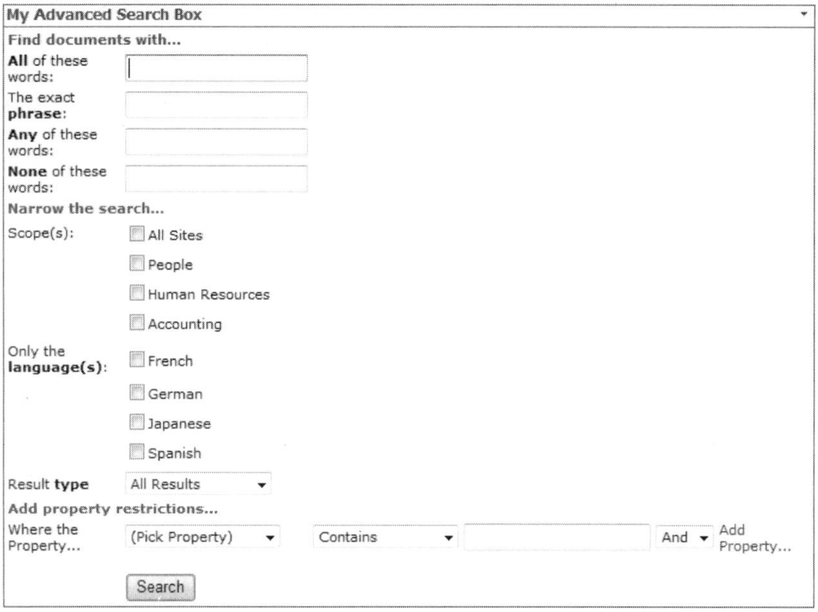

Figure 12-9

Search Box Options

This section enables you to control the text boxes that will be displayed for user input and their description labels. They're fairly self-explanatory. The options included are discussed in the following table:

Item	Description
Search box section label	This option controls the label that appears at the top of this section. The default is "Find documents with . . . ," but you may wish to change it, as not only documents will be returned.
Show "All words" search box	This allows you to turn the field that allows users to search on all entered keywords. This is the default state of search boxes in SharePoint and the one that most users are familiar with.
"All of these words" search box label	This controls what is displayed next to the All words search box.
Show "exact phrase" search box	This allows you to display a text box that users can use to search for a phrase with multiple keywords.
The e phrase search box label	As you could probably guess, this controls what is displayed next to the "Exact phrase" search box.
Show "any words" search box	This allows you to display a text box that users can use to search for results that may relate to one or more of multiple keywords.
Any of these words search box label	This controls what is displayed next to the "Any words" search box.

Item	Description
Show "none of these words" search box	This allows you to display a text box that users can use to exclude search results that contain the included text.
None of these words search box label	This controls what is displayed next to the "None of these words" search box.

Scopes

Though the section title refers to scopes in particular, this section encompasses a bit more. It controls items that relate to how the search results should be filtered, sliced, and diced by SharePoint Search before passing them along to the user. The following table defines the options in the Scopes section.

Item	Description
Scope section label	This controls the text that appears at the top of the Scopes section. The default is . . . wait for it . . . "Scopes."
Show the scope picker	This option will allow you to control whether scopes should be displayed. It will display a checkbox option for every scope that has been included in the *Display group* option below. If this option is not selected, the default scope of the Display group will be used.
Scopes label	Allows you to control the text that appears above the list of scopes.
Display group	This option allows you to set which groups of scopes should appear in the scopes section. A previous section of this chapter details how to set up display groups. This is a very useful option. It allows you to create a custom search Web Part for different core functions of your portal. For instance, you could create a page that allows users to search within a selection of content type based scopes, or search within a selection of search scope-enabled Business Data Catalogs.
Show the languages picker	The languages picker will allow users to limit their search to documents written is a specific language. The items shown here w/are editable in the XML included in the Properties section of this Web Part's options. The next section will go over this in more detail.
Languages label	This option lets you control the text shown with the language picker control.
Show the result type picker	This allows users to limit search results to a specific document type.
Result Type label	This option lets you control the text shown with the Result Type selection control. To add, remove or modify these, you'll need to alter to XML included in the Properties section of this Web Part's options. The next section will go over this in more detail.

Properties

The Properties section provides access to additional means to allow users to be more specific when searching for documents, list items, or other data. The options here are shown in the following table:

Item	Description
Properties section label	This controls the text that appears at the top of the Properties section.
Properties	This option displays as a text box that expands to a text edit control. It contains a chunk of XML that not only controls which items are displayed in the properties dropdown box, but the Language and Result types options as well. The next section will go over this in more detail.

Miscellaneous

Last but not least, there's a Miscellaneous option for the Web Part: Results URL. As you would expect, this dictates the URL that will be used to display the user's search results in a Search Core Results Web Part.

Advanced Search Box Web Part Properties XML

There is a block of XML data included in the Properties section of the Web Part's options. To access the block, click on the " ... " button in the Properties section. This XML data contains four sections and is laid out as follows:

```
<root>
        <LangDefs>  ...  </ LangDefs >
        <Languages>  ...  </ Languages >
        <PropertyDefs>  ...  </ PropertyDefs>
        <ResultTypes>  ...  </ ResultTypes >
</ root>
```

As you can see from the XML block's node names, several functions of the Web Part's fields are controlled by its contents.

Controlling the Language Picker

The first two sections, the `<LangDefs>` and `<Languages>` nodes, contain the information needed to display or hide items in the Language Picker control.

The `<LangDefs>` section contains an entry for every language currently available as a SharePoint Language Pack. It looks similar to this:

```
<LangDefs>
        <LangDef DisplayName="Arabic" LangID="1"/>
        <LangDef DisplayName="Bengali" LangID="69"/>
        <LangDef DisplayName="Bulgarian" LangID="2"/>
        <LangDef DisplayName="Catalan" LangID="3"/>
        <LangDef DisplayName="Chinese" LangID="4"/>
    ... (and so forth) ...
    </LangDefs>
```

There are, of course, many more languages listed in this section, but this should give you a pretty good idea of how languages are defined. Each language is explicitly named in the `DisplayName` attribute and given a number in the `LangID` attribute. The `LangID` value is the internal code that SharePoint uses for each language. This section of the XML will come pre-populated for you, and it's unlikely that you'll need to change much there.

The second node in the Properties XML, the `<Languages>` node, is more interesting from a design aspect. It controls the items in the Language Picker, and will look something like this:

```
<Languages>
        <Language LangRef="12"/>
        <Language LangRef="7"/>
        <Language LangRef="17"/>
        <Language LangRef="10"/>
</Languages>
```

As you can see, each language displayed on the Language Picker has an entry in this block of XML, as referenced by the number in the `LangRef` attribute. In the example shown, the line containing `LangRef = "12"` enables French, the line containing `LangRef = "7"` enables German, and so forth. To add another language, add another entry to the `<Languages>` node with the appropriate number from the `<LangDefs>` section.

Controlling Properties

The next section of the Properties XML block controls the items in the first dropdown that appears in the Properties section of the Advanced Search Box Web Part. It looks similar to this:

```
<PropertyDefs>
 <PropertyDef Name="Path" DataType="text" DisplayName="URL"/>
 <PropertyDef Name="Size" DataType="integer" DisplayName="Size"/>
 <PropertyDef Name="Write" DataType="datetime" DisplayName="Last
    Modified Date"/>
 <PropertyDef Name="FileName" DataType="text" DisplayName="Name"/>
 <PropertyDef Name="Description" DataType="text" DisplayName="Description"/>
 <PropertyDef Name="Title" DataType="text" DisplayName="Title"/>
 <PropertyDef Name="Author" DataType="text" DisplayName="Author"/>
 <PropertyDef Name="DocSubject" DataType="text" DisplayName="Subject"/>
 <PropertyDef Name="DocKeywords" DataType="text" DisplayName="Keywords"/>
 <PropertyDef Name="DocComments" DataType="text" DisplayName="Comments"/>
 <PropertyDef Name="Manager" DataType="text" DisplayName="Manager"/>
 <PropertyDef Name="Company" DataType="text" DisplayName="Company"/>
 <PropertyDef Name="Created" DataType="datetime" DisplayName="Created Date"/>
 <PropertyDef Name="CreatedBy" DataType="text" DisplayName="Created By"/>
 <PropertyDef Name="ModifiedBy" DataType="text" DisplayName="Last
    Modified By"/>
</PropertyDefs>
```

Each item that appears in the list of properties has its own node in this section.

The `Name` attribute refers to the name of the property as listed in the Managed Properties section in SharePoint's Search Settings. The `DataType` attribute describes what kind of data SharePoint should expect. Lastly, the `DisplayName` attribute controls how the property will show up in the list. You can add any attribute that SharePoint manages, including your own custom managed properties, by adding a new `<PropertyDef>` node to the XML block, using the same format as existing items.

This is a particularly powerful feature and is the culmination of all the groundwork that's been laid out for managed properties. The possibilities are endless. Search for items that have a Status of "Incomplete" and a Due Date of "Today." Search for documents assigned to a specific user and flagged as pertaining to a key client. Search for documents assigned to a particular vendor. This is targeted search at its best.

Controlling Result Types

Last but not least is the `<ResultTypes>` section of the XML block. It controls the items listed in the Result Type dropdown box on the Advanced Search Box Web Part. It looks similar to this:

```
<ResultTypes>
<ResultType DisplayName="All Results" Name="default">
        <Query/>
        <PropertyRef Name="Author" />
        <PropertyRef Name="Description" />
        <PropertyRef Name="FileName" />
        <PropertyRef Name="Path" />
        </ResultType>
  <ResultType DisplayName="Documents" Name="documents">
        <Query>IsDocument=1</Query>
        <PropertyRef Name="Author" />
        <PropertyRef Name="Description" />
        <PropertyRef Name="DocKeywords"/>
        <PropertyRef Name="FileName" />
        <PropertyRef Name="Path" />
        <PropertyRef Name="CreatedBy" />
        <PropertyRef Name="ModifiedBy" />
  </ResultType>
  <ResultType DisplayName="Word Documents" Name="worddocuments">
<Query>FileExtension='doc' Or FileExtension='docx' Or
        FileExtension='dot'</Query>
        <PropertyRef Name="Author" />
        <PropertyRef Name="DocComments"/>
        <PropertyRef Name="Description" />
        <PropertyRef Name="DocKeywords"/>
        <PropertyRef Name="FileName" />
        <PropertyRef Name="Size" />
        <PropertyRef Name="DocSubject"/>
        <PropertyRef Name="Path" />
        <PropertyRef Name="Created" />
        <PropertyRef Name="Write" />
        <PropertyRef Name="CreatedBy" />
        <PropertyRef Name="ModifiedBy" />
        <PropertyRef Name="Title"/>
        <PropertyRef Name="Manager" />
        <PropertyRef Name="Company"/>
  </ResultType>
  ...
    </ResultTypes>
```

Each kind of document displayed in the dropdown list has its own `<ResultType>` node. This node contains the information that SharePoint needs to find and display the information the user is looking for. There are a few key bits of information here:

- ❑ `DisplayName`: This is what the user will see. For example, you may see entries such as Word Document, SpreadSheet, or Presentation.

- ❑ `Query`: This is where the display name is translated into the file type. For example, the following code snippet would be used for Word documents:

```
<Query>FileExtension='doc' Or FileExtension='docx' Or
    FileExtension='dot'</Query>
```

The previous query will limit the results to items that have doc, docx, or dot file extensions.

This can easily be modified or copied. For example, to add a section for Adobe Acrobat files, you could add in a section very similar to the Word Document section but updated to match the PDF file extension.

```
<ResultType DisplayName="Adobe Documents" Name="PDFdocuments">
<Query>FileExtension='pdf'</Query>
        <PropertyRef Name="Author" />
        <PropertyRef Name="DocComments"/>
        <PropertyRef Name="Description" />
        <PropertyRef Name="DocKeywords"/>
        <PropertyRef Name="FileName" />
        <PropertyRef Name="Size" />
        <PropertyRef Name="DocSubject"/>
        <PropertyRef Name="Path" />
        <PropertyRef Name="Created" />
        <PropertyRef Name="Write" />
        <PropertyRef Name="CreatedBy" />
        <PropertyRef Name="ModifiedBy" />
        <PropertyRef Name="Title"/>
        <PropertyRef Name="Manager" />
        <PropertyRef Name="Company"/>
</ResultType>
```

The remaining rows in this section, the `PropertyRef` rows, are used by the Search Results Web Part to determine which items should be displayed. Once again, this refers to the Managed Properties list in SharePoint's Search Settings administration and can include any custom managed properties that you've added.

What This All Means

Okay, pay attention. This is the part you've been waiting for. This is where SharePoint Search gets good. Most people come at portal search with the goal of imitating Web search functionality. SharePoint allows you to do so.

Based on the items covered in this chapter so far, you should be able to create as many search pages as your portal needs, each with a specific purpose, anywhere on your portal that you'd like.

Let's imagine, for instance, that you owned a manufacturing company. You make widgets, and lots of them. You've got hundreds or thousands of sites, each of which governs the production of a single widget model.

It would be quite possible to create a search page that allows users to easily find Specification Sheets (a content type), written in Norwegian (a specific language) using MS Word (a result type), for widgets available on a vendors' extranet site (a content source), are in Preproduction (a scope), and are metallic blue (a managed property).

Okay, that's an extreme example, but it's certainly possible. And very, very accurate.

The Search Core Results Web Part

The Search Core Results Web Part is probably why you're reading this chapter. People don't come to a really cool search site to admire your finely tuned scopes or your brilliantly envisioned system of managed properties. They want results. And while you're at it, they better be pretty.

Sigh.

As was noted before, SharePoint returns a chunk of XML every time a search request is issued. The trick is to make that XML look pretty. The Search Core Results Web Part provides two ways to do this. The first is relatively simple: through the Web Part's standard modification options. The second is as complicated as you'll let it be, and that's through the standard method of displaying XML data: an XSL style sheet.

So, to begin, create a new page and drop on a Core Results Web Part. To make things simple, make sure the page has the same URL as you entered when configuring your Advanced Search Box Web Part.

Core Results Web Part Options

The Core Results Web Part, like any other Web Part, has a multitude of switches, toggles and the like for modifying its display. To access these options, place your results page in edit mode and modify the Web Part. As always, the options for this Web Part are broken into sections.

Results Display/Views

The Results Display/Views section governs options that dictate some of the part's high level display options. The available options are shown in the following table:

Item	Description
Results Per Page	As you can imagine, some searches can return a vast number of results. This option dictates how many to display to the user at a time.
Sentences In Summary	This dictates the length of the summary information. This must be a value between 1 and 10.
Highest Result Page	This number puts a cap on how many pages of search results will be made available to the user. As you can imagine, this can get quite large. Putting a limit on how many results are returned can preserve system resources.
Default Results View	This option dictates the default sort order of results, either by *Relevance* (default) or *Modified Date*.

Item	Description
Display Discovered Definition	This is a very neat and underutilized feature in search. When SharePoint is busy indexing everything in your portal, it keeps an eye out for definitions of terms. For instance, somewhere in a document on your portal, there may be a phrase such as "An expense is … " or "a widget is … " SharePoint tries to identify the best of these for each word and mark them as definitions. If this item is checked, an additional link is added at the bottom of the search results that reads "What people are saying about X," where X is the user's search term. Clicking on that link navigates the user to the document that contains the "definition."

Results Query Options

This section dictates a few additional options on which items to include or remove from the search results, as discussed in the following table:

Item	Description
Remove Duplicate Results	This is fairly straightforward. If your search spans multiple content sources, a single result may show up repeatedly. This option eliminates those instances.
Enable Search Term Stemming	SharePoint can use advanced word parsing techniques to try to guess what a user is trying to search for. In this case, SharePoint can extend the range of a search to include additional variations on the word's root. For instance, let's say a user is searching on the word "climbing." If this option is checked, results that match the word "climb," "climbed," or "climber" may also be included.
Permit Noise Word Queries	By default, SharePoint ignores noise words like "the," "and," or "a." Due to their ubiquitous nature, they're usually not very useful in search. Selecting this option, however, allows noise words to be permitted in search.
Selected Columns	This option provides access to an XML block that defines which properties to include in the search results XML.

```xml
<root xmlns:xsi="http://www.w3.org/2001/XMLSchema-instance">
  <Columns>
    <Column Name="WorkId"/>
    <Column Name="Rank"/>
    <Column Name="Title"/>
    <Column Name="Author"/>
    <Column Name="Size"/>
    <Column Name="Path"/>
    <Column Name="Description"/>
    <Column Name="SiteName"/>
    <Column Name="CollapsingStatus"/>
    <Column Name="HitHighlightedSummary"/>
    <Column Name="HitHighlightedProperties"/>
    <Column Name="ContentClass"/>
    <Column Name="IsDocument"/>
    <Column Name="PictureThumbnailURL"/>
  </Columns>
</root>
```

Item	Description
	As you can see, including a `<Column Name>` node for a particular column instructs SharePoint to include that data in its search results set. Note that making the item available for display does not actually add it to the search results. That must be done by editing the XSL code that drives the Web Part display.
Cross-Web Part query ID	In some cases, SharePoint allows results Web Parts to pass search parameters to other results Web Parts. This option helps SharePoint keep track of which Web Part is which.

Fixed Keyword Query

Search Core Results pages don't have to get their input from an Advanced Search Box. You can embed the search terms and parameters directly into the results page and make some very functional interfaces. For instance, suppose you have a scope directed at a specific content type and a managed property. You could display all Contracts that have a status of "Approved." SharePoint could automatically retrieve this list from across countless sites and display the most recently approved contracts automatically. They are discussed in the following table:

Item	Description
Fixed Keyword Query	This text box allows you to enter the search terms that will always be displayed in the search results. It's also possible to include additional parameters here by including a managed property name and a value, separated by a colon. For instance, the text entered might be: Contract IsDocument:1 Status:Approved This would return all documents relevant to the keyword "Contract" that have a status equal to "Approved."
More Results Link Text Label	This is the link text displayed next to the "More Results" link.
More Results Link Target Results Page Url	This is the target for the link that appears next to the "More Results" link.

Miscellaneous

This section covers the remaining options for the Search Core Results Web Part. They are discussed in the following table:

Item	Description
Scope	This option limits search results to a particular scope, and will override any scopes that are set in the Advanced Search Box Web Part. This can become a powerful reporting option when paired with the Fixed Keyword Query option.
Show Messages	This option allows you to show or hide the No Results or No Keyword messages.

Item	Description
Show Search Results	Yes, it's possible to perform a search and not actually display item level results. It may actually even be useful. For instance, you may wish to show a count of search results rather than display each and every item. To go back to our fixed query example, you may wish to display the number of approved contracts but not the full search results.
Show Action Links	Action links are the sorting, alert, and RSS links displayed at the top to the search results. Though you can modify the display of each on an item by item basis, this option allows you to enable and disable the lot of them in a single click.
Display "Relevance" View Option	This option allows you to show or hide the Results By Relevance sorting link at the top of the search results.
Display "Modified Date" View Option	This option allows you to show or hide the Results By Modified Date sorting link at the top of the search results.
Display "Alert Me" Link	This option allows you to show or hide the Alert Me link at the top of the search results.
Display "RSS" Link	This option allows you to show or hide the "RSS" link at the top of the search results.
Sample Data	This field is a place to store a small sample XML block that can be used to test the display XSL.
XSL Link	By default, this Web Part uses an embedded XSL document to render the XML search results. This allows you to reference an external XSL document instead. This can be very useful if you'd like to create a single XSL and reference it from various search results pages around and about your portal.
Enable Data View Caching	To make sure that search results are not constantly changing when paging through results (and to ease the load on the search server), SharePoint automatically caches the set of search results when the search is initially performed. Turning this option off may present more up-to-the minute data, but due to the fact that most Search content sources are set to crawl every 5 to 10 minutes or so, the results are unlikely to change while a user pages through results. The only thing this is likely to change in most scenarios is the amount of processing power the Search server is utilizing as it issues the same query over and over again.
Data View Caching Time-out (seconds)	This sets the duration of the time out for Data View Caching, in seconds.
Send first row to connected Web Parts when page loads	Another neat yet underutilized feature. SharePoint allows Search Web Parts to be connected. They can pass data back and forth. This option allow the search results page to automatically trigger the sending of the first row of results data to another Web Part on the same page.

The Search Core Results XSL

If the Web Part options that the Search Core Results Web Parts provide don't make a pretty enough search page for you, there's one more step, and it's not necessarily for the timid. The Search Core Results Web Part exposes the embedded XSL used to render the XML search results into a Web-friendly format.

XSL is a fairly complicated transformation language that has a fairly steep learning curve. If you're an XSL jock, fire up Notepad and have at it. The rest of us, however, need to tread a little more lightly.

The XSL used by the Search Core Results Web Part is actually three pages in one:

❑   A No Keywords page that will be displayed if no keywords have been passed to the Web Part.

❑   A No Results page that will be displayed if the Web Part received keywords for search, but nothing was returned.

❑   A Results page that renders each search result in a nice tidy list format.

To modify the XSL, open the page in Edit mode; then modify the shared Web Part that is your Search Core Results Web Part. You'll find a section labeled Data View Properties, which, when clicked, reveals an XSL editor button.

Altering the No Keywords Display

Updating the text that is displayed when no keywords have been passed to the Web Part is quite simple. First, find the section of the XSL with the following tag:

```
<xsl:template name="dvt_1.noKeyword">
```

Immediately below that tag, you'll find code that should look similar to this:

```
<xsl:template name="dvt_1.noKeyword">
  <span class="srch-description">
  <xsl:choose>
  <xsl:when test="$IsFixedQuery">
      Please set the ''Fixed Query'' property for the webpart.
  </xsl:when>
   <xsl:otherwise>
      Enter one or more words to search for in the search box.
   </xsl:otherwise>
  </xsl:choose>
  </span>
</xsl:template>
```

You'll notice that two sentences in particular stand out. If your Web Part uses fixed keywords, update the top sentence. If your Web Part does not use fixed keywords, use the bottom sentence.

Altering the No Results Display

This update is a little more complicated, as the page displays additional options. First, find the section of the XSL with the following tag:

```
<xsl:template name="dvt_1.empty">
```

Immediately below that tag, you'll find code that should look similar to this:

```
<xsl:template name="dvt_1.empty">
 <div class="srch-sort">
  <xsl:if test="$AlertMeLink and $ShowActionLinks">
    <span class="srch-alertme" > <a href ="{$AlertMeLink}" id="CSR_AM1"
         title="{$AlertMeText}"><img style="vertical-align: middle;"
         src="/_layouts/images/bell.gif" alt="" border="0"/><xsl:text
disable-output-
         escaping="yes"> </xsl:text><xsl:value-of
select="$AlertMeText" /></a>
    </span>
  </xsl:if>

  <xsl:if test="string-length($SrchRSSLink) &gt; 0 and $ShowActionLinks">
   <xsl:if test="$AlertMeLink">
    |
   </xsl:if>
   <a type="application/rss+xml" href ="{$SrchRSSLink}" title="{$SrchRSSText}"
         id="SRCHRSSL"><img style="vertical-align: middle;" border="0
         src="/_layouts/images/rss.gif" alt=""/><xsl:text disable-output-
         escaping="yes"> </xsl:text><xsl:value-of
select="$SrchRSSText"/></a>
  </xsl:if>
 </div>
 <br/> <br/>

    <span class="srch-description" id="CSR_NO_RESULTS">
    No results matching your search were found.

    <ol>
    <li>Check your spelling. Are the words in your query spelled correctly?</li>
    <li>Try using synonyms. Maybe what you're looking for uses slightly different
         words.</li>
    <li>Make your search more general. Try more general terms in place of specific
         ones.</li>
    <li>Try your search in a different scope. Different scopes can have different
         results.</li>
    </ol>
    </span>
</xsl:template>
```

Okay, if you're not an XSL jock, don't be intimidated. This is still pretty straightforward. There are a few things you update here. The top section (everything within the first set of <div> tags) governs the Action Links. These can be updated using the Web Parts options.

To alter the text displayed, update this section inside the <span> tags as follows:

```
<span class="srch-description" id="CSR_NO_RESULTS">
    No results matching your search were found.

    <ol>
    <li>Check your spelling. Are the words in your query spelled correctly?</li>
    <li>Try using synonyms. Maybe what you're looking for uses slightly different
```

```
        words.</li>
    <li>Make your search more general. Try more general terms in place of specific
        ones.</li>
    <li>Try your search in a different scope. Different scopes can have different
        results.</li>
    </ol>
</span>
```

Altering the "No results ... " code should be fairly self-explanatory. The items below that are a list of suggestions for the user. The <ol> tag starts the list. Each list item is surrounded by <li> and </li> tags. Feel free to modify or delete the text or add new list items if needed. For instance, you might try adding another line item by inserting the following:

```
<li>If you feel your search results are in error, feel free to
    contact Bill Gates at his
        home number (206) 55 . .</li>
```

Altering the Results Display

This is where things can get a little tricky. The search results section of the XSL code gets a bit complex. To directly edit the XSL requires an in-depth knowledge of XSL syntax that is well beyond the scope of this book.

However, all is not lost. There's a bit of sleight of to hand that you can use to get a more attractive layout for search results. If you recall, there are two parts the search results: the XML search results and the XSL that renders the results into a readable format.

Great news: There are free and not-so-free WYSIWYG XSL editors, such as Treebeard (http://treebeard .sourceforge.net/) or <oXygen/> (oxygenxml.com/). All you would need is a chunk of search result XML code to convert.

But, you say, the XML is converted to HTML before it's sent to the browser, before it can be displayed. If only there was some way to get the XML data directly. The Search Core Results Web Part won't run without XSL to translate the XML.

Fortunately, there is. The trick, in this case, is to use a pass-through style sheet. This will allow the XML code to be displayed directly in the Web browser. It's a bit of a hack, but like all other great hacks, it actually works. To implement this hack, do the following:

1. Open the XSL editor in your Web Part's properties menu.

2. Select all the text in the XSL section and delete it. You could save it if you'd like, but if all goes well, you won't need it again.

3. Paste in the following XSL code:

```
<?xml version="1.0" encoding="UTF-8"?>
  <xsl:stylesheet version="1.0" xmlns:xsl="http://www.w3.org/1999/XSL/
Transform">
        <xsl:output method="xml" version="1.0" encoding="UTF-8"
indent="yes"/>
<xsl:template match="/">
```

```
    <xmp><xsl:copy-of select="*"/></xmp>
  </xsl:template>
</xsl:stylesheet>
```

This style sheet simply passes the search results directly to the page.

4. Click OK to exit the XSL editor, then OK again to leave the page's Edit mode.

5. Run a search query. Rather than displaying well-formatted HTML, you'll get something similar to this rather unappetizing chunk of XML:

```
<All_Results>
    <Result>
        <id>1</id>
        <workid>3189</workid>
        <rank>892</rank>
        <title>Search</title>
        <author>Coskun Cavusoglu</author>
        <size>0</size>
        <url>http://www2.mossman.com/Search</url>
        <urlEncoded>http%3A%2F%2Fwww2%2Emossman%2Ecom%2FSearch</urlEncoded>
        <description></description>
        <write>4/15/2008</write>
        <sitename>http://www2.mossman.com/Search</sitename>
        <collapsingstatus>0</collapsingstatus>
        <hithighlightedsummary>
          <c0>Search</c0>  <ddd /> <c0>Search</c0>  <ddd /> <c0>Search</c0>
<ddd /> Advanced
            <c0>Search</c0>  <ddd /> <c0>Search</c0>  <ddd /> <c0>Search</c0>
<ddd />
            <c0>Search</c0>  <ddd /> <c0>Search</c0> </hithighlightedsummary>
        <hithighlightedproperties>
          <HHTitle>
            <c0>Search</c0>
          </HHTitle>
          <HHUrl>http://www2.mossman.com/<c0>Search</c0></HHUrl>
        </hithighlightedproperties>
        <contentclass>STS_Web</contentclass>
        <isdocument>0</isdocument>
        <picturethumbnailurl></picturethumbnailurl>
        <imageurl imageurldescription="Result of type:
            site">/_layouts/images/STS_Web16.gif</imageurl>
    </Result>
    <Result>
        <id>2</id>
        <workid>4087</workid>
        <rank>887</rank>
        <title>Search</title>
        <author>David Drinkwine</author>
  ...
</ All_Results>
```

If you look closely, you start to see a pattern. Each `<Result>` node corresponds to an individual search result.

6. Copy the entire block of XML and paste it into a text file. Save the file with an XML extension.

7. Open up your WYSIWYG XSL editor and go to town. Make whatever changes or modifications that you like.

8. When you're done copy the XSL text to your clipboard.

9. Re-open the XSL section of your Web Part's properties.

10. Delete all text in the XSL section.

11. Paste in your nest XSL text from the clipboard.

12. Save and close.

The Content Query Web Part, Revisited

One of SharePoint's longstanding limitations is its difficulty in sharing information between sites. It's possible to construct custom Web Parts that would function as a crawler and walk through a large number of list items on request, but this approach would be cumbersome and slow.

As you saw in Chapter 10, the Content Query Web Part is a nice way to aggregate information from across your portal. One of the best things about this Web Part is that it pulls information from the search index avoiding the need to crawl portal information in real time.

There are a few key Web Part properties that you can set to leverage your search index customizations. To access the Web Part properties of your Content Query Web Part, change the page to Edit mode, and click the Modify Shared Web Part link on the Web Part's dropdown.

The key areas you'll be interested in will be the Content Type section and the Additional Filters section.

Content Type

At last, you can start to leverage your search customizations. The following table shows available options.

Item	Description
Show items of this content type group:	This dropdown helps pare down the list of selectable content types into manageable chunks.
Show items of this content type:	This dropdown will display a subset of content types, including custom types that may be available on the server. You must choose one and only one content type.
Include child content types	This gives a little flexibility. If the content type you selected has child content types, they also will be included for display. For instance, a *Vacation Request* content type may be a child of an *HR* content type.

Additional Filters

SharePoint allows you to filter based on properties. This functionality looks and acts just like the filter and grouping functionality used to create views for SharePoint lists. Remember, of course, that any custom fields must be manually added.

Content Query Parts vs. Fixed Keyword Core Search Results

As noted previously, the Content Query Web Part can display information that spans your portal, but is extremely limited in how it can refine the data. The Search Core Results Web Part, when configured with a fixed keyword, on the other hand, is extremely robust in its ability to display complex data. The following table compares the functionality of the Search Core Results Web Part with that of the Content Query Web Part:

Feature	Search Core Results Web Part (Fixed Keyword)	Content Query Web Part
Displays information from multiple sites using the search index?	Yes	Yes
Can take advantage of content types?	Yes	Yes
Interface can be customized?	Yes	Yes
Easy to use?	As complex as you'll let it get	Yes
Can limit display to certain list types?	No	Yes
Can limit display to specific scopes?	Yes	No
Can utilize Managed Properties?	Yes	No
Can access Business Data Catalog information?	Yes	No

As you can see, both Web Parts have their advantages. Your needs will determine which Web Part you use.

The Search Center

A brief note on the Search Center site template: This site template is featured prominently in SharePoint's product literature and understandably so. It provides for a prefabricated set of search and search results pages that are conveniently separated into tabs. It can be a real time saver.

However, as you've seen upto this point, the Search Center site need not be the only place for search. Creating a blank SharePoint site and adding a selection of search and result pages would achieve the same results.

Hacking Search Results

Unfortunately, SharePoint doesn't read minds. Let's assume for a moment that you've done everything listed in this chapter and the search results still aren't what you'd like them to be. Fear not; there are still a few things that you can do to override SharePoint's search algorithms.

But first, let's look at how SharePoint ranks search results. There are a large number of variables that go into deciding which end of a set of search results to put any particular item. It is programmatically possible to alter the search algorithm, but that is well beyond the scope of this book. Besides, there are more than a few ways to alter the way that search results are returned without having to crack open Visual Studio.

Search Ranking Factors

First, let's look at some of the factors that the Search uses to rank results:

❑ **Text Analysis:** This is what most people think when they think of search. It uses things like word frequency, variations on words and matching terms to place things with a set of search results. If one document uses the search term three times and another uses a term 50 times, the document with 50 hits is ranked higher.

    ❑ *Hack:* Use Keywords and Best Bets. See the following section on this topic. Make sure your documents use key search terms as many times as possible. This is not necessarily a good hack, but it will work.

❑ **Metadata:** If the search term is featured in the item's metadata, it's more likely to be ranked highly.

    ❑ *Hack:* Train users to use metadata or make the column required in every list.

❑ **Metadata Extraction:** Documents created by Microsoft Office applications (as well as a few third-party applications) automatically tag some document metadata, such as Title or Author. In some cases, the list or library metadata will be populated when the user uploads the document, but not in all cases. SharePoint Search, on the other hand, extracts this metadata when it can and figures it into the search rankings.

    ❑ *Hack:* There's not a lot that can be done in this area, other than training users to enter metadata on their documents.

❑ **URL Depth:** The farther the item is from the top-level site, the farther down the ranking the item will be. The assumption is that top-level sites are more important.

    ❑ *Hack:* Place key document libraries or lists as close to the top-level site as possible.

❑ **URL Matching:** If a search result's URL contains the search term you're looking for, it will be ranked higher than those without the search term. For instance, if a user is searching on the phrase "Accounting," anything on a site that has "accounting" in the URL will win over those placed elsewhere.

- ❏ *Hack*: Name key sites carefully and use descriptive URLS.

❏ **Generically Named Content:** Office documents create a default name if they're saved without intervention from a user. It's a pretty safe assumption that you have a few "document1.doc" or "book1.xls" files on your hard drive somewhere. These are automatically ranked lower. The assumption is that if the user didn't take the time to name the document, it's probably not all that important.

- ❏ *Hack*: Train users to name their documents. SharePoint is all about sharing, and not naming your documents isn't very conducive to this. Strangely, this is still a problem in some organizations.

❏ **File Type Bias:** SharePoint considers some file types to be more important than others. PowerPoint presentations are ranked higher than Excel spreadsheets, and HTML documents are ranked higher than Word Documents.

- ❏ *Hack*: Unfortunately, not very hackable. After exhaustive research, a definitive list of file bias could not be found before this book was completed. Though this can affect search results, most file types are created for a very specific purpose. Presentations work best in PowerPoint, spreadsheets work best in Excel. That being said, testing has shown that Microsoft Office documents consistently ranked higher than PDF equivalents.

❏ **Distance from Authoritative Pages:** SharePoint allows you to define some pages in your portal as more important than others.

- ❏ *Hack*: Not much of a hack, as it's pretty well documented, but making the most of Authoritative Pages can help keep key documents at the top of search rankings. See the following section on this topic.

❏ **Demoted Sites:** Functionally the opposite of Authoritative Pages. SharePoint also allows you to designate some sites as poor candidates for search.

- ❏ *Hack*: Again, not much of a hack, but demoted sites do affect ranking.

Key Words and Best Bets

Keyword and best bets allow you to override SharePoint's built-in ranking algorithms. They let you decide what the best results are, regardless of what data users have put in the portal, and this is not without risk. It removes the dynamic nature of search. So, unless there are documents or pages in your portal that remain fairly static, you may need to manually update keywords, best bets, or both on a fairly frequent basis.

How do you define keywords? Unlike most other search functions, keywords are set in the site collections Site Settings section. Click Search Keywords under the Site Collection Administration section to navigate to the Manage Keywords section, and click Add Keyword. The Add Keyword page shown in Figure 12-10 opens.

Like most SharePoint forms, the Add Keyword page is fairly self explanatory. It allows you to not only define a specific keyword, but also to define synonyms, saving considerable time if you have many keywords that mean essentially the same thing.

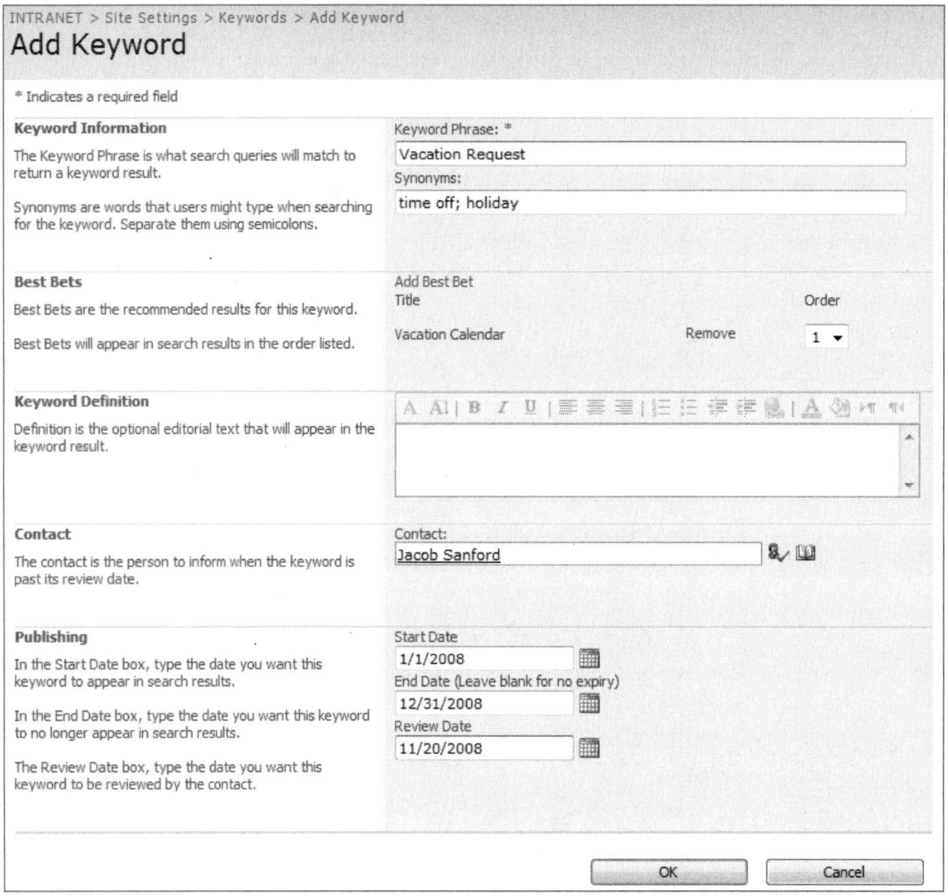

Figure 12-10

The next step is to start adding best bets for the keyword. In the Best Bet section, click the Add Best Bet link and fill out the resulting form. (See Figure 12-11.) Again, the form is fairly simple: Enter the target URL, a Title, and if you'd like, a description for the target page; then save the best bet. Note that you can add multiple best bets as needed.

There are a few other fields on the page that should help you administrate keywords and best bets as you move on, but they are not required.

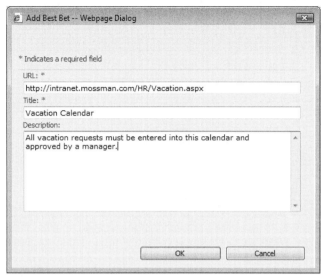

Figure 12-11

That's it. You've successfully overridden SharePoint's search ranking.

Authoritative Pages and Demoted Sites

Kids love playing "Hot and Cold." You probably played it as well. To help find something hidden, one kid (the hider) would yell out "Cold," or "Warm" or "BURNING UP" the farther or closer you were from whatever was hidden. That's what you're doing when you set up authoritative pages and demoted sites. You're yelling "HOT" or "COLD" to SharePoint Search.

To set up an Authoritative Page, open your Shared Service Provider in SharePoint Central Administration and open the Search Settings. Click Specify Authoritative Search Pages. The Specify Authoritative Pages page will appear as shown in Figure 12-12.

To add an authoritative page, simply add its URL to the Authoritative Web Pages section. You can also specify a ranking to your pages by placing them in the second-level and third-level authoritative page sections. These correspond to "Pretty Hot" and "Warm," respectively.

Lastly, the equivalent of "Cold" is the Non-authoritative Sites section. Placing a URL in this box tells SharePoint to rank results lower for items that are on or near the site in question.

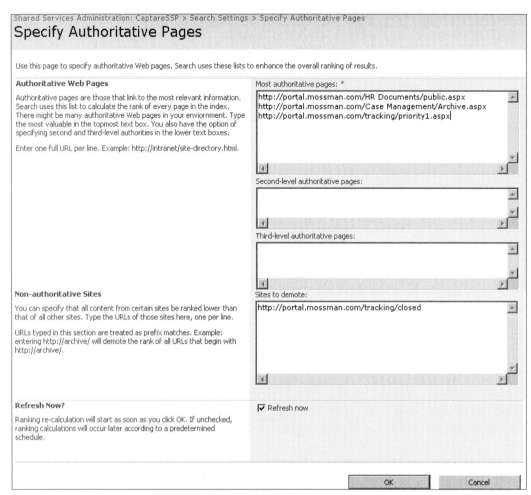

Figure 12-12

Summary

If this chapter teaches you anything, it's that providing great enterprise search capabilities is all about planning. Good preparation should include:

❑ **Getting good data:** Plan ahead to use your company's taxonomy to make the best use of metadata, content types, and managed properties.

❑ **Tell SharePoint how to carve up your data:** Use content sources and scopes to take advantage of segregating your search into logical chunks. The less SharePoint has to pour over every time it gets a search request, the more accurate the results will be.

❑ **Give your users the tools they need to access search:** A Search Center, advanced search and results interfaces, and Content Query Web Parts.

And that, at the end of the day, is how you give your users an *accurate* search.

13

Accessibility in SharePoint

In Chapter 1 you had a brief introduction to accessibility as it relates to Web design. You saw a little bit of the reasons why accessibility should matter and some of the potential consequences of not taking it seriously. But this exposure to accessibility was meant to be merely a cursory overview of this critical element of Web design. It wasn't meant to be a truly deep-dive approach; that is what this chapter is for.

In this chapter, you should hopefully come away with a much more solid understanding of what accessibility means, how it affects today's Web design, how SharePoint measures up, and what you can do as a SharePoint developer to make things better.

As part of this last point, you will be introduced to some free tools that are available that, if used properly and for what they were intended, can really move your SharePoint installations much closer to accessibility compliance. Will you be Priority 3 compliant (don't worry; you'll get to know what that means a bit later in this chapter)? Probably not. But at least you will know where the short-comings are and be able to talk intelligently about them. And maybe work toward new solutions that can help figure some of these problems out.

Accessibility Today

Accessibility, in its simplest definition, would be "making the Web available to everyone." You might be thinking, "The Web is available to everyone already." Is it? Imagine going to your favorite site while blind. Is it still available to you? What happens to all of the flashy graphics and maybe the multimedia functionality of a site that depends on mouse clicks when there is no mouse attached to the computer accessing this site?

The most common perception of what accessibility means are matters that affect those with some sort of impairment (usually visual), so it makes sense to start there. To get an idea of what this might mean to you as a Web developer, consider the study commissioned by Microsoft in 2003 (performed by Forrester Research, Inc.) to look at how many working-age adults could benefit from the use of assistive technology (http://www.microsoft.com/enable/research/workingage.aspx). The numbers, shown in Figure 13-1, might surprise you.

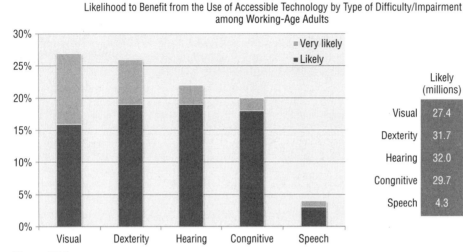

Figure 13-1

So what do these statistics mean? Well, the easy thing to point out is that 45.9 million working-age adults are likely or very likely to benefit from visual accessibility considerations in Web site planning. There are several things to take note of in these results. First, these numbers only represent the US population. That is 45.9 million American working-age adults that are likely to benefit from visual considerations in accessible Web design. Second, these are people who would not considered "disabled" in other studies. In other words, these 45.9 million Americans are not considered legally blind. Finally, these are working-age adults age 18 through 64 years of age. This doesn't include the increasing number of under-18 crowd, as well as senior citizens, who are getting more and more involved in the Internet. So this means that 45.9 million Americans age 18 through 64 who are not otherwise classified as disabled would still benefit from visual assistive technologies in Web design. That is a pretty huge number.

So what do these numbers represent, financially? Most things in business eventually come down to money, after all, so it is worth asking. Can there be a financial impact to not providing accessible Web design? The answer is, of course, yes.

The United States Department of Justice reports that Americans with disabilities have approximately $175 billion in discretionary income (http://www.ada.gov/busstat.htm). Add to that the approximately £45 – 50 billion (almost $100 billion) for the UK reported by the Employers' Forum on Disability (http://www.employers-forum.co.uk) and you have a staggering amount of disposable income from people with disabilities. And, again, those are just the ones classified as disabled; not the ones reported earlier in the Microsoft report. And, maybe more important, that is just from two countries (USA and UK). Project those numbers on a global scale and you begin to get an idea of what this can mean financially. If there are two sites these people can go to in order to get what they want and one is accessible to them and one isn't, guess where those hundreds upon hundreds of billions of dollars are going to go?

A new consideration is getting a lot more attention in the realm of accessibility in today's Web market. Too often, people think of accessibility as only extending to the handicapped (usually the visually impaired), but this is becoming recognized as a short-sighted definition of the topic. To take the mouse-click example at the beginning of this section further. Who has a mouse hooked up to their cell phone? Today's cell phones are capable of accessing the Internet at high-speed rates. But if when they get there, everything looks chaotic, unorganized, and unusable, how long will the mobile user stay there? Not long. And that is a reality of today's world. People surf the Web on the mobile phones or smart phones in airports, in the taxi, or on the commuter train. Basically, anywhere it's not practical to break out the laptop, people are more and more using their phones to do basic Internet browsing. And if your site isn't accessible to these users, they will go somewhere that is.

So how many phones are being used to surf the Web today? A January 2008 report by M:Metrics, a company that specializes in tracking and reporting mobile usage, shows the following statistics (http://mmetrics.com/press/PressRelease.aspx?article=20080318-iphonehype):

Mobile Subscriber Monthly Consumption of Content and Applications
M:Metrics Benchmark Survey: January 2008

	US	EU	FR	DE	IT	ES	UK
Total mobile subscribers (13+)	219m	220.5m	45.5m	48.5m	46.5m	33.5m	46.5m
Watched video	4.60%	5.50%	5.30%	2.80%	6.70%	8.10%	5.60%
Listened to music	6.70%	16.90%	14.70%	15.90%	13.90%	21.10%	19.90%
Accessed news/info via browser	13.10%	9.40%	9.50%	5.50%	7.90%	7.50%	16.50%
Received SMS ads	19.20%	50.60%	64.70%	31.10%	56.00%	73.10%	35.40%
Played downloaded game	9.00%	8.40%	4.10%	7.50%	9.00%	12.30%	10.40%
Accessed downloaded application	4.70%	2.70%	1.40%	2.30%	4.00%	2.40%	3.40%
Sent/received photos or videos	21.90%	28.40%	25.50%	22.10%	33.20%	31.70%	30.60%
Purchased ringtones	9.50%	4.10%	4.30%	3.80%	4.90%	3.90%	3.60%
Used email	12.10%	8.40%	6.30%	6.90%	10.60%	9.10%	9.40%
Accessed social networking sites	4.20%	2.60%	2.20%	1.10%	2.30%	2.50%	4.70%

The first interesting number worth mentioning in this chart is the total number of mobile subscriptions worldwide. If you add up the entire first row of numbers, you will see that there are approximately 660 million global cell phone subscribers. Now, if you do some quick analysis on the numbers, you will also find that there are over 70 million users who access news and information from a browser from their phones while over 20 million users access social networking sites from their phones. Is this surprising? This is the future of the Web. And if your Web site isn't accessible to these devices, many without a mouse and with limited CSS/JavaScript support, you will have unhappy customers (or, likely, lost customers).

Guidelines for Accessibility

The generally accepted authority on accessibility in Web design is the World Wide Web Consortium, commonly referred to as W3C (http://www.w3.org/). This group creates policies and guidelines for creating accessible Web sites. It also provides definitions and links to services that may help you with your own sites. Under this group, a set of guidelines called the Web Content Accessibility Guidelines (WCAG) has been released. The current version (as of writing this chapter) is still WCAG 1.0 (http://www.w3.org/TR/WCAG10/), which was published May 5, 1999.

Generally speaking, most accessibility compliance is measured by compliance with one of three priority levels published by the W3C (copied from their site):

❑ **Priority 1:** A Web content developer *must* satisfy this checkpoint. Otherwise, one or more groups will find it impossible to access information in the document. Satisfying this checkpoint is a basic requirement for some groups to be able to use Web documents.

❑ **Priority 2:** A Web content developer *should* satisfy this checkpoint. Otherwise, one or more groups will find it difficult to access information in the document. Satisfying this checkpoint will remove significant barriers to accessing Web documents.

❑ **Priority 3:** A Web content developer *may* address this checkpoint. Otherwise, one or more groups will find it somewhat difficult to access information in the document. Satisfying this checkpoint will improve access to Web documents.

So, according to these definitions, every site in the world should be, at a bare minimum, complying with the Priority 1 checkpoints, which include things like using alternative text for all non-text elements (images, animations, frames, and so on). When you start looking at Priority 2, you will find things like not using tables for structural layout (for example, only use tables for tabular data, not to lay out your page design). Finally, Priority 3 includes things like identifying the primary language (such as "en-us") of the Web page in the HTML element tag at the top of your page. Many will find Priority 3 difficult, if not nearly impossible, to adhere to. But most people can go to at least Priority 2 compliance if they make a concerted effort to do so.

You can see a full list of the guidelines and their associated priority levels at `http://www.w3.org/TR/WCAG10/Guidelines`. You can see the guidelines grouped by priority at `http://www.w3.org/TR/WCAG10/full-checklist.html`.

WCAG 2.0 is under development and may be in practice by the time you read this book. However, the standards are supposed to be fairly similar and understanding 1.0 is still good for understanding accessibility. You can find more on WCAG 2.0 at `http://www.w3.org/TR/WCAG20/`.

Accessibility in SharePoint

How accessible is SharePoint? The short answer is, honestly, not that great, out of the box at least. Take, for example, the checklist of accessibility guidelines provided in the last section (`http://www.w3.org/TR/WCAG10/Guidelines`) and measure SharePoint up against those guidelines to see for yourself:

Checkpoint	Criteria	Priority	Pass?	Comments
Guideline 1: Provide equivalent alternatives to auditory and visual content.				
1.1	Provide a text equivalent for every non-text element (e.g., via "alt," "longdesc," or in element content).	1	Yes	
1.2	Provide redundant text links for each active region of a server-side image map.	1	N/A	Image maps are not used by default.

Checkpoint	Criteria	Priority	Pass?	Comments
1.3	Until user agents can automatically read aloud the text equivalent of a visual track, provide an auditory description of the important information of the visual track of a multimedia presentation.	1	N/A	Multimedia presentations are not included by default.
1.4	For any time-based multimedia presentation (e.g., a movie or animation), synchronize equivalent alternatives (e.g., captions or auditory descriptions of the visual track) with the presentation.	1	N/A	No time-based presentations are included by default.
1.5	Until user agents render text equivalents for client-side image map links, provide redundant text links for each active region of a client-side image map.	3	N/A	Image maps are not used by default.
Guideline 2: Don't rely on color alone.				
2.1	Ensure that all information conveyed with color is also available without color, for example from context or markup.	1	N/A	Color is not used to convey meaning. But be careful when setting up KPI reports or dashboards that you don't get out of compliance on your own.
2.2	Ensure that foreground and background color combinations provide sufficient contrast when viewed by someone having color deficits or when viewed on a black and white screen.	2 for images; 3 for text	Yes	
Guideline 3: Use markup and style sheets properly.				
3.1	When an appropriate markup language exists, use markup rather than images to convey information.	2	Yes	
3.2	Create documents that validate to published formal grammars.	2	No	No DOCTYPE is included by default. (Blue Band includes it, but default does not.)
3.3	Use style sheets to control layout and presentation.	2	No	Many things are positioned using tables (rather than positioned through CSS). Some pages still use FONT tags.

Checkpoint	Criteria	Priority	Pass?	Comments
3.4	Use relative rather than absolute units in markup language attribute values and style sheet property values.	2	No	Uses pixel (px) and point (pt) measurements in core.css.
3.5	Use header elements to convey document structure and use them according to specification.	2	Yes	For example, <H1> is used for site title and <H2> is used for page title.
3.6	Mark up lists and list items properly.	2	Yes	
3.7	Mark up quotations. Do not use quotation markup for formatting effects such as indentation.	2	Yes	

Guideline 4: Clarify natural language usage.

Checkpoint	Criteria	Priority	Pass?	Comments
4.1	Clearly identify changes in the natural language of a document's text and any text equivalents (such as captions).	1	N/A	The responsibility of the developer to ensure this is done properly in their content.
4.2	Specify the expansion of each abbreviation or acronym in a document where it first occurs.	3	N/A	The responsibility of the developer to ensure this is done properly in their content.
4.3	Identify the primary natural language of a document.	3	No	There is no LANG property of the HTML element by default.

Guideline 5: Create tables that transform gracefully.

Checkpoint	Criteria	Priority	Pass?	Comments
5.1	For data tables, identify row and column headers.	1	Yes	
5.2	For data tables that have two or more logical levels of row or column headers, use markup to associate data cells and header cells.	1	Yes	SharePoint uses scope="col" to identify column headers.
5.3	Do not use tables for layout unless the table makes sense when linearized. Otherwise, if the table does not make sense, provide an alternative equivalent (which may be a linearized version).	2	No	SharePoint heavily relies on many nested levels of tables for layout by default.
5.4	If a table is used for layout, do not use any structural markup for the purpose of visual formatting.	2	Yes	

Checkpoint	Criteria	Priority	Pass?	Comments
5.5	Provide summaries for tables.	3	No	Not all tables, especially formatting tables, provide summaries.
5.6	Provide abbreviations for header labels.	3	No	ABBR is not used by default.
Guideline 6: Ensure that pages featuring new technologies transform gracefully.				
6.1	Organize documents so they may be read without style sheets. For example, when an HTML document is rendered without associated style sheets, it must still be possible to read the document.	1	No	This is fairly subjective. But with nested tables and extensive JavaScript controlling menus and such, turning off CSS provides a totally different experience.
6.2	Ensure that equivalents for dynamic content are updated when the dynamic content changes.	1	Yes	
6.3	Ensure that pages are usable when scripts, applets, or other programmatic objects are turned off or not supported. If this is not possible, provide equivalent information on an alternative accessible page.	1	No	SharePoint is very JavaScript dependent. If you turn off JavaScript, the site does not behave the same and many menus and other functionality is completely disabled.
6.4	For scripts and applets, ensure that event handlers are input device-independent.	2	No	SharePoint uses onmouseover extensively, which is tied to a mouse (obviously). There are no device-independent event triggers provided to counter this.
6.5	Ensure that dynamic content is accessible or provide an alternative presentation or page.	2	No	SharePoint uses JavaScript as the URL of hyperlinks (for example, <A href="javascript: ... >.
Guideline 7: Ensure user control of time-sensitive content changes.				
7.1	Until user agents allow users to control flickering, avoid causing the screen to flicker.	1	Yes	
7.2	Until user agents allow users to control blinking, avoid causing content to blink (changing presentation at a regular rate, such as turning on and off).	2	Yes	

Checkpoint	Criteria	Priority	Pass?	Comments
7.3	Until user agents allow users to freeze moving content, avoid movement in pages.	2	Yes	
7.4	Until user agents provide the ability to stop the refresh, do not create periodically auto-refreshing pages.	2	Yes	
7.5	Until user agents provide the ability to stop auto-redirect, do not use markup to redirect pages automatically. Instead, configure the server to perform redirects.	2	Yes	

Guideline 8: Make programmatic elements such as scripts and applets directly accessible or compatible with assistive technologies.

8.1	Make programmatic elements such as scripts and applets directly accessible or compatible with assistive technologies.	1/2*	No	Much JavaScript provides important functionality to the site but is dependent on mouse events.

Guideline 9: Design for device-independence.

9.1	Provide client-side image maps instead of server-side image maps except where the regions cannot be defined with an available geometric shape.	1	N/A	Image maps are not used by default.
9.2	Ensure that any element that has its own interface can be operated in a device-independent manner.	2	Yes	
9.3	For scripts, specify logical event handlers rather than device-dependent event handlers.	2	No	Many scripts are mouse-dependent.
9.4	Create a logical tab order through links, form controls, and objects.	3	No	Tab order (TABINDEX) is not set by default.
9.5	Provide keyboard shortcuts to important links (including those in client-side image maps), form controls, and groups of form controls.	3	Yes	

Checkpoint	Criteria	Priority	Pass?	Comments
Guideline 10: Use interim solutions.				
10.1	Until user agents allow users to turn off spawned windows, do not cause pop-ups or other windows to appear and do not change the current window without informing the user.	2	No	SharePoint uses pop-up windows for things like people lookup.
10.2	Until user agents support explicit associations between labels and form controls, for all form controls with implicitly associated labels, ensure that the label is properly positioned.	2	No	Controls and associated labels are not necessarily positioned properly according to the guidelines.
10.3	Until user agents (including assistive technologies) render side-by-side text correctly, provide a linear text alternative (on the current page or some other) for all tables that lay out text in parallel, word-wrapped columns.	2	No	When tables are laid out with data presented in parallel, word-wrapped columns, there is no linear text alternative provided.
10.4	Until user agents handle empty controls correctly, include default, place-holding characters in edit boxes and text areas.	3	No	TEXTAREA elements do not contain default text.
10.5	Until user agents (including assistive technologies) render adjacent links distinctly, include non-link, printable characters (surrounded by spaces) between adjacent links.	3	No	Ironically, the accessibility links at the top of a SharePoint page are adjacent and have no printable characters between them.
Guideline 11: Use W3C technologies and guidelines.				
11.1	Use W3C technologies when they are available and appropriate for a task and use the latest versions when supported.	2	Yes	This is excluding any documents uploaded to any libraries.
11.2	Avoid deprecated features of W3C technologies.	2	No	SharePoint uses deprecated tags.

Checkpoint	Criteria	Priority	Pass?	Comments
11.3	Provide information so that users may receive documents according to their preferences (for example, language, content type, and so on).	3	Yes	
11.4	If, after best efforts, you cannot create an accessible page, provide a link to an alternative page that uses W3C technologies, is accessible, has equivalent information (or functionality), and is updated as often as the inaccessible (original) page.	1	N/A	
Guideline 12: Provide context and orientation information.				
12.1	Title each frame to facilitate frame identification and navigation.	1	Yes	These are referring to the IFRAMES created by the Web Viewer Web part.
12.2	Describe the purpose of frames and how frames relate to each other if it is not obvious by frame titles alone.	2	No	The generated IFRAME elements do not contain any description property.
12.3	Divide large blocks of information into more manageable groups where natural and appropriate.	2	No	There is no use of OPTGROUP or FIELDSET to group data together.
12.4	Associate labels explicitly with their controls.	2	No	Use of the FOR property of a label is not consistent.
Guideline 13: Provide clear navigation mechanisms.				
13.1	Clearly identify the target of each link.	2	Yes	
13.2	Provide metadata to add semantic information to pages and sites.	2	No	No metadata is generated to provide things like author, type of content, or the navigation mechanism of the page.
13.3	Provide information about the general layout of a site (for example, a site map or table of contents).	2	No	No sitemap or table of contents is generated by default.
13.4	Use navigation mechanisms in a consistent manner.	2	Yes	

Checkpoint	Criteria	Priority	Pass?	Comments
13.5	Provide navigation bars to highlight and give access to the navigation mechanism.	3	Yes	
13.6	Group related links, identify the group (for user agents), and, until user agents do so, provide a way to bypass the group.	3	No	Links are not grouped through SPAN elements or similar technology.
13.7	If search functions are provided, enable different types of searches for different skill levels and preferences.	3	Yes	
13.8	Place distinguishing information at the beginning of headings, paragraphs, lists, and so on.	3	Yes	
13.9	Provide information about document collections (such as documents comprising multiple pages).	3	No	Previous and next links are not provided for easier navigation.
13.10	Provide a means to skip over multi-line ASCII art.	3	N/A	
Guideline 14: Ensure that documents are clear and simple.				
14.1	Use the clearest and simplest language appropriate for a site's content.	1	N/A	This is fairly subjective. Since this is mostly related to the content of the site, this is largely dependent on the developers that create that content and not as much on SharePoint technologies.
14.2	Supplement text with graphic or auditory presentations where they will facilitate comprehension of the page.	3	No	Where there is text provided by SharePoint, there are no auditory or visual aids provided to assist with comprehension of the text.
14.3	Create a style of presentation that is consistent across pages.	3	Yes	

*1 if functionality is important and not presented elsewhere, otherwise 2.

One thing to keep in mind is that you, as the developer, need to store these checkpoints in the back of your mind for your own development. This checklist only measures the things that SharePoint does by default. So, for example, in checkpoint 2.1, the criterion is, essentially, that the site does not use color-only indicators to convey meaning. So, with the default key performance indicator (KPI) reports SharePoint has, it uses color identifiers that are also distinguishable by their shape. A green circle, a yellow triangle, and a red diamond are examples of the indicators used in these reports. So, even if the user cannot distinguish green from red (common in color-blind individuals), that user should be able to indicate a circle from a diamond. And, even if the images are turned off, appropriate alternative text is provided to convey the meaning of the indicator. So, no matter who accesses those reports, they should be able to get the same meaning from them.

If, however, you go and create your own report and set up the title to be green for good, yellow for warning, and red for noncompliance, you will have a problem. Someone who has visual impairment may not be able to see the colors appropriately and, as such, will not be able to tell which items are okay and which ones are in danger of being out of compliance. SharePoint may meet the guideline on its own, but that doesn't mean you can't go in and manually break it. So be careful. And be informed.

The Checklist in the Real World

While the checklist will be useful for many, it might be more useful to actually see what this means to a typical user. To do this, first take a look at a standard site created using MOSS 2007 using all of the defaults, shown in Figure 13-2.

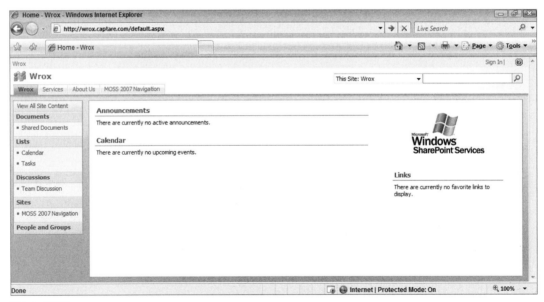

Figure 13-2

Now take a look at the same site as seen in a Windows Mobile 5 Emulator, as shown in Figure 13-3.

It's not the same experience, is it? Now take a look at the site with all CSS and JavaScript turned off (which is typical of some text browsers), shown in Figure 13-4.

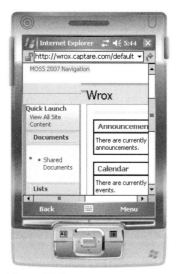

Figure 13-3

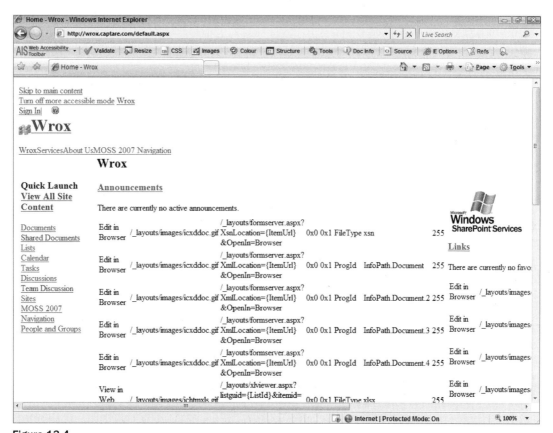

Figure 13-4

You will see that this is, in fact, in the more accessible mode (as evidenced by the link "Turn off more accessible mode" at the top of the page). While it doesn't look completely crazy, there are some things you have to take note of. For one, look at all of the URLs in the Announcements grid. For example, the text reads "/_layouts/formserver.aspx?XsnLocation=–ItemUrl"&OpenIn=Browser" for the first line entry. It is not resolving the –ItemUrl" parameter and is not even creating it as a link. The same is true with the Edit in Browser links. This is not a very usable interface at this point, which means that it scores pretty low in the accessibility department.

One thing to note in this scenario that is not evident in the screenshot is that some of the critical navigation is no longer working. On both the Windows mobile device and the browser with no CSS or JavaScript, the user has no way of getting into, say, the Site Actions menu (if signed in). That menu relies on a mouse event triggering a JavaScript event handler. The mobile device has no mouse and therefore no mouse event, and the browser has JavaScript disabled and therefore no availability of the JavaScript function that brings up the menu.

So this means that, out of the box, SharePoint installations won't display or function properly in mobile clients and probably won't display or function properly in most assistive technology browsers. It is certainly not Priority 2 or 3 compliant but, sad to say, it probably is not even Priority 1 compliant.

In the next sections, you will learn of some of the ways you can get around some of these limitations and make your site a bit better off. You may not be able to get all the way up to Priority 3 compliance, but you should be able to achieve Priority 1 and maybe even Priority 2. Or at least know where your obstacles are and decide if there is a way to get past them in your own projects.

Customizing SharePoint for Accessibility

So, with the information to this point, you might be a little apprehensive. SharePoint, at least out of the box, doesn't even meet the Web Content Accessibility Guidelines (WCAG) Priority 1 level of compliance. Especially if you are in a public sector environment, where accessibility is so vitally important, you might be thinking "Should we really use SharePoint?"

The good news is that, with some diligence and planning, you can make your installations much better. In fact, with enough work, you can certainly meet Priority 1 compliance and maybe even Priority 2 or 3. Those are lofty goals, of course, but if you recognize the issues and know how to integrate some freely available solutions, you can make great strides towards accessibility in SharePoint.

So, in this section, you will be doing exactly that: looking at some of the freely available tools to help with accessibility. The first tool will be the CSS Friendly Control Adapters that are available to all .NET 2.0 Web applications (not just SharePoint). However, the second tool, the Accessibility Kit for SharePoint (AKS), as the name implies, is targeted directly to SharePoint installations and can provide a lot of assistance to the accessibility conscious developer.

The CSS Friendly Control Adapters

One of the most commonly used tools for Web design back in the infancy of the Internet was tables. Using tables provided designers with a matrix for the rendered web page on which they could then lay out the various components of their site in whatever way they wanted. This allowed designers to fairly easily create the header, navigation, sidebar, content, and footer sections that are so predominant in the Web. Tables were easily nested within other tables to allow an even greater level of control over appearance and functionality for the final design. And, unfortunately perhaps (for this discussion), tables pretty much always worked, regardless of what browser a user used to access your site.

However, tables provide a very real problem with regards to accessibility. And this becomes even truer when you start nesting these tables. This is due in large part to the way assistive technology interprets the rendered HTML of a web page. Typically, these browsers read through the HTML in a linear order from the top of the page to the bottom of the page. If your navigation is buried in some nested table halfway down the HTML code, the user won't get to it until the reader goes through all of the preceding code first. These browsers will also often misinterpret the table as a data matrix and render it as such, which can confuse the layout of your final page a lot.

This is why, if you examine the checkpoints for accessibility earlier in the chapter, you will see several references to tables-based criteria. In fact, tables get their own entire Guideline (Guideline 5: Create Tables That Transform Gracefully). And one of the biggest offenses designers make, at least in regards to tables, is against checkpoint 5.3 (Do not use tables for layout unless the table makes sense when linearized. Otherwise, if the table does not make sense, provide an alternative equivalent [which may be a linearized version]). And, as seen earlier, SharePoint is no exception.

For example, look at the following code snippet that showcases the rendered output of a navigation control included in a standard SharePoint site:

```
<table id="zz1_TopNavigationMenu" class="ms-topNavContainer
        zz1_TopNavigationMenu_5
        zz1_TopNavigationMenu_2" CssSelectorClass="PrettyMenu" cellpadding="0"
        cellspacing="0" border="0">
    <tr>
        <td onmouseover="Menu_HoverRoot(this)" onmouseout="Menu_Unhover(this)"
            onkeyup="Menu_Key(this)" id="zz1_TopNavigationMenun0"><table
            class="ms-topnav zz1_TopNavigationMenu_4 ms-topnavselected
            zz1_TopNavigationMenu_10" cellpadding="0" cellspacing="0"
            border="0" width="100%">
        <tr>
            <td style="white-space:nowrap;"><a class="zz1_TopNavigationMenu_1
                ms-topnav zz1_TopNavigationMenu_3 ms-topnavselected
                zz1_TopNavigationMenu_9" href="/" accesskey="1"
                style="border-style:none;font-size:1em;">Wrox</a></td>
        </tr>
        </table></td><td style="width:0px;"></td><td><table border="0"
            cellpadding="0" cellspacing="0" width="100%"
            class="zz1_TopNavigationMenu_5">
        <tr>
            <td style="width:0px;"></td><td onmouseover="Menu_HoverStatic
                (this)" onmouseout="Menu_Unhover(this)" onkeyup="Menu_Key
                (this)" id="zz1_TopNavigationMenun1"><table class=
                "ms-topnav zz1_TopNavigationMenu_4" cellpadding="0"
                cellspacing="0" border="0" width="100%">
            <tr>
                <td style="white-space:nowrap;"><a class=
                    "zz1_TopNavigationMenu_1 ms-topnav
                    zz1_TopNavigationMenu_3" href="/Services.aspx"
                    style="border-style:none;font-size:1em;">
```

```
                    Services</a></td>
                </tr>
            </table></td><td style="width:0px;"></td><td style="width:0px;">
                </td><td onmouseover="Menu_HoverStatic(this)"
                onmouseout="Menu_Unhover(this)" onkeyup="Menu_Key(this)"
                id="zz1_TopNavigationMenun2"><table class="ms-topnav
                zz1_TopNavigationMenu_4" cellpadding="0" cellspacing="0"
                border="0" width="100%">
            <tr>
                <td style="white-space:nowrap;"><a class=
                    "zz1_TopNavigationMenu_1 ms-topnav
                    zz1_TopNavigationMenu_3" href="/AboutUs.aspx"
                    style="border-style:none;font-size:1em;">About
                    Us</a></td>
            </tr>
        </table></td><td style="width:0px;"></td><td style="width:0px;">
                </td><td onmouseover="Menu_HoverStatic(this)"
                onmouseout="Menu_Unhover(this)" onkeyup="Menu_Key(this)"
                id="zz1_TopNavigationMenun3"><table class="ms-topnav
                zz1_TopNavigationMenu_4" cellpadding="0" cellspacing="0"
                border="0" width="100%">
            <tr>
                <td style="white-space:nowrap;"><a class=
                    "zz1_TopNavigationMenu_1 ms-topnav
                    zz1_TopNavigationMenu_3" href="/Navigation/
                    default.aspx" style="border-style:none;font-
                    size:1em;">MOSS 2007 Navigation</a></td>
            </tr>
        </table></td><td style="width:0px;"></td>
        </tr>
    </table></td>
    </tr>
</table>
```

This snippet is the actual rendered code for Figure 13-5.

The code snippet, if you can't tell from reading through it, represents the top-level menu, which, in Figure 13-5, includes "Wrox," "Services," "About Us," and "MOSS 2007 Navigation." For those four little tabs that don't even include any submenus, all of the code in this snippet was generated by the .NET Framework.

This creates at least two problems. One is that it's just sloppy. With that much bloated code, it loads slower and is harder to navigate through if you are, for example, trying to read through the rendered output to see what is going on.

The second problem, and probably more important on a global scale and certainly more important in the scope of this chapter, is its strike against Priority 2 compliance. Examples of how this fails compliance standards might include:

❑ **Checkpoint 5.3 (Priority 2):** Do not use tables for layout unless the table makes sense when linearized. Otherwise, if the table does not make sense, provide an alternative equivalent (which may be a linearized version).

❑ **Checkpoint 5.5 (Priority 3):** Provide summaries for tables.

❑ **Checkpoint 5.6 (Priority 3):** Provide abbreviations for header labels.

❑ **Checkpoint 13.6 (Priority 3):** Group related links, identify the group (for user agents), and, until user agents do so, provide a way to bypass the group.

Figure 13-5

Certainly the way the navigation is rendered makes the page fail Priority 3 compliance but, because the site is using tables to layout navigation, it probably fails Priority 2 compliance, too. So, just because of using the standard out-of-the-box ASP.NET menu control, something not exclusive to SharePoint, the SharePoint site fails Priority 2 and 3 accessibility compliance.

You might be thinking "So what can I do about that? It's out-of-the-box. I can't do anything about out-of-the-box controls!"

Well, actually, you can. One of the greatest traits of the .NET 2.0 Framework is its ability to be modified. While there are several ways to do this, one of the more interesting (and relevant for this discussion) is the introduction of the control adapters. Control adapters allow developers to override the functionality of standard controls to allow complete customization over their behavior. This can mean a lot of things. If, for example, you want to include a custom property for the control that tells the rendering engine, when included, to add a special property to the rendered HTML object, you can do that.

However, for this discussion, it can mean that you can override the non-accessible tables-based rendering of the ASP.NET controls and make them use more accessible standards. Generally, this means using CSS and better linearized HTML (unordered lists, for example).

Fortunately, an initiative was created by Russ Helfand to create a set of adapters specifically targeted at "fixing" the rendering habits of a set of ASP.NET controls to make them more accessible. These adapters are collectively referred to as the CSS Friendly Control Adapters and can be downloaded from their project page on CodePlex: `http://www.codeplex.com/cssfriendly`.

To see how these adapters work, take a look at the same navigation control shown before but now controlled by the CSS Friendly Control Adapters:

```
<div class="PrettyMenu" id="zz1_TopNavigationMenu">
    <div class="AspNet-Menu-Horizontal">
            <ul class="AspNet-Menu">
                <li class="AspNet-Menu-WithChildren  AspNet-Menu-Selected">
                    <a href="/" class="AspNet-Menu-Link  AspNet-Menu-Selected">
                        Wrox</a>
                    <ul>
                        <li class="AspNet-Menu-Leaf  AspNet-Menu-ParentSelected">
                            <a href="/Services.aspx" class="AspNet-Menu-Link
                                    AspNet-Menu-ParentSelected">
                                Services</a>
                        </li>
                        <li class="AspNet-Menu-Leaf  AspNet-Menu-ParentSelected">
                            <a href="/AboutUs.aspx" class="AspNet-Menu-Link
                                    AspNet-Menu-ParentSelected">
                                About Us</a>
                        </li>
                        <li class="AspNet-Menu-Leaf  AspNet-Menu-ParentSelected">
                            <a href="/Navigation/default.aspx" class="AspNet-Menu-
                                    Link  AspNet-Menu-ParentSelected">
                                MOSS 2007 Navigation</a>
                        </li>
                    </ul>
                </li>
            </ul>
    </div>
</div>
```

The first thing you will probably notice is that the code is considerably shorter. It is providing the same information (hyperlinks to other pages in the site collection), but it is all done through more accessibility-friendly methods. In this case, rather than using tables, the navigation menu is using unordered lists (<UL>) to create the navigation hierarchy and then applying CSS classes to everything to allow you, as the developer/designer, to control the look and feel of the menu strictly through CSS style rules.

Just by doing this, you have changed at least four of the "No" answers in the accessibility checklist included earlier in the chapter to "Yes." To answer the four checkpoint items just mentioned in regards to the default table output, this new code solves these issues in the following ways:

❏ **Checkpoint 5.3 (Priority 2):** The navigation menu is no longer using a table to structure its layout.

❏ **Checkpoint 5.5 (Priority 3):** With no table, this is no longer relevant.

❏ **Checkpoint 5.6 (Priority 3):** Again, in the absence of a table for the layout of the navigation menu, this is no longer relevant.

❏ **Checkpoint 13.6 (Priority 3):** The menu is now encapsulated by a CSS <DIV> element with an ID of "zz1_TopNavigationMenu," which groups the set of related links (the navigation menu) into a CSS DIV element.

So, simply by implementing the adapters, you now have a more readable layout in the rendered code (which should load faster) and you have answered some of the accessibility concerns of SharePoint.

Understanding the CSS Friendly Control Adapters

First, it's important to understand what control adapters are, as these are the foundation of the CSS Friendly Control Adapters. Essentially, control adapters, which were introduced in the .NET 2.0 Framework, allow developers to override the behavior of certain .NET controls. More specifically, these adapters are used to modify the rendering behavior of out-of-the-box .NET controls in certain (or groups of) Web browsers.

What this boils down to, though, is that you can modify the rendered output of controls. Basically, this means that you can change the menu control, for example, from outputting tables in its rendered HTML output to outputting DIV, UL, and LI elements that are styled through CSS rules.

So how is this accomplished? Behind the scenes, there are a number of class files with a bunch of methods that override the functionality of the control. For example, take a look at this snippet of code from the menu control adapter:

```
private void BuildItems(MenuItemCollection items, bool isRoot, HtmlTextWriter
        writer)
{
    if (items.Count > 0)
    {
        writer.WriteLine();

        writer.WriteBeginTag("ul");
        if (isRoot)
        {
            writer.WriteAttribute("class", "AspNet-Menu");
        }
        writer.Write(HtmlTextWriter.TagRightChar);
        writer.Indent++;

        foreach (MenuItem item in items)
        {
            BuildItem(item, writer);
        }

        writer.Indent--;
        writer.WriteLine();
        writer.WriteEndTag("ul");
    }
}
```

In this code, the method for building the navigation structure is taken over. Typically, at this stage, the CLR is creating table-based HTML code to store the navigation items. However, as you can see here, the first thing that is happening (of consequence) is this line:

```
writer.WriteBeginTag("ul");
```

This is creating an <UL> element to start the navigation hierarchy. A little later in the code, there is a foreach loop that calls a function called "BuildItem(item, writer)." This method is considerably longer and including the entire thing wouldn't add much to the comprehension of what is going on. However, within this method, you will find a line of code like this:

```
writer.WriteBeginTag("li");
```

If you would like to see the full code of the adapters, you can navigate to http://www.asp.net/ CssAdapters/srcviewer.aspx?inspect=%2fCssAdapters%2fMenu.aspx *and then click "MenuAdapter.cs" on the left-hand menu.*

At this point, the BuildItem method is creating a new <LI> element for each menu item. The method continues on to add class references and other relevant items to the <LI> element but, at this point, you can hopefully get at least the 30,000 foot view of what is going on. This class is overtaking the rendering behavior of the out-of-the-box menu control and forcing it to generate much more accessible HTML elements in the place of its standard tables-based design. This is pretty cool.

So is this done automatically? Meaning, if you have this class file in your project, will it override the menu controls without you having to do anything else? Well, no. There is one other thing you have to play with: the browser file.

In .NET 2.0 projects (and above) there is a protected directory called App_Browsers used to hold *.browser files. The browser files' job is to tell the CLR which controls to override and, when overridden, which class to use to do the job. For the menu control, you would need to have a browser file in the App_Browsers directory with at least this much information in it:

```
<browsers>
  <browser refID="Default">
    <controlAdapters>
      <adapter controlType="System.Web.UI.WebControls.Menu"
               adapterType="CSSFriendly.MenuAdapter" />
    </controlAdapters>
  </browser>
</browsers>
```

The line that does all the magic is highlighted in bold in this snippet. In that line, you are telling .NET to override the control "System.Web.UI.WebControls.Menu" with the class "CssFriendly.MenuAdapter." If you were to go back into the menu class file that the previous snippets were taken from, you would see that it starts off with:

```
namespace CSSFriendly
{
    public class MenuAdapter : System.Web.UI.WebControls.Adapters.MenuAdapter
    {
```

This is how everything ties together. The browser pulls up the page and the .NET Framework looks in the App_Browsers folder to see whether it needs to do anything special. It sees that for all browsers (designated by the refID="Default" property on the browser tag) it should use the CSSFriendly.MenuAdapter class when rendering out the standard menu control. So then it goes into the CSSFriendly namespace and loads the MenuAdapter class and follows the override methods included there for rendering out the control to the browser.

Before you ask, this incurs, at most, a nominal performance hit. In fact, it probably washes because the outputted page will load faster so any hit taken on the rendering will be recovered in the page load. Performance really isn't much of a consideration here; the outputted HTML is the big deal.

For more on control adapters (in general terms), you can read the Microsoft documentation here: http://msdn2.microsoft.com/en-us/library/system.web.ui.adapters .controladapter(VS.80).aspx.

Modifying the CSS Friendly Control Adapters

So, if these are just class files, can I modify them? Yes and therein lies the beauty of these adapters. These files were built with the intention that developers would take them as a starting point but hopefully not a complete solution. These file were, as noted, merely class files with references to them in browser files. As such, the code is very open source. The snippets for this chapter were taken by opening up the class files and copying and pasting them into the manuscript.

You have the full power to manipulate them. For example, say that you had business requirements that every menu control use the order list element (<OL>) rather than the unordered list element used in the adapters. You could simply open up the class file, go to the line in the code that generates the UL code, and change it to OL.

A real world example can be seen by looking at the GridView control adapter included with this tool. It still renders out tables. This is okay because even the WCAG guidelines allow for tables to be used for tabular data, which is really the only purpose of the GridView control. The adapter just cleans up the rendered HTML table (adding things like THEAD, TFOOT, and TBODY sections to the table and eliminating inline styles). However, if your company was determined not to use tables at all for any reason as it still provides an obstacle to readers accessing your site through assistive technology, you could go into the GridViewAdapter.cs file and change the rendering behavior to completely eliminate tables and instead use CSS HTML elements (DIVs, for example) to represent your tabular data. This might be a task more suitable for the intermediate to advanced developer, but it could definitely be done. And, while the WCAG doesn't require you to do this (yet), this would probably provide a better experience for your visually impaired visitors.

This demonstrates that although the CSS Friendly Control Adapters were created and released as a means of combating accessibility concerns that is not their only use. These adapters can be used to do whatever you need to do (with regards to rendering your controls in Web browsers, that is). These adapters, when used in conjunction with other tools like master pages and themes, can be a godsend at creating a .NET Web project framework that allows developers to just drop controls on their page and code against them. Any nuances that you need can be taken care of in a global sense without the developer having to worry about it.

Be warned, though. The adapters are not really for the faint at heart. If you are new to programming, you may not want to get in and tweak the class files much. For example, the C# example for the menu control adapter is 329 lines of code and, without some experience in coding, it will be hard to follow. But, with enough initiative and at least some experience, these adapters can be really fun to dive into headfirst and make some cool things happen in your own projects.

An Overview of the CSS Friendly Control Adapters

The adapters accommodate the following controls:

❑ **Menu:** This is the standard navigation control provided in the ASP.NET 2.0 Framework. SharePoint uses this menu control for its top and side level menus and, as such, this control adapter can be very useful in your SharePoint projects.

❑ **TreeView:** This is the control that provides hierarchy navigation much like you would experience in Windows Explorer (folder with sub-folders and files). This is used by SharePoint for, among other things, the Quick Launch menu.

❑ **DetailsView:** This control is used to display a single record from a data set. This is typically used in conjunction with the GridView control that displays all of the records in a recordset and, when a row is selected, this control displays the details for just that one record.

❑ **FormView:** This control is similar to the DetailsView control in that it is used to display a single record of a dataset. However, this control allows for the customization of how the data is displayed.

❑ **GridView:** This is the standard control for displaying a matrix of data in ASP.NET. This creates a tabular representation of multiple rows of data and allows for things like pagination and sorting of that data. The SharePoint control SPGridView inherits from the GridView control.

❑ **DataList:** This control is used to create a repeater, of sorts, where data bound to the control is repeated using a custom template that the developer creates. The custom template details are rendered out in a matrix of table cells (sort of like the address book in Outlook if you are familiar with that).

❑ **Login:** This is a part of the ASP.NET Membership provider class. This control is the basic means for logging in with the default ASP.NET Membership provider. This provides textboxes for the user's credentials as well as a check box to keep the user logged in.

❑ **ChangePassword:** This is a part of the ASP.NET Membership provider class. This control allows users to update their password by first providing their original password and then creating (and confirming) their new password

❑ **PasswordRecovery:** This is a part of the ASP.NET Membership provider class. This control sends an email with the password for an account to the address used when the account was originally set up.

❑ **CreateUserWizard:** This is a part of the ASP.NET Membership provider class. This control collects the necessary information to create a new account e.g., User Name, Password, Email address, etc. and then creates the new account.

❑ **LoginStatus:** Part of the ASP.NET Membership provider class. This provides a login link to unauthenticated users and a logout link to those that authenticated users.

These adapters were created to fulfill a variety of needs. In the world of SharePoint design, many of these control adapters may not be very useful. For example, all of the login related controls are probably not going to be necessary for most installations because most installations will probably use Windows authentication since it is the default for MOSS 2007 and WSS 3.0. However, if your company chooses a custom authentication mechanism, such as the membership provider included in the .NET 2.0 Framework, then you may need these control adapters.

While most of the adapters are innocuous, meaning that they won't break anything by leaving them in there even if they don't do anything, there is one that is not: the GridView control.

The GridView control is a bit interesting anyway. Its purpose is not to eliminate tables. After all, CSS standards say that tables for data presentation are okay. The purpose of this control is to make the tables it renders better. It includes cleaner table code, as well as THEAD, TBODY and TFOOT tags for the table.

And, in the world of SharePoint, the GridView control probably isn't used that much. For the most part, when you are dropping a grid onto a SharePoint page, it is using the SPGridView control instead. While it is true that the SPGridView control inherits from the GridView control, it is distinctly different from the GridView if only by the namespace reference (Microsoft.SharePoint.WebControls.SPGridView). This means that, if your site is using the SPGridView control, SharePoint won't override it with the GridView control adapter. You would need to create a new control adapter specifically targeted at the SPGridView control to affect this control.

However, if you include the GridView reference in your browser file, you may incur a penalty. As seen in Figure 13-6, if you try to navigate to Manage Content and Structure under Site Actions, you will get an error.

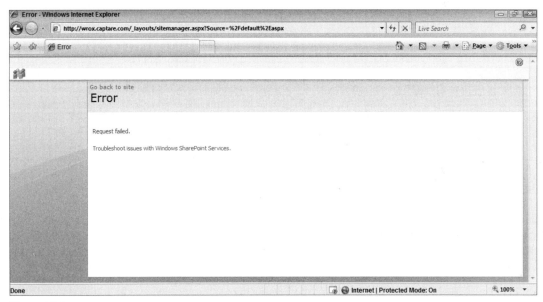

Figure 13-6

So, if using the CSS Friendly Control Adapters in a SharePoint installation, you may want to remove the following line of code from your browser file so that you do not receive this error:

```
<adapter controlType="System.Web.UI.WebControls.GridView"
         adapterType="CSSFriendly.GridViewAdapter" />
```

Or, even better, you might want to figure out what is causing the conflict and fix it. Then share your resolution with the world.

If you find resolution to issues like these, you can help modify the current code base so that others can reap the benefits of your discovery. This truly is an open source project now and will get better and better as more people contribute to its success.

As a final note in this section, many users are finding that they are having problems with the TreeView control as well. The biggest problem lies in the fact that if you navigate to Manage Content and Structure (under Site Actions) and you have the TreeView control adapter in place, you will get an unhandled error. This appears to be a problem with the way the TreeView adapter deals with the ViewState of the TreeView control and one solution (presented at `http://forums.asp.net/t/1052121.aspx`) showcases a way of modifying the adapter to change the way it controls ViewState.

So with this in mind, you might consider turning off the TreeView control adapter as well until a resolution is incorporated. To do this, make sure you remove the following line from your browser file:

```
<adapter controlType="System.Web.UI.WebControls.TreeView"
         adapterType="CSSFriendly.TreeViewAdapter" />
```

While this is only relevant for Publishing sites, this can be a very big problem for those affected so it is worth looking at which solution works best for you in your scenario. While the ViewState solution fixes the problem for some, others found that it caused other problems (for example, the left navigation tree no longer worked when this solution was implemented).

Integration with SharePoint

As stated earlier, the CSS Friendly Control Adapters were engineered to be included in .NET 2.0 (and above) Web projects. And, since SharePoint is built on the .NET 2.0 Framework, it might seem logical that the adapters would easily integrate. But that isn't the case. Take a look at Figure 13-7 and you might get an idea of what the problem is.

Figure 13-7 shows the expanded view of a typical Web site that incorporates the CSS Friendly Control Adapters. There is the browser file in the App_Browsers directory, a bunch of class files (the adapters themselves) in the App_Code directory, some CSS in a CSS directory, and some JavaScript files in the JavaScript directory. There is a WalkThru directory there, too, but that only serves to provide examples on how to implement everything. In a real example, you would probably delete that directory.

Can you spot the problem yet?

If you have worked in SharePoint pages, especially if you have tried to inject any kind of .NET code into the page, you will probably notice the problem pretty quickly. The whole idea of control adapters involves using custom methods in a class file to override behavior. These class files are in the App_Code directory, which is typically fine for .NET applications. And, as such, the code is meant to be compiled into a DLL referenced in the production server. After all, that is generally the point of having class files. (It's bad practice to leave uncompiled source code in a production environment.) However, in the world of SharePoint, this can cause a problem.

So, the first problem is, how do you actually get the compiled class files in your project?

Figure 13-7

There are at least two ways of accomplishing this. You can download the source files and compile your own DLL, which gives you the ability to store the compiled file in your Global Assembly Cache (GAC), which in turn opens up the adapters to all web applications on that server. Alternatively, you can download a precompiled version of the DLL provided through the CodePlex project and, with a little bit of tweaking, install it on an application-by-application basis.

Both of these approaches will be discussed in more detail in the next two sections.

Installing the Adapters in the Global Assembly Cache

If you want to use the adapters on multiple applications on the same server, the best way to do this is to create an assembly and install it into the Global Assembly Cache (GAC) of the server. Once installed there, you will have access to the adapters in any .NET 2.0 application on that server (not just SharePoint).

The first step is to download the latest version of the source code from the CodePlex project at http://www.codeplex.com/cssfriendly. You will need to go the Releases tab and then download the ZIP file, CSSFriendly_1.0.zip, as this contains the source code (the other two files you can download from that page will be discussed in the next section). Extract all of the files to your computer, keeping the path information from the ZIP file. For the remainder of this chapter, it will be assumed that C:\ was chosen, meaning the project is stored in C:\CSSFriendly_1.0\.

Next, you need to open up the solution file that came with the download (CSSFriendly.sln) in Visual Studio (2005 or 2008). With the project open, you will see in Solution Explorer that there are three groupings: Solution Items, CSSFriendly, and the Web project. The first thing you need to do is to sign the CSSFriendly assembly. Expand the CSSFriendly class and you will see that it includes several sub-items, such as CSS and JavaScript folders and several class files. You will also see that there is an item called "Properties." Double-click on this item to get the properties for the CSSFriendly assemblyOnce the properties window opens up, click the "Signing" tab. You should first check the option for "Sign the assembly" located near the bottom of the options. This will enable the "Choose a strong name key file" option. Click the dropdown box and choose <New . . . > to get the Create Strong Key Name dialog box. Enter a name for the file and provide a password (optionally). Now save your project to make sure your changes have been saved (following the good general practice of saving often).

Now build your new assembly by selecting Build from the Visual Studio toolbar and choosing Build CSSFriendly. This will create a new DLL file in the following location (assuming the path used at the beginning of this section): C:\CSSFriendly_1.0\CSSFriendly\bin\Release\CSSFriendly.dll.

The next step is to simply copy this DLL into your GAC. The GAC is a common repository for .NET applications that allows you to copy/install strongly named and signed DLLs for reference by any .NET application on that server. This allows you to have a single source of code to share among multiple applications. It also allows a level of security by keeping the codebase in a server folder rather than a web application subdirectory. So, even if you aren't sharing out your code, it's not a bad idea to store your signed DLL files in the GAC when possible.

The easiest way to install the new DLL in your GAC is to have two instances of Windows Explorer open and to simply drag the DLL from the release folder to the assembly folder (typically C:\Windows\assembly). This will automatically install the DLL and make it available to your applications.

The next thing you need to do is go back into your CSS Friendly project in Visual Studio and open up the CSSFriendlyAdapters.browser file located in the App_Browsers folder of the Web project. This is the file that tells the rendering engine to use the code in the adapters when rendering out the controls rather than the default rendering behavior. This is done through a line similar to the following (this is for the menu control):

```
<adapter controlType="System.Web.UI.WebControls.Menu"
         adapterType="CSSFriendly.MenuAdapter" />
```

The first property, controlType, is telling the .NET compiler what object this applies to. In this case, it is going to override the System.Web.UI.WebControls.Menu control. The second property is telling the compiler what adapter to use. The browser file included with the CSS Friendly Adapters is telling the compiler to use CSSFriendly.MenuAdapter. In the scenario expected in this project, that is fine because this is telling the compiler to look for the CSSFriendly namespace in one of the project class files.

In the scenario this section is working with, the problem is that the namespace will be in the GAC, not in a project class file. So you need to modify this code to something like the following:

```
<adapter controlType="System.Web.UI.WebControls.Menu"
         adapterType="CSSFriendly.MenuAdapter, CSSFriendly, Version=1.0.0.0,
         Culture=neutral, PublicKeyToken=<Your token>" />
```

The part you have added is telling the adapter where in the GAC to locate the namespace you are referencing. You can find the information (Version, Culture, and PublicKeyToken) by right-mouse clicking the assembly in the GAC and selecting Properties.

You need to make this change to all of the controls that you want to override. In other words, if you want to keep using all of the control overrides provided in the default browser file, you need to modify each one to point to the GAC assembly.

Once you have your browser file updated, you need to copy it to the global browser file on your server, typically located here at C:\WINDOWS\Microsoft.NET\Framework\v2.0.50727\CONFIG\Browsers.

Once you have the browser copied to its global folder, you need to compile the browser file and install it in the GAC. Fortunately, there is a tool already installed on your server as part of the .NET 2.0 Framework. So, in order to use the tool, first open up the Visual Studio Command Prompt (Start ⇨ Programs ⇨ Microsoft Visual Studio 2005 ⇨ Visual Studio Tools ⇨ Visual Studio Command Prompt) and type out the following command:

```
aspnet_regbrowsers -i
```

The last thing you need to do is modify the compat.browser file to remove the last four tags included in that file (InfrawareSamSung, InfrawareLG, InfrawareSKY, and InfrawareMotorola). This file is located at C:\Program Files\Common Files\Microsoft Shared\Web Server Extensions\12\CONFIG\.

You need to make this same change to any compat.browser file located in any previously (and future) created SharePoint sites in IIS as well. These files are typically located in a directory using this path: C:\Inetpub\wwwroot\wss\VirtualDirectories\<Your App Pool>\App_Browsers.

At this point, you should have your CSS Friendly Control Adapters installed in the GAC and shared out to all SharePoint installations on that one Web server. Of course, if you are going to use the adapters on multiple servers, you will have to follow these steps on each web server. However, for multiple applications on a single server, this approach has a lot of appeal. On the other hand, if you only have a single SharePoint installation on the server, this might be overkill and you may find that the approach showcased in the next section better fits your needs.

Using the Precompiled CSSFriendly DLL

While installing the adapters in the GAC is a valid approach, it might be overkill for a single SharePoint installation. In such cases, you might find it easier to just use the pre-compiled assembly provided by CodePlex and only apply it to the one installation. This section will highlight exactly how to do that.

Well, first, a little back history. When the adapters were first introduced, they were maintained at the following address: `http://www.asp.net/cssadapters/`. While this address is still valid (and still very useful), the code was moved to its new home at CodePlex in March 2007. It was moved there in an effort to make the code more open source and invite others to participate in its enhancements and maintenance. It is also possible that the project was moved to CodePlex to legitimize the product and make it easier to find. Regardless of the reasons, it was moved there.

While not much has been done to the project since it moved (the release available on CodePlex is still 1.0, which is what was available on the previous site), there is one interesting change that is noticeable: they compiled the DLL for you. Additionally, they provided separate download links to allow you to download only the DLL and/or the browser file (two separate downloads). This means that you can, if you find it useful, just download the bare essentials, set them up to work with SharePoint, and then you are good to go.

While this is a very cool way to use the adapters, especially if you don't have the need to customize anything beyond what is already being customized, there are a couple of problems with this approach. The first, as just stated, is that you can't modify anything since the DLL is already compiled. The second, which is a bigger deal, is that the DLL isn't signed, which means it can't go in the GAC.

So what does that mean? If you can't install it to the GAC, is it useless?

Well, it introduces a new level of complexity, but it is not useless. It would probably be much better if it were signed but, if that is really a huge issue for you, you could certainly download the source file, sign the project, and compile a DLL you could use in the GAC.

However, to avoid doing this, you might consider putting the DLL in the BIN directory of your Share-Point. After all, if you look at the directory structure set up by SharePoint during installation, you can see that there is, in fact, a BIN directory (you will also see that there is an App_Browsers folder as well). You can see these folders in Figure 13-8.

So, if you download the DLL and the browser file, you should be able to put them in the BIN and App_Browsers folders, respectively. And, in some cases, you can do exactly that and be done.

However, in many cases (if not most cases) this won't work exactly as you would hope. The reason is that, by default, your SharePoint site is probably set with a minimal trust level. And, at this level, SharePoint lacks sufficient permissions to execute code in the BIN directory. So, if you simply copy the DLL and browser files as described, you will get the error message shown in Figure 13-9.

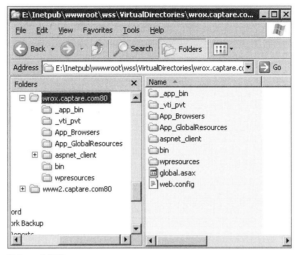

Figure 13-8

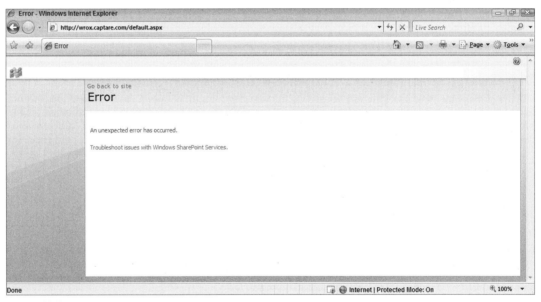

Figure 13-9

If you look in the event log for the error that occurs, it simply gives you this:

> *Request for the permission of type 'Microsoft.SharePoint.Security.SharePointPermission, Microsoft.SharePoint.Security, Version=12.0.0.0, Culture=neutral, PublicKeyToken= 71e9bce111e9429c' failed.*

Since neither of these things is particularly helpful, you might get frustrated and decide this can't be done. However, this can be done, and you have a couple of ways of resolving this issue.

Again, the problem is that SharePoint sites running at the WSS_Minimal trust level cannot execute code in the BIN directory. So what might the logical resolution be? Change the trust level.

In any .NET application, there are the following trust levels:

❑ Full

❑ High

❑ Medium

❑ Low

❑ Minimal

You can read more about these trust levels here: `http://www.microsoft.com/technet/prodtechnol/ WindowsServer2003/Library/IIS/a55fb31b-5b42-476d-9cae-050ab3fae307.mspx?mfr=true`.

However, in addition to these trust levels, SharePoint establishes two additional trust levels:

❑ WSS_Minimal

❑ WSS_Medium

These trust levels were created to extend the "Medium" and "Minimal" trust levels of ASP.NET for SharePoint. By default, SharePoint installations are set to WSS_Minimal. While all of the ramifications for setting various trust levels are not pertinent to this discussion, the one thing that definitely is relevant is which ones allow you to run code in the BIN directory. WSS_Minimal does not; WSS_Medium does.

Changing the permission level is surprisingly simple. Go into the `web.config` file for the SharePoint application and look for a line that looks similar to the following:

```
<trust level="WSS_Minimal" originUrl="" />
```

Now change it to use the WSS_Medium trust level, as such:

```
<trust level="WSS_Medium" originUrl="" />
```

While this does work, it's probably not a good idea. There is a reason the default is set to minimal, and opening up the trust level just so you can get the adapters to run out of the BIN directory isn't a good idea. There are a whole slew of things (such as unrestricted permission on SQLClientPermission and essentially unrestricted permissions on the FileIO) that you will also open up with doing this and it's just not worth it.

So what is the alternative? There are really only two trust levels used by SharePoint? One works but you probably shouldn't use it and the other doesn't work at all (in regards to what you are trying to accomplish in this section at least). So what is the alternative when the only two provided options don't work? Create a third option, obviously.

The nice thing about the trust levels as that they are regulated through a config file stored on the server, typically in the following folder: <<Program Files>>\Common Files\Microsoft Shared\Web Server Extensions\12\config\.

So if, for example, your Program Files directory was stored on your E drive, the configuration file for your WSS_Minimal trust level would be the following: E:\Program Files\Common Files\Microsoft Shared\Web Server Extensions\12\config\wss_minimaltrust.config.

So think about what has been discussed to this point. There are two options, neither of which work. WSS_Medium is too open and WSS_Minimal is too strict. You need to create a new trust level that keeps the strictness of WSS_Minimal but allows you to run code in the BIN directory. This means that you want to start with WSS_Minimal and open up one thing: the ability to run code in the BIN folder.

So, with that in mind, make a copy of WSS_Minimal.config and call it something that makes sense. For the remainder of this section, the file will be called "WSS_cssfriendly.config" and the associated trust level will be referred to as "WSS_cssfriendly." This will let you know that this trust level was created in order to accommodate the CSS Friendly Control Adapters. However, it will also result in allowing code to run in the BIN folder, so if something else like "WSS_Bin" makes more sense to you, feel free to use that. Just substitute your name every time you see "WSS_cssfriendly" in the examples in the remainder of this section.

So, once you have your new file, the first thing you will want to do is add a reference to the SharePoint-Permission class in the SecurityClasses section, as seen below:

```
<SecurityClasses>

...  Other Security Classes omitted for brevity ...

    <SecurityClass Name="SharePointPermission"
    Description="Microsoft.SharePoint.Security.SharePointPermission,
    Microsoft.SharePoint.Security, Version=11.0.0.0, Culture=neutral,
    PublicKeyToken=71e9bce111e9429c" />
        </SecurityClasses>
```

The next step is to add a new permission set that is given the right to access the object model. A permission set is simply a collection of permissions that can be applied to one or more assemblies. The easiest thing to do is to find an existing permission set in the file, copy it, and then modify it slightly. So, in order to do that, search through your config file for a permission set that is called either "ASP.NET" or "SPRestricted" (you probably have one or the other but not both). It will resemble this:

```
<PermissionSet
        class="NamedPermissionSet"
        version="1"
        Name="SPRestricted">
    <IPermission
            class="AspNetHostingPermission"
            version="1"
            Level="Minimal"
    />
    <IPermission
            class="SecurityPermission"
            version="1"
            Flags="Execution"
    />
    <IPermission class="WebPartPermission"
            version="1"
            Connections="True"
    />
</PermissionSet>
```

Now make an exact copy of this section and paste it directly below the copied code. You will need to modify it slightly, as shown below (changes in bold):

```
<PermissionSet
        class="NamedPermissionSet"
        version="1"
        Name="wss_cssfriendly">
    <IPermission
            class="AspNetHostingPermission"
            version="1"
            Level="Minimal"
    />
    <IPermission
            class="SecurityPermission"
            version="1"
            Flags="Execution"
    />
    <IPermission class="WebPartPermission"
            version="1"
            Connections="True"
    />
    <IPermission class="SharePointPermission"
            version="1"
            ObjectModel="True"
    />
</PermissionSet>
```

The last thing you need to do in the configuration file is to add a code group that lets the CLR know which assembly or assemblies the new permission set should apply to. Keeping this in mind, there are two alternatives for setting up the code group: Allow access to a single assembly or to the entire directory. Obviously, the more conservative approach is to only allow access to a single assembly. Short of having a strongly typed name sitting in the GAC, this is the better alternative. It opens up the security you need to access the functionality you need for the adapters without opening up the entire directory to execution rights, which has some security repercussions.

So, to do this, you would need to add the new code group immediately below the "FirstMatchCode-Group" group by adding the following code:

```
<CodeGroup class="UnionCodeGroup"
  version="1"
  PermissionSetName="wss_cssfriendly">
    <IMembershipCondition class="UrlMembershipCondition"
      version="1"
      Url="$AppDirUrl$/bin/CSSFriendly.dll" />
</CodeGroup>
```

Notice that the PermissionSetName property is set to wss_cssfriendly. This is a pointer to the permission step you set up in the previous step. Also notice the IMembershipCondition element and the URL directory. As you can see, it is being set to only open up the CSSFriendly.dll assembly in the BIN directory of the current application. This is fairly tight control over what is specifically opened up beyond the WSS_Minimal Code Access Security level.

However, you may have the need to run multiple assemblies and do not want to set up new code groups for each assembly. If this is the case for you, realize that you do have the ability to turn on code for the entire directory. Just understand that this is not the recommended approach and you are opening up a bigger security hole by doing this. However, if you feel the need to open up the entire BIN directory, you can modify the above code to the following (changes highlighted in bold):

```
<CodeGroup class="UnionCodeGroup"
  version="1"
  PermissionSetName="wss_cssfriendly">
    <IMembershipCondition class="UrlMembershipCondition"
      version="1"
      Url="$AppDirUrl$/bin/*" />
</CodeGroup>
```

You are now finished with the changes to the configuration file. Save your changes and then go back into the web.config file and make the following addition (in bold):

```
<system.web>
  <securityPolicy>
    <trustLevel name="WSS_Medium" policyFile="E:\Program Files\Common
            Files\Microsoft Shared\Web Server Extensions\12\config\
            wss_mediumtrust.config" />
    <trustLevel name="WSS_Minimal" policyFile="E:\Program Files\Common
            Files\Microsoft Shared\Web Server Extensions\12\config\
            wss_minimaltrust.config" />
    <trustLevel name="WSS_cssfriendly" policyFile="E:\Program Files\Common
            Files\Microsoft Shared\Web Server Extensions\12\config\
            wss_cssfriendly.config" />
  </securityPolicy>
```

This step sets up the availability of the newly created trust level, WSS_cssfriendly. You can see that you are simply giving it a name and then giving the physical path to the policy file you just created.

The only step left is to set your site to use the new configuration. So, back in web.config, locate the trust setting and change it to the following:

```
<trust level="WSS_cssfriendly" originUrl="" />
```

You have now created a custom trust level based off of the WSS_Minimal trust level and set your site to use this new trust level. A summary of the steps involved would be:

❑ Create a new policy configuration file (wss_cssfriendly.config)

❑ Create a new trust level in web.config to reference the new policy configuration file

❑ Set the site's trust level to use the newly created trust level in web.config

Now, if you reload your application, it should resemble Figure 13-10.

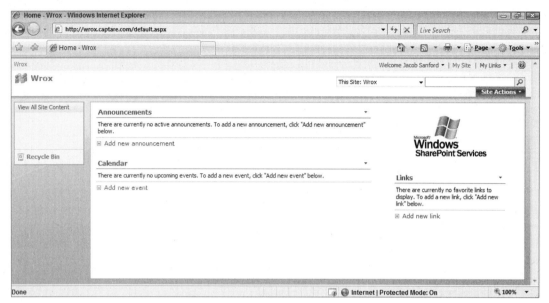

Figure 13-10

At first glance, you will probably think this didn't work. After all, both the top-level navigation and the QuickLinks are missing. However, if you look at the rendered HTML code, you will see the following for the top-level navigation:

```
<div id="zz1_TopNavigationMenu">
    <div class="AspNet-Menu-Horizontal">
        <ul class="AspNet-Menu">
            <li class="AspNet-Menu-WithChildren  AspNet-Menu-Selected">
                <a href="/" class="AspNet-Menu-Link  AspNet-Menu-Selected">
                    Wrox</a>
                <ul>
                    <li class="AspNet-Menu-Leaf  AspNet-Menu-ParentSelected">
                        <a href="/Services.aspx" class="AspNet-Menu-Link
                                AspNet-Menu-ParentSelected">
                            Services</a>
                    </li>
                    <li class="AspNet-Menu-Leaf  AspNet-Menu-ParentSelected">
                        <a href="/AboutUs.aspx" class="AspNet-Menu-Link
                                AspNet-Menu-ParentSelected">
                            About Us</a>
                    </li>
                    <li class="AspNet-Menu-Leaf  AspNet-Menu-ParentSelected">
                        <a href="/Navigation/default.aspx" class="AspNet-Menu-
                                Link  AspNet-Menu-ParentSelected">
                            MOSS 2007 Navigation</a>
                    </li>
```

```
                    </ul>
                </li>
            </ul>
        </div>
    </div>
```

So, this rendered code proves that the adapters are working. The rendered output is now DIV, UL, and LI elements rather than tables. This is the point of the adapters.

So why doesn't it look like it's working? Well, the answer is quite simple: There are no CSS rules set up for this control. Look back at the rendered code again and you will see all kinds of new CSS class references like "AspNet-Menu-Horizontal." There are currently no CSS rules set up for this class. Or, for that matter, any of the class elements rendered out. So you have to set those up. Although setting up the CSS rules is not really the focus of this chapter, some pointers for doing this can be found in the next section. You can also find out where you can get a deeper dive into styling the adapters at the end of that section.

Tips for Styling Your New Controls

While the point of this entire section is to point out the usefulness, especially in regards to accessibility, of the adapters and how to get them integrated into your SharePoint installation, you are going to have to style the controls at some point. This chapter wasn't really intended to be a long CSS tutorial. Even so, it might be helpful to cover a few important styling considerations.

The first thing to think about is to always use the designated custom property of any control you are overriding to set its CSS class. This property has been named "CssSelectorClass." For example, in the top-level menu, you might want to set it up as follows:

```
<SharePoint:AspMenu
    ID="TopNavigationMenu"
    Runat="server"
    DataSourceID="topSiteMap"
    EnableViewState="false"
    AccessKey="<%$Resources:wss,navigation_accesskey%>"
    Orientation="Horizontal"
    StaticDisplayLevels="2"
    MaximumDynamicDisplayLevels="1"
    DynamicHorizontalOffset="0"
    StaticPopoutImageUrl="/_layouts/images/menudark.gif"
    StaticPopoutImageTextFormatString=""
    DynamicHoverStyle-BackColor="#CBE3F0"
    SkipLinkText=""
    StaticSubMenuIndent="0"
    CssSelectorClass="PrettyMenu"
    CssClass="ms-topNavContainer">
<StaticMenuStyle/>
<StaticMenuItemStyle CssClass="ms-topnav" ItemSpacing="0px"/>
<StaticSelectedStyle CssClass="ms-topnavselected" />
<StaticHoverStyle CssClass="ms-topNavHover" />
<DynamicMenuStyle BackColor="#F2F3F4"
BorderColor="#A7B4CE" BorderWidth="1px"/>
<DynamicMenuItemStyle CssClass="ms-topNavFlyOuts"/>
```

```
<DynamicHoverStyle CssClass="ms-topNavFlyOutsHover"/>
<DynamicSelectedStyle CssClass="ms-topNavFlyOutsSelected"/>
</SharePoint:AspMenu>
```

Doing this will change the first DIV element in the rendered navigation menu to the following:

```
<div class="PrettyMenu" id="zz1_TopNavigationMenu">
```

As you can see, this gives a CSS class to the DIV element. Why is this important? Well, if you have more than one horizontal menu, you are going to need more than one class of CSS rules. This allows you to distinguish one control from another in the page. With the menu control, this might not be that big of an issue. But as you begin overriding more controls, this will probably come in handy.

The next thing to remember is something that is fairly unique to SharePoint (that doesn't happen in standard ASP.NET pages). When you create your menu, if you haven't noticed, it has a slightly different hierarchy than you might expect. Specifically, the navigation is set up as follows:

❑   Wrox

❑   Services

❑   About Us

❑   MOSS 2007 Navigation

Even though the navigation comes through in one line in the tables version, in the CSS version, there is one main menu item and then the others come in a second UL list immediately below it. This can cause some unique challenges when styling these menus. It's not as cut and dry as some of the walkthrough examples that assume all of the main menu items are on the same level. So, as you dive into the menu control adapters, make sure you keep this nuance in mind.

The next thing to think about is using the proper DOCTYPE. While this might seem like a master page issue, it has some serious repercussions for how your CSS works in any given browser. For example, you probably will want to use the XHTML Strict Document Type Definition (DTD) to ensure standards parsing mode by your browser. For example, place the following line at the top of your master page (or modify the one that is there) to ensure you are using the XHTML Strict DTD:

```
<!DOCTYPE html PUBLIC "-//W3C//DTD XHTML 1.0 Strict//EN"
    "http://www.w3.org/TR/xhtml1/DTD/xhtml1-strict.dtd">
```

Finally, with all of the styles coming from CSS, make sure you test this a lot and in several different browsers. The thing that makes this tricky is that, not only are you providing cosmetic styling, you are providing positioning, which will always make a CSS developer cringe just a bit. Every browser seems to handle floats and position differently. So you need to make sure that if you get the menu styled the way you want it in IE7 it works in IE6. And then jump over to Firefox and maybe even Safari. If your site passes all of those, you're probably okay. But it wouldn't hurt to hit a few more browsers if you have the time and means.

To get some more tips on CSS, consider picking up *Beginning CSS: Cascading Style Sheets for Web Design, 2nd Edition* (Wrox Press, ISBN: 978-0-4700-9697-0) by Richard York. It has some really great detail on floats and positioning that will probably help you out in this endeavor.

CSS Friendly Control Adapters Resources

Hopefully, if you have gotten this far, you have a fair understanding of what the CSS Friendly Control Adapters do and how they can help you with your own sites, especially in regards to accessibility. As you saw earlier in the book, SharePoint, out of the box, doesn't even meet Priority 1 compliance, which are the guidelines for what every site *must* have. With this in mind, it's important to dissect where Share-Point fails and what you can do about it. As you saw in the checklist provided early in this chapter, there are some very specific points where SharePoint fails that it just shouldn't. Some of these failures are directly related to the rendering behavior of the controls that SharePoint uses. The CSS Friendly Control Adapters help overcome this hurdle. They allow you, as the developer, to take over the rendering habits of these controls and make them provide output that is much more accessible. For example, with the menu control, you saw that you could take a completely tables-based navigation system that fails accessibility compliance and make it provide a CSS navigation system using HTML elements, such as DIVs and ULs, to provide the hierarchy of the navigation system and then CSS rules to provide the styling. This can really help the accessibility-conscious developer move towards a more compliant solution in the SharePoint sites he creates.

However, at this point in your exposure to the adapters, you will almost surely want to find out more. Unfortunately, there aren't a whole lot of places out there yet that deal with the adapters, especially in regards to SharePoint. However, there are a few really good resources.

The first is the original site of the adapters: http://www.asp.net/cssadapters/. This site has some really amazing walk through discussions, code examples, and white papers to help you get started. Granted, it's all targeted towards standard .NET 2.0 Web applications, but the content is really good and you will find a lot of solid examples on how to implement the adapters (which you will probably be able to take directly into your SharePoint installations).

Of course, the CodePlex site where the project is currently maintained is a good source of information as well: http://www.codeplex.com/cssfriendly/. This site has discussions and an Issue Tracker and other relevant tools to help you get started and get you through the difficult scenarios you will almost surely find yourself in. While the adapters take some work to get going properly, it's worth the payload and this site can help you with the work.

There is also a dedicated forum at www.asp.net for the adapters: http://forums.asp.net/1018.aspx. This site is routinely reviewed by the adapters' creator, Russ Helfand and several other experts in the field, not to mention several people that may not be experts but have gone through some of the same things you might be going through and might be able to share some fixes they figured out. This is always a good place to go try to find answers to issues you run into or to ask for help.

Finally, you might also consider picking up *Professional ASP.NET 2.0 Design* (Wrox Press; ISBN: 978-0-4701-2448-2) by one of the co-authors, of this book, Jacob J. Sanford. This book has an entire chapter of the ASP.NET 2.0 CSS Friendly Adapters and discusses them further in the chapter on navigation (using the adapters for the menu control) and then in the "Bringing It All Together – A New Theme" chapter (to show how to turn off the adapters in some scenarios). While this book is targeted at ASP.NET 2.0 Web applications, it provides a solid foundation of the adapters and some real-world advice on their use.

A Final Thought on the CSS Friendly Control Adapters

This majority of this section relied on the assumption that you were going to use the CSS Friendly Control Adapters as some sort of compiled application rather than using open source code on your server. As such, you were first shown how to compile your own code and install it into your Global Assembly Cache so that it is sharable among all of your .NET applications. This approach provides the extra flexibility so that you can adjust the adapters if you like and then compile and share them among all .NET applications, not just SharePoint. You also saw how to use the precompiled version provided in the CodePlex project in a single SharePoint installation. This approach involved adding the DLL to your BIN directory and allowing access to the DLL by creating a custom code access security level.

However, there is at least one other option that is worth mentioning (and will make more sense in the next section): using uncompiled C# source code files in the App_Code folder of your Web project. As stated earlier, this is not a good idea because you are leaving source code on a production server that can be opened by any text editor (such as Notepad). If there is a list of best practices of Web application deployment, on the top of the list there would probably be something like "Never ever leave open source code files on a production server." However, that being said, it is possible.

So, if you want the easy way out, you could simply add the "App_Code" folder to the physical directory for your SharePoint site and add the class files you need in your project there. You can then use the browser file in the same way you have done up to this point.

The final result would be a directory structure that resembles Figure 13-11 on the server and a browser file that resembles the following (this example is only for the menu adapter):

```
<browsers>
  <browser refID="Default">
    <controlAdapters>
      <adapter controlType="System.Web.UI.WebControls.Menu"
               adapterType="CSSFriendly.MenuAdapter" />
    </controlAdapters>
  </browser>
</browsers>
```

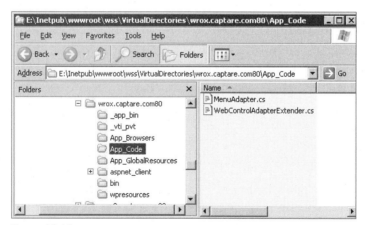

Figure 13-11

As you can see by Figure 13-11, you actually need MenuAdapter.cs and WebControlAdapterExtender.cs in the App_Code folder for things to work. This is because the MenuAdapter class references the WebControlAdapterExtender class so, if they're not both in there, things will break.

This will work. However, it would not be considered a best practice.

The Accessibility Kit for SharePoint (AKS)

One of the nicest things to come out in recent times, at least as far as SharePoint accessibility, is the Accessibility Kit for SharePoint (AKS) created by HiSoftware: http://aks.hisoftware.com. Before this came out, there just wasn't much out there for initiatives in making SharePoint accessible. In fact, most developers were of the mindset "if you want accessible design, SharePoint may not be right for you." But there has been a tangible shift in momentum recently and accessibility is becoming a first-class citizen and the AKS is evidence of that.

So what is the AKS? Well, first, it's important to understand what the AKS is not: It is not a turnkey solution. This means that, while it is great at what it is, you as the developer should understand that it's not something you install on the server and by some dark magic your site is all of a sudden accessible.

Rather, AKS represents a means to make your site more accessible. Not surprisingly, one of its critical components is its own set of control adapters. Similar to the CSS Friendly Control Adapters already discussed, the AKS includes adapters to help override the rendering habits of controls often used in SharePoint. Currently there are more than 50 adapters to help you with a variety of things, including search boxes, blogs, wikis, Web parts, Excel, and more.

The adapters, as described in the discussions of the CSS Friendly Control Adapters, are just C# class files that you can use in your projects. However, one thing of interest is that the description of how to set up each of these adapters that comes with the download tells you to put the class files in the App_Code directory of your Web server for the SharePoint application. As stated earlier, this really isn't a good practice when it comes to production servers. So one thing you might consider is compiling these class files into a single signed DLL and installing that DLL in the server's GAC. This way, you get the benefit of the adapters on all installed applications on that server and also avoid having to leave open source code in the production environment.

The AKS also includes master page and CSS examples to help illustrate how to make more accessible designs. These include changes to the standard CSS files (such as core.css) and master pages (such as BlueBand.master) to modify things like absolute sizing, table structuring, and deprecated elements. These are a much better place to get started than the master pages and CSS files that ship standard with SharePoint.

The AKS even includes a few tools that may help you in your design tasks. For example, there is a tool called the AKS Size Utility that helps you convert fixed sizes to relative ones. For example, if you were using a 50 pixel width for a DIV element, this tool would help you calculate how many Ems (em is a relative unit of measurement used in CSS rules) that would represent. Unfortunately, it doesn't take an existing CSS file and modify it for you. Rather, it has a textbox that allows you to enter a number, a source format (pixel or point), and what the conversion should be to (em or percentage), and it calculates the conversion for you. This tool is kind of neat, but it would be nice if it included a bit more functionality.

And remember, this kit is meant to help you get on your way by showing you some best practices and providing some really useful control adapters specific to SharePoint. But understanding how to implement them is something else. In this chapter, you learned how to implement the control adapters. Similarly, you saw how to appropriately use and modify master pages and CSS rules earlier in this book. With the knowledge gained in this book and the help of the files provided in the AKS, you have a good start on creating a more accessible SharePoint design.

Tools and Validators

Now that accessibility is (hopefully) at the front of your mind, you will probably want to implement some tools to help you in this cause. Fortunately, there are few out there that are free and really helpful.

The Web Accessibility Toolbar was created by Vision Australia: `http://www.visionaustralia.org.au/ais/toolbar/`. This toolbar integrates directly into Internet Explorer (versions 6 and 7) and has some pretty cool features. For example, you can toggle CSS, JavaScript, and even images to get a better idea of how your site might appear to someone accessing your site through assistive technology. One of the best tests it to actually turn off CSS and JavaScript and see what happens. If your site looks unmanageable and un-navigable, then you know you have a problem that needs to be addressed.

Another great free resource is the accessibility validator from WebAIM (Web Accessibility In Mind): `http://wave.webaim.org/`. Using this site, you can enter in the URL of your site, and it will give you a report on how compliant the site is. If your site happens to be inaccessible from the Internet, you can actually copy in the rendered HTML code into a textbox and it will still run the report for you.

And, of course, as the author of accessibility compliance standards, the W3C has its own validator: `http://validator.w3.org/`. This validator, like the one from WebAIM, allows you to validate code based on a provided URL, an uploaded file, or direct input (by copying and pasting the rendered code into a textbox).

Finally, a similar tool is available from HiSoftware, the creators of the Accessibility Kit for SharePoint: `http://www.contentquality.com/`.

While nothing beats planning and thought in your design, these tools should help quantify exactly where you are at with your design. There are probably several other worthy candidates, but these will provide a robust set of tools to help get you on your way.

Summary

This chapter was probably a bit different from some of the preceding ones. While accessibility was mentioned in some of the earlier chapters and brought up here and there in some of the later ones, it wasn't the main focus. For this chapter, it was first and foremost the most important topic on the table. And, as you continue in your career (or hobby) as a Web designer, you will find accessibility will be more and more important as time progresses.

This chapter was also slightly different because it wasn't focused so much on what SharePoint does well, but more on what it could do better at. And then how you can help make it do better with a few free tools in your arsenal.

First, you were introduced to control adapters and their implementation in accessible Web design through the CSS Friendly Control Adapters project. You saw how these adapters can take over the rendering habits of many of your favorite .NET controls, like the menu control, and force it to use much more accessible HTML output than it does by default (no more tables!). You saw a few ways to go about integrating these adapters in your SharePoint sites. You can compile a strongly named DLL and install it in your GAC; you can use a compiled DLL in your BIN directory with a custom trust level; or you could simply use the open source code files in your production environment.

This provided a logical segue to the Accessibility Kit for SharePoint, which relies heavily on the control adapters. You also got a brief overview of what the AKS is and what it isn't and maybe you saw a little on how to use the files included in the kit.

And finally, you saw some free tools that can help you verify your site is accessible after you spend all that time trying to ensure that it is.

But, when it's all said and done, this chapter was meant to point out where SharePoint fails in regards to accessible Web design and how the developers in the world can work to make it better. And hopefully, after reading this chapter, you will go out and do exactly that.

14

Wrapping It All Up

One of the selling points of any portal system, SharePoint included, is that it can create a full Web application for you out of the box. Sure, you have to install it and configure it but, once you have done that, you have a full system up and running, complete with things such as blogs, wikis, and message boards. And this is definitely true with SharePoint. But what can be forgotten or over-looked is that SharePoint can be, and probably should be, a starting point for your Web application. This book's intent is to start with a preconfigured installation of SharePoint and show you how to customize the look and feel to meet business requirements (branding) and accessibility compliance. As a SharePoint developer, you need to understand what SharePoint is really good at and where it needs your help. This book aims at highlighting these things with regard to the interface design of your portal.

Out of the box, SharePoint does an okay job of providing an interface for your site. It is, after all, a portal package and, as such, should provide at least a skeleton for the sites you create. But accepting that is like accepting a new car without a radio. Or air conditioning. Or power steering. Or cruise control. And maybe that is okay for some people. After all, that car will get you from point A to point B, which is the basic requirement of a car. And, like the car, the initial shell will serve the underlying purpose of SharePoint as a Web portal. However, like the car comparison, you'll probably feel better about the ride if you upgrade. And, fortunately, SharePoint was built so that it can be fairly easily "upgraded" if you have the desire and knowledge. Buying this book is a pretty good indicator that you have the desire. After reading it, you will have the knowledge as well.

So what might be helpful now, possibly as a future reference in going forward in your own projects, is to have a summarized list of the ideas presented to this point so that you can make sure they get due consideration in the design aspect of the SharePoint sites you create. To this end, they will be organized as checkpoints (but will not necessarily follow the chapter order of this book) so that you can think through them in a linear fashion and maybe quantify the design aspects of your own projects.

Checkpoint 1: Basic Web Design

One of the first things to take into consideration when planning the design of your SharePoint site is that it is, first and foremost, a Web site. As such, it is susceptible to the same scrutiny and analysis that any Web site would be. For example:

❑ Is this an Internet or intranet application?

❑ If intranet, can you control the browsers that access the site (for example, does corporate policy force all users to have Internet Explorer version 7 installed)?

❑ If Internet, have you decided what browsers and versions you will plan for? Have you thought about the proliferation of various browsers in the Internet community and how big of a hit you will take if you don't, say, plan for Safari? Or Opera? Or Firefox?

❑ What resolution will you target? Will you try to keep a fixed-pixel design? Or a fluid approach?

❑ Will you try to adhere to Web standards, which may prove difficult, or ignore them for the easy road?

To answer these types of questions, you probably will want to try to get as clear a picture as you can on what today's Internet user is using to access the Web. For example, if you want to know what browsers (and versions of those browsers) to target, what analysis could you use to make this decision? You probably couldn't look at your own site statistics, since this is the planning phase of a project and those statistics aren't available before the site is live. So what might be helpful are some generic Web statistics showing what the Web population as a whole (or at least a representative sample of that population) is using.

For this, you might want to consider using statistics like the ones located at TheCounter.com: `http://www` `.thecounter.com/stats/`. TheCounter.com provides analysis tools for Web masters that report on things such as the browsers, resolution, operating systems, and color depth used by the visitors to your site. This is handy, but what is exponentially more useful, at least for this discussion, is that they also aggregate the data monthly and report the global statistics for free to anyone interested. This gives you a much better idea of what is going on in the world of Web surfing. And the price is right.

Of course, if you are targeting your own intranet, this might not be such a big deal. If, for example, you have a corporate network policy that pushes out the latest version of Internet Explorer to all users and you have official protocol that establishes that all employees and visitors to the intranet must use this version, you might not have as big of a need to analyze Web trends for determining browser targets. However, this could backfire on you as well. What if a high-ranking senior staffer uses Firefox even with that policy in place? Are you really going to say, "Well, the company policy requires Internet Explorer, so we're not going to fix the site for you"? Probably not. And believe that, with few exceptions, policies like these don't force people to use the browser you want them to use. People will use what they want.

But remember, these are just the general Web design considerations. In SharePoint, there is always the extra rub that the site is, in fact, also a SharePoint site. So you have to go a bit further than just the basics.

For example, you need to also take into account the level of security you want for your site. Do you want to use Windows-based authentication and tap into an already existing Active Directory system? Or do you want to just use the SQL Membership Provider with forms-based authentication provided as part of the ASP.NET 2.0 Membership Provider? Or maybe a third-party option? Security will definitely be something to consider in the general Web design discussions, since every SharePoint site will have to have some level of security implemented, even if it is planned to be an anonymous Web portal (allowing un-authenticated user access). After all, you have to have some way to administer the site's content, and without security how would you do that? So some discussion about the security ramifications would need to be had, particularly in regard to the way SharePoint uses security.

You will also need to delve into which type of site you want to create. Most companies use SharePoint for one of two purposes: to collaborate with a group of folks or to communicate to them. The distinction between these two types of sites is the number of directions the communication flow of information goes. If it is one-way (from the corporation to all interested parties), it is a communication site and should therefore utilize the MOSS 2007 publishing site templates. If the communication flow is bi-directional (or even multi-directional), where the company is communicating back and forth with interested parties, the site has a more collaborative focus and should use one of the MOSS 2007 collaboration templates. So it is important to understand who your audience is and how they will interact with the contents of the site so that you can make an informed decision as to what type of site you want to create for your portal.

Related to this concept is the topology for the hierarchy of the information you plan to present to the patrons of your site. In other words, how do you want to structure your information? This has a direct result on things such as navigation, since you need to know where the logical breakpoints of your information are and then determine the subsets under each. For example, in a business-based model, you could decide the major categories are areas within your organization, such as Accounting, Marketing, Human Resources, and Information Technology. Then, under each of these classifications, you would have logical subunits of information, such as Accounts Receivable under Accounting and Benefits under Human Resources. Conversely, in a taxonomy-based model, your major headings would be classifications, such as Production or Research & Development with subgroups like Vendors and Factories for Production and Projects and Patents for Research & Development. While this will certainly play a much larger part in the navigation structure of your site (as is discussed later in "Checkpoint 8: Intuitive Navigation"), it is good to start talking about it here as well, as it helps define what the site is and why you are creating it.

If you want to read more about these concepts, they were discussed in more detail in Chapters 2 ("Web Design 101") and 4 ("Communicating or Collaborating?").

Checkpoint 2: Accessibility

Arguably, accessibility could be wrapped up in Checkpoint 1, since it is, in all honestly, a part of general Web design concepts. And, a few years ago, it probably would have been (if it was included at all). But times are changing and accessibility is becoming an increasingly important discussion point for creating Web designs today.

You can see this all around you if you look closely enough. Historically, Internet Explorer metaphorically stuck its nose up at Web standards. If you don't think this is true, try to create a site that is standards-compliant (heavily CSS) and load it in a more standards-based browser like Firefox. Then try to load it in older versions of Internet Explorer. Oh, and by older, that doesn't mean versions and versions ago. No, try loading it in Internet Explorer 6, which still has the major market share in Web browser hits today.

It breaks. Almost inevitably, it breaks. But look now at the latest release, Internet Explorer 7. It is much closer to the other standards-based browsers on the market. And the next version, 8, promises to be even better.

You can also see this trend in some of the information presented in this book. Microsoft engaged a research group to identify exactly how important assistive technology is for today's Web surfer and had some eye-opening results. This might have been what led to a lot of the progress seen in recent years, including, but not limited to, Microsoft's partnering with the community to create the CSS Friendly Control Adapters and the Accessibility Kit for SharePoint in the last few years. As the giants begin embracing this vantage point, you can guarantee it will filter down over the years. Although, honestly, much of the accessibility buzz started at the grassroots level and just worked its way up. But as the above-the-fold companies like Microsoft are embracing it, you know you are at a turning point.

And it's not strictly philanthropic. There are definite business reasons to consider in your reasoning. If not for the hundreds of billions of dollars estimated for discretionary income of the disabled, then for the emergence of litigation for noncompliance. While not widespread yet, if it happens to you, it is widespread enough. And if it can touch companies like Target, it can touch you, too.

So as you start planning your site, it is important to ask, "Is accessibility right for this site?" In every situation, hopefully the answer is "yes." And if it is, you have to decide which level of compliance to hold yourself to.

As you saw in Chapter 13, there are three priority levels of compliance for accessibility. Priority 1 is for all the things that every site has to do and is the bare minimum standard for compliance. Priority 2 includes additional items that every Web site should do. And Priority 3 is more of the nice-to-have features (at least for now). If trends continue the way they are, it won't be surprising to see a lot of Priority 3 items jumping up to 1 or 2. But, for now, they are not the ones that will get you in trouble. So, using this classification schema, all sites should be held to Priority 2 compliance. Again, these are the things that all sites *should* do, which includes Priority 1, which is all the things sites *must* do.

So where does SharePoint fall? Priority 3? Priority 2? Priority 1? Unfortunately, out of the box, SharePoint doesn't even accomplish Priority 1 compliance.

This is not a doomsday sentence, though. This is just an awareness exercise. Consider it a challenge. With enough planning and work, you can surely bring your site to at least Priority 1 and maybe even Priority 2.

Take, for example, the Priority 2 checkpoint of not using tables for layout (only for tabular data, like data grids). This fails all over the place, starting with the basic layout of the page for SharePoint sites, which uses tables. But you can fix that by deciding to create your own standards-based master pages (discussed more in Checkpoint 5) and deciding to use CSS rules to lay out your page rather than tables. You can also implement the aforementioned CSS Friendly Control Adapters (as well as the adapters included in the Accessibility Kit for SharePoint) to override the rendered controls to output CSS rules rather than tables for things like navigation and even blog entries.

The important thing is to understand the limitations you are up against and decide you are going to overcome them. You have to decide to make accessibility a priority and then figure out the tools you need to make that happen.

To read more about accessibility, as well as the CSS Friendly Control Adapters and the Accessibility Kit for SharePoint, turn to Chapter 13 ("Accessibility in SharePoint").

Checkpoint 3: The Design

At this point, you have figured out what type of site you want, what kind of content you are going to provide, and what kind of Web considerations you need to incorporate into the design of your portal. With that information, it's time to mock up the design for your site.

The biggest point to this is: Get inspired. Don't even look at the standard SharePoint templates and sites. You don't really want people thinking, "I've seen that site before. A lot."

Go out and see some really great examples of what other people are doing in SharePoint. Or, even better, go out and see what other people are doing in Web design and see what you can bring back to your own site. Sure, there are limitations for design in SharePoint. It is, after all, a portal. And, as such, there is a need for some basic elements such as navigation, search boxes, and, of course, content. So if you go to a really nice Flash-based site featuring the photographic talents of an artist in the San Fernando Valley, is that going to port directly to a SharePoint site? No, probably not. But can you get some ideas on it? Of course. Maybe the background grabs your attention. Or maybe the layout of the header makes you smile. You can take pieces of that thought and integrate them into your own site.

So maybe search the Web for a while and find some really good sites. Bookmark them. Print them out. Think about what you like about them and what you can use for your own site. Write on the printouts or use some sticky pads. Really put a concerted effort into coming up with the good stuff and the reusable stuff.

Maybe even go to Web sites that have articles on proper Web design. A good site for things like this is Smashing Magazine: `http://www.smashingmagazine.com`. This site is dedicated to providing free commentary on today's Web design. For example, in April 2008, they published the article "Web Form Design: Modern Solutions and Creative Ideas" to showcase different HTML forms and how different designers approached the task of using these forms in their sites. This ranged from clean and elegant to creative and interesting. They also included tips in this article on how to approach something like the standard "Contact Us" form. While this article may not be directly relevant to your project, it certainly can give you some good ideas (and some potential example sites to check out).

Now that you have some ideas of what your site should be, you might consider whiteboarding it to see if you can make everything flow. Sort of lay out, either with pen and paper or, quite literally, on a whiteboard, all of the elements you want to integrate into your site. Maybe cut out some of the examples you printed and stick them in the relevant area of your manual mockup. Try to materialize the intangible idea into something more solid; something you can create in HTML.

Finally, once you've thought about it, get out your graphic editor program and get to work. In this book, this was done using Adobe Photoshop CS3, since that is one of the most common tools for creating Web graphic mockups. But it is certainly not the only tool. In fact, there are some great free resources out there if your means are limited. One popular free graphics program is the GNU Image Manipulation Program (GIMP): `http://www.gimp.org`. GIMP is fairly similar to Photoshop except that it is completely free and open-source. Their Web site contains the free download as well as a slew of free tutorials and documentation. If you don't have the means to get into Photoshop, this is a very viable solution.

So, with your graphic editing program of choice, integrate the planning you have done for your Web site (including things like target resolution) and the visual inspiration you have garnered to this point and make something worth showing off. Create a design that you are proud of and that you would gladly include in your portfolio. Make sure that you include the required elements (such as the navigation and search area), but don't restrict yourself to the portal design of the header and attached navigation with the sidebar and the footer that you see everywhere. Or, at least if you do, make it look special. Make it look so little like standard SharePoint that people need to go into the rendered code of your site to see that it is SharePoint.

To get an idea of how to create your own portal design, you can read Chapter 3, "General Concept Design."

Checkpoint 4: Creating the Mockup

It's finally time to start writing some code. You have all of your planning done and you have made all of your decisions as to what the site will be, who it will serve, and what information will be consumed. You have worked diligently to make your site look as good as possible and have created a reasonable mockup in a graphics editor program. You're probably itching to get some code down and it's finally time to do exactly that.

The next step would be to create the HTML equivalent to the mockup you created in, say, Photoshop. Hopefully, you have decided that you are going to shoot for some level of accessibility compliance and, as such, this means you are going to use CSS. And this is, to be honest, the hardest part of this section.

While CSS isn't the hardest concept in Web design to learn, it also isn't the easiest. In fact, for some developers, its steep learning curve can cause anxiety. But, as accessibility keeps garnering more and more attention (and more and more consequences for noncompliance), CSS will become the standard for which it was created.

But for now, it can prove difficult (especially when having to control position and float elements, as you saw earlier in this book). There is the annoyance that CSS can work differently in different browsers. Your header is positioned perfectly in one, scrunched up in another, and completely out of position in another. So, when you introduce CSS into your design, you introduce another potential fail point.

But it's worth it. The design will load faster and be much more accessible to those who need it to be. It will separate design from code, which is the premise of things like n-tier architecture, and provide a universally central location for style rules that all developers in a project can use.

It makes sense to use CSS. It makes sense on a financial level with the accessibility arguments raised earlier. It makes sense on a performance level because CSS files are cached and only have to load once, which makes pages load faster. And it makes sense on a productivity/reusability level since developers can share the style rules across teams and keep a consistent look and feel for all of the pages.

It makes sense. But it isn't always easy. It will be a struggle if you are new to CSS as a design tool. But it will be worth it in the end.

So, with that in mind, you should begin creating a static HTML page with an external CSS Stylesheet that creates the basic layout of your site. You can use your graphic editing program to create the images you will need for the layout and then position them with the CSS rules that are called in your HTML page.

You will also want to validate (and re-validate) your HTML code throughout the process. You can use tools integrated within the Internet Explorer Developer Toolbar and Firebug (both discussed in Chapter 7) to help you do this. There are also several HTML and CSS validation sites out there that will allow you to enter in your code to see if it validates against universal Web standards, such as the W3C markup validation service, located here: http://validator.w3.org/.

At the end of this process, you should have a static HTML page that will load in the major browsers (at least Internet Explorer, Firefox, Opera, and Safari) and look the same in each. It should be have passed at least some level of CSS and HTML validation and be, say, Priority 2 compliant.

The physical files that you will end this checkpoint with are an HTML page, and external Stylesheet, and several image files.

To read about how to work with creating your HTML/CSS mockup, you can go through Chapter 7 ("Cascading Style Sheets with MOSS 2007").

Checkpoint 5: Creating the Master Page

Now that you have a basic shell for your site, it's time to bring it into the world of SharePoint and create a master page wrapper for your code.

Master pages were introduced as part of the .NET 2.0 Framework and allowed for templating of your ASPX pages. Essentially, a master page creates the shared format of your pages and creates content placeholders for you to use to inject to specific content of any given page into the master page shell. So, this generally means that you create your header, navigation, sidebar, and footer in your master page and then create a placeholder where you want all of the content to go. Then, on any page in your site, you would inherit this master page and throw the content for that page in the provided placeholder. So if, for example, you had a GridView control with the entire inventory for store ABC, you would just inherit the master page, which brings all of the header, footer, and related pieces in, and then add the GridView control to the content placeholder set up by the master page.

And, since SharePoint is built on the .NET 2.0 Framework, it allows for the use of master pages. However, there is a catch. SharePoint requires more than one content placeholder. It requires more like 20 content placeholders. And, if you miss one, you will probably see errors in your rendered pages. So you have to be careful. There are also considerations for where these content placeholders are placed. For example, if you place the "PlaceHolderTitleBreadcrumb" content placeholder in the footer area, it's going to look pretty weird. And with things like page edit mode, placement can get even trickier.

However, if you have set up your HTML mockup soundly, this step shouldn't go that badly. You know where the "PlaceHolderTitleBreadcrumb" will go because, well, you mocked it up beforehand and you will have a pretty good idea where you want the breadcrumb to be located. So, with proper planning in checkpoints 1 through 5, this should go fairly smoothly.

However, it is important to remember that the master page in SharePoint is not a physical file that you can store in a virtual directory. It is a file that is built on the fly from configuration files and database records (everything is virtual). So this means that you will also have to get into SharePoint designer, if you haven't already, to begin creating your file. You will also have to take into consideration the default master page and overriding of the standard site definition of the files you touch.

However, once you have created a SharePoint master page for the first time, all subsequent times seem relatively easy. Like most things in technology, the first time is the hardest.

You can read more about creating SharePoint master pages by going through Chapter 8 ("Master Pages"). Additionally, you may find it useful to read more about using SharePoint Designer in Chapter 5 ("Introduction to SharePoint Designer").

Checkpoint 6: Using a Theme

Another concept introduced in the .NET 2.0 Framework was the idea of themes. Themes allow developers/designers to create skin files that can set defaults for much of the content of a given Web site. For example, a developer could create a skin file that would make every GridView control added to the site have a black header row with a white bold font and then alternating gray and white rows thereafter. With this skin file in place, all any developer on this project would have to do is drop a standard GridView control onto their page and it would automatically be formatted for them. This allows for a really easy way of binding the look and feel of the content of your pages to ensure that all pages are consistent with the prearranged look of your site.

But, beyond that, you also get the power to set up any of the other properties of the controls in your skin file. If, for example, you want all GridView controls to allow pagination and to show 10 records per page, then you can do that in the skin file. So when a developer drops a GridView control on their page, this setting is already made for her behind the scenes. Now, if the business rules require it, the developer can override these defaults and set the properties directly on the control itself. But the fact that she can have preset defaults for any property on the control you want is pretty exciting. This truly allows for consistency among all pages of a site.

While SharePoint themes are essentially the same as ASP.NET 2.0 themes (they are, after all, built off of the ASP.NET 2.0 themes), there are some additional considerations to take into effect. For one, they are applied differently through the site settings of your SharePoint site and require some extra files to work (the theme .INF file, for example). They are also stored in a different location than a typical ASP.NET 2.0 theme, which also introduces potentially new hurdles like sharing themes among server farms.

You can read more about how to set up and apply your SharePoint themes in Chapter 6 ("Themes").

Checkpoint 7: Considering Page Layouts

Especially if you have decided your site should be a Publishing site, you will want to seriously consider creating and integrating page layouts into your Web design schema.

Page layouts actually work hand-in-hand with master pages. In fact, from a very high level, page layouts almost resemble the concept of nesting master pages, which is fairly common in ASP.NET applications.

In a master page, you decide the basic look and feel for all pages in your site. For example, you might have the standard header and navigation at the top, a footer area at the bottom, and the center is basically left wide open for content.

A page layout then comes along and says, "Okay, that's fine, but there will be several different formats for content in that area." For example, you might have one type of page that you would classify as the "welcome" page. You might have another that you would classify as the "articles page." And you might have still another page that you would use for grids of data. While all three types of pages use the basic formatting and layout of the master page, the content for each will be laid out differently. Page layouts allow this distinction between pages that use the master page. Additionally, they define the editable data for different types of pages.

And the really nice thing about page layouts is that they allow for reuse throughout the project. This means that once you create a new page layout other developers can then use that page layout as the template for a new page. So if, for example, you created a page layout for "articles" pages, a developer could then use that page layout to create a new "articles" page for a site he was working on. This allows for better continuity between the sites of your SharePoint portal.

To read more about page layouts, you can flip back to Chapter 9 ("Page Layouts").

Checkpoint 8: Intuitive Navigation

Like a lot of other things pointed out so far in this chapter, life got much simpler for Web developers in respect to navigation with the release of the .NET 2.0 Framework. All of a sudden, navigation became intuitive and easy to implement with the use of standard navigation controls and sitemap datasources, which were typically either XML files or database connections. You could set up globalization as well as security simply by modifying some files in your Web.config (and maybe setting up some resource files). Typically speaking, you could create a very solid navigation schema simply by detailing your site hierarchy in a sitemap XML file and then connecting it to a standard menu control on, say, your master page.

And again, like several other topics in this chapter, SharePoint reaped the benefits of this advancement since it, too, was built on the .NET 2.0 Framework. But, just like those other benefits, integration with the SharePoint environment added a new level of complexity.

First, it matters if you are using a WSS 3.0 or a MOSS 2007 site. Strangely enough, this affects your navigation planning since WSS only offers a subset of the functionality offered in the full MOSS version. Additionally, the idea of an XML sitemap data source is lost on navigation like the Top Link Bar where all navigation, including the order in which the tabs appear, is set through the SharePoint interface. There are also, typically speaking, several navigation controls for a single page. For example, there will almost always be a Top Link navigation bar near the top of the page, but there will also often times be a Quick Launch navigation bar on the left-hand side of the content area. Just by the fact that one of these is typically horizontally aligned and the other one is vertical, you are probably going to need to design these differently.

And while you are looking at all of the properties for styling these controls, you run into one other hurdle: They render tables in your final HTML. This means that, if you use the out-of-the-box navigation provided with SharePoint, you can't achieve Priority 2 accessibility compliance. So what do you do? This brings the CSS Friendly Control Adapters back into the planning. You can integrate these adapters to override the rendering behavior of the navigation controls to render out more accessible code (for instance, DIV, UL, and LI elements as opposed to tables) and continue working toward achieving Priority 2 compliance.

You can read more about navigation considerations in Chapter 11 ("Navigation"). You can also see an example of how to integrate the navigation control overrides of the CSS Friendly Control Adapters in Chapter 13 ("Accessibility in SharePoint").

Checkpoint 9: Content Considerations

While you have certainly, at this point in the checkpoints, given some consideration to the content area of your portal through things like page layouts and themes, it's time to really hammer down on what your site needs to provide to be successful, and the design considerations for these elements.

One of the main elements to consider is the search functionality of your site. Search is probably one of the most sought-after features when considering implementing SharePoint. It is powerful and fairly easy to modify and customize if you know what you are doing. And, as part of this customization, you can style the results to fit along with your site.

Additionally, since most content of a SharePoint site is delivered through Web Parts in some form or another, it is critical that you have a solid understanding of at least some of the major Web Parts available with a standard installation and how they can be used in your own sites. You can then use these Web Parts strategically in your content areas to allow users to provide the information for your site, as well as maybe sneak in a little JavaScript functionality to help make your site a little better. You can even use these Web Parts to bring in data from unrelated sites to add more value to the users that consume the content of your portal.

While most of the other areas of the book were talking about how to style components of a SharePoint portal to integrate with your design, the chapters on Web Parts were more aimed at making sure you were aware of some of the Web Parts you could integrate into your content areas as part of the design of your site. In other words, when planning out how your site will look, you can decide which Web Parts to include and where, to facilitate this design best.

You can read more about styling your search results, as well as the Search Web Part, in Chapter 12 ("Customizing Search"). You might also want to read Chapter 10 ("Working with Out-of-the-Box Web Parts") to help you better plan the Web Parts to use in creating the content areas of your final portal design.

Checkpoint 10: Checks and Validation

Now that your site is set up, you can sit back and admire your work, right? The site looks cutting edge and maximizes the controls and features of SharePoint to create content worth talking about. Everything is laid out perfectly and intuitively and you are ready to pass it on to your users.

Or are you?

If you really wait to test until Checkpoint 10, you are going to probably regret it. Hopefully, as you implement new design aspects to your site, you are testing them along the way. However, as a final step, you should recheck everything.

What does this mean?

Well, to start with, it means testing in as many popular browsers as you can. This would probably include, at a minimum:

- ❑ The latest version of Microsoft Internet Explorer (`http://www.microsoft.com/windows/downloads/ie/getitnow.mspx`)
- ❑ The latest version of Mozilla Firefox (`www.mozilla.com/firefox/`)
- ❑ The latest version of Opera Web Browser (`http://www.opera.com/download/`)
- ❑ The latest version of Apple Safari (`http://www.apple.com/safari/download/`)

If you have it available to you, you should also test against Microsoft Internet Explorer version 6 since it is still one of the most popular Web browsers. In fact, according to the statistics at TheCounter.com, IE6 continually beat IE7 until February 2008 and, even through March 2008, was still running almost neck-and-neck with the more advanced browser. So it makes a lot of sense to keep testing with IE6 until it is no longer accessing pages on the Internet, which will probably not be anytime real soon.

Is that enough? Well, it depends. But, generally speaking, the answer is probably "no."

What about mobile devices? Will your portal ever be accessed by mobile devices? If so, have you tested to see how it works? While this might seem hard to test with, there are emulators you can download for pretty much any mobile operating system to test against and run from within Visual Studio. This includes Palm, Blackberry, and, of course, Windows Mobile.

Is that enough? Well, again, it depends. And, again, the answer is probably "no."

Why not consider testing your application against one of the most popular assistive technology browsers, JAWS (`http://www.freedomscientific.com/fs_downloads/jaws.asp`). While the full version costs money, there is a free demonstration version you can download that will work in a limited capacity and will let you know pretty quickly how your site *sounds*. (JAWS actually reads out all of the content of your site from your browser.)

And of course, you should give some consideration to validation just to make sure you didn't miss anything. Some popular validators would include:

❑ The W3C Markup Validation Service (`http://validator.w3.org/`)

❑ The W3C CSS Validation Service (`http://jigsaw.w3.org/css-validator/`)

❑ WAVE by WebAIM (`http://wave.webaim.org/`)

If everything looks okay in all of the listed browsers, sounds okay in JAWS, and passes the validation tests, you are probably okay. But if you change anything along the way, you should retest against all of these tools.

In fact, go ahead and retest anyway. You can never be too safe.

Summary

So, as the final chapter wraps up, what have you learned so far?

Hopefully you learned that the standard SharePoint installation is just a starting point for your design, not a finished product. You saw in this book how to use various tools, many of which came with the introduction of the .NET 2.0 Framework, to customize the look and feel of your site while at the same time keeping that look and feel consistent across all pages. You also saw how just because something worked one way in a standard ASP.NET page doesn't mean it will work the same way in SharePoint. In fact, it probably won't.

But more basic than that, hopefully you got to a point where you are thinking about SharePoint, at least in a designer's eye, as simply being some HTML that is there for you to manipulate. You can now see it as a Web site, not a portal. And a Web site you can design; portals are what seem hard.

And, in this chapter, hopefully you gained a bigger picture of how all of these concepts come together. In fact, you could almost take this chapter and use it as your own checklist for the SharePoint sites you develop. Will it be exhaustive? Of course not. Every project has its own nuances that must be considered as part of the planning phase. But this is a good place to jump off from. And that should be the point of any good programmer's book — helping you take the leap into something new. As this book comes to an end, we hope we have provided that for you.

Introduction to Deploying SharePoint Designs

— *by John Ross*

A number of very important topics have been covered in this book relating to professional Share-Point design. Your head is probably filed with ideas that you are ready to implement as soon as you finish this book. You have probably come up with an idea for a design and even have an idea about how to make it. Before you run off, there is still one big question remaining: How do you implement your design/brand into production? Better yet, how *should* you implement your design/brand into a production environment?

This appendix will discuss the final piece of the design process called deployment. You might be thinking "Isn't this a topic for developers?" The answer to that question is yes; traditionally the topic of SharePoint deployment is covered in texts for developers and administrators. But this is exactly why the topic of deployment is important to designers; the way that the design elements for a SharePoint site are created will directly impact both developers and administrators.

Specifically, this appendix will explore the various options available for deployment of design elements and the pros and cons of each option and how it can affect your SharePoint implementation now and in the future. And no discussion on deployment would be complete without mentioning file customization, including what it is and why it matters to you as a designer. Best of all, this appendix will give you some perspective into how the other members of your team might be thinking and help to shed some light on their world.

Customized and Uncustomized Files

Before you start reading about deploying your SharePoint design, it is probably best to clarify the differences between customized and uncustomized files. While this might not be the first time you have seen these terms, you might have heard them referred to as ghosted (uncustomized) and unghosted (customized) files. These terms (ghosted and unghosted) were used in WSS 2.0 and SharePoint Portal 2003 but have since been deprecated. However, if developers were around back then, they might still use these terms, so it's good to understand what they mean in today's Share-Point installations. And, after all, it's all semantics anyway.

Uncustomized Files

All of the files used to create the out-of-the-box sites in SharePoint are uncustomized. This means that the source of the file lives on the file system and not in the content database. However, an uncustomized instance of the file resides in the content database and acts as a pointer to the file on the file system. This means that when an uncustomized page is rendered, SharePoint will first look to the content database, but since the instance of the page does not include a source, the file will be rendered from the file system.

Uncustomized files make it possible to have many copies of a file point to the same source, similar to how a template for a document works. For example, if you had many sites that used the same page layout, you could make modifications to a single file and every place that the uncustomized page layout was used would be updated. This is very helpful from a design perspective because it allows you to make changes very easily.

For a more information on customized and uncustomized files, see Andrew Connell's MSDN article at: http://msdn.microsoft.com/en-us/library/cc406685.aspx

Customized Files

A customized file is one where the source of the file lives in the content database. A file becomes customized if it is modified in any way through the SharePoint user interface or by using Share-Point Designer 2007. When a file becomes customized, a version of that file is saved to the content database even if the file was originally uncustomized. Once a file has been customized, the source of the page is saved to the instance. When the customized page is rendered in the browser, the source is being pulled from the content database. As discussed in Chapter 5, files can be reverted to an uncustomized state easily with SharePoint Designer.

An example of how this might occur in the real world is looking at the default master page of your site collection, typically default.master. In your project, you might have a business need that requires you to add some custom code to the page, which is typically done through the code-behind file for the page. This might be something as simple as needing to perform some calculations on data in the background to report at the top of the content area for all pages. It could also be something considerably more complicated. The point is that you need to add custom code to your master page.

In this example, default.master starts off as an uncustomized page. However, to implement your custom code, you will open up the page in SharePoint designer and change the @Master directive for default.master to point to a custom class file in the Global Assembly Cache you created with the custom code. As soon as you save the file in SharePoint Designer, it becomes customized.

Conversely, a file created using SharePoint Designer or through the SharePoint user interface will be a customized file and cannot be reverted to an uncustomized state. To continue the previous example, you could revert default.master to its original, uncustomized, state by right-mouse click-ing the file name in the Folder List pane of SharePoint Designer and selecting Reset to Site Definition in the options presented. Doing this would remove the new @Master directive property you set and, consequently, remove the ability to use the custom code-behind file you created for default.master. In other words, default.master would reset back to its original code.

Key Considerations

The initial implementation of a SharePoint site will likely require time from designers, developers, and administrators to deploy the site into production. The decisions made prior to going live will directly impact how the site is updated in the future and this is especially important to administrators. For example, as a designer you might create a custom master page, custom CSS, and custom page layouts using SharePoint Designer and then save everything customized in the content database. Once completed you will have an attractive custom branded SharePoint site. However, what happens in a few months when requests for changes come from the business or when Microsoft releases a future version of SharePoint? It is the responsibility of the designer to have an idea about how this will happen and what the level of effort required to do ongoing maintenance to the various design elements is.

Many companies have a person who wears the SharePoint administrator hat exclusively. Others take a more hybrid approach. In either case, the administrator's perspective is the same on the topic of deployment of design elements. As long as the chosen approach does not take up too much of their time, require them to compromise server security, or modify any SharePoint system files, they are fine with just about anything.

Be prepared to answer the following questions from your administrator:

❑   Where do you need me to put the files?

❑   How long will it take to deploy everything?

❑   What happens if we need to make changes to the files in the future?

❑   Did you modify any of the system files?

Developers will play a very different role in the implementation process. The instinct for most developers seems to be to set up SharePoint to work as they go through the development process and then replicate the same thing when they are ready to take their code to production. Most developers do not realize how important a role they will play in the deployment of design elements. If your team decides to deploy your design files in an uncustomized manner, then it will be the developer who will need to learn how to do it. To create this deployment package, the developer will use a combination of Windows SharePoint Services solutions and Features.

Learning how to create deployment packages can be a daunting task, even for experienced developers. The process is very time consuming and also can be very frustrating. We will talk more about solutions and Features in the next section. However, as a designer it is important for you to have a good working relationship with your developer because every time you make a small change to any of your design files, you will need to send them to your developer.

If you would like to learn more about the specific tasks that are required for creating solutions and Features, refer to Wrox's Real World SharePoint 2007, specifically Chapter 4, "Developing Publishing Sites the Smart and Structured Way."

Also note that if your team decides to use customized files, the role of deploying design elements will lie almost entirely with you, the designer. Regardless of the decision, it is important to include all members of the team as part of the discussion.

Creating Uncustomized Files with Features and Solutions

If files created by SharePoint Designer and the SharePoint user interface are always customized, then how are uncustomized files created? The mechanism used to provision uncustomized instances of files in SharePoint is called a *Feature*. It is difficult to define what a Feature is, but it is easy to describe what they do. A Feature allows a developer to deploy site customizations or functionality to a site collection or individual site by placing files on the SharePoint server's file system. The Feature can then be activated through the user interface, which deploys the files in an uncustomized state.

To create a Feature, you need to collect all of the files you want to deploy and place them in a new folder in the Features directory in the 12 Hive (\\Program Files\Common Files\Microsoft Shared\Web server extensions\12\TEMPLATE\FEATURES). So if, for example, you wanted to create a new Feature to deploy a new Master Page, you might create the following folder: C:\Program Files\Common Files\Microsoft Shared\Web Server Extensions\12\TEMPLATE\FEATURES\MyMasterPage\.

The primary file of every Feature is its feature.xml file, which provides basic information (title, description, scope of deployment, and so on), a unique ID, and the name and location for the element manifest file. So, to continue the previous example, you would need to create a new XML file in the MyMasterPage directory called "feature.xml" that might have code similar to the following in it:

```
<?xml version="1.0" encoding="utf-8" ?>
<Feature xmlns="http://schemas.microsoft.com/sharepoint/"
  Id="13b88dd0-29be-11dd-bd0b-0800200c9a66"
  Title="My Master Page"
  Description="This Feature contains a new Master Page."
  Hidden="FALSE"
  Scope="Site"
  Version="1.0.0.0">
<ElementManifests>
  <ElementManifest Location="MyMasterPage.xml"/>
</ElementManifests>
</Feature>
```

This file just defines the Feature and tells SharePoint where to find the manifest XML file, which defines the components of the Feature. In this case, feature.xml has referenced the Feature manifest as "MyMasterPage.xml." So, in the MyMasterPage directory created earlier, you would need to add a new file called MyMasterPage.xml and give it code similar to the following:

```
<?xml version="1.0" encoding="utf-8" ?>
<Elements xmlns="http://schemas.microsoft.com/sharepoint/">
  <Module Name="MyMasterPage"
    Url="_catalogs/masterpage"
    Path=""
```

```
              RootWebOnly="TRUE">
              <File Url=" MyMasterPage.master"
                Type="GhostableInLibrary">
                <Property Name="ContentType"
                  Value="$Resources:cmscore,contenttype_masterpage_name;"/>
                <Property Name="PublishingPreviewImage"
                  Value="~SiteCollection/_catalogs/masterpage/Preview Images/
                        MyMasterPage.jpg,
                        ~SiteCollection/_catalogs/masterpage/Preview Images/
                        MyMasterPage.jpg" />
                <Property Name="Description"
                  Value="New Master Page provisioned from the MyMasterPage
                        Feature."/>
              </File>
            </Module>
            <Module Name="MyMasterPagePreviewImage"
              Url="_catalogs/masterpage"
              Path="">
              <File Url=" MyMasterPage.jpg"
                Name="Preview Images/MyMasterFile.jpg"
                Type="GhostableInLibrary"/>
            </Module>
          </Elements>
```

This is a fairly simple example, but it is doing two things. First, it is provisioning the new master page, MyMasterPage.master, as part of this Feature. That is the purpose of the first module. The second thing it is doing is provisioning a new image for the Feature, MyMasterPage.jpg. This Feature will be used as the preview image for the Master Page and is referenced as such in the Master Page module (look at the PublishingPreviewImage property reference). You will need to add these physical files (MyMasterPage.master and MyMasterPage.jpg) to your Feature directory (MyMasterPage), but upon doing so your Feature is ready to be deployed. Doing it this way allows you to introduce modified pages to your site without turning them into "customized" files. This means that, when you deploy MyMasterPage.master to your site, it will be treated as an uncustomized file, even though it includes custom code (potentially).

Features are very powerful and can be used to provision other SharePoint elements such as site columns, content types, and lists. Features can even call custom code.

By themselves, Features allow you to deploy elements in an uncustomized state, but in an environment with multiple Web front ends (WFEs), you still need to get the files to each of the servers. Also, what if you have multiple environments for development, testing, and production? How can you easily move files between environments or servers? To address this issue, Microsoft added the solution framework to the latest release of SharePoint. A solution is simply a cabinet (.cab) file with a .wsp extension. To create a solution, you need to include all of the files to be deployed along with another file (manifest.xml) which tells SharePoint where everything needs to go.

Once the solution package has been created, it is then added to the farm and deployed. In a farm with multiple WFEs, this allows you to simultaneously push all of the files it contains to all of the servers in the farm. So there is no need to manually drop the files on each server; the solution does it for you. When you combine solutions and Features together, the solutions deliver the files to the server and the Features enable the functionality. The result is that all of your files are deployed in an uncustomized manner.

Appendix A: Introduction to Deploying SharePoint Designs

The process to create uncustomized files is certainly more complex than the process to create customized files. Typically, design elements are created by a designer in SharePoint Designer (or Visual Studio, Dreamweaver, a text editor, or so on) and then exported to a file. Next, the designer gives the files to the developer to create the deployment package, which typically includes a combination of Features and solutions. Then, the completed solutions are given to the administrator, who deploys them to the appropriate instance of SharePoint and activates the Features, which results in uncustomized files in all the places you need them. Figure A-1 shows a diagram of the process for creating a deployment package.

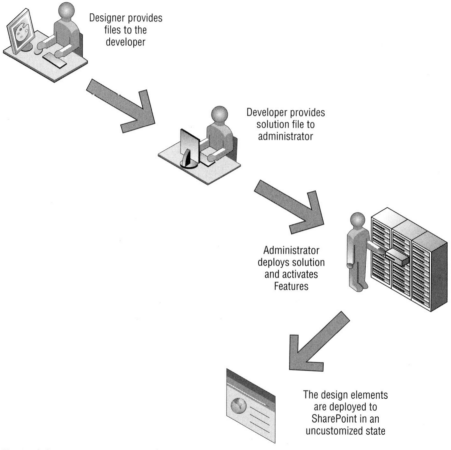

Designer provides files to the developer

Developer provides solution file to administrator

Administrator deploys solution and activates Features

The design elements are deployed to SharePoint in an uncustomized state

Figure 1-1

After the initial deployment, changes can be made by providing the new or changed files to the developer, who simply adds or updates their existing project in Visual Studio. The developer then provides a new solution to the administrator, who upgrades the existing solution with the new one.

For more information on the commands you use when actually upgrading solutions, see http://technet.microsoft.com/en-us/library/cc262014.aspx.

The Designer's Role in Solutions and Features

As mentioned earlier the process of deployment of design elements begins with the designer. But how exactly does a designer give files to the developer to make them into a solution and Feature? You might think it's a silly question, but try it without reading the rest of this section. This seemingly simple task has given heartburn to many SharePoint designers and developers alike.

To create a solution or Feature, the developer needs all of the files used in the design including:

- Master pages
- Page layouts
- Cascading style sheets
- Images
- JavaScript files
- Pre-configured web parts

In addition to getting all of these files, they are also going to ask where they need to put them. All of this information should be simple to provide; by the time they ask for it, you will probably have a version of the site running in a development environment. Just be prepared ahead of time to save yourself the extra time and energy on email.

If you stopped at the beginning of this section and attempted to figure out the easiest way to give your files to the developer, how did it go? You might have opened SharePoint Designer and attempted to publish the files to a local drive. Or you might have tried to export the files from SharePoint Designer. Or you might have opened up the SharePoint site and downloaded the files from the various document libraries. Most graphic, CSS, and JavaScript files will exist outside of SharePoint and can easily be saved to a ZIP file. However, the best practice for pulling custom master pages and page layout files is to open SharePoint Designer and use the Save As function from the file menu. Although other methods may seem to work, they are much more cumbersome and less reliable.

After providing the files to the developer, all you have to do is sit back and wait for them to complete their deployment package. Once it is completed, you will need to review all of the sites to make sure everything looks as it should. Don't expect that developers or administrators have the keen design eye that you do!

It is also important to remember that like developers, you will want to make sure to version the design elements you are working with. Whether you choose to use one of the many options for source control software or simply use a folder structure with a naming schema, it is important to use something! You never know when someone will realize that some later version of a master page caused some strange behavior that definitely wasn't there in the version from two weeks ago.

The Downside to Solutions and Features

The case for using solutions and Features sounds compelling, but it is not perfect. There are some big disadvantages to using solutions and Features for deployment.

The biggest is that the process is more complicated. Learning to create solutions and Features can be a difficult task even for the most seasoned ASP.NET developer. This fact alone can rule out the possibility of using this option for deployment, causing project timelines to simply become too long. However, once a developer gets the hang of it, the speed at which solutions and Features can be created will increase dramatically.

Another drawback is that the process just takes longer. Once the designer finishes creating all of the design elements, the files need to be given to the developer to create the solutions and Features. The additional step to create a deployment package is something that would need to be figured into project plans. Over time this process will go much faster. It isn't magic, but it does require that hours are allocated to the task to accommodate this step in the SharePoint development lifecycle.

Finally, there is no real mechanism for debugging. If an error occurs when you are installing or activating your Feature/solution, it will likely be a generic error that gives you no real detail that will allow you to figure out what went wrong. This means that you have to modify your XML files (Feature and manifest files) and keep retrying until you figure out where it is breaking. In other words, you use trial-and-error and hope for the best. Hopefully your Features and solutions will deploy without incident, but in the cases where they do not, this can be a real headache.

Deployment Scenarios

There is no single answer for the right way to deploy content in a SharePoint environment. Every company is going to have a unique set of circumstances that are going to directly impact the decision that is made. For example, if you only have a designer and an administrator and neither are interested in learning how to write solutions and/or Features, then you probably won't be using solutions and Features.

Small Farm and Single Server Installations

Small farm and single server installations seem to make up the majority of the installations in the wild. In this case, there is only one Web front end and often only one SharePoint environment. The deployment scenario is wide open with this type of implementation since moving files between servers is not much of an issue. Although the deployment scenario is not as critical for this scenario, SharePoint designers should still be aware of the files they are customizing.

Medium Farms and Multi- Level Server Environments

Companies that have more than one Web front end and/or server environments should carefully consider solutions and Features as a deployment option. This would make moving files between servers and environments much easier, but companies have to weigh the ramp-up costs associated with learning the more complicated process. For simple implementations that will only be done once, you still might choose to use a more manual deployment method. But keeping the manual process in a multi-server farm can produce some deployment and maintenance headaches since each change would have to be manually uploaded and installed on each server. For example, take a custom master page. Without Features and solutions, you will probably manually modify the default master page for every site on every server. However, with Features and solutions, you have one handy package that you can install to as many sites and servers as you need to. In fact, once a solution has been added to a SharePoint solution store, administrators can deploy that solution to as many sites as necessary through the Central Administration application. Obviously, with a multi-server farm, this makes things much simpler.

Large Farms

The large farm environment will include several Web front ends and a multi-tiered server environment. Companies that invest in large farm architectures will benefit greatly from the deploying files with solutions and Features. Manually moving files between servers and environments is simply not a practical option.

> *Microsoft strongly recommends the use of Features and solutions for deploying files in medium and large farm architectures.*

Summary

Now that you know a little more about the topic of deploying SharePoint design elements, you should have enough information to determine what will make sense for your projects. Each project presents its own unique set of requirements that need to be carefully considered with all members of your team. It is important to talk about deployment issues relating to the initial implementation as well as issues that might arise during post implementation, including changes to the design and upgrades.

If your project has the time, it is recommended that you use solutions and Features to deploy your design elements, regardless of whether you have a single server installation or a large farm. The benefits of this method greatly outweigh the negatives. Additionally, the negatives will soon become insignificant after your team becomes familiar with the process. If your project is on a tight timeframe or you simply don't have a developer, that is just fine, too. The most important thing is to understand the deployment story for your implementation so that you can plan accordingly.

Index

A

A List Apart, 245
<a> tag, 287
absolute positioning, 260
accessibility, 535–575
  AKS and, 10, 548, 573, 575
  Americans with Disabilities Act, 8
  browser text and, 102
  checkpoint, SharePoint design, 579–580
  Content Editor Web Part and, 437
  CSS Friendly Control Adapters and. *See* CSS Friendly
    Control Adapters
  definition of, 535–536
  hearing-based issues, 3
  legal battles and, 8, 9
  MOSS and, 10
  priority levels, 538
  Section 508, of Disabilities Act, 3
  SharePoint customization for, 548–574
  Target Corporation and, 8
  tools, 574
  validators, 574
  vision-based issues, 3, 8
  WCAG guidelines, 537–538
    SharePoint accessibility *v.*, 538–546
  WebAIM and, 574, 587
Accessibility Kit for SharePoint (AKS), 10, 548, 573,
  574, 575
accuracy, search, 498–499, 534
ActiveX control message, 365, 366
ad fatigue, 34
Add and Customize Pages (permission), 147
Add Items (permission), 146
Additional Filters section (CQWP), 529
Add/Remove Personal Web Parts (permission),
  148
administrative pages, MOSS, 184, 185
Adobe Dreamweaver, 169, 594. *See also* **SharePoint**
  Designer
Adobe Photoshop CS3. *See* **Photoshop CS3**
adoption, of design, 15–16
Advanced Search Box (Web Part), 512, 513–520
  Properties section, 516
  Properties XML, 516–518
  Results URL, 516

  scope options, 515
  search box options, 514–515
aesthetics, 2–3, 34–35
AJAX, 39, 436
AKS (Accessibility Kit for SharePoint), 10, 548, 573,
  574, 575
alerts
  Create Alerts permission, 146
  Manage Alerts permission, 147
All Content scope rule, 510
Almost Standards mode, 247
alpha transparency, 102
Alternate CSS, setting, 275–276
alternative text, 449, 538, 546
Americans with Disabilities Act, 8
anonymous access, 341
Apple Safari, 570, 578, 583, 586
application pages, 206
Apply Style Sheets (permission), 147
Apply Styles pane, 188
Apply Themes and Borders (permission), 147
approval workflows, 160, 176, 178–179
Approve (permission level), 145
Approve Items (permission), 146
Article Pages, 377
artistic *v.* surgical approach, 79–81
ASP.NET 2.0
  controls. *See* controls
  master pages, 312, 313
    structure, 313–316
  Professional ASP.NET 2.0 Design, 571
  themes, 207. *See also* themes
  WSS on top of, 313
assistive technology, browsers, 548, 587
Audiences, 485, 486
authoritative pages, 531, 533–534
automatic line breaks, 118

B

Background Contents property, 60, 66, 76, 77
Background Gradient layer
  navigation area, 94–95
  welcome area, 88–90
background property, 265
background-attachment, 264

background-color, 262–263
background-image property, 263
background-position, 264–265
background-repeat, 263–264
backgrounds
   CSS and, 262–265
   sliced, 282–285
bad design, 8
BDC (Business Data Catalog), 10, 506
50 Beautiful CSS-Based Web-Designs in 2006, 40
Beginning CSS: Cascading Style Sheets for Web Design 2nd Edition (York), 570
Beltown theme, 202
best bets, 531–533
best practices
   collaboration/team site, 167–168
   communication/publishing site, 160–161
10 best-designed Web sites in the world, 40
BIN directory, 562, 564, 565, 566
Black Bar layer group, 126–127
   Gradient Overlay settings, 126
   Inner Shadow settings, 126
   Stroke settings, 126, 127
black box , Free Transform tool and, 69–72
   height/width settings, 71
   Paint Bucket tool, 69
   reference point, 70, 71
   X/Y coordinates of, 70, 71
black gradient box, in photo area, 107–109
   Gradient Overlay settings, 109
   Inner Shadow settings, 109
   photo for. *See* photo area
BlackBand.master, 155, 326
BlackSingleLevel.master, 155, 326
BlackVertical.master, 155, 326
blank space. *See* white space
Blank/Team site template, 164–165
blind Internet users, 3, 8
Blog site template, 167
blogs, 167, 168
Blue Band master page, 155, 275, 277, 278, 280, 281, 282
BlueBand.master, 155, 276, 326
BlueGlassBand.master, 155
BlueTabs.master, 155, 327
BlueVertical.master, 155, 327
<body> tag, 287
book list (XML Web Part example), 441–445
borders
   Apply Themes and Borders permission, 147
   CSS, 265–266. *See also* Stroke settings
brain activity
   artist *v.* surgeon and, 79–81
   left, 68, 80
   right, 68, 79, 130

branding, 3
   communication sites and, 168
   custom. *See* master pages
   Publishing Portal site template and, 154
   themes for, 205–206
Breeze, 202
Broken Hyperlinks report, 199
Browse button, 485
Browse Directories (permission), 147
Browse User Information (permission), 147
Browser Display Statistics, 74
browsers
   Apple Safari, 570, 578, 583, 586
   assistive technology, 548, 587
   CSS support, 246
   Internet Explorer, 586, 587
      Name ActiveX control message in, 365, 366
      version 6, 548, 570
   JAWS, 587
   Mozilla Firefox, 179, 244, 247, 586
      Almost Standards mode, 247
      anonymous access and, 341
      Firebug, 273–274
      HTML Validator, 274, 275
      testing in, 570, 586
   Opera, 578, 583, 586
   portal testing in, 586–587
   text, accessibility and, 102
Business Data Catalog (BDC), 10, 506
business-based portal topology, 19–20

C

caching, 33–34
Calendar, 164
calendar control, MOSS, 339, 340
Calibri font, 97, 101, 102
Candara font, 97, 106, 114, 121, 122, 126
CAPITAL LETTERS, 34
caption box layer, in photo area, 113–114
   Color Overlay settings, 113
   Stroke settings, 113, 114
   text for, 114
Cardinal, 202
cascade, 270
Cascading Style Sheets. *See* CSS
Change Screen Mode button, 45, 49
ChangePassword control, 556
check-in/check-out, 173–174
checking/testing portals. *See also* validation tests
   in browsers, 586–587
   against JAWS, 587
   mobile devices and, 587
checklist, accessibility. *See* accessibility

checkpoints (SharePoint design), 577–587
#1- basic Web design, 578–579
#2- accessibility, 579–580
#3- design mockup, ideas for, 581–582
#4- design mockup, creation of, 582–583
#5- master pages creation of, 583
#6- themes, using, 584
#7- page layouts, using, 584–585
#8- navigation, intuitive, 585
#9- content considerations, 585
   search functionality, 586
   Web Parts, 586
#10- checks and validation, 586–587
Citrus, 202
class selectors, 251
classes, pseudo-, 252–253
Classic theme, 202
classifications. *See* **taxonomy**
cleanness, of Web page design, 29–30
Client Integration Features (permission), 147
ClosingDate, 382
Code View, 170, 174, 180. *See also* **Design View**
CodePlex. *See also* **CSS Friendly Control Adapters;**
   CSSFriendly DLL
   CSS Friendly Control Adapters, 551, 571
   CSSFriendly DLL, 562
   Stramit SharePoint 2007 Master Picker, 311
coding methodology, CSS, 268
collaboration, 162, 168
Collaboration Portal site template, 154
   intranet and, 154, 160
   master pages for, 155
collaboration/team sites, 161–168
   best practices, 167–168
   Blog site template, 167
   communication sites *v.*, 168
   content, 163
   defined, 161
   Document Workspace site template, 165–166
   effective usage of, 163–164
   goal of, 162, 163
   information flow in, 162
   look/feel consistency in, 168
   project management sites as, 162–163
   Quick Launch and, 164
   site templates, 164–167
   Team site template for, 162, 164–165
   when to use, 162
   Wiki site template, 166
color keywords, 261
Color Overlay settings
   caption box layer, 113
   Green Bar layer group, 124
   logo text, 103
color picker tool, 91, 96

colors
   background-color, 262–263
   CSS and, 260–262
   foreground
      content area, 120
      setting of, 77
   for gradient stops, 84
   hexadecimal, 261
   RGB, 261
   W3C page on, 261
   Web-safe, 84
   for welcome area, 91
columns, docking panel, 53
   customization of, 53–54
   icon-only view of, 54
combined portal site map provider, 492
comments, in CSS, 268–269
common sense, design and, 13, 36
communication/publishing sites, 131–161
   best practices, 160–161
   branding and, 168
   collaboration sites *v.*, 168
   corporate identity guidelines, 138–140,
      160
   corporate policy and, 140–142
   effective usage of, 136–152
   goal of, 133, 160
   information flow in, 132
   intranets as, 133–135
   look/feel consistency in, 137–138
   master pages and, 137
   News Site template, 159–160
   page layouts and, 138
   public Web sites as, 135–136
   publishing pages, 142–144
      security, 145–146, 147, 148
   Publishing Portal site template, 154–157
   Publishing Site template, 157–158
   security, 142, 145–146, 147, 148
   site hierarchy, 146, 148
   site variations, 148–152, 160
   when to use, 133, 160
concept design, 37–130. *See also* **design**
ConnectTimeout, 508
Connell, Andrew, 590
consistency
   in collaboration/team sites, 168
   in communication/publishing sites, 137–138
   in site/page/portal design, 31–32
content, 585–586
   added to MOSS site, 174–178
   checkpoint #9, 585–586
   collaboration site, 163
   intranet, 134
   search functionality, 586. *See also* search

content (continued)

Web Parts as, 403, 452, 586. *See also* Web Parts

without Web Parts, 452

content area, 118–124

dummy text, 122

font properties, 122

foreground color, 120

gradient background, 119

header sections

Excellence, 121, 123

font properties, 121

Latest News, 121, 123

layer groups for, 123–124

Quality of Service, 121, 123

layer groups for, 78, 79

Content Editor Web Part, 190, 191, 192, 193, 194, 195, 433–437

accessibility and, 437

fun with, 437

content fields, 375

Content Management Server, Microsoft, 136

content pages

creating, 185

editing, 185–186

master pages and, 312

as *pages*, 312

structure, 314–315

content placeholders, 314

ASP.NET panel and, 325

list of, 324–325

Content Query Web Part (CQWP), 195–198, 404–421

Additional Filters section, 529

Content Type section, 528

'Latest News'

adding, to Internet site, 410–411

additional fields added to, 413–415

announcements list, creation of, 405–409

custom item style for, 415–421

online information, 421

presentation settings, customization of, 413–421

query for, 411–413

online information, 421

search and, 528–529

Search Core Results Web Part *v.*, 529

Content Source scope rule, 510

content sources, 504–506

adding, 505–506

Business Data Catalog, 506

Exchange Public Folders, 506

File Shares, 506

SharePoint Sites, 505

Web Sites, 505–506

Content Type section (CQWP), 528

content types

creating, 379–380

features and, 593

inheritance and, 372

page layouts and, 185, 371–373

search and, 500

site columns in (list), 371

contextual selectors, 252

Contribute (permission level), 145

contributors, 132

readers and, 162, 168

control adapters, 553–555, 574. *See also* **CSS Friendly Control Adapters**

controls. *See also specific controls*

ASP.NET, 175

master pages and, 315–316

in CSS Friendly Control Adapters, 556–558

(list), 556

styling, 569–570

SharePoint, 175

copyright notification, 125, 126, 128

Core Results Web Part. *See* **Search Core Results**

corporate identity guidelines, 138–140, 160

corporate policy, communication sites and, 140–142

Coskun's Data View Web Part. *See* **Data View Web Part**

Coskun's Theme, 214, 219, 224. *See also* **project**

crawler (gatherer/indexer) service, 504

settings, 506–508

Create Alerts permission, 146

Create Groups (permission), 147

Create Page link, 138, 139

Create Subsites (permission), 147

Create Variation Label screen, 151, 152

CreateUserWizard control, 556

CSS (Cascading Style Sheets), 186–190, 245–309

Alternate, setting, 275–276

backgrounds (of HTML elements) and, 262–265

Beginning CSS: Cascading Style Sheets for Web Design 2nd Edition, 570

borders, 265–266

browsers and, 246

cascade in, 270

classes, overriding, 241, 244, 246

coding methodology, 268

colors, 260–262

comments, 268–269

DOCTYPEs, 246

HTML/XHTML and, 247–248

in MOSS, 248

elements, 246–248

Firebug and, 273–274

floating in, 257–259

font faces, 254

font sizes, 254–257

forcing the footer technique, 289

in HTML, 249–250

HTML Validator and, 274, 275
IE Developer Toolbar and, 271–272
!important in, 269
limitations of, 311
margins, 266–267
in master pages, 276–280
master pages and, 329
mockup, 282–307. *See also* project
in MOSS, 275–282
overview, 245–248
padding, 266–267
positioning in, 259–260
project mockup converted to, 282–307
properties, 244–267
  inheritance and, 269–270
rendering modes
  Almost Standards mode, 247
  Quirks mode, 245, 246
  Standards mode, 246–247
rules, 250
selectors and, 250–254
SharePoint Designer and, 186–187
tables *v.*, 248
text decoration, 257
text wrapping, 262
tools for, 271–275
W3C CSS home page, 245
W3C CSS Validation Service, 587
W3C Property Index, 254
Web info on, 245
working with, 249–275
CSS Friendly Control Adapters, 548–573, 574
control adapters in, 553–555, 574
controls in, 556–558
  (list), 556
  styling, 569–570
CSSFriendly DLL and, 562–569
in GAC, 560–562
modifying, 555
.NET 2.0 Framework and, 553, 558
open source code files and, 571–573
overview of, 556–558
Professional ASP.NET 2.0 Design and, 570
resources for, 571
SharePoint integration with, 558–569
CSS Properties pane, 188–190
CSSFriendly DLL, 562–569
trust levels and, 564–567
current portal site map provider, 492
Current Web style, 40
custom code, features and, 593
custom themes, 218–242
custom trust levels, 564–569
customContentMain section, 303–305
customFooter section, 305–306

customHeader, 297–298
customization
Data View Web Part, 426–433
debate. *See also* deployment
  customized files *v.* uncustomized files, 179–180,
    333, 589–590
  master pages, 333
  page layouts/content types/site columns, 379
MOSS 2007 navigation, 489–494
Quick Launch, 478–481
search. *See* search
SharePoint
  for accessibility, 548–574
  checkpoints, 577–587
themes, 218–242. *See also* project
Top link bar, 461–472
Tree view menu, 482–483
customized files, 179–180, 333, 589–591. *See also*
  deployment
as unghosted files, 179, 416, 590
Customized Pages report, 199
customLogo, 297–298
customMainTitle, 305
customNav, 299–300
customShadow section, 302–303
customSlantedPhoto style, 303
customSloganText style, 302
customTop, 296
customTopNavFlyOut, 358
customTopNavFlyOutHover, 358
customTopNavFlyOutItem, 358
customTopNavItem, 301

D

data providers, in MOSS 2007 navigation, 492
Data View Web Part, 421–433
adding, 421, 422
conditional formatting in, 430–432
data source
  insertion of, 424–426
  selection of, 422–424
grouping items in, 428–430
look/feel customization of, 426–433
paging properties, updating, 432–433
XSLT customization in, 427–428
DataList control, 556
DataTimeout, 508
deafness, and accessibility, 3
Default Colors icon, 62–63, 77
Default Theme, 202
Default theme, custom themes as, 242
default.master, 155
Define Pattern, 65
Delete Items (permission), 146

Delete Versions (permission), 146

demoted sites, 531, 533, 534

deployment, 179, 333, 379, 589–597

features for

  content types and, 593

  creation of, 592

  custom code and, 593

  defined, 592

  designer's role in, 593

  disadvantages of, 595–596

  functions of, 592

  master pages and, 592–593

  site columns and, 593

ghosted files, 179, 589, 590

key considerations, 591–592

master pages and, 333

page layouts and, 379

Real World SharePoint 2007, features/solutions and,

  591

scenarios, 596–597

  large farms, 597

  medium farm/multi level server environments, 596

  small farm/single server installations, 596

solutions for

  defined, 593

  designer's role in, 595

  disadvantages of, 595–596

  upgrading, 594

uncustomized files

  creating, 592–594

  customized *v.,* 179–180, 333, 589–591

unghosted files, 179, 416, 590

descendant selectors, 252

Design (permission level), 145

design (Web site/page/portal), 26–35, 37–130. See

  also customization; Photoshop CS3; SharePoint

  Designer

accessibility in, 3. *See also* accessibility

ad fatigue and, 34

aesthetics, 2–3, 34–35

artistic *v.* surgical approach to, 79–81

bad, consequences of, 8

50 Beautiful CSS-Based Web-Designs in 2006, 40

10 best-designed Web sites in the world, 40

blank space in, 30

brain activity and. *See* brain activity

branding, 3

changes in, 35

checkpoints, 577–587

  #1- basic Web design, 578–579

  #2- accessibility, 579–580

  #3- design mockup, ideas for, 581–582

  #4- design mockup, creation of, 582–583

  #5- master pages creation of, 583

  #6- themes, using, 584

  #7- page layouts, using, 584–585

  #8- navigation, intuitive, 585

  #9- content considerations, 585–586

  #10- checks and validation, 586–587

cleanness of, 29–30

clients and, 9

common sense in, 13, 36

concept, 37–130

consistency in, 31–32

Current Web style, 40

defining, 6

deployment and. *See* deployment

60 Elegant and Visually Appealing Designs, 40

evolution of, 13

examples, 4–7

feature creep in, 13

financial benefits of, 1, 7–8, 9

508, 3

45 Fresh, Clean and Impressive Designs, 40

F-shaped page scanning pattern in, 30–31

functionality *v.,* 2

goal of, 17

goal-oriented, 14–15

important information at top, 30

inspiration and, 37–41

Keep It Simple, Stupid, 40

Kroger Company, 5

learning, 1

liquid, 74, 76

managers and, 8–9

Migros, 5, 6

mockup. *See also* project

  creation of, (checkpoint #4), 582–583

  ideas for (checkpoint # 3), 581–582

MOSS for, 10

navigation, ease of, 9, 32, 95

101, 13–36

page loading in, 32–34

pride in, 7

project. *See* project

quantification of, 1

Redesigns from Scratch and, 40

referrals and, 8

SendTec, 5, 6, 7

simplicity, 29–30, 32

site templates and, 27

Smashing Magazine and, 39–40

storyboarding and, 16–17

target resolution, 27–29

templates and, 6

uniqueness, 3, 5, 6, 7

usability, 2, 18

user adoption of, 15–16

user driven, 27

Web 2.0 hot-to design guide, 40

Web Design from Scratch, 40
Web Parts and, 403
design project. *See* **project**
Design View (WYSIWYG editor), 170, 174, 180–182
Code View *v.*, 180
XSLT customization with, 427–428
DetailsView control, 556
development site
creating, 219
theme applied to, 219
diagonal pattern, 58–67
gradient pattern and, 88
on logo area, 85–86
name for, 66
painting, 63–65
Pencil tool for, 61–62
saving, 65–66
thickening of, 63–65
using, 66–67
dimensions, of project, 72–74. *See also* **resolution**
Disabilities Act, Section 508, 3
<div> tag, 287
DLL. *See* **CSSFriendly DLL**
docking panel, 50–54
columns, 53
customization of, 53–54
icon-only view of, 54
palettes and, 50–52
reduced footprint version of, 54
DOCTYPEs, 246
HTML/XHTML and, 247–248
in MOSS, 248
Document Library Settings, 141
Document Workspace site template, 165–166
double-checking master pages, 338–341
down arrow, on Top link bar, 470–471
Dreamweaver, 169, 594. *See also* **SharePoint Designer**
Drop Shadow effect, 88, 102
logo text, 102, 103
navigation area, 95, 97
for photo, 113
welcome area, 90
Duck Island, 122
dummy text
generator, 122
Hillbilly, 122
Marketing, 122
Techno Babble, 122
DynamicChildLimit attribute, 492

E

ease, of navigation, 9, 32, 95
ECM (Enterprise Content Management), 164, 417

Edit Items (permission), 146
Edit Personal User Information (permission), 147
effective usage
collaboration/team sites, 163–164
communication/publishing sites, 136–152
60 Elegant and Visually Appealing Designs, 40
elements, pseudo-, 252–253
Elliptical Marquee tool, 45, 68
em-based font sizes, 256–257
'empowering knowledge workers,' 26
'enabling communities,' 26
Enterprise Content Management (ECM), 164, 417
enterprise search, 497, 534. *See also* **search**
Enterprise tab, WSS and, 167
entry point **search Web Parts, 512**
Enumerate Permissions, 147
errors
401/404, 184
robust, 331–332
Excellence header section, 121, 123
Exchange Public Folders (content source), 506
Expression Web, 169. *See also* **SharePoint Designer**
Extensible Markup Language. *See* **XML**
Extensible Stylesheet Language. *See* **XSL**
Extensible Stylesheet Language Transformations. *See* **XSLT**
external style sheets, 249–250
external Web sites, 135–136
eye icon, 57

F

farms (deployment scenarios)
large, 597
medium, 596
small, 596
feature creep, 13
features, 333
content types and, 593
creation of, 592
custom code and, 593
defined, 592
designer's role in, 593
disadvantages of, 595–596
functions of, 592
master pages and, 592–593
Real World SharePoint 2007 and, 591
site columns and, 593
uncustomized files with, 592–593
field controls, page layout with, 384–386
50 Beautiful CSS-Based Web-Designs in 2006, 40
File Shares (content source), 506
File Type Bias, 531
files. *See* **customized files; uncustomized files; specific files**

Fill, 88
financial benefits, of design, 1, 7–8, 9
Find and Replace tool, 225, 237, 241, 244
Firebug
    CSS and, 273–274
    IE Developer Toolbar v., 273
    themes and, 244
Firefox. *See* Mozilla Firefox
508 design, 3
fixed keyword, in Search Core Results Web Part, 529
Fixed Keyword Query text box, 522
Flickr RSS feeds, 445, 446
floating (in CSS), 257–259
fluid designs. *See* liquid designs
fly-out menus, in Quick Launch, 479–480
Folder List pane, 172–173
font faces (CSS), 254
font sizes (CSS)
    em-based, 256–257
    percentage, 255
    pixel-based, 255
    values, 254–255
fonts, 34–35
    Calibri, 97, 101, 102
    Candara, 97, 106, 114, 121, 122, 126
    choices, for project, 97
    color, 34
    dummy text and, 122
    Gray Bar layer group, 126
    header sections, 121
    sans serif, 97
    simplicity in, 35, 97
    Tahoma, 93, 97
footer area, 124–127
    copyright notification, 125, 126, 128
    layer groups, 78, 79
        Black Bar, 126–127
        Gray Bar, 125–126
        Green Bar, 124
footer, forcing the (CSS technique), 289
forcing the footer (CSS technique), 289
foreground color
    content area, 120
    setting of, 77
Foreground to Transparent, 120
<form> tag, 285, 287
FormView control, 556
45 Fresh, Clean and Impressive Designs, 40
401/404 error, 184
Free Transform tool, 68–72
    black box and, 69–72
    control of, 68
    precision of, 68
FrontPage, 169, 170. *See also* SharePoint Designer
F-shaped page scanning pattern, 30–31

"F-Shaped Pattern for Reading Web Content"
    (Neilson), 30
Full Control (permission level), 145
Full Property Table, W3C, 269
Full Screen Mode, 48–50
Full Screen Mode With Menu Bar, 48–50
Fulltime, 382
functionality, design v., 2

G

GAC (Global Assembly Cache), CSS Friendly Control
    Adapters in, 560–562
gatherer (crawler/indexer) service, 504
    settings, 506–508
Gecko open source browser rendering engine, 247
gel effect, 94, 97
generator, dummy text, 122
Generically Named Content, 531
ghosted files, 179, 589, 590. *See also* uncustomized
    files
Global Assembly Cache (GAC), CSS Friendly Control
    Adapters in, 560–562
Global Breadcrumbs, 319
global portal site map provider, 492
Google
    search engines and, 497, 498
    white space and, 35
gradient background
    content area, 119
    diagonal pattern and, 88
    welcome area, 93
Gradient brush, 119
Gradient Editor settings, 120
Gradient Editor tool, 120
Gradient Overlay Editor, 96
Gradient Overlay settings
    Black Bar layer group, 126
    black gradient box, in photo area, 109
    Gray Bar layer group, 125
    logo area, 81–84
    logo text, 103
    navigation area, 96
    welcome area, 91
gradient stops
    colors for, 84
    for navigation area, 96, 97
Granite, 202
graphic design. *See* design
Gray Bar layer group, 125–126
    font properties, 126
    Gradient Overlay settings, 125
    Inner Shadow settings, 125
Green Bar layer group, 124
    Color Overlay settings, 124

Stroke settings, 124
GridView control, 556
Gueury, Marc, 274. *See also* HTML Validator
guidelines, accessibility, 537–538
SharePoint accessibility *v.*, 538–548

H

H. *See* height setting
hacking search results, 530–534
header sections. *See also* content area
Excellence, 121, 123
font properties, 121
Latest News, 121, 123
layer groups for, 123–124
Quality of Service, 121, 123
hearing-based accessibility issues, 3
Heather Solomon's minimal master pages, 328
height setting (H), 71
for project, 75, 76
final, 127
Helfand, Russ, 551
Help Icon, 320
Hewitt, Joe, 273. *See also* Firebug
hexadecimal colors, 261
hidden layers, 57–58
hide/show links, 488–489
hide/show subsite feature, 488
Hillbilly dummy text, 122
HiringEmail, 382
**HiSoftware, 10, 573, 574. *See also* Accessibility Kit
    for SharePoint**
horizontal menu, two level, 492–494
Horizontal Type tool, 91–93, 117
hover effect, 100–101
HTML
CSS in, 249–250
DOCTYPEs and, 247–248
internal style sheets added to, 249
mockup design. *See* project
in page layouts, 375
    improvement from, 390–393
tables. *See* tables
<html> tag, 287
HTML Validator, 274, 275
**Hue/Saturation tool, 226, 227, 228, 231, 233, 240,
    241, 244**
Hunt, B., 40
hybrid portal topology, 24–25

I

icons
column view, 54

Default Colors, 62–63, 77
eye, 57
Help, 320
Logo, 320
underline, 122
ID selectors, 251–252
IE Developer Toolbar, 239
CSS and, 271–272
Firebug *v.*, 273
themes and, 243–244
IFrames, 437, 438, 440, 544
Image Web Part, 447–452
example, 447–450
Images List added to, 450–452
supported image formats, 447
Images, 173
Images List, added to Image Web Part, 450–452
<img> tag, 287
!important, 269
IncludeAuthoredLinks attribute, 492
IncludeHeadings attribute, 492
IncludePages attribute, 492
IncludeSubSites attribute, 492
indexer (crawler/gatherer) service, 504
settings, 506–508
indexing features, search, 501–511
INF file, Vintage theme, 210–211
information, at top of Web page, 30
information flow
in collaboration/team sites, 162
in communication/publishing sites, 132
**Information Management Policy Settings page, 141,
    142**
inheritance
application pages and, 206
content types and, 372
CSS properties and, 269–270
Top link bar and, 473
inline styles, 249
Inner Shadow settings
Black Bar layer group, 126
black gradient box, in photo area, 109
Gray Bar layer group, 125
hover effect, 101
inspiration, design and, 37, 41
interface, Photoshop CS3, 42–54
internal style sheets
added to HTML, 249
added to MOSS pages, 280–282
Internet Explorer
developer toolbar. *See* IE Developer Toolbar
Name ActiveX control message in, 365, 366
testing in, 586, 587
version 6, 548, 570
Internet Information Services console, 13, 14

Internet Site welcome page example. *See* welcome
page layout
internet.css, 286
Internet-facing Web sites, 135–136
intranets, 133
Collaboration Portal site template and, 154, 160
as communication/publishing sites, 133–135
content, 134
master page design, 366
mockup project
HTML, 307–308
Photoshop, 128
intuitive navigation, 585. *See also* navigation

J

Jacob, Neilson, 30
JAWS, 587
Jet, 202

K

Kay, Michael, 198, 447
keywords, 531–533
color, 261
fixed, in Search Core Results Web Part, 529
knowledge workers, empowering, 26
Kroger Company, Web site design for, 5

L

labels, variation, 151–152
Lacquer, 202
Language Picker control, 516–517
large farms (deployment scenario), 597
'Latest News' CQWP
adding, to Internet site, 410–411
additional fields added to, 413–415
announcements list, creation of, 405–409
custom item style for, 415–421
online information, 421
presentation settings, customization of, 413–421
query for, 411–413
Latest News header section, 121, 123
layer groups
Black Bar, 126–127
footer area, 78, 79, 124–127
Gray Bar, 125–126
Green Bar, 124
header sections, 123–124
logo area, 78–79
navigation area, 78, 79
photo area, 78, 79
for project, 78–79
Layer Style dialog box, 81, 82, 84, 96

layers, 55–58
approach, for project, 81
basic concept of, 56
examples of, 56–57
eye icon and, 57
folders in, 57
hidden, 57–58
masks for, 88
non-destructive editing of, 58
pattern fill, 88
Layers palette, 52, 57, 75
layout design project. *See* project
Left Navigation, 320
left-brain activity, 68, 80
legal battles, accessibility and, 8, 9
Lichen, 202
Limited Access (permission level), 145
line breaks, automatic, 118
Line tool, 98
link to external file option, 437
links
reordering, 489
showing/hiding, 488–489
sorting, 489
on Top link bar
adding, 458–459
deleting, 458
modifying, 457–461
reordering, 460–461
liquid designs, 74, 76
list permissions, 146
list views, 32
Login control, 556
LoginStatus control, 556
logo area, 81–88
diagonal pattern on, 85–86
Gradient Overlay effect, 81–84
layer groups for, 78–79
search area and, 104–106
text for, 101–103
Logo Icon, 320
look/feel
consistency
collaboration/team sites, 168
communication/publishing sites, 137–138
themes and, 205–206
customization
of Data View Web Part, 426–433
of Quick Launch, 478–481
of Top link bar, 461–472

M

Main Content, 320
Manage Alerts permission, 147

Manage Hierarchy (permission level), 145
Manage Lists, 146
Manage Permissions, 147
Manage Personal Views (permission), 148
Manage Styles pane, 187–188
Manage Web Site (permission), 147
managed properties, search and, 502–504
managers, design and, 8–9
margins, 266–267
Marketing dummy text, 122
Markup Validation Service, W3C, 587
masks, 88
Master Page Gallery, 173, 176, 177, 325,
    326
master pages, 137, 311–367, 583
    ASP.NET, 312, 313–316
    Blue Band, 275, 277, 278, 280, 281, 282
    checkpoint #5, 583
    for Collaboration Portal site template, 155
    communication sites and, 137
    content pages and, 312
        structure, 314–315
    content placeholders in, 314
    controls in, 315–316
    CSS added to, 276–280
    defined, 312
    design, from HTML mockup. See project
    double-checking, 338–341
    downloading, 164
    features and, 592–593
    minimal, 327–328
        Heather Solomon's, 328
        implementing, 333–341
        Microsoft's, 316–318, 328
        wrox.com, 328
    MOSS, 311, 313, 318–341
        challenges with, 329–332
        content placeholders (list), 324–325
        CSS and, 329
        ending of, 320–323
        functional areas, 319–320
        location of, 325–326
        nesting, 330–331
        out-of-the box, 326–327
        robust errors (turning on), 331–332
        safe mode, 330
        sample, 316–318
        system pages and, 329–330
        Web Part Zones in, 330
    nesting, 330–331
    page layouts v., 312, 313, 370, 402
    for Publishing Portal site template, 155
    resetting to site definition, 472–473
    SharePoint Designer and, 182–186
    structure, 313–316

themes and, 206–207
    WSS sites and, 201, 311
Master Picker, Stramit SharePoint 2007, 311
Maximized Screen Mode, 46–48
MaximumDynamicDisplayLevels, 469–470
medium farm (deployment scenario), 596
menu bar, 43
Menu control, 556
Metadata Extraction, 530
metadata, search and, 499–500, 530
Microsoft Content Management Server, 136
Microsoft Office SharePoint. See MOSS 2007;
    SharePoint Designer; WSS 3.0
Microsoft's minimal master pages, 316–318, 328
Migros, Web site design for, 5, 6
mini portals, 25–26
minimal master pages, 327–328
    Heather Solomon's, 328
    implementing, 333–341
    Microsoft's, 316–318, 328
    wrox.com, 328
mission statement, in photo area, 116–118
mobile devices
    portals and, 587
    Visual Studio and, 587
mockups (design). See also project
    creation of, (checkpoint #4), 582–583
    ideas for (checkpoint # 3), 581–582
models, site. See portal topologies
More Results Link Target Results Page Url, 522
More Results Link Text Label, 522
MOSS 2007 (Microsoft Office SharePoint
    Server 2007), 1
    accessibility and, 10
    administrative pages, 184, 185
    calendar control, 329, 330
    content added to, 174–178
    CSS in, 275–282
    customizing, with SharePoint Designer, 170–180
    for design, 10. See also design
    DOCTYPEs in, 248
    internal style sheets added to, 280–282
    limitations of, 10, 17
    master pages. See master pages
    navigation, 483–494
    opening, with SharePoint Designer, 171–172
    page layouts in, location, 376, 377
    RSS feeds, 159
    security. See security
    strengths of, 10, 17, 27
    12 hive, 179, 208, 212, 214, 330, 333, 470, 592
    VPC image, 171
    WCM and, 136, 483–484, 494
    WSS 3.0 site v., 455–456
mossExtension.CSS file, 209–210

Mossman & Partners, Inc. project. *See* **project**
Move tool, 43, 93, 94, 97, 99, 105, 115
Mozilla Firefox, 179, 244, 247
  Almost Standards mode, 247
  anonymous access and, 341
  Firebug
    CSS and, 273–274
    IE Developer Toolbar *v.*, 273
    themes and, 244
  HTML Validator, 274, 275
  testing in, 570, 586
multi level server environments (deployment
    scenario), 596
My Links, 320
My Sites, 319
MyMasterPage directory, 592, 593

N

Name ActiveX control message, 365, 366
NAPP (National Association of Photoshop
    Professionals), 129
National Association of Photoshop Professionals
    (NAPP), 129
navigation, 455–495, 585
  checkpoint #8, 585
  intuitive, 585
  MOSS 2007, 483–494
    customizations, 489–494
    data providers in, 492
    enabled for WSS sites, 494
    links, reordering, 489
    links, showing/hiding, 488–489
    links, sorting, 489
    links/headers, modifying, 484–488
    maintaining, 484
    Quick Launch, 484
    show/hide subsite feature, 488
    Top link bar, 484
    two level horizontal menu, 492–494
    WCM and, 136, 483–484, 494
    WSS navigation *v.*, 483–484
  relative paths in, 459
  simplicity in, 9, 32, 95
  WSS 3.0, 456–483
    MOSS navigation *v.*, 483–484
    Quick Launch, 473–481
    Top link bar, 457–473
    Tree view menu, 481–483
navigation area, 94–101
  Background Gradient layer, 94–95
  Drop Shadow effect, 95, 97
  gel effect, 94, 97
  Gradient Overlay effect, 96
  gradient stops for, 96, 97

  hover effect, 100–101
  layer groups for, 78, 79
  separator bars, 98–99
  text for, 97
navigation, ease of, 9, 32, 95
nesting master pages, 330–331
.NET 2.0 Framework. *See also* **ASP.NET 2.0**
  ASP.NET themes, 207. *See also* themes
  CSS Friendly Control Adapters and, 553, 558
  modification of, 551
  SharePoint built on, 558
  trust levels, 564
New Fill Layer, 85
new project, 75. *See also* **project**
New Web Part Zone button, 192
News Site template, 159–160
No Keywords Display, 524
No Results Display, 524–526
Non-authoritative Sites section, 533
non-destructive editing, of layers, 58
Notepad, 169, 170. *See also* **SharePoint Designer**

O

Obsidian theme, 38, 39, 202
Offset of sub-menu, 468
On-object User Interface (OOUI), 182
OOUI (On-object User Interface), 182
Opacity, 88
Open (permission), 147
Open Items (permission), 146
Open Link in new Window check box, 485
open source code files, CSS Friendly Control Adapters
    and, 571–573
Opera browser, 578, 583, 586
Options toolbar, 43
OrangeSingleLevel.master, 155, 327
Override Check Out, 146
overriding CSS classes, 241, 244, 246

P

padding, 266–267
Pages (directory structure), 173
pages, as content pages, 312. *See also* **content**
    pages; *specific pages*
Page Breadcrumbs, 320
page fields, 375
page layouts, 138, 369–402, 584–585
  Article Pages, 377
  checkpoint # 7, 584–585
  communication sites and, 138
  content in, 375–376
    content fields, 375

HTML, 375
  page fields, 375
  Web Part Zones, 375–376
  Web Parts, 375
content types and, 185, 371–373
creating, 383–384
defined, 369–370
editing, 185–186
field controls added to, 384–386
improving, with HTML, 390–393
location, in MOSS, 376, 377
master pages v., 312, 313, 370, 402
out-of-the-box, 377–378
publishing, 388
publishing pages detached from, 185–186, 390
Redirect Page, 377
SharePoint Designer and, 185
structure, 373–375
Web Parts added to, 386–388
Welcome Pages, 377
page loading, 32–34
  caching and, 33–34
  data intensive information and, 33
  image sizes in, 33
  list views in, 32
  simplicity in, 32
  Web Parts and, 33
Page Viewer Web Part, 438–441
Pages Document Library, 141, 390
Pages library, 139
Paint Bucket tool, 69, 78, 105, 113, 119
palettes, 50
  docking panel and, 50–52
  dragging, 52–53
  Layers, 52, 57
  reduced footprint version of, 54
panes. *See also* task panes
  Apply Styles pane, 188
  CSS Properties pane, 188–190
  Folder List pane, 172–173
  Manage Styles pane, 187–188
PasswordRecovery control, 556
Paste, 94, 113
pattern fill layer, 88
patterns, 58–67
  diagonal
    examples of, 58–60
    for project, 58–67
  reusable code v., 58
Pencil tool
  color selection for, 62
  hardness of, 62
  pixel size of, 62
  selection of, 61
People Search Box (Web Part), 512

People Search Core Results (Web Part), 513
percentage font sizes (CSS), 255
performance, site variations *v*., 160
permissions. *See also* specific permissions
  levels, 145
  list, 146
  personal, 148
  site, 147
personal permissions, 148
Personal User Information, Edit (permission), 147
Personal Views, Manage (permission), 148
Petal theme, 202
photo area, 107–118
  black gradient box, 107–109
  caption box layer, 113–114
  layer groups for, 78, 79
  mission statement, 116–118
  photo
    Drop Shadow effect for, 113
    positioning/rotating, 115–116
    preparation of, 110–112
Photoshop CS3, 37
  docking panel, 50–54
  education, 129
  Free Transform tool, 68–72
  Hue/Saturation tool, 226, 227, 228, 231, 233, 240, 241, 244
  interface, overview of, 42–54
  layers, 55–58
  mockup design. *See* project
  new project, 75
  patterns, 58–67
  PSDTuts-Photoshop Tutorials and Links, 129
  resources, 129
  screen modes. *See* screen modes
  toolbar, 43
  toolbox, 43–50
  tools. *See* tools
  tutorials, 129
***Photoshop User* magazine, 129**
PhotoshopCAFE, 129
pixel-based font sizes (CSS), 255
PlaceHolderMain, 320, 385
Placeholders, 181. *See also* content placeholders
Planet Photoshop, 129
Plastic theme, 202
policies, corporate, 140–142
Polygon tool, 104
portal site map provider
  combined, 492
  current, 492
  global, 492
portal topologies, 19–26
  business-based, 19–20
  hybrid, 24–25

portal topologies (continued)
  process-based, 20–22
  publishing, 23–24
  taxonomy-based, 22–23
portals. *See also* sites
  defining, 14
  design. *See* design
  goals for, 14–15
  growth plan for, 18, 19
  marketing of, 14
    internal, 16
  mini, 25–26
  MOSS as, 10
  reasons for, 17
  selling point of, 577
  successful, 36
  testing, in browsers, 586–587
  uncontrolled, 17
  user adoption of, 15–16
PortalSiteMapDataSource attributes, 491
PortalSiteMapProvider attributes, 492
PositionDetails, 382
positioning (in CSS), 259–260
pride, in design, 7
priority levels, accessibility, 538
process-based portal topology, 20–22
***Professional ASP.NET 2.0 Design* (ISBN:**
    978-0-4701-2448-2), 571
project (Mossman & Partners, Inc.)
  CSS mockup, 282–307
  HTML mockup design
    added to welcome page layout, 395–397
    intranet version, 307–308
    to master page design, 341–365
    from Photoshop mockup, 282–307
  master page design
    from HTML mockup, 341–365
    intranet, 366
    welcome page layout, 369
  Photoshop mockup design, 41–129
    artistic *v.* surgical approach, 79–81
    completed, 41–42
    content area, 78, 79, 118–124
    creating/setting up, 75–79
    diagonal pattern for, 58–67
    dimensions of, 72–74
    font choices for, 97
    footer area, 78, 79, 124–127
    height, 75, 76, 127
    to HTML mockup, 282–307
    intranet version, 128
    layer approach to, 81
    layer groups for, 78–79
    logo area, 78–79, 81–88, 101–106
    new project creation, 75
    photo area, 78, 79, 107–118
    resolution for, 73–74
    saving, 79
    toolbar of, 94
    welcome area, 88–94
    width, 75, 76
  theme design, 218–242
    color schemes, applying, 224–240
    color schemes, creating/mapping, 223–224
    creating, 214–217
    design environment for, 219–222
    finalizing, 241
    moving to server, 242
  welcome page layout, 394–402
    content added to, 400–402
    creating, 395
    field controls added to, 397
    HTML design added to, 395–397
    page layout specific CSS in, 399
    publish/approve, 399
    switching, 399
    Web Part Zones added to, 397–398
project management sites, 162–163. *See also*
    collaboration/team sites
Properties section, 516
Properties XML, 516–518
Property Query scope rule, 509–510
PSDTuts-Photoshop Tutorials and Links, 129
pseudo-classes, 252–253. *See also* selectors
pseudo-elements, 252–253
public Web sites, 135–136
publish, to communicate, 160, 161. *See also*
    communication/publishing sites
publishers, 132
publishing (defined), 132
publishing pages
  creating, from page layouts, 389–390
  detaching, from page layout, 185–186, 390
  publishing process and, 142–144
  security management with, 145–146
Publishing Portal site template, 154–157
  branding and, 154
  master pages for, 155
publishing portal-based topology, 23–24
Publishing Site template, 157–158
Publishing Site with Workflow template, 158–159
Publishing tab, WSS and, 167

Q

Quality of Service header section, 121, 123
quantification, of design, 1
Quick Launch, 473–481
  collaboration sites and, 164
  fly-out menus added to, 479–480

headings, 476–478
  creating, 476, 477
  reordering, 477–478
links
  adding, 475–477
  deleting, 474–475
  modifying, 474–478
  reordering, 477–478
look/feel customization of, 478–481
MOSS navigation and, 484
orientation, modifying, 480
View All Site Content, hiding, 480–481
Quirks mode, 245, 246

R

ranking factors, search, 530–531
rasterizing, 99, 104–105
Read (permission level), 145
readers, contributors and, 162, 168
real world scenario, for CQWP. *See* **Content Query**
  Web Part
Real World SharePoint 2007 (Wrox), **591**
Rectangular Marquee tool, 43, 44, 68, 100, 105, 111,
  113
Redesigns from Scratch (Hunt), **40**
Redirect Page, 377
reference point, 70, 71
referrals, design and, 8
Reflector theme, 202
relative paths
  defined, 459
  in navigations, 459
relative positioning, 259–260
relevancy, search, 498–499
Remote Interfaces (permission), 147
rendering modes
  Almost Standards mode, 247
  Quirks mode, 245, 246
  Standards mode, 246–247
reordering links, 489
reports (SharePoint Designer), 198–199
  Broken Hyperlinks, 199
  Customized Pages, 199
  Style Sheet Links, 199
  Unlinked Files, 199
Reset to Site Definition, 472–473
resolution, 27–29
  Browser Display Statistics and, 74
  determining, 73–74
  liquid designs and, 74, 76
  for project, 73–74
  TheCounter.com and, 73
Restore Down button, 48
Restricted Read (permission level), 145

result display **search Web Parts, 513**
Result Types, 518–519
Results display, 526–528
Results URL, 516
reusable code, 58. *See also* **patterns**
RGB colors, 261
Rich Text Editor, 434, 435
right-brain creative activity, 68, 79, 130
RobotThreadsNumber, 508
robust errors, turning on, 331–332
RSS feeds, 445, 447
  Flickr, 445, 446
  MOSS, 159
  XML Web Part example, 445–446
rules (CSS), 250

S

Safari (Apple), 570, 578, 583, 586
safe mode, MOSS master pages, 330
San Filippo, David R., 207
sans serif fonts, 97. *See also* **fonts**
Saturation tool. *See* **Hue/Saturation tool**
scopes (search), 19, 508–511
  creating, 508–510
  make available to users, 510–511
  options, 515
  rules, 509–510
    All Content, 510
    Content Source, 510
    Property Query, 509–510
    Web Address, 509
Scratchmedia, 40
screen modes
  Change Screen Mode button, 45, 49
  Full Screen Mode, 48–50
  Full Screen Mode With Menu Bar, 48–50
  Maximized, 46–48
  Standard, 45–46
  toggling, 49
screen resolution. *See* **resolution**
search (SharePoint), 18–19, 497–534
  accuracy, 498–499, 534
  authoritative pages and, 531, 533–534
  best bets, 531–533
  checkpoint # 9, 586
  content sources and, 504–506
  content types and, 500
  CQWP and, 528–529
  demoted sites and, 531, 533, 534
  enterprise, 497, 534
  gatherer (crawler/indexer) service, 504
    settings, 506–508
  Google and, 497, 498
  key words, 531–533

search (SharePoint) (continued)
managed properties added to, 502–504
metadata and, 499–500, 530
planning for, 534
ranking factors, 530–531
relevancy, 498–499
results, hacking, 530–534
scopes, 19, 508–511
  creating, 508–510
  make available to users, 510–511
  options, 515
  rules, 509–510
search indexing features, 501–511
user interface, 511–530
Web Parts and. *See* search Web Parts
search area, 104–106
textbox area for, 105–106
triangle button for, 104–105
Search Box
functional area, 320
options, 514–515
Web Part, 512
Search Center site template, 529–530
Search Core Results (Web Part), 513, 520–528
CQWP *v.*, 529
fixed keyword in, 529
Fixed Keyword Query text box, 522
options
  miscellaneous, 522–523
  Results Display/Views, 520–521
  Results Query, 521–522
XSL and, 524–528
  No Keywords Display, 524
  No Results Display, 524–526
  Results Display, 526–528
search data **Web Parts, 513**
Search High Confidence Results (Web Part),
  513
Search Paging (Web Part), 513
Search Statistics (Web Part), 513
Search Summary (Web Part), 513
search Web Parts, 512–528
Advanced Search Box, 512, 513–520
entry point, 512
People Search Box, 512
People Search Core Results, 513
result display, 513
Section 508, of Disabilities Act, 3
security
communication/publishing sites, 142, 145–146,
  147, 148
MOSS, 18
permissions
  levels, 145
  list, 146

personal, 148
site, 147
publishing pages and, 145–146
'Select stop color' selector options, 84
selectors, 250–254
class, 251
contextual, 252
descendant, 252
ID, 251–252
pseudo-classes, 252–253
pseudo-elements, 252–253
type, 251
universal, 253–254
Self-Service Site Creation permission, 147
SendTec, Web site design for, 5, 6, 7
separator bars, 98–99
server environments (deployment scenarios)
multi level, 596
single installations, 596
Servé's SharePoint Theme Generator, 243
Shared Documents, 164
SharePoint
accessibility. *See* accessibility
AKS, 10, 548, 573, 574, 575
built on .NET 2.0 Framework, 558
checkpoints. *See* checkpoints
controls, 175
deployment. *See* deployment
integration, with CSS Friendly Control Adapters,
  558–569
limitations, 10, 17, 311, 528, 575
navigation. *See* navigation
portals. *See* portals
products/versions. *See* MOSS 2007; WSS 3.0
search. *See* search
sites. *See* sites
Skinner tool, 243
Theme Generator, 243
themes. *See* themes
trust levels, 564–565
'upgradability' of, 577
WCM, 136, 483–484, 494
SharePoint Designer, 169–199
Apply Styles pane, 188
approval workflow, 178–179
check-in/check-out files, 173–174
Code View, 170, 174, 180
CSS and, 186–187
CSS Properties pane, 188–190
Design View (WYSIWYG editor), 170, 174, 180–182
  XSLT customization with, 427–428
Dreamweaver *v.*, 169, 594
Expression Web *v.*, 169
Folder List pane, 172–173
functionality, overview of, 170

Manage Styles pane, 187–188
master pages and, 182–186
MOSS sites
  content added to, 174–178
  customization of, 170–180
  opening, 171–172
Notepad *v.*, 169, 170
page layouts and, 185
reports, 198–199
Split View, 170, 181
trial download, 169
Visual Studio *v.*, 17, 169, 170, 313, 333
Web Part Zones and, 190–195
Web Parts and, 190–195
XSL and, 195–198
SharePoint Sites (content source), 505
show/hide links, 488–489
show/hide subsite feature, 488
showing/hiding links, 488–489
ShowStartingNode, 491
Silverlight, 436
Simple theme, 202
simplicity
  in approval workflows, 160
  in fonts, 35, 97
  Keep It Simple, Stupid, 40
  in navigation, 9, 32, 95
  in Web page design, 29–30, 32
single server installations (deployment scenario), 596
site(s). *See also* collaboration/team sites;
    communication/publishing sites; MOSS 2007;
    portals; WSS 3.0
  10 best-designed Web sites in the world, 40
  content, Web Parts as, 403, 452. *See also* Web Parts
  demoted, 531, 533, 534
  models. *See* portal topologies
  project management, 162–163
  public, 135–136
  skinning, 201. *See also* themes
Site Actions, 320
Site Column gallery, 382
site columns, 371–372
  creating, 380–383
  features and, 593
  list of, 371
  spaces and, 381, 382
site hierarchy, communication site, 146, 148
site map data source, 465–467
site permissions, list of, 147
site templates, 27
  Blog, 167
  collaboration, 164–167
  Collaboration Portal, 154
  Document Workspace, 165–166
  News Site, 159–160

Publishing Portal, 154–157
Publishing Site, 157–158
Publishing Site with Workflow, 158–159
publishing subsite, 157
Search Center, 529–530
Team/Blank, 162, 164–165
top-level publishing, 153
user training about, 168
Wiki, 166
WSS and, 167
Site Title, 320
site variations, 148–152, 160
  performance *v.*, 160
  variation labels, 151–152
  Variation settings, 150–151
60 Elegant and Visually Appealing Designs, 40
Skinner tool, SharePoint, 243
skinning SharePoint sites, 206. *See also* themes
skins, 201
sliced background, 282–285
small farm (deployment scenario), 596
Smashing Magazine, 39–40
solutions, 333
  defined, 593
  designer's role in, 595
  disadvantages of, 595–596
  Real World SharePoint 2007 and, 591
  uncustomized files and, 593–594
  upgrading, 594
sorting links, 489
Source Editor, 436
spaces, site columns and, 381, 382
Split View, 170, 181
SPNavigation, 325
SPTHEMES.XML file, 211–212
Standard Screen Mode, 45–46
standardized metadata, 499–500
Standards mode, 246–247
StartFromCurrentNode, 491
StartingNodeOffset, 491
StaticDisplayLevels, 469
storyboarding, 16–17
Stramit SharePoint 2007 Master Picker, 311
Stroke settings, 91
  Black Bar layer group, 126, 127
  caption box, 113, 114
  Green Bar layer group, 124
  logo text, 103
  textbox, 105
Style Library, 173
Style Sheet Links report, 199
style sheets. *See also* CSS
  Apply Style Sheets permission, 147
  external, 249–250
  internal, 249

subsites
Create Subsites permission, 147
publishing subsite templates, 157
show/hide feature, 488
surgical precision. *See* **artistic** *v.* **surgical approach;**
Free Transform tool
Switch Foreground and Background Colors button, 77
system pages, 329–330

T

Tables, CSS *v.*, **248.** *See also* **CSS Friendly Control**
Adapters
tabs, Top link bar
adding, 458–459
deleting, 458
modifying, 457–461
reordering, 460–461
tags. *See specific tags*
Tahoma font, 93, 97
Target Corporation, accessibility and, 8
target resolution. *See* **resolution**
task panes
Apply Styles pane, 188
CSS Properties pane, 188–190
Folder List pane, 172–173
Manage Styles pane, 187–188
Tasks, 164
taxonomy, 22, 168, 500, 534
taxonomy-based portal topologies, 22–23, 579
Team Discussion, 164
team sites. *See* **collaboration/team sites**
Team/Blank site template, 162, 164–165
Techno Babble dummy text, 122
templates, design and, 6. *See also* **site templates**
10 best-designed Web sites in the world, 40
testing portals. *See also* **validation tests**
in browsers, 586–587
against JAWS, 587
mobile devices and, 587
text
browser, accessibility and, 102
caption box layer, 114
dummy, 122
hover, 101
logo area, 101–103
mission statement, 116–118
navigation area, 97
welcome area, 91–94
text analysis, 530
text decoration (in CSS), 257
text wrapping, 262
CSS and, 262
textbox controls, 105
TheCounter.com, 73

Theme Generator, SharePoint, 243
Theme.Css file, 209–210
Theme.INF file, 210–211
themes (ASP.NET), 207
themes (SharePoint), 201–244, 584. *See also*
specific themes
Apply Themes and Borders permission, 147
applying, 203–205
site contents and, 212–213
branding with, 205–206
caveats, 242
checkpoint #6, 584
creating, 214–217
tools for, 243–244
custom, 218–242
Default theme and, 242
defined, 201, 208
designing, 218–242
files
mossExtension.CSS, 209–210
SPTHEMES.XML, 211–212
Theme.Css, 209–210
Theme.INF, 210–211
Firebug and, 244
functionality of, 208–213
IE Developer Toolbar and, 243–244
issues, 242
limitations of, 311
list of, 202
master pages and, 206–207
Mossman & Partners. *See* project
moving, to server, 242
reapplying, 242
SharePoint Skinner utility, 243
SharePoint Theme Generator, 243
working of, 208–213
Themes folder, 208–211
_themes folder, 212, 213
thickening, of diagonal pattern, 63–65
toggling screen modes, 49
toolbar, 43
IE Developer. *See* IE Developer Toolbar
Options, 43
of project, 94. *See also* navigation area
toolbox, 43–50
two-column view of, 45
Toolbox pane, 175
tools
accessibility, 574
color picker, 91, 96
for CSS, 271–275
Elliptical Marquee, 45, 68
Find and Replace, 225, 237, 241, 244
Free Transform, 68–72
Gradient Editor, 120

Horizontal Type, 91–93, 117
Hue/Saturation tool, 226, 227, 228, 231, 233, 240, 241, 244
Line, 98
Move, 43, 93, 94, 97, 99, 105, 115
Paint Bucket, 69, 78, 105, 113, 119
Polygon, 104
Rectangular Marquee, 43, 44, 68, 100, 105, 111, 113
Skinner, 243
Top link bar, 457–473
down arrow, changing, 470–471
inheritance and, 473
levels, displaying, 468–470
links (tabs) on
adding, 458–459
deleting, 458
indenting, 468
modifying, 457–461
reordering, 460–461
look/feel customization of, 461–472
MOSS navigation and, 484
Offset of sub-menu in, 468
orientation, modifying, 468
site map data source for, 465–467
style of, changing, 471–472
Top Navigation, 320
top-level publishing site templates, 153. *See also*
Collaboration Portal site template; Publishing Portal site template
TopNavigation area, 240–241
transparency, 102
alpha, 102
foreground to, 120
TreatStartingNodeAsStart, 491
Tree view menu, 481–483
Tree View Navigation, 320
TreeView control, 556
triangle button, for search area, 104–105
TrimNonAncestorDecendantTypes, 491
TrimNonAncestorTypes, 491
TrimNonCurrentTypes, 491
trust levels
CSSFriendly DLL and, 564–567
custom, 564–569
.NET, 564
SharePoint, 564–565
12 hive, 179, 208, 212, 214, 330, 333, 470, 592
two level horizontal menu, 492–494
type selectors, 251

U

uncustomized files. *See also* deployment
creating

with features, 592–593
with solutions, 593–594
customized files *v.*, 179–180, 333, 589–590
as ghosted files, 179, 589, 590
underline icon, 122
unghosted files, 179, 416, 590. *See also* **customized files**
uniqueness, design, 3, 5, 6, 7
universal selector, 253–254
Unlinked Files report, 199
Update Personal Web Parts (permission), 148
'upgradability,' of SharePoint, 577
URL Depth, 530
URL Matching, 530–531
usability, 2, 18
Use Client Integration Features (permission), 147
Use Remote Interfaces (permission), 147
Use Self-Service Site Creation (permission), 147
users
adoption of design by, 15–16
site template info for, 168

V

validation tests
checking and (checkpoint #10), 586–587
W3C CSS Validation Service and, 587
W3C Markup Validation Service and, 587
WAVE and, 587
validators, accessibility, 574
variation labels, 151–152
Variation settings, 150–151
Variation Settings screen, 150, 151
variations. *See* site variations
Verdant theme, 202
Version History, 174
View All Site Content link, 140
hiding, 480–481
View Application Pages (permission), 146
View Items (permission), 146
View Pages (permission), 147
View Usage Data (permission), 147
View Versions (permission), 146
Views (SharePoint Designer)
Code View, 170, 174, 180
Design View (WYSIWYG editor), 170, 174, 180–182
XSLT customization with, 427–428
Split View, 170, 181
Vintage theme, 202, 205, 208, 210
folder, 212
INF file, 210–211
vision-based accessibility issues, 3, 8
Visual Studio, 594
mini portals *v.*, 25

Visual Studio (continued)
mobile devices and, 587
SharePoint Designer *v.*, 17, 169, 170, 313, 333
VPC image, MOSS 2007, 171

W

W. *See* **width setting**
W3C (World Wide Web Consortium)
colors and, 261
CSS home page, 245
CSS Validation Service, 587
Full Property Table, 269
Markup Validation Service, 587
Property Index (CSS), 254
XSLT and, 441, 447
W3Schools.com, 74
WAVE, 587
**WCAG (Web Content Accessibility Guidelines),
537–546**
**WCM (Web Content Management), MOSS and, 136,
483–484, 494**
Web 2.0 hot-to design guide, 40
Web Accessibility in Mind (WebAIM), 574, 587
Web Address scope rule, 509
**Web Content Accessibility Guidelines (WCAG),
537–546**
**Web Content Management (WCM), MOSS and, 136,
483–484, 494**
Web design (checkpoint #1), 578–579. *See also*
design
Web Design from Scratch, 40
Web front ends (WFEs), 593
Web logs. *See* **blogs**
Web metrics, 9
Web page design. *See* **design**
Web Part Zones
added to welcome page layout, 397–398
defined, 375
in MOSS master pages, 330
New Web Part Zone button, 192
in page layouts, 375–376
SharePoint Designer and, 190–195
Web Parts, 190–195, 403–452, 586
adding, to page layouts, 386–388
Add/Remove Personal Web Parts permission,
148
checkpoint #9, 586
as content, 403, 452, 586
Content Editor, 190, 191, 192, 193, 194, 195,
433–437
CQWP, 404–421
Data View, 421–433
design and, 403
Image, 447–452

out-of-the-box, 403–452
in page layouts, 375
Page Viewer, 438–441
role of, 452
search, 512–528
Advanced Search Box, 512, 513–520
entry point, 512
People Search Box, 512
People Search Core Results, 513
result display, 513
Search Box, 512
Search Core Results, 513, 520–528, 529
search data, 513
Search High Confidence Results, 513
Search Paging, 513
Search Statistics, 513
Search Summary, 513
SharePoint Designer and, 190–195
Update Personal Web Parts permission, 148
Web portals. *See* **portals**
Web sites. *See also* **collaboration/team sites;
communication/publishing sites; MOSS 2007;
portals; sites; WSS 3.0**
as content source, 505–506
design. *See* design
Manage Web Site permission, 147
public/external/Internet-facing, 135–136
10 best-designed Web sites in the world, 40
WebAIM (Web Accessibility in Mind), 574, 587
Web-save colors, 84
welcome area, 88–94
Background Gradient layer, 88–90
color for, 91
Drop Shadow effect, 90
Gradient Overlay effect, 91
text for, 91–94
Welcome Menu (functional area), 319
welcome page layout, 394–402. *See also* **project**
content added to, 400–402
creating, 395
field controls added to, 397
HTML design added to, 395–397
page layout specific CSS in, 399
publish/approve, 399
switching, 399
Web Part Zones added to, 397–398
Welcome Pages, 377
WFEs (Web front ends), 593
What You *See* Is What You Get editor. *See* **Design
View**
Wheat theme, 202
white space, 30, 35
Google and, 35
width setting (W), 71
for project, 75, 76

Wiki site template, 166
Windows SharePoint Services 3.0. *See* WSS
wrox.com, minimal master pages, 328
WSS 3.0 (Windows SharePoint Services 3.0)
  Enterprise tab and, 167
  master pages and, 201, 311
  MOSS navigation enabled for, 494
  MOSS on top of, 7
  MOSS site *v.*, 455–456
  navigation, 456–483
    MOSS navigation *v.*, 483–484
    Quick Launch, 473–481
    Top link bar, 457–473
    Tree view menu, 481–483
  Publishing tab and, 167
  site templates and, 167
  on top of ASP.NET 2.0, 313
WSSDesignConsole, 325
WSS_Medium, 564, 565
WSS_Minimal, 564, 565
WYSIWYG editor. *See* Design View

X

X coordinate, of black box, 70, 71
XHTML, DOCTYPEs and, 247–248
XML (Extensible Markup Language), 441

XML Web Part, 441–447
  examples
    book list, 441–445
    RSS feed, 445–446
  XSLT and, 441–447
XSL (Extensible Stylesheet Language), 195–198. *See also* **Content Query Web Part; Data View Web Part**
  Search Core Results Web Part and, 524–528
  SharePoint Designer and, 195–198
XSLT (Extensible Stylesheet Language Transformations), 441
  customization, in Data View Web Part, 427–428
  information on, 447
  tutorials (online), 447
  W3C and, 441, 447
  XML Web Part and, 441–447
XSLT 2.0 Programmer's Reference (Kay), 198, 447

Y

Y coordinate, of black box, 70, 71
York, Richard, 570

Z

Zink, Tony, 171